FOR REFERENCE

Do Not Take From This Room

William Shakespeare

HIS WORLD · HIS WORK
HIS INFLUENCE

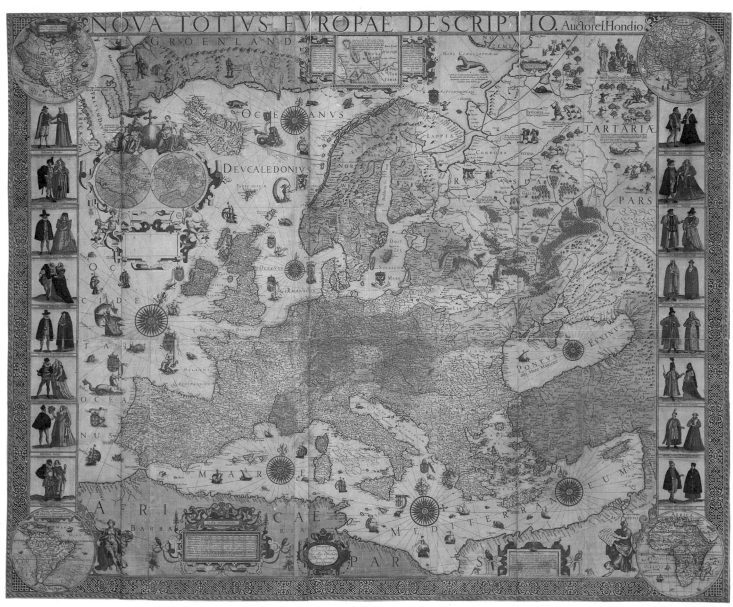

A wall map of Europe, by Jodocus Hondius and Petrus Kaerius (1595).

WILLIAM SHAKESPEARE

His World · His Work

His Influence

VOLUME I

HIS WORLD

John F. Andrews

EDITOR

CHARLES SCRIBNER'S SONS · NEW YORK

PJC LEARNING RESOURCES CENTER

All credits for illustrations are included in Volume III in the *List of Illustrations.*

Copyright © 1985 Charles Scribner's Sons

Library of Congress Cataloging in Publication Data

Main entry under title:

William Shakespeare: his world, his work, his influence.

Includes bibliographies and index.
Contents: v. 1. His world—v. 2. His work—
v. 3. His influence.
1. Shakespeare, William, 1564–1616—Criticism and
interpretation. 2. Shakespeare, William, 1564–1616—
Contemporary England. 3. Shakespeare, William, 1564–1616
—Influence. 4. Great Britain—Civilization—16th
century. 5. Great Britain—Civilization—17th century.
I. Andrews, John, 1942–
PR2976.W5354 1985   822.3'3   85-8305
ISBN 0–684–17851–6 (Set)
ISBN 0–684–18773–6 (Volume 1)
ISBN 0–684–18774–4 (Volume 2)
ISBN 0–684–18775–2 (Volume 3)

Published simultaneously in Canada
by Collier Macmillan Canada, Inc.
Copyright under the Berne Convention.

All rights reserved. No part of this book
may be reproduced in any form without the
permission of Charles Scribner's Sons.

3 5 7 9 11 13 15 17 19   V/C   20 18 16 14 12 10 8 6 4

PRINTED IN THE UNITED STATES OF AMERICA

90-0911

Editorial Staff

STEVEN A. SAYRE, *MANAGING EDITOR*

JONATHAN G. ARETAKIS, *Editorial Assistant*

ELIZABETH ELSTON, *Associate Editor*

JOHN F. FITZPATRICK, *Associate Editor*

NORMA FRANKEL, *Associate Editor*

PATRICIA FOGARTY, *Associate Editor*

JOEL HONIG, *Associate Editor*

LELAND LOWTHER, *Associate Editor*

W. KIRK REYNOLDS, *Associate Editor*

SANDRA D. KNIGHT, *Administrative Assistant*

EMILY GARLIN, *Proofreader*

EVA GALAN SALMIERI, *Proofreader*

DEBBIE TAYLOR, *Photo Researcher*

JOYCE ANNE HOUSTON, *Indexer*

ANJU MAKHIJANI, *Production Manager*

G. MICHAEL McGINLEY, *DIRECTOR, REFERENCE DIVISION*

Introduction

In the early years of the seventeenth century, Ben Jonson eulogized William Shakespeare as the "soul of the age" his works had reflected and adorned. Coming from an erstwhile rival, this was extravagant praise; but Jonson didn't stop there. He went on to proclaim that Shakespeare was a writer whom posterity would acknowledge as "not of an age, but for all time." In the next century Samuel Johnson confirmed the accuracy of his predecessor's prophecy: "This therefore is the praise of Shakespeare," he observed, "that his drama is the mirror of life." Within a few years, the eighteenth century's preeminent actor was speaking in even more emphatic terms: "Shakespeare had a genius," argued David Garrick, "perhaps excelling anything that ever appeared in the world before him." By the nineteenth century, the playwright's stature was verging on deity. Samuel Taylor Coleridge called him "the greatest man that ever put on and off mortality." And Ralph Waldo Emerson accorded him a unique position in the pantheon of history's deepest thinkers: "He was inconceivably wise," asserted Emerson, "the others conceivably." Owing in part to George Bernard Shaw's dismissal of such Bardolatry, our own century has been somewhat less hyperbolic in its critical estimate of the great Renaissance playwright. But that has not prevented such testimonies as that of the author of *Ulysses* and *Finnegans Wake;* James Joyce referred to the creator of Hamlet and Prospero as the poet who "wrote the great Folio of the world," and his favorite name for this peerless artist was "Shapesphere."

No other dramatist, in English or in any other language, can approach Shakespeare's primacy as poet, psychologist, and philosopher; and no one else in any humanistic endeavor has projected a vision as comprehensive or commanded an influence as all-pervasive. Shakespeare's phrases and cadences have become so familiar to us that it is sometimes with a start that we realize how many of our everyday expressions were first minted in his fertile mind. When we utter a cliché like "one fell swoop" or misapply a sentiment such as "more honored in the breach than the observance," whether we recognize it or not, we are speaking Shakespeare. And when we attend a performance of *Kiss Me Kate* or *West Side Story* and participate in the lives and loves that Shakespeare's characters continue to enjoy outside the dramatic settings in which they first thought and spoke and moved, we are benefiting from just a few of the other ways in which Shakespeare has enlarged our world by imitating it. His poems and plays have inspired more than 800 symphonic and operatic scores, and his themes have enriched the repertories of composers as varied as Berlioz and Copland and Tchaikovsky and Verdi.

Shakespeare's resonance can be felt in the writings of hundreds of subsequent authors. We delight in the hilarious (and not always sweet) uses to which the Duke and the King put Shakespeare in Mark Twain's *Huckleberry Finn.* We wince at political lampoons like *Macbird* (an anti-LBJ polemic of the 1960s) and *Dick Deterred* (a 1970s satire on Richard Nixon). We ponder William Faulkner's *The Sound and the Fury,* which can be approached, among other things, as a sustained allusion to Macbeth's "tomorrow and tomorrow and tomorrow" soliloquy. Or we savor such theatrical spinoffs as Edward Bond's *Bingo* (a "biographical drama" about Shakespeare the man) and Tom Stoppard's *Rosencrantz and Guildenstern Are Dead* (an absurdist redaction of *Hamlet* from the perspective of two innocents for whom the court of Renaissance Elsinore is as bewildering as the world their twentieth-century counterparts might encounter in a play like Samuel Beckett's *Waiting for Godot*).

Meanwhile, if we consider the dozens of Shakespearean scenes that have enriched the canvases of painters like Henry Fuseli and Eugene Delacroix and Pablo Picasso, we realize that Shakespeare has also expanded our visual horizons. No matter where we turn—whether we find ourselves chuckling over a New Yorker drawing in which a queen asks her husband "You gave your kingdom for a what?" or pausing for a doubletake at a Superbard T-shirt—we are continually reminded of the omnipresence of Shakespeare. In well nigh every nation that has a dramatic or literary tradition, Shakespeare is the playwright whose works are most frequently performed, the poet whose writings furnish the most accessible source of allusion. As ideological symbol or as standard of excellence, then, as literary model or as universal language, Shakespeare is part of us. And because he is so central to our lives, sooner or later we feel a desire to know and understand him better.

And that is the rationale behind this collection. *William Shakespeare: His World, His Work, His Influence* is designed to provide a multifaceted twentieth-century view of Shakespeare for the same kind of audience the compilers of the First Folio addressed in 1623 as "the great variety of readers." Most of us are familiar with the Shakespeare that students encounter in school. Others know the playwright who can still astonish us in the theater, or thrill us at the cinema, or fill our homes with enchantment through the technology of television and stereo. Many of us value Shakespeare as the supplier of wise saws and modern instances, a seemingly inexhaustible fountain of well-turned phrases for every occasion. Some of us draw on Shakespeare in our professional lives—as teachers, scholars, directors, actors, designers, critics, writers, lecturers, journalists, lawyers, or public servants. And millions of us treasure him as the companion we can beckon from our nearest bookshelf. But no matter how we respond to him, few if any of us are in a position to apprehend him from more than one angle. The historian who can elucidate a Shakespearean reference to Isis may be totally unaware of the echoes of Shakespeare in a given day's comic pages, popular song lyrics, or magazine advertisements. The theater professional who can perform Shakespeare's dialogue with metrical sophistication and fluid stage movement may be oblivious to what his words and gestures signify in the iconographic framework of a Renaissance art form. And the teacher who can analyze the image patterns of a Shakespearean soliloquy may sometimes feel at a loss to convey how those patterns relate to a dramatic design that is fully realized only in performance.

Hence the justification for a reference set that gathers into one convenient place a collection of essays on virtually every aspect of the phenomenon we refer to as Shakespeare. It is not enough to be acquainted with the few surviving biographical records of Shakespeare the man; we need to be able to interpret those records in the context of the institutions, customs, and modes of thought and feeling that gave the era of Elizabeth and James its peculiar form and pressure. It is not enough to know Shakespeare's poems and plays as individual texts; we must also be able to understand them in relation to one another and in relation to the other literature and drama of the period in which they were produced. Nor, for many of us, will it suffice to have a general notion of the vicissitudes of Shakespeare's reputation over the four centuries since he made his first entrance on the London theatrical scene; we also want to know the particulars of his reception in and influence on the various languages and cultures that have been affected by his life and work.

The twenty articles in Volume I of this collection are intended as an introduction to the world that conditioned and is to some degree mirrored in the poems and plays of William Shakespeare. For if the last four hundred years have demonstrated that Shakespeare was indeed for all time, they have also helped us see that he was very much a man of his own age. The more we know about government and society under the two monarchs who ruled England during Shakespeare's lifetime, the more likely we are to register the nuances of political maneuvering in plays like *Richard II* and *Henry V.* The more we know about patronage of the arts during this period, the more we are able to infer about Shakespeare's own professional career from such evidence as the dedications to the Earl of Southampton that precede his two narrative poems of the early 1590s. The more we know about daily life in city, town, and country, the more we are able to garner from those scenes in which we see Shakespeare's characters engaged in ordinary activities like eating, drinking, attiring themselves for courtship, and hunting for game.

The articles in the first half of Volume I are focused primarily on the institutions and professions that shaped the age: the church, the legal system, the schools and apprenticeship programs that prepared young people for entry into adult life, the economic and social constraints on getting and spending, the health standards of the time and their effect on everyday commerce, the military establishment and the modes of warfare that would have been familiar to Shakespeare and his fellow citizens, and the two industries that most directly concerned Shakespeare himself, theater and publishing. Building on these articles as a foundation, the second half of Volume I provides an overview of the many facets of life and thought in Shakespeare's England. The first three essays gauge the intellectual climate of the period: its sense of history, its literary culture, and its fascinating mixture of what we would now classify as science, magic, and folklore. The remainder treat subjects as diverse as travel, dress and decorum, sports and recreations, and farming and gardening.

Volume II is devoted to an examination of Shakespeare's work. Once again, the first half of the volume is intended to lay a broad foundation for the ten essays that comprise the second half. Beginning with an article on the problems involved in reconstructing a life of Shakespeare, this part of the collection proceeds to studies of Shakespeare's thought and sensibility, his professional career, his relationship to his fellow poets and playwrights, and his deployment of the tools of his chosen trade: his language, his poetic techniques, his prose strategies, his dramaturgical devices, his use of music, and his appropriation of the visual arts in his poems and plays. The second half of the volume then takes up Shakespeare's work both generically—with articles on the sonnets, the nondramatic poems, the English history plays, the plays on Roman history, the comedies, the tragedies, and the tragicomedies and romances—and topically—with articles on Shakespeare's audiences, his treatment of ethical and theological questions, and his insights into human behavior. Taken together, the twenty articles in Volume II should place the reader in a position to deal intelligently with all of Shakespeare's writings, both in terms of the characteristics of individual poems and plays and in terms of the larger motifs that link one work to another.

Volume III offers a variety of perspectives on Shakespeare's reception and influence. The first half of the anthology surveys the growth of Shakespeare's reputation from his time to ours, with articles on such subjects as the editing and publishing of his works, the fortunes his plays have had in the theaters of Great Britain, North America, and the rest of the world, his emergence as a literary figure of international standing, his penetration of such twentieth-century media as film and television, and his impact on art forms like painting and music. The second half of the volume features a series of personal viewpoints on Shakespeare today. Anthony Burgess talks about Shakespeare and the modern writer; Peter Ustinov muses on Shakespeare and the modern playwright; Jonathan Miller comments on Shakespeare and the modern director; Sir John Gielgud ponders tradition, style, and the Shakespearean actor today; and John Simon considers the ways in which Shakespeare tests the mettle of the modern critic. Along with Ralph Berry's assessment of today's major Shakespearean institutions, Joseph Price's study of Shakespeare as a cult object, and Jacques Barzun's reflections on Shakespeare and the humanities today, these personal observations should prove especially engaging. And they should set the stage for the two articles that round out the collection, Homer Swander's meditations on past and present in the teaching of Shakespeare and Maurice Charney's speculations about where current trends in Shakespearean interpretation are likely to lead us in the years ahead.

Appropriately, many of the essays in this collection elicit at least as many queries as they answer, for it is not the purpose of *William Shakespeare: His World, His Work, His Influence* to attempt definitive solutions to any of the problems that the study of such an unfathomable subject occasions. As Matthew Arnold observed in his famous sonnet about Shakespeare, "Others abide our question. Thou art free." This reference set will have achieved its aims if the reader emerges with an enhanced awareness of the complexity of Shakespeare's world and an expanded appreciation of the playwright's incomparable mastery of the means to immortalize that world through the writings for which we continue to turn to him. Ideally, that awareness and appreciation will carry with it the impulse to pursue the quest for Shakespeare beyond the confines of these pages. There, no doubt, the artist who inspired Arnold's sonnet will remain just as elusive as ever. But that is as it should be. Meanwhile, it may be hoped that future readers will be helped to the same discovery that Arnold wrote about— the revelation that one of life's most liberating experiences is the privilege of falling under the spell of William Shakespeare.

A concluding word about the image of Shakespeare that adorns the dust jacket. A derivative of the Chandos portrait, it comes, fittingly enough, from the collection of the Folger Shakespeare Library, under whose auspices it toured the country several years ago as part of the exhibition "Shakespeare: The Globe and the World." The original is painted on a large mahogany oval, and it found its home at the Folger through the generosity of the distinguished scholar and collector Mary C. Hyde. What makes this rendering of the poet especially suitable as the cover illustration for *William Shakespeare: His World, His Work, His Influence* is that for more than a decade it served as the shop sign of the Shakespeare Head, Jacob Tonson's eighteenth-century printing establishment in the Strand. As the publisher of several significant collections of Shakespeare's works, including Nicholas Rowe's seminal multi-volume edition of 1709, Tonson symbolizes an august tradition with which it is an honor for a new undertaking to be associated.

Among the dozens of people to whom this reference set is indebted, I wish first to thank the sixty distinguished authors who were kind enough to join me as contributors to the pages that follow. Many have provided indispensable counsel not only about their own articles but also about other aspects of the project; in this regard I think especially of Leeds Barroll, Geoffrey Elton, John Pocock, Sam Schoenbaum, and

Lacey Baldwin Smith. And then I think of a number of scholars who offered encouragement and advice even though they were finally not able to accept my invitation to contribute to the collection: Stephen Booth, Stephen Greenblatt, O. B. Hardison, Stephen Orgel, and Norman Rabkin are among those who will remember conversations in which they helpfully responded to my questions about one matter or another. I'm grateful to Terry Barker for her assistance in transcribing the interview upon which the article by Jonathan Miller was based. I've profited from the support and good judgment that Eileen McWilliam has provided at many points along the way. And I've found it valuable to keep my family and friends ever before me as potential readers. My greatest debts, however, are to the wonderful people at Scribners who have labored so tirelessly to bring this collection into being. I enjoyed working with Marshall De Bruhl and Christiane Deschamps in the early going, and in recent months it has been a pleasure to work with Steven Sayre. But more than anyone else, Charles Scribner, Jr. is the grand progenitor of *William Shakespeare: His World, His Work, His Influence.* I shall always be grateful to Charlie for asking me to serve as Editor in Chief, and it will give me immense satisfaction if the result is as he likes it.

JOHN F. ANDREWS

Contents

VOLUME I

hIS WORLD

CONTENTS

VOLUME III

hIS INFLUENCE

CONTENTS

xvii

William Shakespeare

HIS WORLD · HIS WORK
HIS INFLUENCE

The State:
Government and Politics
Under Elizabeth and James

G. R. ELTON

Central Government

The England of Shakespeare's day was a monarchy, but a monarchy of a special kind. Though the king or queen ruled without question and stood isolated at the apex of the social and political pyramid, that rule had to be exercised within quite well defined limitations: it was in no sense despotic, though it could be autocratic. The most formal conditions of restraint existed in the law of the land, called the common law, and its accepted conventions. Though the monarch possessed special rights not available to his subjects, these so-called prerogatives themselves received definition in terms of the law.

Royal prerogatives—rights enjoyed by that person whose duties were special and could not be discharged without such rights—were usually divided into two kinds, ordinary and absolute, which refer to the relationship between royal rights and the law. *Ordinary* (meaning ordained) signified "defined in the law of the realm"; *absolute* (free of the law) meant "not so defined," the implication being that they could not be defined because they touched upon unpredictable needs of the state that the ruler must be able to meet. Ordinary prerogatives included the fiscal rights of the crown, the power to appoint to office, the right to dispense justice, and the regulation of trade. Absolute prerogatives included the making of peace and war, but also (more ominously) the taking of necessary action against alleged enemies of the common-

wealth, as for instance imprisonment and examination under torture. The absolute prerogative unquestionably had autocratic and even tyrannous possibilities; it needed to be used with tact and without arousing dangerous dissatisfaction, the more so because this monarchy disposed of only a minimal establishment of armed force. That is to say, political action, as it always does, required skill and good sense.

The legal doctrine that the king can do no wrong sounds like despotism. In reality it meant only that, since no man can be sued in his own court, and since the courts of the realm were the king's, it was not possible to bring an action at law against the king; being unremediable in a court, the king's actions must be presumed never to do wrong. As a judge put it in a case tried in 1562: "The king cannot do any wrong, nor will his prerogative be any warrant to him to do an injury to another." This was all very well in principle, but suppose the king—or his agents—did do such a wrong, perhaps inadvertently, and no remedy lay against him in a court of law: what redress was there in such a case? On the death of a man possessed of land whose heir was a minor—a very common event at the time—an inquiry might discover that a part of the dead man's real estate was held of the crown in knight's service. The heir and all his property then became subject to the very burdensome royal right of prerogative wardship, and, as the phrase went, the lands were immediately taken into the king's hands, so that their income was lost to the heir's family. The verdict of the inquiring jury might be wrong—malevolently so, through corruption or intimidation, or quite innocently through ignorance or error—yet the king could not be sued for illegal entry, forcible disseisin, or any of the other ways in which such injustice could be remedied between two of his subjects.

The law nevertheless provided a remedy to prevent the king from "doing wrong"—a remedy derived from every subject's right to petition the king. The law knew two kinds of petition. A petition of grace asked the king to do something that lay within his free choice, such as granting an office or bestowing a piece of land. Such a petition asked for something that the petitioners wanted but had no existing right to have until the king had responded favorably. A petition of right, on the other hand, declared that a right already existing at law had been offended and asked that the right so lost be restored to the petitioner. Such a petition obviously applied if the grievance concerned an erroneous verdict that had transferred some lands from the petitioner to the king. There was a standard procedure for these petitions that produced a proper review of the case and a restoration of the property if the investigation showed that the petitioner had indeed been wronged.

Thus the subjection of the crown to the law had positive reality, and the English monarchy, though often described as absolute and manifestly powerful, was a law-defined and therefore a law-restrained monarchy. Cases arising out of these circumstances were naturally not common, and as a rule the power of the crown showed more plainly than the limitations upon it. Kings reigned and ruled; government and politics flowed from the personal position and actions of the monarch. However, in these respects, too, kingship was not unrestrained both in theory and in fact. The government of the realm was indeed in the fullest sense royal, but it had to be exercised in ways that limited the power of the monarch to do as he pleased. These ways appear in two kinds: the formal limitations of the instruments of government, which dictated the shape that political action could take; and the informal but all-pervasive conditions imposed by the mutual relations between ruler and ruled. First we shall consider the former: the structure of government and its agencies.

Elizabeth and James bore titles that defined them as monarchs of England (not to mention France and Ireland, and in James's case of Scotland too) as well as supreme governors of the Church of England. This duality raised no problems because it simply described royal rule over one set of people who in their bodies constituted the commonwealth of England ruled by the king, and in their souls made up the Church of England ruled by its supreme governor. For both purposes, kings commanded machinery for the exercise of these supremacies, while beyond and behind them, in the Parliament of England, there stood machinery that united commonwealth and church, as well as king and governor.

The chief instrument of rule was the Privy Council. Technically a body of advisers chosen by the monarch and sworn to his service, it had in fact a corporate existence of its own as well. It emerged during Thomas Cromwell's reform of the administration in the 1530s, replacing the very large medieval king's council that Henry VII had reconstituted as the center of a highly personal government. The reformed Privy Council constituted one of the clear indications that such personal rule was to be replaced by government through established institutions. Composed of the leading officers of state, including the top officials of the Royal Household whose posts were sinecures, it in fact consisted of politicians engaged in governing the realm. Elizabeth followed Cromwell's example by using a small Council of never more than twenty members, reduced at the end to thirteen by her failure to replace old men who died before her. James, pressed by men of ambition, understandably found it advisable to enlarge the body, even to unmanageable size. At all times, some privy councillors carried more weight than others—men of outstanding abilities or in the monarch's special confidence, but, above all, men sufficiently devoted to the work to attend meetings regularly. The chief active councillors were the (commonly two) principal secretaries, or secretaries of state, who usually prepared the agenda and carried out most of the decisions taken. Under Elizabeth, the secretaries included such leading councillors as the two Cecils—William Lord Burghley and his son Robert, later earl of Salisbury—and Sir Francis Walsingham; but even so, the office never enjoyed the highest formal standing that rested rather with the three great officers of state—the lord chancellor, the lord treasurer, and the lord privy seal. Under James, leading statesmen spurned the secretaryship, which came to be held by working bureaucrats of relatively low standing. During the reigns of Henry VIII and his two successors, the problems of the Reformation had made it essential to have leading bishops on the Council, but Elizabeth kept them off it until she found a congenial churchman in John Whitgift, archbishop of Canterbury from 1583 to 1604; thereafter the spirituality had always at least one man on the Council.

The councillors exercised their nominally chief function of advising the monarch as individuals or, more commonly, as a body. Elizabeth generally relied on advisers who had been formally appointed to the Privy Council. James resorted to the older practice of obtaining extraconciliar advice from court favorites and even from foreign ambassadors; altogether his government could be said to be more distinctly personal, even quirky, than his predecessor's.

The Tudor-Stuart Privy Council had independent powers unusual in the administrations of the age. Unlike the councillors of the kings of Spain and France, who could only advocate actions all of which required formal sanction by the king, English privy councillors discharged many tasks of government on their own authority. It would not be far wrong to say that while the making of policy (especially in foreign affairs) involved the monarch's direct participation, the running of the country was supervised by the Council, which activated executive agencies by means of instruments—Privy Council letters—in which the monarch played no part. In fact, the Council did many things, especially in the supervision of justice and finances, of which the sovereign remained ignorant. So long as the Council was purposeful and efficient, this was a sensible arrangement: kings and queens of England saw no reason why they should involve themselves in every detail, and government was not, as in Spain, subjected to the endless delays that resulted from having to seek the king's signature on every act of state. Privy councillors, then, were men of very superior standing in the realm, often independent actors in matters political and social, rather than mere creatures of the royal will. Their personalities and opinions mattered; what mattered especially was their inclination to pursue personal advancement and to promote particular policies by forming associations within the Council. Elizabeth on the whole succeeded in balancing these so-called factions (about which more later on) against one another and in maintaining the principle that the service of the state overrode other concerns, but the enlargement of the Council and the decline

of respect for the monarch that came with the next reign meant that the standing of the councillors deteriorated together with their efficiency. As James encouraged political dominance by court favorites, the Council, though never negligible, became an arena of personal rivalry rather than a formidable instrument of royal government.

The Council worked through regular government departments charged with particular functions. The oldest, and in its way the most important, was the Exchequer, first organized in the reign of Henry I and most recently reformed in a general review of the financial offices under Mary I. In Elizabeth's reign it underwent piecemeal and never entirely successful reforms at the hands of Lord Treasurer Burghley. The Exchequer was a ministry of finance in the narrow sense, responsible for collecting, spending, and accounting for the revenues of the crown, but not responsible for financial policy, the province of the Council.

The crown (always in this age underfinanced) enjoyed certain revenues as of right, all but one of which were administered by the Exchequer. The crown lands, a mainstay of early Tudor finance and enormously augmented by the dissolution of the monasteries under Henry VIII, now represented a wasting asset. After her first few years, Elizabeth tried to avoid selling this capital but had to countenance leases favorable to the lessees. In the war years at the end of her reign, she was forced to resume selling, and James made no effort to hold the vast landed estate together. By the early seventeenth century the crown was no longer a major national rent-collecting landowner, though of course some lands continued to generate income. By then, the most important because most buoyant sources of revenue were the customs on imports and exports, granted to each monarch for life in the first Parliament of every reign. This income was augmented, especially under James, by new "impositions," which the government justified rather speciously as a means to control trade (a right vested in the prerogative) rather than raise revenue (which required parliamentary consent). Impositions, declared lawful in a collusive action arranged with a cooperative merchant in 1606 (Bate's Case), caused an uproar in Parliament in 1607 and 1610 but remained embedded in the customs. The post-Reformation church contributed to the royal coffers an annual 10 percent income tax (the clerical tenth) as well as the "first fruits" payable by every cleric (from parish priest to archbishop) appointed to a new benefice and valued as a rule as equal to one year's income from that benefice.

All these and a variety of lesser sources—especially the fines, forfeitures, and amercements arising from legal suits—fell within the province of the Exchequer. The one item that did not was what we call the "feudal revenue," which was based on the principle that the sole owner of all land in England was the king, from whom the real owners technically "held" their properties on various terms. Feudal revenue is best described as a collection of death duties, because it fell due only on the death of a crown tenant. If there was no heir, the property returned to the crown (escheat). If there was an heir, and he was of age, he had to pay a standard sum (the relief) for the formal confirmation of his inheritance. If he was under age, he became a royal ward and the revenues of his lands were either administered by the crown or (more commonly) sold to a purchaser, often but not always a relative of the ward. This revenue constituted the province of the Court of Wards and Liveries. Wardship, which could threaten disastrous consequences to a family estate, always benefited the crown, but it was attractive also to others because it represented a potentially profitable area for investing surplus capital. Thus, though often resented, very haphazard in occurrence, and a cause of much uncertainty for landowners, it survived as a fiscal remnant of feudalism until the earl of Salisbury tried to increase its yield. His plan to amortize feudal rights in exchange for a parliamentary tax (the Great Contract of 1610) failed, but a start had been made on removing an awkward fossil. The Court of Wards was abolished in 1646 and not revived at the Restoration (1660), when an arrangement similar to that proposed by Salisbury a half-century before came into existence.

During the years under discussion here, the notion that the state should be financed as the public but personal concern of the crown, by means of money due to the prerogative, endured despite its manifest inadequacy. In fact, actual government financing increasingly depended on parliamentary taxes, on borrowing in anticipation of revenue, and on such windfalls as the capture of Spanish treasure ships or pensions (bribes) obtained from foreign powers. By dint of a frugality that rarely extended to her personal needs but in the realm at large looked like miserliness, Elizabeth avoided bankruptcy even in the war that left a legacy of debts both owed and owing. James, who evidently believed that in England money grew on trees, never came within hailing distance of making ends meet, a folly that, more than anything else, undermined the stability of monarchic government.

War apart, the greatest drain on royal resources —the largest spending department financed out of the Exchequer—was the Royal Household, or, in the reign of James, who had a wife and children to look after, the several Households. The Household maintained the king's court, that political center of England; it comprised a vast inner bureaucracy ranging from kitchen boys to gentlemen of the Privy Chamber, lord chamberlains, and lord stewards. In the reign of Henry VII it had also been the center of the actual government of the realm; that role had disappeared in the wake of Cromwell's administrative reform in the 1530s, though some functions of state (especially those connected with war) remained in the charge of Household officials, as did the Privy Purse, the monarch's private financial reserve. By the reign of Elizabeth, the normal government of the realm was managed by a regular bureaucracy of agents employed by the crown in organized departments. Two kinds of departments call for mention here—the secretarial offices and the courts of justice.

The secretarial offices were responsible for conveying the decisions of government in writing to others—officers in the localities, envoys abroad, foreign powers, and private individuals. The oldest and largest of these offices was the Chancery, which occupied the better part of its time in the conduct of judicial business.

In matters secretarial it acted by this time only as the issuer of formal documents that required the application of the Great Seal of England. It produced the letters patent that certified grants of the royal patronage—awards of offices, lands, and so forth—and the transfer of executive powers by royal commissions. It also kept the massive rolls on which these activities of the crown were registered.

Its clerks received their instructions mainly from the Office of the Privy Seal, a lesser royal seal that had at one time been the crown's chief executive instrument but now mainly carried out formal and really superfluous duties—receiving and transmitting orders for the making of letters patent. Its only effective function was financial: while routine payments out of the Exchequer relied on standardized writs under the Great Seal, special disbursements were usually authorized by Privy Seal letters on the orders of the Privy Council or the lord treasurer.

The Privy Seal also authenticated the bonds used in raising repayable loans to the crown negotiated within the realm.

Behind the Privy Seal stood the king's third seal, the Signet, kept by the secretary of state. Most regularly its clerks wrote out orders to the Privy Seal on instructions embodied in petitions to the crown that had been approved by the royal signature (sign manual bills), another of the strictly superfluous links in the chain that produced letters patent. The Signet retained original powers, however: in particular, it authenticated the monarch's "private" letters, especially correspondence with foreign rulers and with English ambassadors. Thus the Signet was the instrument of diplomacy and the formal emblem of the secretary's function as a minister for foreign affairs. Furthermore, letters under the Signet could convey specially important decisions in domestic matters (the secretary's other province)—items for which Privy Council letters or the secretary's private correspondence were thought insufficient, more particularly orders for arrests in matters of state. The three seals and their staffs thus formed an interlocking but flexible series of instruments for executing the will of government.

The courts of law dealt with conflicts that arose either between the crown and a party or between party and party. The central courts at Westminster comprised the ancient courts (or courts of record) and the more recent courts sprung from the duty of the Council to respond to appeals for justice withheld or unobtainable, and therefore commonly called the conciliar courts.

The three ancient courts, in order of repute, were the King's Bench (theoretically for cases involving the crown and therefore, among other things, the chief criminal court), the Common Pleas (for disputes between party and party, by this time concerning mostly debts but also titles to land), and the Exchequer (for disputes arising out of the royal revenue, especially so-called debts to the crown that were really revenue unaccounted for). These courts applied the common law of England.

The conciliar courts practiced what was known as equity, originally a means for doing justice if the law failed to provide it, but by the period under review settling into a subsidiary system complementing the common law. The conciliar courts were the Chancery (civil pleas, especially over landed property, contracts, and the personal rights of people ill protected by the law, such as women and children), the Star Chamber (in effect the Privy Council sitting as a court and controlling public order with jurisdiction over violent breaches of the peace, perjury, slander, corrupt juries, and miscreant officials), and the Court of Requests (for lesser equitable matters). The Exchequer also developed an equity side from the middle of the sixteenth century. In addition, the Court of Wards adjudicated disputes arising out of lands held in wardship, and the Duchy Chamber of Lancaster dealt with litigation over its large and scattered properties vested in the monarch as duke of Lancaster.

Local Government

Common law and equity were not hostile to each other but complementary, and the working of both systems lay altogether in the hands of people trained as common lawyers at the Inns of Court. Only Requests used judges from the ranks of both the common lawyers and the practitioners of the Roman law (as taught at the universities), called civilians. (The chief resort for civilians as working lawyers was the High Court of Admiralty, which heard litigation over maritime and commercial disputes occurring outside the realm and therefore not triable at common law.) Though important differences existed between the two sets of central courts in matters of procedure and power, these did not lead to confrontation. Generally speaking, the conciliar courts acted more directly and swiftly, but in civil pleas they could issue only intermediate orders technically reviewable at common law if the unsuccessful party liked to go on. Thus Chancery could prevent a man from taking another man's lands but could not safely settle title. Similarly, Star Chamber, although widely regarded as the most formidable of courts, could fine and imprison a rioter or a perjured juryman, but it could not hang a thief or a murderer, rights reserved to the common law.

These courts were financed by fees payable by litigants and therefore needed to compete for business. In the earlier part of the sixteenth century the equity courts had prospered because the older courts had failed to keep up with changes in society and the evasive devices of attorneys, so that they became useless in a great number of cases. In particular, the ancient courts could offer no remedies for disputes arising out of property arrangements largely invented to evade the rules limiting a man's right to dispose of lands (by sale or bequest) that technically he did not own but held from a superior lord (especially the crown). The backwardness of common law then made the fortunes of Chancery and Requests. The old law reacted in two ways: it invented new remedies for new situations, and its courts—especially King's Bench and Exchequer—developed various fictions to empower themselves to hear cases that technically were outside their purview. Thus by the end of the century there was a marked recovery in the business handled by those courts at the expense of Common Pleas and Requests.

This competition for litigants could be dressed up as a battle of principle. When Sir Edward Coke became chief justice of Common Pleas he set himself to limit the activities of Chancery, whose attraction to litigants constituted the heaviest drain on the business of his court. In 1616, however, thanks to the king's personal intervention, Coke lost that battle with Thomas Egerton, Lord Ellesmere, one of the founding fathers of the established court of Chancery.

The Tudor-Stuart machinery for waging war remained somewhat underdeveloped. There existed a Royal Navy—ships belonging to the queen—and a somewhat rudimentary administration for it: the Navy Board, which consisted of officers separately responsible for building ships, staffing and victualing them, and supplying ordnance. But the running of the navy came under a lord admiral and his deputies, appointed for each of the coastal counties. They had no link with the Navy Board, and there was no career system for naval officers, though the experience of the long war with Spain began to produce professional captains out of the amateur gentlemen (often trained in careers of exploration and piracy) who commanded the queen's ships. In actual war, the Royal Navy was always augmented by privately owned vessels licensed by the crown.

The army, such as it was, had even less organization, though the Ordnance Office was created early in Elizabeth's reign to administer the newly important weapon of artillery. Military administration had traditionally been the task of the Royal Household and, in a manner, remained so, with the Master of the Horse providing a species of military expertise, but in reality defense and war were managed by the Privy Council. Tudor and early Stuart armies consisted of contingents raised by commissioners of array in the counties, and of mercenaries hired at home and abroad. The general militia duty imposed on all males between the ages of sixteen and sixty, and supposedly supported by regular county musters and exercises supervised by the lords lieutenant and their deputies, produced only troops for domestic defense; these largely imaginary forces could not be compelled to fight abroad, though they provided material for the real armies recruited by the array.

Military administration was a thicket of malpractice, involving much inefficiency and vast corruption, though it should be remembered that the reality cannot have been quite as desperate as many accounts suggest—or as Shakespeare caricatured it in Falstaff's recruiting efforts in *Henry IV, Part 2.* Soldiers quite often went ill-shod and poorly fed, long waits at ports of embarkation resulted in regular and often massive desertions, contractors made their usual illicit profits, and captains of companies cheated the crown by drawing pay for nonexistent soldiers on their roster (dead pays). Nevertheless, by the end of the century English armies were fighting quite effectively in the Netherlands, Normandy, and Ireland, proving a severe drain on the resources of the crown and the taxpayer but also displaying a gratifying degree of professional competence.

From the point of view of the common man, the agencies of local government mattered more immediately, and more frequently, than those at the center. Most of these authorities belonged to the royal machinery, though some did not. In the reign of Henry VIII, efforts to control the particularly troublesome parts of the realm along the Scottish border and in the Welsh Marches (along the Severn and on to Cheshire) had produced two supervising bodies—the Council of the North (at York) and the Council in the Marches of Wales (at Ludlow). Both were created by royal commission, with powers of civil and criminal jurisdiction; they were not offshoots of the Privy Council but subject to its authority. In the shires under their charge they acted by Elizabeth's time simply as superior courts of law, also receiving pleas remitted from the center; they had powers both at common law and at equity. Wales itself had its own system of established courts—the four courts called Great Sessions—that was set up during the reorganization of 1536 to 1543, when Wales was incorporated into England. These, however, were the exceptional means of local government, designed to deal with unusual areas and problems.

The ordinary diffusion of royal authority throughout the country flexibly and very successfully employed the principle that the king could delegate his rule by commissions empowering named persons to do specified work in his name. At the top of this system stood the assizes. Twice a year, judges of the central courts perambulated one of the six circuits into which the country was divided for this purpose. Usually associated with leading gentlemen from the counties in question, the judges carried three commissions (assize, oyer and terminer, jail delivery), which authorized them to try both civil and criminal pleas at the sessions resulting. In civil pleas, always decided by the verdict of local juries, a case had much better expectations of completion if the plea was brought to that jury in its county than if efforts were made to bring the jury to Westminster. Also, crimes had nearly always to be tried in the shires in which they were committed, which meant that, after the King's Bench settled at Westminster in the early fourteenth century, it had to exercise that jurisdiction by delegation.

The best known of all the commissions was that of the peace, a regular annual instruction that set up courts of quarter sessions in every shire. For reasons of prestige privy councillors and bishops were included in the list where suitable, but most justices of the peace were local gentlemen; some were chosen for their legal experience. Between sessions, individual justices had powers to police the shire and collect material for trials at quarter sessions and assizes. By the 1590s, all felonies were tried at assizes, before a royal judge and his associates. Sessions dealt with lesser misdemeanors as well as the enforcement of controlling statutes, such as those concerned with the fixing of wages and the organizing of apprenticeship. In effect, justices of the peace managed the counties for the crown, and since membership on the commission constituted an important aspect of local standing, the crown's control over the composition of the commission helped to preserve its hold over localities.

The executive officer of all these local bodies was still the sheriff. Though no longer the master of his shire, he remained responsible for finding juries, guarding prisoners and producing them for trial, hanging convicted felons, executing all royal writs sent down to the shire, and arranging elections of members of Parliament for the county. A serious study of the Tudor sheriff is overdue.

These were the standing commissions for carrying out local government, but special commissioners abounded—to deal with a particular case, to control river navigation, to investigate complaints, to assess and collect taxes, and so on. Writs of commission provided for a flexible and inexhaustible transfer of authority from the center to the localities and therefore for the extension of royal rule over all the realm. Of course, their effectiveness depended on the willingness of the amateur and unpaid gentlemen so commissioned (often, as at assizes and sessions, assisted by a paid and professional clerk) to carry out the burdensome work demanded by the crown. Though lapses occurred and private favor could frustrate justice, there is no reason for doubting that the system generally worked very well.

We should also note the multiplicity of local courts independent of any exercise of the royal will at least in their existence and powers, though not necessarily in the work they did. Cities and boroughs ruled themselves under mayors and aldermen who held regular courts for their towns. Those feudal remnants, the courts of the leet and the manor, provided rule and justice (as well as much ordinary administration, for instance over admission to manorial landholding) at the level of the village. They settled the small disputes over boundaries, casual violence, or neighborly hostility that, to the people at large, mattered more than the occasional greater crimes or litigious disputes that reached the king's courts. In these village tribunals, leading local men—peasants often of small property acting as guardians of the rules (the custom of the manor)—conducted a measure of self-government for the common man that has been insufficiently recognized in social studies of the period.

Two things become apparent as one surveys the working of this sometimes well organized, sometimes haphazard structure of authorities for the government of England. Though the ultimate control vested in bodies such as the king and the Privy Council, whose function and ethos were political, the instruments charged with the application of political power were all in form courts of law—agencies for the settlement of disagreements and claims of right according to known rules. Even the Privy Council, quite apart from its alter ego appearance in Star Chamber, often acted as a quasi court, as it responded to petitions put before it by individuals seeking justice. This was government not only under the law but by the law.

Parties to a dispute often tried to avoid the costs

and delays involved in using the courts by agreeing to abide by the decision of one or more persons of eminence whose oracular pronouncements carried no powers of enforcement but nevertheless quite frequently terminated a dispute. Arbitration is another subject so far insufficiently studied.

Civil Servants

Although many government administrators were unpaid amateurs, the system also provided for a considerable number of salaried professionals. The great Royal Household, the offices of Chancery, the Exchequer, the secretaries of state, and the central courts between them employed men by the hundreds. Most of them had other personal interests and wished to set themselves up as landed gentlemen, investing the profits of office in the only form of wealth that gave social status. Many of them went in and out of office in the wake of their superiors. Some of them, in fact, behaved like members of an American-style spoils system, while others more closely resembled the officials of nineteenth-century Britain, but all were nonetheless civil servants of the crown. Their kind is also found in the localities: officers of the Exchequer (customers and their colleagues in the ports, receivers of land revenue), representatives of the Court of Wards, and clerks of assizes and sessions. In the greater departments definite career courses can be discerned as men rose through the ranks, whereas some offices provide interesting evidence of dynastic practices: men would get patents of survivorship or reversion, which enabled them to associate their sons in the office with themselves and thus to create a family preserve that could extend over several generations.

This civil service drew its income from two sources. The crown paid salaries, but these were never meant to be adequate and always lagged behind the steady inflation of prices. The major profits of office arose from the fees paid by people who used the offices. Fees were payable for the issue of all government documents solicited by the public (writs, letters patent), for all enrollments, for every step taken in the paying of revenue. In a case at law, litigants owed regular payments to the officers of the courts as well as to their own attorneys and counsel. Fees were supposedly fixed and indeed were posted in offices, but throughout the period complaints multiplied that officers arbitrarily in-creased the official scales—as they had to do if they wished to keep up with inflation. In James I's reign, many officers overcharged for their services, but efforts to control their greed achieved very little, while the value of crown office increased markedly.

Though unauthorized increases should not have been tolerated, the fees system by itself constituted no sort of corruption; it reflected the principle that at least a part of the costs incurred by the king's government should be borne by those who specifically made use of it for their own purposes. It has been calculated that around 1625 the official fees collected amounted to about £50,000 a year, or close to a sixth of the regular income of the crown. In addition, beyond any doubt, improper gifts and bribes were paid by people who sought to tip a decision in their favor or at least accelerate the operations of government, but it is understandably difficult to get firm evidence for this. Gifts were no doubt frequently of money, but what we can learn of them shows that presents in kind—a bolt of cloth, a cheese, a quantity of wine, or a piece of venison—very often served, changing manifest corruption into kindnesses bestowed on friends. Frequently promises of compensatory services sufficed, or even kind words about prayers offered or memories recalled.

Some historians have wildly exaggerated the extent of true corruption. While probably fairly rampant at the top, it seems to have played far less part within the civil service proper. Thanks to the survival of the correspondence of Sir Michael Hickes, secretary to Lord Burghley and later assistant to Robert Cecil, we know that the sale of wardships put money that should have gone to the crown into ministers' pockets, and we learn of the sizable gifts they expected to receive for their favors, though many of these gifts really did represent a proof of personal attachment. But the Cecils' opportunities were exceptionally great. The indications are that truly corrupt behavior increased at the much looser court of James I, where several genuine scandals came to light. Unquestionably privy councillors and men of influence thought it right to exploit the help they could give to applicants, and the general ethos of the day supposed that friendly services from one side justified expectations of friendly appreciation from the other.

The line of propriety excluded excessive greed (which was with reason charged against some of the favorites of James I), strikingly biased actions in return for bribes (the charge that ruined Francis

Bacon in 1621), and blatant robbing of the royal till (the misbehavior that brought down Lord Treasurer Suffolk in 1618). Though the worst cases did occur after 1603, it is plain that things improper by the standards of the time (not just by ours) happened under Elizabeth, too. The most systematic suppliers of bribes were foreign envoys intent on buying both favor and information; they found English courtiers exceptionally open to such offers, which the English seem to have treated as an agreeable and amusing way of fleecing the foreigner.

Moralizing judgments about "wholesale corruption" not only go well beyond the evidence but also obscure the realities of a system that incorporated the demands made by close personal acquaintance and relations, with palpable exchanges of favors, in the structure of civil government. The society involved in this work was small, and its members knew one another too well to remove all temptation to exploit acquaintance. Consequently, those less well acquainted needed to use more obviously corrupt methods to attract the attention of the men at the heart of government. Finally, it must be noted that successful careers in the civil service depended not only on favor but also very much on ability, though this encouraging aspect of the scene deteriorated as the monarch and Council distanced themselves from administrative affairs in the 1610s.

The Church

The king, as head of the commonwealth, thus disposed of a complex structure of government; as supreme governor of the Church of England, he similarly commanded a wide and well-articulated instrument of rule. Like the secular offices, those of the church were inherited from the medieval past but had gone through important transformations that testified to the end of medieval kingship some time in the 1530s. In the church, these changes had been called for after the Henrician Reformation removed the foreign authority of the papacy.

The two provinces of the English church, Canterbury and York, presided over by archbishops, consisted of bishoprics—eighteen in the south and four in the north—themselves divided into archdeaconries. The parishes, the lowest rung in this chain of command, were grouped in rural deaneries. The cathedrals, seats of the bishops, were independently managed by deans and chapters, whose members held "prebends" and were termed "prebendaries." The relative simplicity of this hierarchic order was slightly complicated by the existence of "peculiars"—parishes and manors lying within one diocese but subject to the bishop or archbishop of another. The archbishop of Canterbury, as primate of England, ranked above his brother of York but had no governmental means of control over him; the traditional organization of the English church provided for no single instrument of unification, since before the Reformation that function had been exercised by the pope and his court at Rome.

Each province possessed a representative assembly called a convocation, which consisted of an upper house of bishops and a lower house of proctors (elected representatives) of the clergy. By this time the convocations, though they still commonly met during parliamentary sessions, retained no significant powers. If they passed laws for the church, these had no authority without parliamentary enactment. Even the taxes of the clergy, which it required their grant to make available to the crown, were always further embodied in an act of Parliament.

In terms of government, the church, like the state, operated essentially as a system of law courts, presided over by bishops and archdeacons, or in the first case usually by deputies (chancellors, vicars general, official principals) appointed for the purpose. The courts were linked in a regular sequence of appeals from the lower to the higher, something the state did not possess. The law administered in the church courts stood in some confusion. In 1535 the study of the canon law of the universal church was prohibited as popish at the universities, and in 1545 lawyers trained in the civil (Roman) law were authorized to take the place of canonists as practitioners in the courts. Several attempts to provide a reformed code of law suitable to a Protestant church failed to gain authorization, until the canons of 1604, agreed by the convocations but never enacted by Parliament, came, as a case of necessity, to be treated as applicable.

The church courts in the main dealt with four categories of cases. They enforced discipline on the clergy in matters of personal behavior and uniformity of worship; they asserted the claims of the clergy on the laity in matters of money (especially the tithe); they adjudged the moral delicts of the laity, a competence that brought within their grasp not only such sins as adultery and fornication but also all matters arising out of marriages and defamation; and they presided over the probate of testaments so far as movables were concerned. (Land devised by will came under the common law after the Statute of Wills of 1540.) Because they impinged in many, often intimate ways on the life of the people, the church courts were not popular. Though their powers had declined since pre-Reformation days, they remained very active, especially in matrimonial, testamentary, and moral cases. The sanctions they could apply included excommunication (rarely used) and penances, very commonly commuted for money payments. These courts were necessary aids in the affairs of men, as well as somewhat oppressive instruments of social coercion; and clerical lawyers, civilians now rather than canonists, continued to do good business.

The system was inadequate in two important respects. The supposedly ultimate cause for the attention of the church courts—the matter that most concerned the church as an instrument of salvation—was the assurance of spiritually sound means of grace and the prevention of heresy; and by the time that Elizabeth settled her Protestant church, these courts found that they had effectively relinquished jurisdiction over such matters. The second weakness lay in the removal of papal authority, with the consequent loss of a unifying umbrella above the archbishops and a unifying court of appeal above their courts. In both areas, the new pope—the supreme head, and after 1559 the supreme governor, of the Church of England—intervened. The experiment by which Henry VIII delegated the whole of his quasi-papal authority to a vicegerent in spirituals was never repeated after the fall of Thomas Cromwell in 1540, but the statutory creation of an ad hoc court of ultimate appeal, called the High Court of Delegates and appointed each time such an appeal came forward, survived quite usefully into the nineteenth century.

For the rest, the crown predictably resorted to its well-tried power to delegate authority by commission. Royal commissions were created within the government of the church for specific occasions before the Reformation, but it was only in the reign of Elizabeth that their existence was regularized by the creation of occasional ecclesiastical commissions over dioceses and especially the setting up of Courts of High Commission for each archiepiscopal province. Possessed of powers to fine and imprison, the high commissions (composed of clergy and laity) dealt with the more serious offenses triable at spiritual law and acted as general supervisors of order and uniformity within the church.

The problem of uniformity, however, proved insoluble. Doctrine was plain and simple: since all Englishmen composed one church, all should in matters of the faith behave alike, accepting the doctrines defined in the Thirty-nine Articles (1563), worshiping according to the rites laid down in the Book of Common Prayer (1559), and obedient to the queen, the bishops, and the rest of the established order. Not all Englishmen were willing to do so. Those who refused to accept the restoration of a Protestant church in 1559 and adhered to Roman Catholicism proved no problem for the church courts: their refusal to attend the services of the church (recusancy) and their involvement in actual or potential treasons were matters for the secular courts. Deviance among Protestants, however, called for rectification by the bishops and their courts. These were the instruments available for tackling the many and various failures to conform—ranging from a refusal to use the Prayer Book or some part of it to demands for a presbyterian church government in place of an episcopalian one—which are nowadays summed up under the name *Puritanism.* These courts also dealt with the more extreme departures from the form of religion laid down in law, namely the growth of separatist sects that rejected the principle of a national church and regarded themselves as the only true Christian congregations ("gathered churches").

The term *Puritanism* should be reserved for those English Protestants who accepted the existence of a uniform, national church but who in one way or another regarded that set up by the settlement of 1559 as inadequately scriptural and therefore in need of further reform, whether that reform touched the wearing of clerical vestments, the role of prayer and sermon, the use of certain ceremonies reckoned to be "rags of popery" (for instance, the use of the ring in marriage, the sign of the cross in baptism, or kneeling at communion), or the structure of church government. Few Puritans really looked for revolution, and the attempt made in the 1580s to set up a presbyterian government was easily repressed by Archbishop Whitgift and the high commission. But deviation short of revolution, fed by the ardent Calvinism of a younger generation of clergy coming from the universities, remained ineradicable because it often represented an active spiritual zeal that many in authority welcomed and wished to see at work in the church.

Elizabeth herself always implacably opposed all visible signs of nonconformity while remaining indifferent to deviant opinion so long as it caused no public scandal. James, once persuaded that the Puritans did not seek to do away with bishops or undermine his own authority in the church, showed himself more receptive to the disputatious ardor of those preachers. In his reign a strongly Protestant, very Calvinist state of mind sufficiently dominated the church, especially after the death of Archbishop Richard Bancroft in 1610, to inhibit energetic action against minor manifestations of nonconformity within the church. Separatists and sectarians were another matter: it was at this time that the English refugee congregations (from which sprang the Pilgrim Fathers of 1620) settled in the Netherlands.

The government of England, secular and ecclesiastical, was very monarchical in its fundamental principles: everything derived from the king, and all lines led back to him. Even if this monarch was supposed to govern under and by the established law, and even though he commonly did so, he resembled a truly absolute king very closely. Jacobean theorists, from the king downward, regularly emphasized this quality in English kingship, though by *absolute* they meant not superiority to the law but only unlimited exercise of power within that law.

Political realities, however, made the king rather weaker in practice than in theory. He had no means of his own to alter the law. His proclamations, theoretically issued with the advice of his Council, could not, it was universally agreed, make new law or abrogate old. If on occasion Elizabeth transgressed this principle when urgent dangers to the state required action against dissidents, she always took care to have such innovatory breaches of the rules ratified as soon as possible by the only lawful means available—by act of Parliament. Though on occasion James favored a very free doctrine of monarchy and would speak of giving ultimate authority to his proclamations, he never attempted to turn such claims into reality.

The making of law lay with the English Parliament. (Scotland and Ireland, being separate kingdoms, though from 1603 all under one monarch, had their own parliaments.) It used to be thought that everything about that body had been fully worked out, especially by two historians of the previous generation—Sir John Neale and Wallace Notestein—but in the last twenty years their coherent and systematic account has pretty well totally collapsed. A new look, unencumbered by ancient

presuppositions, at the various sorts of evidence has shown that they got things very wrong indeed, but the new look has not yet found expression as complete as theirs, for which reason old error persists in some places. Neale and Notestein really confined their attention to the House of Commons, which they regarded as engaged in a struggle for independence and power; they believed that what mattered in the history of Parliament was the alleged rise of an opposition to the crown, achieved by developments in parliamentary procedure and privilege, and expressed in battles over religious and constitutional principles. They put the emphasis on very exceptional occurrences, which, in addition, they misread by evaluating them as signs of a conflict between autocratic rulers and constitutionalist leaders in the Commons—conflicts that supposedly grew steadily more serious and in the end produced the confrontation of the civil war. Convincing though this picture could be at a very superficial level, and reflecting though it did propagandist explanations first put forward by the parliamentary side in the war, it simply falsifies what really went on and has proved as misleading as it has proved persistent. The Parliament of England was a part of the king's government, brought into intermittent existence by his summons and dismissed or prorogued at his will. It constituted the ultimate manifestation of government in action, with total competence over all affairs of state and church. Parliamentary law defined not only treason but also the sole lawful form of religion. Although the initiative in legislating for aspects of government remained with the crown, the existence and role of Parliament certainly meant that in this ultimate exercise of his powers the monarch was associated with a representative of the whole governing order sitting in assembly. Although Parliament originated in the thirteenth century, it underwent a transformation between about 1484 and 1536. Out of this transformation came the familiar institution of three equipollent partners—king, Lords, and Commons, each a part of the Parliament. The king, as head, had a place of formal preeminence, and the Lords were socially and politically superior to the Commons. In parliamentary terms, however, they were all equally essential to the existence and the work of the institution: while the king could veto what the other partners had agreed, so could either house kill bills passed by the other or urgently put forward by the crown. In constitutional principle, therefore, all three entities stood on one level, though in political reality the Commons came last and mattered least—true throughout the period in question.

The three parts had to agree for anything to be achieved, and of the three two consisted of scores or even hundreds of people. The necessary agreement, therefore, could be easily upset by even minor disagreements, so that Parliament required regular management and careful guidance by the king's ministers. Councillors always sat in Parliament, in one house or the other, responsible for seeing to it that the purposes for which the crown had called a Parliament were carried through. In this task they had the help of the Speaker of the Commons (then invariably a government appointee), of the judges and other lawyers who sat as assistants in the upper house, and of men in both houses who, though not formally officeholders, were attached to leading councillors and worked on their behalf. We now call these unofficial leaders "men of business," a term familiar in parliamentary history down to the later nineteenth century. They were regular attenders at sittings—a fact that distinguished them from the larger part of the Commons and a not negligible part of the Lords—and they made themselves responsible for seeing to it that the business of the session got done. No one, of course, could guarantee such success: opinion and interest varied greatly within Parliament, which could be managed but not coerced. Difficulties and conflict certainly occurred, but such incidents arose from immediate and often factious explosions; they did not constitute the really important history of Parliament as a body.

True to the conventional language of the day, Parliament was called a court—the highest royal court in the land—but its activities rarely resembled those of a genuine court, and when it acted curially it was the Lords who carried out that function. Its actual purposes were of two kinds: the granting of taxes and the making of laws. It had established its control over both functions in the middle of the fourteenth century. Taxes, supposedly for extraordinary needs (war or defensive preparation for war), had since the 1530s been regularly requested for the general costs of government. They consisted of the customs duties (voted in this age for the monarch's life in the Tunnage and Poundage Acts passed in the first Parliament of each reign) and the special income taxes (subsidies) granted as demanded on occasion. Elizabeth asked for money in all but one of the thirteen ses-

sions of her ten Parliaments. James's four Parliaments and eight sessions voted only three grants of taxation, though his demands on those three occasions ranged higher. The penury of government and the consequent "power of the purse" vested in the Commons have traditionally been regarded as the greatest bulwark of parliamentary freedom and the greatest weakness of the crown in facing the representatives, but it should be noted that these grants rarely caused any dispute at all and became something of a routine, provided they remained at the traditional level. They did, however, begin (in 1571) to provide an opportunity for bringing forward complaints and requests for remedies, which by the eighteenth century was to make tax bills an opportunity for general political discussion.

The making of laws took up most of the time of Parliament. Invariably the majority of bills presented failed to pass, usually because their originators abandoned them in the course of the proceedings or for lack of time. Bills originated with a great variety of promoters: the Privy Council, towns, particular mercantile or manufacturing interests, or individuals interested in matters of both general and personal concern.

Acts were either public (printed at the end of the session and thus deemed to be universally known) or private (not printed and therefore needing to be presented in a certified copy if pleaded in litigation). Public acts dealt mainly with the affairs of crown and state: confirmation of royal powers; settlement of religion; treasons and other crimes; the control and promotion of husbandry, manufacture, and commerce; and reforms of the law. Private acts, according to a ruling of 1607, could not affect more than three counties. They attended to the needs of the localities (for instance, the levying of town rates for bridge building or road repairs, or the embodying in statute of private agreements touching such things as riparian rights or the enclosing of open fields), or of individuals and their families (naturalization, removal of disabilities, marriage settlements).

Thus the ordinary business of Parliament involved the interests of a great many people, individuals as well as communities (not to mention the community of the whole realm), and for obvious reasons the individuals in question tended to be propertied and therefore influential. A long absence of Parliament probably caused more annoyance because it prevented private legislation than because it was perceived as some sort of a threat to the liberties of the subject. Until 1628, any mention of liberty and privilege in Parliament almost always signified the liberties and privileges of its members, not of the community at large.

The making of laws, however, could have a wider political side to it, a fact that emphasizes a further function of Parliament beyond the normal business of the session. In the common constitutional theory of the day, Parliament was the nation in assembly, present in person (king and lords, including the bishops) or by representation (knights for the shires, citizens and burgesses for cities and boroughs). The principle had been exemplified in the reign of Henry VIII when the creation of a unitary realm had been accompanied by the calling of members from hitherto unrepresented regions (Calais, Wales, Cheshire; only Durham was, inexplicably, left out). From its earliest days, the announced purpose of the assembly had included the bringing up of problems by the localities and the presentation of urgent matters by the crown; not without reason was Parliament often called the great council of the realm. For the king, it was an efficient national forum for hearing complaints and disseminating information. Inevitably, however, Parliament came to be involved in issues that concerned government—inevitably, naturally, and justly, since it was itself a special instrument of royal rule. Thus all parts of Parliament cooperated in settling the Church of England (1559), considered the political problems raised by the treasons hatched around Mary Queen of Scots (1572, 1587), found themselves exercised over the prosecution of the Spanish war and its economic consequences (in 1597 and 1601 the cause of angry exchanges over burdensome monopolies granted by the crown), were approached when James wished to promote his dream of a union of England and Scotland (1606), and debated iniquities committed by the ministers of the crown (1621, 1624).

Normally these issues were brought forward by the crown managers, as were all but the third example mentioned above. Elizabeth, however, found that some members of the Commons were eager to initiate discussions on touchy subjects, such as the further reform of the church or the uncertainties of the succession. She therefore invented a distinction between matters of the common weal, properly raised in Parliament by anybody, and matters of state, which could be discussed only with her permission. By the next reign this distinction—untenable because the line of demarcation rested with the sovereign's arbitrary decision—had ceased to operate, though it should be noted that matters of state (Edward I's "grosses besoignes") continued to be put before the houses by members of the king's government. Privy Council initiatives unleashed the troublesome parliamentary demand of 1566 that the queen should secure the succession to the throne, and Privy Council politics promoted the so-called impeachments of royal servants in James I's last two Parliaments.

Such controversies, and the constitutional debates occasionally arising from them, do not testify to the existence of opposition parties or the rise of the Commons, but to the fact that Parliament was not only a legislative body but also an important arena of politics—a place where problems of state and nation could be discussed, fought over, and sometimes resolved by legislation. Parliament offered a convenient instrument for the antagonists in real politics, the politics of the king's Court and Council. So-called opposition nearly always turns out to be a maneuver of councillors against councillors, or a more united attempt to force the sovereign into decisions that pressure in Council had not succeeded in making him adopt. The very occasional cases of opposition by one man or a small group not associated with government never got anywhere at all and were stifled by majority opinion in one house or the other. It is only toward the end of the period and really only in the reign of Charles I that a new kind of opposition began to make itself felt—the opposition of ambitious politicians seeking service under the crown and compelled by the monopoly of favor enjoyed by the duke of Buckingham to show themselves enough of a nuisance for king and duke to decide that buying them off with office was worth the candle.

So much for the structure of government. The discussion has now brought us to the highly complex and confusing problems that a systematic analysis of the means of rule tends to hide. Politics used the system but also altered and even perverted it.

Politics

The structure of courts, offices, secretaries, bishops, and high commissions worked effectively only insofar as it took account of the existing social structure and the distribution of power within it. This society was plainly hierarchic: every man's place and function were defined in relation to those above and those below him. Only the king had no superiors (except God), and only landless and masterless men had no inferiors. Movement up and down the scale was certainly possible for individuals and their families; fortunes in this "mobile" society notoriously rose and fell, either through changes in a man's wealth or through the crown's ability to raise inferiors to higher places. But individuals moving upward, or for that matter down, did not alter the ladder on which their climbing and falling took place. By the later sixteenth century there was no truly unfree man left in England; serfdom had in fact disappeared under the pressure of economic facts, though it was never formally abolished. But the free men of England differed widely in status: each had a position in a many-layered structure of social degrees in which a term like *class* has no meaning. This structure is conveniently illustrated in the range of correct forms of address, from a duke's or archbishop's "grace" to the husbandman's "goodman."

One great dividing line separated those who exercised rule from those who did not, the latter on the face of it composing the great majority of Englishmen; but since trial juries and village adjudicators included husbandmen, even this distinction lacked genuine precision. Another line divided men and women, for women in the theory of the law lacked all independence and stood permanently in the tutelage of their fathers or husbands; however, in practice many women, especially widows but also spinsters and even wives, controlled their own affairs and property despite the law and with the frequent assistance of the court of Chancery. One of the more piteous but not uncommon figures of the age was the great landowner whose mother survived his inheritance of the estate by thirty years or more, during which time she by law possessed at least a third of what was nominally his and in the process very likely ruined him.

Such a structure by degree is theoretically coherent but in practice needs a social glue if ambition and ruthlessness are not to make it fly apart. And what held it together is commonly called the patronage system. This familiar term is usually interpreted as either a bond of loyalties or a form of pervasive corruption, but in fact it was neither. It meant simply that the relations between superior and inferior were anchored in the possession by the former (the patron) of desirable goods that the latter (the client) sought to attain in return for supporting his patron's causes. The desirable goods ranged from outright gifts to the bestowal of profitable offices and landed possessions to protection and assistance in any difficulties the client might find himself in. The returns made by the client included both active aid—for instance, by voting in parliamentary elections or by supplying physical force for the patron's proceedings—and the less substantial but equally important support that the possession of a large following gave to a patron's standing. Every man of substance depended for his influence on attracting the services of inferiors and therefore on his ability, exercised or potential, to satisfy his clients' requirements.

These relationships and their political maneuvers pervaded all society, especially among the ruling elite. In no sense did they amount to corruption, though abuse of the system had led in the fifteenth century to the emergence under the crown of lesser rulers with private armies and the means to subvert the instruments of the law for private advantage. Of this kind of corruption very little survived into the later sixteenth century, by which time the crown had firmly reestablished its overall control of society. This control was possible because, of all patrons, only the king was nobody's client, and he possessed far and away the largest reservoir of the goods that clients wished to obtain.

Thus the patronage system underpinned the monarchy, but it also qualified the dominance of the monarch in two ways. In the first place, if the central government wished to make itself felt in the provinces, and especially if it wished to carry through the enforcement of law and order or the maintenance of religious uniformity, it needed to retain the active cooperation of the hierarchically ordered society over which it presided. Government might be "bureaucratic" at the center, with civil servants doing more or less as they were told, but its exercise in the localities meant using men who could not be ordered about in this fashion. The power of these men to carry into effect the commands received from the center depended on their standing at the point of action: though possession of a royal commission enhanced their status, they could exact obedience as noblemen or leading gentlemen rather than as servants of the crown. This fact gave them a measure of independence and something of a bargaining counter when they wished to secure the recompenses of the patronage system in return for doing the government's work.

The real power in the shires rested with the local

aristocracy and gentry, often deliberately pro-moted by the crown against some hostile interest. They had to be kept reasonably content with fa-vors, and their deeper convictions needed regard and respect. Much the same conditions, in a smaller way, applied to the oligarchs who ruled the towns, though few towns—London being the great excep-tion—could afford to do without the patronage of some great man in the neighborhood, who in turn derived prestige from holding an honorific sine-cure in the towns within his patronage structure. The earl of Leicester picked up high stewardships of boroughs with the same zest that Lord Burghley applied to the high stewardships of the two univer-sities. Royal power was thus clearly, if often unsys-tematically and unpredictably, limited by the need to carry "the country" along in the framing and execution of policy. If orders were issued that went counter to the interests of the local rulers, they were either ignored or, if the government insisted on their execution, produced the sort of relentless pressure that threatened future loyalties.

In this respect a real difference should be noted between the age of Elizabeth and that of her succes-sor. Elizabeth's government kept carefully in touch with the localities and knew both men and public opinion throughout the realm very well. Lord Burghley decorated a wall of his house with a map of the English counties that showed the leading families in every region, and his correspondence was in great part a continuing flow from and to the people who ruled locally. The inflow offered de-tailed information on what was going on or being said, as well as requests for favor; the outflow re-sponded with exhortations, instructions, promises, and reassurance. In consequence Elizabethan gov-ernment could expect its orders (which it tailored to circumstances) to be obeyed. It rarely needed to pander to independent men in the shires; it worked on known ground and through familiar people, preventing opposition or noncooperation by an-ticipating such difficulties rather than by confront-ing them when they showed themselves.

James I and his ministers, especially after the decline of the earl of Salisbury in the later 1600s, lost this close touch with the people on whose cooperation they so manifestly depended. The re-sults were uncertain relations, an inability to get orders carried out, a widening split on such basic issues as those of religious diversity, and ultimately an increasing alienation of the country from the court—an alienation that, as the next reign was to

show, could easily supply disaffected court politi-cians with disquieting support in their political struggles at the center.

Politics in the Elizabethan counties characteris-tically revolved around the efforts of local rivals to secure crown favor, a state of affairs that clearly improved the crown's freedom of action. All men of ambition wooed the court, which in return had very little wooing of its own to do, provided it continued to use its advantage with instructed care and informed good sense. In the next reign, shire politics increasingly testified to the existence of local parties, only one of which had much hope of enjoying court favor. The other tried vainly to break into what had become a charmed circle and thus came to regard king and court not with greed and loyalty, but with disappointment and distrust.

The other circumstance that limited the mon-arch's power of patronage sprang from the elemen-tary fact that kings could grant only such requests as came to their knowledge. Petitions had to be presented before they could be answered. This gave great importance, at times amounting to polit-ical control, to the normal channels for such com-munications, and in the first place this meant the secretary or secretaries of state. Apart from prepar-ing the Council's business and carrying most of its decisions into effect, apart from managing foreign affairs by their conduct of the necessary correspon-dence and their collection of intelligence, the secre-taries enjoyed great power by virtue of their regu-lar access to the sovereign.

Their only real rivals in this matter were the monarch's personal attendants—ladies and a few gentlemen of the Privy Chamber under Elizabeth (who quite deliberately withheld political power from her female companions), gentlemen of the Privy Chamber and Bedchamber under James I. Of course, men specially favored—such as the earl of Leicester (Robert Dudley) under Elizabeth or the earl of Somerset (Robert Carr) under James—could at times bypass normal channels and offer a good service to urgent clients, but in the total oper-ation of the royal patronage their interventions played a minor part. Even they quite often worked through the secretary or the Privy Chamber. It may be supposed that, as royal favorites, they could hope for a more compliant response from those necessary intermediaries than could most men, but the intermediaries remained necessary.

The rule of the Cecils at court (unsuitably un-glamorous though their personalities were) extended with mild interruptions from 1558 to 1612, and it rested upon the possession of the secretaryship, alternating with solid alliances with other secretaries, such as Francis Walsingham. Walsingham died in 1590, and when the queen delayed for six years before appointing Robert Cecil to his place, old Burghley, while training his son for the job, reassumed duties he had formally dropped in 1572. Jacobean secretaries—generally men of lesser mettle, truly executive officers rather than leading politicians—did not forget the lesson taught by the Cecils. Their lack of luster has been mistaken for a lack of importance: behind the scenes, through their control of access to the king, they maintained an influence that historians seem to have failed to notice. James, admittedly, made himself generally more accessible than Elizabeth had done; he could be petitioned directly while on horseback, hunting at Royston or Newmarket.

This aspect of the patronage system subjected the king to the maneuvers, desires, and even conspiracies of men who were nominally servants but in practice could become masters. In the 1620s George Villiers, duke of Buckingham, worked to monopolize control of the king and with it control of the royal patronage. Buckingham's success proved disastrous because it alienated the neglected sector of the ruling caste, probably the chief single cause of the crisis of 1640–1642. He secured his influence by the ruthless exploitation of the two things that shaped court politics—royal favor and the building of factions.

Factions were the visible organization (perhaps too strong a word) of patrons and their followers for securing political and financial benefits. Factional organization ran through the whole of this hierarchic society but became most manifest at court (where it organized the exploitation of patronage) and much less evident in Council (where it could supposedly organize the promotion of rival policies). In the shires, factions appear to have shifted rather loosely with personalities and in response to events, but family alliances at times gave them stability and endurance. Elizabeth, well aware of the difficulties that her dependence on others for information about the realm created for her, liked to balance her factions. James tended to fall into the hands of his factions, though for much of his reign he also managed to keep them dangling and to preserve some real freedom of action. The factions of court politicians stretched through the realm by the attachment to them of people and factions in shires and boroughs, and many political struggles of the day cannot be understood unless that fact is kept in mind.

At the same time, the prevalence and especially the permanence of factions can be exaggerated. The power of a leader depended entirely on his ability to produce the goods, and no following ever felt bound to adhere to a patron in adversity. Moreover, these followers included too many men themselves of weight and influence, both at court and in the country, for the nominal leaders to be able to act as they pleased. Even as the patronage system limited the power of the crown, so it also forced politicians to observe the limitations set by their clients' individual strength and status.

The influence of faction, weakened by the willingness of followers to switch allegiance if it seemed prudent to do so, was further reduced by the readiness of wiser politicians to address also men who technically did not belong to their clientele in terms of friendship, favor, and consideration. The Cecils throughout made a point of offering assistance to anybody willing to respond, without insisting that everyone so favored should regard himself as a Cecilian: in a way, they copied the crown in refusing to confine themselves to a fixed set of useful acquaintances. On the other hand, people like Leicester, the Howard clan under James, and ultimately Buckingham, who tended to demand a firm attachment from those they aided, in the end ruined the usefulness and flexibility of the faction system. Efforts to create monopolies over benefits and to make them available only to those who humbly acknowledged their service to the patron put too high a premium on self-interest and too low a premium on friendship. Few even of Buckingham's clients had sufficient respect for him to give him loyalty, and he came to depend solely on the king's favor.

An earlier danger signal had appeared with the entry upon the political stage of Robert, earl of Essex, in the late 1580s. Essex tried far too blatantly to create a national network of faction for himself, a hectic enterprise that shocked solid politicians, surrounded him with men of neither weight nor sense, and aroused the fatal suspicions of the queen. His faction-building forced Robert Cecil to practice similar tactics, though it was largely Cecil's refusal to appear in public as a leader of a faction that gained him his victory at court and with his sovereign. If Essex had been successful, faction would have hardened into party, a state of affairs that no tenant of the throne could have tolerated—Elizabeth allowed Essex's fate to demonstrate that truth for the benefit of other ambitious men. The ruin of Essex enabled Cecil to return to the wiser policy of treating faction as only one element (and a fluid one at that) in the power structure upon which he rested his government of the realm in the first years of James's reign.

Faction both local and central thus grew out of the search for influence by means of which power and profit might be obtained. Because factions rather obviously embodied plain self-interest, despite all the professions of undying friendship, they never could be anything but fluid so long as kings avoided putting themselves into fetters by giving sole favor to one faction leader. Men calculating the advantages of the Tudor and especially the Stuart courts could not afford to let themselves be moved by loyalties and sentiments. Faction was therefore a poor instrument for the working out of policy; those who followed power in the search for wealth used faction, those who sought power for the purpose of directing affairs knew that faction by itself could not aid them.

Royal policy dealt in effect with two areas of government: relations with other kings and nations, and the control of the realm. It is quite evident that in the minds of kings and queens the former came first, which distinguishes royal concerns from those of modern historians. Both Elizabeth and James saw themselves above all as members of an international clan of monarchs; the problems raised by these relations—diplomacy and war—preoccupied them. Internal policy necessarily included the assuaging of "grievances" (that is, balancing of rival interests seeking wealth and welfare), though it should be noted that enough of these demands involved the protection of domestic trade and manufacture to have international implications. More strictly internal were the issues of public order and obedience, usually left entirely to the Council and its subordinate agencies. Aside from all this, there were the problems of the church —uniformity and dissent—which, thanks to the aggressive policies of the Counter-Reformation papacy and the European Calvinist network, also had their international aspects.

In these matters faction should have played little part: policy, it was generally agreed, was the work of a monarch presiding over a united nation in whose interest he or she governed, and successful monarchs managed to make a reality of the ideal, as Elizabeth usually did and the Stuarts usually failed to do. But policy also, of necessity, produced differences of opinion concerning both what should be done and how it should be achieved. Policy therefore supplied the one element to faction that made it more than a device for seeking power and wealth, the one constituent part that could give it endurance. That element was principle, or (as we are now taught to call it) ideology. Relations with other powers involved basic principles of alliance or opposition and always entailed the possibility of armed conflict; thus one can usually find peace and war parties at court and in Council who held to their convictions with persistence and assurance. In an age of religious wars, both foreign relations and the internal problem of uniformity infused policy with principles of the faith, and divisions among makers of policy often arose out of varying zeal for the Protestant cause. In the 1570s and 1580s, the threat of Spain, seen by some as an overbearing and by others as a Catholic power, created a real rift on the Council between those (Leicester, Hatton, Walsingham) who called for active resistance and war, and those (Burghley in particular) who regarded peace as essential to the survival of England and held that the cause of Protestantism could be better protected by diplomacy and guile. From about 1587 all policy was profoundly affected by the long war with Spain, complicated by the equally prolonged endeavor to reestablish English rule over all of Ireland. Though James concluded the former and inherited the accomplishment of the latter, his policies consisted in great part of reactions to the strains produced by the continued hostilities in the Netherlands, by the rivalry of Spain and France, and from 1621 by the outbreak of what was to become the Thirty Years' War, in which England was directly (though very ineffectually) involved through the marriage of James's daughter Elizabeth to the elector palatine, briefly king of Bohemia and thereafter (1620) an exile at The Hague.

High politics, then, responded much less to domestic issues or power struggles within the gentry and aristocracy than to the international stresses of a much disturbed age—stresses in which religion played a leading role. Even though some statesmen might try to write religion out of politics and pursue national or dynastic interests in bare purity, those whom they governed and on whose cooperation they depended very often made religion a principle that transcended self-interest. A typical effect of these complications can be seen when James made peace with Spain: he immediately and irreversibly aroused anger and distrust both among ardent Protestants and among those (especially the organizers of maritime war and plunder) who had found the war profitable—sometimes, of course, the same men. The religious (or indeed the economic) concerns of the nation, represented at court by politicians who were more than faction leaders but less than independent statesmen, formed one of the conditions for policy. Another arose from the equally principled concerns of other powers, usually represented by strictly unprincipled agents; the politics of the English court derived in no small measure from the conspiratorial activities of foreign ambassadors seeking to exploit faction and to influence the English monarch's decisions.

There is still much to be learned about the manner in which policy was actually made, and since the process often took place either in the monarch's mind or in unrecorded conversations, much of it will always remain obscure. Yet it seems clear that the role of faction can easily be overestimated. The Elizabethan and Jacobean factions found it difficult to accommodate principle because their whole essence lay in the pursuit of interest that an excessive devotion to principle could only hinder; it might easily tie a man to a declining patron and therefore destroy for him the very virtue of faction.

The so-called factions arrayed in the Council for the pursuit of policy ought not to be given that name. They were really groupings of individuals —leaders, not followers—that rested on perceptions of political problems and on genuine personal convictions that often derived from faith. Zeal for the Reformation animated many of them, and even more were certain that they faced a popish plot of one kind or another, an apprehension that became well entrenched after the arrival in England of Mary Queen of Scots (1568) and, thanks to the Spanish war and the Gunpowder Plot, easily survived her execution (1587). These attitudes determined much of the advice the monarch received and acted on. They pushed people into cooperation with like-minded colleagues and led to confrontations in Council and elsewhere, but they operated against the sort of factions that derived from local connections and purely mate-

rial ambitions. The politics of the age revolved around two fundamental pivots—power and principle—and according to the problems faced were directed either by unprincipled aspiration or by inner convictions of an ideological kind. Only Queen Elizabeth seems to have been entirely immune to ideology, unless her vanity and self-assertion deserve that name; she alone conducted policy with an eye solely to her success as a monarch and a symbol of national unity. James, in person much less suited to act as such a symbol, shared her vanity, but in his case it took the form of claims to intellectual eminence, which made him an ideologue in matters of religion.

Thus the structure of its government made England a monarchy limited by the rule of the law, but not a constitutional monarchy limited by the counterweight of Parliament, which was really an instrument of royal government. In actual practice, the real limitations on monarchy sprang from political realities that rendered the king dependent on others for advice, cooperation, and effectiveness in rule; without the willingness to act shown by a hierarchy of people over whom no real means of compulsion existed royal government hardly existed. The Tudors knew how to make their government much more effective than such generalizations might suggest; their control of patronage enabled them to hold the nation together and secure loyalties. Despite divisions and serious disagreements (visible at times in Parliament but more commonly in the everyday operation of political ambition and strife), the sentiments of nationalism and Protestantism were powerful bonds within the nation as well as between the nation and its head.

Doubts and more than doubts concerning this system of government have often been expressed, and some would call it ramshackle. This it never was, though by the standards of the twentieth century it was loose and flexible: it worked, provided it was operated with political awareness and skill. No king could afford to act as though the theory of absolute monarchy really described its practical possibilities, and no king could safely ignore the claims, rights, and demands of powerful groups or individuals within his society. Yet by the standards of its own day, the England of Elizabeth and James was a coherent and much governed country, improving in internal order, in wealth and standing, and (not to be forgotten) in the production of a high culture.

BIBLIOGRAPHY

Items marked * contain useful bibliographies.

Gerald E. Aylmer, *The King's Servants: The Civil Service of Charles I* (1961). John H. Baker, "Criminal Courts and Procedure at Common Law 1550–1800," in James S. Cockburn, ed., *Crime in England 1500–1800* (1977). Thomas G. Barnes, *Somerset 1625–1640* (1961). Bernard Beckingsale, *Burghley: Tudor Statesman* (1967). Nicholas Canny, *The Upstart Earl: A Study of the Social and Mental World of Richard Boyle, First Earl of Cork* (1982). Charles H. Carter, "Diplomatic Intervention in English Law Enforcement: Sarmiento and James I," in DeLloyd J. Guth and John W. McKenna, eds., *Tudor Rule and Revolution* (1983). Maria Cioni, "The Elizabethan Chancery and Women's Rights," ibid. Patrick Collinson, *The Elizabethan Puritan Movement* (1967) and *English Puritanism* (1983). Mary Dewar, ed., *De Republica Anglorum by Sir Thomas Smith* (1982).

*Geoffrey R. Elton, *England Under the Tudors* (1955; rev. 1974) and "Parliament in the Sixteenth Century: Functions and Fortunes," in *Studies in Tudor and Stuart Politics and Government,* III (1983). *Geoffrey R. Elton, ed., *The Tudor Constitution* (1960; rev. 1982). Michael A. R. Graves, "Thomas Norton the Parliament Man: An Elizabethan M.P., 1559–1581," in *Historical Journal,* 23 (1980). Rudolf W. Heinze, "Proclamations and Parliamentary Protest, 1539—1610," in DeLloyd J. Guth and John W. McKenna, eds., *Tudor Rule and Revolution* (1983). Ralph Houlbrooke, *Church Courts and the People During the English Reformation, 1520–1570* (1979). Joel Hurstfield, *The Queen's Wards: Wardship and Marriage Under Elizabeth I* (1958) and "Church and State, 1558–1612," in *Freedom, Corruption and Government in Elizabethan England* (1973).

William John Jones, *The Elizabethan Court of Chancery* (1967). *John P. Kenyon, ed., *The Stuart Constitution* (1966). Sheila Lambert, "Procedure in the House of Commons in the Early Stuart Period," in *English Historical Review,* 95 (1980). David M. Loades, *Politics and the Nation 1450–1660: Obedience, Resistance and Public Order* (1974). Roger Lockyer, *Buckingham* (1981). Wallace T. MacCaffrey, "Place and Patronage in Elizabethan Politics," in S. T. Bindoff, Joel Hurstfield, and C. H. Williams, eds., *Elizabethan Government and Society* (1961). Ronald A. Marchant, *The Church Under the Law: Justice, Administration and Discipline in the Diocese of York 1560–1640* (1969). John E. Neale, "The Elizabethan Political Scene," in *Essays in Elizabethan History* (1958).

Linda L. Peck, *Northampton: Patronage and Policy at the Court of James I* (1982). Menna Prestwich, *Cranfield: Politics and Profits Under the Early Stuarts* (1966). Conrad Russell, "Parliamentary History in Perspective, 1604–29," in *History,* 61 (1976). Kevin Sharpe, ed., *Faction and Parliament: Essays on Early Stuart History* (1978). Alan G. R. Smith, ed., *The Reign of James VI and I* (1973). A. Hassell Smith, *Court and Country: Government and Politics in Norfolk 1558–1603* (1974). Penry Williams, *The Tudor Regime* (1979). Frederic A. Youngs, Jr., *The Proclamations of the Tudor Queens* (1976).

The Church:
Religion and Its Manifestations

PATRICK COLLINSON

The world into which William Shakespeare was born was fragmented, with, in John Donne's telling phrase, all coherence gone. Shakespeare and countless others of his generation did not know what to believe or, if they did, could not tell when they might be called on to believe contrary things. Like all human systems, the medieval church had been wracked with strife and occasionally plunged into constitutional crisis. Head and members were chronically discordant, and for forty years in the late fourteenth and early fifteenth centuries there had been two and even three heads. But apart from a handful of heretics who put themselves outside society there had been an underlying unity of belief, which, if anything, was strengthened by diversity and debate among the theological schools and tendencies.

The major conflict of the sixteenth century was sufficiently deep-seated and complex to shatter the unity of Western Christendom irreparably because it concerned matters of belief that either were fundamental or were perceived to be fundamental, especially by Martin Luther. This German Augustinian canon boasted that whereas others before him had assaulted the corrupt life of the church (and none more recently or devastatingly than Erasmus of Rotterdam), he was the first to attack church doctrine. Luther did so first in the private agony of his religious and theological consciousness as a monk, a pastor of souls, and a university professor at Wittenberg in Saxony; later, in public challenges to the prevailing schools of systematic

theology; and finally, in questioning the principle and abused practice of granting indulgences, whereby the pope offered to reduce the penalties of sin, not only temporally but eternally—at a price. This protest, articulated in the Ninety-five Theses of October 1517, sparked the conflagration of the Reformation, for it drew Luther ever deeper into controversy that sharpened the edge of his own critical convictions, deepened the gulf separating him from the magisterium of the church, and aroused immense public interest and sympathy.

At a debate in Leipzig in June and July 1519, Luther set the individual conscience grounded in Scripture above pope and council. In 1520, in *De Captivitate Babylonica Ecclesiae Praeludium* (*The Babylonian Captivity of the Church,* to which Henry VIII of England wrote a rejoinder), he denounced as a conspiracy and a fraud the entire sacramental scheme of attaining grace. Excommunicated, he burned the papal bull that banned him and added the canon law to the flames. In 1521 he refused to recant before the emperor at Worms, a moment that the nineteenth century saw as the most pregnant in human history. At an imperial diet in 1529, a formal protest (the *Protestatio*) by Luther's supporters among the German princes gave rise to the new designation *Protestant.* The next year, the new Lutheran theology was codified by Luther's orderly colleague Philip Melanchthon in the Augsburg Confession. When Rome responded to the challenge by convening the Council of Trent, which met intermittently between 1545 and 1563, Catholicism agreed with Luther that the differences between them were past healing and paid him the compliment of defining itself by a series of confutations of what was now known as Protestantism.

At the heart of Protestantism was Luther's conviction, which he equated with the Gospel itself, that man is justified in the sight of God not by any virtue inherent in himself or by any striving on his part but by God's unmerited grace, made available by Christ's death and appropriated by faith, understood as a deeply trustful commitment to God's mercy of the whole being, itself an act of which man was incapable until enabled by the Holy Spirit and enlightened by the Word of God contained in the Bible. Justification was an instantaneous transaction. Thereafter, the justified man, still burdened with his sinful nature but seen by God as just, served God and his neighbor, not slavishly in order to gain a reward but in a spirit of free thanksgiving. The strong stress of Luther's dialectic excluded any compromise of these evangelical principles. The Reformation slogans were "Grace alone," "Faith alone," and "Scripture alone."

The immediate effect on those who responded to this theology was the destruction of the motivation with which almost all pious acts, individual and corporate, had been undertaken. Salvation was not to be earned through continual attendance at mass, by the daily sacrifice of Christ's body and blood at the altar, in pilgrimage and prayers to saints, or least of all in the ascetic disciplines of the monastic life. There was no room in Protestantism for the spiritual rule of a priestly hierarchy that controlled these things and claimed a special competence in them. The church was now to consist of a listening people, a flock, as Luther once said, that hears its shepherd's whistle. The place occupied in Catholic worship by the altar, half-hidden from the congregation by a screen, was now taken by the Bible on a lectern and by the pulpit. Ears and voices were exercised rather than eyes.

Protestants retained the two sacraments of the Lord's Supper and baptism, and Luther invested them with great material value, as the means by which God ratifies and even conveys himself to the believer. Luther is often said to have taught "consubstantiation" rather than the "transubstantiation" of Roman Catholicism. In fact he eschewed all philosophical explanations of the real presence of Christ's body in the sacrament and simply asserted it as a mysterious fact, to the offense not only of Catholics but of other Protestant reformers for

whom it was a merely spiritual and symbolic presence. For in the secondary reformations that sprang up in Switzerland and South Germany, initially under the inspiration of the Zurich preacher Huldreich Zwingli, the spiritual, invisible properties of God and his service were strongly emphasized and a more drastic, iconoclastic approach to traditional images and forms was taken. This "best reformed" branch of Protestantism developed in theological and geographical isolation from the Lutheran, or "Evangelical," branch and was set in order, doctrinally and institutionally, by John Calvin in the model of a Christian society that he built up in Geneva and in his great theological work *The Institutes of the Christian Religion* (1536).

The English church would eventually veer toward, and even anchor itself in, the Calvinist, or "Reformed," tradition, but only after many changes of course. In the 1530s, in the midst of a dynastic and political crisis, it was detached from Rome by Henry VIII and his minister Thomas Cromwell and placed under royal supremacy, but without at first committing itself doctrinally or liturgically to Protestantism. That followed in the reign of the boy king Edward VI (1547–1553), when the Swiss model began to prevail, especially in the second version of the new English service book, the Book of Common Prayer of 1552. The English Reformed Church received its confession of faith in the Forty-two Articles of Religion of 1553, revised in the reign of Elizabeth as the Thirty-nine Articles, but an attempt to revise the canon law of the church in a reformed sense in the *Reformatio Legum* was abortive. In the reign of Edward's elder half sister Mary (1553–1558) there was virtually a complete reaction and Catholic restoration, accompanied by active persecution of Protestants of all persuasions. But on 17 November 1558, Mary died, to be succeeded by Elizabeth (1558–1603), who was the child of her father's breach with Rome.

In 1564, the year of Shakespeare's birth, the bishop of the diocese in which Stratford-upon-Avon lay wrote, "The right waie to stablishe a kingedome is first to rectifie religion: where god is trulie Sought, there is greate Safetie" (Bateson). The Catholic Mary would not have dissented. But Mary had been dead for five years, and Bishop Sandys' advice was now to be understood in a contrary sense. Queen Elizabeth's Act of Uniformity of 1559 required the clergy to make exclusive use in all ministrations of the 1552 Book of Common Prayer, with a few stipulated changes, and further required "all and every person and persons inhabiting within this realm" to resort to their parish church on Sundays and holy days "and then and there to abide orderly and soberly during the time of the common prayer, preachings, or other service of God."

The statute invoked sanctions as severe as life imprisonment for obstinate and persistent refusal to use the Prayer Book or for denouncing it, while those neglecting to come to church and having no valid excuse for absence were subject to ecclesiastical censure and pecuniary fine. Yet in the second Parliament of the new reign the lord keeper, Sir Nicholas Bacon, complained that the act was not in force: "How commeth it to pass that the common people in the country universally come so seldom to common prayer and divine service?"

The Preface to the Prayer Book declared its intention to "appease" diversity of practice so that "all the whole realm shall have but one use." In principle, at a certain hour on a Sunday morning, the entire population should have been occupied in the same action, hearing and repeating the same words. It is often said (Francis Bacon said it first) that Queen Elizabeth had no desire to open windows in men's souls. However, the Elizabethan formularies imply a uniformity of mentality no less than of behavior. Notorious and extreme heretics were still occasionally burned at the stake, and Catholics and some extreme Protestant dissenters were executed for reasons hard to disentangle from their sectarian beliefs. Lesser heterodoxies, even those disclosed in casual speech, were dealt with in the ecclesiastical courts.

Yet, after the queen had reigned for more than forty years, the West Country was reported by its bishop to be very far from the godly uniformity that the law envisaged: "Few or none come to church to pray to God for her Majesty, and for the good estate of the realm; but they will follow rattle headed preachers from town to town." Rank atheism was on the increase: "A matter very common to dispute whether there be a God or not." In contempt of religion, a goose and a gander were profanely married. At Launceston a horse's head was baptized, and in another place a whole dead horse was brought to receive the sacrament. "Every day complaints are made by ministers who are railed on and shrewdly beaten by lewd persons. A minister was made to kiss the bare hinder parts of a man" (Historical Manuscripts Commission, *Calendar of the MSS. of the Marquis of Salisbury,* 10 [1904], 450–451).

These sound more like fictions than sober fact. Scholars debate whether it was possible, in the sixteenth century, to be an atheist in any philosophical sense. Yet the historian of Tudor England who supposes that the Act of Uniformity was effectively and universally in force has failed to cross the *pons asinorum* of his subject, which is to grasp that the statute book is evidence of the aspirations of government, not a record of social reality. One has no sure means of knowing how uniform in religious practice Shakespeare's generation was. As for religious knowledge and experience, that is retrievable only for a tiny, well-documented minority. It may be that the York citizen who in the late 1570s crossed himself (and was in trouble for it) indicated thus that he still believed what Catholics believe about the pope, the saints, the Mass; on the other hand, it may just have been an old habit. Since the publication in 1971 of Keith Thomas' ambitious reconstruction of early modern mentalities, *Religion and the Decline of Magic,* it has been clear that an adequate account of Elizabethan religion must include the beliefs and practices associated with witchcraft and the fear of witchcraft, and the many forms of magic and astrology that both competed with "religion," in the modern sense, and were coexistent with it. But the extent and influence of this not yet demystified world view is strictly immeasurable.

The only available record of the religious sentiments of large numbers of Shakespeare's contemporaries is found in the preambles to wills. But such statements were copied from formularies or were contributed by the scribe who wrote the will. Shakespeare's own will is no exception to this rule. There is abundant testimony of Shakespeare's religious knowledge, of his familiarity with both Bible and Prayer Book, of his capacity to turn to dramatic effect the common themes of religion and morals. Yet his use of these resources was eclectic and aesthetically controlled, so that recent scholarship has declared his private religious views "inaccessible" (Gless), and the evidence "simply inconclusive" (Frye).

An anthropologist whose task was, as it were, to take a snapshot of the religious dimension of Elizabethan civilization at a given moment would face formidable difficulties. But the historian has a more daunting job to do, for he must trace across a century complex changes in religion and the concomitant alterations in other aspects of life. In a formal sense, England became a Protestant church and realm when the new services came into legal use on Saturday, 24 June 1559. The Act of Supremacy of 1559 had removed England from papal jurisdiction, subjecting the church to the monarch as "Supreme Governor" and to no other power on earth. The Act of Uniformity enforced church services that were vehicles of the Protestant doctrines of grace, faith, works, and sacraments, which in 1563 were to be explicitly articulated in the Thirty-nine Articles of Religion. This version of Protestantism approximated more closely to the Swiss and South German model, which claimed to be "best reformed," than to Lutheranism. (Shakespeare was to make Anne Boleyn a "spleeny" Lutheran.) To put it a little too crudely, the Church of England was now to favor Calvinism. Only in respect of ecclesiastical organization and government was the religion of England not thoroughly reconstructed in the early years of Elizabeth's reign or, indeed, subsequently. But at first few Elizabethan Protestants found episcopacy anomalous. Many early Elizabethan bishops were themselves Protestants of an advanced reformed persuasion and had spent Mary's reign in Strassburg, Zurich, or Geneva.

Beginning in the summer of 1559 with a royal "visitation" (or tour of inspection), the newly established religion was taught and enforced by "injunctions," royal and episcopal; by the catechism; by officially sanctioned sermons, or "homilies"; and by the more spontaneous word of the sermon itself, although preachers were still scarce. The legal enforcement of the official religion was entrusted in part to the Court of High Commission (or the Ecclesiastical Commissioners), a mixed tribunal of clerics and lay magistrates that exercised the powers of the royal supremacy directly. The new ways were defended against their Catholic detractors at the famous pulpit of Paul's Cross in London and in such polemical publications as Bishop John Jewel's *Apologia Ecclesiae Anglicanae* (1562), the defense of a faith allegedly not new at all but primitive and apostolic. In the anonymous interlude *New Custome* (*ca.* 1571), a character of that name repudiates her title and insists that she be called Primitive Constitution.

But none of this activity could convert England overnight into a Protestant nation. The full internalization of Protestantism was to have very far-reaching implications—negative in the abandonment of belief in religious "works," the mediation of the saints, the pains of purgatory, and related pious practices and institutions, many of which centered on the Mass and on pilgrimage to the shrines and images of saints. Protestants who were more than formal in their profession would relinquish the ingrained habit of punctuating their speech with the old familiar oaths "By the mass" and "By God's body." Outwardly, a good Protestant would be identified by his "conscionable" attachment to "godly exercises" and by regular reading of the Bible in the version prepared by English exiles in Geneva. Almost the entire Reformation process might be summarized as the reception of the English Bible by a population previously denied any direct encounter with Scripture. John Foxe's *Actes and Monuments of These Latter Perilous Days* (1563, popularly known as *The Book of Martyrs*), which carried the sacred story of God's dealings with his people into the recent past, was read "throughly" and "as a book of credit." The godly man sought out sermons and, as he went to and from them, sang psalms with his family. Inwardly, such a life was sustained by a settled belief in Providence and by that alert and anxious "walking in God's ways" commonly recorded in some of the earliest English diaries.

Communities in which the Protestant religion was taken seriously were strict observers of Sunday, the Christian Sabbath. Traditional ways of passing time on that day were reprehended. So it was that absorption of the full implications of the new faith led to a withering of the rich culture of "Merrie England," with the gradual disappearance of dancing, maypoles, and church ales. In Coventry it was decreed in 1591 that maypoles should never be set up again. But at Stratford the issue was not confronted until 1619.

Meanwhile, the medieval urban drama, consisting of mystery, miracle, and morality plays and having close ties to both religion and the social order, was coming to an end. At Coventry an exceptionally rich dramatic tradition was all but dead by 1591, although the young Shakespeare may have borrowed from some of the later performances the idea in *Hamlet* of "out-Heroding Herod." The Chester plays, which were staged for the last time in 1574, were said by a local chronicler to be of no use "excepte it be to showe the Ignorance of oure forefathers" (Clopper). In early Elizabethan York the great Corpus Christi cycle was first stripped of the more offensive plays concerning the Virgin Mary and then replaced by a more homiletical piece, the Creed Play. But even this was declared inadmissible by the dean of York and future archbishop, Matthew Hutton: "Ffor thoghe it was plausible 40 yeares agoe, and wold now also of the ignorant sort be well liked: yet now in this happie time of the gospell, I knowe the learned will mislike it and how the state will beare with it I knowe not." Presently, the York mysteries, in spite of their popularity, were finally suppressed by Archbishop Edmund Grindal, who also stopped the Wakefield plays.

As the religious drama was stifled, its place was taken by shows of a more secular character at midsummer and by the performances of troupes of strolling players. But the city fathers of York soon turned against the players; while at Chester, where the magistrates were "exclaimed upon" from the pulpit for tolerating them, citizens were even fined for going elsewhere to witness such "obscene and unlawful" entertainments. The players visited Stratford regularly in the years of Shakespeare's youth; but by the end of the century they were no longer welcome, and seven years after the poet's death they were paid to go away. By that time the itinerant drama had changed its character. The interludes brought to Elizabethan country towns seem to have been moralities, which would have reinforced municipal godliness, but now the frank secularity of the stage seemed to its critics "filthy." In spite of his coauthorship of *Gorboduc,* Thomas Norton thought theatergoing "unnecessarie and scarslie honest."

So it was that a mimetic civilization of image and myth, symbol and ritual, gave way to a more patently moralistic culture of the printed and authoritatively pronounced word. The records of the last days of the old ceremonies suggest the gulf separating old from new: in Coventry payments were recorded "to Pilate 4s. 8d." and "to God 16d."; in Chester, the cost of "guildinge of litle Gods face"; in York, an explanation that the nuts distributed by the figures of Yule and Yule's Wife in their annual procession were "in rememberance of that most noble Nut our sauiors blessed body." "Most noble Nut" indeed! In 1572 the Ecclesiastical Commissioners terminated this "very rude and barbarouse custome." In Chester in 1599, the mayor cleaned up the midsummer show, causing the "giants" who used to go in procession to be broken and substituting the martial figure of a

knight for the traditional "dragon and naked boys." The divines had complained. But later the giants came back and, with them, the devils attending men in women's costume, "to the greate dislike of them which are well disposed" (Clopper).

When can it be said that England had become a predominantly Protestant, rather than some kind of Catholic, society? The question is much debated, some authorities believing that the Reformation happened quickly by political imposition from above. Others agree on an early date but give more credit to social and genuinely religious forces, or reformation from below. Another school of thought believes that the Reformation was forced on a reluctant populace, but not effectively before the reign of Elizabeth; while others identify the "real" Reformation with Elizabethan Puritanism, a popular and irrepressible movement, equivalent to the internalization of Protestant religious values in some sections and levels of society (Haigh, 1982).

The question seems to turn on the reign of Mary. If Mary had lived, would Catholicism have stuck as both the legally enforced and willingly professed religion of most Englishmen? According to both Scarisbrick and Haigh, there was no reason for it not to have stuck. Does our impression of a popular revulsion from the Marian burnings depend entirely on John Foxe's power as a grand historical mythmaker? Perhaps. Yet it was not Foxe but W. Cunnyngham's *1564: A New Almanack*—the almanac was the most popular form of Tudor literature —that, a year after Foxe was first published in England, attributed the recent outbreak of the plague to the blood of God's martyrs crying out for revenge. And J. R. Green, in his *History of the English People* (1876), thought that it was only in the period between the middle of Elizabeth's reign and the civil war of 1642–1652 that "England became the people of a book, and that book was the Bible." He adds, "No greater moral change ever passed over a nation."

The question cannot be answered without recourse to local and regional history, for the lack of synchronization in the process of Protestantization is very marked. Many places in Essex and East Anglia were precocious in their acceptance and practice of the new religion, as was the Suffolk cloth town of Hadleigh by the reign of Mary. The same stage was probably not reached anywhere in the north until a full half-century or more later, while far into the seventeenth century a large tract of Lancashire remained frontier territory, hostile to

Protestantism. And the extreme northwest and much of Wales seemed impervious to any stirring and evangelistic religious influence, whether Protestant or Catholic. Such "dark corners of the land" were of active concern to the Long Parliament in the mid-seventeenth century.

If broad regional distinctions can be drawn, it is equally necessary to recognize that local differences of environment and occupation influenced, perhaps even determined, the response to Protestant evangelism of parishes and of individuals and groups within parishes. Just as literacy was very unevenly distributed through the social hierarchies (for example, thatchers and fishermen were almost generally illiterate; tailors and yeomen, partially literate; and printing workers, wholly literate), so it appears likely that skilled craftsmen and cloth workers responded more readily to a religion of Bible-reading and sermons than peasants and agricultural laborers. And woodland and highland zones, with their patterns of scattered settlement, diverse livelihoods, and absence of close social surveillance, provided a more fertile soil for forms of religious independence than corn-growing villages, which lived under the watchful eye of squire and parson.

In tracing and measuring the acceptance of the reformed religion, one may make a rough-and-ready distinction between, on the one hand, the almost imperceptible penetration of the language of Bible and Prayer Book as heard and absorbed in parish worship by a majority of the population, and, on the other, a more deliberate, active, instructed response to the propositions of preachers and other evangelists and to the Bible read at first hand. The first kind of exposure and response can be located in church and attributed to the reading ministry of the bulk of the clergy, disparaged by Puritans as a "bare" reading ministry without saving force, rather than to the "powerful" and "edifying" sermons of the preachers. After 1568 what was heard in church was a revision of Miles Coverdale's "Great Bible" (1539) known as the Bishops' Bible, since the episcopal bench and its chaplains shared the labor of preparing this authorized version. The more energetic response of thoroughly indoctrinated Protestants, which in many cases is describable in terms of religious conversion, was nourished as much in the home as at the parish church. "His house he endeavored to make a little church," wrote John Geree in *The Character of an Old English Puritane* (1646). It was a commonplace.

Recently, historians have increased their interest in what may be termed Prayer Book Protestantism or parish Anglicanism—the habitual, relatively unexacting religion probably characteristic of the majority of Jacobean Englishmen. To devote too much attention to the strident minorities at both religious extremities may exercise a false sense of historical priority. Moreover, there is impressive evidence from the seventeenth century of massive public resistance to religious innovations—"Arminian" or "Laudian" in the 1630s, Puritan and Presbyterian in the 1640s—which argues for deep attachment to the Prayer Book and to all that it symbolized and safeguarded in the traditional scheme of things. Yet relatively low levels of religious commitment are not in practice easy to penetrate, and it is understandable that the history of the Elizabethan church should have been written very largely with respect to the minorities, Catholic and Puritan, which stood on either side of the official via media.

Virtually no public proponent of religion in Elizabethan England believed in, or found it possible to approve of, a state of religious pluralism. It was assumed to be dangerous and unnatural for more than one religion to be tolerated within one commonwealth. Sir Nicholas Bacon, the lord keeper, voiced a common fear when he spoke of the danger that "religion, which of his own nature should be uniform, would against his nature have proved milliform, yes, in continuance nulliform" (*Remains of Edmund Grindal,* W. Nicholson, ed., 1843). If anything, the Tudor state, having eliminated all duality from government by placing authority over both church and state in the same royal hands, laid a greater and more practically enforceable stress on religious unity than had been associated with the medieval Catholic polity.

Yet the fact could not be avoided that there was more than one religion in the realm that Elizabeth inherited in 1558. One writer accurately described the church of the Elizabethan settlement as a "constrained union" of papists and Protestants. It was not possible by "one blast of Queen Elizabeth's trumpet," as another critic wrote, to turn lifelong Catholics into faithful gospelers. Neither was that necessarily Elizabeth's immediate aspiration. Insofar as the settlement of religion was based on a coherent plan, the strategy of the queen herself and her closest advisers (and this, as will be shown, is a matter still in dispute) was to comprehend the entire nation in a church somewhat of the middle way, essentially Protestant but not so nakedly Protestant as to alienate confused Catholics, of whom there were many.

A philosophical and ethical principle was implied, a version of the Aristotelian via media or golden mean, first adumbrated in the apologies for the Henrician Reformation of the 1530s made by humanists and destined to become, in a somewhat different guise, the hallmark of the Church of England in its maturity, the essence of what would later be called, but was not yet known as, Anglicanism. The via media lay between having too much, as in too great an exuberance of religious ceremony, and having too little, a denuded and degraded religion. In George Herbert's words, it was "A fine aspect in fit array,/Neither too mean, nor yet too gay." It was also a ground on which those whose opinions were in fact divergent could in some measure agree, at least in an outward harmony. When Sir Nicholas Bacon, in a closing speech at the 1559 Parliament, defended the settlement that had just been made, he warned off its detractors with these words: "Amongst thease I meane to comprehende aswell those that be to swifte as those that be to slowe, those I say that goe before the lawe or beyond the lawe as those that will not followe" (British Library, MS Harley 5176, fol. 113ᵛ).

For those reluctant to follow, the Elizabethan settlement contained some encouragement. The words with which the sacrament of the altar was communicated to the faithful were not hostile to belief in the real presence of Christ's body in the elements, thus making of this rite more than a Protestant communion for those who wished so to regard it. The queen's intention was that the form of the thing communicated should be an unleavened wafer thicker than heretofore and without the impressed marks of the passion, but otherwise not unlike the "singing cakes" of the recent past, whereas most Protestants preferred to use common bread. The sacrament should, in the queen's view, be celebrated at a kind of altar, adorned with a cross —or so the example of her own royal chapel suggests. A clause in the Act of Uniformity, with a corresponding rubric in the Prayer Book, required the clergy to wear vestments and other attire that tended to align them with the massing priesthood of Catholicism rather than with the Protestant ministry of Switzerland and South Germany. The queen wished her clergy to remain celibate, a desire she shared with many old-fashioned people;

and while most Elizabethan clerics were in fact married, the law took only grudging cognizance of the fact.

Those "reluctant to follow," for whom such concessions were intended, were very numerous. Whereas virtually all the surviving Marian bishops refused to endorse the new settlement and were removed from their positions, their example was not followed by the great majority of the inferior, parochial clergy. Most early Elizabethan parishes were therefore served by former Marian priests, accustomed to the old Latin service. Even Bishop Grindal had to say on one occasion, "I have said mass. I am sorry for it." Many were not sorry. And if the early Elizabethan church contained so many clerics who were still Catholic priests at heart, why should one suppose that the laity was any differently disposed? The likelihood is that a majority of those in the church of Shakespeare's infancy were "church papists," as they were commonly called. If not "rank papists," wrote the Essex preacher George Gifford (*The Countrie Divinitie*, 1581), such people retained "still a smack and savour of popish principles." Yet the expectation was that such "survivalists," as A. G. Dickens has called them, would in the course of time be absorbed into a broadly Protestant consensus.

Although it was something that Queen Elizabeth could scarcely admit, the success of her religious settlement depended on the preparedness of her subjects to limit the depth of their religious commitment. The paradoxically counterproductive effect of a more aggressive Protestant evangelism and apologetic, which was asserting itself even in the relatively unenthusiastic 1560s and to greater effect in the 1570s, was to stiffen the resolve of those who were still Catholic in sympathy and to inspire these stalwarts to stand up and be counted as recusants; they refused to attend Protestant services and, by this act, indicated their rejection of the queen's religion. As an enthusiastic form of Protestantism gathered strength, so by a polarizing process an authentic, resistant Catholicism began to flex its muscles. As Arnold Oskar Meyer remarked, the Reformation and Counter-Reformation coincided in Elizabethan England as mutually exacerbating forces.

The lines had been drawn in the 1560s in a battle of the books between Protestant apologists, notably John Jewel, and exiled Catholics, such as Oxford scholars like Thomas Harding, himself a former Protestant. These hostilities were on such a massive scale that they have been called the Great Controversy. Nevertheless, the real watershed was later and political. In 1569 the conservative affinities of the northern aristocracy rose, albeit without marked enthusiasm and unsuccessfully, in open revolt against the Elizabethan regime. They were encouraged by the presence in England since 1568 of the captive Scottish queen, Mary, a plausible claimant to the English throne, and by their reading of certain international signals. In the bull *Regnans in excelsis* (1570), Pope Pius V excommunicated Elizabeth and forbade her subjects to obey her laws. These were perplexing developments for English Catholics, who had hoped that it might prove possible to reconcile their faith to their political obligations as Englishmen.

Practically, the papal sentence of deposition was a futile gesture, for it did little but increase the insecurity of English Catholics. Yet from 1570 on, the well-informed knew that the pope required that they continue to profess their religion at all costs, a religion not to be confused with what went on in the queen's churches, even if this ran counter to their ordinary duty as the queen's subjects. Within four years the English Catholic seminary founded at Douai, France (then the Spanish Netherlands), by William (later Cardinal) Allen began to dispatch into England priests charged with a mission "for the preservation and augmentation of the faith of the Catholics." Later, other missionaries would arrive from Rome itself, where the English pilgrim hospice had been converted into another college. The capture of this institution by the Society of Jesus and its way of life under the Jesuits were matters shared with a fascinated and duly horrified English public by Anthony Munday in *The English Romayne Life* (1582): "After supper, if it be wintertime, they go with the Jesuits and sit about a great fire talking, and in all their talk they strive who shall speak worst of Her Majesty." The English Counter-Reformation, so long delayed, had begun.

According to the brilliant thesis advanced by John Bossy in *The English Catholic Community, 1570–1850,* that community has no history, only a prehistory before the watershed of 1570. The death of the medieval English church was a principal condition for the emergence of a new kind of Catholicism, one practiced by a minority community in a non-Catholic England. But, in the view of Bossy's critics, this idea has been allowed to run out of control. The history of the Catholics for many decades after 1570 must take account of an untold

but far from insignificant number of church papists who were not recusant and did not necessarily identify with a self-consciously isolated "community." The most often quoted description of a church papist, that composed by John Earle for his *Microcosmographie* (1628), is cited as if it provides a firsthand description of the religious conditions prevailing in the 1560s, but Earle wrote six decades later. Moreover, both the survival of church papists and the existence and health of a community of separated, recusant Catholics in good standing with their church depended on perceived continuities with the past history of the church in England and on links with the Catholic Continent. To be fair to Bossy, he is by no means unaware of the paradox that brought out of these wider connections in space and time a somewhat insular and withdrawn religious community.

Important though the church papists were, it is inevitable that historians of post-Reformation Catholicism should have focused their attention on individuals, households, and other groups whose practice of Catholicism was relatively complete and coherent, not merely the debris of redundant folk beliefs. Bossy has created a rich landscape of a hidden world, describing the disciplines, the calendar, and the social rhythms of feast and fast that characterized the larger Catholic households. There is much more of this in the contribution made by local historians of the subject. Yet the most certain means of identifying Catholics in Elizabethan England has always been negative: their refusal to attend Protestant services in the parish church, or at least to receive the Protestant communion. And the historian remains very dependent on the recognition of that refusal by the authorities, their application of the label *recusant,* and their punitive responses to it.

The responses of the authorities were not universally or uniformly energetic. Like all processes of Tudor government, they arose from personal initiatives and motives and from intermittent governmental pressures prompted by events and contingencies. The two decades following the papal excommunication and deposition witnessed a great increase in missionary activity, as exiles trained in the English seminaries abroad made their reentry, and as the Society of Jesus took a belated interest in the conversion of England with the well-publicized arrival of the Jesuit fathers Robert Parsons and Edmund Campion in 1580. These years also saw a worsening of the international situation and the intensification of threats to the security of the Elizabethan regime. At last, in the late 1580s, came open war with Spain, whose King Philip II was thought by English Protestants to vie with the pope himself as the archenemy of their queen and their religion. These two lines of development were woven together in the public mind. While the earl of Leicester lived (he died in 1588), it was later remembered, it went for current that papists were traitors, either in action or in affection. The earl personified a strong political commitment to a robustly anti-Catholic Protestantism.

The consequences are reflected in the statute book. Parliament had already passed the Treasons Act of 1571, which made it treasonable to follow the dictates of the papal bull and which imposed severe penalties for importing such bulls or other objects of devotion. In 1581, to convert or suffer conversion to Catholicism with the intent of withdrawing allegiance from the queen became treason, and the fine for nonattendance at church rose to £20 a month, with provision for the sequestration of the estates of those failing to pay. This last measure was aimed at the Catholic landed gentry, whose patronage and social and political support were all but essential to the survival of the old faith and who were numerous, not only in the north but in such southern counties as Hampshire and Sussex.

By an act of 1585, a Jesuit or seminary priest apprehended in England was by definition a traitor, and those harboring or assisting such traitors were themselves liable to execution. One such harborer, the York housewife Margaret Clitherow, was crushed to death for refusing to plead at her trial. The fate of 123 priests (making up two-thirds of the total of Elizabethan martyrs) was the equally fearful death of hanging, drawing, and quartering. In 1593, Parliament debated, but failed to pass, a bill that would have deprived Catholics of virtually all legal rights. The statute actually passed in that year reduced the penalties for being a priest or Jesuit but confined all recusants to within five miles of their homes. However, many priests and most lay Catholics seem to have escaped the full rigors of this ferocious penal code, only a very few recusants paying their fines in full. In Essex more than half the money collected came from the pockets of one individual, the unfortunate Ferdinando Paris.

For centuries, the victims were celebrated by the historians of one tradition as blessed martyrs and saints, but by those of the other as political offenders who were not unjustly punished for activities that were a threat to the state at a moment of acute danger. The rights and wrongs of these contrary points of view have dominated the literature. More recent studies have benefited from the broadening scope of modern social, cultural, and religious historiography and have acknowledged that the topic of Elizabethan Catholicism transcends the limited themes of both hagiography and political history. The matters of most abiding and absorbing interest to Catholics were peculiar to themselves; only at moments of danger were Catholics absorbed in their relations with the government. Thus, the serious differences that divided English Catholics toward the end of the sixteenth century, which were gathered up in a cause célèbre known as the Appellant, or Archpriest, Controversy, were once interpreted as a dispute about the political obligations of Catholics, the problem of allegiance. But for Bossy, this was "an ecclesiastical, not a political argument," having to do with questions of internal organization and authority. This is not to deny that the tensions between the Jesuits and their opponents, and between the clerical and lay points of view, which were near the heart of it, were cleverly exploited by the government, which encouraged the anti-Jesuit party of the Appellants to advance its cause by a policy of pragmatic cooperation with the authorities.

Nevertheless, the question of allegiance was inescapable and critical to the survival of the Catholic community. Usually it has seemed to historians that most Catholics were politically quiescent. The bull of 1570 was canonically and procedurally a dubious document, and in 1580, Pope Gregory XIII declared it to be for the time being practically inoperative, although binding in conscience. Catholics might be feared as a potential fifth column, but in spite of occasional scares such as the Babington plot (1586), there is little evidence of their readiness to rise in support of England's foreign enemies, not even in 1588.

Bossy has provided this analysis with a sociological dimension. Noting that the most significant dividing line in Catholicism is normally that which separates priests and laity, he has proposed two ideal types: on the one hand, the gentleman, pragmatic, antiheroic, old-fashioned in his politics; on the other, the missionary priest, an advanced, radical intellectual, idealist and activist, capable (as the gentleman was usually not) of political as well as spiritual adventures. The Jesuit Robert Parsons answers most closely to this second type. But Parsons' career was a failure. Given the dependence of the mission on its lay patrons (an inevitable dependence according to Bossy, a preferred and avoidable dependence in the hypercritical view of Haigh), the gentleman had the last word over the devoted priest. The final chapter of Elizabethan Catholicism, like its first, was a story of inertia.

More recently, Peter Holmes has doubted some parts of this scenario. Study of the casuistry of Elizabethan Catholics suggests that a greater number were prepared to contemplate political resistance to the queen than historians have supposed. There were no lifelong, consistent "Catholic loyalists" and few matters on which priests and laymen are known to have differed. Resistance was the cause not of particular groups or kinds of Catholics but of particular moments in their history. There was a "chronological rhythm" to the development of the political ideology of Elizabethan Catholics. In the 1580s the prospect of a successful political intervention against the regime appeared good and seems to have aroused a wide interest. It is hardly surprising that after 1588 interest diminished. Two years after the Armada, the Northamptonshire gentleman Sir Thomas Tresham (often cited as a typical loyalist and the most articulate of lay Catholic spokesmen) wrote fulsomely to the Privy Council of God's benefits bestowed "under the government of so Christian a prince and council." But there is reason to believe that Tresham's loyalty was more expedient than sincere.

Expediency of many kinds was a way of life for persons as exposed and subject to contradictory pressures as the Elizabethan Catholics. Bossy has written of "the optimum line," which provided the maximum in self-determining capacity and the minimum in destructive isolation. Haigh has described —and censured—that expediency which led many priests to neglect the fruitful mission fields of the north and far west, where the greatest numbers of retrievable church papists were to be found, in order to enjoy the protection and patronage of Catholic gentry in less remote regions. Priests were not immune to the Elizabethan craving for "civility," even when they mentally prepared themselves for the ultimate incivility of death by hanging and drawing. In the north of England one-fifth of all the Catholic clergy in England ministered to two-fifths of the detected recusants. In 1580 half the missionaries deployed in England were in Essex, London, and the Thames Valley, where only a fifth of recusants were to be found. Cumbria and much of Wales were to prove total and perhaps unnecessary losses. The gentry expected to hear Mass daily. Their social inferiors would be lucky to have it monthly.

Whether or not it is possible to imagine a different kind of mission, living precariously among the people and nourishing a more popular, resistant, and Irish type of Catholicism, there is no disagreement among historians that the mission as it operated in fact, and as they must therefore describe it, had a different character and different consequences. It sustained a distinct religious community numbering perhaps 200,000, or some 5 percent of the population. As an authentic product of the Counter-Reformation, this community was faithful in the seriousness of its religious commitment and the regularity of its practice. It was also productive in the early, heroic years of a rich alternative culture nourished by Counter-Reformation piety, notably the fervent poems of the martyred Robert Southwell ("Tender my suite, clense this defiled denne,/Cancell my debtes, sweete *Jesu,* say Amen") and the poignant music of William Byrd and many other Catholics among the composers of English music's golden age.

The community grouped itself around the great houses of Catholic nobility and gentry and was sometimes hard to distinguish from the servants and tenants of these magnates. The lay leaders were in principle and often in practice totally excluded from the public offices normally attendant on their dignities, such as university positions and many others that might have drawn them toward the mainstream of polite society. Their children were sent to foreign schools and convents. Yet only occasionally, as in the late 1630s and 1680s, did a minority of these outsiders entertain the political ambition of overcoming the disadvantages that were the penalty of their faith. And although an elaborate and apocalyptic mental fabric of anti-Catholicism became almost a world view in its own right for Protestant England in the seventeenth century, it was only from time to time that this form of collective paranoia became a physical threat to English Catholics. More typically, it served as an ideological stiffener against foreign threats and foreign tyrannies, real and imagined.

Puritan was a term of stigmatization, which in Shakespeare's England was bandied about freely and loosely as a weapon against a certain kind of excessive religiosity and scrupulous morality. The

90-09/1

mayor of Chester who in 1600 reformed the mid-summer pageants was called "a godly, over-zealous man" and might well have been called a Puritan. Such "busy controllers" were pilloried with the full vituperative virtuosity of Elizabethan street rhetoric: they were "precise fools," "saints and scripture men," "curious and precise fellows who will allow no recreation." "It was never merry world since that sect came first among us." In the same spirit Chaucer's contemporaries had exclaimed against "Lollards," and Henry VIII's subjects against "you fellows of the new trickery." Only in the mid-seventeenth century would *Puritan* be owned and acknowledged by the godly themselves as an honorable flag under which to sail—"the good old English Puritans."

It follows that there is little profit in attempting to invest such a loosely pejorative term with exact definitional meaning and not much more in debating whether a certain individual was or was not a Puritan. Stigmas tell us more about the stigmatizer than the stigmatized, or rather they tell us about the entire dynamic and stressful situation that gave rise to the stigma. In the later years of Elizabeth, when the stigma became a topic for sophisticated investigation, on the stage as well as in literature and commonplace books, the question of definition became in itself a kind of game and a means of heightening the polemical voltage: "Long hath it vexed our learned age to scan/Who rightly might be termed a Puritan." It is somewhat in this vein that Maria in *Twelfth Night* says of Malvolio, "sometimes he is a kind of Puritan" (II. iii. 128). A popular jest assumed the form of a mock definition, accentuating the hypocrisy that, in literary treatments of the subject, became Puritanism's outstanding feature: "A Puritan is such a one as loves God with all his soul, but hates his neighbor with all his heart." Historians engaged in their own struggles to delineate Puritanism have not always understood the point of these by no means disinterested satires.

Perennial though the qualities attributed to it were, it is unlikely that the term *Puritan* would have been invented but for a set of specific historical circumstances arising from the Elizabethan religious settlement. The ideal content of Puritanism is elusive, but its meaning within these circumstances perfectly clear. In the perception of the Puritans themselves, the church had been "but halfly reformed" by the legislation of 1559. Things having proceeded "but halfly forward and more than halfly

backward," there was need for "further reformation"; and it was in promotion of this concept that Puritan publicists, politicians, and preachers labored. Two radical Puritan preachers, John Field and Thomas Wilcox, issued the manifesto *An Admonition to the Parliament* (1572), which complained that "we in England are so fare of, from having a church rightly reformed, accordyng to the prescript of Gods worde, that as yet we are not come to the outwarde face of the same." But the authors thought better of what they had written and altered *not* in this statement to *scarce*—"scarce come to the outwarde face of the same." The space between *not* and *scarce* was the space occupied and exploited by Elizabethan Puritanism.

The Church of England exhibited the marks of a true church, rightly reformed. It professed sound, biblical doctrine, its sacraments were pure, and so it was not to be lightly rejected as a false church. Some extreme Puritans in extreme circumstances would from time to time reject the church and separate. Their cause was reformation "without tarrying." These were, toward 1580, the "Brownists," followers of Robert Browne, who was to give his name to Separatism for a hundred years, and, toward 1590, the new wave of schism called "Barrowist" after Henry Barrow, which transplanted from London to Amsterdam a separatist colony that, surrounded and beset as it was by splinters of further secession, came to be known as the "ancient church" of the separatist way. But Separatism or Brownism became another scene, and except for later denominations that trace their origins from it and for American Christianity, to which it made an important contribution, it was of minor importance for the immediate future.

It was almost of the essence of Puritanism to remain within the national church. But the marks of a true church were barely exhibited, and in practice little was being done to teach and instill the doctrines and principles of a reformed church in the population at large. Thus, the Puritans seemed a race apart, isolated by their dissatisfaction with things as they were and by their full and enthusiastic participation in Protestant religion and its concomitant morals and habits. A distinct and peculiar subculture in an England that still expected a high degree of social conformity, they were almost a church within the church.

Puritans found objectionable in the Elizabethan church precisely those features that Anglicans later proudly celebrated as the virtues of the via media, notably its forms of worship, which in overall structure and many specific details retained a strong measure of continuity with the services of the Roman Catholic Church. One extreme critic, the London preacher John Field, spoke of the Prayer Book as encapsulating "a certaine kynde of Religion, framed out of mans owne braine and phantasie farre worse then that of Poperie (if worse may be), patched and peeced owte of theirs and ours together" (Cambridge University Library, MS Baker 32, pp. 442–443). Among as many as a hundred points, or "dregs," of popery allegedly retained in the Prayer Book, the Puritans took exception to the provisions for ecclesiastical vestments, including the white linen surplice, which was the standard attire for all Elizabethan ministers; the sign of the cross in baptism; and the giving of the ring in marriage.

More fundamentally, Field objected to what he called the "general inconvenience" of the book, to its liturgical character. The constitution of the church, which was episcopal and hierarchical and retentive of the elaborate and still unaltered infrastructure of its Catholic constitution (episcopal courts, archdeacons, cathedral churches and their deans and chapters), was equally hard for many Puritans to stomach. More generally, the Puritans thought of the church as coming into being by means of the preaching of the lively word of the Gospel, which literally "edified" its membership in an authentically Pauline sense; that is, the church was a building composed of living stones. But the church in a non-Puritan perception, which we may attribute to the queen for one, was an institution already complete, a legacy of the past, requiring only repair to some parts of its fabric. Under the broad and accommodating roof of this structure, *edification* meant nothing more than the process of instructing the people in their religious duties, the program of the official sermons known as the *Homilies*. Puritanism was a religious dynamic contained within a rather static set of values.

The character of the Elizabethan settlement, which provided the Puritan movement with its agenda for further reformation, was determined by political motives and even by political forces. Traditionally, the critical decisions that led to a decisive but moderate commitment to Protestantism have been ascribed to the queen herself and to her secretary of state, William Cecil, and lord keeper, Nicholas Bacon. In making the settlement, Parliament proceeded on a governmental blueprint designed to establish Protestantism but in a form not too offensive to Catholic consciences.

In 1950, John Neale reexamined the sparse evidence and argued that the true story of 1559 was different. Elizabeth had not intended to legislate a Protestant prayer book, at least not in this first parliamentary session. One of the factors that persuaded her to change her mind was the obstructive pressure exerted by advanced Protestants (or Puritans) both within and without the membership of the House of Commons, led by recently returned religious exiles. These political tactics won for the radical Protestant interests less than they had desired but more than they would have secured without them. Neale saw the long-running political contest between the queen and the Puritans in later Elizabethan Parliaments as arising from the inconclusive round fought in 1559. The Puritans believed that the strategy that had won some ground on that occasion could win still more. But Elizabeth, who had been forced to yield more than she was originally willing to concede, turned that defeat to advantage by digging into a position from which she was never subsequently dislodged.

Recently doubts have been cast on the plausibility of Neale's account of the parliamentary religious settlement. It appears likely after all that the queen obtained the settlement that she and her advisers had originally intended and that only the opposition of Catholics, especially in the House of Lords, had posed any serious threat to her policy (Jones). Be that as it may, two things are not in doubt. First, the queen, while committed by birth, education, and policy to Protestantism, was more conservative in her Protestantism than many of her subjects. The single fact that she was not well disposed to a preaching ministry and considered three or four preachers sufficient for a shire is enough to establish that. Second, more advanced Protestants, having no sense that a permanent and irrevocable settlement had been made, continued to press for progressive reform, regarding each new Parliament as an opportunity to renew the campaign.

It is important not to attribute every religious bill introduced into the House of Commons to a highly organized Puritan high command. Further religious legislation was favored by a broad and loose coalition of interests, including highly placed politicians and public servants and many of the early Elizabethan bishops, whose outlook on many matters was not different from those labeled as Puritans. But there was tension between the regime, certainly in the person of the queen, and these interests, and it was out of that tension that the stigma of the term *Puritan* arose. Moreover, we need not doubt that it was in the character of the Calvinist form of Protestantism, in England no less than in other parts of Europe, to convey to its adherents a sense of involvement in a movement and a cause, the cause of "the godly," or God's cause.

Puritanism assumed a more definite profile as a movement of nonconformity, protest, and political pressure as it became clear that Elizabeth had no plans to complete the limited settlement of 1559 but rather intended to exact a strict conformity to every detail of the settlement as made. In 1565 she demanded that any cleric who did not wear the prescribed vestments (often, it appears, on the insistence of the "simple gospellers" in their congregations, who in the aftermath of the Marian persecution were deeply offended by "the pope's attire") was to be disciplined. According to a fashionable doctrine of the time, which became the ideological basis of Elizabethan conformism and Anglicanism, articles of clerical attire such as the surplice and square cap were *adiaphora* ("things indifferent"), which had no doctrinal value and which in their neutrality were legitimately ordered by the political authority of the queen, as governor of the church. The episcopal constitution of the church was originally viewed in the same light, not as a divine ordinance.

The first Puritans (for it was in the context of this controversy that the term appeared) either doubted whether such things were indifferent at all or held that if they were indifferent, then the individual conscience was at liberty to use them or not, according to its own sense of what was consistent with the biblical revelation of God's will. St. Paul had said that all things were lawful to him, but not all things were expedient. Certainly to impose things indifferent with legal sanctions was to deprive them of any indifference they might have had.

Matthew Parker, the first Elizabethan archbishop of Canterbury and a moderate and scholarly divine who had not joined the Marian exile, proved capable of the disciplinary measures that the queen's policy required; he composed and published in 1566 a new code of conduct, the "Advertisements," and persuaded his more radically evangelical colleagues to follow his lead. In the course of the ensuing "Vestiarian Controversy," some parts of which had been anticipated in the Edwardian church and in the churches of the Marian exile,

ministers were suspended from duty and even deprived of their livings; books and pamphlets were published on both sides; and in London lay Puritans reverted to meeting in conventicles as they had done in Mary's time and found themselves in prison, the victims of a new "popish tyranny." A sectarian fault line had opened into a narrow crack, later to become a chasm and destined never to close over in subsequent centuries.

All agreed that the surplice was not in itself a matter of great moment. But as a character in Trollope reminds us, "Wars about trifles are always bitter, especially among neighbours." In the years after the Vestiarian Controversy, some Puritans, especially the younger men, were encouraged by the bitterness and by the train of their own thinking to call greater things in question. On the Continent, the embattled Calvinist movement was assuming a more rigid and intolerant attitude toward everything that appeared to deviate from its own understanding of the mandates of the New Testament. Any bishops who lorded it over their fellow pastors were now condemned by the ranking Geneva minister, Theodore Beza, as instruments of the devil and so not acceptable for the exercise of that godly "discipline" which Beza insisted on as a necessary mark of the church. In Cambridge in 1570 these "Presbyterian" principles were explored in the lecture hall by a young professor of divinity, Thomas Cartwright. In London they justified the harsh judgment now pronounced on the English church by the even younger Field and Wilcox, authors of the *Admonition.* In a private letter, Field complained that the godly had hitherto confined their attention to the "shells and chippings of popery" while neglecting "that which beareth up Antichrist chiefly."

Not all those who were dissatisfied with the extent of the reforms already achieved in the Elizabethan church agreed with Cartwright and Field in their drastic diagnoses of its structural faults. Only a minority were hard-line Presbyterians. The first priority of many and perhaps of most was to establish universally a learned, godly preaching ministry in every parish and so to make the church in reality what in principle it already was—a godly people. Edward Dering, the model and prototype of the Puritan divine, complained, "Scarce one of a great many can give an account of their fayth. . . . A very small number have tasted of the beginnings of the Gospell of Christ." To pray "thy kingdom come" and to do nothing about the scandal of the ignorant ministry was to "speak like parrots" (Collinson, "A Mirror of Elizabethan Puritanism"). So Dering shared the indignation of the Presbyterians, but he suspected that their preoccupation with structure was to mistake the shadow for the substance of reformation. He also doubted whether their pessimistic alarmism was justified. Many bishops were godly and sympathetic. And religion had still more powerful friends in high places, including the earls of Bedford, Huntingdon, and Warwick, and above all Warwick's brother, the immensely potent favorite of the queen, Robert Dudley, earl of Leicester.

Among churchmen, Edmund Grindal was the most able and respected. As bishop of London (1559–1570) he had coerced the Puritan clergy with great reluctance. As archbishop of York (1570–1575) he had begun an effective program of Protestantization in the north. When this notable father of the English Reformation was transferred to Canterbury on Parker's death, it seemed to be a time to call for a truce in "civil wars of the Church of God." But within little more than a year, a confrontation occurred between Grindal and his royal mistress that led to his effective suspension from office, the greatest of all setbacks to progressive Protestantism. The queen had declared her dislike of the preaching conferences held in provincial towns and known, somewhat misleadingly, as exercises of "prophesying" (a term borrowed from St. Paul writing to the Corinthians). She now demanded their suppression and proposed a general curtailment in the number of preachers. This was to put the Reformation into reverse; and in a courageous letter, which proved fatal to his career, Grindal told the queen that he could have no part in such a policy.

On his death in 1583, Grindal was succeeded by John Whitgift, who in the 1570s had engaged Thomas Cartwright in a running battle of the books arising from the *Admonition.* Whitgift was a more than willing instrument in repressing not only acts of nonconformity but the Puritan conscience, from which such acts arose. The entire clergy was required to subscribe, on pain of suspension and ultimate removal, to a schedule of three articles that included an affirmation that the Prayer Book contained nothing contrary to God's Word. Resistance to this demand became a common cause for Puritans of all complexions and so played into the hands of Presbyterian extremists. John Field, as secretary of a Puritan cell in London, aspired to play the same role nationally. Ministers in the country were exhorted to resist subscription, to group themselves in conferences, or "classes," which already resembled the constituent units of a Presbyterian, nonepiscopal church, and to maintain an active liaison with their friends among the parliamentary gentry.

These internal developments coincided with a period of acute danger, as it was perceived, to religion, the queen's life, and the Protestant establishment from its Catholic enemies, internal and external. In the Netherlands, William the Silent fell victim to an assassin's bullet in 1584. The members of the English Parliament of 1584 went to it committed to applying lynch law to the person most likely to benefit by their queen's violent death—Mary Stuart. Their speeches complained of the untimeliness of the archbishop's onslaught against the godly preachers and dwelt on the deplorable condition of the clergy at large. In this mood, many were willing in this and the following Parliament to give a hearing to bills that would have dismantled the existing constitution of the church at a stroke, replacing it with a form of Presbyterianism.

It was not to be. Elizabeth stood in the gap, and presently the Presbyterian moment passed. After the defeat of the Armada in 1588 there was some shift in public attitudes. The great patrons of Elizabethan Puritanism were dead or dying, Leicester among them. Puritan extremism reached its limits, so far as literary exchanges were concerned, in the virulently antiepiscopal pamphlets known as the Martin Marprelate tracts of 1588–1590, which were almost certainly written by Job Throckmorton, a Warwickshire gentleman and member of Parliament. Marprelate provoked a severe reaction in the form of an exemplary Star Chamber prosecution of Thomas Cartwright and other notorious Presbyterians (but not Field, who, like Leicester, had died in 1588). In the 1590s, Richard Hooker elevated anti-Puritan polemics to philosophical heights previously unknown in his *Laws of Ecclesiastical Polity* (1593–1597). He defended the existing constitution of the church not on the rather weak grounds of the *adiaphora* but as broadly consistent with the intentions of the Apostles and of Christ himself and as inherently reasonable. Meanwhile, Puritanism as an organized, political movement lay low, waiting for a better day.

That day seemed to dawn with the accession in 1603 of King James I. Unlike Elizabeth, whose motto, especially in matters ecclesiastical, was *Semper eadem* ("Always the Same"), James was prepared to envisage change where he was convinced that it was called for; and as a well-informed Calvinist Protestant, he was in sympathy with at least some parts of the agenda of moderate Puritanism. In particular, he needed no persuasion that the ministry of the church ought, as a matter of course, to be a learned preaching ministry. And, like the church's Puritan critics, James perceived that its pastoral effectiveness was gravely damaged by the alienation, or "impropriation," of the revenues of thousands of parishes into lay hands and sought, albeit unsuccessfully, a remedy. Consequently the Millenary Petition (so called because a thousand ministers were said to have put their hands to it) and the many other addresses that greeted the new king were not entirely unrealistic.

However, as a veteran campaigner against hardline Presbyterianism, which in his Scottish kingdom was the principal political problem with which he had to contend, James was an even more resolute opponent of the Puritan threat to royal supremacy than was the old queen. The mere fact that the Puritans were capable of organizing and applying political pressure rendered them odious and dangerous in the king's perception, regardless of the content of their program.

These two sides of James's mind on ecclesiastical questions were displayed at the Hampton Court conference that the king held with the bishops and a small group of Puritan spokesmen in January 1604. This was a kind of round-table conference in which the king was willing to explore, with an open mind and with a variety of points of view represented, remedies for acknowledged ecclesiastical abuses and failings. But in other episodes the conference was made an occasion for James to issue a public warning to the Puritans that if they maintained a posture that implicitly defied his royal prerogative in matters of religion, he would "harry them out of the land, or else do worse" (Collinson, "The Jacobean Religious Settlement"). In the event, the conference was not very productive, except that the Authorized, or King James, Version of the Bible (1611) came out of an idea floated at Hampton Court.

Whitgift was now succeeded as primate by Richard Bancroft, who had built his career on the literary and forensic exposure of Martin Marprelate and other Puritan extremists. Bancroft proceeded to codify the canon law of the Church of England and, with the king's endorsement, to impose the canons by a subscription campaign that had a far more devastating effect than the one conducted by Whit-

gift twenty years earlier. Some Puritans were driven out of the church altogether into a separatist exile in the Netherlands. Many more towed the line and ceased to be Puritans, at least in the original and most proper sense of that elastic term. Historians used to see in this profound reaction the origins of the "Puritan Revolution," their term for the great political crisis and civil war of the mid-seventeenth century. According to S. R. Gardiner, the greatest of the modern historians of these events, what Charles I reaped, his father had sown at Hampton Court. "James went his way, thinking little of what he had done." The Puritans were to have a terrible revenge.

However, the perspective implied in that analysis is so foreshortened as to be false. Although the Puritans were endlessly frustrated in their hope of political satisfaction in the shape of a new religious settlement, many of their ends were well on the way to achievement by the time of James's death. Most of the more able and energetic of the Jacobean bishops were the children of Grindal rather than of Whitgift or Bancroft: Calvinists, firm in their detestation of Catholicism, promoters of the godly preaching ministry, and often regular preachers themselves. Under George Abbot of Canterbury and Tobias Matthew of York, both primatial sees were for long held by churchmen of this caliber. The formal qualifications of the clergy had by now so far improved that in many dioceses more than half were licensed preachers. By the 1620s, the great majority of those ordained and instituted to livings in all dioceses were university graduates.

As for society at large, in many parts of England it had now advanced some distance along the road of moral change traced by J. R. Green. Jacobean provincial life was often dominated by the twin commanding figures of godly ministry and grave magistracy, those two "optic pieces" of the commonwealth, as one preacher put it. Shakespeare was expressing his misgivings about this overtly and excessively righteous kind of government when he drew the figure of Angelo in *Measure for Measure.* In the towns, sermons drove out plays and other "obscene" entertainments, and the "rude multitude," the "base rabble," was obliged, however reluctantly, to knuckle under to a bleakly Sabbatarian regime. In printed form, the kind of divinity known as "practical" sold briskly, as the increasingly literate middle classes warmed to its edifying themes. Hooker and Shakespeare were not the best-selling authors of Jacobean England;

far more popular were the physicians of the soul, Richard Rogers, John Dod and William George Gouge, and above all William Perkins, and Lewis Bayly *(Practise of Pietie)*.

In all this there were seeds of future conflict. "The war was begun in our streets," wrote the great divine Richard Baxter, "before the king and the Parliament had any armies." But it is not likely that that "war" would have breached the outward casing of Protestant provincial society if power had not passed, in the disastrous reign of Charles I, into the hands of an ecclesiastical party whose policies were detrimental not only to Puritanism but also to the religious values of a moral majority of Protestants, values that in the years of Shakespeare's maturity had not been much questioned but that were now, in a revival and extension of the old stigma, denounced as puritanical by the new men in power. This party—sometimes labeled Arminian after Jacobus Arminius, the Dutch proponent of a theology of grace divergent from the doctrine of double predestination taught by strict Calvinists, and sometimes Laudian after Archbishop William Laud—set itself against the "orthodoxy" of the prevalent Calvinism, promoted unwelcome "innovations" in ritual and ceremony, gave new and disturbing emphasis to the exalted status of the clergy and its material rights and claims, and seemed to be prepared to betray the Reformation and England itself into the hands of its Romish enemy (Tyacke). But these developments, with their catastrophic consequences for the Church of England, extend beyond the lifetime of Shakespeare and the scope of this article.

The final task of this essay will be to investigate the local and particular impact of religious change in Warwickshire, in Stratford-upon-Avon, and in William Shakespeare's immediate family circle. A report made to the Privy Council by the bishop of Worcester in the year of Shakespeare's birth says that of forty-two justices of the peace and other officers resident in his Warwickshire jurisdiction, twenty-two were "adversaries of true religion" and twelve "indifferent" or "of no religion." Only eight were identified as "favourers of true religion" (Bateson). According to an earlier bishop of Worcester, that founding father and martyr of the English Reformation, Hugh Latimer, Stratford lay at the "blind end" of his diocese. So although Edgar Fripp thought that in Mary's reign the town was "a protestant stronghold" and was "encircled

by the martyr fires," this seems most unlikely. Latimer's editor, Augustine Bernher, may well have had Stratford in mind when he wrote in 1562 from the south Warwickshire town of Southam of "great parishes and market-towns . . . utterly destitute of God's word."

The early corporation records of Stratford contain none of the telltale clues to the precocious Protestant enthusiasm found in the annals of Ipswich, Leicester, or, indeed, Coventry, within a day's ride of Stratford. Almost no payments or gifts of wine for visiting preachers are listed, no expressions of anxiety about church attendance or Sabbath observance. Evidently violent affrays, unregulated muck hills, and stray dogs troubled the magistrates more than sin. Only in 1564, with the departure from the town of the influential Catholic Clopton family, were the images defaced and the rood loft taken down in the guild chapel, the principal religious edifice in the town of Stratford. These measures should have been taken in 1560, and in southeastern England they generally were.

In 1566 the curate composed a will for an alderman in which he bequeathed his soul to God "to be in joy with our Blessed Lady and with all the Holy Company of Heaven." It is probable that most members of this community were church papists. John Bretchgirdle, the vicar who baptized Shakespeare, was a learned man who left behind him a distinguished little library. It was the library of a humanist but not necessarily that of a convinced Protestant. His successor fell under suspicion at the time of the Northern Rebellion and lost his position, while both the curate and the schoolmaster left town at the same time and evidently under the same cloud.

The next vicar to be installed, Henry Heycroft, was not a cryptopapist. Yet not until the mid-1580s are there any signs of a watershed in the religious culture of Stratford or evidence of any local influence that could have brought about such a conversion. Simon Hunt, the schoolmaster who must have taught Shakespeare, withdrew to Douai in 1575, moved on to Rome, and became a Jesuit. One of Hunt's pupils and Shakespeare's schoolfellow, Robert Dibdale, took the same route. He reentered England as a priest in 1580 and died on the scaffold in the aftermath of the Babington Plot in 1586. So the evangelical credentials of early Elizabethan Stratford are anything but convincing. Bishop Bayly's *Practise of Pietie* continued through countless editions and as far away as Hungary (where it was translated) to indict Stratford as a town meriting God's visitational wrath for profaning the Sabbath and "contemning his Word in the mouth of his faithful ministers."

In 1586, as part of the groundwork for the presentation of petitions and bills for further reform in the House of Commons, the organized Puritan movement mobilized its supporters in the country to draw up surveys of the condition of the parish clergy at a time when Archbishop Whitgift and the High Commission were continuing to harry with subscription and suspension the minority of "faithful" and "sufficient" ministers. In Warwickshire, this undertaking was very likely inspired by two local Puritan notables, Thomas Cartwright, installed by the earl of Leicester as master of his hospital in Warwick, and Job Throckmorton of Haseley, the future Martin Marprelate.

Doubts have often been cast on the value of the Warwickshire survey as sober historical evidence. Yet comparison with an episcopal inquiry of about the same time in which the clergy were required to assess themselves suggests that it is factually accurate (Barratt). The Puritan surveyors found the vicar of Warwick to be "unsound in some pointes of christian religion" and "verie much subiect to the vice of good felowshippe." The curate of the Shakespeares' ancestral parish of Snitterfield was a nonpreacher, conceded to be "honest" but "far unfit for the ministerie"; "he teacheth to plaie on instrumentes and draweth wrought workes." A pluralist who held three livings, including Henley-in-Arden, was encouraged by the prospect of a French and Catholic royal marriage to shave off his Protestant beard. The incumbent at Honiley "could not one daie read the commandementes for want of his spectacles"—a touch worthy of Marprelate. At Grafton the vicar, John Frith, was an aged Marian survivor, "unsound in religion." "His chiefest trade is to cure hawkes that are hurt or diseased, for which purpose manie do usuallie repaire to him." This is the man who is thought to have married Shakespeare and Anne Hathaway, and he is sometimes linked with the figure of Friar Laurence in *Romeo and Juliet,* a herbalist who corresponds to the popular stereotype of the "massing" priest as "conjurer."

But at Stratford, the Puritan surveyor had high praise for the newly installed vicar, Richard Barton: "a preacher, learned, zealous, and godlie, and fit for the ministerie. A happie age yf our Church were fraight [with] manie such." Barton had been vis-

ited on the town by the godly earl of Warwick, and with his advent in 1585, Stratford at last embarked on the first steps of J. R. Green's path of moral transformation, which would reach its climax, in a sense, in the magistrates' decision in 1623 not to entertain the visiting players. In 1591 the corporation was anxious lest the poverty of the living would mean that "the word" would be taken from them and "able and learned" ministers discouraged from accepting the cure. Barton had been offered more money as an inducement to stay. Their anxiety was groundless. Barton was the first of a line of zealous preachers, rarely interrupted. In 1587 and 1588, Cartwright himself preached at Stratford, accompanied by Throckmorton, the town marking these notable visits by gifts of wine and sugar.

Ecclesiastical life in Stratford was self-contained and self-sufficient to an unusual degree. The tithe income was enjoyed by the corporation, which paid the vicar an annual stipend of £20. In 1591 the town petitioned for the right of appointing to the vicarage, which was vested in the crown. In one respect, Stratford already approximated to the model of ecclesiastical organization and discipline desired by Cartwright and Throckmorton. Instead of the normal oversight of its faith and morals by bishop and archdeacon, the town was ecclesiastically a "peculiar," subject in the first instance to the jurisdiction of its own vicar, who sat in judgment over his parishioners in his own court of correction.

Much of the business of this little tribunal resembled that of archdeacons' courts elsewhere—the detection and punishing of sexual and marital offenses, which explains their familiar title of "bawdy courts." (At Stratford, Thomas Faux "scandalized" the court by calling it the bawdy court.) There are several recorded instances of the court's provoking a spirited resistance to its discipline by the townspeople. On 1 October 1595, Elizabeth Wheeler "brawled" in the court itself—crying out, "Goodes woondes, a plague a God on you all, a fart of ons ars for you"—and was excommunicated. On 26 March 1616, Shakespeare's son-in-law Thomas Quiney was ordered to do public penance for copulation with Margaret Wheeler (perhaps the daughter of the impenitent Elizabeth?), who had died in childbirth with her baby eleven days earlier. This is a most intriguing episode, for Quiney had married Judith Shakespeare (irregularly according to church law, as it happens) on 10 February. Had Margaret died because she refused to tell the midwives until it was too late who the father of her child was? It was understandable that so recent a bridegroom as Quiney should have asked to have the humiliation of public penance commuted to a payment of 5 shillings into the poor box.

From the late sixteenth century, the records of Stratford's bawdy court document a creeping Sabbatarianism. In 1590 the court ordered the churchwardens and constables to go through the inns and alehouses in time of divine service to detect those engaged in gaming and tippling. Presentments for such offenses subsequently occur with regularity. In 1622, Thomas Canning admitted to playing at ball on the Sabbath, said that it was the first time that he had done so, and promised that it should be the last. In the same year, two parishioners were interviewed for the offense of striking noisy children in church who were disturbing the sermon. They were told that they ought to have complained to the magistrate, who would have had the children whipped. On the same occasion, four morris dancers and "the Maid Marion" were in court. Two years later Stephen Lea was in trouble for singing "profane and filthie songs" and for deriding ministers and the profession of religion. In 1619 a rather unsatisfactory vicar, John Rogers, was squeezed out of office by the corporation to make way for a stirring preacher in the Puritan mold, Thomas Wilson. *A Satire to the Chief Rulers in the Synagogue of Stratford* was scattered in the streets, complaining against the dominant Puritan oligarchy: "Stratford's a town that doth make a great shew,/But yet it is governed but by a few . . ./Puritants without doubt" (quoted in Fripp, *Shakespeare, Man and Artist*). Here was "the war in our streets" referred to by Baxter.

And what of the Shakespeares? It has been argued that the family tradition was conformable and Anglican, that it was crypto-Catholic if not fully recusant, and that it was Puritan. Of these incompatible theories, the suggestion that Shakespeare's father was a Puritan, even an extreme Puritan and Separatist, is the most implausible and weakly supported. It rests on deeply mistaken and anachronistic perspectives of Elizabethan religious life. Those writers who regard John Shakespeare as a conformable citizen who, as a chamberlain (treasurer) of the Stratford corporation, willingly presided over the Protestantization of the guild chapel believe that his withdrawal from all civic responsibilities after 1576 contains no suspicious circumstances but was prompted by genuine business and financial embarrassment. It was reported in 1592 that he (and some others) stayed away from church only "for

fear of process for debt," and many authorities believe that this was the simple truth.

However, this writer agrees with De Groot that some explanation of John Shakespeare's withdrawal from public life must be found in other than business failure and that that reason is likely to have been religious. Shakespeare's father was most probably an unreconstructed Catholic of the old sort who was a potential and perhaps an actual "convert" of the missionary priests who had penetrated to the vicinity of Stratford by 1580. He had had no formal schooling and whether or not he was literate is an old controversy. The family into which he married, the Ardens, had many links with recusancy; and it is not unlikely that Mary Arden, the poet's mother, was more consistent in her Catholicism than her husband, a common and understandable state of affairs. That John Shakespeare was a municipal officer when the guild chapel was Protestantized proves nothing. Indeed, the fact that the great doom painting was whitewashed over rather than destroyed suggests the kind of crypto-Catholic conduct of which Puritans often complained.

In 1583 the extended family to which Shakespeare belonged was placed in great jeopardy when their cousin John Somerville was arrested on his way to London to assassinate the queen. The response of Warwickshire Catholics was to clear their houses "of all shows of suspicion." So it was probably at this time of danger that John Shakespeare concealed in the roof of his house in Henley Street the copy of St. Charles Borromeo's "Last Will of the Soul" to which he had apparently set his name, article by article, fourteen in all, making it the personal confession of "John Shakspear, an unworthy member of the Holy Catholick religion." This document bemused scholars when it was discovered by chance two centuries later. But the Jesuits Campion and Parsons are known to have asked for thousands of copies of this little classic of Counter-Reformation piety to distribute in England, and in 1580 Campion stayed in a house only twelve miles from Stratford (De Groot, Milward, Schoenbaum). There is no conclusive evidence of John Shakespeare's Catholicism, but this is very nearly conclusive.

As for William Shakespeare himself, the late-seventeenth-century report of Richard Davies that Shakespeare "died a Papist" is unsubstantiated. Yet since the dramatist avoided all parochial office and responsibility, in both Stratford and London, failed to receive the communion in Southwark (on the surviving evidence of the distribution of communion tokens), and is only assumed to have attended church in that he was never presented for recusancy, he may well have leaned in that direction. The plays themselves contain no reliable pointers to the dramatist's private religious convictions, tastes, or prejudices; although there is a persistent and well-informed use of Catholic terminology and imagery (as there is in the thoroughly Protestant Edmund Spenser), which is a little intriguing, unless Shakespeare employed them for the mere sake of artistic authenticity. The point has often been made that he did not exploit the stories of either King John or Henry VIII as a robustly Protestant dramatist (such as John Bale) would have exploited them. Again, while not a virulently anti-Puritan dramatist, Shakespeare made use of some features of the stage Puritan in constructing two of his least appealing characters, Malvolio and Angelo, and always represented the parish clergy of the Elizabethan church as figures of fun. But it is to Ben Jonson's *Bartholomew Fair* and *The Alchemist* and to Thomas Middleton's *The Family of Love* that we must turn, not to Shakespeare, to find unambiguous Puritan parodies.

Shakespeare's plays are replete with points of religious reference and resound with echoes of the Bible, Prayer Book, and Homilies, texts with which he was thoroughly familiar. No less than forty-two biblical books are refracted in his dramatic corpus. But whereas proponents of Shakespeare's supposed bias toward Puritanism suggest that the poet learned the Bible in the Genevan version at his mother's knee, this seems most unlikely. Richmond Noble thought it "reasonable to doubt that Shakespeare was grounded in the Bible in his home." Some biographers believe that his knowledge was of the kind acquired almost by a process of osmosis, as Bible and Prayer Book were heard again and again, in church. A. L. Rowse has remarked, "The rhythms of the majestic phrases of the Bible and Prayer Book, heard all the days of one's youth, enter into the blood-stream: one cannot get them out of one's head if one would." Even if atheism or agnosticism lies ahead, it is an atheism or agnosticism nourished and made tolerable by those mighty words. So "a tale told by an idiot" derives from the Psalmist: "We bring our years to an end, as it were a tale that is told." Henry VI declares, "Blessed are the peacemakers" (*2 Henry VI*, II. i. 34), and Marcus in *Titus Andronicus*

quotes, "To weep with them that weep" (III. i. 244).

But Noble points out that the Bible was not yet so resonant with this generation and argues that Shakespeare's knowledge was so accurate and so aptly applied that it could have been acquired only by reading. "It is sufficiently clear that Shakespeare read the Bible in adult life and it may be that he did so fairly frequently." However, this may underestimate the capacity of the memory in a culture that was still more aural than literate. As the Bible itself puts it, "Faith cometh by hearing." The fact that the Bishops' Bible is the version most heard in the earlier plays and the Geneva Bible is more frequently echoed in the later suggests that it was only in his maturity that Shakespeare owned a Bible and read it at first hand. This is precisely what the general historical picture would lead us to expect. There is also interesting evidence that Shakespeare appreciated and borrowed from one of the greatest of the godly preachers of the Elizabethan church, Henry Smith, called by Thomas Nash "silver-tongued" (Milward).

So Shakespeare may have been himself part of that creeping "moral change" which Green located within his lifespan, the complicated track of which this essay has attempted to traverse. Shakespeare's father was probably a Catholic of the old stamp, whereas the more respectable of the poet's two sons-in-law, the successful physician John Hall, was an impeccable Jacobean Protestant whose published casebook bears the motto "Health is from the Lord." But as for Shakespeare himself, we cannot say.

BIBLIOGRAPHY

General. Horace Gundry Alexander, *Religion in England, 1558–1662* (1968). Patrick Collinson, *Archbishop Grindal, 1519–1583: The Struggle for a Reformed Church* (1979) and *The Religion of Protestants: The Church in English Society, 1559–1625* (1982). Arthur G. Dickens, *The English Reformation* (1964). Harold C. Gardiner, *Mysteries' End: An Investigation of the Last Days of the Medieval Religious Stage* (1946). Christopher Haigh, "The Recent Historiography of the English Reformation," in *Historical Journal,* 25 (1982). William Haller, *Foxe's Book of Martyrs and the Elect Nation* (1963). Felicity Heal and Rosemary O'Day, eds., *Church and Society in England: Henry VIII to James I* (1977). Norman L. Jones, *Faith by Statute: Parliament and the Settlement of Religion 1559*

(1982). Peter Milward, *Religious Controversies of the Elizabethan Age* (1977) and *Religious Controversies of the Jacobean Age* (1978). John E. Neale, "The Elizabethan Acts of Supremacy and Uniformity," *English Historical Review,* 65 (1950). Rosemary O'Day, *The English Clergy: The Emergence and Consolidation of a Profession, 1558–1642* (1979). Records of Early English Drama: *York,* Alexandra F. Johnston and Margaret Rogerson, eds., 2 vols. (1979); *Chester,* Lawrence M. Clopper, ed. (1979); *Coventry,* R. W. Ingram, ed. (1981). J. J. Scarisbrick, *The Reformation and the English People* (1984). Keith V. Thomas, *Religion and the Decline of Magic* (1971).

Catholicism. John Bossy, "The Character of Elizabethan Catholicism," in *Past and Present,* 21 (1962) and *The English Catholic Community, 1570–1850* (1975). Alan Dures, *English Catholicism, 1558–1642* (1983). Christopher Haigh, "The Continuity of Catholicism in the English Reformation," in *Past and Present,* 93 (1981). Peter J. Holmes, *Resistance and Compromise: The Political Thought of the Elizabethan Catholics* (1982). Arnold Oskar Meyer, *England and the Catholic Church Under Queen Elizabeth* (1916). Arnold Pritchard, *Catholic Loyalism in Elizabethan England* (1979).

Puritanism. Patrick Collinson, *The Elizabethan Puritan Movement* (1967); *English Puritanism* (1983); *Godly People: Essays on English Protestantism and Puritanism* (1983); and "The Jacobean Religious Settlement: The Hampton Court Conference," in Howard Tomlinson, ed., *Before the English Civil War* (1983). John S. Coolidge, *The Pauline Renaissance in England: Puritanism and the Bible* (1970). Walter H. Frere and Charles Edward Douglas, eds., *Puritan Manifestoes* (1907; rev. 1954). William Haller, *The Rise of Puritanism* (1938). Christopher Hill, *Society and Puritanism in Pre-Revolutionary England* (1964). William P. Holden, *Anti-Puritan Satire, 1572–1642* (1954). Marshall M. Knappen, *Tudor Puritanism: A Chapter in the History of Idealism* (1939). Peter Lake, *Moderate Puritans and the Elizabethan Church* (1982). A. F. Scott Pearson, *Thomas Cartwright and Elizabethan Puritanism* (1925). Albert Peel, ed., *The Seconde Parte of a Register: Being a Calendar of Manuscripts Under That Title Intended for Publication by the Puritans About 1593,* 2 vols. (1915). N. R. N. Tyacke, "Puritanism, Arminianism and Counter-Revolution," in Conrad Russell, ed., *The Origins of the English Civil War* (1973).

Stratford-upon-Avon, the Shakespeares and William Shakespeare. Dorothy M. Barratt, ed., *Ecclesiastical Terriers of Warwickshire Parishes,* 2 vols. (1955–1971). Mary Bateson, ed., "A Collection of Original Letters from the Bishops to the Privy Council, 1564," in *Camden Miscellany,* n.s. 53 (1893). Henry S. Bowden, *The Religion of Shakespeare* (1899). Thomas Carter, *Shakespeare: Puritan and Recusant* (1897). John Henry De Groot, *The Shakespeares and "The Old Faith"* (1946). Edgar I. Fripp, *Minutes and Accounts of the Corporation of Stratford-upon-Avon and Other Records, 1553–1620,* 4 vols. (1921–1929); *Master Richard Quyny, Bailiff of Stratford-upon-Avon and Friend of William Shakespeare* (1924); *Shakespeare Studies, Biographical and Literary* (1930); and *Shakespeare, Man and Artist,* 2 vols. (1938). Roland M. Frye, *Shakespeare and Christian Doctrine* (1963). Darryl J. Gless, *"Measure for Measure," the Law and the Convent* (1979). George Wilson Knight, *Shakespeare and Religion* (1967). Peter Milward, *Shakespeare's Religious Background* (1973). Heinrich Mutschmann and Karl Wentersdorf, *Shakespeare and Catholicism* (1952). Richmond Noble, *Shakespeare's Biblical Knowledge and Use of the Book of Common Prayer* (1935). Samuel Schoenbaum, *William Shakespeare: A Documentary Life* (1975). John Semple Smart, *Shakespeare: Truth and Tradition* (1928).

Law and Legal Institutions

J. H. BAKER

Shakespeare's familiarity with legal vocabulary has been the subject of several books and much comment. It has led some writers to suppose that he must have had some legal education; and in truth it would not be altogether surprising to find that, like so many of the minor gentry, he had once heard the chimes at midnight in one of the Inns of Chancery. Yet the assumption that only men with legal training knew anything about the law is anachronistic. There were few Elizabethans or Jacobeans who stayed out of law courts. Writs and plaints, latitats and subpoenas, citations and presentments were part of the lives of great lords and lowly countrymen alike. An owner of land had to be familiar with entails and uses, fines and recoveries, and actions of ejectment. Even the humble and landless needed to know about archdeacons and apparitors, about the justices of the peace and their sessions, about the ways of enforcing petty debts and resolving squabbles with their neighbors. English men and women in Shakespeare's time used courts more regularly and with less trepidation than do their descendants. Indeed, it has been credibly supposed that this was the most litigious period in English history. Certainly it was a fine time in which to be a lawyer. Small wonder, then, that legal terms occur often in Elizabethan literature. The dramatists may sometimes have had an Inns of Court audience in mind, but it is doubtful whether legal allusions were aimed at impressing the elite: they were a natural reflection of everyday life.

Litigation and Courts

Private parties who went to law with each other had an enormous range of tribunals to choose from. Sir Edward Coke listed over 100 different species, though only a few of them had general jurisdiction throughout the country in civil suits. Some were essentially organs of government, such as the Court of Wards and Liveries, the Duchy Chamber, the Council Table, and indeed the high court of Parliament. The Exchequer, too, was still chiefly a revenue department and only incidentally a court of law. The word *court* was deemed appropriate for any body whose decisions affected the lives or property of others. Even local government, such as it was, fell to courts, particularly the quarter sessions of the county justices, the commissions of sewers, and the courts leet of boroughs. Some courts had solely criminal jurisdiction. Others had jurisdiction only in particular places (for example, palatinates, liberties, or cities), or over privileged litigants (for instance, members of the royal household or of the universities), or over specialized subjects (such as the admiralty, fairs, or forests). Some courts were ecclesiastical: the archdeaconry courts of correction, the consistory courts of bishops, the provincial courts (the Court of Arches for Canterbury and the Prerogative Court of York), the Court of Delegates, and the High Commission. And some courts were manorial: courts baron and customary, courts leet, and views of frankpledge.

At this lowest level, as at the highest, courts often performed administrative as well as judicative functions.

The central royal courts of King's Bench, Common Pleas, Chancery, and Star Chamber were all located (with Parliament) in the Palace of Westminster. For centuries Westminster Hall had been the center of the English judicial system, and so it would remain until 1882. On entering the great north door, a visitor would see the vast hammer-beamed roof soaring above the milling crowd of lawyers, litigants, shopkeepers, and spectators in the body of the hall. A passage at the right led to the Exchequer Chamber. Further inside, on the right, was the Court of Common Pleas (or Common Bench), a court held "in a certain place" so that (in the words of the Great Charter) "common pleas should not follow the king." At the far end of the hall were steps leading to the Council and Parliament chambers. On the left of the steps sat the Court of King's Bench, theoretically held before the queen or king and confined to pleas affecting the crown. In practice, by Elizabethan times it had become permanently resident at Westminster and another central court for common pleas. On the right of the steps was the High Court of Chancery, presided over by the lord chancellor or lord keeper of the great seal. This court had been established to hear petitions in exceptional cases where no remedy was available in the two benches (Common Pleas and King's Bench). By Elizabethan times it had become a regular part of the legal system, with a settled procedure of its own and a growing body of principles (called equity) to govern its decisions. The last of the superior courts was the Star Chamber, which Coke called "the most honourable court (our parliament excepted) that is in the Christian world." It took its name from the room in which judicial sessions of the King's Council had been held, a room formerly adorned with gilded stars on the ceiling. Since 1540 the High Court of Star Chamber had been separate from the Privy Council, which usually met elsewhere. The court dealt with criminal informations and heard private suits involving public disorder, forgery, perjury, or such other matters as either prevented justice from being attained through the usual channels or otherwise invited intervention from on high.

A plaintiff's choice of tribunal was guided chiefly by the preferences and attachments of his lawyer but was also affected by his place of residence, the subject matter of his case, and the kind of remedy he sought. Plaintiffs did not always limit their activities to one court: a full-blooded lawsuit often involved subsidiary actions in all the central courts and sometimes in local courts as well. As a result, it is not easy for historians to gain a clear overall picture of the patterns of litigation.

Certainly the King's Bench and Common Pleas had far more work than any other courts, with tens of thousands of suits commenced every year. Only a fraction of suits reached the trial stage, but it seems that by 1600 as many as 20,000 suits a year proceeded as far as an appearance by the defendant or outlawry. In Chancery only about 2,000 actions were begun every year, though by 1617 the backlog of cases pending without determination was said to have reached 8,000. In the Star Chamber the number of suits begun each year was around 500. In a flourishing local court, such as that of Battle Abbey liberty in Sussex, there could be as many as 100 new suits every year; in a smaller local court, perhaps five to fifty. Ecclesiastical courts entertained civil suits at a similar rate, besides granting probate of wills and punishing sins. All in all, the number of cases brought before courts was enormous.

Sir John Davies attributed the increase in litigation to greater prosperity and luxury. "If we were a poor and a naked people, as many nations in America be, we should easily agree to be judged by the next man we meet, and so make a short end of every controversy," he wrote; but when a country "begins to flourish, and to grow rich and mighty: the people grow proud withall, and their pride makes them contentious and litigious." Modern writers have not come up with a better explanation. Indeed, research has shown that the distribution of cases broadly matched the distribution of wealth throughout the country. In the royal courts, fewer than a third of all litigants were from the gentry class; as many plaintiffs were yeomen as gentlemen; and at least a quarter were tradesmen.

Civil Procedure

The most basic tenet of common-law procedure was that, in actions other than those to recover land, there could be no trial or judgment without an appearance by the defendant or his attorney. As a result, the system depended on the efficacy of the means of procuring that appearance. In the central courts of common law, the means used were writs issued by the courts to the sheriff of the appropriate county; in the local courts, precepts issued by the courts to their bailiffs. The basic sequence of these "judicial" writs or precepts was that the defendant was first to be summoned by summoners, then attached by pledges (if anyone was willing to stand surety for his appearance), then distrained by seizing cattle or other movables (if any could be found), then distrained again—perhaps repeatedly —and only in the last resort arrested. If the defendant could not be found at all, the plaintiff could proceed to outlaw him, a long-winded process requiring proclamations at five successive county sessions, yet still not resulting in a judgment on the merits. In many local courts this ancient system of repeated distress, usually without the ultimate sanction of outlawry, lingered on into the Elizabethan period. Its shortcomings may well have driven more litigants into the central courts, which had striven to find ways of making an arrest (followed by release on bail) the first step in as many actions as possible.

To sue in the Common Pleas it was necessary first to purchase an "original" writ from the Chancery, authorizing the court to proceed. The plaintiff had to choose the correct writ to suit his case, and much learning had been expended on this subject in medieval times. Anthony Fitzherbert's *New Natura Brevium* (1534), a summary of that learning, was still a student primer in Shakespeare's day. When the writ was sealed it was delivered to the sheriff, who returned it into the Common Pleas: a purely formal exercise performed in the central offices. The original writ was then taken to a filazer (or philacer) of the court, who made out the judicial writ—perhaps a *distringas* (to distrain the defendant) or a *capias* (to arrest him). It might take several judicial writs to produce any effect, since sheriffs did not always do what they were told.

There had to be at least fifteen days between each writ, which had to be issued and returned in term time; and since the four law terms (Michaelmas, Hilary, Easter, and Trinity) occupied only around 100 days of the year, mesne process could easily occupy a year or two. Outlawry could begin only after the third *capias,* and then the appropriate writs were obtained from an "exigenter." In reality outlawry was not as terrible as it sounds. So few were the disabilities that many otherwise respectable persons did not trouble to pay the pound or two needed to obtain a pardon or reversal. Indeed, Queen Elizabeth I is said to have complained at the number of outlaws serving as members of Parliament.

In the King's Bench a slightly more effective process had been discovered in the fifteenth century and enlarged by the employment of fictions. The court could entertain bills of complaint from the county in which it sat, without an original writ. It had therefore become common form for plaintiffs to sue their adversaries by bill, complaining of a fictitious trespass in Middlesex (the county where Westminster Hall was situated), whereupon the sheriff of Middlesex was immediately ordered to arrest the defendant. If the defendant was in fact from another county, a writ of *latitat* was issued to arrest him there. Once the defendant had been arrested and released on bail, the plaintiff dropped the fictitious complaint (so that its falsity was never revealed) and preferred his true complaint against the defendant as a prisoner of the court.

Under another old rule, prisoners could be sued by bill in any kind of personal action: a rule designed to protect third parties, who would otherwise be delayed. When coupled with the fictional "bill of Middlesex," this device enabled King's Bench litigants to evade Magna Carta and commence "common pleas" without the expense of a Chancery writ. By undercutting the costs of the Common Pleas and providing speedy process to arrest defendants, the King's Bench greatly expanded its business in the sixteenth century.

When the defendant appeared in either court, the pleadings commenced. Pleading does not mean arguing: it is the technical procedure by which the issue between the parties is defined. Pleadings were drawn up in Latin, following strict rules; and when settled on paper they were entered by the prothonotaries (or their clerks) on parchment plea rolls. (Latin was the language of all common-law records until 1731.) The plaintiff began, with his count or declaration, setting out the details of the cause of action specified in the writ. The defendant then entered his plea, either challenging everything in the declaration (and so taking the "general issue") or taking issue on some particular point. If the defendant's plea introduced new facts, the plaintiff had to reply to them. Pleadings were exchanged until issue was reached, either when a fact was affirmed by one and denied by the other or when the parties agreed on the facts and disagreed on the law. If issue was joined on the law (a "demurrer") it was decided by the judges.

Most issues were issues of fact. Since the court itself was unable to decide such questions, an issue of fact resulted in the issue of a writ of *venire facias* to summon a jury of twelve to find the truth. It was usually arranged that the jury would give its verdict not in Westminster Hall but "at nisi prius" before the assize judges. The trial was thus conducted, for the convenience of all concerned, in the locality where the matter arose. Trials were very brief, because the few witnesses were left to tell their stories themselves, without elaborate examination and cross-examination. In the 1610s it was not unknown for more than 300 civil cases to be disposed of on a single assize circuit, which would have left an average of about twenty minutes for each trial.

If difficulties of law arose, the jurors might be directed to determine the facts alone in a special verdict, leaving the law to be argued at Westminster. When the circuit had ended, the clerks entered each verdict in Latin on the plea rolls in the central offices, and judgment followed after a due interval unless a motion was made to the full court to prevent it. Once judgment had been given, it could be reversed only for error on the face of the record. In the absence of any true appellate system, much of the legal argument in the central courts of law therefore took place upon special verdicts or motions to arrest judgment after trial.

Procedure in Chancery was markedly different from the common-law system just outlined. The plaintiff began by filing a petition (called a "bill") addressed to the lord chancellor, setting out his complaint. The defendant was then summoned by a *subpoena ad respondendum,* a writ served by the plaintiff himself, not by the sheriff. In the medieval Chancery a personal appearance had been expected, followed by a personal examination; but by Elizabethan times appearance by attorney was allowed. If the subpoena was ignored, a writ of attachment could be issued to arrest the defendant for contempt; and if that failed, a commission of rebellion could be issued to apprehend him. Besides making threats, the court could also encourage appearance by enjoining the defendant from continuing a suit at law or even by ordering interim possession of land in dispute.

After appearance, pleadings followed a similar course to those in the two benches; but they were in English and often ranged much further into the facts than pleadings at common law. The basis of

equitable proceedings was that positive rules of law could not provide for every eventuality, and so conscience required an allowance to be made in special circumstances. A court of conscience had to know more of the facts than were disclosed by procedure at law. But there was no trial as such.

Issues of fact were often complex, but instead of using juries the court collected the information in writing, a procedure evidently inspired by the inquisitorial system associated with Roman law. The medieval viva voce examination of the parties had largely given way to written interrogatories, administered in town by official examiners and in the country by commissioners. Depositions could be taken in the same way from witnesses. The fact-gathering process was controlled by the masters in Chancery, who also heard interlocutory motions and conducted inquiries on behalf of the court. Contentious issues were commonly referred to commissioners to arbitrate in the country, the nearest Chancery equivalent to jury trial. Questions of common law could be referred to the judges.

Only a small proportion of cases came to hearing before the lord chancellor himself, but those that did imposed an intolerable burden on a busy officer of state, and every pretext was sought to delegate questions whenever possible. When a decree was given, it did not have the finality of a judgment at law: until it was enrolled it was tentative, in that it could be set aside on motion, and even enrolled decrees could in some circumstances be rescinded. There were many complaints of delays and uncertainty. A system designed for the disposal of extraordinary cases before the king's chief minister was not easily adapted to cope with 1,000 plaintiffs a year.

The procedure of the Star Chamber was the same, in essence, as that of the Chancery. Hearings were conducted before an imposing array of peers and councillors, including very often (besides the lord chancellor) an archbishop, the lord treasurer, the chancellor of the Exchequer, and the chief justices; but much use was made of commissions and arbitration. Unlike the Chancery, the Star Chamber could award damages and could also inflict corporal penalties or fines.

Criminal Law and Procedure

The criminal courts shared in the general increase of business already noted with respect to private litigation. Elizabethans believed that there was a major crime wave and were inclined to attribute it to the same causes as the rise in lawsuits: greater plenty bred more envy and greed among those who felt excluded. Precise figures are unobtainable, but historians have found evidence of an increase in prosecutions for crimes against property, especially in the 1580s and 1590s.

The most serious offenses were treason, murder, and felony. Felonies included manslaughter, rape, buggery, arson, burglary, robbery, and grand larceny (stealing goods worth at least twelve pence). All these carried a mandatory death sentence, though execution was frequently avoided. Such serious offenses were triable only on indictment, which meant that the accusation (in the form of a bill of indictment) had to be found "true" by a grand jury before the accused could be tried before a petty jury of twelve.

Besides these capital offenses there was a wide range of lesser crimes, later called misdemeanors. These could be prosecuted either on indictment or in a number of other ways: for instance, by information in the King's Bench (where the accusation was made by an individual but tried by jury) or the Star Chamber (where it was tried by the court), by presentment in courts leet (where the presentment itself operated as a conviction), by presentment in archidiaconal courts (where trial was by oath), or by summary conviction before justices of the peace (who had statutory powers to convict after making investigation). These miscellaneous jurisdictions overlapped. The church courts were mainly concerned with sexual misconduct, which accounted for about half the cases they dealt with; but similar cases could be dealt with by the justices of the peace. Church courts also punished nonconformity and failure to attend church (offenses sometimes prosecuted on indictment at the assizes), as well as spiritual shortcomings as diverse as drunkenness, golfing on Sunday, or consulting wizards. The inferior secular courts were more concerned with disorderly behavior or public nuisance, though insofar as these involved sin (as in the case of bawdy houses or drunkenness) their jurisdiction overlapped with that of the church courts.

The most varied criminal jurisdiction, if numerically one of the smallest, was that of the Star Chamber. It took a particular interest in forgery, perjury, riot and unlawful assembly, maintenance, fraud, libel, breach of statutes and proclamations, and misconduct by public officials. It developed (or invented) new crimes when occasion required. Some of its inventions, such as the inchoate crimes (attempts and conspiracies), became firmly embedded in the common law. Others, such as "inveigling of young gentlemen and entangling of them in contracts of marriage to their utter ruin" or "drawing of young gentlemen into security for commodities of tobacco and phillizellas and such unnecessary stuffs," have remained more obscure. Yet the Star Chamber did not develop an exclusive jurisdiction, like the equity of the Chancery, because the crimes it recognized could in theory be prosecuted elsewhere.

Apart from the occasional state trial in Westminster Hall, such as that of Sir Walter Raleigh in 1603 and of Guy Fawkes in 1606, most serious offenses were tried at the assizes. Once or (more usually) twice every year all the English counties were visited by pairs of commissioners, appointed from the justices of the two benches, the barons of the Exchequer, and the serjeants-at-law. The commissioners were divided into six circuits (the Northern, Western, Oxford, Norfolk, Midland, and Home) and heard both civil and criminal cases. In London and Middlesex there were no assizes, but similar commissions for both counties were executed at Newgate (later called the Old Bailey) and at the Middlesex Sessions in Clerkenwell, where a new courthouse (called Hicks Hall) was built in 1612. At each assize town there might be between twenty and a hundred prisoners awaiting trial. On average, three-quarters of them were charged with some form of stealing, and the number charged with homicide was usually in single figures. Though most of the charges were capital, only about one prisoner in twelve would ever be executed.

In every county there were also four general quarter sessions of the peace each year, held by authority of the county commissions of the peace. At these quarter sessions prisoners could be tried on indictment between the assizes. The justices of the peace had in theory much the same jurisdiction as the assize judges, but in practice they dealt with fewer and less serious cases, and only one in thirty or forty of their prisoners went to the gallows.

Procedure at assizes and quarter sessions was much the same, although the assizes were conducted with more pomp. After the opening ceremonies, the bills of indictment (drawn up in advance, in Latin, by the clerk of assize) were considered by the grand jury; and then the prisoners who had been duly indicted were arraigned at the bar. On arraignment the clerk of assize read over the indictment, or rather paraphrased it in English, transposing from the third to the second person. The prisoner was asked how he would plead. In contrast with civil procedure, only the general issue was permitted. After pleading not guilty, the prisoner was asked, "How wilt thou be tried?" To this the only acceptable answer was, "By God and the country," meaning by jury. Trials were so short that up to a dozen prisoners might be thus arraigned before a jury was impaneled to try them, and each jury was usually expected to sit through several cases before being asked for its verdicts. The prisoners who were convicted of felony were taken away by the jailer and brought up for sentence at the end of the assizes. Before sentence was passed, the prisoners were asked whether they had "anything to say why sentence of death should not be pronounced." This was an opportunity for prisoners to produce pardons or pray clergy, the two principal means of avoiding the death penalty.

Pardons could be granted by the crown under the great seal, on the authority of a secretary of state. They were granted as a matter of course in cases of homicide by misadventure or in self-defense; they were issued by discretion on grounds of clemency or favor; and it seems they could be purchased by money. Some prisoners obtained pardons in advance of trial, and some were given respite of execution by the judge in order to apply for a pardon.

An even more common means of escape was benefit of clergy. Thomas à Becket's martyrdom had secured for the clergy exemption from secular punishment for felony, and medieval royal judges had extended this privilege to the literate laity as a way of qualifying the otherwise rigid death penalty. The extension had been achieved by making the test of clergy the ability to read rather than written evidence of ordination. The practice was to hand the convict who prayed clergy a copy of the psalter and to require him to read from it. His performance was assessed by the "ordinary," or bishop's representative. The ordinary alone could decide whether the man read "as a clerk," but he could be fined by the judge for an unreasonable decision. In practice, rejection was uncommon. It became usual to assign the same verse every time (the beginning of the Miserere), so that even illiterate prisoners could learn to act the part of clerks well enough to pass the examination. But the judge retained the discretion to assign an unexpected text and prevent prompting if he felt the death penalty appropriate.

Benefit of clergy led to anomalies. It excluded not only unfavored illiterates but also women, who could not possibly be clerks even if they could read. (It seems that the exclusion of women from the privilege led to greater leniency for them, in that there was a distinct reluctance to prosecute women for crimes that were normally clergiable.) Another defect of clergy was that it allowed the literate criminal to escape punishment altogether, as if literacy excused murder and theft. It was therefore enacted in 1490 that laymen could pray clergy but once, their second felony being capital. To make this measure effective, convicts who read as clerks were branded on the brawn of the thumb with an *M* (for manslayer) or *T* (for thief); but even this indignity could be pardoned for "persons of quality." In the sixteenth century, Parliament declared certain serious crimes (such as murder, burglary, and robbery) unclergiable and therefore subject to the death penalty, thus making the legal distinctions between different kinds of felony important for the first time.

For misdemeanors the usual punishment was a fine or whipping. Imprisonment was not yet in general use as a punishment, because there were no public funds available for the maintenance of indigent prisoners. The Star Chamber occasionally prescribed more inventive punishments, such as cutting off of ears, slitting noses, branding in the face, or wearing papers; but these were relatively uncommon in Shakespeare's time.

The church courts had very limited powers. Their usual sentence was penance, an act of contrition sometimes performed in a white sheet. The only ultimate sanction of the church courts was excommunication. In theory this penalty could be enforced by arrest, through secular process, but in reality excommunication was too awkward or expensive to be regularly invoked. Perhaps as much as 5 percent of the Elizabethan population remained obstinately excommunicate as a result of disobeying sentences in church courts.

The system of criminal justice in Shakespeare's time was somewhat primitive by modern standards. There was no regular police force, unless we so reckon the apparitors of the church courts, whose efficiency in investigating private lives led to frequent complaints. The town and parish constables, the Dogberrys and Verges, and the magistrates (who had the prime responsibility for detecting and punishing wrongdoers) attained widely varying standards of efficiency across the country. Trials, as noted above, were very short. There was no sophisticated law of evidence; and in state trials hearsay evidence, depositions, and dubious confessions were admitted indiscriminately. Even torture was sometimes used, by authority of the Privy Council, to induce confessions; though it was never, as on the Continent, a recognized part of legal procedure.

In ordinary cases, on the other hand, a lack of prosecutorial zeal was more typical than an excess: at the assizes many prisoners were discharged "by proclamation" because no accusers were forthcoming. Another surprising defect is that prisoners accused of capital offenses were not allowed counsel to present their case. Moreover, there were no appeals except for errors on the face of the record; and since the record contained very little, mistakes at the trial could not be corrected. These shortcomings were offset by the double protection of the grand jury and petty jury, and by the various opportunities for clemency.

The substantive criminal law was slow to achieve uniformity. There were few pronouncements from the central courts other than those regarding the form of indictments. Even in the time of Elizabeth I there was judicial uncertainty on elementary points: for instance, taking lead from a roof was held by the assize judges at Lancaster to be no felony (on the grounds that things affixed to the realty could not be stolen) and yet held to be a felony by the assize judges at York. The York prisoner had no right of appeal, and his only hope was that the judge might stay execution until he could consult his brethren. Most prisoners did not know enough law to be aware of such points.

The judges themselves, by reserving difficult cases for discussion in Serjeants' Inn, did much to bring about a uniformity of principles in the criminal law. There was also a steady flow of authoritative textbooks: Sir William Stanford's *Plees del Coron* (1557), William Lambarde's *Eirenarcha* (1581), Richard Crompton's enlarged edition (1583) of Anthony Fitzherbert's *New Book of Justices of Peace,* Ferdinando Pulton's *De pace regni et regis* (1609), Michael Dalton's *Countrey Justice* (1618), and Sir Edward Coke's *Third Institute* (written before 1630 but not published until 1644). No other branch of the law was so well served by legal writers, chiefly because no other major branch of the law was so poorly served by case law.

The Legal Profession

The increase in litigation in the sixteenth and seventeenth centuries was matched by an expansion of the legal profession. Lawyers were wont to say that a greater harvest required an increased work force, but many preferred to blame the lawyers themselves for not controlling admission to the profession more strictly. The number of attorneys of the two benches grew from about 300 in the 1560s to over 1,000 in the 1610s, though the increase was partly offset by the decline and disappearance of an older class of unqualified attorneys in local courts. The number of barristers also increased dramatically in the sixteenth century, from a few hundred to about 1,000, though it is not certain what proportion of them engaged in practice. The superior judges repeatedly exhorted the Inns of Court to reduce the number of calls to the bar, lest a glut of lawyers bring the profession into disrepute; but the pressure to expand was too strong to be withstood.

The number of officials of the central courts also increased significantly. There were about fifty superior officials in the two benches, each with underclerks; but a whole range of new officials had arisen since 1500 to cope with the increase in business, especially in the Chancery. The entire Westminster bureaucracy, including the revenue departments and the civil service, probably reached 1,000 in the early seventeenth century. In addition, there were the practitioners in the central ecclesiastical courts and a large body of students at the Inns of Court and Chancery. Scholars may differ as to the proper definition of the term *legal profession,* but no one can doubt that the number of men connected with the practice, administration, or study of the law in Shakespeare's time was very large, perhaps 3,000 at any one time. All claimed by custom the title of gentleman, though many were relatively lowly persons. At the top of the profession, a leading advocate or a senior court official in 1600 could earn as much as £1,000 a year, enough to build a great house such as Montacute or Blickling, enough indeed to join the ranks of the nobility and found a dynasty. The law still provided the best opportunities for social mobility, at least for men of outstanding ability.

The most glittering prize was the great seal of England, possession of which entitled the holder to be lord keeper or lord chancellor. The holders of that office in this period were Sir Nicholas Bacon (1558–1579), whose son Francis became lord chancellor in 1617; Sir Thomas Bromley (1579–1587); Sir Christopher Hatton (1587–1591); Sir John Puckering (1592–1596); and Sir Thomas Egerton (1596–1617), created Lord Ellesmere in 1603 and Viscount Brackley in 1616. All except Hatton had risen to office from practice at the bar. Next in order came the judges: four each (or thereabouts) in the King's Bench and Common Pleas, four barons of the Exchequer, the master of the rolls and eleven masters in ordinary of the Chancery, the masters of requests, the dean of Arches, and the judge of the Admiralty Court. The "twelve judges" of the common law belonged to the order of serjeants, which also included the most distinguished members of the bar.

Serjeants at law had a degree of dignity, with special robes and a distinctive headdress called a "coif," and they were created with much ceremony and expense. Only eighty-eight serjeants were created during Shakespeare's lifetime, and two-thirds of them became judges. The practicing serjeants had the monopoly of audience in the Common Pleas; but in the other courts they shared audience with the readers and benchers of the Inns of Court and, increasingly, with mere barristers. All ranks of the bar performed functions other than advocacy, such as giving counsel in chambers, drawing conveyances, and keeping manorial courts. A few were retained by the sovereign, the principal queen's counsel being the queen's serjeants, attorney general, and solicitor general. Sir Francis Bacon was given the special rank of queen's counsel extraordinary by Elizabeth I, but the rise of king's counsel as a distinct branch of the profession lay far ahead.

The ordinary litigant might see the great men in action in court, but he was likely to have more personal contact with the attorney who advised him and managed his lawsuits. Attorneys were of relatively low social standing, because their work was deemed to be administrative rather than intellectual, and in this period the Inns of Court did their best to exclude them from membership. The increase in work had also produced an even lower order of general practitioner, the "solicitors," men who, without formal training or qualification, made a living by soliciting lawsuits through their various stages in different courts, retaining attorneys or counsel if need be. The courts took a dim view of solicitors, who were often accused of stirring up and prolonging suits for their own gain: needy solicitors, said Serjeant Davies, "are loath to quench the fire that maketh them warm." Lord Ellesmere called them "caterpillars of the common wealth" and often railed against them in the Star Chamber. But all efforts to abolish them were in vain.

The Inns of Court and Chancery

The intellectual and social home of the legal profession was the little legal university situated on the Westminster side of the City of London. It was not a university in the strict sense, for the constituent colleges were not formally linked with each other and there were no charters of incorporation. But contemporaries had good reason to call it the third university of England, for a large part of the gentry passed through it and it probably had more influence on the secular life of the nation than Oxford and Cambridge. There were four major colleges, called Inns of Court.

Two of them, the Inner Temple and Middle Temple, occupied the "New" Temple, originally built for the Knights Templar in the twelfth century. The Templars' round church, with effigies of cross-legged knights on the floor, still survives. It was connected by old cloisters to the medieval hall, used by the Inner Temple. The Middle Temple erected a grand new hall (1562–1574), and both societies built busily in Tudor times:

Those bricky towers
The which on Thames broad aged back do ride,
Where now the studious lawyers have their bowers,
There whilom wont the Templar Knights to bide,
Till they decayed through pride.

(Spenser, *Prothalamion,* 132–136)

The gardens running down to the river provided quiet solace for the men of law. Shakespeare himself must have seen the rosebushes there, for they inspired the famous scene in *Henry VI, Part 1,* in which the emblems of Plantagenet and York are plucked from the briars in the Inner Temple garden, a quarrel that would "send, between the red rose and the white, a thousand souls to death and deadly night" (II. v. 126–127).

On the west side of Chancery Lane stood Lincoln's Inn, once the town residence of the bishops of Chichester and largely rebuilt in brick by Tudor lawyers. Its chief architectural glory was to be Inigo Jones's neo-Gothic chapel, built in 1619–1623, when John Donne was preacher to the inn. The fourth and largest Inn of Court in Shakespeare's period, taking one-third of all entrants, was Gray's Inn. The site had been an old townhouse of the Lords Grey de Wilton, on the north side of High Holborn, which lawyers had inhabited since the fourteenth century. Like the other inns, it had been largely reconstructed: the fine hall and screen were completed early in Elizabeth's reign, and the gardens (or "walks") were beautified by Sir Francis Bacon.

In the "bricky towers" and garrets of these four houses lived nearly 1,000 students. Most of them did not intend to pursue legal careers. Their brief stay at best acquainted them with such legal knowledge as they would need in the shires. The inns provided an opportunity to meet people, to learn the ways of polite society, and to indulge youthful fancies. Many were the young gallants who spent more on dancing lessons and silk doublets than on law books. They were fond of lively entertainments, ranging from the courtly medieval revels to the latest plays and masques. *The Comedy of Errors* was performed at Gray's Inn in 1594, and *Twelfth Night* at the Middle Temple in 1602. Those who tried to keep Inns of Court men at their books would doubtless have been shocked to know that such distractions would one day be an academic study in themselves.

The inns were, first and foremost, law schools. The law was not taught in any systematic way, but it could not easily be learned elsewhere, for (in the words of Sir John Davies) it was "learned by tradition as well as by books." For books, the student began with Sir Thomas Littleton's *Tenures* and Fitzherbert's *New Natura Brevium,* and then progressed to the cases. Reports of medieval cases (the "year books") were kept in print by Richard Tottel, the law printer, but many students used the printed abridgments of Fitzherbert and Sir Robert Brooke. Recent cases were available in Edmund Plowden's *Commentaries* (1571) and Sir James Dyer's *Ascuns Novel Cases* (1585), followed in the 1600s by Sir Edward Coke's *Reports.* All these books were in law French. The student read, pen in hand, collecting the nice, sharp quillets of the law into alphabetical commonplace books. He also attended Westminster Hall and sat in the wooden galleries of the King's Bench and Common Pleas, making notes on the proceedings.

In addition, law students attended learning exercises at the Inns of Court. In the two learning vacations, during Lent and in August, a member of at least sixteen years' standing was appointed to "read" in each house. Many notes of these readings (which were lectures on particular statutes) and of the accompanying discussions have survived. Upon reading, or sometimes shortly before doing so, a barrister became a bencher of his inn and, as such, a member of its governing body. The members of the inns also engaged in disputing law at moots, which were set cases pleaded and argued in the same way as real cases at Westminster. The benchers had acquired their name from their role as judges at moots, and barristers likewise from their place as advocates at the bar of the inn. The exercises (performed daily) were tough and weeded out the unsuitable without any need for written examinations. By 1600, call to the bar of an Inn of Court was a qualification for practice, subject to a waiting period. Such was the status of these societies that admissions trebled between 1560 and 1620.

Besides the four Inns of Court were the eight Inns of Chancery: Barnard's Inn, Clement's Inn, Clifford's Inn, Thavie's Inn, Furnival's Inn, Lyon's Inn, New Inn, and Staple Inn. These housed the younger students, straight from the universities, who were acquiring the rudiments of law before progressing to an Inn of Court; gentlemen such as Shallow, Pickbone, and Squele, who were finishing their education without gaining admission to an Inn of Court; and the many attorneys and court officials who kept chambers there and were barred from the Inns of Court. The latter were the governors, or "ancients," but they did not provide any teaching. The Inns of Court sent readers each year to lecture for four terms and also to help with the moots. The "grand moots" in the Inns of Chancery were apparently open to young students (or "mootmen") from all the societies.

These inns were all close to one another, wrote Sir Edward Coke in 1604, "and altogether do make the most famous university, for profession of law only, or any one humane science, that is in the world." England was, indeed, unique in having schools of purely national law, schools where Justinian held no sway. Without them the history of English law and of English culture would have been very different.

Law and Legal Change:
The Recovery of Debts

So widespread was moneylending and dealing on credit that actions to recover debts were the commonest actions in nearly every lay court. In this period, debt cases increased from about two-thirds to three-quarters of the work of the Common Pleas, and from nearly one-quarter to nearly one-half of the work of the King's Bench. After 1600 two-thirds of all cases begun in the two benches were actions of debt. In local courts, one-half to three-quarters of the cases concerned unpaid debts. Yet, despite their frequency, debt cases gave rise to few legal problems. The main practical difficulty was that debtors could not pay, would not pay, or needed more time to pay. Even if a debt was contested, the usual problem was not theoretical but evidential—the problem of proving the contract or payment.

Actions of debt were usually brought either on a contract or on a bond ("obligation"). In debt on a contract, the plaintiff relied on an oral transaction (such as a sale, loan, hiring, or employment). If he had performed his side, payment was due from the other party. The defendant could ask for a jury trial if he denied the debt, but he also had the option of waging his law. This ancient method of proof involved swearing that he did not owe the money and bringing with him a set number of compurgators to swear that his oath was trustworthy. In local courts wager of law was still practiced with some reliability in early Elizabethan times: the persons concerned all knew each other, and it seems that many defendants who waged law either failed to find enough support or were unwilling to risk damnation when the time came to swear. In the central courts, however, the impracticability of bringing the requisite eleven compurgators to Westminster had resulted in a strange concession: the defendant still swore the main oath but could hire compurgators for a few pence from the court porter.

This system may nevertheless have had some merits in comparison with jury trial, in which neither party was allowed to give evidence. Many defendants preferred jury trial, both because it gave them more time and because it relieved them from having to take an oath. Yet it was a snare for plaintiffs with just claims, so sixteenth-century lawyers invented a form of trespass action called *assumpsit* to enable debts to be recovered in the form of damages for breach of a promise to pay. In trespass, trial was always by jury, so the defendant could not swear himself out of debt. *Assumpsit* as an alternative to the action of debt was developed by the King's Bench, but because it deprived alleged debtors of their ancient right of waging law, it was attacked by the more conservative Common Pleas. A dispute between the courts raged until 1602, when it was resolved by a bare majority of the justices in the Exchequer Chamber in favor of the new action. Wager of law went rapidly into obsolescence.

The more secure method of contracting was the money bond. A simple (or "single") bond was a written acknowledgment under seal that the debtor (the "obligor") owed a sum of money to the creditor (the "obligee"). In an action of debt this deed would be conclusive proof (in the absence of duress or forgery) that the money was owed, unless the defendant could produce an acquittance or release under seal. A more elaborate form was the conditioned bond, or penal bond, which was a deed of the same character endorsed with a condition destroying the main obligation in the event of performance. In this form the main debt operated as a penalty on failure to perform the condition. Suppose Antonio owed Shylock £50. Shylock might require Antonio to make a bond for £100 endorsed with the condition that if the £50 was paid by a certain day the bond would become void. If Antonio paid in time, the £100 debt was extinguished; but if he defaulted, even by a day, the penalty was forfeited and Shylock could sue for his monetary pound of flesh. The conditioned bond provided a means of enforcing all manner of contracts, and it was in very wide use, despite the availability of relief against unconscionable penalties in Chancery. By 1600, conditioned bonds accounted for perhaps half of all the cases begun in the courts of common law.

Debts recovered by judgment could be levied by writs of *fieri facias* (to seize and sell goods) or *elegit* (to levy the sum on half the land and half the goods of the debtor). If a debtor sought to evade execution by making a collusive conveyance of his land, the conveyance could be set aside under a statute of 1571. If there was insufficient property to satisfy the creditor, the debtor could as a last resort be arrested by *capias ad satisfaciendum* or, if he could not be found, be outlawed and made subject to arrest by *capias utlagatum*. This was a last resort, because the plaintiff who chose this course waived all other remedies. Moreover, it did not facilitate the earning of money by an impecunious debtor, because the debtor could not be released on bail; indeed, if the sheriff released him or permitted his escape, the sheriff became personally liable for the debt. The main object of arresting judgment debtors was to induce third parties to stand surety, so that the debtors could be released. Actions of debt against sureties were therefore common. Special provision was also made in this period for the insolvency of tradesmen, thereby laying the foundations of the English law of bankruptcy.

Law and Legal Change: The Land Law

Although the most frequent cause of action in the central courts was debt, from the point of view of bench and bar nine-tenths of the law was concerned with property in land. Land law had always dominated legal literature and the learning exercises in the Inns of Court. Littleton's elementary treatise on *Tenures* went through more than fifty editions between 1481 and 1600 and was perhaps the most successful legal textbook ever written in England. All gentlemen of property needed to know the first principles and maxims of land law, yet complete mastery was attained by few lawyers. Coke's commentary on Littleton, published in 1628 as *The First Part of the Institutes,* shows how recondite the subject had become, and there were many areas he left untouched.

Land law had never been simple. The worst medieval complexities had been procedural, since there was a wide range of original writs for the recovery of property in different circumstances, and a corresponding variety of procedures rooted in the distant past. By the 1560s a new and simpler remedy (the action of ejectment) had rendered most of this abstruse learning obsolete. In its place new complexities and uncertainties had arisen from the transfer of so much property litigation to the Chancery. But, as far as jurisprudence was concerned, most of the intellectual complexity of property law had shifted to conveyancing and, in particular, to the problems involved in settling land on a succession of owners. Conveyancing had long been an important aspect of practice in chambers; but in Shakespeare's time it led more and more often to disputes in court.

Family settlements were intended to ensure the devolution of real property from eldest son to el-

dest son and, incidentally, to make suitable provision for other relatives. The main ingredient of a settlement was the entail (or fee tail), which resulted from land being given to a person "and the heirs of his body." Entailed land could not pass to collateral heirs, and the direct descendants of the donee had a sufficient interest to enable them to prevent the heir in possession from giving away or charging the land beyond his own lifetime.

Had there been no escape from entails, most of the land in Elizabethan England would have been rigidly shackled to the wishes of long-dead medieval settlors. The deceased could not be allowed so much power over the living, and in the fifteenth century means had been found of "barring entails" by fine or recovery. Shakespeare mentions fines and recoveries in at least three plays (*Hamlet,* V. i. 98–99; *Merry Wives of Windsor,* IV. ii. 183–184; *Comedy of Errors,* II. ii. 73). The common recovery was a fictional lawsuit brought against the tenant in tail, which by an ingenious misuse of long-established principles resulted in the plaintiff's recovering the land free of the entail. The future issue in tail were cut off with a theoretical right to compensation from the land of a person who had been called in to warrant the title. This "common vouchee" was always a minor official of the Common Pleas who took care to own no land and suffered countless unenforceable judgments to be given against him for a fee of four pence a time. The fine (or final concord) was another fictional lawsuit, ending in a compromise, the effect of which (with statutory approval and safeguards) was likewise to bar the entail. As a result of these devices the entail had little more than moral force: the prodigal heir could "sell the fee simple . . . and cut th' entail from all remainders" (*All's Well That Ends Well,* IV. iii. 261–263).

If the entail would not by itself safely ensure devolution to the intended descendants, conveyancers tried other devices. The simplest was to make the first tenant (for instance, the husband in a marriage settlement) a tenant for life, so that the entail started with his sons. This common arrangement tied the land for one generation. But sixteenth-century conveyancers experimented with more ambitious and complex schemes, which began to vex the courts in the second half of the century. The principal doubts arose from the Statute of Uses (1536) and the Statute of Wills (1540), which solved certain revenue problems by the invention of a neat legal fiction. Lawyers turned this fiction to unforeseen ends, and abstract logic trapped the courts in a position from which they were soon seeking every pretext to escape. The result was utter confusion. Sir Francis Bacon, reading on the Statute of Uses in Gray's Inn in 1600, said it was "a law whereupon the inheritances of this realm are tossed at this day like a ship upon the sea." Even Sir Edward Coke, who thrived on legal niceties, criticized settlements "so extravagant that no one will know any rule to decide the questions that will arise upon them." It was finally settled in 1613 that any device which sought to make an entail unbarrable was void, and the courts also introduced various rules preventing "perpetuities," or unbreakable settlements. The classical strict settlement was devised later in the century.

One major achievement of the Elizabethan courts was the assimilation of copyhold tenure to freehold. Copyhold tenure had been associated with villeinage and was "unfree": the tenant held at the will of the lord of the manor. Unfree tenures had been divorced from unfree status in medieval times, and there were few if any villeins left by 1600. But a great deal of land was held "by copy of court roll" (the new name for villein tenure), and it was held by persons in no way servile. In the changed social circumstances there was no reason to deny copyholders the security of tenure long given by the common law to freeholders. Chancery led the way, and by the 1580s the common-law courts had agreed that copyhold land could be recovered by an action of ejectment. At the same time, the central courts extended many of the rules of land law to copyholds, including some of the law relating to entails and settlements. Except in manors where distinct customs were preserved, such as inheritance by youngest sons, copyhold came to be little different from freehold except in the mode of conveyancing. "Time," said Coke, "hath dealt very favourably with copyholders in divers respects."

Two important contributions to the law of property were made in this period by the Court of Chancery. The first arose from the creation of interests in land not recognized by the common law or affected by the Statute of Uses but imposing on the legal owner a "trust" that bound him in conscience. Trusts were employed in order to achieve various technical objectives in conveyancing and were received under the shelter of equity by stages that cannot readily be discerned in the law reports. Trusts encountered the criticism that they created more uncertainty, but they were to become an essential feature of English property law.

The second contribution of the Chancery was the recognition of the equity of redemption. The court set aside strict legal rights when conscience so required; on grounds of fraud or hardship, the Chancery had long protected debtors against penalties in bonds and lessees against forfeiture clauses in leases. During the first decades of the seventeenth century, the court also began the routine protection of mortgagors who for various reasons had not paid their debts on time. There were complaints that Chancery mercy was not always sufficiently restrained, but by the time of Francis Bacon's chancellorship (1617–1621), the mortgagor's equity had probably become a recognized doctrine.

Law and Legal Change: The Crises of 1616

The year of Shakespeare's death was also a year of turmoil in the legal world—a year, wrote Bacon, "consecrate to justice," though in hindsight that may not have been the most apt description. The central character was Sir Edward Coke (1552–1634), chief justice of the King's Bench, a judge of oracular learning and integrity. Coke's memory has been understandably tarnished by his intemperate speeches as a crown prosecutor prior to 1606, though by the standards of the day he does not seem to have greatly exceeded his duty. As a judge his contemporary reputation was unquestioned, and his every word was law.

On 14 November 1616, Coke received with dejection and tears a writ dismissing him from office, an outrage without recent precedent. The occasions for his dismissal were various. "The common speech," according to John Chamberlain, "is that four p's have overthrown and put him down—that is, pride, prohibitions, praemunire and prerogative." Pride was a vice not confined to Coke. Bacon, his old rival, was ambitious and determined to destroy Coke. Lord Ellesmere was opinionated and favored a somewhat totalitarian legal system: he had, for instance, advised the king that he could decide cases in person, whereas Coke had provoked James to physical anger by asserting that the king was not learned in the law and was subject to the law. Coke could not compromise on issues that he saw in absolute terms. His campaign to control new and extraordinary jurisdictions (particularly the broad powers of the High Commission) by issuing writs of prohibition had brought him into conflict with Archbishop Bancroft and other members of the Privy Council. Coke had also attacked the controversial practice of reopening cases in Chancery after judgment had been given in one of the benches, and in 1615 he had taken to releasing Chancery prisoners by *habeas corpus,* even suggesting that the terrible (and obsolete) penalties of *praemunire* might properly be invoked to discourage such suits.

This intervention provoked Ellesmere to complain to the king, and in 1616 the matter was resolved (for the time being) in favor of the Chancery. At the same time, Coke had taken a stand against the prerogative power of staying suits in which the government (or a royal favorite) was interested. Bacon argued that the king might better lose Windsor Castle than this prerogative, adding that "the twelve judges are as the twelve lions under Solomon's throne: they must be lions (that is, stout) but beneath the throne (that is, with all obedience)." The principal case was settled, but in 1616 the judges were asked in the king's presence whether they were not bound to stay suits at the king's direction. All gave in except Coke, who replied that "when that case should be, he would do that should be fit for a judge to do." One lion had not stayed under the throne, and within a week he was suspended from sitting as a judge.

Coke was not alone in perceiving this threat to the rule of law. A young barrister of Gray's Inn, Timothy Tourneur, was probably expressing a widespread sentiment when he jotted down in 1616 his worries about "the high power of chancellors who persuade the king that they are solely the instruments of his prerogative, and insinuate with the king that his prerogative is transcendant to the common law":

> By such means they will enthral the common law, which yields all due prerogative, and by consequence the freedom of the subjects of England will be taken away and no law practised on them but prerogative, which will be such that no one will know the extent of it. And so the government will in a short time lie in the hands of a small number of favourites, who will flatter the king to obtain their private ends, even if the king remains indigent. If these breeding mischiefs are not redressed by Parliament the body will soon die in every part: but some say that no parliament will be held in England again, *et tunc valeat antiqua libertas Angliae.*
>
> (British Library, Add. MS 35957, fol. 55ᵛ, translated from law French)

Thus was the scene set for a greater conflict to come.

History has vindicated the supporters of the common law on almost every issue. Coke's influence on the development of constitutional principles is widely recognized on both sides of the Atlantic. His opinions are the foundations of judicial review of legislation in the United States and of administrative law in England. No other judge did as much to establish the principle that in England no man is above the law and that the law protects the individual against arbitrary government. That this position would eventually be acknowledged by kings and governments could not, perhaps, have been easily foreseen in 1616. But it was surely the most important long-term achievement of Jacobean jurisprudence.

BIBLIOGRAPHY

John H. Baker, "The Common Lawyers and the Chancery: 1616," in *Irish Jurist,* 4 (1969); John H. Baker, ed., *Legal Records and the Historian* (1978); and *An Introduction to English Legal History,* 2nd ed. (1979). Desmond S. Bland, *A Bibliography of the Inns of Court and Chancery* (1965). Lloyd Bonfield, *Marriage Settlements 1601–1740* (1983). James S. Cockburn, *A History of English Assizes, 1558–1714* (1972); James S. Cockburn, ed., *Crime in England 1550–1800* (1977). Edward Coke, *Les Reports,* 13 pts. (1600–1659) and *Institutes of the Laws of England,* 4 pts. (1628–1644). John Davies, "A Preface Dedicatory" to *Le Primer Report des Cases . . . en Ireland* (1615).

Charles M. Gray, *Copyhold, Equity and the Common Law* (1963); "Bonham's Case Reviewed," in *Proceedings of the American Philosophical Society,* 116 (1972); and "The Boundaries of the Equitable Function," in *American Journal of Legal History,* 20 (1976). Edith G. Henderson, "Relief from Bonds in the English Chancery," in *American Journal of Legal History,* 18 (1974). William S. Holdsworth, *History of English Law,* 17 vols. (1903–1972), esp. vols. IV and V. William Hudson, "A Treatise on the Court of Star-Chamber" (*ca.* 1620), in Francis Hargrave, ed., *Collectanea Juridica,* II (1791–1792). Eric W. Ives, "The Law and the Lawyers," in Allardyce Nicoll, ed., *Shakespeare in His Own Age* (1964). William J. Jones, *The Elizabethan Court of Chancery* (1967).

Louis A. Knafla, *Law and Politics in Jacobean England: The Tracts of Lord Chancellor Ellesmere* (1977). Brian P. Levack, *The Civil Lawyers in England 1603–1641* (1973). Mortimer Levine, *Tudor England 1485–1603* (1968). Ronald A. Marchant, *The Church Under the Law: Justice, Administration and Discipline in the Diocese of York 1560–1640* (1969). Stroud F. C. Milsom, *Historical Foundations of the Common Law,* 2nd ed. (1981). O. Hood Phillips,

Shakespeare and the Lawyers (1972). Thomas Powell, *The Attourney's Academy* (1623). Wilfrid R. Prest, *The Inns of Court Under Elizabeth I and the Early Stuarts 1590–1640* (1972); Wilfrid R. Prest, ed., *Lawyers in Early Modern Europe and America* (1981).

Walter C. Richardson, *A History of the Inns of Court: With Special Reference to the Period of the Renaissance* (1978). A. W. Brian Simpson, *An Introduction to the History of the Land Law* (1961) and *A History of the Common Law of Contract: The Rise of the Action of Assumpsit* (1975). Samuel E. Thorne, "History of Law," in Conyers Read, ed., *Bibliography of British History: Tudor Period, 1485–1603,* 2nd ed. (1959). Percy H. Winfield, *The Chief Sources of English Legal History* (1925).

The records of the central courts and of some others are preserved at the Public Record Office, London. Records of various local and ecclesiastical courts are to be found in repositories throughout England. There are collections of manuscript law reports, readings, and tracts in the British Library; the Bodleian Library, Oxford; the University Library, Cambridge; the Inns of Court libraries; the libraries of the Harvard and Yale law schools; the Folger Shakespeare Library, Washington, D.C.; and numerous other libraries.

Education and Apprenticeship

ANTHONY GRAFTON

The play within the play in *A Midsummer Night's Dream,* "Pyramus and Thisbe," is apparently fantastic in plot and language; yet it vividly reveals some of the realities of the England that Shakespeare knew. The scene presents noblemen and artisans, separated by an enormous difference in wealth and standing but linked by their shared ability to read and write. It reveals that aristocrats and commoners alike were literate enough to use their skills for recreation as well as for practical ends. But it also shows powerfully that merely knowing about mythological characters—or performing in plays—could not make one a learned man. The smallest details of vocabulary, syntax, and pronunciation could betray one's lack of real cultivation. And the educational system as a whole acted simultaneously as an aid to social advancement and as a bar against it. Here, as in other areas, Shakespeare's image of his society both matches and enriches the one reconstructed by modern historians from archival sources.

Sixteenth- and seventeenth-century England invested a great share of the national wealth in education and vocational training. By the standards of the preindustrial world or the modern Third World, people spent a large proportion of their time receiving instruction instead of engaging in economically productive activities. An astonishing number of both men and women could sign their names or read a simple printed text. Government officials and the ruling elite took an extraordinarily serious interest in both the theory and practice of education.

Yet any comparison with the national educational systems of modern Europe or the United States, for example, risks falling into fallacies of exaggeration and anachronism. For all its obsession with education, England had no educational system in the modern sense but a series of educational institutions that often overlapped in function. Some of them tried to tailor their offerings to the needs and abilities of children of a specific age; others tried to fit pupils, whatever their age or aptitude, to the requirements of a curriculum. Still others—the universities above all—tried to do both. Furthermore, early-modern English institutions rarely enforced their rules with rigor and consistency, and their records were inefficiently kept and imperfectly preserved. Whatever the complexities of the data, we can define the chief levels at which education was offered, reconstruct the social origins of the clientele for each, and gain a taste of the different flavors of pedagogical practice. The story may not be complete or accurate, but it is colorful and varied. And, in a number of important respects, it enlarges our understanding of late Tudor and early Stuart society and culture.

The Petty School

For modern students of premodern times, the lowest level of education is the hardest to imagine. The elementary school, called the petty school, was crucial. It provided basic instruction in reading, writing, and arithmetic. But it was run for the most part by private enterprise, and pupils came voluntarily instead of being required to do so by binding and effective legislation. Teachers, though perhaps no more badly paid than their modern counterparts, came and went with little ceremony—or scrutiny of their credentials. If the modern primary school is a complex, organic being centrally controlled and elaborately articulated, the petty school of Shakespeare's day was a primitive, unstable creation.

The petty school was normally headed by a man, though in some cases by a woman. Its students often included both boys and girls. For most children the term of study began at the age of five or six and did not last long, for the children of the poor became economically indispensable at seven or eight and joined their parents in agricultural or domestic work; the children of the gentry and those few poor boys whose ability won attention and support could enter a grammar school at age seven.

The petty-school curriculum did not reach a high level of sophistication. Contemporary illustrations show children learning together in one large (and presumably noisy) room. Most petty schools were run not by trained teachers but—as Francis Clement said (1576)—by "men and women altogether rude, and utterly ignorant of the due composing and iust spelling of words," or, as Edmund Coote put it in 1596, "men and women of Trade, as Taylors, Weavers, Shop keepers, Seamsters, and such others, as have undertaken the charge of teaching others." Pitiful salaries and miserable working conditions ensured that elementary schoolteaching did not attract the ambitious. The best-educated teachers were university graduates who had lost jobs in grammar schools for drunkenness or misbehavior of other kinds.

Although the petty school's organization was chaotic, its aims and curriculum were well defined. It was expected to train boys and girls to read English, to pronounce it properly, to write legibly, and to do simple arithmetic. The pupil began with a hornbook, a single sheet, protected by a slice of transparent horn, mounted on a wooden plank with a handle. On the sheet were printed an alphabet, generally in Old English, roman, and italic type; a short prayer; and, perhaps, the various possible combinations of vowels and consonants. The use of the hornbook is vividly described by the Spanish humanist Juan Luis Vives in a dialogue (originally in Latin):

[Teacher] Take the ABC tablet in your left hand and this pointer in the right hand, so that you can point out the letters one by one. Stand upright; put your cap under your armpit. Listen most attentively how I shall name these letters. Look diligently how I move my mouth. See that you return what I say immediately in the same manner, when I ask for it again. Attention. Now you have heard it. Follow me now, as I say it before you, letter by letter. Do you clearly understand? [Boy] It seems to me I do, fairly well. [Teacher] Every one of these signs is called a letter. Of these, five are vowels: A E I O U.

(*Colloquies,* 1538)

From reading and pronunciation—the latter no simple matter at a time when dialects sprouted in every town and experts disagreed violently in their attempts to formulate standard English—the child moved on to learn his primer, a set of English prayers established by statute as the proper beginning text; his catechism; and the copybook hand, a formal script mastered by imitating models in a printed copybook.

The content of instruction was overwhelmingly religious; its purpose, as enunciated by statutes from the time of Henry VIII on, was to enable children to take a proper part in church services. Yet the manner of instruction was often much less orderly than this purpose might lead one to expect. The harried schoolmaster or schoolmistress was hardly likely to find gentleness an effective aid to leading twenty or thirty children over these unattractive pedagogical hurdles, and discipline was enforced by a switch applied to a pupil's bottom. Contemporary accounts confirm that petty schools did not aspire to what would now be considered reasonable standards of decorum. In a play by a St. Paul's master (1530s), Idleness teaches Ignorance:

Idleness. Coomme on, ye foole!
All thys day or ye can cum to scoole?
Ignorance. Um! Mother wyll not let me cum.
Idle. I woold thy mother had kyst thy bum! . . .
Say thy lesson, foole.
Ign. Upon my thummes?
Idle. Ye, upon thy thummes. Ys not there thy name?
Ign. Yeas.
Idle. Go to, then; spell me that same.
Where was thou borne?
Ign. Chwas i-bore in Ingland, mother sed.
Idle. In Ingland?
Ign. Yea.
Idle. And whats half Ingland?

[pointing to first one thumb and then the other]
Heeres "ing" and heeres "land." Whats tys? . . .
Ign. Tys my thum.

This rich and bizarre mixture of insult, obscenity, and half-understood mnemonic was no doubt typical.

Yet, we must not underestimate the effectiveness of these strange and fragile institutions. For all their noise, dirt, and disorder they turned out an astonishingly literate population. For example, almost half of those condemned to death for petty theft by the Middlesex justices in the period 1612–1614 proved able to read aloud a verse from a printed Bible—and thus to plead the ancient right of benefit of clergy (which enabled them to get off with a branded thumb while their less literate colleagues were hanged). In some southern counties, a third or more of the male population signed the protestation of loyalty circulated by Parliament in 1642. Although recent work has shown that the ability to sign varied greatly between regions, on the whole one can only be astounded by the extent of functional literacy in England by the middle of the seventeenth century.

Above the petty school, paths were expected to diverge. Boys with ability or rich parents went next to the grammar school; ordinary boys, to less refined institutions or directly to apprenticeship in an adult occupation; girls, to a wide variety of fates less clearly defined by statutes and formal institutions. We turn first to the ideal—and highest—of these forms of secondary education.

The Grammar School

The grammar schools varied almost as much as the petty schools in size, wealth, and composition. At the top, the great, late-medieval colleges like Winchester (founded 1387) and Eton (founded 1440–1491) possessed buildings, endowments, and facilities comparable to those of Oxford and Cambridge. In the middle, prosperous city schools like Merchant Taylors' and St. Paul's catered to the sons of elite businessmen. At the bottom, a single small-town grammar master, with a handful of boys and without benefit of charter or statutes, might prepare several entrants to Oxford or Cambridge every year with little fuss and less expense. Yet these schools were alike in key respects.

In the first place, all grammar schools were the product of a single, coherent movement for the expansion of educational opportunity. That movement began, for reasons that remain obscure, in the late Middle Ages. Throughout England, even in the north, schools flickered into life in the fourteenth and fifteenth centuries. Simultaneously, at the great schools, the aristocratic descendants of the founders' families demanded entrance for their sons, elbowing aside the poor future clerics for whose education the colleges had been established.

After the 1530s, the Reformation powerfully reinforced this trend. By eliminating monasteries, chantries, and the buying of indulgences, it did away with the schools' main competition for charitable gifts and bequests. By emphasizing the need for a literate laity and an educated clergy, the Reformation furthered secondary as well as primary schooling. By fostering the transfer of a limited amount of property directly to schools, it increased their resources and effectiveness. And by defining curricula and selecting authoritative textbooks, royal statutes confirmed the importance of the grammar schools and imposed some measure of uniformity upon them.

In the second place, the grammar schools relied for their raison d'être on a well-established and uniform body of educational theory forged by the humanists of fifteenth- and sixteenth-century Italy and imported into sixteenth-century England by theorists and translators. The new theory held that neither the traditional curriculum of the medieval Latin school, with its barbarous Latin and emphasis on the philosophy of language, nor the traditional training of the nobility, with its vernacular poetry and emphasis on strength and courage, could adequately train the social elite to serve the needs of the state, which was taking on ever-increasing responsibilities and spawning governmental bodies of growing complexity. The new wave of educators insisted that a training in the best of Greek and Roman literature, read in the original languages, would equip men with the political and social insight, the command of detail and mastery of historical precedent, the fluency in speech and writing that would make them fit to rule. A rigorous classical training that emphasized history, moral philosophy, and politics would produce an elite of learning and culture as well as of birth. This body of theory, expounded in varying forms by men as different as Thomas Elyot and Roger Ascham, made the grammar schools attractive to parents and guardians of noble boys and young gentlemen.

In the third—and most important—place, the grammar schools possessed a solid, coherent, and long-established curriculum that appeared to instill some of the virtues claimed for it by its theorists. In the early sixteenth century, to be sure, the nature of a grammatical curriculum appropriate for rulers had seemed less clear. Innovative teachers were more worried about making their charges literate in Latin at quite a basic level. Experimental, non-classical tools like the *Vulgaria* of John Stanbridge and of William Horman taught the schoolboy how to say in Latin:

> His nose is like a shoeing horn.
> He is the veriest coward that ever pissed.
> Would God we might go play!

More advanced exercises enabled him to clothe some of his experiences in vivid if unclassical Latin: "I had an hevy hede in the mornynge when I sholde aryse and a slepy, and if I myght for my maister I wolde have leyn an hour more, but he was very hasty upon me." Exercises like this, practiced at Magdalen College School and elsewhere, produced boys who could express their feelings but were hardly future guardians of the state in the Platonic sense.

By Shakespeare's day, however, these early— and, in their own wit and fluency, rather Shakespearean—innovators had been crowded off the stage. The schoolboy was now insulated from reality by a series of carefully compiled and chosen texts and exercises. He began by memorizing the Latin grammar of William Lily, approved by statute and widely disseminated, and moved on to direct reading of such classical works as the comedies of Terence, the dialogues of Cicero, and the moral distichs attributed to Cato. He learned to parse— separating a Latin sentence into its component parts of speech and analyzing each word in terms of its grammatical and syntactic function. He learned to translate from Latin into English and back into Latin and to imitate the best authors' styles. And he learned a variety of means for improving his active knowledge of Latin more quickly than he could have through direct study of the classical authors. Manuals of composition like Erasmus' *De duplici rerum ac verborum copia* (*On Copiousness in Style and Subject Matter* [1512]) showed how to build any simple, declarative sentence into an elegant set of balanced clauses and how to amplify any subject by adding vaguely relevant similes, historical exam-

ples, and quotations. The famous tour de force by which Erasmus shows 150 different ways to say "Thank you for the letter" in correct Latin provided both a stock of useful expressions and a magnificent example to emulate. Similarly, reading aloud from Erasmus' *Colloquies* and performing newly written as well as ancient Latin plays made the boys fluent in speaking as well as in writing.

The object of this arduous preparation was, as Erasmus' title indicates, *copia;* the boy had to be not only correct but also articulate. To this end he accompanied his work in texts and manuals with systematic study of the ancient rules of oratory and the modern rules of letter writing. At first he might write mock Ciceronian letters, recombining bits extracted from Cicero. Later he would learn the ancient schemes for writing essays and speeches. By the end of his training, he would know how to show, for example in a funeral oration, that a noble man had been born of the right sort of parents, had performed the proper scholastic miracles, had married the right sort of woman, and had died the right sort of death. And he would know exactly how to enrich the treatment of these standard topics by introducing set-piece comparisons and other stock devices. The exercise was obviously highly artificial, as Shakespeare shows by parodying it with vicious accuracy:

> [Fluellen] . . . If you mark Alexander's life well, Harry of Monmouth's life is come after it indifferent well; for there is figures in all things. Alexander, God knows and you know, in his rages, and his furies, and his wraths, and his cholers, and his moods, and his displeasures, and his indignations, and also being a little intoxicates in his praines, did, in his ales and angers, look you, kill his best friend, Cleitus.
> Gower. Our king is not like him in that. He never killed any of his friends.
> Fluellen. It is not well done, mark you now, to take the tales out of my mouth ere it is made and finished.
>
> (*Henry V,* IV. vii. 28–39)

Only someone who had the formal techniques of rhetorical composition entirely at his command could have produced Fluellen's mock comparison of the two heroes and Gower's brilliant, destructive interruption of it. Also, only a dramatist who expected the parody to be intelligible to a large segment of his audience would have incorporated it in a play. In any event, Shakespeare reveals more vividly than any real example could the nature of traditional rhetoric as late Tudor and early Stuart schoolboys had come to know it.

The curriculum was not rigorously confined to Latin grammar and rhetoric. The larger schools offered Greek as well, beginning with the New Testament and a grammar, and proceeding to the moral verses of Theognis and Phocylides and short selections from Plutarch, Plato, and Homer. A few schools even offered Hebrew. Yet even instruction in Greek was designed primarily to foster fluency in Latin. Boys were really being instructed less in the expressive possibilities of Greek than in those of Latin when they were taught to take a single Greek epigram, two or four lines long, and produce multiple Latin versions of it. One popular anthology offers ten ways of translating the distich "If you're slow to walk and swift to eat, then run with your mouth and eat with your feet."

This, then, was the grammar school. For five to ten years, from six in the morning until half past five in the afternoon, unrefreshed by vacation or systematic physical exercise, the boys learned Latin grammar, formal rhetoric, and poetics. In the upper forms, Latin was spoken at all times. Lapsing into English was a breach of rules, which other students were expected to report and the master to punish. Immured in a curriculum that would have been largely familiar to that great rhetoric professor of a millennium earlier, St. Augustine, the boy learned to move chunks of Latin about as a chess player moves pieces, following set rules that could be neither altered nor questioned.

Despite their fluency, the boys read little. The master led them through their texts, generally for two hours a day, and thus can have covered no more than ten pages a week or a few hundred in a normal education. What the boys read, they knew. They parsed, translated, adapted, and copied out salient bits into their own systematic notebooks (John Foxe, the martyrologist, printed up a notebook with ready-made headings to make the task easier). But their culture was narrowly restricted, in scope and content, to a small segment of the literature produced by an ancient society that they did not attempt to study in its historical or cultural context.

For all its limitations, the grammar school proved continually attractive to parents. Theorists denounced its drudgery, the years wasted on learning an ancient language. Efforts were made to introduce such modern subjects as French, Italian, and drawing into some curricula and even to set up alternative schools. But few well-to-do parents were induced to abandon the rigorous, traditional grammar schools. Even those entrusted with the training of future monarchs opted not to give them the formerly traditional nobleman's indoctrination in manners and arms or a modern training in science and practical skills. The tutors of Edward VI and Elizabeth I praised them not for their fiery spirits or original minds but for their command of Latin.

Evidently, then, the grammar-school curriculum did provide some valuable elements of education, according to the expectations of the day. In the first place, a classical education instilled discipline. And the fact that men like Dr. Busby of Eton taught the classics by breaking their charges' wills with drudgery seemed to ensure that the victims of such schooling would be docile and polite. In the second place, classical education meant exposure to the right sort of culture. The Tudors, James I, and their ministers were well-educated men and women. They forced their wards and children to undergo a sound, elaborate training and offered preferment to others who had heard the Cambridge and Oxford muses sing. The ability to give a striking Latin speech or write an elegant Greek poem was an eminently practical skill between the late 1550s and 1640, as it would be again in the nineteenth century for Englishmen hoping to enter the Indian civil service. In the third place, the grammar school seems to have filled a profound, if obscurely felt, need of English society. At a time of rapid social, economic, and religious change, the grammar school offered a well-known and clearly defined way to produce adults.

Wrested from their normal place in society, instructed in the wisdom of the ancients, and physically maltreated, schoolboys developed a strong sense of loyalty and attachment to those who had undergone the tribulations with them. The school thus provided a kind of puberty rite, a way for its pupils to order and make sense of the passage to manhood. Although the society's standards of value and behavior seemed to be shifting, the young knew at least where they stood.

The rhetorical curriculum had powerful and unforeseen consequences. Whatever its failings when judged by the standards of modern liberal education, the grammar school had enormous virtues as a hotbed for literary talent. The emphasis on verbal variation finds its consummation in the wonderfully rich lexicon of late Elizabethan and Jacobean prose.

Learning the set piece proved a good way to attain the larger artistic discipline that gave shape to sonnets and tragedies. Paradoxically, an education obsessively dedicated to the details of a dead language proved to be a uniquely successful groundwork for mastering the elements of English style. For this alone the grammar schools deserve respectful attention.

Apprenticeship

Boys not enabled by talent or inheritance to attend the grammar school met a variety of educational fates. The most common one was to attend, for periods too various and informal to be specified, a secondary school at which reading, writing, and arithmetic were taught at a higher level than at the petty school, and then to receive training in a craft or mercantile endeavor, generally as an apprentice. The parents or guardians of each boy signed a contract with a guild master, who was required by law to accept apprentices. He took responsibility not merely to introduce the boy to the technical "mysteries" of his trade but also to bring him to adulthood. The apprentice lived in his master's house, ate meals with his family, and—most important of all, in theory—attended family prayers and underwent catechetical examination. The master, expected to serve as the just, strict, and pious head of a Christian household, was meant to replace the parent in moral as well as educational matters. Only after seven years of training and labor in the master's house and shop was the boy released into adult freedom.

In theory, the system was designed to produce conscientious and well-trained craftsmen, adept with tools and knowledgeable about the technical standards of their trade, disciplined by constant supervision and religious instruction, and guaranteed to be honorable and law-abiding adults. In fact, practice rarely matched this elevated ideal. On the one hand, too many masters fell below the moral and religious standards that they were expected to meet. Court records document the cases of masters who allowed or forced their apprentices to enter debauched company and who mistreated them physically.

On the other hand—since the system resulted in the proximity in urban centers of large numbers of adolescents—the apprentice's experience was less that of membership in a hierarchical and orderly Christian household than of membership in an egalitarian and disorderly corporation of apprentices with money and free time at their disposal. Apprentices met, told the traditional stories of their station in life (Dick Whittington and his cat was a special favorite), went to plays (though they were not supposed to), chastised prostitutes and created disorder in the streets on holidays. To some extent, even this apparently violent and raucous behavior enforced the norms and values of the larger society: when a crowd of apprentices noisily serenaded a family in which a wife consistently mistreated her husband, they were expressing the general tenet that wives should properly be subordinate. Apprenticeship also provided a powerful training in acceptable forms of behavior, although apprentices in the street were far less amenable to discipline than were boys in school. Especially in London, where great numbers of apprentices were concentrated, they amounted at times to an independent political force, vulnerable to radical influences because of the piety of its members: radical preachers rightly saw them as likely recruits. On the memorable occasion in 1647 when the London apprentices purged Parliament itself, it was clear that this system of labor discipline was neither draconian nor even consistently effective.

The substantive training that apprentices received is harder to reconstruct than the general process of socialization. A craftsman's training involved a large measure of hands-on instruction in the nature of materials, the use of tools, and standards of finishing; a merchant needed more abstract education in rates of exchange and the weights and measures used in the countries with which England traded. Certainly, the advent of printing and of humanism greatly enlarged the range of ideas and historical experiences with which an apprentice and his master came in contact. An example is revealing. From 1570, when Henry Billingsley's translation of Euclid appeared, with its famous polemical preface by John Dee, English architects and builders had access to a fascinating and provocative set of ideas, derived from the ancient treatise on architecture by Vitruvius and modern treatises on magic and cosmology by the Neoplatonists. Emphasis was on architecture as a mathematical discipline and on the practitioner as a learned man who understands the mathematical rules that govern the stars and, through them, life on earth. These works offered the modern craftsman not only high ideals but also concrete names of, and details about, ancient role models for the practice of architecture as a learned profession. The impact of such works cannot be known precisely; yet Shakespeare's play-acting apprentices, with their knowledge of ancient myths and theatrical methods, seem to show that interest in the higher culture filtered down, via books in the vernacular, to artisans as well. Moreover, the vagaries of individual families' fortunes, the growing belief of merchants and craftsmen that solid, formal education would benefit their sons, and the growth of limited but genuine scholarship support for poor schoolboys all ensured that some of them would undergo both grammar school and apprenticeship. Ben Jonson—to choose a famous example—had direct experience of every level of schooling we have so far discussed. As a boy he received a rigorous grounding in Latin at Westminster School; as a young man without means or patronage he became apprenticed to his stepfather, a mason, and worked —according to Thomas Fuller—with "a *trowell* in his hand . . . [and] a book in his pocket." As a mature dramatist he employed in his work the most recondite humanist learning and the most down-to-earth artisanal humor. His career illustrates the system's potential for flexibility—though the scorn he often underwent for his low birth and low employment also illustrates the limits of that flexibility.

The Education of Women

The third, and most amorphous, set of educational paths beyond the petty school was that provided for girls. Some formal education was available to those who lived near grammar schools that would accept them, as a few did for the ages from seven through nine. Aristocratic young ladies and the daughters of scholarly individuals (like Thomas More) occasionally mastered, by private tuition, the classical languages and tools of formal rhetoric and poetics. In the seventeenth century boarding schools for girls were founded on the outskirts of London, especially at Putney and Hackney. But there seems to have been little progress over time in opportunities for more technical and literary kinds of education. Greek-reading ladies tended to become extinct in the sixteenth century, and the new girls' boarding schools emphasized not the ideal of young women as humanists but the value of fashionable attainments: modern languages, dancing, fancy needlework. For such advantages, parents paid as much as

£32 a year, more than the salary of many petty-school masters.

Far more important for most parents than anything their daughters could learn in school was training in running a household and entrée to social circles where they might find a husband. Far more than any other European nation, the English attained this end by placing their daughters in situations outside the family. At the lower levels of society, girls became domestic servants or, if more adventuresome, worked in shops. Daughters of the gentry went to live in families connected to theirs by blood or friendship where, by participating in the work of the household, they learned the manifold skills required of its mistress. Even noble girls were often sent away to serve as ladies-in-waiting and thus acquire a more elevated set of social skills. This method was anything but irrational. The complex of skills required of the mistress of a household was so large, so diverse, and so tied to the learning of specific, traditional techniques that it would have been virtually impossible to devise a curriculum that included all or even most of them. It was far more efficient to allow the girl to learn cooking, preserving, sewing, needlework, pharmacy, cleaning, and estate management by watching a successful practitioner at work—especially, so the English thought, one who was not her mother and, perhaps, could therefore impose discipline more effectively. This departure from the parental household to attain the status of—as it were—an apprentice to a mature woman formed the basis of female education at virtually every social level.

Since a large number were literate, women of every social level could enlarge their knowledge and mastery of important techniques by reading. A flood of advice literature about everything from social behavior to child-rearing guaranteed women access to a vast body of detailed, if sometimes contradictory, advice.

The spread of basic literacy among women affected English society far more profoundly than did the few cases of women reaching a high level of formal scholarship: access to the Bible, printed sermons, and other religious literature underlay women's rise to prominence in the deviant religious sects of the seventeenth century. The pious sixteenth- and early-seventeenth-century founders of petty schools would have been shocked to think that they were planting the seeds from which the Quakers and other more radical groups grew. To this extent, the rise of women's schooling did help women to escape the subordinate social position to which they were confined. Again, the unintended consequences of educational change appear almost more significant than the planned results.

The Universities and the Inns of Court

Atop the hierarchy of formal educational institutions stood the two sets of collegiate bodies that had traditionally governed entrance into the professions: the universities and the Inns of Court. Oxford and Cambridge were rich and venerable institutions that had long offered solid instruction in the scholastic liberal arts and higher training in theology, law, and medicine. They had consistently attracted support from notables throughout England for their building needs and the financial support of needy students. Their graduates had long held many of the highest offices in the state as well as in the church. In the political disorder of the fifteenth century, Oxford and Cambridge had been able to take advantage of the newly invented printing press to publish educational books efficiently; Oxford had managed to build the spectacular Schools of Liberal Arts; and the dons of both universities had done sophisticated and original work on difficult problems of technical logic and natural philosophy.

The sixteenth century transformed the universities radically. Even before the Reformation, new colleges like Corpus Christi, Oxford, and Cardinal (which became Christ Church) had offered training in the grammar and rhetoric that formed the core of the humanist curriculum, and in the Greek and Hebrew needed to read the Bible in its original form. John Colet and Erasmus had offered a new approach to the Bible that emphasized not its doctrinal content but its direct moral message. After the Reformation, change came even more quickly. Canon law was eliminated, Roman law deemphasized, and Scholastic theology challenged more directly. And while the curriculum came to include more and more advanced work in the subjects studied at humanist grammar schools, the social foundations on which it rested also began to shift. The noblemen, gentry, and rich merchants who had patronized the grammar schools began to think that a few years at the university would also benefit their sons. Places were opened for boys who had no intention of becoming clerics or civil lawyers. Some colleges deliberately set out to win a segment of this new lay population—as St. John's, Oxford, did by reserving a large number of places for boys from Merchant Taylors' in London. By 1600, the universities were no longer ecclesiastical corporations for young clerics in training.

Rapid growth in student numbers and the advent of a new kind of student required major changes in the universities' structure and methods. The lower-class boys who came on scholarships or worked their way through university as servants wanted an updated version of the traditional curriculum. They fully intended to attend the lectures, participate in the disputations on knotty philosophical problems, and take the traditional degrees; for only so could they make their way as ministers or schoolmasters. But the well-born boys who attended for a few years normally did not expect either to undergo the rigors of intensive training in logic and theology or to earn degrees by the approved exercises. They—or their parents—wanted more drill in grammar and rhetoric, more instruction in manners, morals, and history, more training in socially useful skills. As the old curriculum did not supply this, a new one, not formalized by degrees and exercises, evolved within the interstices of the old.

Tutors and coaches came to dominate the teaching of the upper classes. They took the boys into their personal charge and oversaw their meals, their lives outside the classroom, and their studies; indeed, the boys usually slept in their tutors' rooms. They taught the classical Latin, rhetoric, and poetics slighted by the formal curriculum. They arranged for instruction in such extracurricular subjects as dancing, fencing, riding, and modern languages. And they arranged the pupil's work in accordance not with university statutes but with the pupil's abilities and interests and his parents' or guardians' requirements and beliefs—which were made plain in extended, detailed correspondence. The new university structure, then, was two-tiered. Though there was constant, informal interplay between them—as tutors took on poor boys and made them classical Latinists or as well-to-do boys like Simonds D'Ewes eagerly took part in the formal exercises of the standard curriculum—the tiers remained basically distinct in goals, methods, and social composition.

The universities in Shakespeare's day had become prosperous and attractive beyond their wildest dreams. Pupils and benefactors abounded, and a building boom produced much of the Oxford and Cambridge of today, as new colleges were founded and old ones extended to make room for enlarged student bodies. The Bodleian Library, new institutions like Sidney Sussex, Cambridge, and Wadham College, Oxford, and the Renaissance quadrangles added to most of the older colleges attest to the universities' success in capturing not only the sons but also the admiration and active support of England's elite.

The intellectual life of the universities had proved more contentious than their social history. On the one hand, students and nonuniversity educators complained bitterly about the sterility of the formal curriculum. It was imprisoned in a dead language, obsessed with technical points of logic and theology, and erected on boring books by deservedly obscure authors:

Hang Brirewood and Carter, in Crakenthorps garter,
Let Keckerman too bemoan us;
I'll be no more beaten for greasy Iacke Seaton
or conning of Sandersonus—

So ran the "Catch Against the Schoolmen" in the early-seventeenth-century comedy *Aristippus;* and such ridicule and satire reappeared buttressed by much learning and solid argument in more serious works like the *Novum organum* of Francis Bacon. Proposals were continually floated for the creation of new educational institutions, which would devote themselves systematically to instructing young gentlemen either in the pursuits appropriate to their station or in modern science. In his will Thomas Gresham (d.1579), a graduate of Caius College, Cambridge, founded a set of lectureships (in the vernacular) in astronomy, geometry, physic, law, and other subjects, to be delivered in London. Earlier studies of the universities of Shakespeare's time have concentrated on these reform proposals and accepted their portrait of the sterility of the universities.

More recent research, however, has demonstrated that this view is one-sided. Direct study of the curriculum actually taught at Oxford and Cambridge has revealed that the new science of the seventeenth century flourished within the universities as well as outside them. As early as 1570, at Oxford, the young Henry Savile delivered lectures on astronomy, based on Ptolemy's *Almagest,* that showed a full command of Copernicus' recent revolutionary work. Seventeenth-century Oxford was the spawning ground for much original work in physiology and other natural science. Even in the central fields of the statutory curriculum, changes

can be detected. By the middle of the sixteenth century the logic curriculum at Cambridge had come to emphasize not the traditional, rigorous instruction in formal logic and semantics but a much broader and less technical introduction to the forms of argument that appear in literary texts and serve the purposes of ordinary, practical men. Even at Oxford, where Aristotle underwent fewer direct attacks, by the end of the sixteenth century it was acknowledged that a serious Aristotelian scholar had to read the texts in Greek, study them in the light of humanist textual criticism, and master the ancient Greek commentaries as well as the modern Latin ones. And in those colleges—like Emmanuel, Cambridge—that embraced Puritanism, the full range of new theological questions about doctrine, ecclesiology, and church services was subjected to vigorous debate.

It would be as wrong to exaggerate the universities' receptivity to new books and ideas as it was to denounce them for their sterility. Few students mastered both the old and the new curriculum at an equally high level. Perhaps none of them ever grasped that terrifying range of learning demanded by contemporary guides to reading in the main fields of scholarship. Yet, it is clear that the universities participated fully in both the social and the intellectual changes of their age. And, insofar as they probably produced many more learned men than the church and state could employ, they too perhaps contributed to the political and religious discontent that would lead to the civil wars and the destruction of Shakespeare's England.

The other collegiate institutions, the four Inns of Court in London, were both institutions for training barristers and professional associations of practicing barristers. Their curriculum, like that of the universities, rested on formal exercises: lectures and disputations. As at the universities, senior students taught junior ones. Unlike the universities, however, the Inns offered not a systematic introduction to a body of Latin scholarship and thought recognized as valid throughout Europe, but an unsystematic introduction to the bizarre and unique common law of England. The student had to learn to read law French, the artificial language of the law and the courts. He had to learn from listening to lectures how to analyze a statute and its application. And, by reading law reports and observing his elders in court, he had to learn to plead a case. Education proceeded less by inculcation of clear, abstract principles than by total immersion in a body of chaotic axioms, dicta, and facts, the interrelationships of which became clear as the student forced his way to greater proficiency. From the 1520s on, to be sure, systematic manuals began to appear that tried to impose some order on the pullulating mass of English law. But there is little evidence that they had a significant impact on the nature of instruction at the Inns.

What did happen, as at the universities, was a dramatic growth in numbers of students and the rapid development of a two-tiered system of instruction. Alongside the future professionals stood more and more young gentlemen, who came to spend a year or two. Like the gentry who went to the university—and indeed, many new students came to the Inns after a year or two at Oxford and Cambridge—they came not for technical training but for useful skills. They sought to learn enough law to manage their properties and escape damage when threatened by litigation. But they generally did not seek to master the intricacies of the legal system as professionals. Instead, they devoted themselves to rhetoric, poetry, dancing, fencing, tennis, business arithmetic, and other unofficial studies. The Inns served as their base in London and in some cases facilitated their extracurricular studies. Yet, given the upper-class demand for education, even this not very active cooperation was enough to win the Inns an enormous increase in students and to finance a rebuilding program as ambitious and successful as the Oxbridge ones. The great new brick-and-stone buildings, like Middle Temple Hall, rivaled anything in the universities for grandeur and served as models for imitation there.

One final kind of education, difficult to describe without imposing a spurious precision on scattered evidence, enabled sons of the richest families to put a final gloss on the polish acquired at grammar schools, universities, and Inns of Court. This was the grand tour, systematic travels guided by a tutor, during which the boy perfected his military skills, attained fluency in the modern languages, visited courts, sketched fortifications, or consulted libraries as his talents and interests dictated. Those young nobles and gentlemen who had gone on the grand tour and had come to know continental cultures, tongues, and habits later served as England's diplomats. Their range of knowledge and experience could be extraordinary. In the 1590s, young Henry Wotton met the greatest scholars in northern Europe, Joseph Scaliger and Isaac Casaubon; consulted the greatest manuscript collections in Italy; and spent so much time pretending to be a German Catholic in Italy that he was later able to pose successfully as an Italian Catholic in England. He, perhaps more than any of his more famous contemporaries, can be seen as an ideal product of English education in Shakespeare's day.

No capsule assessment of these complex phenomena can possibly do them justice. What was most distinctive about the educational system in Shakespeare's England was not any single social, institutional, or intellectual development. Native precedents and foreign parallels could be found for almost every Elizabethan educational custom except, perhaps, the wholesale exile of children from their homes and the local world of the Inns of Court. What cannot be found in any other early-modern society is a population so avid for learning of every kind. "Every man strains his fortune to keep his children at school; the cobbler will clout it till midnight, the porter will carry burdens till his bones crack again, the plowman will pinch both back and belly to give his son learning; and I find that this ambition reigns nowhere so much as in this island." There is hyperbole in James Howell's assessment but truth as well. Shakespeare's England sought access to knowledge, not for everybody but for a larger segment of the population than any other western European nation had done. That is a worthy epitaph for the systems of education and apprenticeship that it built.

BIBLIOGRAPHY

The most recent general survey is provided by Rosemary O'Day, *Education and Society, 1500–1800* (1982), chs. 1–10, which is especially good on social history. Lu Emily Pearson assembles a great deal of relevant detail and anecdotes in *Elizabethans at Home* (1957). Lawrence Stone, "The Education Revolution in England, 1560–1640," in *Past and Present,* 28 (1964), which marked the beginning of modern work on the impact of education on early-modern English society, still deserves close study even though many of its conclusions have since been modified. For the petty-school curriculum see Thomas Whitfield Baldwin, *William Shakspere's Petty School* (1943); David Cressy, *Literacy and the Social Order* (1980); and Margaret Spufford, *Small Books and Pleasant Histories* (1981).

Fritz Caspari admirably describes the ideology of the grammar schools in *Humanism and the Social Order in*

Tudor England (1954). Thomas Whitfield Baldwin assembles a monumental body of material about the nature of grammar school teaching in *William Shakspere's Small Latine and Lesse Greeke* (1944). A classic case study in the theory and practice of rhetoric in the English Renaissance is Wilbur Samuel Howell, *Logic and Rhetoric in England, 1500–1700* (1956). An elegant essay on the teaching of scansion is Derek Attridge, *Well-Weighed Syllables* (1974). On the social and ritual functions of classical education see Walter J. Ong, *Rhetoric, Romance and Technology* (1971), ch. 5.

For the world of the apprentices see Steven R. Smith, "The London Apprentices as Seventeenth-Century Apprentices," in *Past and Present,* 61 (1973). For the importance of Billingsley's translation of Euclid and similar works see Frances A. Yates, *Theatre of the World* (1969). The best treatment of education for women is offered by O'Day, *op. cit.,* ch. 10.

On the universities, the literature is already profuse and rapidly increasing. For the social background see the articles by Lawrence Stone, Guy F. Lytle, James McConica, and Victor Morgan in Lawrence Stone et al., eds., *The University in Society,* I (1974). On the transformation of the curriculum see Mark H. Curtis, *Oxford and Cambridge in Transition, 1558–1642* (1959); Charles B. Schmitt, *John Case and Aristotelianism in Renaissance England* (1983); and Mordechai Feingold, *The Mathematician's Apprenticeship* (1984). For the impact of new methods on core subjects see especially Lisa Jardine, "The Place of Dialectic Teaching in Sixteenth-Century Cambridge," in *Studies in the Renaissance,* 21 (1974); and James McConica, "Humanism and Aristotle in Tudor Oxford," in *English Historical Review,* 94 (1979). On the overproduction of men with higher education see Mark H. Curtis, "The Alienated Intellectuals of Early Stuart England," in *Past and Present,* 23 (1962). Wilfrid R. Prest has surveyed *The Inns of Court Under Elizabeth I and the Early Stuarts, 1590–1640* (1972). Lawrence Stone describes the grand tour in *The Crisis of the Aristocracy, 1558–1641* (1965).

Economic Life
in Shakespeare's England

D. C. COLEMAN

The People and the Land

The material and economic circumstances of Shakespeare's world had few features in common with those of the present age. Shakespeare lived in an England that was overwhelmingly rural and had virtually no mechanized industry. Nobody could travel on land faster than by horse, or on water faster than by sail. The average life expectancy at birth was about thirty-seven years, roughly half of what it is in Britain and the United States today.

Between Shakespeare's birth in 1564 and his death in 1616, the population of England and Wales rose from about 3 million to about 4.8 million, less than a tenth of the present population. This rate of growth was formidable: it would not be reached again until around 1800, when a population explosion combined with the industrial revolution to change the face of the country. Such a rate of increase made for a youthful population (about one-third was under fifteen years of age), though it does not necessarily mean that people married when they were very young. Shakespeare's Juliet may have married at fourteen, and there were instances of child marriage, especially in aristocratic circles, but the average age at which women married in Elizabethan England was about twenty-five.

The reasons for this rapid population growth are not immediately obvious. Richard Hakluyt wrote in 1584 that "through our long peace and seldom sickness . . . we are grown more populous than ever heretofore." This explanation may not be wholly accurate, but there is no doubt that relative freedom from bubonic plague, typhus, influenza, and other killing diseases aided growth, just as the continuance of high infant mortality limited it. (On the average, about one child in seven died before reaching the age of one.) This was a society in which death and disease were the common experiences of all families but also one in which a vigorous and youthful population was growing with unusual rapidity. Such growth generated economic and social problems and provided an impetus for economic development. If England was not quite bursting at the seams, it did have solid demographic reasons for expansion.

How, then, did these people earn a living, where, and with what results? In seeking answers to such questions it is useful to start by drawing an imaginary line from Bristol in the southwest to Hull in the northeast. To the north and west of the line the land was higher and wetter. Here agrarian life was mainly pastoral, towns were fewer, and the population was more thinly scattered; this was generally the poorer part of the nation. To the south and east lay drier and lower land, mainly concerned with grain growing. Its population density was greater, it had more towns and ports, it was richer, and, above all, it had London. Of course, this division is very rough: the north had the prosperous and expanding port of Newcastle, and sheep-rearing was widely practiced in the south. In most of the country agriculture had some elements of mixed farming, and everywhere the land was far more heavily wooded than today.

The traditional picture of the English countryside at this time is that of a village with arable holdings in strips divided roughly into two or more large open fields. The strips are held by the villagers as tenants of the manorial lord, the villagers enjoy common annual rights of pasture over the open fields, and the lord of the manor exercises power through the manorial courts. In some areas and to some extent this vision coincides with reality, particularly in parts of the Midlands and the southeast.

But as often as not, arrangements were quite different. Substantial areas in Kent, Essex, and Devon, for example, had already been enclosed with hedges or fences; others had never known open fields. In some Midland counties common rights had been extinguished and fields enclosed by landlords or prosperous peasants in pursuit of higher rents, whether from sheep-rearing or grain-growing; in other parts of the same region, however, they survived to await enclosure in the eighteenth century. In the uplands of the north and west, different and more flexible field systems prevailed: many people lived in scattered pastoral communities, and the nucleated village of the traditional pattern was less common, though examples could be found, especially in Durham. There were still substantial layers of freeholders and small copyhold tenants (sometimes known in Elizabethan usage as, respectively, yeomen and husbandmen), and the lordship of a manor could be important. But the reality of power rested on control of a landed estate, much of it let at economic rents to tenant farmers who worked the land with agricultural laborers. This pattern of landownership and management was not yet predominant, but Shakespearean England was moving rapidly in that direction. The rising landowning gentry, whose political forum was the House of Commons, was challenging the peers for control of the shires.

Most people worked within this agricultural economy as laborers, small farmers, or rural craftsmen—tilling the fields, tending cattle or sheep, and making everyday wares, ruled by landlords and the weather. They lived mainly in villages of some two hundred to five hundred souls. The much smaller urban population—not directly engaged in agriculture though often indirectly dependent on it—lived in numerous market towns ranging in size from five hundred to five thousand people, a category that included Shakespeare's birthplace. Only about 8 percent of the population lived in towns of over five thousand people, and London accounted for most of that percentage.

England was far less urbanized than many parts of continental Europe. In *The Cause of the Greatness of Cities* (1589), the Italian author Giovanni Botero observed that "in England, London excepted, . . . there is not a city that deserves to be called great." In 1600, only three towns—Norwich, Bristol, and York—had populations between ten thousand and fifteen thousand. London, with a population of about two hundred thousand, exercised a powerful influence over the whole kingdom, especially the richer south and east. When Shakespeare left Stratford to seek his fortune in London, he was only doing what many others did. London's rate of growth was two or three times that of the population as a whole. As the center of government, the seat of the law, the focus of cultural life, and the commercial and financial capital of the realm, it attracted all sorts: the politically ambitious, the budding young lawyer, the merchant and the businessman, the courtier and the courtesan, the poet and the playwright.

The city also drew in goods by sea and land, by river and road. Grain, butter, and cheese came in by coastal trade from ports in the south and east, from King's Lynn round to Poole. The metropolis consumed coal from Newcastle; timber, stone, lead, and glass for its houses; and a variety of raw materials for its export trade.

Industries

Those exports were dominated by woolen cloth, the manufacture of which was the country's largest industry. Like so many industries at that time, the making of woolen cloth was essentially a matter of processing an agricultural product, and most of that processing was carried out in the homes of workers. Large-scale sheep-rearing had long been an important part of the English economy, and the fine wools of the Cotswolds had been exported to supply the industries of continental Europe, but since the middle of the fifteenth century, more and more English wool had been made into cloth at home. By the time Elizabeth I came to the throne, her kingdom included 10–11 million sheep. They provided the raw material for an industry that had become concentrated in four or five main areas.

The most important of these areas was the west country, embracing Gloucestershire and parts of Somerset and Wiltshire, chiefly producing fine broadcloth. The southwest region, centered on Devonshire and stretching into the adjacent counties of Cornwall and Somerset, made coarser and cheaper woolens and some worsteds. Across the country lay the prosperous industrial region of East Anglia. Here quantities of colored broadcloths of varying quality were made in numerous villages, chiefly around the Essex-Suffolk border, where massive churches (such as those at Lavenham and Dedham) bear witness today to the wealth of fifteenth- and sixteenth-century clothiers. In the northwest, coarse and cheap woolens were produced in Lancashire and parts of Cumbria, and a rapidly expanding industry in Yorkshire was turning out quantities of cheap "kersies" and similar light woolens. Fabrics of one sort or another were made in many other areas, from Kent to the Welsh borders. The geographical location of the woolen industry depended not so much on local wool supplies as on available labor able to combine semipastoral agriculture with carding, spinning, weaving, and other processes of woolen manufacture.

By Shakespeare's day, many of the traditional types of cloth were being supplemented or even replaced by what contemporaries called "new draperies." These were lighter and more colorful fabrics, often worsteds, the manufacture of which was much stimulated by the immigration of Protestant artisans from the Spanish Netherlands. Driven out by religious persecution, they had settled mostly in East Anglia.

In some areas, such as Yorkshire, the manufacturing processes were in the hands of independent weavers who bought the wool, wove the fabrics, and sold the product to merchants. In other regions, as in the west country, the industry was dominated by merchant clothiers who put out the wool to spinners and weavers in their employ and who then sold the cloths (sometimes after they had been dyed and finished) in the main cloth market at Blackwell Hall in London. No single pattern of organization ruled, but for most of the workers in the industry the workplace was the home: women and children carded the wool, women spun it into yarn, and men wove the fabric or carried out the finishing processes. For many, spinning or weaving was a part-time activity combined with farming; for others, and their numbers were growing, it provided the main livelihood. Either way, woolen

manufacture had come to be regarded (in the words of an Elizabethan commentator) as "one of the pillars of our commonwealth."

Domestic manufacture of a similar type produced small quantities of other fabrics. Linen and canvas from locally grown flax or hemp were made in many parts of the country. The hand-knitting of hosiery, to be found in sundry pastoral regions from Devon to the Yorkshire dales, was given a fillip by the invention (about 1590) of the stocking frame. When Doll Tearsheet calls Pistol "a fustian rascal" (*Henry IV, Part 2,* II. iv. 173), she is figuratively alluding to imported fabric made of linen and cotton; but by that time fustian manufacture was well under way in Lancashire, using imported cotton and local flax yarn. At the other end of the scale of prestige, a small amount of weaving and hosiery-knitting of silk was to be found in London, Norwich, and Canterbury, where Protestant refugees were giving some stimulus to the silk industry.

The ancient tin-mining industry had its center in Cornwall, and its high-quality product enjoyed renown both at home and overseas. Lead, mined in the Mendip hills in Somerset as well as in the Pennines and the Welsh mountains, also entered into the export trade.

The country's iron industry was growing rapidly as a result of the introduction from continental Europe of the water-powered and charcoal-fueled blast furnace. During Elizabeth's reign many furnaces were at work, especially in the Weald of Sussex and Kent, where iron ore, waterpower, and woodland for the charcoal were all found in close proximity. Iron-smelting was one of the very few industries needing sizable amounts of fixed capital, and many of the ironworks were set up by peers or landowning gentry such as the Sidneys in Sussex or the earls of Rutland in Yorkshire.

The nation's coal resources were also being developed, mainly in Northumberland, Durham, the Midlands, and south Wales. The use of coal in industry was limited, largely confined to blacksmithing, soapmaking, and the production of salt by the evaporation of brine. The main use of coal, in areas where it could compete economically with wood, was for domestic heating.

In 1600 much English industry was still catching up on continental Europe, often with the aid of immigrant artisans. Woolen cloth aside, English industrial techniques and products were often inferior to those found in the richer areas of France, Spain, Italy, or Flanders. England was still dependent on imports for such wares as writing paper and good-quality glass or silk. Talk of "industry" should not lead one to suppose that there was a recognizable "industrial sector," as in modern industrialized communities. England, like the rest of Europe, was a preindustrial society: manufacture was still closely linked to agriculture, and industrial activity was subject to the forces of nature and the whims of the weather. Watermills were halted by frozen rivers or floods or drought. Harvest labor invariably took priority over manufacturing, and the quality of the harvest determined the income of many people and so affected the demand for goods. Also, most manufacturing was still carried out by artisans and craftsmen—bakers and brewers, masons and thatchers, weavers and tailors, carpenters, blacksmiths, and shoemakers. In many towns artisans were still organized in guilds, though the power of the guilds was waning: they exercised little or no authority over many rural workers in textiles or in some of the new industries that were getting under way.

Trade

The towns, with their markets or fairs, formed part of a network of trade that went far toward making England a single national economy. Some towns were stagnant or even decaying, such as Coventry, Chester, and indeed Stratford. Others, like Leeds and Manchester (still tiny but beginning to grow), were prospering or, like Colchester and Exeter, becoming cloth-trading ports. The towns were collection and distribution centers for the products of agriculture, rural industry, and the processing and manufacturing activities within their own walls, be it leatherworking in Leicester or woolen-weaving in Norwich. Buyers came to town for imported wares, and sellers came to start their goods on the journey to distant markets overseas.

England was not yet a great commercial nation, but it was well set on that path. Nothing could be further from the truth than the myth that Shakespeare's England was a subsistence economy based on self-sufficient peasants innocent of the profit motive and devoid of commercial acumen. Contemporary writers reckoned that England had some six hundred market towns, tiny though most of them were. In addition, there were special fairs, of which one of the most notable was Stourbridge Fair, held just outside Cambridge. Lasting for three weeks

each year, it was described in 1589 as "by far the largest and most famous fair in all England . . . [used] by the merchants dispersed throughout the whole realm." Here a great variety of wares were traded: fish, cloth, grain, groceries and spices, silks and furs, wood, charcoal and coal, pewter and brass, and all sorts of household goods.

Without the river linking Cambridge to the port of King's Lynn, the fair could not have existed; many other markets also depended on waterborne transport. Because no part of England was more than about seventy miles from the sea, many goods were shipped by the flourishing coastal trade, which was linked to such navigable rivers as the Thames, Severn, and Trent.

Water transport was most economical for bulky goods—grain, coal, stone, timber—but horse-drawn wagons and trains of packhorses carried much, probably most, of the country's internal trade. The network of roads converged on London and varied greatly in quality. Many highways were often impassable in winter; others, especially in the south, were capable of sustaining regular carrier services by the early seventeenth century. As the volume of business grew, the roads were under increasing pressure; and the parishes, which by an act of 1555 had formal responsibility for road maintenance, often proved unequal to the task. The increased traffic was in turn a result of rising population, the astonishing growth of London, and the long-term expansion of England's overseas trade.

Outside London the commerce of the main ports that were engaged in foreign trade—Bristol, Hull, Newcastle, and Exeter—was largely regional in character. In common with some lesser east-coast ports, Hull and Newcastle traded mainly to the Baltic or to Dutch and German ports, and also took part in North Sea fishing. Similarly, the merchants of Bristol, Exeter, and, to a lesser extent, Chester traded with France, Spain, Portugal, and Ireland.

Only London was a truly international port. Its extraordinary dominance of the country's overseas commerce was of relatively recent origin. At the beginning of the sixteenth century London brought in not much more than half of the total revenue from customs duties on foreign trade; by the 1580s that proportion was approximately 90 percent. The relative decline of the "outports" did not pass without complaint. Around 1575 the merchants of Hull grumbled, with some pardonable exaggeration, that "the whole trade of merchandize is in a manner brought to the City of London . . . and other ports . . . falleth to great decay."

The predominance of London resulted from two interrelated developments from the later fifteenth century onward. One was the growth of Antwerp, which became the commercial and financial capital of western Europe. The other was the rise of the London trading organization known as the Fellowship of the Merchant Adventurers. This guildlike body had successfully challenged the power of the Hanseatic merchants, who had controlled much of English trade at the end of the fifteenth century. Enjoying a crown-authorized monopoly of the export of English cloth by Englishmen, the Merchant Adventurers operated from headquarters in London and Antwerp. To Antwerp came merchants from many countries, who marketed English cloth all over Europe, from the Baltic to the Mediterranean, from Poland to Portugal. Likewise, linens and other textiles, dyestuffs, salt and spices, wines and dried fruits, and a miscellany of manufactured wares were imported to England along the Antwerp-London axis. The Merchant Adventurers sat profitably astride that axis and were the very opposite of adventurous.

In the span of Shakespeare's lifetime that situation was substantially changed by external events. In the 1550s and 1560s the long upswing in English exports of traditional types of woolens came to an end. Political relations with the Hapsburgs worsened, and the Merchant Adventurers left Antwerp in 1564. They settled in various German ports until they were expelled from Stade in 1597; the Hanseatic merchants were driven from London in reprisal. Meanwhile, religious revolts in the Netherlands and the ferocity of the ensuing Spanish repression had, by the 1580s, smashed Antwerp's commercial preeminence and imparted momentum to the rise of Protestant Holland. By the first decade of the seventeenth century, Amsterdam had assumed Antwerp's former role. So long as English resources were heavily committed to the London-Antwerp axis and so long as Spain and Portugal were able to exclude foreigners from their new empires in America and Asia, the English role in European expansion remained minimal.

It was the crumbling of the Iberian powers—of which the defeat of the Spanish Armada in 1588 was merely a symptom that had the secondary effect of stimulating English patriotism—that let in the Dutch, the English, and the French. The Hansards and the Italians were in decline, unfavorably placed for profitable participation in the new European adventures. At the time of the writing and production of *The Merchant of Venice,* in the 1590s, it was highly improbable that Antonio would have had "an argosy bound to Tripolis, another to the Indies . . . a third at Mexico, a fourth for England" (I. iii. 16–19). He would far more likely have been grumbling at English poaching and piracy in the Mediterranean, just as twenty or thirty years earlier Spaniards had grumbled at the escapades of Sir John Hawkins and Sir Francis Drake in the West Indies.

These events marked the beginning of English mercantile expansion. It took three main forms: larger numbers of individual merchants or ships trading or carrying in markets hitherto dominated by Spaniards, Portuguese, Italians, or Hansards; attempts to found "plantations" or colonies in the Americas (preceded by some successful trial runs in Ireland); and the establishment, with crown support, of chartered monopolistic companies designed to foster trade with particular areas. Although Londoners played the major part in these endeavors, expansion also brought new opportunities for the provincial ports. For example, of all the English ships entering the Baltic through the Sound (between Denmark and Sweden) in about 1600, some 70 percent were registered at Hull, Newcastle, and other provincial ports, and only 30 percent at London. By that time English ships were busy trading not only in the western Mediterranean, where many of them used the port of Livorno as a base, but also with the Turkish empire in the Levant.

The establishment of colonies in America was advocated in tracts and pamphlets that flowed from the printing presses in a steady stream from the 1580s to the 1630s. In practice, after the various voyages of exploration and the abortive attempts to found colonies by Humphrey Gilbert, Walter Raleigh, and others in the 1580s, the piecemeal settlement of the West Indian islands and the North American coast made significant progress only in the first three decades of the seventeenth century.

Thus, the first British Empire began precariously in Shakespeare's lifetime, with the first American colonies and the foundation of the East India Company in 1600. Most of the chartered companies formed in the second half of the sixteenth century were for trading in Europe—for example, the Eastland Company in 1579 and the Levant Company in 1581. Around the turn of the century similar companies were formed to promote more distant ventures, such as the Virginia Company in 1606. When the Portuguese opened up the sea route to eastern Asia, imported spices from the East Indies, and briefly created a commercial empire, the jealousies of other maritime powers were aroused. The Dutch were the first effective predators in the 1590s, followed by the English, thus fomenting a fierce rivalry that was to endure throughout the seventeenth century, leading in time to British rule over India.

Economic and Social Policy

Tudor and Stuart governments were for the most part disposed to support, rather than to initiate, these sundry acts of economic expansion. Such a body as the Eastland Company was seen by the government as worthy of encouragement because it opened up the possibility of securing better supplies of "naval stores" (timber, hemp, tar, and canvas) from the Baltic. Moreover, trading companies could be, and were, made to pay for their monopolistic charters, and they were leaned on for loans in time of war.

Elizabeth's famous chief minister, Lord Burghley, made genuine efforts to encourage industrial enterprise by granting patents of invention. Unfortunately, such endeavors degenerated, to some extent during Elizabeth's later years and much more notably under James I, into the granting of monopoly rights to courtiers and other favorites. This did little but worsen relations between the crown and the business community and help to raise prices.

Inflation was indeed one of the few features of the age that give it some resemblance to the present. Between approximately 1500 and 1620 prices in general rose about fivefold, industrial prices rather less than that, but those of cereals almost sixfold—not nearly so rapid an inflation as that experienced in some countries in the twentieth century, but enough to have serious repercussions. Why prices behaved thus, not only in England but in Europe as a whole, is a matter of debate among historians. Suffice it to say that responsibility lies partly with population growth and partly with an increase in the money supply, itself largely the result of the influx of silver from the Spanish conquests in Peru and Mexico. In Shakespeare's own lifetime food prices doubled. In the bad harvest years of 1587 and 1596–1598 they reached still higher levels. The disastrous crop failure of 1597 in particular brought soaring prices and famine to some areas, especially in the north.

This was an economic matter of central concern to the governments of the day, not so much because they were moved by a benevolent paternalism as because they knew that food shortages and consequent high prices—"dearth" in Elizabethan usage —represented potential threats to public order. The maintenance of order and social stability, the provision of an adequate supply of foodstuffs, and the ability to raise money and men to fight wars were the economic and social priorities of the government. Rising prices for food and wool stimulated enclosure and the elimination of common rights, and these in turn sometimes sparked off riots. The rapid growth of population was not always matched in the right place and at the right time by comparable growth in employment, and wages did not move up as fast as prices. If prosperity came to the enterprising or the lucky, be they gentry or yeomen, merchants or craftsmen, poverty worsened and vagrancy increased among the poor, the unfortunate, the dispossessed, and the feckless.

An awareness of these problems helped to bring into being the main props of Tudor economic and social policy. That policy sought, inter alia and by sundry statutes and proclamations, to regulate the supply and hence the price of grain by prohibiting exports when shortage threatened; to require local magistrates to fix the level of wages as well as the price of bread and ale; to restrict the movement of labor and ensure an adequate work force in agriculture; to demand a seven-year term of apprenticeship in certain specified occupations; and to require all parishes to levy a local tax for the relief of the poor. Not all these ends were achieved, but the aims typify the reaction of the rulers of the state to the multifarious threats to stability and order posed by economic and social change. We should be foolish to seek instant reflections in Shakespeare's writings of either the problems or the reactions. But there can be little doubt that when, in *Troilus and Cressida,* he gave to Ulysses his celebrated eulogy of "degree, priority and place," he was echoing a widespread view of the social order—and still more so in this eloquent warning:

Take but degree away, untune that string,
And, hark, what discord follows.

(I. iii. 109–110)

BIBLIOGRAPHY

Andrew B. Appleby, *Famine in Tudor and Stuart England* (1978); Peter J. Bowden, *The Wool Trade in Tudor and Stuart England* (1962); K. N. Chaudhuri, *The English East India Company* (1965); Peter Clark and Paul Slack, *English Towns in Transition, 1500–1700* (1976); D. C. Coleman, *The Economy of England, 1450–1750* (1977); Ralph Davis, *The Rise of the Atlantic Economies* (1973); William Harrison, *The Description of England,* Georges Edelen, ed. (1968); D. M. Palliser, *The Age of Elizabeth: England Under the Tudors, 1547–1603* (1983); G. D. Ramsay, *The City of London in International Politics at the Accession of Elizabeth Tudor* (1975); Lawrence Stone, *Family and Fortune* (1973); Joan Thirsk, *Economic Policy and Projects: The Development of a Consumer Society in Early Modern England* (1978), and, as ed., *The Agrarian History of England and Wales,* IV: *1500–1640* (1967).

Medicine and Sanitation

MARGARET PELLING

The relationship between human beings and their physical environment is an area of great historical interest and wide extent. It has fairly consistently been assumed that Elizabethan people were closer to the natural world, the soil, the seasons, and even to death than their twentieth-century western counterparts. This greater intimacy has been made to look alternately romantic or primitive, just as the mentality of the period itself has been seen as vibrant or melancholy. Shakespeare's contemporaries were perhaps better able than modern people to comprehend, if not to resolve, contradictory experience, to express the sense of spring as well as the bitterness of winter, to describe beauty as well as degradation.

Their relationship with the natural world was at once closer and more casual, but closeness did not preclude cruelty or fear. Thus, an early-modern woman might suckle a young puppy to keep herself in milk until it was proper to put her baby to the breast. Animal (including human) excrements, properly treated, were used in medicine as well as agriculture and industry (urine, for example, being used as a bleach). But the greater intrusiveness of the natural world was also an object of fear, as in the suspicion of small animals kept as pets or in the notion of many sick people that their symptoms were akin to, or even caused by, the invasion of their bodies by worms, insects, or even small mammals such as moles. Living and organic matter of all kinds was thus at once more useful and more intrusive. This situation aptly bears out the contention of anthropologists that pollution can best be defined as material in the wrong place, and is thus not only relative to the society in which it occurs but also likely to vary within that society (Douglas).

Shakespeare's England was still largely a rural society, including hinterlands such as the forest and fenlands. Even the largest provincial towns, such as Norwich, and London itself, included open space, river meadows, orchards, and walled gardens, although these more natural areas were not necessarily idyllic. Most interiors were plain, dark, and sparsely furnished. Living space for the most part did not as yet show a material artificiality that implied a necessary separateness from the unadorned world outside. By contrast, the dress of the wealthier classes displayed an extreme artificiality that distinguished individuals from their surroundings. At the same time, the style of dress and accessories adopted was one in which most of the body was concealed from view unless it could be satisfactorily presented. Some habits were becoming less communal; in the case of eating habits this may have been, at least in part, a response to the prevalence of venereal disease.

The Physical Environment

The Elizabethan period was markedly one of change and of conscious awareness of mutability. The artificial environment was being transformed as the result of the "great rebuilding," which occurred toward the end of the sixteenth century. For certain classes there was a rising standard of material comfort and even luxury. The classical theme of the dichotomy between urban and rural life was finding a new relevance with the enormous growth of London, which was among the four largest cities in Europe by 1600.

Contemporaries were disturbed by evidence of social mobility and rifts in the social order. As a whole the population was much more mobile than is customarily believed, traveling on business, to marry, in search of work or subsistence, and for or during apprenticeships or service. Although adolescents and young adults were the most mobile, both the very young and the very old could become rootless, and young children habitually changed households even among the less prosperous. Pressure from substantial population growth gave a new dimension to this situation, increasing the gulf between rich and poor. By the end of Elizabeth's reign, England's population may have been 35 percent higher than at its beginning. The Elizabethan poor law evolved to meet apparent threats to economic and social stability from resident as well as vagrant poor. Sickness and disability were perceived as creating poverty as well as danger from contagious disease; and local authorities invested in a wide range of medical services, as well as in clothing and diet, to change the physical state and dependency of the poor.

The easy impression that public and private standards of cleanliness were especially low during this period has been challenged but not systematically investigated (Thomas). Comparisons drawn between the eighteenth and nineteenth centuries from conflicting points of view have overshadowed the investigation of earlier periods, but it is clear that the element of public provision in towns of relevant services such as street cleaning and paving should not be underestimated. We should no longer assume that the development of these amenities was necessarily dependent upon the emergence of strong centralized government. Most commentators have accepted uncritically, and extrapolated backward from, the denunciation of prevailing urban conditions by late-seventeenth-century reformers of manners who aimed at a "polite society." Local geography—the state of natural drainage, rivers, brooks, types of soil, and even prevailing winds—had a major influence on local conditions, in particular the sources and degree of contamination of water supply. In many respects

sixteenth-century urban life merely provided variations on problems inherent in any extensive human settlement, problems that were consequently provided for from an early period. The detailed regulation of markets included constant attention to the quality of provisions exposed for sale—especially meat, grain, bread, and ale or beer. Trades, especially those related to food and clothing, were still producing locally for local consumption, and municipal authorities were concerned by the effects on the public health of the activities of butchers, dyers, glovers, curriers, fishmongers, tanners, and the like. These tradesmen were normally restricted in different ways, being required to operate outside the city walls, to burn their waste only at night, to divide it into a form suitable for disposal at certain sites, or to filter their contaminated effluents in sumps, or "sinkers." Some domestic industries (such as brewing, soap boiling, and sugar refining) were beginning to move onto an industrial scale of operation, to use coal rather than wood as fuel, and thus to change the nature of urban pollution.

The economic situation of a town could mean considerable variation in its physical condition, and some major sixteenth-century towns felt themselves to be less populated, less well paved and cleaned, and generally less well "edified" than at earlier periods. Many of the larger corporate towns undertook more thorough paving in the course of the century, which provided raised footways and a central drainage channel. In legal terms, the cleaning of all but the widest streets was effected by some variation on the ancient device of responsibility of the householder or tenant for that part of the highway coextensive with the house frontage. Like other responsibilities, the duty of overseeing street cleaning tended in the later sixteenth century to devolve onto parish officials. The more feudal system of contributed labor was being replaced by contracts with individuals or by the direct employment of labor by the municipality. But (as in the case of medical relief for the poor) many sixteenth-century experiments of this kind were short-lived. Sweeping and refuse collection could take place weekly or even twice as often, financed by rates paid to "scavengers," with tradesmen having to make special arrangements. Charitable bequests for municipal improvements sometimes provided for services like a "common cart" for rubbish removal.

Whereas gardens or open spaces remained within cities, rubbish was disposed of in fenced-off private tips as well as "common laystalls," which were usually, for health reasons, outside the city walls. Often the latter were placed so that they could be drawn upon for agricultural purposes. Present-day commentators are well placed to appreciate the possibility that more waste was recycled—or was at least biodegradable—in the early modern period than in later phases of industrialization. Animal hair, bone, dung, decaying fish, offal, blood, sawdust, malt dust, soot, soap ashes, leather scraps, and rags were all applied to the land. In London this occurred systematically: dung was carried by barge to the Hertfordshire market gardens which supplied the capital. In smaller towns contaminated water from the streets was fed by ditches into the fields. In some rural areas road repair and agriculture were linked: bracken, cut to preserve pasture, was laid on the roads in autumn and put on the fields in the spring after it had been broken down by traffic (Thirsk). Because of the dominance of agriculture, towns are unlikely to have festered passively in their own wastes.

It would seem inevitable that for Shakespeare's contemporaries odor was as ubiquitous as defect and sickness; in neither case, however, should it be assumed that this led to crassness or indifference. In the medical theory and natural philosophies of the time, odor had a substantial existence and was consequently taken seriously both as a cause of disease and as a means of its prevention or cure. Thus, when there was a threat of epidemic disease, municipal authorities prohibited the normal cleaning and dredging of ditches and rivers, to prevent the corruption of the air by ill odors. For the same reason, they were especially vigilant about the quality of foodstuffs exposed for sale in markets. The quality of the stuffings of mattresses and pillows was a matter of concern, because if inferior, these stuffings released foul odors when warmed by sleeping bodies. It is not surprising that odor often formed the major part of the definition of a nuisance, which was the main concept involved in legal proceedings against unsanitary conditions.

In terms of legislation, Elizabethan codifications were to dominate the future maintenance of highways, as they did methods of poor relief. It is significant, however, that national bodies were created not for the maintenance of roads but for the proper management of rivers and harbors. Freely running water was still of the greatest economic as well as social importance. Any scheme to tap rivers and brooks met with opposition from those dependent upon the flow for transport, power, or fishery.

Apart from diversion to agriculture, the main vehicle of waste disposal was still running water. Riverbanks were carefully maintained and divided into areas specified for transport, waste disposal, manufacturing processes, and washing. Householders were responsible for brooks and ditches, as they were for highways, and could be persuaded to take on this responsibility in exchange for a cheap lease; but, as with rubbish removal, sixteenth-century urban authorities also experimented with special taxes and direct labor. An inability to maintain rivers and harbors could be an important part of a vicious cycle of economic decline, and it often prompted direct intervention.

Although the water supply of towns varied, it was probably better than is usually imagined. The different projects culminating in the practically (but not economically) successful New River, which brought water to the northern parishes of London, are well known (Gough), but by 1600 most provincial towns had some kind of extramural supply, usually from springs; this water was brought in to a few centrally sited cisterns or conduit heads. Some towns, in confiscating monastic property, also acquired a relatively sophisticated system of water supply. Direct connection to private houses (by "quills," or pipes of lead) was fairly unusual and, where wells were plentiful, not sought after even by the prosperous; trade and public-health purposes, and especially fire prevention, were paramount. The Plymouth "Leat," which antedated London's New River, was intended primarily to victual, clean, and prevent fire in the fleet. Nonetheless, Shakespeare's contemporaries were served with water by an increasing body of entrepreneurs, or "projectors," as well as by wells, water carriers, waterbutts (in which roof water could be collected), and domestic cisterns.

Many commentators on the physical conditions of sixteenth-century life have allowed themselves to be guided partly by the robustness of contemporary description and partly by the incidence of devastating outbreaks of epidemic disease. However, it should be noted that the "sweating sickness," bubonic plague, and syphilis are not "filth diseases" in the nineteenth-century sense. It is also important in the present context to remember that the England of Shakespeare's time consisted of a large number of small settlements; increased human contact inevitably heightened mortality, but it was only in the largest towns and in London that traditional methods of sanitation were obviously inadequate.

Even in London it was partly the existence of private latrines that made it necessary to consider culverting brooks and ditches. Careful collation of scattered information is likely to show that public latrines were both more numerous and more substantial in London than is usually assumed (Sabine). The alternative was cesspools, some very large and others only the circumference of a barrel; the dangers of these to public health depended upon the surrounding soil. In any event, the failure of Shakespeare's contemporaries to adopt Sir John Harington's valvular water closet at least meant that cesspits did not usually overflow or need constant emptying.

Latrines and cesspools were often the site of accidents. Latrines tended to be built in alleys and to multiply at the riverside end of narrow lanes, which were in any case likely to be used for "easement." Relieving oneself in the street might be tolerated in children under twelve years old, but citizens could be rewarded for informing against older offenders, and fines were often levied on parents or on masters in the case of servants. Indoors, chamber pots were common, and closestools were becoming increasingly so in better-furnished households. These were usually emptied either into cesspools or at night in the channel of the street outside. However, effective connections between private latrines, rainwater cisterns, and external drainage systems were not unusual even at an earlier period.

Obviously, habits and tolerance varied, between localities as well as nations. The connections between circumstantial evidence and contemporary views on the nature of man (for example, the notion that defecation became necessary only after the Fall) are still a matter of conjecture. It is worth stressing that Shakespeare's contemporaries, preoccupied with the threats posed by the rootless poor and by immigrants from the Continent, inevitably expressed these fears in terms of environmental pollution or concern about personal habits or cleanliness. This can be seen most clearly in the widespread apprehension over the growth of London's suburbs.

Demography, Death, and Sickness

Recent work has done much to establish the importance of demographic factors in historical change (Wrigley and Schofield; Palliser). A number of presumptions, many of them based on literary evidence, have been shown to be ill founded, although it is worth noting, first, that even on such questions as age at marriage literary sources may reflect some important aspect of contemporary culture or experience, and, second, that local variation could be considerable. In general, families in early-modern England were rather more nuclear than extended; large numbers of children were unusual; and marriage after the age of twenty was the rule, even among the aristocracy, and took place comparatively late in life, given the age's shorter life expectancy. Old people were often found living alone or not with their immediate families; and many people remained unmarried, though remarriage was common. The average life expectancy was affected primarily by the frequent loss of infant lives: a person surviving to the age of thirty could expect to live another thirty years. As for mortality rates in general, Shakespeare's blessed plot compared favorably with the rest of Europe and with modern non-Western societies. On the other hand, compared with the twentieth century's profound shift to an aging society, the Elizabethan period was dominated by young people: over half the population was under twenty-five. This has plausibly been given considerable sociological importance; for example, with respect to political unrest or to the period's increase in the provision of higher education.

Many of these generalizations have been developed with reference to rural populations and are less likely to be true of towns. It has customarily been assumed that in crowded urban areas, and above all in London, family life was less stable, marriages took place earlier, and death and decay came sooner. Most literature, especially satire and plays, was produced in London for London audiences and may faithfully mirror perceptions of life in the capital without being true for the country as a whole. The assumptions of historians as to high levels of mortality in towns, which have tended to rest too comfortably on aggregate statistics and on a paucity of information about sanitation, have only recently begun to be tested.

Famine was a real cause of death, particularly during the disastrous years 1596–1598, and "starvation" (this term being used to include exposure as well as lack of food as a cause of death) is sporadically recorded as such in the parish registers of London churches (Appleby; Forbes). As with epidemics, the desire to determine when there were crises of national importance (which do not seem to have been frequent) should not be allowed to obscure the significance of devastation on a local scale. The relationship between dearth and disease remains unclear. A still mysterious crisis of mortality in the 1550s was followed by a period of demographic recovery lasting into the 1580s; the ensuing decades were punctuated by urban epidemics of plague that exceeded in severity, if not in notoriety, the "great plague" of 1665. There are considerable difficulties involved in identifying epidemic outbreaks, and even the term *plague* had, like *ague,* a generic as well as a specific meaning.

Much attention has been paid to epidemic crises or peaks of mortality, partly because such incidents are more discrete than other demographic phenomena and partly because of the view, first systematically put forward by nineteenth-century medical historians, that great epidemics not only are characteristic of the age in which they occur but also bring major features of society into high relief. In demographic terms, this emphasis implies a neglect of the major subject of the causes of infant death. Little attention has been paid, moreover, to endemic or chronic disease. Yet it is arguable that such conditions are likely to have had a greater effect on the *mentalité* of the time, and certainly a greater part in everyday experience for all classes, than did the occasional outbreaks of plague.

More specific conditions, of great consequence but less visible as causes of death, include malaria; scurvy (which was seen most clearly among sailors but also affected urban populations); stone, or calculus (which had a wide incidence among small boys as well as old men and affected both sexes); and venereal disease, notably syphilis (which was a major social phenomenon of the sixteenth and early-seventeenth centuries). Of these conditions, the prolific metaphors, euphemisms, and symptomology of venereal disease most directly affected the extremely physical language of the urban satirists and playwrights, the celebrated outburst of Shakespeare's Timon being only one example (*Timon of Athens,* IV. iii). It is increasingly recognized that many of the major diseases of the period were as important for their influence on morbidity as for their mortality levels.

A high incidence of serious disease did not induce a state of apathy toward everything but the immediate threat to life itself. Case records show that people constantly monitored their own state of health and were profoundly concerned about the significance of apparently trivial symptoms. It is not surprising that skill in prognosis was sought for as well as ability to cure. The inexorable process of physical degeneration from small beginnings was as familiar in the body as it was in crops and foodstuffs. Physical disability could lead to immediate economic and social reclassification. Contemporaries feared any threat to the senses, especially the eyesight. Anxious attention was paid to the normal and abnormal functioning of the generative organs. As in later periods, maternal disability consequent upon childbirth was a hidden enormity; more women consulted physicians than men. There is increasing evidence that medical attention was sought even for very young babies. The relief of pain was an object; backache, headache, and toothache were not suffered in silence.

Modern medicine pays little attention to the surface of the skin, but in earlier periods this was in both theory and practice a major area of concern, equivalent in cosmological terms to the surface, as opposed to the unknown interior, of the earth. The probable incidence of dietary deficiencies and the number of serious diseases (including plague) that resolved themselves on the surface of the body justify this stress on cutaneous appearances; but Elizabethans also sought remedies for pimples and boils, and made extensive use of cosmetic aids and disguises. (It is consequently perverse to ascribe Shakespeare's attention to apparently minor defects to his superior powers of observation.) Accidents (especially drownings) and violence caused many deaths; but burns, scalds, dog bites, and fractures also had long-term consequences, as did strains caused by work, especially rupture. Stoicism did not even extend to congenital deformity: the treatment of harelip and wryneck was a recognized specialization.

To these physical causes of anxiety must be added the Elizabethan obsession with mood and state of mind. Melancholy was not only a traditional symptom but also a mental disorder regarded as particularly afflicting the English. Not surprisingly, anxiety about physical disease itself emerges as a cause of mental disturbance, especially among women. Insomnia was a commonly reported complaint. Among ordinary people, the importance of family life was reflected in the main causes of mental stress as reported by patients: troubled courtships, marital problems, bereavements, and economic problems. The last factor—significantly expressed as "loss of estate"—is a measure of the contemporary sense of social and economic precariousness (MacDonald).

Medical Practice and Practitioners

These circumstances created a situation in which the demand for all kinds of medical attention was very high. To a considerable extent this demand was met in the first instance within the family circle. Procedures now formally thought to be "neutral" or merely hygienic, like bathing, changes of clothing, dietary variation, and avoidance of heat or cold, were then regarded as much more strongly medicinal. Herbal remedies were widely used, but laymen were also alert to novel remedies and constantly exchanged such information. Books of recipes enjoyed a steady sale. Servants, equivalent in the household hierarchy to the master's children, were consequently as likely to receive treatment at his or his wife's hands. It was not unknown for individuals to study medicine for years in order to deal with their own persistent complaints.

Outside the household, demand was met by a wide variety of medical practitioners, who may have been present on a ratio to population as high as 1:200. This estimate is based on the adoption of a broad definition of *practitioner,* as justified by the practices of the time. Other criteria, such as effectiveness or level of formal education, are either impossible to apply historically or irrelevant to actual practice (Webster, 1979). Sick people chose freely from among the range of practitioners according to their own and their friends' judgment of the nature and seriousness of their condition. A scale of fees and of practitioners existed to meet the needs and expectations of different social classes, although some sought-after practitioners could charge low fees and the venality of others was bitterly resented. An unmeasured but probably important amount of medical services was provided for nothing or was paid for in kind. The former practice had an official existence in statutes and the ordinances of barber-surgeons' companies; it survived into the twentieth century, but motives altered radically according to social changes; much more investigation is required to document its history.

The high level of lay expertise and involvement in medicine in the early modern period has been explained in terms of medicine being then more elementary and more dependent upon traditional shared knowledge (Poynter). This perhaps oversimplifies both the social structure of medicine and the variety of schools of thought available at the time. It is also possible to argue that the relations between doctor and patient were more evenly balanced than is the case today. Patients bargained with practitioners as in a commercial transaction and settled on an agreed product or "cure." Contracts were used in which a portion was paid on account and the rest reserved conditionally upon completion of the cure. Physicians and some surgeons were just beginning to resist this system, although some of their fees were so high that they were paid in stages during the cure or even in the form of annuities.

The social status even of academically qualified practitioners was not particularly high, although at the same time gentry or nobility who practiced medicine or surgery did not lose caste by so doing. Further consideration of the economic framework of medicine as an occupation in the early-modern period reveals the inappropriateness of the modern ideal of the full-time dedicated member of the professional classes. Large numbers of practitioners existed, but many, if not most, of them engaged in other activities of economic significance (Pelling). Physicians and apothecaries could also be merchants; landowners, the clergy, and schoolmasters practiced medicine; medicine was a frequent resort for clergy who were poor, unlikely to rise, or deprived of their livings. The versatility of Timothie Bright, physician, cleric, pioneer on the subject of melancholy as well as in the development of shorthand, reflected not only personal abilities but also the contemporary social and economic structure. Quite prosperous, as well as poor, practitioners diversified into the food and drink trades. Barber-surgeons were regularly trained in netmaking or musicianship and were likely to become involved in the textile trades where these were dominant. The better-known side of this coin is the way in which other trades drifted into medicine. In rural areas, where "by-employments" and seasonal working were the rule rather than the exception, medicine was equally likely to be a part-time occupation. Even in the context of the ecclesiastical licensing structure dating from 1511, medicine was a skill in which experience and good character were regarded as adequate qualifications. The English universities themselves granted licenses in physic and in surgery on this basis.

As in the case of other established occupations,

medicine was traditionally subject to restrictive practices that suggest a tripartite division into physicians, surgeons or barber-surgeons, and apothecaries. It follows from the competitive situation described above that this division of labor was observed only according to social and economic circumstances. The division existed more as a weapon in conflicts between practitioners than as an agreed framework. Different strategies were adopted, that of the academically qualified physician being closest to the modern definition of a professional, although enjoying only a limited success at the time. The College of Physicians of London, founded in 1518, insisted on a level of humanist culture available only to a few, thus raising the level of mystique of their occupation. (It did not, however, invariably attract those with a high level of academic accomplishment.) In essence this strategy was also that adopted by many empirics. The London barber-surgeons at first imitated the college's strategy but then came to appeal directly to the laity and to lesser practitioners by contributing to the increasing body of medical literature being published in the vernacular. The tripartite division was explicitly rejected by Protestant critics who praised the empirical efficiency of primitive and Hippocratic medicine, in which all parts of practice were combined within a religious and moral framework.

Anxiety about health and the high level of demand for medical services produced simultaneously a concern for standards and a fixity of belief on the part of the sick person in the practitioner of his or her choice. To regard the patient of this period as especially "gullible" is rather to miss the point. Skepticism as to the morality and expertise of practitioners in general was equally widespread. The forms of medical regulation demanded by the College of Physicians had the undesirable implication of severely restricting the range and amount of medical assistance available to the public, and the college's claims were never wholeheartedly upheld by the state. In the so-called Quacks' Charter of 1542–1543, London surgeons were also criticized by the state for their venality and their attempts to restrict the public's access to effective remedies for important conditions such as venereal disease.

Medical regulation was also integrally related to broader economic and religious factors. The ecclesiastical licensing system was at its most rigorous, particularly for midwives, during the regime of Archbishop Laud in the 1630s. Puritans were increasingly accusing learned medicine, as well as the law and the church, of being a professional monopoly. The London medical corporations that emerged in the sixteenth and early-seventeenth centuries drew on continental models but were also part of a wider economic trend toward companies and corporations. The College of Physicians encouraged the separation of the apothecaries from the Grocers' Company in 1617 in the hope of being able to supervise the monopolistic sale of drugs in London. Slightly later, two royal physicians, ex officio fellows of the college, were granted a monopoly in distilling strong waters and vinegars that subsequently evolved into the Distillers' Company. This interest related to the profitability of the drink trade but also to the role of distillation in chemical therapy (Webster, 1975).

Medicine and Culture

Medicine during Shakespeare's lifetime was notable both for its eclecticism and for struggles between the exponents of different schools of thought. These struggles were an integral and important part of a major shift at the end of the sixteenth century toward a Neoplatonic philosophy, consistent with reformed religious views and symptomatic of the increasing cultural assertiveness of northern Europe. This, rather than any "simplicity" of medical theory, explains the degree of knowledge found among the laity, poets, playwrights, and intellectuals. The rational and skeptical Galenism embodied by the humanist Thomas Linacre in the London College of Physicians remained entrenched in the medical facilities of the universities but increasingly lost ground as a philosophical system. The revival of anatomy led by Andreas Vesalius (1514–1564), while having little immediate relevance to medical practice, was associated with more orthodox views; nonetheless, its tendency was to undermine the self-sufficiency of classical medicine. Therapeutic effectiveness became an important criterion and prepared the way for the favorable reception of the teachings of the religious and medical reformer Paracelsus (*ca.* 1493–1541) and a revitalized alchemy. Academic physicians were seen as having become aloof from their patients and from therapeutics; their outlook was fatalistic, and they had little to say to either the diseases or the remedies of the modern age.

The initiative lay instead with those who had

knowledge of the plants and minerals of the New World or who arrived at the quintessential secrets of nature by chemical means. Their practice, which included the use of mercury in syphilis, explicitly revived the Hippocratic principle of extreme measures in extreme cases and was compatible with Protestant diagnoses of the world's ills. For Protestants, physical degeneration was linked to spiritual corruption as a result of the Fall; but by painful endeavor man's original powers could be regained and his span of life extended. The pace was forced by immigrant iatrochemists (many of whom were also involved in mining projects) and by empirics pressing the claims of a narrow range of chemical remedies. These innovations gained a sophisticated intellectual framework with the influence of Paracelsian medical philosophy, which began in England as early as 1560. Francis Bacon, John Donne, and Ben Jonson all wrote for an audience that had fully assimilated Paracelsianism. Unlike Galenism, Paracelsianism had something to offer all levels of practitioners; the London medical corporations were eventually forced to compromise with both its commercial and its intellectual success (Webster, 1975, 1979).

English medicine of the sixteenth century was not remarkable for major innovations or discoveries. The achievements of William Harvey and other English physiologists belong to the revolution in natural philosophy that occurred in the seventeenth century. Instead, the liveliness of English post-Reformation culture was dependent upon a new receptiveness to continental developments, fruitfully combined with an increasing sense of national identity. A large number of minor figures, working in close collaboration with printers and publishers, produced translations and paraphrases of continental works for the English market, often adding their own material or urging attention to the native tradition. Thus, continental herbals were copied, but observations were also made of the local flora. As in other areas of economic life, the growth of imports was met by schemes to supply the desirable commodities from the colonies or to promote the native product. Timothie Bright's treatise on the "sufficiency of English medicines" (1580) urged the extraction of chemical essences from plants and an improved knowledge of local flora.

Similar parallels could be drawn with respect to the response of English poets and dramatists to con-

tinental models, a process also involving minor figures and complex bibliographical problems, although the flowering of the native tradition arguably took place earlier in literature than in medicine. The emergence of a literature in the vernacular was a major feature of both developments, although it should be noted that the book trade is an imperfect summary of either, since many works circulated in manuscript. However, it is not surprising that the intermingling of science, literature, and medicine that characterized the intellectual life of the Tudor period should also be represented at the economic level, especially in bookmaking and bookselling. Neither is it surprising that some literary figures, such as Robert Greene and Thomas Lodge, turned to medicine as a means of supporting a literary career. This is perhaps best interpreted as an example of the occupational diversification or economic flexibility attributed to medicine earlier in this article, but it has also been seen on a more elevated plane as characteristic of the "Renaissance man" or as an example of the enduring humanist sympathies of educated physicians.

Estimates of the intellectual and scientific content of Shakespeare's works have varied according to the historical context in which they were made. The eighteenth century, rediscovering Shakespeare and admiring polymaths, tended to see him as especially learned. By the end of the nineteenth century, professionalization, specialization, and the ideal of the humanist physician had given a new and often ludicrous dimension to "bardolatry." While it was still possible to feel that a physician might be steeped in literature, by this time extensive lay knowledge of medicine had become an ideological, if not a practical, impossibility. The Tudor age had receded and become primitive, albeit illumined by such selected intellectual giants as Bacon, and the broadly based philosophical and religious preoccupations of the period were no longer understood. Hence, medical lovers of Shakespeare could not comprehend his erudition, given, as they saw it, the age in which he lived. They asserted that his degree of acquaintance with medical matters was such that he must himself have been a physician or at least an apothecary. More rationally, some of them proposed that Shakespeare must have depended upon his physician son-in-law, John Hall. In their turn, representatives of emerging medical specialisms have predictably found in Shakespeare's writings clear evidence of particular knowledge of their specialty. Above all, links have been forged between the twin humanist and scientific ideals of modern medicine: it has even been found necessary that Shakespeare, somehow, must have known about the circulation of the blood, with or without the assistance of Harvey himself.

While both medicine and Shakespeare remain in high esteem, it is likely that such claims will continue to be made, in spite of effective criticism (Edgar). Even in the 1950s it was asserted that "the medical reference frequency" of Shakespeare's works could be used as a yardstick to determine authorship. It is doubtful if any historian of English literature would agree with this judgment now. With respect to the body, the mind, health, and disease, Shakespeare's language fully participates in the physicality that was characteristic of Elizabethan satire and is thus a confirmation of contemporary preoccupations. Although frequently misinterpreted, the relevant references have been constantly quoted. But even enthusiasts are obliged to admit that there are relatively few references to medical treatment and that these lack detail. Practitioners of medicine, like practitioners of law, are not represented in Shakespeare according to their ubiquity in contemporary life. It is indicative of the lack of civic or "citizen" content in Shakespeare's plays, for example, that they make no substantial reference to barbers or barber-surgeons, who can be identified as carrying the main burden of "general practice" in towns. Similarly the poor apothecary who makes a brief appearance in *Romeo and Juliet* is unrepresentative of the often wealthy retailers, associates of merchants and goldsmiths, who were frequently found as members of Elizabethan urban elites.

More physicians appear as characters in the plays than do representatives of any other kind of practice, but even these are for the most part fairly dim appendages of aristocratic or royal households. Shakespeare's nurses are similarly situated but more definite in character. The physicians are appropriate to their context, especially the vigorous Dr. Butts *(Henry VIII)*, but their comparative ineffectuality is perhaps a reflection of contemporary skepticism about these practitioners, "whose skill is mere opinion" (John Earle, *Microcosmography* [1628]).

Suspicion of poisoning as a result of the involvement of medical practitioners was another Elizabethan motif that is reflected in Shakespeare. Xeno-

phobia and official paranoia received their well-known expression in the case of Roderigo Lopez, the Jewish physician to Elizabeth; he was hanged in 1594 for allegedly plotting against the queen's life. But the reality may also be seen, in the murder of Sir Thomas Overbury in the Tower in 1613 at the instigation of Frances Howard, countess of Essex and Somerset (McElwee). Physicians and other practitioners close to officers of state were used as spies or pawns in diplomatic maneuvers, most notably by Elizabeth in respect of the Russian court. Royalty and the nobility followed a notably independent line in their choice of practitioners or, as in the case of James I, brought their attendants with them. When their choice fell on foreigners or unorthodox practitioners, as it frequently did, this could arouse resentment.

The success of immigrant practitioners in establishing themselves in Shakespeare's society finds a mocking echo in Dr. Caius *(Merry Wives of Windsor)*, although it seems unlikely that this figure was intended to represent any individual immigrant practitioner. Dr. Caius is the only reminder in Shakespeare that the medical practitioner was a stock figure in traditional comedy, reinforced in the sixteenth century by imitations of continental models, such as the Italian *dottore*. Many lesser-known plays, as well as such playwrights as Massinger, Middleton, and Beaumont and Fletcher, made greater use of these conventions. Other regions of practice that Shakespeare chose to represent in far less depth than did some of his contemporaries are alchemy and astrological medicine. The obvious contrast is with Jonson, who portrayed the adept; Heywood and others used as characters the cunning men and women who practiced in towns as well as rural areas. Shakespeare's allusions to these complex subjects are in general terms and demonstrate his comparative lack of interest in contemporary intellectual debates.

Literary sources are indispensable for the study of the society that produces them, even with respect to supposedly esoteric areas such as medicine, but it cannot be expected that their coverage will be comprehensive or even that information will be conveyed directly. Many of Shakespeare's contemporaries give a fuller and more literal account of medicine and disease than does Shakespeare himself. A balanced view of the role of medicine and health in society can be attained only by attention to the broader social and economic context, and it is within such a view that the contribution of any given writer can most safely be interpreted.

BIBLIOGRAPHY

Andrew B. Appleby, *Famine in Tudor and Stuart England* (1978); Robert Burton, *The Anatomy of Melancholy* (1621), Holbrook Jackson, ed., 3 vols. (1964); George Norman Clark, *A History of the Royal College of Physicians of London,* 2 vols. (1964); Charles Creighton, *A History of Epidemics in Britain,* 2 vols. (1894; repr. 1965); Mary Douglas, *Purity and Danger: An Analysis of Concepts of Pollution and Taboo* (1966; repr. 1976).

Irving I. Edgar, *Shakespeare, Medicine and Psychiatry* (1970); Norbert Elias, *The Civilizing Process, I: The History of Manners* (1939), E. Jephcott, trans. (1978); Thomas Rogers Forbes, *Chronicle from Aldgate: Life and Death in Shakespeare's London* (1971); John W. Gough, *Sir Hugh Myddleton, Entrepreneur and Engineer* (1964).

John Harington, *A New Discourse of a Stale Subject, Called the Metamorphosis of Ajax* (1596), Elizabeth Story Donno, ed. (1962); Harriet Joseph, *Shakespeare's Son-in-Law: John Hall, Man and Physician,* with a facsimile of the 2nd ed. (1683) of Hall's *Select Observations on English Bodies* (1964); John J. Keevil, *Medicine and the Navy,* 2 vols. (1957–1958); Michael MacDonald, *Mystical Bedlam: Madness, Anxiety and Healing in Seventeenth-Century England* (1981); William McElwee, *The Murder of Sir Thomas Overbury* (1952); Jane O'Hara-May, *Elizabethan Dyetary of Health* (1977).

David M. Palliser, *The Age of Elizabeth: England Under the Later Tudors, 1547–1603* (1983); M. Pelling, "Occupational Diversity: Barber-Surgeons and the Trades of Norwich, 1550–1640," in *Bulletin of the History of Medicine,* 56 (1982); D'Arcy Power, *The Elizabethan Revival of Surgery* (1902); F. N. L. Poynter, "Medicine and Public Health," in Allardyce Nicoll, ed., *Shakespeare in His Own Age* (1964).

Reginald Reynolds, *Cleanliness and Godliness; or the Further Metamorphosis: A Discussion of the Problems of Sanitation Raised by Sir John Harington . . .* (1946); George Rosen, *A History of Public Health* (1958); E. L. Sabine, "Latrines and Cesspools of Mediaeval London," in *Speculum,* 9 (1934); Herbert Silvette, *The Doctor on the Stage: Medicine and Medical Men in Seventeenth-Century England* (1967); Owsei Temkin, *Galenism: Rise and Decline of a Medical Philosophy* (1973); Joan Thirsk, ed., *The Agrarian History of England and Wales,* IV: *1500–1640* (1967); James Henry Thomas, *Town Government in the Sixteenth Century* (1933).

Charles Webster, *The Great Instauration: Science, Medicine and Reform, 1626–1660* (1975); ed., *Health, Medicine and Mortality in the Sixteenth Century* (1979); and "Medicine as Social History: Changing Ideas on Doctors and Patients in the Age of Shakespeare," in Lloyd G. Stevenson, ed., *A Celebration of Medical History* (1982); Frank Percy Wilson, *The Plague in Shakespeare's London* (1927); Edward A. Wrigley and R. S. Schofield, *The Population History of England 1541–1871: A Reconstruction* (1981); Sidney Young, *The Annals of the Barber-Surgeons of London* (1890; repr. 1978).

Shakespeare and Warfare

JOHN RIGBY HALE

The Range of Shakespeare's Interest in War

In choosing, from the beginning of his career, to cater to the public's lively interest in dramatized history, Shakespeare was accepting war as a major theme. Staged English history was royal history. And what was interesting about kings—apart from their personalities—was not the economic or administrative histories of their reigns but their foreign wars and the armed crises they had to deal with at home. It was against a background of wars (gains and losses of territory) and of domestic faction (treachery, usurpation, and punishment) that audiences defined their relationship to the England of their day-to-day existence. And it was against such a background that they related to foreigners and to the polity whose drama, with its long line of actor-monarchs, conditioned the way in which they thought of themselves as subjects of a Tudor and, less spiritedly, of a Stuart ruler.

In fleshing out this scenario from the reign of John to that of Henry V (Henry VII's studious husbandry of his inheritance was matter for a Bacon, not a Shakespeare, and the postscriptlike *Henry VIII* is the most war-free of the historical plays), Shakespeare was forced to bring war onto the stage. For princes capable of shouldering aside the justice of the courts, the battlefield was the tribunal before which they were judged. For over-mighty subjects, such a tribunal was the judicial duel that, in the theater, often took the form of a single-combat episode epitomizing a larger conflict being waged offstage.

War was still seen by some as part of the divine historical plan. It is clear, moreover, that audiences relished stage violence and its accompanying tuckets and explosions. Theatrical wardrobe masters took for granted the need for military costume, as did actors living in a city of fencing teachers and habituated to the speedy doubling of parts that was part of the working life of small repertory companies essaying large themes.

For Shakespeare, albeit increasingly interested, after the hurly-burly of *Henry VI, Part 1,* in the politics rather than in the armed punctuation points of war, an army had additional dramatic virtues. Among other things, it offered in microcosm an analogy to the Elizabethan ideal commonwealth, which should be united in common self-discipline under a single, respected leader. Within an army, examples of divided command, insubordination, cowardice, or corrupt self-seeking were the more telling for occurring in a version of a polity that was stripped to the essentials needed for its survival. "Who does i' th' wars more than his captain can / Becomes his captain's captain," warns Ventidius in *Antony and Cleopatra* (III. i. 21–22).

Another advantage of dramatizing war was that the variety of army life prompted the deployment of a notable gallery of military character studies. If we focus only on Shakespeare's English history plays in the order of their composition, we can see that no other dramatist of his age offered so wide a range of men recognizably shaped by the exigencies of war service. There is the blunt aristocrat Talbot, to whom soldiering is one of the automatic duties that fall to conscientious members of the second estate and whose pride of birth will not allow him to accept exchange for a prisoner of common birth. Then there is Hotspur, whose impetuous embracing of war as the finest of all sports not only allows Shakespeare to depict the soldier's impatience with the differing brands of caution associated with his confederates—the go-slow wizard Glendower and the bluffly careful Worcester—but also provides an occasion for Lady Percy to report on a considerable repertory of soldier's dream thoughts:

> In thy faint slumbers I by thee have watched,
> And heard thee murmur tales of iron wars,
> Speak terms of manage to thy bounding steed,
> Cry "Courage! to the field!" And thou hast talked
> Of sallies and retires, of trenches, tents,
> Of palisadoes, frontiers, parapets,
> Of basilisks, of cannon, culverin,
> Of prisoners' ransom, and of soldiers slain,
> And all the currents of a heady fight.
>
> (*1 Henry IV,* II. iii. 44–52)

The range broadens to include Falstaff's transmogrification into the most roistrously cynical of recruiting captains. And the brief sketch of his most poignant recruit, the woman's tailor Feeble, is followed, in *Henry V,* by the more rounded figures of those thoughtful other-rankers John Bates and Michael Williams. Indeed, in this play, with a historical theme straightforward enough in time and place to leave room for detail, Shakespeare's interest in the social and professional life of armies expands. His earlier portraits of war leaders are revealed as sketchy adumbrations of the omnicompetent, almost mawkishly conscientious king-commander. Moreover, the dramatist's interest flows down the military hierarchy all the way to that trio of captains Fluellen, Macmorris, and Gower (compellingly differentiated, in national temperament and professional approach), on past the ad hoc NCO's Pistol, Nym, and Bardolph, to Bates and his colleagues, and outward to the pilferer that Bardolph made of his young servant and even to the sutler-provisioners whose ranks Pistol decides to enter after his discomfiture. And there is even a reference to those noncombatants Henry warns his men not to alienate by theft or acts of violence.

From *King John,* with its opening French challenge of "fierce and bloody war," countered by the king's resoundingly anachronistic response that "the thunder of my cannon shall be heard," Shakespeare carried his story forward through the reigns of Richard II, Henry IV, Henry V, Henry VI, and Richard III. In these plays there is scarcely an act that is not motivated by the reality or the threat of civil or foreign war or where the tension at some point is not increased by one or more of several stage devices: parleys with the defenders of a town or castle; marches and countermarches; episodes from battle or siege; or the arrival of news about battles won or lost, about lands in revolt, about rebel forces mustering, or about exiles returning in arms. No wonder the Prologue to *Henry VIII* warns that there is to be no fighting, lest "they that come to hear . . . a noise of targets . . . will be deceived."

Shakespeare's interest in social and professional military manners had by then waned from its climax in *Henry IV, Part 2,* and *Henry V.* But the later plays with British historical settings kept stage armies on the move, with the predominant private themes contained within envelopes of war. *Macbeth* opens with Duncan asking news of "our captains, Macbeth and Banquo" from that most dauntingly eloquent of Shakespeare's NCO's the Sergeant, who describes how Macbeth had fought "the merciless Macdonwald . . . till he unseamed him from the nave to th' chops." A moment later Ross emphasizes the fact that Macbeth, throughout his closet intensities and hesitations, is to be thought of as a Mars, "Bellona's bridegroom, lapped in proof." And this image of Macbeth persists until the final act of crisscrossing armies and single combats. Lear's most painful griefs are bracketed within the landing of a French army and the march and camp scenes—plus the Edgar-Edmund judicial duel —of Act V.

Even in *Cymbeline,* the play most instinct with tenderness toward characters trapped mistily in the past, Shakespeare starts by setting out the military qualifications of Posthumus and the king, invokes the challenge of Roman invasion at the play's midpoint, and moves toward the unique gentleness of its close (for war has here at last served to reveal the truth about individuals and to reconcile nations) across the familiar terrain of march, skirmish, and single combat. *Cymbeline* is a reminder that Shakespeare had, quite early in his career, identified in potential audiences and in himself an interest in ancient Roman, as well as in "British" and (from John's reign) English, warlike settings and characters.

In *Titus Andronicus,* his first Roman play, Shakespeare's awkwardly zestful reworking of his horror script involved such a welter of palace plottings, murders, and mutilations that the armies depicted, whether Roman or Goth, are little more than stage properties. The only true military moment in the play occurs when Titus vainly begs the senators, in the name of the ten years of generalship during which he has saved Rome from its enemies, and "for all the frosty nights that I have watched," to pardon the crimes of his (framed) sons. This anticipates the equally vain appeal, in the much later classical play *Timon of Athens,* that Alcibiades makes to the Athenian senators to pardon a comrade-in-arms who has killed a man in a duel of honor. Both men believe that the hazards and hardships of professional military life justify special treatment under civil law. Alcibiades comments bitterly:

> I have kept back their foes
> While they have told their money and let out
> Their coin upon large interest, I myself
> Rich only in large hurts.
>
> (III. v. 105–108)

This theme of mutual resentment, in which soldiers expect special treatment from civilians, and civilians fear the pretensions of the soldiery, becomes in *Coriolanus* a major motif. Marcius has only intemperate scorn for self-regarding, stay-at-home politicians and the unreliable cowards they pandered to:

> Being pressed to th' war,
> Even when the navel of the state was touched,
> They would not thread the gates. This kind of service
> Did not deserve corn gratis. Being i' th' war,
> Their mutinies and revolts, wherein they showed
> Most valor, spoke not for them.
>
> (III. i. 122–127)

These issues—the incompatability of the military and political temperaments, and the professional's scorn for the civilian part-time soldier—were then much in men's minds, but for reasons of tact, they could not be raised so bluntly within the context of the English history plays. On the other hand, the distance in time and place that enabled them to be raised in plays set in antiquity meant that there was less immediate interest in (and less available information about) the texture of military life as a whole. In *Julius Caesar* and *Antony and Cleopatra,*

we get studies in the perennially interesting topic of military leadership. We see generals—Brutus, Cassius, and Antony (the perfect antidote to Henry V)—who move to war primarily conditioned by the nonmilitary situations that are the plays' major concerns. In both plays battle violence is kept to a visual minimum. In the first, the battle at Philippi is fought offstage, its fortunes explained by brief episodes of dialogue and a single skirmish. In the latter, the sea battle at Actium is fought necessarily offstage, after the only discussion in Shakespeare of a strategic choice (III. vii). And in spite of the heavy use of military costume on both sides, the only forms of violence shown in the play are suicides.

Yet it is in the classical play remotest in time, *Troilus and Cressida,* that we get, if only by fits and starts, the fullest representation of military themes and manners outside of *Henry V.* The battles are represented as sour charades, episode following episode like the frames in a black-comedy cartoon. Yet, though some of the large cast of warriors are but animated suits of armor, a notable assembly of recognizable military types emerges, from the bluffly conscientious Agamemnon and his intellectual aide Ulysses, to those classicized quasi-Hotspurs Ajax and Hector and the martial prima donna Achilles, pouting with wounded dignity, to the fascinatingly equivocal figure of Troilus, brave but sickened by a war whose public cause has come to seem so much less urgent than his personal campaign to win Cressida. Linking the audience to the cause, conduct, and personalities of the war is the figure of Thersites, a brilliant blending of the stock braggart soldier of Plautine and Terentian comedy with the native tradition of the licensed fool. Moving with an unaccustomed freedom from his sources, Shakespeare takes the interminable siege of Troy and produces a sardonic grisaille to set beside *Henry V,* necessarily the more glamorously colored side of the diptych, portraying as it does an unwontedly successful phase in England's interminable wars with France.

By choosing historical themes with political contentions dramatic in themselves or within the frame of which personal dramas could be all the more tensely explored, Shakespeare was committing himself to a treatment of, or at least a continual reference to, military events. If I have labored so obvious a point, it is for two reasons. One is that it is easy, when under the spell of one play, to forget the many other plays that also have military content. The other is that in his dramatization of wars set in the past Shakespeare never forgets his audience's interest in the way in which wars were being waged in the present.

Shakespeare was deterred from writing plays about contemporary military and political events. These were matters over which censorship—whether that exerted on traveling companies by justices of the peace under statute law or by the master of the revels in London—was especially sensitive. And Shakespeare, connected as dramatist, actor, and, eventually, shareholder with serious, well-established companies under august patronage, was unlikely to choose a theme that might give offense to the government or to any powerful individual associated with it. Like most of his fellow playwrights, he left current events to balladeers and newssheet writers or to ad hoc companies—"the quick comedians" who, Cleopatra says with such scorn, "extemporally will stage us, and present our Alexandrian revels" (V. ii. 217–218).

But it may well be, too, that Shakespeare was perfectly content to satisfy his audiences' strong liking for patriotic nostalgia and "romantic" escapism. There is no clear evidence that he wished his plays to be seen in terms of current political or military events (unless *Othello* was an oblique compliment to James I as the poet of *Lepanto*), though the inevitability of parallelism has made attempts to do this a beguiling game. The single clear exception occurs in the context of the Chorus' invitation to the audience at the beginning of Act V of *Henry V* to compare Henry's triumphal return from France to the scene that might greet Leicester's return from his military governorship in Ireland.

Presumably Shakespeare's classical soldiers were armed in accordance with Aufidius' order to those bearing Coriolanus' body offstage to "trail your steel pikes." Or they may have carried the "partisan" of *Antony and Cleopatra* or the "pistol" of *Pericles.* From King John's cannon to the reworking of Shakespeare's sources that enables Fluellen to discuss the mining operations at Harfleur in terms of gunpowder, a plethora of such references to modern weapons would have drawn the audience's attention to the military practice of their own times. But anachronisms of this sort were habitual in Elizabethan drama; they do not suggest that Shakespeare was covertly nudging his auditors into the ꞏent.

ꞏt, as reflecting his interest in warfare, they can ꞏed to the range of military characters in

Shakespeare's work (not excluding the negative example of Hamlet), some of whom are so vivid that they have even tempted editors to look for historical models, like the Sir Roger Williams and Thomas Digges who have been suggested as providing hints for Fluellen. And this interest appears all the more intense in that it is even reflected in the comedies, as in the army whose officers are identified by the Widow for Helena as they parade through Florence in *All's Well That Ends Well* or the war in the same play in which "the gallant militarist" Parolles, who "had the whole theoric of war in the knot of his scarf, and the practice in the chape of his dagger," (IV. iii. 134–135) is so drastically ridiculed. Above all, it is seen in the military images or references that occur with a spontaneity that seems to reflect an instinctive familiarity with both the practice and the theory of contemporary warfare.

In *Love's Labor's Lost,* for instance, Berowne rues his enforced service as a "corporal" in the army of General Love and advises his similarly smitten colleagues how to attack their mistresses:

> Advance your standards, and upon them, lords!
> Pell-mell, down with them! But be first advised,
> In conflict that you get the sun of them.

> (IV. iii. 362–364)

Falstaff in *Merry Wives* likens his cramped position in the laundry basket to a well-tempered sword blade bent "hilt to point." In *The Winter's Tale,* Leontes refers to the point-blank range of cannon in his bitter complaint that Polixenes "is quite beyond mine arm, out of the blank and level of my brain" (II. iii. 5–6). And similar images flow through the whole range of Shakespeare's works. There is Friar Laurence's reproach to Romeo that his "wit,"

> Like powder in a skilless soldier's flask,
> Is set afire by thine own ignorance.

> (III. iii. 131–133)

And there is the anticipation of what Lady Percy overheard from the sleeping Hotspur, in Mercutio's description of Queen Mab:

> Sometimes she driveth o'er a soldier's neck,
> And then dreams he of cutting foreign throats,
> Of breaches, ambuscadoes, Spanish blades.

> (I. iv. 82–84)

There are casual references in *Hamlet* to those with a hair-trigger ("tickle o' th' sere") laugh and to the false alarm which is likened to the "false fire" that flashes up from the priming pan of a caliver.

To glance outside the plays, in *The Rape of Lucrece,* Shakespeare's description of the rape in terms of the siege of a fortress is conventional enough, but in describing the painted siege of Troy, Shakespeare's writing is very much his own. So also with the references to "the labouring pioneer begrimed with sweat, and smeared all with dust," and to reluctant recruits, "Pale cowards marching on with trembling paces."

Taken together, there is a broad sweep of military interest about such images that, considered in conjunction with the surrealistic nonchalance with which Shakespeare could liken the infectious miasma arising from the rotting bodies of Henry V's soldiers to a bullet's ricochet (IV. iii. 104–106), makes it natural to wonder about the nature of the writer's personal relationship to the military events of his day.

Was Shakespeare a Soldier?

Those "lost" years between the last documented references to Shakespeare's residence in Stratford and his emergence as a player and playwright in London (1585–1592) have still to be accounted for. Had he been himself a soldier? The idea is at least less bizarre than trying to deduce a professional basis for the wealth of his allusions to horticulture, medicine, and the law. The soldiering explanation was first suggested in 1865 in a *Notelet* by William Thoms. His conjecture received a little more color when J. W. Fortescue, in the first volume of *A History of the British Army* (1910), wrote of Shakespeare that he was "truly the painter of the English army in his own day. . . . Not in these poor pages but in Shakespeare's must the military student read the history of the Elizabethan soldier." And it was presented as a near certainty in Duff Cooper's beguiling *Sergeant Shakespeare* (1949). All those military portraits, all those military images and allusions, those evocations of military service, rang true to Cooper, who reread Shakespeare while serving in World War II. What more natural, Sir Duff asked, than that a restless young man, burdened with an infant daughter he had had to legitimize and a pair of twins who had arrived two years later, and apparently in trouble with the law over

a matter of poaching, should go to nearby Kenilworth and enlist with the earl of Leicester, his natural lord, appointed in 1585 to raise a military expedition to the Netherlands?

The idea is gruffly dismissed by scholars. Yet it does not run totally counter to possibility. In 1591–1592, Ben Jonson had served as a soldier in the Netherlands before turning dramatist, and his plays, too, are strewn with military allusions. Such Shakespearean contemporaries as Thomas Churchyard, Barnabe Rich, and George Gascoigne were writers, albeit at Grub Street level, whose works drew heavily on their experience in camp and field. So it is not solely in the interest of polemic that the question is put again: Was Shakespeare a soldier? It is a possibility that gives added interest to a review of the nature of warfare and the military profession in his lifetime.

Warfare in Shakespeare's Age

The European peace treaty of Cateau-Cambresis was signed in 1559, four years before Shakespeare's birth. It brought to an end a series of international conflicts that had been fought on the Continent but had had repercussions that had drawn English contingents across the Channel in 1512, 1544–1545, and 1557–1558 and that had effected a drastic reformation of the ways in which armies were raised and organized and campaigns were fought. Gunpowder had at last transformed the conduct of war. Challenged by cannon, military engineers had evolved bastioned defensive systems that produced stalemates more frequently resolved by starvation than by storming. The need to maintain forces adequate to blockade enemy cities as well as to provide a mobile battle force led to the raising of larger armies, at greater cost, than formerly. And with firearms now the chief missile weapons, the majority of troops within these larger armies were infantrymen. The reduced proportion of cavalry was now employed to scout, harass, and skirmish rather than to operate as heavily armored shock troops.

Throughout western Europe, armies had come to consist of a permanent core, garrisoning towns and frontier fortresses in peacetime, and a native militia trained (in theory) to relieve them and to provide a defense force while the professionals were fighting abroad. These were supplemented—for there were never enough of them—by mercenaries raised on the international military manpower market and by the recruitment of natives not already enrolled in militias. This last category was a mixed bag. There was a minority of volunteers; the rest, while not conscripted on a named basis, were men forced by their local communities to fill quotas set by government and scoured out by licensed recruiters—"scoured out" because the military wage was a subsistence one, because government control of the profits of war made enrichment by loot or ransom practically impossible for the common soldier, and because long campaigns and large concentrations of men in unsanitary conditions in camp or siege lines made for higher casualty rates off the battlefield than on it. Boult, the pimp in *Pericles,* asks a not unnatural question: "What would you have me do? go to the wars, would you? where a man may serve seven years for the loss of a leg, and have not money enough in the end to buy him a wooden one?" (IV. vi. 161–164).

Then, during Shakespeare's boyhood, a new and nearly continuous series of wars began in 1572 in the Netherlands, with Spain trying to prevent its rebellious Protestant provinces from breaking away from Catholic Hapsburg rule. By the long-deferred truce of 1609, campaigns in what was increasingly referred to by contemporaries as a "school of war" had produced further changes in cavalry tactics, infantry dispositions, and the proportioning of arms (pike, arquebus, musket). Against a background of training projects and a heavily classicizing military literature, this series of changes has been dubbed by modern historians the "military revolution." Constantly refreshed by mercenary and voluntary free lances with experience of the civil wars in France and the long standoff campaigns in eastern Europe against the Turks, the Netherlands theater, as the chief pressure point in the European political-religious system, stimulated intense discussion of the theory of war, even if the majority of underpaid, underdrilled, and often reluctant soldiers could not match it in practice.

From 1585, the first of Shakespeare's "lost years," England sent troops to fight on the Protestant side in this conflict. Uninvaded (though from 1588, the Armada year, living in fear of invasion), Elizabethan England also raised armies and amphibious forces to deal with wider aspects of the threat from the Hapsburgs and the papacy, pouncing now on Spanish ports, now harassing Spanish fleets and possessions in the Caribbean. And at intervals from 1562, English forces intervened in the civil-religious wars in France, most notably through Essex's Rouen campaign of 1591–1592. Between 1585 and 1597, some 47,000 soldiers were sent to fight in various European theaters. Moreover, insurgency in Ireland, especially dangerous as providing Spain with a back door to the realm, led to a continual need for troops. In 1601, England had 12,600 men in Ireland, the largest single force raised during the reign for a single theater.

It is useful to compare this figure with the 48,000 men raised for his Boulogne campaign by Henry VIII in 1544. Shakespeare's was not an age of aggression. The late sixteenth century was an era of precautionary interventions, police operations, gadfly stings abroad, and preparations against invasion at home. Because of the occasional nature of its forays into the continental war scene before 1559 and the modest and intermittent role played there under Elizabeth (and still more modest under James I), England was, in the main, a military backwater, with much to learn from the "revolution" but without the military structure or involvement to be much affected by it.

Shakespeare's Knowledge of Contemporary Warfare

It is against this background that a further review of the military topics dealt with, or touched on, in Shakespeare's plays may lead from a consideration of his interest in warfare to a reconsideration of the suggestion that he may have played a part in it.

Nothing save service in the military brought war so much to mind as being taxed to pay for it. In all the English history plays apart from *Richard III* and *Henry IV,* Shakespeare shows himself aware of the role of the wallet in war, from King John's easy decision that "our abbeys and our priories shall pay this expeditious charge," to Queen Katherine's accusation of Wolsey in *Henry VIII:*

> The subject's grief
> Comes through commissions, which compels from each
> The sixth part of his substance, to be levied
> Without delay; and the pretense for this
> Is named, your wars in France.
>
> (I. ii. 56–60)

The concern is even carried back to antiquity in Brutus' outburst against Cassius' apparent withholding of gold for the soldiers' wages:

> For I can raise no money by vile means.
> By heaven, I had rather coin my heart
> And drop my blood for drachmas than to wring
> From the hard hands of peasants their vile trash.

> *(Julius Caesar,* IV. iii. 71–74)

With money assured or promised, mobilization could begin. Inspired by his love of "sherris," Falstaff, in *Henry IV, Part 2,* evokes the hilltop early-warning system of bonfires that called out the English militia:

> It illumineth the face, which as a beacon gives warning to all the rest of this little kingdom, man, to arm, and then the vital commoners and inland petty spirits muster me all to their captain, the heart, who, great and puffed up with this retinue, doth any deed of courage, and this valor comes of sherris. So that skill in the weapon is nothing without sack, for that sets it a-work.

> (IV. iii. 103–110)

But the militia in England or elsewhere was—though the convention could be forced aside—mainly a home guard. On the Continent, a permanent army, a professional force maintained in peacetime, was at once put on alert with notice to move off. But England had the smallest such force of any European state, basically only the yeomen of the guard, and Shakespeare refers neither to them nor to mercenaries, whom Henry VIII had hired in large numbers but who were considered both too dangerous and too expensive for Elizabeth's small-scale operations. So in England volunteers were called for first, those against whom Chatillion (in *King John*) warns the French monarch:

> Rash, inconsiderate, fiery voluntaries,
> With ladies' faces and fierce dragons' spleens,
> Have sold their fortunes at their native homes,
> Bearing their birthrights proudly on their backs,
> To make a hazard of new fortunes here.

> (II. i. 67–71)

Because volunteers came forward in small numbers, the majority of men had to be rounded up and pressed into service. In *Troilus and Cressida,* Achilles, reproaching Thersites for accepting a beating by Ajax, establishes the difference: "Your last service was sufferance, 'twas not voluntary.

. . . Ajax was here the voluntary, and you as under an impress" (II. i. 92–94). And in the recruiting scene (III. ii) in *Henry IV, Part 1,* Shakespeare depicts indelibly and accurately how recruiting captains like Falstaff could proudly claim: "I have misused the king's press damnably. I have got, in exchange of a hundred and fifty soldiers, three hundred and odd pounds" (IV. ii. 12–14).

In England the lowest, but crucial, officer in the recruiting mechanism was the parish constable, charged by the justice of the peace to order adult males to present themselves for selection. For those wishing to dodge the press, the solution was to bribe or browbeat this officer. In *Much Ado About Nothing,* Privy Council complaints about him and his minions suggest that Dogberry was no fiction:

> *Dogberry.* You are to bid any man stand, in the Prince's name.
> *2. Watch.* How if 'a will not stand?
> *Dogberry.* Why then, take no note of him, but let him go . . . and thank God you are rid of a knave.

> (III. iii. 23–28)

And if good men were presented who were unwilling to serve, they could still have recourse to bribery. Falstaff's release of Mouldy and Bullcalf constitutes no exception. "Take heede that none be discharged for anie monies," the council admonished recruiters in 1597. The press operated best in London or in areas where magnates were charged to serve along with men raised from their estates. As the son who has killed his father exclaims in *Henry VI, Part 3:*

> From London by the king was I pressed forth;
> My father, being the Earl of Warwick's man,
> Came on the part of York, pressed by his master.

> (II. v. 64–66)

Audience interest in the press is reflected in such plays as the anonymous *The Lamentable Tragedie of Locrine* (1595) and Robert Wilson's *The Coblers Prophesie.* In both the press got its man. But the verisimilitude of Falstaff's settling for those who were too poor or cowed to bribe their way out is further demonstrated by—it is one instance among many—a comment from the mayor on recruits mustered in Bristol in 1602: "Few of them have any clothes, small, weak, starved bodies, taken up in fair, market, and highway to supply the place of better men kept at home."

There is, then, a ready explanation for the contempt for the common soldier shown in so many of the plays. Falstaff's "Food for powder, food for powder. They'll fill a pit as well as bitter"; Pandarus' "Asses, fools, dolts; chaff and bran, chaff and bran"; Coriolanus' "Base slaves. . . . Down with them"; and the scorn expressed elsewhere, and qualified only by the portrayal of the soldiers Henry V talks to on the eve of Agincourt (IV. i), were calculated to ring true not only to the gentry in Shakespeare's audiences but to practically everyone who could afford a place in the theater.

The scraping up of wastrels, dropouts, and the feeble was a European phenomenon, as were the corrupt practices of recruiters. It is interesting that Shakespeare does not follow the trail of their corruption beyond the recruiting process and into the field, for it was thanks to recruiters' falsification of company numbers (commanders never had accurate numbers of the men they could deploy), their illegal withholding of pay (which encouraged desertion and ruined discipline), and their negligence about maintaining the due proportion of NCO's (which inhibited the use of tactical subdivisions) that the evolutions so neatly set out by theory could seldom be carried out in practice.

While a commander like Richmond in *Richard III* could call for ink and paper so that he might

> draw the form and model of our battle,
> Limit each leader to his several charge,
> And part in just proportion our small power
>
> (V. iii. 24–26)

and though Calphurnia could be oppressed by the portent of heavenly warriors arrayed "in ranks and squadrons and right form of war," formations were seldom, if ever, drawn up with textbook precision. Humanism, in one of its utilitarian guises, created the aim of rivaling the feats of Alexander and Caesar by imitating their tactical dispositions, as outlined in description and diagram, in the burgeoning European literature of war. Fluellen, as a convert to ancient example, accordingly praises Gower because he is "a good captain and is good knowledged and literatured in the wars" and commends Jamy because "he will maintain his argument as well as any military man in the world in the disciplines of the pristine wars of the Romans." But quite apart from the no-nonsense philistinism of such warriors as Ajax and Achilles, who, as Ulysses complained, wrote off paperwork preparation for

combat as "bed-work, mapp'ry, closet-war" (in 1599, Essex warned Elizabeth's council against sending Mountjoy to Ireland as a man "too much drowned in book-learning"), army command structure inhibited niceties, save on the parade ground or on paper, and in no forces perhaps as much as in those raised, always from scratch, in England.

In large permanent garrisons or in sizable mercenary contracts, military rank in the infantry was fairly consistently defined in all countries. Under a colonel there were captains of companies (some 150 men) each assisted by a sergeant, six corporals, and a drummer. Each colonel had a personal captaincy in one of these companies, which had on its payroll his staff lieutenant and ensign, who acted not within the company structure but as his personal assistants. In a field army the colonels were subordinate to the commander in chief (variously termed colonel, governor, or captain general) and his tactical officer, the sergeant major. Leaving aside the separate cavalry and artillery services and the officers responsible for law enforcement, provisioning, and pay, this was, with small regional variation, the professional structure on which rates of pay were based. Finally, it was common for commanders in chief also to have companies of their own, either within a colonelcy or as a personal staff and guard.

The building block within an army was, then, the company, and the key officer, the captain. Apart from the personal salaries and expense accounts of general officers, all pay was distributed through captains. In theory, from 1586 on, English pay was to be given out by muster masters, but as armies came to be strung out on service, after the initial general muster, at which NCO's were checked, the understaffed and inexperienced pay corps gave little attention to the composition of companies, save for an occasional check on their overall numbers. So, not unnaturally, captains retained as few NCO's as was practicable, pocketing the difference between their pay and that of the rankers. This tendency resulted in fluidity throughout the army, as experienced NCO's became casualties and were not replaced, and as rankers were named, if not paid, as NCO's for favor's sake or gained kudos by referring to themselves as such when off duty.

One result of this organizational malaise was that the small-unit tactics called for by the proponents of the "military revolution" failed for lack of enough experienced NCO's. Another was that military nomenclature became vague, especially in the armies of Shakespeare's maturity, which had no organizationally defined permanent forces to draw example from and no mercenary companies to offer a working model of professional, long-standing military structure. "Regiment" meant only a force placed temporarily under a single subcommand.

It is, then, not surprising that Henry V is referred to as "the royal captain" or that Philo calls Antony a general and a captain in the same speech. There are no colonels in Shakespeare because outside the muster lists and pay sheets, colonels came alive only as captains. That Bardolph should figure now as a corporal and now as a lieutenant, Pistol as an ensign (or ancient), and Nym as a corporal is also readily understandable against this background. If there is no English sergeant, it is because Pistol had selected the more prestigious if less well paid rank. We do not know what the company rank of Cassio was before Othello promoted him to be his personal lieutenant or second in command, above Iago's company rank as an ensign (which it seems he was forced to retain when detached to the garrison governor's staff), but promotion by favor rather than by service experience was an old—and frequently criticized—fact of military life. So was Iago's plain-soldier-man outburst against "the bookish theoric" and "great arithmetician" Cassio,

> That never set a squadron in the field,
> Nor the division of a battle knows
> More than a spinster.
>
> (I. i. 22–24)

No speech in Shakespeare so clearly calls up the conflict between, on the one hand, the student of those diagrams and mathematical formations devised to facilitate the marshaling of ranks and files in a given area of ground, and, on the other, the fierce believers in experience as the only true preparation for combat. All the same, what rankled more was Othello's preference for a man whose breeding and ease of manner, rather than his experience, would commend him to the citizens of a city garrisoned by an occupying power. Pistol queries Henry V:

> Discuss unto me, art thou officer;
> Or art thou base, common, and popular?
>
> (IV. i. 37–38)

This and his acceptance that his interlocutor is a gentleman, albeit a ranker pikeman (as Henry let

him understand), explains much concerning the feeling about rank, as opposed to its logic, in the patched-together armies of Elizabethan England.

As for the armament of foot soldiers (England raised few cavalrymen and sent none abroad, though their role in continental armies remained important), his stories do not call on him to itemize it, but there are scattered references to all the standard weapons: dagger; sword; partisan (or halberd); pike; musket; and the commonest hand-held English firearm, the matchlock caliver. It may be revealing that in non-English military contexts Shakespeare never refers to the arquebus, which on the Continent was almost universally used in preference to the caliver. The pistol was used exclusively as a cavalry arm or as the much legislated-against weapon of an assassin (like Thaliard in *Pericles*).

Once in service in the Netherlands and, to a lesser degree, in France, English units found themselves serving in the mongrelized forces characteristic of European warfare. Exaggerated as it deliberately is, Parolles' dilemma when taken prisoner does reflect the polyglot flotsam washed into wars:

> I know you are the Muskos' regiment,
> And I shall lose my life for want of language.
> If there be here German, or Dane, Low Dutch,
> Italian, or French, let him speak to me.
>
> (IV. i. 66–69)

Shakespeare takes no advantage of the comic, satiric, or purely generic opportunities offered by the corrupt practices of captains on active service: the doubling-up of live men along the line to collect the pay of dead ones, the pay clerk's identification of men by warts and other deformities as a check on the names in the muster list, the hasty borrowing of body armor to qualify for the bonus payable to heavily armed men. Even more surprising (if he had served himself) is his virtual omission of the whole company of camp followers who clustered about armies, at times in numbers almost equal to their own. These included not only vendors of the fresh cheese, eggs, vegetables, and meat not available from the commissariat but dealers in captured (or pawned) equipment, wine sellers, professional gamblers, and real and soi-disant laundresses.

Shakespeare's vision focuses on the soldier himself. Given governments' inability or reluctance to pay their troops on time, commanders were often forced to dig into their own pockets to prevent desertion. Timon's observation to Alcibiades, "Thou art a soldier, therefore seldom rich," would have been greeted with a grim acknowledgment of its justice. But so would Timon's later challenge to the pillagers: "Now, thieves?" "Soldiers, not thieves." "Both two." Theft, indeed, was rife in armies whose pay was often late and whose rations were too often reduced to a basis of that "hard cheese" which has remained a phrase of offhand commiseration ever since. It was all the more so because of the thieves who were enlisted or caught up into armies—men, as Henry V put it, "making the wars their bulwark, that have before gored the gentle bosom of peace with pillage and robbery." The portrayal of soldiers as thieves was all the more telling because audiences knew that armies not only contained them but produced them. The disgraced Pistol says:

> To England will I steal, and there I'll steal;
> And patches will I get unto these cudgelled scars
> And swear I got them in the Gallia wars.

> (V. i. 79–81)

This but paraphrased a Privy Council denunciation of "such as had been employed in the wars in foreign parts and others that did pretend and bear a show to have served in the wars as soldiers."

To audiences most of whom would have dodged military service if they could (as the sluggish response to the Armada mobilization showed), more interesting than social details of service life abroad were reminders of the military fallout they knew from their own streets. War increased the number of beggars. "I have led my rag-of-muffins where they are peppered," reflects Falstaff. "There's not three of my hundred and fifty left alive, and they are for the town's end, to beg during life" (V. iii. 35–38). And war magnified that Elizabethan bugbear roguery. Gower's portrait of Pistol is as near as Shakespeare got to the nondramatic genre of the "character," and it was surely essayed in the full knowledge that it would sink instantly home:

> Why, 'tis a gull, a fool, a rogue, that now and then goes to the wars to grace himself, at his return into London, under the form of a soldier. And such fellows are perfit in the great commander's names, and they will learn you by rote where services were done: at such and such a sconce [field fortification], at such a breach, at such a convoy; who came off bravely, who was shot,

who disgraced, what terms the enemy stood on; and this they con perfitly in the phrase of war, which they trick up with new-tuned oaths; and what a beard of the general's cut and a horrid suit of the camp will do among foaming bottles and ale-washed wits is wonderful to be thought on.

> (III. vi. 66–77)

And such fellows, together with their betters, brought back news and views that could tell much to a man who, like Shakespeare, could readily have been at ease—through his trade, standing, and connections—with a wide variety of those who had seen service overseas.

The Sources of Shakespeare's Military Knowledge

From what we have seen of what Shakespeare included and omitted, it does not seem necessary to posit actual service to explain his interest in, and knowledge of, war. These arose from his plots and were sustained by the scares, the mobilizations, the issuing of arms to citizens, the demands for war taxes and loans, and the flow of news and men from Ireland and the Continent that colored London life during his most productive years. He took such impressions and transmuted them into poetic images and hints of character. On the basis of Tasso's epic poem *Gerusalemme Liberata*, with its range of military information, metaphor, and character, it could be argued that Shakespeare's Italian contemporary had been a soldier. But, with no missing year in his biography, we know that Tasso had not been. The sermon literature of the age, at times so buoyantly full of up-to-date military jargon, provides an even more pertinent warning against equating knowledge with experience. Like the stage, the pulpit also drew on two other sources whence Shakespeare might have derived his information without crossing the Channel: the parades and training sessions of the "trained bands" (instituted in 1572 to provide regularly drilled units to stiffen the lackadaisically supervised national militia), and the ever-increasing number of books dealing with the art of war.

That Shakespeare knew the weapons training at Mile End, the favored practice ground for the London bands, is clear enough. Consider a passage on handling the caliver: "I remember at Mile-end Green," quavers Justice Shallow, in a speech that is one of Shakespeare's most explicit gifts to a comic actor, ". . . there was a little quiver fellow, and 'a would manage you his piece thus, and 'a would about and about, and come you in and come you in. 'Rah, tah, tah,' would 'a say, 'Bounce,' would 'a say, and away again would 'a go, and again would 'a come" (*2 Henry IV,* III. ii. 262–268). Also revealing is the reflection in the plays of the emphasis placed, as we know from training manuals dating from as early as 1562, on drawing up and drilling men in formations of different shapes—squares or rectangles, basically—determined by the number of men in rank and file. No memoir or chronicle reports this sort of drill as being carried out by English troops in the course of a campaign or refers to "squares" of men.

Yet, time after time, *file* and *square* are used by Shakespeare in the context of campaign soldiering: Aufidius, wishing to placate Coriolanus, says, "Let him choose/Out of my files . . ./My best and freshest men." Antony is introduced as a man who—before his dotaged surrender to a tawny front—had "goodly eyes/That o'er the files and musters of the war/Have glowed like plated Mars" (I. i. 2–4). Antony mocks the Brutus who (shades of Iago's scorn of Cassio) "dealt on lieutenantry, and no practice had/In the brave squares of war." It was a term that came so automatically to the dramatist's mind that Antony could apologize to Octavia for his Alexandrian liaison with the admission that "I have not kept my square." Indeed, when the terrified Parolles denigrates Captain Dumain, it is tempting to think that Shakespeare is in part making a wry reference to his own assumption of military expertise (though he also reflects the unpopularity of the foreign captains hired to instruct the militia):

Faith, sir, has led the drum before the English tragedians—to belie him I will not—and more of his soldiership I know not, except in that country he had the honor to be the officer at a place there called Mile-end, to instruct for the doubling of files.

(*All's Well That Ends Well,* IV. iii. 250–254)

And this calls to mind the remark of Sir Roger Williams, a professional soldier who knew the London players, in his *A Briefe Discourse of Warre* (1590) that "divers play *Alexander* on the stages, but fewe or none in the field."

If the file and square references did not come only from the later plays (including *Cymbeline*), we might indeed think of the Shakespeare of the lost years as perhaps a sergeant, but in the trained bands. There were, however, other everyday hints that could add verisimilitude to the portrayal of military life: the workshops of armorers, gunsmiths, and swordsmiths; the near-craze for fencing with rapier and dagger or poniard as a gentlemanly accomplishment; and the traffic of soldiers to and from the London docks. And for a man with a youth and a continued stake in the Warwickshire countryside, there was also the experience of the huntsman and the poacher. It did not take military service to sympathize with sentinels who are "when others sleep upon their quiet beds,/Constrained to watch in darkness, rain, and cold," or to bring to mind the familiar military advice that when closing in on a quarry it is wise to "have the wind."

It is true that there are scenes and speeches whose atmosphere strongly suggests military service—the midnight relief of the guard in *Hamlet,* or the off-duty carouse in *Othello,* which leaves Cassio so vulnerably drunk. Most suggestive of all is the night scene evoked by the chorus (*Henry V,* IV. i) before the battle of Agincourt: the watch fires, the neighing of horses and the clink of armorers' hammers, the troops playing dice or waiting silently for dawn, the king on his rounds while "the hum of either army stilly sounds." But much of this has been shown to have been prompted, in phrases and situations, by the description of Agamemnon's night round before Troy in George Chapman's translation of Homer, *Seaven Bookes of the Iliades of Homere* (1598).

The clues Shakespeare could have followed from books were indeed manifold. Between the publication in 1581 of Thomas Styward's comprehensive *The Pathwaie to Martiall Discipline* and the appearance in 1616 of John Bingham's *The Tactiks of Aelian,* there were twenty-two new works, original or translated (including classical texts heavily commented on to bring out their relevance to the present), that dealt directly with the art of war, some of them to an almost encyclopedic extent, covering everything from martial law, fortification, and ballistics to definitions of military duties, rank by rank, and diagrams of troop formations.

It has not yet been proved that Shakespeare used any literary sources. In *An Arithmeticall Militare Treatise, Named Stratioticos* (1579), Leonard and Thomas Digges had roundly claimed that the "antique Roman and Grecian discipline martial does far exceed our modern." It seems clear that Shakespeare, too, was interested in classical precedent, just as, like Bingham, he was also interested in the place to be accorded theory in the training of the soldier and in the need during peacetime to be prepared for the next war. But these topics were not restricted to books. In his *Observations upon Caesars Commentaries* (1600), Sir Clement Edmondes emphasized the role of "discourse" as well as reading and experience in shaping the soldier's education. When Sir John Smythe, author of *Certain Discourses Military* (1590) and *Instructions, Observations, and Orders Militarie* (1595), had brought his Essex men to the Tilbury musters of the Armada year, the earl of Leicester noted that "he entered again into such strange cries for ordering of men and for the fight with the weapon as made me think he was not well." London must have resounded with such strange cries, conveying information and opinion all the more suggestive of character and situation for not being in cold print. Tempting as it is to trace Iago's outburst against Cassio's promotion to a passage like Giles Clayton's "None to be captains unless first a lieutenant, none lieutenant except first an ensign" (in *The Approved Order of Martiall Discipline,* 1591), it is more likely to have been borrowed from some spoken grievance. Yet there were many lively, popular debates that found no reflection in his plays, such as the proper treatment of serving and discharged soldiers and the rival merits of mercenary and native troops, of bows and firearms, or of arms and letters.

Of course, this is not to say that Shakespeare read no books on war. *Henry V* suggests that he had used some of the published descriptions of the ideal commander to guide his transformation of Hal into Henry, but his information was probably collected in the nontraceable, skimming manner of the swift reader who seeks suggestion rather than statement. Most of the military literature he had access to was irrelevant to the strobe-like treatment of staged battles and to the drama's greater interest in the bangs and trumpets of warfare, as distinguished from the methods of making war. There is, for instance, no extended passage in Shakespeare resembling that speech in *Tamburlaine, Part 2,* where the conqueror lectures his sons on the art of war, a speech that commentators have traced to Paul Ive's *Practise of Fortification* (1589) as Marlowe's source.

We can, then, to round out this consideration of the "lost years" with reasonable assurance, listen to Petruchio's rhetorical question in *The Taming of the Shrew:*

> Have I not heard great ordnance in the field
> And heaven's artillery thunder in the skies?
> Have I not in a pitched battle heard
> Loud 'larums, neighing steeds, and trumpets' clang?
>
> (I. ii. 200–203)

And, on Shakespeare's behalf, we can answer no.

Shakespeare on War and Peace

And the dramatist's attitude to war itself? While England produced reckless amateur commanders in chief like Leicester and Essex, free lances of the gallantry of Sir Philip Sydney, and tough professional leaders like Sir John Norris, Sir Francis Vere, and Sir Roger Williams, there were never enough militant gentry even to keep the militia in training; and the great majority of ordinary soldiers and NCO's served reluctantly. But if the English were unwarlike—save for the "coursing snatchers" whose raids across the northern border were referred to by Henry V—they were not opposed to the idea of war. The growing Tudorization of the public mind and the threat from a papacy-backed Spain had caused Erasmian pacifism to wither and the remnants of Anabaptist pacifism to go underground. Dean Matthew Sutcliffe's statement in *The Practise, Proceedings and Lawes of Armes* (1593) was unchallengeable:

> It is needeless (as I suppose) to dispute whether it be lawfull, either for Christian princes to make warres or for Christians to serve in warres. Those that think it unlawfull, as men devoyd of iugement in religion and state, are declared long since to be both heretical and phrenetical persons.

It is a very rare instance in Elizabethan drama when someone such as Tamburlaine's son Calyphas refuses to serve from "remorse of consciences"— and Calyphas' father speedily kills him for expressing such a sentiment.

There is no hint of Shakespeare's dissenting from the received opinion that monarchs had the right to order their subjects to war in a just cause and that, if it were just, God would favor it. As Henry VI exclaims:

> What stronger breastplate than a heart untainted?
> Thrice is he armed that hath his quarrel just,
> And he but naked, though locked up in steel,
> Whose conscience with injustice is corrupted.
>
> (III. ii. 232–235)

And before Bosworth, Richmond's "God and our good cause fight upon our side" is sharply contrasted with Richard III's "Our strong arms be our conscience, swords our law." Shakespeare does focus on the grimness of the consequences of a royal decision to declare war. In *King John* he has the Bastard say to King Philip:

> Ha, majesty! how high thy glory towers
> When the rich blood of kings is set on fire!
> O now doth death line his dead chaps with steel!
> The swords of soldiers are his teeth, his fangs;
> And now he feasts, mousing the flesh of men
> In undetermined differences of kings.
>
> (II. i. 350–355)

But it is within the context of his own just cause that the disguised Henry V discusses with Bates and Williams the responsibility of the individual soldier to prepare his soul for death (IV. i).

In endorsing—though not without the Bastard's shading—the monarch's right to wage war, Shakespeare was satisfying his audience and the censor at the same time. In similar fashion, the corruptions in army organization that he dramatized (like those of Falstaff) were already covered by official censure of the sort that was published in proclamations. Yet, in thus playing it safe, there is no suggestion in the plays that Shakespeare was suppressing strong feelings, one way or another, about the role of war in human life. Shakespeare was never a chauvinist, and he was certainly not a fanatic in religion. No "view" on war emerges from the evenhandedness with which he has his characters express sentiments appropriate to their roles. If for Timon war is "beastly," for Othello it is "glorious."

In *Henry V,* the Duke of Burgundy deplores the fact that among war's victims are "arts" and "sciences." But this was one of the consequences of wars so long prolonged that children grew up in their atmosphere "like savages." The concept of the just war, like that of the judicial duel, envisaged a short, sharp conflict, with God as umpire. It was perfectly orthodox to approve war as contest while deploring it as condition. And it was generally agreed that the habits of war should not be carried over into peace. The most Machiavellian moment in the plays comes when Volumnia urges Coriolanus to gain political power with the guile forced on a commander by the exigencies of war:

> If it be honor in your wars to seem
> The same you are not,—which, for your best ends,

> You adopt your policy—how is it less or worse,
> That it shall hold companionship in peace
> With honor, as in war; since that to both
> It stands in like request?
>
> (III. ii. 46–51)

Volumnia's is a subtler point than those usually made at the time about the difficulty of reabsorbing into civilian society those who had learned violence, wenching, and peculation in the wars, but it is firmly related to them.

Though Shakespeare could, in the private world of the Sonnets, refer to the resolution of a conflict in such a way that "incertainties now crown themselves assured,/And peace proclaims olives of endless age" (Sonnet 107, 7–8), in the plays he also reflected his age's doubts about the quality of a long-lasting peace.

The discernible chivalrous revival in later Elizabethan England prompted the question of how valor can be claimed if it cannot be demonstrated:

> He wears his honor in a box unseen
> That hugs his kicky-wicky here at home,
> Spending his manly marrow in her arms,
> Which should sustain the bound and high curvet
> Of Mars's fiery steed.
>
> . . . .
>
> Therefore to th' war!
>
> (*All's Well That Ends Well,* II. iii. 273–279)

True, this is Parolles speaking, the soldier of mere *paroles,* "words." But in an earlier scene, when the King of France grants leave to the gentlemen of his court to join the Duke of Tuscany's army as volunteers, the Second Lord comments that "it well may serve/A nursery to our gentry, who are sick/For breathing and exploit" (I. ii. 15–17). And it is the same current within contemporary aristocratic self-definition that breaks out in Hamlet's envy of Fortinbras' ability to prove his valor in action, even in a conflict over an eggshell.

The dying Henry IV's advice that his son forestall the civil strife that can arise in peacetime with diversionary "foreign quarrels" drew on advice given by writers on politics from the early sixteenth century on, advice that came to be more widely offered by observers of the French civil wars during Shakespeare's lifetime. And equally familiar to Shakespeare's audiences from a wide variety of sources would have been references to peace's tendency to corrupt the moral fiber of a people. "Plenty and peace breeds cowards" is the comment

97

given, somewhat surprisingly, by the gentle Imogen in *Cymbeline*. When *Coriolanus* opens with the news that the Volsces are in arms, he replies, "I am glad on't. Then we shall ha' means to vent/Our musty superfluity"—by which he means what Falstaff referred to as "the cankers of a calm world and a long peace": men made slothful, dissolute, and criminous by years of security. In his *Piers Penilesse His Supplication to the Devil* (1592), Thomas Nashe, remarking that "there is a certain waste of the people for whom there is no use but war," went so far as to suggest that the theater itself could serve, if need be, as a second-best disciplinarian:

> If the affairs of the state be such as cannot exhale all the corrupt excrements, it is very expedient they have some light toys to busy their heads withal. . . . [Plays] show the ill success of treason, the fall of hasty climbers, the wretched end of usurpers, the misery of civil dissention, and how just God is evermore in punishing of murder.

But in the matter of warfare Shakespeare never preached from the stage or allowed an ideology to slant his delineation of military characters or blur the immediacy of the images he derived from what he knew of the Renaissance art of war.

BIBLIOGRAPHY

Frederick S. Boas, *Queen Elizabeth in Drama and Related Studies* (1950). Lindsay Boynton, *The Elizabethan Militia, 1558–1633* (1967). Duff Cooper, *Sergeant Shakespeare* (1949). Cyril Bentham Falls, *Elizabeth's Irish Wars* (1950). J. W. Fortescue, *A History of the British Army,* I (1910), and "The Soldier," in *Shakespeare's England,* I (1932). John Rigby Hale, *The Art of War and Renaissance England* (1961). T. R. Henn, "A Note on Shakespeare's Army," in *The Living Image: Shakespearean Essays* (1972).

Paul A. Jorgensen, *Shakespeare's Military World* (1956). G. Geoffrey Langsam, *Marital Books and Tudor Verse* (1951). John Smythe, *Certain Discourses Military,* J. R. Hale, ed. (1964). William J. Thoms, *Three Notelets on Shakespeare* (1865). Henry J. Webb, *Elizabethan Military Science: The Books and the Practice* (1965). Sir Roger Williams, *The Works of Sir Roger Williams,* John X. Evans, ed. (1972).

Patronage of the Arts

F. J. LEVY

Had the young earl of Rutland leafed through the copy of Aristotle's *Nicomachean Ethics* bought for him at the close of 1599, he would have found a passage defining the lordly virtue of Magnificence as one's "suitable expenditure of Wealth in large amounts" not only on public objects but even "to furnish his house in a way suitable to his means, for that gives him a kind of distinction." Indeed, at that date the earl's expenditures were far outrunning his income. His entourage—the servants who attended his person, his castles, and his estates—numbered around 150. In his family's account books could be found the names of William Shakespeare, Inigo Jones, the miniaturist Nicholas Hilliard, and the Flemish portraitist Paul Van Somer; the same accounts record visits to Belvoir Castle by groups of strolling actors and by musicians belonging to other gentlemen of the neighborhood. Of strictly literary patronage, however, only one example comes readily to hand: the £3 given to Randle Cotgrave when he presented his French dictionary to Lady Rutland.

The Rutland accounts are probably fairly representative in their depiction of noble patronage. The family was well educated and literary in its interests —indeed, Roger Manners, the fifth earl, had gone on the grand tour and had married the daughter of the poet Sir Philip Sidney. They spent lavishly on books as well as on the customary clothes and furnishings. Yet Ben Jonson could remark rather bitterly that "one day being at table with my Lady Rutland, her husband comming in, accused her that she keept table to poets" (*Ben Jonson,* I, 142).

Aristocratic families of the period spent huge amounts on building and decorating their houses. Building became a veritable mania, and some of the "prodigy" houses that resulted—such as the earl of Suffolk's Audley End or the earl of Salisbury's Hatfield—were the equal in size and magnificence of anything going up on the Continent. The house once built had to be appropriately furnished, preferably with that most coveted commodity, suites of tapestry hangings. Bess of Hardwick, countess of Shrewsbury, in building Hardwick House, designed her great chamber specifically to display the tapestries she had bought from the estate of Lord Chancellor Christopher Hatton. James I, in emulation of the French king Henry IV, established a royal tapestry works at Mortlake by importing Flemish arras workers and a first-rate Danish designer; the products of this bit of enlightened royal patronage were so greatly sought after that it was necessary to obtain royal favor merely to get on the waiting list.

Where the walls were not hung with woven pictures, they might be covered with portraits. This was true especially in the long gallery, a most modish and up-to-date room in which the master of the house could take exercise and in which he and his guests might stroll beneath the painted visages of the host's powerful friends and relations. Supplying the portraits provided work not only for such great painters as Marcus Gheeraerts, Paul Van Somer, and Daniel Mytens (and, a little later, Sir Anthony Van Dyck) but also for lesser production workers in London shops. Some of the great houses would also have resident musicians. The Kytsons at Hengrave Hall provided a home for the madrigalist John Wilbye, whose entire career was spent in the family's service, not only as music teacher and composer but also as estate agent and friend. The family supplied as well, for Wilbye's use and their own, viols, violins, recorders, flutes, sackbuts, cornets, hautboys, an organ, several virginals, and music books in abundance. But such great houses would also have a resident preacher, and its owners might well have the right of appointment to other pulpits in the neighborhood; these positions were as much the result of patronage as any gifts to artists or performers.

The proprietors of the magnificent household dealt with the outside world either by outright purchase, a one-time arrangement, or by patronage, an exchange of favors and services involving a more permanent relationship. Anthropologists have told us that these "patron-clientele networks may be seen as strategies for the maintenance or aggrandisement of power on the part of patrons, and of coping and survival on the part of clients" (Waterbury), a definition that fits the situation around the end of the sixteenth century fairly well. The system resembled a pyramid, with the monarch at its apex. Queen Elizabeth had in her gift the right of appointment to a myriad of positions in church and state, ranging in importance from minor curacies and canonries, through keepers of castles and forests, to the major offices of government. She could award lucrative patents and monopolies—for example, the earl of Essex's control of sweet wines was worth perhaps £10,000 a year—and she could grant honors and titles of nobility. Ranged around the queen were her councillors and officers, her favorites, her ladies-in-waiting. Some of these had appointments in their own gift, but all of them traded on their access to the queen and their ability to influence her patronage. As Shallow reminded Falstaff, "A friend i' th' court is better than a penny in purse" (*2 Henry IV,* V. i. 27–28).

The queen, by a skillful use of her rights, could play her courtiers off against each other. Moreover, these same courtiers depended for their power on their ability to perform favors for lesser men. Thus, an Essex or a Burghley built up his faction by a judicious exercise of influence at court, but that influence in turn depended to some extent on the number of his supporters. So, too, an earl of Huntingdon exerted his power and prestige on behalf of the town of Leicester when the corporation needed a royal favor, but the town then found it expedient to appoint the earl's nominees to positions in its gift. The system worked on the basis of a series of quid pro quos.

In these exchanges, each gentleman parlayed his access to those above him on the ladder into a way of granting favor to those below him; but, of course, this system worked only if those below were willing to give up some of their independence. So the clergyman who had accepted aristocratic patronage to become a bishop might then find himself forced to repay his benefactors by granting away episcopal lands on beneficial leases —and this could occur even when the queen arranged the appointment. The benefits to be gained were not always material: a devoted Puritan like the earl of Huntingdon used his patronage at Leicester to ensure that his version of Protestant theology would be publicly taught in the town. Many a local gentleman used his rights of appointment the same way.

But what of the artists or poets? What increase of power could they offer their patrons? The aristocratic ideology of the day insisted that a gentleman be learned, well versed in Latin, and able to write his own language eloquently in poetry and prose. Many a courtier used his poetic ability to create or further a career at court—Elizabeth especially seems to have battened on versified flattery. In addition, as Aristotle had remarked and Baldassare Castiglione was to repeat, while a gentleman had no need to be an architect or painter, he had to understand those arts well enough to employ their practitioners sensibly. So a reputation as a patron of poets did no harm and might even do some good; and when collecting and connoisseurship became de rigueur at the courts of James and Charles, the gentleman unable to keep up the pace hired assistance.

Thus, the minor Flemish painter Balthasar Gerbier parlayed his expertise into a position as artistic adviser to the duke of Buckingham. Buckingham impressed everyone with his art collection at a time when such things mattered at court, and Gerbier became Sir Balthasar. Similarly, Sir Henry Fanshawe, a member of a gentry family that had attained a virtually hereditary position at the Exchequer, achieved an influence disproportionate to his wealth because of his reputation as an artistic patron and bon vivant. His gardens at Ware Park were famous, and invitations were much sought after. His collection of paintings aroused envy even in the hearts of connoisseurs like the earl of Arundel. Fanshawe's household found room for the composer John Ward, himself a minor gentleman, who exercised his talent in the family's service until his death. Even a country gentleman like Sir Nicholas Saunderson of Fillingham, Lincolnshire, found it expedient to make a lease with Giles Farnaby, the composer, performer, and instrument-maker, by which Farnaby's son Richard was indentured to Sir Nicholas for seven years to instruct the Saunderson children in the arts of music and playing on instruments. Gentlemen needed help to fill out their roles.

The arrangements of patronage could, of course, be damaging to the artist. Only the rare patron was himself expert in the art, as practitioner or even as connoisseur. How often was it true, as Thomas Nash said of Sidney, "thou knewst what belongd to a Scholler, thou knewst what paines, what toyle, what travell, conduct to perfection: wel couldst thou give every Vertue his encouragement, every Art his due, every writer his desert" (Sheavyn, p. 13). Even when such praise was merited, the patron might well try to bend the poet to his, or her, will. Honest Samuel Daniel spent some years at Wilton in the service of the earl and countess of Pembroke, probably as tutor to their children. At the same time, however, the countess (Sidney's beloved sister, Mary) involved Daniel in her plans to revitalize and "correct" the English drama by bringing it more closely into line with the best continental models. Converting "sweete hony dropping Daniel" (as he was called in the second *Parnassus* play), the lyrical poet of the *Delia* sonnets, into a soberminded tragedian, straining him to a higher pitch, may well have seemed (and even been) a good idea, but it is no surprise that the poet offered some resistance. Relations between patron and poet collapsed for a time, with the result that Daniel, already given to self-doubt, had to be rescued and revived by new, more generous, and wiser patronage: Lord Mountjoy took him in, and Fulke Greville procured him a sinecure that could be converted to ready cash. Similarly, Sir John Hos-

kyns admitted that he changed his style with the seasons of courtly taste:

Whilst Mathematics were in requests, all our similitudes came from lines, circles and angles; whilst moral philosophy is now a while spoken of, it is rudeness not to be sententious. And for my part I'll make one. I have used and outworn six several styles since I was first Fellow of New College, and am yet able to bear the fashion of the writing company.

(Saunders, p. 39)

For many an artist, bowing to the taste of his patron meant survival.

Whether the artist had any independence depended to a great extent on the status accorded his art. As long as painters were considered artisans, their status was correspondingly low. Thus, in England as in Italy, painters labored mightily to convince their public of the gentility of their art—and that of its practitioners. Some emphasized the intellectual content of the work. Others emphasized the absence of the least tinge of the grime associated with manual labor. Hilliard the miniaturist made a point of performing his small miracles in settings intended to resemble as closely as possible the houses of the aristocracy, and conversed with his sitters as equals. As the "architect" gradually separated himself from the ranks of the master masons —again largely by elevating the "idea" of a house above the mere details of execution—his status and prestige rose. But painters and architects, whatever their status, did not enter into permanent relations with their customers. Theirs was, in the end, an art of the market, and their achievement was to raise the market price of their product.

The same, however, was not true of most writers, least of all the poets. Only those poets who were also great gentlemen could afford independence. Provided he did not venture into the forbidden lands of sedition or heresy, a Sidney or a Greville could say more or less what he pleased. But when Sidney wrote a letter of unsolicited (and unwanted) advice to the queen, he was rusticated for his pains (and wrote *Arcadia* to console himself). When Walter Raleigh found himself in the Tower for his injudicious marriage, he thought flattering poetry might yet restore him to his queen's good graces. For poetry, as we have already noted, was a mark of education, a way to show a man was fit for more important things. As the literary theorist George

Puttenham had noted, even in ancient times poets had gained a reputation not only because of their ability to please princes but also because they were thought for their universal knowledge to be very sufficient men for the greatest charges in their commonwealths, both for counsel and for action, skills that could coexist in one person. The poet using his skills for advancement (as Spenser) and the courtier turning poet for the same reason (as Raleigh) were equally constrained in subject matter. Paradoxically, the courtier faced one additional obstacle, for his very gentility was seen as a barrier to print:

> It is ridiculous for a lord to print verses; 'tis well enough to make them to please himself, but to make them public is foolish. If a man in a private chamber twirls his band-string, or plays with a rush to please himself, it is well enough; but if he should go into Fleet Street, and sit upon a stool and twirl a band-string, or play with a rush, then all the boys in the street would laugh at him.
>
> (John Selden, quoted in Sheavyn, p. 166)

Yet the pursuit of fame and reputation, and the hope of position, meant that one's writing had to be circulated somehow—a situation that led to a great deal of hypocrisy.

Those writers who, unencumbered by social position, were driven by poverty and the absence of patronage to seek their fortunes elsewhere could turn only to the printers and the theatrical impresarios. In the absence of authorial copyright, their dealings with the printers were likely to be unsatisfactory. A "best-selling" pamphleteer like Robert Greene could write quickly enough to keep himself in drink and pickled herring, but he died in poverty all the same. William Elderton could scrape together a living by writing broadside ballads—and he was the best of a bad lot. Proper poets had a much harder time of it. Thomas Bastard, peddling his epigrams around the publishers just when such goods were popular, nonetheless discovered that

> The Printer when I askt a little summe,
> Huckt with me for my booke, & came not nere.
> Ne could my reason or perswasion,
> Move him a whit; though al things now were deere.

And so he was driven to ask, as poets have before and since,

> Hath my conceipt no helpe to set it forth?
> Are all things deere, and is wit nothing worth?
>
> (quoted in Miller, p. 150)

In fact, it was not altogether uncommon for a writer to be forced to subsidize the publication of his work. Even if he escaped that indignity, he might still be paid in copies of his own book, to be hawked about the streets by the author himself.

Grub Street filled the imagination more than the belly, and most of those condemned to live there at some time made their way to the theaters. Even here, they could soon find themselves in a form of indentured servitude, borrowing money from owners like Philip Henslowe and then writing furiously to repay it; a few had even to promise that they would write for no one else. Usually, one of Henslowe's authors came to him with the germ of an idea; Henslowe consulted with the members of the Admiral's Company, whose agent he was; if they agreed, he advanced some cash to the author. But as like as not, to speed the drama to the boards, the task of writing it was divided between a multitude of playwrights, who had then to share out the payments, which came to around £5 or £6 for a play, sometimes even less, rarely much more. So a Thomas Dekker, a John Day, or a Michael Drayton would receive perhaps a pound for some weeks' work, more than the wages of a skilled artisan, but not by much. The fortunate among the playwrights were those whose skills ran also to acting or, better yet, who managed to become a sharer in one of the successful companies of players. It was thus that Shakespeare became a gentleman and retired to Stratford as a sober householder.

Yet even so public an activity as the drama could come within the patronage system. The laws of the realm equated an actor with a vagrant, and the only way to avoid prosecution was to come under the protection of some great nobleman or official. In exchange, the company had to be ready to perform for its patron during the holiday season or on special occasions (royal visits, weddings, and the like). Traveling companies regularly sought such employment, turning up at the door of some great establishment (Prince Hamlet's, perhaps) and asking to play. They did the same at the market towns, often first putting on a special performance for the mayor and aldermen and being paid out of the town funds. The best of the companies were invited to play at the royal court: since payment here could run easily to £10 or more (double or triple what an evening at the playhouse would bring in), royal patronage was well worth having. It would be more lucrative still had a new play to be prepared for the occasion: if it is true that Queen Elizabeth asked to see Falstaff in love, the Lord Chamberlain's Men and their playwright Will Shakespeare did well out of it.

Various corporate bodies also used the skills of the dramatic companies. The lawyers of the Inns of Court sometimes produced their own entertainments, but they were known to hire professional players to enliven the Christmas festivities. Sometimes interested groups of Londoners might hire a company for a special evening—as the friends of the earl of Essex did on the eve of his revolt, when they had *Richard II* revived, presumably as a way of working up within themselves the wrath of the righteous. On gala occasions, such as a royal entry into London or the annual lord mayor's pageant, professional writers prepared the scripts and the actors took time off from their usual work to perform them.

In the end, then, most artists had to work within the patronage system, at least some of the time. Musicians seem to have been most bound to it—and were fortunate that, for reasons of prestige and magnificence, there were so many public occasions for their art. Even Queen Elizabeth, whose direct patronage of artists was negligible, had a number of musicians on her rolls, including the great composer William Byrd as her organist. London and many of the larger provincial towns had their own town "waits," musicians on the municipal payroll to herald and entertain at the frequent ceremonial occasions (though one notes that the waits eked out their stipends at neighboring great houses). As we have seen, some musicians became music masters to the aristocracy, just as some writers became tutors.

It was more difficult for writers. Not many families were prepared to support indefinitely a resident poet; but a poet, his foot once in the door, might easily advance within the larger, political patronage system. Spenser comes to mind as an example: his poetry brought him to the attention of the Sidneys and of Lord Grey, whose secretary he became. Grey's influence, and probably Sir Henry Sidney's as well, procured him a post in Ireland, where he spent (perhaps reluctantly) the remainder of his life. It is customary to lament with Spenser that his rewards were so few; in fact, the poet did remark-

ably well from the system. A poor Londoner who had gone to Cambridge on a scholarship, whose connection with the lordly Spencers was probably more imaginary than real, he advanced to a substantial estate in Ireland and the rank of sheriff. Nor, as legend once had it, did he die in poverty after his lands were ravaged by Irish rebels; on the contrary, Elizabeth uncharacteristically eased his difficulties with a substantial pension of £50. Spenser lived well on patronage organized for him by great men with access to the distribution of offices. Other poets, like Drayton and Daniel, would have been envious.

Or consider the career of Thomas Hobbes. When young William Cavendish, heir to the earl of Devonshire, was ready to go on his grand tour, his father sought for him a tutor who would be only a few years senior to his charge and thus might be able to influence him through friendship rather than authority. Friends at Oxford suggested Hobbes, a poor boy from Malmesbury whose academic attainments seemed appropriate. The plan worked brilliantly. Tutor and student became firm friends and remained so for the rest of the young lord's unfortunately short life. Hobbes served as his amanuensis and agent, voted his stock in the Bermuda Company, and lived with him at Hardwick and Chatsworth. After his patron's death, Hobbes continued with the Cavendishes for almost all of the remainder of his very long life, and he wrote most of his works while he was in their service. The family protected him and sustained him; his position with them was so secure that he could survive even a quarrel with the strong-minded widow of his old friend. Family patronage supplied all his needs.

Hobbes and Spencer were exceptionally successful in their (rather different) uses of the patronage system. Most writers had perforce to seek their patronage piecemeal. Typically, one followed Cotgrave's path and dedicated a book to some great person (like the countess of Rutland) in the hope of reward—and the £3 that Cotgrave received was not atypical. But the game of dedications led to abuses. Some men tried the trick of multiple dedications (Thomas Lok seems hardly to have omitted any of the great ones in the kingdom); some had the dedication page printed with a blank line where the patron's name could be inserted in manuscript; some even went to the trouble of having several dedicatory leaves printed up. And some hoped to succeed by simple flattery: "Fayre sister of Phoe-bus, & eloquent secretary to the Muses, most rare Countesse of Pembroke," said Nash to Philip Sidney's sister,

> thou art not to be omitted; whom Artes doe adore as a second Minerva, and our Poets extoll as the Patronesse of their invention; for in thee the Lesbian Sappho with her lirick Harpe is disgraced, & the Laurel Garlande which thy Brother so bravely advaunst on his Launce is still kept greene in the Temple of Pallas. Thou only sacrificest thy soule to contemplation, thou only entertainest emptie handed Homer, & keepest the springs of Castalia from being dryed up.
>
> (Miller, p. 107)

Since the dedication prefaced a surreptitious edition of Sidney's *Astrophel and Stella,* even Nash's extravagantly ladled butter was probably insufficient to gain him anything.

So many others tried the same thing that, ultimately, the elaborately complimentary dedication became matter for derision. "I compiled a pleasant Pamphlet, and dedicated the same unto him," laughed Ulpian Fulwell of some lordling he had gulled,

> in the preface wherof I fed his vayne glorious humor with magnificent Tytles and termes. . . . I waited opportunity to deliver my sayd Pamphlet unto the Patron when I found him in a mery moode (which is a thing specially to bee regarded of all suters) it pleased him so wel to read his owne commendacions, that hee vouchsaved to peruse the rest, and gave mee his rewarde and good countenance which was the thinge for the which I fished.
>
> (Miller, p. 99)

Before long, most such fishing expeditions returned home empty-handed. In begging help from Raleigh, Thomas Churchyard, the long-lived soldier and poet, told the story of his efforts to find enough patronage. A most honorable personage to whom he had dedicated a volume named *Churchyardes Choise*—Sir Christopher Hatton—got him two royal grants under the Great Seal; Churchyard presumably sold the privileges embodied therein and lived a season on the proceeds. Raleigh himself, he recollected, had some six years past spoken in his behalf at court, and benefits had accrued. But now, Churchyard complained,

> I have sixteene severall bookes printed presently to bee bought (albeit they are but trifles) dedicated in sundrie seasons to severall men off good and great credite, but to be plaine not one among them all, from the first day of my labour and studies, to this present yeere and hower, hath anie waye preferred my sutes, amended my state, or given mee anie countenaunce.
>
> (Miller, p. 119)

How was a man to live on that?

The most successful artists mixed the several sorts of patronage, avoiding a complete dependence on any one of them. Shakespeare turned to the earl of Southampton for a brief time only, and that when the theaters were closed because of plague; the dedication to the *Rape of Lucrece* suggests that the playwright did not do badly from the relationship. For the rest of his career, Shakespeare remained within the orbit of the theater, and his contact with aristocratic patronage came through his association with the Lord Chamberlain's (later the King's) Men. The only recorded exception was a payment to him of 44 shillings for composing an impresa—a sort of illustrated motto, here placed on a banner—for the earl of Rutland's entry into a tournament. (To keep matters in perspective, one should perhaps add that Shakespeare's friend Richard Burbage received the same amount for painting and gilding the impresa, and one Tyler, a painter, got nearly £4 for decorating the tilt staves.)

But Shakespeare was unusual in his willingness to seek a fortune largely within the theatrical world; he emerged only when the theater failed him. Drayton and Jonson were, in this sense, more typical: both used their associations with the great families, made much of their dedications, and sold their talents to the theater. Drayton seems never to have suffered abject poverty; still, after years of labor, culminating in his mighty geographic epic *Poly-Olbion* and a folio of poetic works, he died without a will, leaving an estate inventoried at less than £25.

As a young man, Jonson established for himself a base in the popular drama. At the same time, despite his low birth, he made a reputation as a classical poet and playwright, a reputation that gave him access to aristocratic and courtly patronage. For years, he wrote most of the royal masques and was much in demand to perform the same task for private festivities. King James I granted him an annual pension of 100 marks. Each year the earl of Dorset gave him a grant to buy books and did it so unostentatiously and with such kindness that the poet did not labor under the obligation:

And though my fortune humble me, to take
The smallest courtesies with thankes, I make
Yet choyce from whom I take them; and would shame
To have such doe me good, I durst not name:
They are the Noblest benefits, and sinke
Deepest in Man, of which when he doth thinke,
The memorie delights him more, from whom
Then what he hath receiv'd. Gifts stinke from some.

    ("An Epistle to Sir Edward Sacvile, now Earle of Dorset")

Yet, in spite of all, by the beginning of King Charles I's reign, Jonson was near poverty. No longer able to pick and choose from among those offering him money, he addressed to the king "The Humble Petition of Poore Ben . . . ," begging that his pension be raised by a third, from 100 marks to as many pounds. Johnson also sent to the lord treasurer "An Epistle Mendicant," telling him that

    Disease, the Enemie, and his Ingineeres,
    Want, with the rest of his conceal'd compeeres,
    Have cast a trench about mee, now, five yeares.

Further, he suggested that relieving such distress was as honorable as relieving a besieged town. So Jonson, too, it seems, was never able to achieve a steady and reliable source of income, though he could write popular plays and had better access to the resources of patronage than almost all of his contemporaries.

Yet Jonson's career, more than that of any other Elizabethan, points to the future. The poet who was welcome at the houses of his noble patrons—the earl of Rutland's curt remark was much more the exception than the rule—and who was treated as an equal by scholars and courtiers alike foreshadows such Augustans as Alexander Pope. But Pope had his own villa at Twickenham, and could compete in garden-making with this patrons. Jonson's independent base, despite the bravado of the poem to Sackville, was never that sound, at least partly because the opportunities for earning wealth by the pen were still so limited.

In the Elizabethan period new elements mixed with old, and the results were volatile and unstable. The printing press and the public opportunities it represented had become available to authors, but the profits still accrued largely to the printers and publishers. Grub Street may have been invented in the sixteenth century, but the successful Grub Street hack had to wait until the eighteenth. Yet patronage in the medieval style was gradually disappearing as it became more and more rare for noblemen to support individual artists for any length of time.

Two things saved the situation. First, the general expansion of magnificence and display meant that there were simply more occasions for artistic commissions of all kinds. Second, the increasing importance of the court under the first two Stuarts (especially noticeable after the Elizabethan dearth) protected the arts against the growing opposition of the Puritans. The Stuart court also dispersed a steady and by no means insignificant stream of money among the artists, and its patronage provided as well some focus for their activities. Nevertheless, for most artists the golden age had not yet arrived.

BIBLIOGRAPHY

Malcolm Airs, The Making of the English Country House, 1500–1640 (1975). Erna Auerbach, Tudor Artists (1954). John Buxton, Sir Philip Sidney and the English Renaissance (1954; rev. ed., 1964). John F. Danby, Elizabethan and Jacobean Poets (1952; 1965). Richard Helgerson, Self-Crowned Laureates: Spenser, Jonson, Milton, and the Literary System (1983). Daniel Javitch, Poetry and Courtliness in Renaissance England (1978). Ben Jonson, C. H. Herford and Percy and Evelyn Simpson, eds. (1925–1952).

Guy F. Lytle and Stephen Orgel, eds., Patronage in the Renaissance (1981). W. T. MacCaffrey, "Place and Patronage in Elizabethan Politics," in S. T. Bindoff et al., eds., Elizabethan Government and Society (1961). Eric Mercer, English Art, 1553–1625 (1962). Edwin H. Miller, The Professional Writer in Elizabethan England (1959). David C. Price, Patrons and Musicians of the English Renaissance (1981).

J. W. Saunders, The Profession of English Letters (1964). Phoebe Sheavyn, The Literary Profession in the Elizabethan Age (1909; rev. by J. W. Saunders, 1967). Lawrence Stone, The Crisis of the Aristocracy, 1558–1641 (1965), and Family and Fortune (1973). John Waterbury, "An Attempt to Put Patrons and Clients in Their Place," in Ernest Gellner and John Waterbury, eds., Patrons and Clients in Mediterranean Societies (1977).

Theaters and the Dramatic Profession

ANDREW GURR

The Rise of Commercial Acting

Shakespeare was ten years old when, in 1574, the English government began to license professional playing companies for the first time. He was twelve when the first playhouse built in London exclusively for the commercial showing of plays came into existence. By 1590, he had made himself one of the first generation of playwrights to earn a living from writing for the commercial stage. At the age of thirty, he became a shareholder in one of the two companies licensed to perform in London and probably at the same time became the first playwright in England to be contracted on a regular basis to write playscripts for a major company. Shakespeare and commercial theater grew up together.

English theater and Shakespeare's novel profession as a poet who was paid to write plays for the commercial stage came into existence together in the last decades of the sixteenth century in London. In those years London, growing rapidly as the social face of England was transformed by the force of new economic pressures, began for the first time to provide a regular audience ready and eager to frequent and to finance a popular theater. The hectic inflation that followed Henry VIII's release of church property into England's markets for land and trade, the influx of gold bullion filched by Francis Drake and others from the Spanish who mined it in the Americas, and the broaching of new opportunities for profitable trading ventures abroad all helped to focus wealth in the twin cities on the Thames, London and Westminster. For both the merchants of London and the nobility of Westminster, inflation accelerated a change in the idea of what wealth was. From the simple fact of owning land, which needed care and residence if it was to yield a good living, wealth became increasingly the possession of gold, which was portable and indestructible, and gave much easier access to the pleasures of city life. In the sixteenth century, wealth increasingly became concentrated in London. So, for the first time a strong market developed that was ready and able to cater to the pursuit of leisure. Ben Jonson and his fellow playwrights, who observed with scorn and moral disapprobation the young men of the country selling their land for gold and flocking into London to spend it, were condemning a major source of their own livelihood.

When, in 1572, Queen Elizabeth's Privy Council attempted to regulate the flood of social change and to control the tide of landless people who washed around the cities and towns in the wake of the inflationary surges of the midcentury, they included all unauthorized entertainers in their category of "Vacabondes," including "all Fencers Bearewardes Common Players in Enterludes & Minstrels . . . all Juglers Pedlars Tynkers and Petye Chapmen" (quoted in Chambers, IV, Appendix D). Acting companies were lumped in with other fairground and marketplace salesmen and entertainers, whether they entertained with dancing bears, juggling, or sword-fighting displays, or performed plays and interludes. In 1572 playacting was a fairground activity. The playing companies traveled from town to town, taking their plays to their audiences and collecting their fees by carrying a hat through the throng in the marketplace. London, which later offered auditoriums with doors, where no fee meant no show and where the audiences traveled to the plays, was then only one of an endless sequence of stopovers for the traveling companies.

The 1572 act against vagabondage attempted to license the best companies so as to simplify the operations of the law officers who had to control vagabonds. The only players authorized to perform in public were those who belonged to lords of the realm. For several decades noblemen of the great houses had been accustomed to maintain companies of players paid to perform as the great households' entertainers, in imitation of the custom at court. Such entertainments were infrequent, and the pay was rarely enough to sustain a player for much of the year. Thus, for most of the time these legitimate companies would travel with their plays and interludes, advertising themselves under their noble patron's name, secure through its influence from the harm otherwise promised them by the law officers of the towns they visited. The greatest lords had the best entertainers, and the reputation of the best companies grew rapidly.

In 1574, two years after this attempt by the government to separate the worthily performing sheep from the vagabondish goats, a more positive move was made that effectively began to open the way for companies to base themselves permanently in London. The queen issued a license specifically for the company of players who traveled under the patronage of the earl of Leicester. It authorized them by name (five of them) to perform where they pleased "as well within oure Citie of London and liberties of the same, as also within the liberties and fredomes of anye oure Cities, townes, Bouroughes &c whatsoever as without the same, thoroughoute our Realme of England" (quoted in Chambers, II, chapter 13). The only limits imposed in return for this license were a prohibition on performing in times of common prayer or plague, and approval by a censor of the texts to be performed. With such a license in his hands, the leading player of Leicester's company, James Burbage, promptly set about building the first commercial playhouse. This for the first time gave the acting companies a profitable

base in London. That development in turn gave Shakespeare his opportunity, and succeeding ages the priceless benefit of his plays.

What Burbage constructed was an open-air amphitheater, about 100 feet in diameter, capable of cramming up to 3,000 people into its wooden circle. It was a polygonal building similar to the structures built for displays of bull- and bearbaiting, amphitheaters that themselves ultimately derived from Roman models. Like the baiting houses, the first theater had three ranges of galleries with seating, but most of the audience stood for the performance in the yard surrounding the stage platform. The stage, the locus of the action and the focus of all attention, was a rectangle projecting from one side into the middle of the yard and measuring more than forty feet across and twenty-seven feet in depth. Behind it was a wall with two or three entry doors fronting the "tiring-house," or players' dressing room. Above the stage doors was a balcony usually reserved for the wealthiest of the audience to sit in, though part of it was sometimes used for acting and in later years became a musicians' gallery. The stage design was powerful but not elaborate, since staging needs had to be kept simple. To Burbage the chief value in building a theater was the control it gave him over the spectators and their money.

Throughout the sixty-six years when theaters like Burbage's existed in London, the prices charged to spectators never changed. One penny (in the old system, one-twelfth of the shilling that a skilled craftsman could expect to earn in a day) gained access to the yard, where you could stand next to the stage in whatever weather London skies might choose to offer. To sit with a roof over your head in the galleries cost a further penny, or two if you chose the "twopenny rooms" closest to the stage. The wealthy, who enjoyed being seen as well as seeing, took over the "lord's rooms" on the balcony above the stage doors.

Burbage's theater, which, appropriately enough for the first such building in England, was called the Theatre, opened in 1576 on one of the two main roads to the north of the city, just outside the city boundary. Despite the government's license, locating the Theatre clear of the city was a sensible piece of caution. The mayor and the Corporation of London did not want players inside their territory and throughout Elizabeth's reign made efforts to stop plays from being performed there. They believed that plays were immoral and unhealthy (they drew crowds, and crowds helped to spread diseases such as the plague) and that they seduced men from their work. England always had a strong faction that objected to plays, and it was principally the favor given to players by the court that allowed them to flourish in Shakespeare's time. When the court fell from power in 1642, all of England's theaters were promptly closed. Hostility to playing was never far away. The hostility was so strong that for the first decades the commercial London theaters had to lurk in the suburbs of Middlesex to the north, and later in Surrey to the south of the city.

Burbage's Theatre acquired a neighbor, the Curtain, in 1577. Ten years later Philip Henslowe, a wealthy impresario and bear owner, opened a third amphitheater, the Rose, across the Thames in Surrey next to the major bearbaiting arena. The marshy land of the Bankside was close to the southern end of London Bridge and was easily accessible with the help of the boatmen who provided the chief form of public transport around the two cities and their royal palaces. The south bank of the Thames proved then as it does now a fertile ground for public entertainment. Eight years after the Rose was built, a speculator named Francis Langley built the Swan on Bankside; and two years after that, Burbage acquired a plot of land nearby to which he transferred his dismantled Theatre. His lease of the ground in the north on which the Theatre was originally built had expired, and the Bankside seemed a good alternative site. The rebuilt Theatre became Shakespeare's Globe. It provided a third amphitheater south of the river and the fourth or fifth in London altogether. That number amply reflects the size of the commercial market to which plays and playmakers were now catering. And that was by no means the limit either for spectators or for the finance they brought with them.

The Globe opened in 1599. Within a year Henslowe had moved in the opposite direction, replacing his Rose with the Fortune, which opened in 1600 in Golding Lane, due north of St. Paul's. Two more amphitheaters followed, the Red Bull in Clerkenwell to the northwest and the Boar's Head to the east. Both of these theaters were converted from inns. By this time, however, the speculators had overreached themselves. Six or seven amphitheaters were more than even the court was willing to tolerate. Officially up to 1600 no more than two companies had been licensed at any one time to

perform daily within reach of London, so some theaters had to suffer. In the event success went to Shakespeare's company at the Globe, Henslowe's company at the Fortune, and a third company, licensed when James came to the throne in 1603, that took up residence at the Red Bull. The other playhouses were used only occasionally for shows like fencing displays or for occasional visits by traveling companies. In any case, by the time James came to the throne, a new kind of theater and a new kind of acting company were in existence. The adult actors now had competition from the boy companies who performed at indoor, or "private," theaters.

England had a rigorous and extensive social hierarchy in Shakespeare's time. The new forms of wealth, especially in the merchant classes of the cities, gave rise to some social mobility when cash began to replace land as the chief mark of status. Once cash started flowing into the theaters and their footing in London became firm, the theatrical profession began to climb socially, too, and two previously distinct traditions merged. Entertainment in midcentury had existed on two quite distinct social levels. The higher level existed at court and in the halls of the great country houses. The lower level worked in the fairgrounds and marketplaces of the principal towns, where the highest aspiration of the players would be to perform in a town's guildhall before an indulgent mayor and citizenry. Only the very best of the traveling companies would ever be asked to include performances at court in their itinerary. And the court was by no means entirely dependent on these companies, because the choir schools of the Chapel Royal at Windsor and St. Paul's were also trained to offer plays to court audiences.

Up to 1590 the boy choristers were serious rivals to the companies of adult players as providers of plays for the aristocracy. Acting in plays was a respectable part of a child's education, since it helped his skills in the art of oratory, which was the chief objective at the higher levels of the Tudor school syllabus. Witnessing a play performed by children was socially more respectable than seeing one played by professional adults, because it was less frankly commercial and could be passed off as a display of educational skills instead of mere entertainment for idle pleasure. The boy players were "amateur" in that superior class-conscious sense which made them as socially respectable as the law students who occasionally put on special shows at the Inns of Court or the students who performed in plays at Oxford and Cambridge. Nonetheless, the interests of the boy companies certainly were commercial. And they were entertaining London with plays well before the adult players gained full acceptance. Sebastian Westcott, who was master of the St. Paul's children for nearly thirty years until his death in 1582, besides providing entertainment at court, regularly staged plays for Londoners in the small theater adjoining the cathedral. These were openly commercial shows. The Children of the Chapel Royal's choir school opened a playhouse in the Blackfriars at about the same time as Burbage opened his Theatre in Shoreditch and with the same object. Adult companies and boy companies then competed for paying customers for fifteen years, from 1576 to 1590, when the boy companies were closed down and London was left to the adults.

It was the boy companies, no doubt partly because their social status was more secure, who really opened London to commercial theater in the second half of the sixteenth century. Their controllers included such playwrights as Richard Edwardes, who was master of the chapel children in the 1560s, and John Lyly, who led the competition against the adult companies in the 1580s. But it was always going to be an unequal struggle, boys against men; and the 1580s saw the adult companies taking over from the boy companies the function of entertaining both city and court. The boys of St. Paul's were invited to perform plays at court for every year but one of Westcott's long rule, but by the time the adult players built their first theater in London, they were being summoned to court much more often than the boys. Elizabeth openly acknowledged the growing power of the adult companies in 1583 when she ordered the formation of her own adult acting company, the Queen's Men. Not until 1599, when the adult companies were prospering hugely, did the boy companies return to the fray. In the first decade of the seventeenth century, two boy companies performed at the smaller indoor theaters, called "private" to differentiate their social status from the common "public" stages. But by then they were fighting against heavier odds than their social status could compensate for, and in 1609 they left the stage for good. The adult companies reigned royally for the next three decades. The principal jewel in their crown, and indeed the chief agent in their coronation, was their stock of Shakespeare's plays.

The Acting Companies and Their History

The story of the acting companies of Shakespeare's time, including the company for which he wrote all his great plays, really begins with the queen's decision in 1583 to cream off the best talent from the adult companies of the day and make one supremely good company, which would receive her personal patronage. This was recorded by Edmond Howes, a chronicler of the time, in his expansion of John Stow's *Annales* (1615):

Comedians and stage-players of former time were very poor and ignorant in respect of these of this time: but being now grown very skilful and exquisite actors for all matters, they were entertained into the service of divers great lords: out of which companies there were twelve of the best chosen, and, at the request of Sir Francis Walsingham, they were sworn the queens servants and were allowed wages and liveries as grooms of the chamber: and until this yeare 1583, the queene had no players. Among these twelve players were two rare men, viz. Thomas [i.e., Robert] Wilson, for a quicke, delicate, refined, extemporall witt, and Richard Tarleton, for a wondrous plentifull pleasant extemporall wit, he was the wonder of his time.

(page 697)

The new company, the most talented in the land, spent the next five years consolidating the status of adult playing companies. The royal name now helped to secure the London theaters against the hostility of the city fathers, and the queen's company's affluence stimulated such new playwrights as Thomas Kyd and Christopher Marlowe to start writing for the popular stage. In so doing, they created a new style and began the trend that brought the heroic roles into prominence ahead of what Marlowe dismissively called the "jigging veins of rhyming mother-wits" (*1 Tamburlaine,* Prologue).

Howes recorded two clowns as the leading Queen's Men in 1583. Richard Tarlton was the most famous player of his day and the star of his company. A story by Thomas Nashe offers a neat cameo of the Queen's Men and their clown on their travels:

A tale of a wise Justice. Amongst other cholericke wise Justices, he was one, that having a play presented before him and his Towneship by Tarlton and the rest of his fellowes, her Majesties servants, and they were now entring into their first merriment (as they call it), the people began exceedingly to laugh, when Tarlton first peept out his head. Whereat the Justice, not a little moved, and seeing with his beckes and nodes hee could not make them cease, he went with his staffe, and beat them round about unmercifully on the bare pates, in that they, being but Farmers & poore countrey Hyndes, would presume to laugh at the Queenes men, and make no more account of her cloath in his present.

(*Pierce Penilesse,* 1592)

It was a nice paradox for the judge. The dignity of the queen's own players was bestowed on a company that made its living by clowning.

Tarlton's clowning turned out to be the company's mainstay, because after his death in 1588 its fortunes fell and other companies quickly took its place in the royal favor. These companies gained their reputation in a new way, by the speaking of "majestic" verse and Marlowe's "mighty line" instead of by their clowns.

The brightest new star was Edward Alleyn. Twenty-two years old when Tarlton died, he took all of Marlowe's greatest roles, the most famous parts of Elizabeth's last years: Tamburlaine, Faustus, and the Jew of Malta. At this time the predominant fashion in men's clothing, particularly among the hated Spanish, was for thickly padded doublets with hugely enlarged sleeves. Skeptical contemporaries took the name for the coarse cotton fabric used for such clothes, fustian, and the padding, bombast, and applied them to the inflated language of the poets who wrote for the new stages. Even Alleyn called himself derisively in a letter "the fustian king," because his living and his reputation came from the way he spoke the inflated verse of the new plays. He could well afford to mock himself. In 1592 he married Philip Henslowe's daughter and became a partner in Henslowe's enterprises, helping to run his theater as well as leading its companies of actors, and taking a share in the bull- and bearbaiting that Henslowe also promoted. After 1602, when he finally retired from acting to work full time as an impresario, he became rich enough to found Dulwich College and make himself the most respectable ex-actor England was to know before the twentieth century.

The years 1589–1594 were difficult ones for the acting companies, particularly the last two years, when visitations of the plague kept the London theaters closed for long periods. All the companies had to travel for their living, a course they found

1. A contemporary portrait of Richard Tarlton with his pipe and drum.

more painful than ever now that they had sampled the comforts of a permanent base. Alleyn's company even petitioned the Privy Council in 1592 to allow it to stay in London despite the plague, though without any noticeable response. But in the midsummer of 1594 the plague cleared away, and the two companies that then established themselves enjoyed a run of unprecedented freedom and consequent prosperity. The two companies that secured this benefit became so prosperous in the next few years that they dominated the London scene, in one case until 1621 and, in the other, right up to the closure in 1642. The first of these companies was Alleyn's company, the Admiral's Men, playing at Henslowe's Rose theater, and the other was the company Shakespeare joined, the Chamberlain's Men, playing at James Burbage's old Theatre.

The two companies that monopolized London theater in 1594 were composed rather differently, and in the long run this told. Alleyn led the Admiral's Men and helped to finance their purchases of playbooks, costumes, and other properties. But his partner Henslowe was a playhouse-owning financier, and his participation in company affairs was consequently rather ambiguous. Alleyn withdrew from acting in 1597, after a tremendously profitable run of three years in which his company played uninterruptedly six days a week for nearly fifty weeks in each year. He returned to acting during 1600–1602, but even then he was more the impresario and financier than the acting star. He ceased to be a sharer in the company and became an employer instead.

Under King James, companies regularly occupied Alleyn's theaters, but they generally lasted as little as three years each before moving on. Each new company needed to borrow money to finance its run, and none ever managed to free itself from obligation to its landlord. Dulwich College has, in a nicely pious tribute to its founder, preserved a large quantity of Henslowe's and Alleyn's accounts, which show an extraordinarily complex pattern of financial dealings between the financiers and their tenants. The Chamberlain's Men left no such records of their finances, but there is enough evidence about them to show that their organization was rather different. Its peculiarities undoubtedly helped them to survive in an unbroken and unrivaled flow of prosperity from 1594 to 1642.

The Chamberlain's Men began life as an amalgamation of players from different companies, performing at James Burbage's Theatre in conditions not unlike those of the Admiral's Men at the Rose. Just as the Admiral's leading man was their landlord's son-in-law, so the Chamberlain's leading man was Burbage's son, Richard. But the principle of sharing or team spirit or whatever it was that held the traveling companies together helped to keep the Chamberlain's actors in a better relationship with their landlord and financier. Moreover, their financier operated differently. In 1596, James Burbage, responding to City and Privy Council restraints that forbade the use of inns inside the City for playing, built a replacement for the City inns, a new theater in a hall in the Blackfriars. The Blackfriars was a "liberty," an area free from the City's control, inside the City walls west of St. Paul's. Building an indoor theater in the liberty was a clever scheme, because it secured an ideal site in a wealthy residential area between the two cities of London and Westminster. It offered several advantages over the old amphitheater built in the northern suburbs twenty years before. The smaller size of the hall was offset by the fact that it was roofed against the weather and higher admission prices could be charged.

Sadly, though, in setting up such a novel scheme Burbage overreached himself. The wealthy residents of Blackfriars objected. They petitioned the Privy Council, and the Chamberlain's Men were forbidden to use it. Their own patron, a resident in Blackfriars, signed the petition to stop them. So the £600 that Burbage had spent on converting the hall was tied up uselessly. And soon he would need more cash because the lease of the land on which the old Theatre stood was expiring, and a new theater was already a pressing need. The solution that was found for this problem not only brought Shakespeare's Globe into being but also introduced a new financial arrangement that did as much as anything besides Shakespeare's plays to secure the Chamberlain's Men a long and prosperous future.

Old Burbage died in 1597, and the problem of finding a new theater fell to his sons, Cuthbert, who inherited the major assets, and Richard, the actor. They decided to pull down the Theatre and rebuild it on the Bankside, and in 1599 they did so, creating the Globe out of the timbers of the Theatre. That took money, so, uniquely, they turned to the sharers of their acting company for help. The two Burbages put up half the capital; and Shakespeare, together with three other sharers among the actors, put up the other half. Thus, the Chamberlain's Men became not only shareholders in the fortunes of their acting company but also shareholders of the building they performed in. In one function they were tenant sharers, and in the other, landlord householders. They were thus freed from the endless drain the other companies suffered in making repayments of cash to a landlord-impresario. They were masters of their house and therefore more nearly of their fate than any other company. Shakespeare stood on both sides of the financial fence, owning a one-tenth share of his acting company and a one-eighth share of their playhouse.

When King James came to the English throne in 1603, he lost little time in declaring his support for the adult players. The Chamberlain's Men became the King's Men. The Admiral's Men were also adopted, as Prince Henry's Men, and a third company for which Thomas Heywood was resident playwright secured something better than its former toehold in London and gained a place as the third resident company under the name of the Queen's Men. The queen also lent her name to the principal boy company, which became the Children of the Queen's Revels.

The boy companies had disappeared in 1590 and did not reappear for another nine years. Their reappearance was in the long term another stroke of good fortune for Shakespeare's company. Although in *Hamlet* (II. ii. 332) he gave Rosencrantz a comment about the "little eyases" (baby eagles) who were putting the adult actors out of favor, they had already done the Burbages some financial benefit by taking a twenty-one-year lease of the empty Blackfriars theater. The more respectable social status of the choir-school boys, plus most likely their habit of performing only once a week instead of daily, allowed Evans to slip in where the adult players had been balked. From 1600 to 1608 the boy company at the "private" playhouse in the Blackfriars and, for most of that time, the Paul's Boys at their smaller theater by the cathedral ran in competition with the three adult companies. The names for the two types of theater, "private," meaning indoor halls, and "public," the larger open-air buildings, indicate the difference in their social status, which no doubt helped the boys to ease their way into the theater, which was barred to the adults.

Five companies competing for the same audiences in London proved more than the market could bear. In the 1590s two companies did well; in the 1620s four companies made a living. But five companies, even with royal approval, meant a hard struggle. In the event, the adult companies prevailed. The boy companies, aiming at the wealthier end of the audience range, were drawn into offering more and more audacious satire. They pandered to the higher social classes with "girds at citizens" and mockery of the lower-class adult company repertoire in plays such as Francis Beaumont's *The Knight of the Burning Pestle* (1607). They satirized King James and his entourage of greedy Scotsmen in plays like *The Isle of Gulls* (1606) by John Day and *Eastward Ho!* (1605) by George Chapman, Ben Jonson, and John Marston, and of course in the end they paid the price of their audacity. In 1606 the Paul's enterprise folded, and in 1608 the same thing happened to the Blackfriars boys when they so infuriated the king that he "vowed they should never play more, but should first begg their bred" (Chambers, II, chapter 12). The boys being now mostly fully grown, the company continued on the fringes as a young-adult group, but they had to relinquish the private Blackfriars theater to the adults. In 1609, after a pause for the plague, Shakespeare's company finally took possession of the indoor theater that old Burbage had built for them thirteen years before.

What the King's Men now did was to use both venues. The public Globe was occupied for the summer months, when the light was brightest and the city was largely empty of the upper end of the audience range, the courtiers and lawyers. The private Blackfriars, seating only 600 compared with the Globe's 3,000, supplied the needs of the city gallants, lords, ladies, merchants, and lawyers in the eight months of the English year that were less favorable for outdoor shows.

The pattern that the King's Men thus established in 1609 dominated London theatergoing until 1642. The only new theaters to be built after 1609, apart from an unsuccessful attempt by Alleyn in 1614 to introduce a dual-purpose amphitheater for both acting and bearbaiting, were private venues. Audiences began to divide, with the citizenry continuing to frequent the amphitheaters while the more moneyed classes preferred the indoor theaters. As the antiquary James Wright summarized it in his *Historia Histrionica* (1699):

> Before the Wars, there were in being all these Playhouses at the same time. The Black-friers, and Globe on the Bankside, a Winter and Summer House, belonging to the same Company called the King's Servants; the Cockpit or Phoenix, in Drury-Lane, called the Queen's Servants; the private House in Salisbury-court, called the Prince's Servants; the Fortune near White-cross-street, and the Red Bull at the upper end of St. John's-street: The two last were mostly frequented by Citizens, and the meaner sort of People. All these Companies got Money, and Liv'd in Reputation, especially those of the Black-friers, who were Men of grave and sober Behaviour.

The Cockpit or Phoenix private theater was built in 1616 by Christopher Beeston, and the Salisbury Court in 1629 by Richard Gunnell, each founder being an actor turned impresario like Alleyn. At the old amphitheater playhouses, the Fortune and Red Bull, the companies generally offered a staple of conservative plays. The newer and more fashionable work appeared at the indoor playhouses.

The King's Men and the various groupings that made up the other three of the four companies in the decades prior to 1642 enjoyed rather mixed fortunes in these years. Twice a fire completely destroyed one of the amphitheaters and put the owners to the expense of rebuilding and the players to the cost of restocking their resources in costumes and playbooks. In 1613 it was the Globe, when smoldering wadding from a cannon lodged in the thatched roof of the galleries. Within two hours it had burned to the ground. There was no loss of life, though one man's trousers caught fire and had to be doused with a bottle of beer. There may have been time to save some properties and playbooks, or perhaps enough were stored at the Blackfriars, because the company was able to carry on even though rebuilding the Globe (with tiles this time) cost £1,400, more than two years' takings. When the Fortune burned down in 1621, it cost Alleyn £1,000 to rebuild in brick and tile, and the company resident at the time of the fire did not survive its losses. Pestilence added its troubles to fire on several occasions, and closures because of plague in 1625, 1630, 1636–1637, and 1640 proved long enough to break every London company except the King's Men. But there were always new companies ready to move in and impresarios ready to finance them. As the country moved toward civil war, London society became increasingly polarized, and the court party's insistence on lavish displays of the virtues of royalty and aristocratic honor was reflected in the intense popularity among courtiers of the indoor theaters. Parliament's closure of the London theaters in 1642 was designed as an emphatic signal of the way power had shifted away from the court and its supporters. That was the price the actors had to pay for their share in social polarization.

Company Organization

The history of the companies that acted in London in the seventy years up to the general closure of 1642 is an account of a commercial enterprise in which, not surprisingly, the names of the impresarios or financiers stand out as strongly as the leading actors. They all figure in the records as hardheaded businessmen who supported and exploited the players in varying degrees. The players were by no means innocent victims of the system: they had their tight and hardheaded organization, too, survival techniques evolved in their traveling days, precisely adapted for the new kind of livelihood that London now offered.

The boy actors were completely under the rule of their financial controllers. Officially they were schoolchildren, their masters serving as teachers and choirmasters, their commercial acting only a sideline in their education. The income their performances earned went to their master for the upkeep of their singing school and theater. The adult players, on the other hand, shared their work and its rewards equally among themselves. The impresarios financed them, but the relationship was that of moneylender and borrower, not master and servant. The players worked as a mutually interdependent ensemble. They made their living exclusively from playing, and the better they worked together the more money they made for themselves. The best of them secured patronage to make their activities legitimate, but even the best were totally dependent on their paying customers, whether the payers, like royalty, demanded candlelit evening performances at court or, like city apprentices, wanted an afternoon's pennyworth of entertainment in the suburban amphitheaters. Adult companies were tight-knit groups that rose together and fell together. They shared all expenses, in playscripts, costumes, and properties, and they shared their profits. It was not a system that encouraged strong individualists. The whole company was needed to perform every play, and every member of the group shared that collective responsibility. Their organization reflected that common need.

The average traveling company consisted of six or eight players in the sixteenth century and ten or even twelve in later years, plus perhaps a boy or two for female parts and the occasional hanger-on who did not share any of the financial responsibilities. They carried all their gear with them, and since they rarely performed in the same place twice, it had to be thoroughly portable property. That in itself was, no doubt, a strong incentive for them to establish a base, a permanent theater in London where they could rest both their properties and their feet. In London they could work in larger groups with more hangers-on, or "hired men," as they were called to distinguish them from the sharers. In Shakespeare's time a total of well over twenty men and boys was needed to mount a full performance of a Shakespeare play. The same play taken on the road would be trimmed so that it could be performed by eleven or twelve at most.

The permanent theaters in London offered all kinds of advantages to the adult companies and only one major disadvantage. Control of the audience at the entry points meant not only much bigger crowds paying more money but also that the crowds were more docile and the income guaranteed. An audience paying at the door is both more rewarding to entertain and more willing to be entertained than a crowd casually assembling in a market square and consenting to listen, tossing its pennies into the circulating hats only if the show distinctly pleases them. A permanent theater also allowed a company to accumulate costumes and properties and to store them securely as the profits began to mount. Even the hired men could expect more money in London, 10 shillings a week (half a pound, a better wage than a skilled carpenter could earn) as against 5 shillings when they were with a traveling company. In the last years of the 1590s theaters were taking £20 a week just from the galleries, and the total annual income could be as much as twice the value of the building. The one disadvantage of operating on this scale was in the repertory. A traveling company could exist on a very small range of plays, since its travels would take it fifty or a hundred miles in a week, and thus, the same play could be offered to a new audience each day. In London, playing at the same venue, the companies had to offer something different every day of the week.

One of the most difficult feats of all in trying to envisage Shakespeare's plays as they were staged in his own time is grasping the effects of the repertory system. In good times Shakespeare and his fellows could expect to perform on almost every afternoon of the week throughout the year except for a short break at the government's insistence in Lent, when the playhouse would be redecorated and Shakespeare could gallop off on the three-day journey to Stratford. Each day of the working week demanded a different play. The Admiral's Company's records for the good years 1594–1597 show that in their first season they put on thirty-eight plays, twenty-one of them new to the repertory and added at fortnightly intervals. Two new plays were performed only once, and only eight of the twenty-one stayed in the repertory through the following season. The most popular play, Marlowe's *Tamburlaine, Part I,* was staged fourteen times in the year; his *Faustus,* twelve; and *The Jew of Malta,* nine. Nineteen more plays were added in the following year and another fourteen the year after that.

Thus, at any moment the players had to keep at least thirty parts in their memory (more if they had minor parts and were doubling roles), while learning a new part every two weeks. Each morning they would rehearse that fortnight's new play while conning their parts in that afternoon's play and making sure that costumes and properties were on hand. Leading actors, such as Alleyn with the Admiral's Men and Richard Burbage with Shakespeare's company, would automatically take the leading parts in each play. This would entail memorizing as many as 800 lines for each play, nearly 5,000 lines in a week. They had, moreover, to rattle them off much faster than modern actors and with only rudimentary rehearsal. The "parts" written out for each actor to memorize included only single cue lines from other actors' speeches, and it was left to the "book-keeper," or prompter, to ensure that each man was ready to enter on cue and was equipped with the right accouterments.

What the actor did when he went out onstage, apart from reciting his lines, was left to him and his reservoir of experience from playing in so many different plays with the same fellows. The scale of human effort involved was acknowledged in the early years of the established London companies by such comments as this one from Kyd's *Spanish Tragedy* (1587):

> The Italian tragedians were so sharp of wit
> That in one hour's meditation
> They would perform anything in action.
>
> (IV. i. 163–165)

Perhaps the English tragedians were not yet so sharp. The Prologue to the anonymous *Wily Beguiled* (before 1606) demands:

> What ho! Where are these paltry players? Still in their papers, and never perfect? For shame, come forth. Your audience stay so long their eyes wax dim with expectation.

Such a hectic performing program had to be streamlined. The companies managed this primarily by typecasting so that each player took the kind of part he was most familiar with. The company clown usually improvised in the manner he knew best, ending the afternoon's entertainment with a jig, a farcical knockabout rhyming piece or song-and-dance act that had nothing to do with the play proper. If he acted in the play itself, it was often only a small cameo role. Will Kempe, the first of the Chamberlain's Men's clowns, played the nurse's man Peter in *Romeo and Juliet* and Dogberry in *Much Ado About Nothing,* both parts that called for a couple of scenes of broad comedy and no more during the two hours that the play required in performance. The leading man similarly took the role that was obviously his. Burbage, who took over from Alleyn the reputation of leading actor for his day, is known to have played Richard III, Hamlet, Lear, Othello, and Ferdinand in John

Webster's *The Duchess of Malfi* (1613–1614). We can reasonably assume that he also played Romeo, Prince Hal, Prospero, and all the other leads. Every sharer in the company was expected to take his part in every performance; and parts were allocated—indeed, plays were written—on the assumption that every sharer in the company would contribute his share to every performance.

The pressures this must have imposed even on the sharers who doubled in the fringe parts was enormous. They could hardly afford to be ill, let alone idle or drunk. A contract that Philip Henslowe got Robert Dawes, one of his actors, to sign in 1614 when he joined a company playing at Henslowe's theater clearly announces the price of backsliding:

> . . . that he the said Robert Dawes shall and will at all tymes during the said terme duly attend all suche rehearsall, which shall the night before the rehearsall be given publickly out; and if that he the saide Robert Dawes shall at any tyme faile to come at the hower appoynted, then he shall and will pay to the said Phillipp Henslowe and Jacob Meade, their executors or assignes, Twelve pence; and if he come not before the saide rehearsall is ended, then the said Robert Dawes is contented to pay Twoe shillings; and further that if the said Robert Dawes shall not every daie, whereon any play is or ought to be played, be ready apparrelled and—to begyn the play at the hower of three of the clock in the afternoone, unles by sixe of the same company he shall be lycenced to the contrary, that then he, the saide Robert Dawes, shall and will pay unto the said Phillipp and Jacob or their assignes Three [shillings]; and if that he, the saide Robert Dawes, happen to be overcome with drinck at the tyme when he [ought to] play, by the judgment of ffower of the said company, he shall and will pay Tenne shillings; and if he . . . shall [faile to come] during any plaie, having noe lycence or just excuse of sicknes, he is contented to pay Twenty shillings. . . . And further the said Robert Dawes doth covenant, [promise, and graunt to and with the said Phillip Henslowe and Jacob Meade, that if he, the said Robert Dawes], shall at any time after the play is ended depart or goe out of the [howse] with any [of their] apparell on his body, or if the said Robert Dawes [shall carry away any propertie] belonging to the said company, or shal be consentinge [or privy to any other of the said company going out of the howse with any of their apparell on his or their bodies, he, the said] Robert Dawes, shall and will forfeit and pay unto the said Phillip and Jacob, or their administrators or assignes, the some of ffortie pounds of lawfull [money of England].

(quoted in Chambers, II, chapter 13)

The size of the forfeits, at a time when 10 shillings a week was an extremely good wage, indicates how much profit there was to be made from plays. No doubt there was always a queue of would-be sharers waiting to buy the backslider's share in the company.

To buy a share in a company of players was expensive. It was an investment to be made in the expectation of substantial returns, and the better the company, the higher a share was valued. To be a sharer in the Queen's Men in 1592 or in the Red Bull company in 1612 was worth rather more than Shakespeare paid in 1597 to buy the second-best house in Stratford. The price of a share in the Chamberlain's Men when he joined them in 1594 would have been about the same, though he, of course, had the priceless asset of his plays to contribute. When his fellow sharers in the King's Men decided in 1622 to issue a memorial volume of all the plays of his that they possessed, at least seven of the thirty-six plays they published had been onstage with other companies before 1594. Presumably Shakespeare had kept possession of these early playbooks—usually they remained the property of the company that performed them—and took them with him to the Chamberlain's Men. The price of a new play in manuscript in 1594 was as little as £5. With seven plays in his knapsack Shakespeare might still have needed another £40 or so in cash to become a Chamberlain's sharer.

Each London company had a considerable outlay. Besides the rent of their playhouse, which in the amphitheaters normally amounted to one-half of the take from the galleries, the company covered the cost of playbooks and costumes and paid the wages of the hired men, musicians, stagekeepers, and bookkeeper, not to mention the "gatherers," who collected the admission fees from the audience. The only extensive accounts of this system that have survived, Henslowe's, suggest that the impresario took a direct part in buying plays and costumes and paid most of the wages, debiting the company for its share in all the costs and extracting what was due to him from the receipts, which he usually handled himself. He tended to keep plays, costumes, and properties on his own account and lend them out to whatever company he had in residence at his various playhouses. He is reckoned to have spent £1,317 between 1597 and 1603 on company assets, half of them playbooks. From his records we know that a newly written play could be bought for as little as £5 and that costumes were a much bigger item of expense. In both cases the quantity needed was substantial. The Queen's Men in 1592 valued their stock of costumes at £80, more than a company share.

Henslowe once spent £20 on a single item, the dress for the heroine of Thomas Heywood's *A Woman Killed with Kindness* (1603). Hired men, and presumably most of the other helpers, cost about 10 shillings a week. The gatherers especially had to be good men in one sense or another, judging from a comment on how some of them "seeme to scratch their heads where they itch not, and drop shillings and half croune-pieces in at their collars" (quoted in Chambers, I, chapter 11, note 1). And there was a stock of boys in each company, playing the women's roles and learning from their masters among the sharers. Such boys were employed in a form of apprenticeship, and they received little besides their board and lodging so long as they were officially learners.

The rewards of playing were great by Elizabethan standards. Most of them went to the impresarios, Henslowe and Alleyn, Beeston and Gunnell, and their imitators. But Richard Burbage, who resisted the temptation to turn impresario and made his living entirely from his shares in his acting company and its playhouses, died in 1619 with an estate worth more than £300. His associate Shakespeare owned 240 acres of land around Stratford, one of the town's biggest houses, and a pied-à-terre in the Blackfriars when he died in 1616. Nobody worked in that hectic repertory system solely for love of the art.

During all the years when the London companies prospered, the government kept a watchful eye on them. The statutes of the 1570s were designed to restrict the number of companies to a manageable few, a restriction to which the lucky and monopolistic few would hardly object. Their license or patent authorizing them to play was their only real security. A warrant sent to all major towns in 1616 and copied into the records for the town of Norwich shows how precious and how much in demand such patents were:

> Whereas Thomas Swynnerton and Martin Slaughter beinge two of the Queens Ma^{ts} company of Playors having sep[ar]ated themselves from their said Company, have each of them taken forth a sev$_{e}$rall exemplification or duplicate of his ma^{ts} Letters patente graunted to the whole Company and by vertue thereof they severally in two Companies with vagabonds and such like idle p[er]sons, have and doe use and exercise the quallitie of playinge in div[er]se places of this

> Realme to the great abuse and wronge of his Ma^{ts} Sub^{ts} in generall and contrary to the true intent and meanings of his Matie to the said Company . . . [the warrant names three other duplicated documents] Wherefore to the end such idle p[er]sons may not be suffered to continewe in this course of life These are therefore to pray, and neatheless in his Ma^{ts} name to will and require you upon notice given of aine of the said p[er]sons by the bearer herof Joseph More whome I have speciallye directed for that purpose that you call the said p[ar]ties offendo^{rs} before you and thereupon take the said sev[er]all exemplifications or duplicats or other ther warrants by which they use ther saide quallitie from them, And forth with to send the same to me.

> (quoted in Bentley, 1942–1968, I, chapter 4)

The man who issued this warrant was the master of the revels, a royal servant appointed by the lord chamberlain specifically to control the playing companies. He issued their licenses to play, he licensed the playhouses, and above all he censored the plays. The commission issued to him in 1581 puts heavy emphasis on his function as censor:

> We have and do by these presents authorize and command our said servant, Edmunde Tilney, Master of our said Revels, by himself, or his sufficient deputy or deputies, to warn, command, and appoint in all places within this our realm of England, as well within franchises and liberties as without, all and every player or players, with their playmakers, either belonging to any nobleman, or otherwise, bearing the name or names or using the faculty of playmakers, or players of comedies, tragedies, interludes, or what other shows soever, from time to time, and at all times, to appear before him with all such plays, tragedies, comedies, or shows, as they shall have in readiness, or mean to set forth, and them to present and recite before our said servant, or his sufficient deputy, whom we ordain, appoint, and authorise by these presents, of all such shows, plays, players, and playmakers, together with their playing places, to order and reform, authorise and put down, as shall be thought meet or unmeet unto himself, or his said deputy in that behalf.

> (quoted in Adams, Introduction)

Tilney and his successors had ample power to enforce their requirements over censorship. Besides their control of licensing, they ran the program of entertainment for the court, and it was the master of the revels who chose the companies to be honored by an appearance at court. Such honors gained them only £10 for each performance, which was not a great deal more than a good day's take at the Rose or Fortune; but it involved no cost in rent for a playhouse and was a bonus, since it took place at night, after the usual hours of public performance. Following their afternoon's work at their amphitheater, the company would pack such costumes and properties as they needed and transport everything, either by water (if the destination was one of the riverside palaces) or by cart (if they were headed for Whitehall), to the theater prepared for the occasion by the yeoman of the revels and his assistant. A summons to perform at court was a genuine advertisement of the company's quality. It was in the hands of the master of the revels to decide who would be acknowledged as the best company of the year. No acting company cared to get into dispute with such a powerful controller.

Censorship is a difficult matter to see clearly, partly because its chief function was to eliminate the evidence for its existence and partly because much of it must have been tacit. Knowing that the master of the revels was going to review a play, no playwright would willfully choose to offer him anything open to objection. Sometimes, certainly, the master did object. Manuscript texts of four plays that were thoroughly censored survive, from 1594, 1613, 1619, and 1628. In all of them the censor's objections amount to quite drastic revision, and the 1628 play was banned altogether. Several other plays show signs in their printed texts of having been altered by censorship, notably Shakespeare's *Richard II,* which was printed three times in 1597 and 1598 without the central section of the scene (IV. i) in which Richard gives up his crown. This section was included for the first time in a 1608 reprint with a title page advertising its inclusion. Some of the more satirical boy-company plays of 1600–1608 also survive only in versions that have clearly been molested by the licensing authority.

This is not the place to examine the vexed question of what was thought to be censorable material in the Shakespearean drama. By its very nature such material is intriguing but also elusive. All we can note here is the conspicuous banality of most of the details that we know to have been censored. A statute of 1606, for instance, forbade profanity of any kind, with the result that wherever Shakespeare wrote *God* the King's Men's bookkeeper after 1606 dutifully altered it to *heaven.* Most of the other troubles over censorship, including an extraordinary scandal in 1624 when the King's Men staged Middleton's anti-Spanish play *A Game at Chess,* grew out of insults to foreigners, especially insults to those nations with a powerful ambassador at the English court.

The other restraint that the master of the revels exercised over his licensees was his prohibition on performing during the religious season of Lent and during times of plague. Although bubonic plague is in fact principally transmitted by the rat flea, Elizabethans assumed that, like most diseases, it could be caught through human contact, and they tried to control outbreaks by prohibiting any large gatherings of people. They gauged an outbreak by simply counting the number of plague deaths each week. When the count rose to fifty bodies a week, the playhouses were ordered to close. In 1604 this total was reduced to thirty a week, though the patents issued to the King's Men in 1619 and 1625 specify forty. Plague periods were always difficult for the players. The city fathers of London were quick to demand a closure, and at such times there would be no work for the players except for traveling. Even then a provincial mayor or justice might well prefer to see the Londoners pass by rather than run the risk of catching the plague from them. Sometimes the closures lasted fifteen months or more, and the players starved. In an obvious way, the players were parasites. When the society from which they made their living was sick, they suffered, too.

The Theaters

The nature of the places in which plays were staged was of less importance to Elizabethan companies than Shakespeare's use of them makes them to us today. Basically all that the players needed was an open space with a curtained-off room behind it. While they were on their travels, they performed wherever they could attract a crowd. In London they divided their time between the open-air amphitheaters, the enclosed halls, the stages at court or in noblemen's houses, and, until the 1590s, even innyards or the drinking rooms of the bigger taverns. They put on the same plays at whatever venue offered them financial reward.

The little solid evidence we have about Shakespearean playhouses suggests that through the fifty-three years when new theaters were being built, the chief developments took place not in stage design but in the auditorium, to economize on the cost of collecting the spectators' pennies. In the first playhouses one penny was taken for admission to the yard and its standing room by the stage platform. A second penny was handed over at the stairs from the yard into the galleries (probably the stairs marked "ingressus" in Johannes De Witt's much-reproduced drawing of the Swan). A third penny would grant admission to the "twopenny galleries" nearest the stage, while the lordly patrons would enter through the actors' tiring-house and pay six-pence, half a shilling, for one of the rooms shown above the stage in the Swan drawing. As William Lambarde reported shortly before the Swan was built, "Such as goe to Parisgardein, the Bell Savage, or Theatre, to beholde Beare baiting, Enter-ludes, or Fence play, can account of any pleasant spectacle, [if] they first pay one pennie at the gate, another at the entrie of the Scaffolde, and the thirde for a quiet standing" (quoted in Chambers, II, chapter 16). In the later playhouses, including the Globe and Fortune, admission to the galleries was not through the yard but directly up the staircases at each entrance. Thus, one gatherer could collect for the yard and the galleries at the same time, and the wealthier spectators avoided the crush in the yard. No such innovations, except possibly in the number of stage doors, were made for the acting area.

The basic configurations of the open-air play-houses did not vary widely. Mostly they were round or polygonal buildings about one hundred feet in outside diameter and fifty-five feet inside, with three levels of galleries. The total capacity of spectators standing in the yard and sitting in the galleries, more than 3,000, gave on average no more than an eighteen-inch square to each stander or sitter. In the yard it must have felt more like a crowd than an audience. When John Marston cele-brated the reopening of the St. Paul's theater in 1600, he claimed, no doubt with some feeling, that seated there you ran less risk of being "pasted to the balmy jacket of a beer-brewer" (*Jack Drum's Entertainment*, V. i.).

Among the Henslowe papers are preserved two sets of builders' contracts for playhouses, one for the Fortune and one for the Hope, the dual-pur-pose playhouse and bearbaiting house constructed close to the Globe in 1614. From these and other pieces of evidence, we can make some reasonable deductions about the design of a playhouse such as the Globe. On entering the yard past the gatherers at one of the two doors set in the base of the two stair-turrets you would find yourself in a polygon fifty-five feet in diameter, with three ranges of gal-

2. Johannes de Witt's sketch of the Swan playhouse (1596).

leries rising to a roof height of about thirty-six feet all around. The timber fronts of the galleries were pilastered and decorated with carved figures, all brilliantly painted. The galleries had ranks of wooden seating, or "degrees," with a corridor at the back running around the whole circle as far as the tiring-house. The first gallery had a higher ceil-ing height than the upper two, twelve or more feet as against the ten and nine feet of the upper galler-ies, to allow access underneath from the entrance-ways and to raise the spectators higher than the crowd standing in the yard. The topmost gallery was roofed with thatch at the first Globe and with tile at the second, after the fire of 1613.

Inside the yard the theater's dominant feature was the stage, a platform occupying nearly half the available space in the yard, extending out from the tiring-house wall into the middle of the yard and taking up two-thirds of its width. It was surrounded by wooden palings and was about five feet above yard level, so that the heads of the crowd standing in the yard were level with the players' feet. Sarcas-tic playwrights called the yard audience "under-standers." The only ornamentation on the stage

3. Wenceslaus Hollar's drawing of the second Globe, made from the tower of Southwark Cathedral (1647).

platform itself consisted of two Corinthian pillars made of wood and possibly painted to look like marble, rising more than twenty feet up from the stage to support the cover, or "shadow" or "heavens" as it was variously called. This cover not only sheltered the players and their expensive costumes from London's rain but also contained a ceiling trapdoor from which such objects as a boy playing Cupid could be lowered to the stage. The stage itself had a trapdoor for use as a grave or a dungeon cell; it could also represent hell just as the ceiling represented heaven. Malvolio's dungeon in *Twelfth Night* and Ophelia's grave in *Hamlet* would have been down the stage trap.

At the back of the stage the tiring-house wall contained the doors and the "discovery space" from which the players emerged to play their parts. The blank two-door frontage shown in De Witt's Swan drawing may be deceptively plain. Contemporary pictures of indoor stages show the rear covered by curtains, or "hangings," painted or embroidered with classical figures. Between

the doors there might well have been alcoves housing sculptured plaster or wood figures such as appear in the hall screens that served as backdrop for plays staged in the halls of the great houses of the day. De Witt's pencil sketch certainly gives no indication of how brilliantly all the details would have been colored. The actors in their lavish costumes would have moved against an equally colorful background.

How many doors the Globe's tiring-house wall contained, and what size they were, we cannot be sure. Most likely there was a set of impressively massive double doors in the center, providing a large opening that could be curtained across to make the discovery space, which might serve as a study (with table, book, and candle), a monk's cell, the countinghouse piled with Volpone's gold, or the private chapel where Claudius tries to pray in *Hamlet.* Flanking this wide doorway on each side would be single wooden doors for normal entries, and through these doors the processions so loved by the actors would march on. A procession gave a fine opportunity for the actors to show off handsome costumes. They would either enter two by two through one door before gathering in position —around the royal throne if it was a scene at court like the second scene of *Hamlet*—or march around the perimeter of the stage before exiting by the door on the other side of the discovery space. A play written by Heywood for the Red Bull company required a procession of more characters than the company had actors. Presumably there was some quick changing in the tiring-house while the rest of the procession was still doing its round of the stage.

Above the tiring-house doors was the stage balcony. Probably divided into five bays at the Globe, it accommodated the most lordly among the spectators, those who came not so much to see as to be seen and who could therefore more easily tolerate watching the players' backs and being unable to see into the discovery space beneath them. For rather less than half the plays that we know were staged at the Globe, one of these "lords' rooms," presumably the central one, was used by the actors as a balcony. Variously called a "tarras" or merely "above" and later a "balcone," this room rarely took more than two or three actors, and action there was always supplementary to the main action on the stage platform, which was always the focal point for audience attention. In the later years of the Globe, when the King's Men also had use of the private theater at the Blackfriars and consequently had acquired the consort of musicians who provided extra entertainment there, one room on the balcony was turned into a musicians' room. Before that, when the demand for music at the Globe usually asked only for the heraldic military trumpet and drum and an occasional recorder, the sounds came from behind the tiring-house hangings at stage level.

A structure of rooms or huts above the stage cover was necessary to house the machinery, a windlass and pulleys, by means of which the boy-gods descended to the stage. The surviving illustrations of London playhouses are not entirely consistent about what shape they had. The clearest, Wenceslaus Hollar's drawing of the second Globe, shows a pair of large huts with parallel roof ridges running inward from the gallery roof and a tall turret or cupola between the huts. Possibly the cupola was designed to admit light to the huts, and most likely it provided the place for the two main

devices that the players used to signal the commencement of a performance. On playing days a large flag was flown from a flagpole surmounting the highest point of the building. (De Witt's Swan drawing shows one with a large swan painted on it.) As the play was about to begin, the company hastened latecomers along with a trumpet blast sounded from a platform above the gallery roof level. The Swan drawing also shows that happening. Both of these devices were signals to people outside the amphitheater, so clear access from above roof level was necessary. Hollar's cupola would provide such a place.

A visit to the indoor theaters once the Blackfriars opened in 1600 offered an experience different in many ways from a visit to the Globe. Where a single penny secured a standing position next to the stage itself in the open-air amphitheater, at the Blackfriars the cheapest place cost six times as much and gained the spectator only a bench in the gallery located farthest from the stage. The auditoriums of the indoor theaters reversed the amphitheaters' priorities. Instead of receiving the poorest closest to the stage and secluding the wealthier at a distance in the galleries, they set the more expensive places closest to the stage. The boxes that flank the stage in Inigo Jones's 1616 design for an indoor theater like the Blackfriars cost half a crown, thirty times the minimal Globe penny. The price of a bench in the "pit," equivalent to the Globe's yard, was a shilling or eighteen pence. The minimal sixpence gained access to the "topmost" gallery, equivalent to the top balcony, or "gods," of a modern theater. In fact, the Blackfriars auditorium replaced the populist Globe pattern of auditorium, which derived from the marketplace origins of the players, with something very like the modern kind of auditorium. The chief difference between the Blackfriars design and a nineteenth-century opera house lay in the positioning of the former's boxes behind what became known as the proscenium arch, the picture frame characteristic of post-Restoration scenic staging, and in the peculiar practice of allowing some spectators to sit on stools on the stage itself.

This extraordinary indulgence is well documented by some of the people who suffered from it. The point was essentially for wealthy young gentlemen to show how fashionable they were by sitting in full view on the stage platform itself to watch the play. Even though the height of the indoor

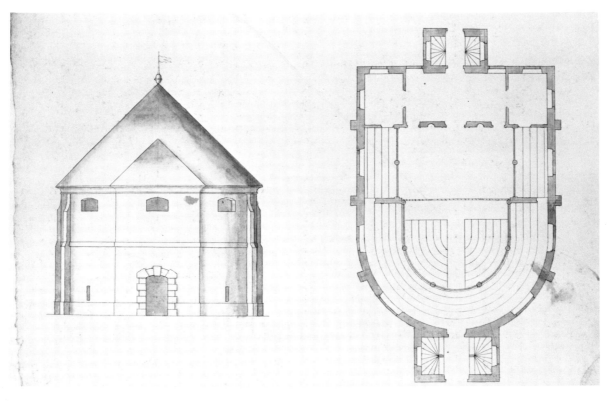

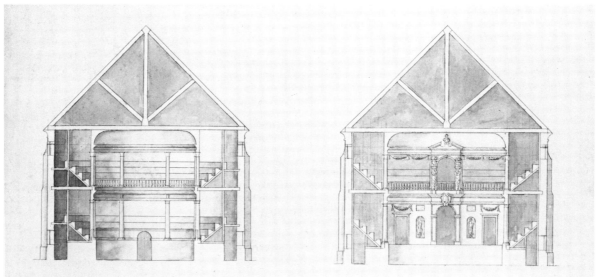

4. Drawings by Inigo Jones for an indoor playhouse (1616).

theater stages was less than the height of the Globe stage, the position of audience heads in relation to the stage was the same because in the pit they were sitting down while at the Globe they were standing. Thus, a young man in an expensive cloak puffing clouds of tobacco smoke could obscure the view of quite a number in the audience. And he could do worse than that. Thomas Dekker wrote a splen-didly caustic mock treatise for such foolish young men, *The Gull's Hornbook* (1609):

Present not your selfe on the Stage (especially at a new play) untill the quaking prologue hath (by rub-bing) got culor into his cheekes, and is ready to give the trumpets their Cue, that hees upon point to enter: for then it is time, as though you were one of the properties, or that you dropt out of the Hangings, to creepe from behind the Arras, with your Tripos or three-footed stoole in one hand, and a teston mounted betweene a forefinger and a thumbe in the other: for if you should bestow your person upon the vulgar, when the belly of the house is but halfe full, your apparell is quite eaten up, the fashion lost, and the proportion of your body in more danger to be devoured then if it were served up in the Counter amongst the Powltry: avoid that as you would the Bastome. It shall crowne you with rich commendation, to laugh alowd in the middest of the most serious and saddest scene of the terriblest Tragedy: and let that clapper (your tongue) be tost so high, that all the house may ring of it: your Lords use it; your Knights are Apes to the Lords, and do so too: your Inne-a-court-man is Zany to the Knights, and (mary very scurvily) comes likewise limping after it: bee thou a beagle to them all.

(chapter 6)

In general, audiences at the Blackfriars were more respectful than Dekker's young gull. The playwright James Shirley, writing a preface to the 1647 collection of Beaumont and Fletcher's plays, which were the staple of the King's Men's repertory once they occupied the Blackfriars, made a large claim for their value in educating those same young gulls:

The three hours' spectacle, while Beaumont and Fletcher were presented, was usually of more advantage to the hopeful young heir than a costly, dangerous foreign travel, with the assistance of a governing monsieur or signor to boot; and it cannot be denied but that the young spirits of the time, whose birth and quality made them impatient of the sourer ways of education, have from the attentive hearing these pieces got ground in point of wit and carriage of the most severely employed students.

This claim was made when the "academy" at Black-friars had been closed by government order. Shirley was overstating his case, perhaps, but we need not question his assumption that most gallants attended the theater to see as well as be seen.

As the King's Men continued their tenure of the Blackfriars into the 1620s and 1630s, some changes in staging seem to have evolved between what they offered there and what the Globe presented. The Blackfriars stage, of course, was only half the size of the outdoor stage, and being enclosed, its noise levels also varied. Where the Globe could fire off cannon, the nearest Blackfriars

5. A vignette from the title page of *Roxana* (1632) showing an indoor theater stage.

imitation might be a pistol shot. Fireworks were much less popular at the indoor theater and music much more so. The outdoor instruments, trumpet and drum, were replaced by concert wind and string instruments, and concerts replaced jigs in the interludes. Battles and duels were dangerous on the smaller, less well lit stages, and wordplay gradually supplanted swordplay. William Davenant's *News from Plymouth* (1635), first performed in summer at the Globe, contains a heavy-handed prologue saluting the Blackfriars element in the audience:

A Noble company! For we can spy
Beside rich gaudy sirs, some that rely
More on their judgements than their clothes, and may
With wit as well as pride rescue our play.
And 'tis but just, though each spectator knows
This house and season does more promise shows,
Dancing, and buckler fights, than art or wit.

Fencing was totally dependent on good light. The fencing matches that were popular in the 1590s, when the rapier was first becoming a fashionable weapon, always took place at the open-air theaters or innyards. The Blackfriars and the other private playhouses were lit by candelabra. What difference that might have made to the staging of *Hamlet* there we do not know. Certainly Burbage managed to survive his duels with Laertes for a good ten years at the Blackfriars.

Spectators and Auditory

The twenty or so years that Shakespeare spent working in London witnessed radical changes in what a spectator could buy for his penny or sixpence. The playwright began when the stage was ruled by the fustian king and Marlowe's mighty line. He left it when his company was in possession of the two finest theaters in the country and a repertory of unrivaled sophistication. Both "spectacle" and "wit," the two extremes of Jacobean playing, were at their command.

In the later years of this first great run of professional theater, playgoers looked back on the early times as barbaric. Conscious of their superior social status and sophistication and unaware of the troubles to come, they saw Shakespeare's early years as the heyday of crudely popular knockabout clownage. Richard Brome in *The Antipodes* (1638) made a Hamlet-like lord reprove an actor for adopting the tricks of the great clowns "in the days of Tarlton and Kemp, / Before the stage was purged from barbarism / And brought to the perfection it now shines with" (II. ii).

Even as early as 1611, Thomas Middleton could be derisive about the fashion for mighty lines that followed the clowns with Alleyn in the 1590s:

> The fashion of play-making I can properly compare to nothing so naturally as the alteration in apparel. For in the time of the great crop-doublet your huge bombasted plays, quilted with mighty words to lean purpose, was only then in fashion. And as the doublet fell, neater inventions began to set up. Now in the time of spruceness our plays follow the niceness of our garments, single plots, quaint conceits, lecherous jests, dressed up in hanging sleeves.
>
> (*The Roaring Girl,* Epistle)

By 1611, when Shakespeare retired from writing for the stage, the range of fashion in his own plays,

6. An engraving of an Elizabethan Tamburlaine, probably Edward Alleyn.

from *Titus Andronicus* to *The Tempest,* fairly reflected this change in audience taste. What is perhaps too rarely noted is how comprehensively responsible for those changes he himself was.

Plays with historical subjects existed before Shakespeare wrote the first of his plays about the reign of Henry VI. Nobody, however, had planned a sequence of four plays following the historical accounts so carefully and dramatizing the political conflict with such delicate precision. He made the genre of history play popular. He was similarly an innovator in social and romantic comedy with *The Comedy of Errors* and *The Taming of the Shrew,* in Jonsonian gulling comedy with *Love's Labor's Lost,* in romantic tragedy with *Romeo and Juliet.*

In the 1590s he extended the range and transformed the quality of almost every kind of play. In 1600 and the years of the great tragedies that followed, his plays made Burbage the successor to Alleyn's reputation with a series of magnificent character parts. And in 1607 with *Pericles* he started the fashion that made Blackfriars into the so-called academy of Beaumont and Fletcher's plays. *Pericles,* which came to rival the Falstaff plays in popularity, was the first play to offer the type of Arcadian romantic drama that Beaumont and Fletcher took up in 1609 with *Philaster* and *The Maid's Tragedy,* and on which the reputation of the King's Men at the Blackfriars came to rest through the 1620s and 1630s. In the twenty years of his writing life Shakespeare took the fashion in plays all the way from the clownage and bombast of 1590 to the Beaumont and Fletcher academy that ruled until 1642.

Spectacle and wit were the two contrasting staples of theater entertainment, and Shakespeare excelled in both. They differed substantially from what modern audiences are accustomed to, and study of them tells us more than anything else what it was like to be an Elizabethan or Jacobean spectator at a performance by Shakespeare's company. The spectacle was less realistic and the wit more complex, more deeply implicating the audience in the shared game of theatrical illusion. For all the commercial motivation of the players, a performance at the Globe was a community ritual.

Realism on the stage of the Globe was of a kind different from the scenic effects and their extreme form, cinematic realism, that are the available forms of illusion today. At the opening of *Hamlet,* the dark midnight on the battlements of Elsinore, with sentries who cannot identify each other and a ghost about to walk, was staged in the broad daylight of a London afternoon. One sentry had to announce the time (" 'Tis now past twelve") before the audience could understand they were watching a midnight scene. The ghost similarly had to walk in broad daylight, leaving the audience to do what the Prologue in *Henry V* asks for: "Piece out our imperfections with your thoughts." No night scene could be presented realistically at the Globe. There was no scenic illusion, because not only was there no control of lighting but there was no scenery.

Plays ran continuously without any act or scene pauses. The scene changed when all the players left the stage and new players entered. Locales for each scene were usually a matter of verbal references, which the audience took up and responded to with their imaginations. Some visual realism there certainly was. Antony could have told Cleopatra, "I am dying, Egypt, dying," while showing her his blood. Fights and duels onstage were prolonged and realistic displays by skilled swordsmen. But in its scenic aspects staging was representational or emblematic rather than realis-

tic, and the players had to rely on a visual symbolism familiar to everyone.

Hamlet, that most openly theatrical of all of Shakespeare's plays, exploits to the full the Globe's standard symbolic properties. Hamlet stood on the stage platform of the earthly globe with the stage cover, or "heavens," above him and the understage area, or "hell," beneath. In his second soliloquy, when he admits himself "Prompted to my revenge by heaven and hell" (II. ii. 570), he would have gestured upward to the cover and then downward to the stage floor as he spoke. "Hell," or more specifically the stage trap, would have been the ghost's point of entry. He would rise probably wreathed in smoke like the figure of Night in *The Maid's Tragedy,* which "arises in mists." The same trapdoor to hell would later in the play have received the body of Ophelia, with the "maimed rites" of a suicide. Neither Shakespeare nor his audience would have missed the poetic symbolism that the use of such standard devices made possible.

In the throne room scene immediately following the opening on the battlements, the central feature would have been the great "chair of state" that symbolized the court. Claudius sits in the chair to make his speech from the throne and uses it for a little joke. Speaking of the danger of Fortinbras invading Denmark while the country is in disarray over the late king's death, he pats the arm of his chair while he says that Fortinbras thinks "by our late dear brother's death / Our state to be disjoint and out of frame" (I. ii. 19–20). His chair of state is properly in its frame, its joints secure, as anyone can see. Only later does Marcellus suggest that, however substantial its carpentry, "Something is rotten in the state of Denmark" (I. iv. 90). It may look right, but it still might fall to pieces under the king.

The throne or chair of state was carried on stage for all scenes at court. Similarly the canopied bed on which Desdemona and Othello lie together in death was pushed out to signify a bedroom scene. Night scenes, apart from those indicated by words, might be signified by characters entering with flaming torches, or wearing nightgowns and nightcaps. For travel scenes the men would be booted and spurred, and for battle scenes, dressed in armor. Such symbolism was economical, and offered no check to the rapid flow of the scenes. Visual splendor was principally a matter of costuming. At the first court scene in *Hamlet,* all the courtiers appear dressed for the wedding of the king

7. Queen Elizabeth on her chair of state in 1586.

126

and queen, in the sharpest possible visual contrast to Hamlet himself, who enters still dressed in the black of his father's funeral. The newly married couple and the courtiers enter in procession in the order of their rank; but Hamlet, who should immediately follow the royal pair, instead (according to the stage direction in the Second Quarto) enters a reluctant last, alone amid the splendor.

Equally potent is the symbolism of the throne in *Richard II.* At the beginning of the play Richard occupies it with his spectacular Sun King regalia, using it as his judge's seat for the official hearing of the complaints between Bolingbroke and Mowbray (I. i) and later when he umpires their duel (I. iii). At the end of the play Bolingbroke occupies it, and his ally Northumberland greets his "sacred state" (V. vi. 6). But in the central scene of Richard's deposition (IV. i), the throne remains empty while Bolingbroke and Richard maneuver uneasily around it. The scene (in "Parliament") opens with a series of complaints and challenges, with gauntlets being thrown down in an exact repetition of the opening scene. But this time there is no royal judge to hear the complaints, only an uneasy Bolingbroke standing beside the chair he would like to occupy but dare not. The loss of authority that went with Richard's deposition is thus signaled by the empty throne of justice, and Bolingbroke's position as no more than one among many is made visually apparent by his stance in the scene.

The playwrights regarded this symbolic exploitation of staging, which we can properly call poetic, as secondary to their words, and there was always a latent antagonism between what the players provided for the eye and what the playwrights made for the ear. Some playwrights, notably Ben Jonson, openly scorned the idle audiences who wanted only spectacle. In a special prologue written for a performance of *The Staple of News* (1626) at court, he described his play as "writ to the Meridian of your Court," and

> offered as a Rite,
> To Schollers, that can judge, and fair report
> The sense they heare, above the vulgar sort
> Of Nut-crackers, that onely come for sight.

Shakespeare writes in the Induction to *The Taming of the Shrew* about an innocent who had "never heard a play."

Given that the playwrights insisted on the prior-

ity of their words over the players' spectacle, we can appreciate the depth of their sarcasm in calling the audience in the yard "understanders." The boy-player in *The Knight of the Burning Pestle,* welcoming the grocer who has come with his family to the Blackfriars instead of his usual public playhouse, calls him "an understanding man." The grocer and his wife consistently misunderstand the play and demand instead that the hero, their apprentice Rafe, should

> travel over great hills, and let him be very weary, and come to the King of Cracovia's house, covered with black velvet, and there let the King's daughter stand in her window all in beaten gold, combing her golden locks with a comb of ivory, and let her spy Rafe, and fall in love with him, and come down to him, and carry him into her father's house, and then let Rafe talk with her.
>
> (IV. i. 36–42)

Spectacle first, words after. That, at least as Beaumont saw it in 1607, was the taste of the citizen class in the theater.

Wit was far more than a matter of punning wordplay that an "understanding" man would not bother to understand. At its best, it entailed a game of theatrical illusion played with extraordinary sophistication. Hamlet's second soliloquy (II. ii. 533–591) shows an actor complaining about an actor acting a fiction. In a speech pregnant with the technical language of acting ("cue," "prompted," and that most ambiguous of terms for playacting, "action"), he complains that the player reciting the speech about revenging Pyrrhus has been so possessed by the "fiction" of his words that he has behaved as if his passion were real:

> all his visage wanned,
> Tears in his eyes, distraction in his aspect,
> A broken voice, and his whole function suiting
> With forms to his conceit? . . .

Hamlet is outraged that a mere player could imitate a passion so completely as to lose himself in the fiction, when he himself is forced to be silent in face of a monstrous reality:

> What would he do
> Had he the motive and the cue for passion
> That I have? . . .

There is a nice piece of wordplay for the "auditory" in those words. Hamlet's motive and cue are not for passion but for "action," the word that meant both the acting of a stage role and the action of revenge. An Elizabethan audience would have noted the change and understood the evasion when Hamlet goes on to condemn himself for the fact that he, unlike the player, speaks like John-a-dreams, "And can *say* nothing." Hamlet needs words—passion and saying—more than action at this point in his gradual adjustment to the ghost's command that he revenge his father's death.

Behind that piece of wordplay, exploiting the language of the profession of acting, lies another neat theatrical irony. Hamlet objects to the player being moved by an unreal passion, a fiction. His own passion is all too real. But, of course, it is not. Hamlet was Richard Burbage the player objecting to the playing of his fellow actor. The theater was all around them, and players and audience shared the complex game that operated in the gulf between the reality of the stage illusion and the reality of the real world. When Hamlet refers to "this distracted globe" (I. v. 97), he means his own head and the world it has to live in, but he also means the theater and its audience whom he is addressing.

If you stood on your feet on wet cobblestones for two hours or more, pasted to the jacket of your neighbor, the smell of everyone else's garlic in your nose, wondering whether to buy apples or bottled beer from the vendors who circulated while the play was going on, and wondering whether you would miss a good piece of the play while you pushed your way through the crowd to urinate against a quiet wall, you would inevitably be more conscious of your surroundings than a modern audience needs to be, relaxed in armchairs in the dark and with decent intervals for drinking and other comforts. The passive acceptance of cinematic realism was neither practical nor desirable on Shakespeare's stage. Elizabethan spectators joined in the game of playing far more vigorously than moviegoers, piecing out the imperfections of the symbolic staging with their active thoughts. They gave their positive assent to the request that the Prologue in *Henry V* makes for his players: "Let us, ciphers to this great accompt, / On your imaginary forces work." Actors are like the single figure (cipher) that represents a million in the reality that the "great accompt" describes. "Into a thousand parts divide one man, / And make imaginary puissance." Elizabethan spectators could not, either for the negative reason of physical discomfort or for the positive reason of imaginative engagement, remain passive at a play. It was a game of imaginary puissance that everyone shared.

BIBLIOGRAPHY

Joseph Quincy Adams, ed., *The Dramatic Records of Sir Henry Herbert* (1917). John Leeds Barroll, Alexander Leggatt, Richard Hosley, and Alvin Kernan, *The Revels History of Drama in English,* III: 1576–1613 (1975). Charles Read Baskervill, *The Elizabethan Jig* (1929). Gerald E. Bentley, *The Jacobean and Caroline Stage,* 7 vols. (1941–1968), and *The Profession of Dramatist in Shakespeare's Time, 1590–1642* (1971). Herbert Berry, "The Playhouse in the Boar's Head Inn, Whitechapel," in *The Elizabethan Theatre,* 1 (1969); "The Boar's Head Again," in *The Elizabethan Theatre,* 3 (1973); and *The First Public Playhouse: The Theatre in Shoreditch, 1576–1598* (1979). Muriel C. Bradbrook, *The Rise of the Common Player* (1962).

Edmund K. Chambers, *The Elizabethan Stage,* 4 vols. (1923). Ann Jennalie Cook, *The Privileged Playgoers of Shakespeare's London, 1576–1642* (1981). Reginald A. Foakes, ed., *The Henslowe Papers,* 2 vols. (1978). Reginald A. Foakes and R. T. Rickert, eds., *Henslowe's Diary* (1961). Reavley Gair, *The Children of Paul's* (1982). David George, "Shakespeare and Pembroke's Men," in *Shakespeare Quarterly,* 32 (1981). Andrew Gurr, *The Shakespearean Stage, 1574–1642* (1970; rev. ed., 1980). Michael Hattaway, *Elizabethan Popular Theatre* (1982). Harold N. Hillebrand, *The Child Actors* (1926). George L. Hosking, *The Life and Times of Edward Alleyn* (1952). Richard Hosley, "A Reconstruction of the Fortune Playhouse: Part I," *The Elizabethan Theatre,* 6 (1978), and "Part II," 7 (1980).

William Ingram, *A London Life in the Brazen Age: Francis Langley* (1978). Thomas James King, *Shakespearean Staging, 1599–1642* (1971). L. C. Knights, *Drama and Society in the Age of Jonson* (1937). Scott McMillin, "Simon Jewell and the Queen's Men," in *Review of English Studies,* n.s. 27 (1976). Edwin Nungezer, *A Dictionary of Actors and of Other Persons Associated with the Public Representation of Plays in England Before 1642* (1929). John Orrell, *The Quest for Shakespeare's Globe* (1983). George F. Reynolds, *The Staging of Elizabethan Plays at the Red Bull Theater, 1605–1625* (1940). Ernest L. Rhodes, *Henslowe's Rose: The Stage and Staging* (1976).

Samuel Schoenbaum, *William Shakespeare: A Compact Documentary Life* (1977). Michael Shapiro, *Children of the Revels* (1977). Charles J. Sisson, "Notes on Early Stuart Stage History," in *Modern Language Review,* 37 (1942). Peter Thomson, *Shakespeare's Theatre* (1983). Karl P. Wentersdorf, "The Origin and Personnel of the Pembroke Company," in *Theatre Research International,* 5 (1979). Glynne Wickham, *Early English Stages, 1300–1660,* 4 vols. (1959–1985).

Printing and Publishing in the Tudor Age

ARTHUR J. SLAVIN

From Manuscript to Print

Shakespeare seldom mentions either printers or publishers, and when he does, his words often mock their work. In *The Winter's Tale,* Mopsa rhapsodizes about her love for ballads when they are in print, swearing that "then we are sure they are true" (IV. iv. 254–255). The subsequent wordplay between the Clown and Autolycus is our guarantee that they are not. In *Henry VI, Part 2,* Jack Cade, the rebel leader, condemns a nobleman to death for treason and the corruption of youth. On what evidence? The lord has built a grammar school and has also been a publisher: "Whereas, before, our forefathers had no other books but the score and the tally, thou hast caused printing to be used, and, contrary to the king his crown and dignity, thou hast built a paper mill" (IV. vii. 30–33).

Shakespeare may reflect here the ambiguity in popular attitudes toward printing. He may also be alluding to the fact that English monarchs had oscillated in their own attitudes toward the press. The very conditions under which the technology of printing reached England encouraged diverse responses. But to grasp why this should have been so requires that we go back to Gutenberg's invention itself and to William Caxton and his successors, who set up the craft and trade in London.

The art of making books by writing on vellum (sheepskin smoothed by scraping until it was thin and fine) had dominated European publishing for centuries. Monastic writing rooms called scriptoria had met all the needs of churchmen for religious works, the needs of governments for documents, and the needs of literate folk for devotional manuals, books of husbandry, and such literary and scientific publications as there were. From about the year 1100 on, the revival of towns and of commerce and the rise of cathedral schools and universities sharply increased the demand for books. The growth of learned professions such as law and medicine, the need for student texts, and the development of wider lay literacy among the urban classes engaged in manufacture and trade expanded the publishing market.

The men who met those demands were stationers, meaning merchants who sold things from a fixed location, such as a stall in an open market or a shop. Stationers were usually also publishers, men who used an old text or commissioned a new one and then coordinated the work of book production. This meant obtaining skins, finding craftsmen to scrape and smooth them, and then hiring such additional craftsmen as ink-makers, scriveners (copyists), illuminators (who provided decorated capital letters and pictures), and binders (who sewed the finished work in covers, which they sometimes lettered and decorated lavishly). When it was a matter of providing a very large edition, particularly one in which accuracy counted for a great deal, then a stationer would engage in mass production. Once in possession of a good copy, called the exemplar, he employed a legion of copyists under license from a bishop or university, often working in a place adjacent to school or university buildings. This factory system

8. A sixteenth-century printing shop, showing two presses with compositors and proofreaders at work.

was competent to meet some very large demands, as we know from the survival of more than 2,000 copies of works of Aristotle produced between 1200 and 1400.

As this system was reaching its highest point of development, European woodcutters began to print some items on paper, at least as early as 1380. Their original purpose had been to make trial sheets for designs that they would then print on cloth, a technique that had reached Europe from the East. But this new application of print to paper spread rapidly, providing cheap products such as playing cards, alphabets, calendars, and even small booklets of religious pictures with very simple texts. The only hindrance to printing more complex works was that carving a page of text in woodblocks was very time-consuming and hence expensive. And because of the pressure on the surface of the raised design as the image was being transferred, these early printing blocks were not very durable. Experiments to achieve a stable mold for a whole page in metal also proved economically unfeasible. Another limiting factor was that through the fourteenth century, paper—which had reached Europe from China by way of Arab merchants active in Spain some two hundred years earlier—was still very expensive and was usually too coarse to take ink well enough to yield the clarity needed in printing texts.

The importance of improvements in the surface of paper and in its price as a competitor with vellum cannot be too strongly stressed if we are to grasp the situation in which Gutenberg and others were seeking to reproduce texts at competitive prices. Until the fifteenth century the supply of paper was not large and its price remained high—perhaps high even relative to vellum in countries like England, which had very large numbers of sheep to supply the wool trade and clothing industries. The main cause of the paper shortage lay in the absence of a suitable supply of rags made from such vegetable fibers as hemp and flax.

9. A 1607 engraving of a large paper mill in operation.

Only a very steep rise in the standard of living among survivors of the Black Death caused a shift away from wool to linen for underwear in Europe. To meet this demand for linen garments, farmers near big towns and cities increased their acreage in hemp and flax, thereby guaranteeing the supply of rags the papermakers required to make a pulp that would hold together in the drying frames and provide a smooth and fast surface for ink. The availability of good cheap paper was one of the necessary conditions of Gutenberg's invention of printing from movable type. Demand by itself was not enough.

Making a page of print from individual pieces of movable type (called sorts) required the solution of many technical problems. The most fundamental of these was the manufacture of sorts in an alloy of metals strong enough to stand up to repeated use under the pressure of the actual press itself. By the late 1440s, German goldsmiths had learned to make effective punches, or engraved relief devices, which were used to stamp an impression in a matrix of softer metal. The resultant impression or die could then cast many images. If the engraving was a single letter, the resulting casts would then be used to make up a text, provided they could be held in line under pressure.

Evidence suggests that before Gutenberg these difficulties were not overcome. Gutenberg's knowledge of chemistry enabled him to make matrices stable enough to hold molten metals in casting and casts strong enough for reuse. Moreover, he improved the press and the forms of lead to hold the sorts. He also made a fatty ink high in iron and lead content, which would make a clear and durable impression without running. Gutenberg was not a printer himself, and no book that survives has his colophon, but every printed page bears his mark in a historical sense.

The Printshop

A publisher who wanted to produce a book from moving type, like the stationers of manuscript books, had to assemble the materials and skilled labor required; but now his business was much more capital-intensive. He needed one or more presses, as many as 100,000 sorts, or letters, fatty ink, vast quantities of paper, devices to assemble the type into pages, woodcut designers or copperplate engravers to make illustrations or page frames

and borders, and of course binders (if he did not ship the assembled pages "white," or unbound, to save on transport costs). He also needed two new species of skilled labor: a compositor to make up an accurate page from the sorts and a printer to make the actual impression on every sheet of paper with rapidity and the least possible spoilage, for paper represented about half the cost of producing a book throughout the period from Caxton's first 1476 printed indulgence to the First Folio edition (1623) of Shakespeare's plays.

Assuming the publisher was himself the printer, he had to make certain that the page of sorted type held together under pressure in the press itself. He wanted to keep the type in line, and he wanted to see to it that the elevation of each face of type was identical with that of every other sort to be printed. Otherwise, he could not guarantee that the inked type would print or that the impression would be whole and uniform.

The compositor who made up the pages sat at a table or desk. He had before him at a slight tilt the cases into which the sorts or letters had been distributed. Until the eighteenth century there were no standard type sizes anywhere in Europe, and although there had been aliens who cast type even earlier in England there was no native type foundry at all until 1597, when Benjamin Sympson established one; consequently, compositors often worked with types of uneven sizes and heights. Because the compositor was often an itinerant journeyman, he might find himself working in a strange environment, unfamiliar with any peculiarities in the house's distribution system. The workday was frequently from twelve to sixteen hours, which meant much labor in conditions of poor light.

Under handicaps such as these, a Tudor compositor had to read from the copy before him and place into his slotted composing stick a line of text. He next transferred this line into a tray called a galley, holding it fast with small pieces of lead too low to print even if inked. After he had done enough such lines to make up a page, he grouped them into the frame, holding the ensemble firmly in place by a system of wooden retaining wedges. Dabbers then inked the standing type, and it was ready for the pressman or printer.

The pressman began his work by placing a large paper sheet in contact with the inked standing type in the form on the stone bed of the press. He then activated the press itself, making a sharp pull on a bar or lever. This pull activated a screw connected to a flat weight, called the platen, which was poised above the bed. The turn of the screw pressed the platen down hard on the type in the form, causing the inked faces to leave their impression in the paper. By the late sixteenth century most presses were double-action devices of either French or Dutch design and manufacture, with the bed on rails. The inking could be done out of the way of the platen, and a printer actually moved the bed and platen simultaneously. This was a tricky operation: a platen of the wrong size or not parallel with the plane of standing type would mar the page, as would any movement of the form or looseness in the ink. Under such conditions a good Tudor team working a sixteen-hour day might run off as many as 1,700 sheets printed on both sides.

This productivity was remarkable, because even as many as 100,000 sorts would enable a team to set and print only a dozen or so full sheets before it became necessary to break up the forms and distribute the type to set up new pages. If the author or editor of the work in hand was not in the shop to correct the galleys, the composed errors ran. If the size of an edition required that pages of the same number be run from more than one form, errors multiplied. Another source of irregularity was in determining the sequence of pages to be set in a form. Unless a single page filled the whole sheet, a situation rare in a book but common in broadside ballads and royal proclamations, pages had to be imposed on the form in the proper order. In a folio book, for example, the compositor had to set pages one and three on the front of the paper sheet, with pages two and four on the back. When the sheet was then folded once from left to right, the four pages would appear in proper sequence.

After shipping a book white and gathered into groups of pages called quires, the publisher was ready to face the market. Over most of the sixteenth century, the English printer was at some serious competitive disadvantages. Not only was there no type foundry in the country before 1597, but (apart from a short-lived experiment at Stevenage from 1495 to 1498) there was no paper mill in operation before 1589, when John Spilman set one up at Dartford in Kent. This lack may reflect the tremendous influence of the merchants who traded in wool: they had no wish to encourage competition from linen and cotton cloth or garments, and we know how the availability of rags affected the supply and price of paper. In any event, English

10 and 11. Two woodcuts by Jost Amman, showing form making and compositors and pressmen at work.

133

12. This woodcut clearly shows the nature of the double action press, with the platen down and the rails having carried the form in.

13. Death Among the Printers. The earliest known illustration of a printing press, showing a two-page form, the compositor's stick, and the inking balls.

134

printer-publishers had higher shipping costs than their continental competitors.

The Pioneer Printer-Publishers

The men who made the printing trade in England were, however, courageous enough to operate in a freewheeling situation of very high risk. Not only were labor and materials expensive; money was too. England lagged behind France, Italy, and the German states in developing credit machinery until at least the middle of the Tudor age. This meant that the pioneers had to be either self-financed or under the patronage of a wealthy merchant, a bishop, a lay lord, or the crown. William Caxton was himself a rich merchant who had risen to prominence and great wealth in the wool trade at Bruges. When he returned to London in 1476—having financed his own education as a printer in Cologne—he had powerful court patrons with an interest in his products. Caxton rented quarters from the monks at Westminster Abbey, near the palace, in what was a western suburb of London.

Caxton established a pattern for the printer-publishers who followed him. If they were native Englishmen, they made money in another trade—for example, as drapers, haberdashers, or mercers—and then tried their fortunes with the new art. Two-thirds of all craftsmen and publishers at work in England between 1476 and 1540 were foreign-born, but in this also Caxton set the pattern, for he probably had brought with him the man who took over his premises after his death in 1491. Wynken de Worde was from Lorraine, and when he began to print books at Westminster, before moving into the City in 1500, he began a long period of foreign domination of English publishing.

This was partly a matter of necessity because of the inadequacy of English labor, technique, and capital accumulation, but it was also a result of government policy. Richard III had been anxious to promote the new craft, and in 1484 he made a statute that framed efforts for more than fifty years. He relaxed prohibitions on the entry of foreign craftsmen and supplies into England, and his successors continued this policy until 1523, when Henry VIII, perhaps under pressure from a growing number of English craftsmen and booksellers, gave scope to native enterprise. Henry ruled that each foreign master printer could have no

foreign apprentices and no more than two foreign journeymen.

In the meantime, foreign masters had come to dominate the production and sale of books in England. The master printers following Caxton and de Worde were William Machlinia from Flanders, John Lettou of Lithuania, and the Frenchmen William and Richard Faques, Julian Notary, and Richard Pynson. Only the naturalized Welshman Thomas Berthelet broke the line of foreigners. In addition to these great printer-publishers from abroad, major international publishers like Christopher Plantin of Antwerp and the Frenchmen Antoine Vérard and François Regnault held most of the rest of the market. Even in midcentury it was difficult to compete with Plantin, who kept twenty-four presses running in his factory at Antwerp and maintained depots and shops in the main European fairs and towns. European masters also formed leagues of stationers to control both the market and the upstart bands of compositors and printers, whose teamwork in the printing shop promoted a solidarity that the masters considered dangerous.

The impetus toward a native English publishing industry came from the Reformation. As early as 1529, Henry VIII forbade aliens to set up any more printing shops in England. In 1534, Thomas Cromwell promoted an act forbidding the importation of books of foreign manufacture, apparently to keep out continental books hostile to Henry VIII and his new church. The king reinforced this exclusionary measure by proclamation in 1538. In the meantime Cromwell had become deeply engaged in publishing himself, arranging the importation of Bibles in 1537. In the following year, with his partners Richard Grafton, a grocer, and Edward Whitchurch, a haberdasher, he produced the authorized English-language Bible known as the Great Bible of 1539. Cromwell assembled not only the translators and editors but the craftsmen as well. He also contracted to print at Paris in the workshop of Master Regnault—an arrangement necessary because of the backwardness of English shops, he admitted in a letter.

Cromwell also took another step fateful for the development of the English printing industry. In his effort to convince his merchant friends to put up the vast sum of £500 for the project, he had to give them some security in the marketplace. He therefore obtained a royal patent of privilege, or what we might call a monopoly, to sell the Great Bible. This patent gave security to publishing investors for the first time, awarding them exclusive rights to sell a book for which the demand was guaranteed by another requirement: that every curate buy a copy and set it up in his church. Here was the germ of the idea of copyright—but, significantly, for the publisher and not the author. In fact, with *Paradise Lost,* Milton became the first great English writer to have any interest in the sales of a book made from a manuscript after he sold it for the first edition. There was no general copyright for authors until 1709.

The privileges accorded the patentees in the 1530s were enlarged in the 1540s, when Grafton and Whitchurch achieved a monopoly for printing and selling prayer books and other religious manuals. Thus ended the phase of free competition in the industry; now there would be a period of linkage between royal control and a market governed by privileged printers, publishers, and booksellers. The crown was interested in seeing that what was printed was not heretical, seditious, or blasphemous. Those in the trade were interested in finding hedges against the risks of an uncertain market in which pirates operated freely. (The pirates set up illegal presses and ran off very large editions of works in which they had invested nothing other than the printing costs.)

In 1557, Queen Mary gave a new charter to the Stationers' Company, which was at that time a group of just over 100 entrepreneurs: master printers, publishers, and booksellers. Not even the licenses in the 1530s or prohibitions of the 1540s had reached as far as this charter, which gave the stationers in London the sole right to print and publish licensed works. Elizabeth I tightened this system of royal license and control of the market in 1586, in a Star Chamber decree that forbade the setting up of any press outside London and its suburbs except for the presses in the university towns of Cambridge and Oxford. This measure dealt a death blow to provincial presses of the kind that had been established at St. Albans, York, Tavistock, Abingdon, Ipswich, Worcester, Norwich, and Canterbury. Printing was not to be undertaken again on a regular basis even in so important a city as York until 1662. James I tightened the system still further in 1615, when he limited the number of printing shops in London to twenty-two, a provision not repealed until 1695.

The stationers were right to celebrate their new charter in 1557, for what had been a decentralized industry now became centralized in their hands. Their privileges crippled overseas competitors, and by the end of the century an industry that had once been dominated by foreigners was entirely in English hands. The area around Paul's Yard and Fleet Street, where the printshops and publishers were gathered together with the booksellers, attained a unique character that made it synonymous with both wit and deceit.

Let us now look back some eighty years from 1557 to the beginning of English printing. When Caxton published his first book in England in 1477, unlike any other printer in Europe he made his first title a vernacular work, his own translation of *The Dictes or Sayengs of the Philosophres.* Caxton seems to have known that the invention of printing would serve a much wider market than the traditional form of publishing based on the church, the law, and a literate lay public with a taste for chivalric stories and translations of a few classical authors. He undertook job printing in such things as indulgences, and he printed and sold popular religious works; but his chief contributions were his editions of allegories, romances, and histories.

In this area Wynken de Worde far surpassed Caxton, for the Alsatian was a very hardheaded businessman who realized that the market would absorb cheap, portable books more readily than monster folios and large quartos. De Worde sought to reduce costs by helping John Tate to establish a short-lived paper mill in Hertfordshire. He enlarged his profit margin by squeezing more type onto a page through the introduction of Italic type in 1528, and he published many editions in small page sizes. Moreover, in opening new markets, he showed the way to later publishers who would specialize in those markets. For example, de Worde published not only music but also cheap law books, school texts, liturgies, primers, and even a book with the first English translations of the Creed and the Lord's Prayer (1523). He first tested the market for Lutheran pamphlets in 1524, before earning the summons of his bishop for a tract that he published in 1525. Before he died in 1534, de Worde had devoted 40 percent of his output to texts for grammar schools and other books with a potential market beyond 500 copies, which was the limit for larger, expensive works.

De Worde's most important competitor was Richard Pynson from Rouen. Pynson had shown his willingness to innovate as early as 1509, when

14. Earl Rivers presents his *Dicts of the Philosophers* to Edward IV.

he printed the first book to use Roman type in England. He also published the first English arithmetic in 1522. But of far greater importance from the standpoint of specialization was the systematic investment he made in publishing the yearbooks. All in all, he printed more than 150 editions of texts basic to the law, pointing toward a rich market also developed by his native-born competitors Richard Redman and John Rastell. Pynson also brought job printing to a very high level of development through his many indulgences, form letters, advertisements, royal proclamations, and statutes; and he pioneered the publication of guides to government offices and other practical manuals.

When Pynson died, only Thomas Berthelet among all the French masters survived him. Hence, the 1530s mark yet another important watershed in the development of the industry in England. The master printers and publishers who worked with Thomas Cromwell down to 1540 and shared his Protestant leanings were mainly Englishmen: Grafton and Whitchurch, of course, but also de Worde's assistant, Richard Copland, and Richard Bankes, who had assisted Copland, not to mention John Byddell, William Bonham, and Henry Dabbes. Cromwell had to go abroad to find a good printer able to do texts in Greek, Latin, and Hebrew—the German, Reyner Wolfe, for example—but Grafton and Whitchurch were the dominant figures right into the 1550s. It was Grafton who published Cranmer's *Book of Common Prayer* in 1549, after Edward VI elevated him to king's printer in place of Berthelet.

The displacement of Berthelet by Grafton shows the importance attached to printing by sovereigns. Grafton's own life is a perfect illustration, for on

Caxton's Type 3, from his Advertisement for the Sarum Ordinal (1479).

her accession Queen Mary dismissed Grafton, who had been imprudent enough to support Lady Jane Grey by printing a proclamation in which he styled her the queen of England. Grafton never printed again.

His successor, John Cawood, was a Catholic, though also circumspect enough to be retained by Elizabeth. In granting Cawood his patent as royal printer, however, she took the precaution of associating him with the strongly Protestant Richard Jugge. Jugge first came to notice in 1551, when he obtained license to print Tyndale's once-proscribed version of the New Testament. He produced an attractive edition that sold at the low price of 22 pence. With Cawood, Jugge was responsible for a very large output, accounting for 153 entries in the *Short Title Catalog* on his own and another 204 with Cawood. He is worthy of notice because of his friendship with Richard Tottel, who had married Grafton's daughter Joan and had first printed Tottel's famous *Miscellany* in 1557 as *Songes and Sonettes.*

The Great Stationers

Jugge and Cawood mark a turning point in publishing history. It was Cawood who had the reversion to Reyner Wolfe's patent to print in the classical languages, thus ending yet another form of English dependence on the European humanist-printers. Jugge, who was a King's College, Cambridge, man with a humanist education, made editions noteworthy for their excellence in layout, typography, and illustrations. His classic work was the Bishops' Bible (1568): its 143 maps and portraits had no precedent for quality and quantity in an English book.

Jugge was also associated with John Day, a university graduate who, under Archbishop Parker's patronage, cut the most elegant type made in England. His font of Anglo-Saxon type for an edition of Aelfric's homily *A Testimonie of Antiquitie* (1567) is still a landmark in typography. Day was on close terms with John Foxe the martyrologist, who actually lived with the printer after working on his *Book of Martyrs.* No other book apart from the Great Bible and the Book of Common Prayer did as much to shape the language and thoughts of Elizabethan men and women.

In the years between the Marian patent and the 1590s, only the Huguenot refugee Thomas Vautrollier had anything like the influence of the major English stationers. He had first come to notice as Plantin's agent about 1567, but a few years later he was printing and trading on his own account. Vautrollier made his impact on the university curriculum with such works as his editions of Théodore de Bèze's New Testament, John Calvin's *Institutes,* and Petrus Ramus' *Dialectics.* Perhaps his most impor-

Epiftola.

Petrus Gryphus:Nuncius apoftolicus:Reueredo patri Dño Thome Rontal Regio Secretario Salutem plurimam.

Xegifti a me tantopere:vt oratione quam habere inftituerā coram fereniffimo Rege Hérico feptimo : intēpeftiua ipfius morte præuentam/ad te mitterem. Quod feci tardius ac cūctatius/quā vehemētiores hortatus tuí depofcebant.Dubitabā eni/an effet fatis cōgruens: vt quæ mors vetuerat/me publice recéfere: priuatim nunc legēda exhiberem/ne ex editione nō recitati fermo nis fpeciē ambitionis icurrerem. Accedebat etiam quod cū in ea oratione cōmunibus potius commo dis & effectui iniūcti mihi muneris/quam priuatæ vel laudi/vel iactantiæ ftuduiffem:ftilus tanq̃ præf fus demiffufq̃ argui poffe videbatur.Cū præcipue gratia et calor ille quem fumit oratio ex actione/ge ftu/voceq̃ dicētis: ficut audiendo accenditur & ani matur/fic legēdo deprimaͬ et relāguefcat: dū nullo extrifecus actu vel fono/legentiū intētio excitatur. Suftulifti tamen tua efflagitatione oēm exhibendi verecundiam. Cum videam me & tua auctoritate/ et meo obfequio poffe excufari apud eos: qui et dicunt & fcribūt accuratius.Non habitā igiͭ oͬonem ea fimplicitate/qua incolumi Regi dicendā propo=

A.ij.

16. A page from Richard Pynson's 1509 printing of *Oratio* by Petrus Gryphus, showing the elegance of even a mediocre Roman type face.

tant works for the wider reading public were his Cicero, his Ovid, and Sir Thomas North's translation of Jacques Amyot's French version of Plutarch, set up in a huge folio with very good Italic and Roman typography and some handsome copperplate portraits. Vautrollier also published the music of Thomas Tallis and William Byrd. By the 1590s such ventures were in the hands of English masters. Noteworthy among them was Thomas East, who worked closely with the major publishers of the Stationers' Company, preferring to collaborate rather than compete. East produced vernacular works and music especially.

Perhaps East's decision to avoid being his own publisher may be explained in part by crises involving Christopher Barker and John Day. Barker was an interloper, a draper who came to publishing at the age of forty and chiefly through the patronage of the powerful politician Sir Francis Walsingham. Walsingham procured for Barker the patent to publish the Geneva Bible and other works in 1577. Archbishop Parker had kept the work from lawful

17. The Bishops' Version (1568) with portrait of Queen Elizabeth, illustrating a well laid out page.

print while he lived, but it was so popular that it ran into 140 editions by 1640 and had replaced the Great Bible as the text people most wanted before the King James version of 1611. This patent was a great privilege, but Walsingham so managed his suit in favor of Barker to get in the license all other rights to sell New Testaments and any other service books. This engrossment of the market was so flagrant that other stationers, led by John Wolfe, flatly said they would defy the patent.

A few years later John Day's patent to sell the *A.B.C. with the Little Catechism* revealed even more interesting complications of the trade. In 1582, while the fight over Barker's patent lingered, Day went into Star Chamber to sue one Roger Ward, a printer. He alleged that Ward had pirated the *A.B.C.* in an edition of 10,000 copies. Day won a judgment and execution against Ward. Three years later, however, a syndicate of illegal printers brought a Day to the defense of his rights again, in the person of his heir, Richard. He proved that the syndicate had printed and sold more than 10,000 copies of the primer in little over eight months. Soon thereafter the Star Chamber issued its decree restricting the location of presses. Only a few days later, Ward was in defiance, with the result that he was imprisoned and his presses and stock destroyed.

One piece of evidence is particularly pertinent to the monopolists' troubles with Ward. In 1585, Ward had set up shop in Shrewsbury, where the sheriff seized his inventory to pay off debts that he owed. In the shop Ward had more than 2,500 books, ranging from the *Iliad* to Thomas Wilson's *Discourse on Usury.*

In 1587, the stationers made a regulation limiting editions of all but a few very popular kinds of books to 1,250 copies, ostensibly to protect the employment of journeymen, while allowing runs of 3,000 copies of primers, prayer books, grammars, and almanacs. These surefire best-sellers were the heart of what became known as the English stock. In 1603, James I gave the stationers collectively the absolute monopoly to produce and sell this English stock, embracing the once scattered patents and thereby appearing to settle rivalries within the company. By doing so, the king also completed the transition from free competition to total monopoly in the printing trade. Many scholars believe that this privilege discouraged members of the company from risking much in the way of new techniques to improve the appearance of English books.

Others point out that such privilege encouraged piracy and therefore led to the debasement of texts, as the poet Thomas Heywood reminds us in his *Queen Elizabeth* (1605): "That some by stenography drew the plot: put it in print: (scarce one word trew).''

But regulation did not discourage diversity in the products of the press. English presses had produced less than 1 percent of the total European output before 1500, but 7 percent in the sixteenth century. The average annual output in 1550 was less than 100 titles, whereas in 1600 it ran close to 260. Of all English books published before 1500 nearly 75 percent were in Latin and 45 percent were either theology or systematic treatises concerned with religion. By 1600 the proportion of Latin or other learned languages to English had been reversed, and the ratio of religious books to others was declining. Whereas in 1500 the libraries of clerics outnumbered those of lawyers by more than twenty to one, a century later there were three times as many lawyers' libraries as there were clerical collections.

Arguments continue as to whether the press was a force for revolutionary change. But however the terms are defined, it does seem that printing created new tastes as well as serving those already in existence. The printed book was a factor in social mobility as well as in the movement of ideas. Also, it seems beyond debate that printing changed both the curriculum and the methods of teaching in schools at every level. Lord Bacon and the poet Samuel Daniel agreed that printing had been a force for radical change, the one welcoming it and the other regarding it as a force for instability.

Shakespeare more than once reminded his listeners and readers of the impact of printing on ordinary lives. We may recall the passage in *The Merry Wives of Windsor* where Alice proudly produces a letter of proposal of marriage. She asks whether Mrs. Ford has ever seen a similar proposal. Here is her answer:

Letter for letter, but that the name of Page and Ford differs.—To thy great comfort in this mystery of ill opinions, here's the twin brother of thy letter. . . . I warrant he hath a thousand of these letters, writ with blank space for different names—sure, more—and these are of the second edition. He will print them . . . for he cares not what he puts into the press, when he would put us two.

(II. i. 63–71)

18. An initial letter cut from William Cuningham's *The Cosmographical Glasse* (1559), showing the sorts of things illustrators did to enliven a page.

BIBLIOGRAPHY

Henry Stanley Bennett, *English Books and Readers, 1475–1640,* 3 vols. (1952–1970; vol. 1, 2nd ed., 1969). Cyprian Blagden, *The Stationers' Company* (1960). Curt Ferdinand Bühler, *The Fifteenth-Century Book: The Scribes, the Printers, the Decorators* (1960). Colin Clair, *A History of Printing in Britain* (1965). David Cressy, *Literacy and the Social Order: Reading and Writing in Tudor and Stuart England* (1980). Gordon Duff, *A Century of the English Book Trade* (1905). Elizabeth L. Eisenstein, *The Printing Press as an Agent of Change* (1979). Lucien Febvre and Henri-Jean Martin, *The Coming of the Book: The Impact of Printing, 1450–1800,* David Gerard, trans. (1976).

Stanley Lawrence Greenslade, "English Versions of the Bible, 1525–1611," in *Cambridge History of the Bible,* III, Greenslade, ed. (1963). Walter Leo Heilbronner, *Printing and the Book in Fifteenth-Century England* (1967). Rudolf Hirsch, *Printing, Selling and Reading, 1450–1550* (1967; rev. ed., 1974). Sears Jayne, ed., *Library Catalogues of the English Renaissance* (1956; rev. ed., 1983). Marjorie Plant, *The English Book Trade,* 2nd ed. (1965). *A Short-Title Catalogue of Books Printed in England, Scotland, and Ireland, and of English Books Printed Abroad, 1475–1640,* A. W. Pallard and G. R. Redgrave, eds. (1926). Frederick S. Siebert, *Freedom of the Press in England, 1476–1776* (1952). D. B. Updike, *Printing Types, Their History, Forms, and Use,* 3rd ed. (1962).

The Sense of History
in Renaissance England

J. G. A. POCOCK

Articles elsewhere in this set deal with Shakespeare's use of history in the two eras that interested him most, Lancastrian England and republican Rome. Many other eras of history were known in Renaissance England, and in reviewing their full range, one necessarily enters into modes of historical awareness in which Shakespeare seems not to have been interested or that he did not exploit as a dramatist. It is possible, however, that traces of some of these other modes may be found in his writings, and it may be instructive to consider why he did not exploit fields of history that were otherwise important to his countrymen.

The sense of history in Renaissance England was a regional variation of that available in Latin Christendom generally, when Latin Christian culture was beginning to undergo the changes accompanying the Protestant Reformation. It was derived from three principal traditions: Christian, classical, and vernacular (or national). It was in many ways more late-medieval than early-modern in character. Though already deeply affected by the impact of Renaissance humanism, it was not yet secularized or unified. We find ourselves at a great distance from the modern sense of history as a mode of understanding the past, applicable to human life in all its manifestations, or the sense that the meaning of human life is found in the changing patterns of social existence. The Renaissance English had a sense of tradition but hardly any sense of either progress or revolution. Their thought was still ruled by the Christian perception that human action

means little apart from the workings of God and by the classical perception that history is a branch of rhetoric, in which the moral and political deeds of men are exhibited for praise or blame, as examples to be imitated or avoided. History was not in the full sense an art, nor was it a science; it was written, read, and studied but not yet taught in any curriculum. There was a muse of history—Clio—but not a distinctive discipline of the mind. The word *history* was used in many ways, some of them remote from ours and not all of them consistent with one another; some ways of thinking that we consider essential to historical understanding were not present at all, while others were present but not yet known as "history." When Sir Philip Sidney discusses the nature of "history," he is concerned only to compare it with "poetry"; characters in Shakespeare's plays do not discuss it at all.

In discussing the sense of history in Renaissance England, we have to consider what Shakespeare's contemporaries meant by "history" and what kinds of awareness and discourse they grouped under this title; and we have to consider what kinds of awareness we mean by a "sense of history," in what forms they were present, by what terms they were known, and how they were related to one another, if indeed they were present in Renaissance England at all. These are two distinct inquiries, but it is not practicable in a single article to separate them completely. We must confine ourselves to examining the chief modes of historical awareness present in Shakespeare's England and to asking in what forms they were present, how they were expressed and used, whether they were recognized as "history," and in what ways the word *history* was emphasized and understood.

"Sacred history" consisted of a history of God's actions with respect to man (though the idea of a history of God himself would have been theologically unacceptable). The chief events of this history were the Creation of the world and of man; the Fall of Man and the condemnation under which he still lay; the birth of Christ as God incarnate; his Crucifixion and death; his descent into hell, where he began the Redemption of man by setting free certain actors in past history; his Resurrection and ascension; and the descent of the Holy Ghost upon the Apostles. History thus conceived possessed a future: it was promised that Christ would come again, that there would be a general resurrection, a Last Judgment, and an end of all earthly things. The medieval drama—as in the York Cycle—found it possible to present all the events of this history, with human actors speaking in the person of God himself. The Shakespearean drama confined itself to secular, if not always to profane, history. To the increasingly (though incompletely) Protestant mind of Shakespeare's England, the actions of God were contained in his Word, which could be read and expounded, and which could edify the spirits of worshiping congregations; but the actions themselves could not be enacted or reenacted except by communication of the Word. There was only one book of sacred history, and it did not furnish material for Elizabethan staged drama.

This book—the Bible, or Scripture—was divisible into many books, some of which were recognizable as histories; the ways in which it was divided furnished a further schematization of sacred history. The books of the Old Testament provided a complex history—heroic and political, as well as sacred and covenantal—of that first people whom God had chosen to make peculiarly his own. The books told of the patriarchs, the covenants, and the captivity in Egypt; the Exodus and the conquest of Canaan; the judges and high priests, and the kingdom in the manner of the Gentiles; the failure of the kings of Israel and Judah, and the captivity in Babylon. At this point, Jewish history, as presented in writings organized by the Christian church, gave way to prophecy: to the Exilic foretellings of a Messiah and Suffering Servant, which the Christians insisted had been fulfilled in the incarnation of Christ. The Christian church, proclaiming itself the true Israel, characterized the events of Jewish history as merely the establishment of prophetic patterns that Christ and his church were to fulfill together with proofs that the Jews themselves were unworthy to fulfill them. The history of Israel became the history of the Old Dispensation; it had been written only once, under divine inspiration, and could not be written again. It was to be studied only by means of those interpretive techniques—prophetic, allegorical, analogical, typological—which reduced it to symbolizing the New Dispensation that was to fulfill and supersede it. The history of Israel, thus presented, ended with the Exilic prophecies on which the Christians rested their case.

The Christians did not give much attention or authority to the history of the Second Temple; the books of Maccabees were apocryphal, not canonical. The Christian insistence that the guilt of deicide rested with the Jewish people as a whole was powerful but historically undeveloped. And the works of Josephus, which alone were admitted as evidence on matters otherwise biblical, belonged more to Roman than to sacred history. How the Jews of the Diaspora interpreted their past very few in Shakespeare's England knew or wanted to know; Shylock is not much of a Talmudist. Perhaps because the narrative lives of Joseph, Moses, and David were not written or rewritten as secular history, the rich materials they might have offered a dramatist were not exploited in the Shakespearean theater. Since they belonged to sacred history, they could belong only to sacred drama, which was a bookish and academic affair, of minimal importance compared with either the liturgy or the sermon.

After the ascension of Christ and the descent of the Spirit, sacred history continued, but in a special and, to our minds, elusive sense. The sixteen centuries separating those events from Shakespeare's lifetime formed part of the interval, of unknown duration, that separated the last recorded event in sacred history from the next prophesied: the Pentecost, when the Holy Ghost had descended upon the Apostles, from the Parousia, or Second Coming, when Christ would return. The time and space separating that past from that future were occupied by the church, the *ecclesia militans* or *peregrina*, the struggling and suffering body that was the vehicle of Christ's mystical presence "always, even to the end of the world."

It might seem that the actions and sufferings of

the church during those centuries constituted the sacred history that Christians shared and studied. But it was not in fact generally held that events in the history of the church constituted the history of the processes of redemption; the church as the body of Christ was not a historical body. Arguing against the Donatist heretics at the end of the fourth century, St. Augustine had laid down that, while the church was the vehicle of human salvation, it did not lead men to salvation through the adventures that it might undergo in earthly time. Christ's promise to the church meant that there was that about it which history could not corrupt and need not reform; the church effected salvation not in time but alongside time. Individual souls lived out their earthly lives, which led to salvation or damnation, in time but also in the body of a church that was a visitor from outside time altogether. Each soul discovered salvation or damnation at the moment of leaving time to enter eternity. Prophecies of the General Resurrection and Last Judgment, of the sufferings and triumphs of the church in the last days, while held to be literally true, were at the same time to be read as figurative of the salvation or damnation of the individual soul. No event in secular history, or in the fortunes of the church as it belonged to secular history, formed any part of the sacred history of the redemption of mankind. From Pentecost to Parousia, salvation was in history, but history was not of salvation; there was no necessary reason why the Christian should concern himself with history at all.

Augustine's position had always been debatable. The church was a body and communion on which salvation depended, and when the church as a visible social institution seemed vicious or corrupt—which in the course of human events was often enough—it was natural for concerned worshipers to feel that its corruption imperiled their salvation. Such reformers declared that the church must be reformed in time and that salvation depended on membership in the church as it would be reformed at the end of time; apocalyptic or millennial expectations made themselves heard. When the reformers identified corruption with the power of an ancient and deep-rooted institution like the papacy, they constructed histories that showed how human or diabolical action had set up the institution or instigated the corruption, and that prophesied how human and divine action would reform the church and bring about salvation in a historical future. Heresy in the church regularly produced this kind

of counterhistory, part secular and part sacred. It was secular because certain events in past history appeared crucial in determining whether or how the church had become corrupt. One such event was the conversion in the fourth century of the Emperor Constantine to Christianity and his proclamation that the Roman Empire was a Christian body; another was the relationship that he had set up between the empire and the church. There was a legend that Constantine had conceded great powers to Pope Sylvester and that a voice from heaven had cried out that the Body of Christ had received poison.

But heretical history was also sacred history, because it expected reformation through the actions of God and his agents in a prophesied or apocalyptic future. It was possible for both orthodox and heretical minds to construct scenarios of such apocalyptic happenings, based on the books of Daniel in the Old Testament and Revelation in the New, and to organize sacred history around a series of fulfillments of prophecy. The great (and, on the whole, orthodox) Joachim of Fiore in the twelfth century had written that, as the Age of the Father, in which God revealed himself to Israel through the Law, had given place to the Age of the Son, in which he revealed himself to the church through Christ's body, so there would come an Age of the Spirit, in which he would reveal himself in all men through their own redeemed bodies. A revolutionary vision, in which both the church and the Law would be overthrown by a sanctified humanity, could be developed from this point. Anabaptists had done so not long before Shakespeare's birth; Diggers and Ranters were to do so not long after his death.

From the time of the English Reformation—that is, of the drastic reconstitution of the English church by Henry VIII's legislation—it became increasingly necessary to decide what the church was: to distinguish between, and perhaps to recombine, the view of the church as an invisible body, an association of worshipers in communion with God outside of time, and the view that it was a visible body, formed by divine agency in this world and subject to human authorities acting in this life. The latter view could have many meanings but necessarily implied that the church possessed a history that could be studied and traced through secular time; the former view could mean that there had existed false churches or false systems of religious authority, whose history should be unmasked as the his-

tory of corruption and usurpation. The history of
the Christian church, the Roman church, and the
church in England came to be much studied from
both points of view, with important consequences
for the history of those systems of secular authority
—the Christian empire founded by Constantine,
the Christian kingdom that had taken shape in England—with which the church visible or invisible
had interacted.

The conversion of Constantine was both an event
in church history and the last act in the history of
classical antiquity. The reigns of King John and
King Henry VIII were events in both the history of
the English church and in that vernacular history of
the English nation which forms the third tradition
of English historical knowledge. We must review
both the classical and the national traditions before
returning to the general state of historical consciousness in Shakespeare's England.

The classical tradition embraced a copious
knowledge of the history, literature, jurisprudence,
and mythology of Roman and Greek (in part,
derived through the Roman) antiquity, as well as a
limited amount of information about the Egyptian,
Syrian, and Persian civilizations with which Greeks
and Romans had been in contact. What little else
was known about Egyptian, Babylonian, and As-
syrian civilizations was associated with Hebrew and
scriptural antiquity. A principal aim of scholarship
was to devise systems of chronology by which the
history of all these peoples could be reconciled with
the biblical history of mankind before and after
Noah's Flood and Abraham's Covenant. Attempts
to incorporate Arabic, Hindu, and Chinese myth-
ography and history with this chronology began
soon after Shakespeare's death and were developed
by later generations, while pre-Columbian American antiquity did not play much part in the history
of that essentially literary and documentary form of
scholarship to which the term *archaeology* was then
confined.

Antiquity, therefore, meant classical antiquity,
with the partial exception of churchmen to whom
it might mean biblical history and the history of the
early church. Greek and Latin supplied sixteenth-
century Englishmen and western Europeans with
nearly all that they knew about the secular past of
mankind. The centrally important characteristic of
the Elizabethan classical tradition is that it was
knowledge of certain deeply admired values which
were pursued, practiced, imitated, and studied, and
yet were set apart from Christian study by the ines-

capable fact that they had been formulated, practiced, and expressed before the birth of Christ
(which marked the true end of antiquity in secular
history, as it did that of the Old Dispensation in
sacred history). Christian civilization was in love
with its pagan past, in more ways than with its
Hebrew.

History, the mirror in which antique values
could be seen, entailed processes—the recurrent
patterns of the rise and fall of republics, empires,
and civilizations—and European and English readers might perceive themselves to be part of these.
But, for most readers, what counted was the enactment of values in individual lives. The rise and
fall of states merely underlined the lessons that
history taught; a humanist cliché stated that history was "philosophy teaching by examples." In
classical antiquity were to be found exemplary
achievements in the visual and literary arts, in philosophy, and in the linked practices of war, politics, and social living. Insofar as these activities
were reconcilable with Christian faith and worship, the purpose of history was to study the
achievements of antiquity and to learn to reenact
them. Historiography, the writing of history as a
literary form, was itself an invention of the ancients. Though its subject matter was overwhelmingly military and political, its purposes were didactic and mimetic—to teach lessons and furnish
examples. Its competitors in carrying out these
functions were oratory, poetry, and philosophy.
Renaissance cultural debate asked whether these
rivals had equaled or surpassed historiography.

The classical and neoclassical conception of history did more than supply Renaissance Europeans
with their knowledge of the human cultural past; it
told them what elements of this past they should
consider significant and provided the aesthetic,
moral, and practical reasons for considering them
valuable. It taught them that history was a storehouse of examples rather than of processes. At the
same time, it instructed the individual who wished
to write history regarding what manner of social
actor he was to be and in what manner he was to
write. The historian was to provide narratives of
human action for didactic and mimetic purposes,
and he was to imitate specific literary models from
antiquity. He might further be, or draw close to
being, any one or any combination of the following: a rhetorician, a poet, a counselor, or a philosopher. A rhetorician employed speech, typically in
the form of oratory, to move men to admirable

actions and the practice of the virtues. A poet did the same, with the admixture of a component of fantasy or imagination, which was to raise difficult questions about the nature of the historian's art. A counselor used exemplary materials in urging moral and practical prudence on those who governed in society: his fellow citizens if he lived in a republic, his superiors if—as was far more typical—he lived under the authority of magistrates or a prince. A philosopher might engage in rhetoric or counsel (it was far less likely that he would be a poet) with the additional function of reflecting on the foundations of knowledge itself and on the relationship between knowledge (or contemplation) and moral or practical action. A historian did not have to be either a poet, a counselor, or a philosopher, though he almost certainly was some kind of rhetorician; but he supplied all four roles with so much of their exemplary material that he might not avoid—and should not fear—being drawn into any of them.

Literary, rhetorical, and social problems arose for the sixteenth-century historian from the variety of roles presented to him. In the first place there was the problem of truth, or rather factuality. A historian was expected to adhere strictly to what he knew to be true, either from having witnessed events himself or from information supplied him by other witnesses. If he was a modern following the narrative of an ancient historian, he should follow the latter as his authority and not presume to add anything. Yet the value of the facts he recounted lay in their exemplary and moral character, and to expound this was essential to moral art; the historian had to decide how far he might go in representing the facts as being of the moral character which good men saw them as possessing.

Aristotle in his *Poetics* had observed that history was limited to recounting what Alcibiades did and suffered, whereas poetry might represent Alcibiades as an actor among the eternal verities and as doing those things which were merely signified by the things he (or others) actually did. Was the historian justified in acting as a poet, rhetorician, or philosopher and in presenting his narrative in terms of its true moral significance? It was the perdurable problem of interpretation. There might arise a form of legitimate historical fiction in which the protagonist was depicted as having really committed acts typical of the sort of person to which he had really belonged. Richard III, represented as a classical tyrant by both Sir Thomas More and William

Shakespeare, may have undergone this kind of transformation. And what was truth? Or rather, what kind of truth mattered? Tyrants throughout history had been murderers of children; did it matter more to display this truth or to determine what had really happened to the princes in the Tower? Those chiefly concerned with questions of the latter kind were sometimes said to have written out of "curiosity," often a word of reproof.

There was, therefore, more to history than factual truth, and the latter need not always be regarded. Classical and neoclassical critics often distinguished between histories that were true, in the sense of rigorous factuality; histories that were probable, in the sense that they sometimes enlarged the meaning of the facts (the best-known example being the placing of speeches in the mouths of historical actors, in which they were made to articulate the premises on which they had probably acted); and histories that were false, in the sense that they were exemplary fictions about characters who were not fictitious. None of these genres was illegitimate; the only lying historian was one who sailed under false colors, offering as true that which he knew to be true in some other sense, probable or fictitious. But this analysis approximated history to what Aristotle meant by poetry, in which the significance of the facts takes control of the facts themselves; and this problem has never been eradicated from historiography.

In sixteenth-century English, the word *history* often retained its Greek meaning of a methodical inquiry, as in "natural history," which might have nothing "historical" about it; it could also mean (and was sometimes spelled) *story,* in the sense of a tale that did not even pretend to be true, such as the "tragical history of Pyramus and Thisbe." Somewhere between the poles lay "histories" that paid attention to both facts and the meanings of facts, though fantasy and imagination might help in establishing both moral and factual truths. Romances were narratives that were nothing more than fantasies or fables; when a sixteenth-century explorer found himself in a land so remote as to seem fabulous, he might give it a name from romance, such as "California." Utopia itself might yet be discovered somewhere.

The concept of the historian as counselor, even more than as poet, presented the Renaissance writer with a series of problems regarding the historian's social role. Whether as senator in a republic or confidential adviser in a prince's cabinet, a counselor was supposed to be a grave and weighty statesman capable of making events as well as reporting on them; this formed part of the classical image of the historian as one who had taken part in great events and later retired to write their history. In the space beyond the counselor and historian revolved the figure of the philosopher; but here the role of counsel became problematic. From Plato's *Republic* to More's *Utopia,* the question had been asked whether the man of wisdom, practical as well as moral, did not endanger and degrade himself in giving advice to those less wise than himself. Socrates and Cicero typified the philosopher as citizen in a corrupt city; Seneca, the philosopher as adviser to a tyrannous prince in a corrupt court. Was not the business of wisdom the contemplation of truths beyond this world, rather than the attempt to advise on actions within it? The historian was not a philosopher; the truths he imparted were not arrived at by contemplative reason but were discovered in the significance of actions performed and narrated, so that his role (whether or not that of the counselor) was closer to that of the poet. For this reason the problems of counsel and the tensions between contemplation and action were in his case peculiarly acute, so that the classical figure of the historian became that of a man of action in retirement, abdication, or even disgrace, analyzing the inner meaning of events that he could no longer control.

From Thucydides, Sallust, or Tacitus in antiquity to Machiavelli or Guicciardini in the sixteenth century—even to Milton or Clarendon in the generation after Shakespeare—the dominant image of the historian was as a man in retirement. There is nothing less true than the adage that history is written by the victors; most of these great figures wrote in defeat, to analyze failure. There came indeed a point where the exemplary function of history itself broke down; the great historical realists, Tacitus and Guicciardini, thought that events were too knotted and recalcitrant to be reduced to lessons capable of easy imitation, and they ceased to be moralizers in order to become tragic artists.

By the end of Shakespeare's career the archetype of the historian as counselor seemed to be Tacitus, though this had more to do with the writings of Jonson and Bacon than with those of Shakespeare. Given the social realities of Elizabethan and Jacobean England, the role of counselor to which men aspired in a humanist culture—that of providing advice in a literary form—was less likely to be filled by statesmen and senators than by the lay clerisy, who were the educated dependents of leading courtiers, literati often motivated by bitter ambition and disappointment. A literature arose that described the courtier's life in tones of obsessed revulsion and dwelled on the servility to which men were condemned by their ambition to win favor and shape events. Disappointed counselors found their imaginations satisfied by Tacitus' terrible accounts of how an emperor, his senators, and his favorites had degraded and corrupted one another. Ben Jonson (who knew the historical scholars of his day) wrote drama with a Tacitean theme; Francis Bacon wrote his *History of Henry the Seventh* as he was about to fail as chancellor. Tacitism was a widespread European phenomenon, perhaps part of what H. R. Trevor-Roper has termed the "general crisis of the seventeenth century." The effect of this revulsion against courts, of this despair of the humanist ideal of counsel, on the English understanding of history did not become apparent until the civil wars and the Puritan revolution.

The classical perception of history thus focused on the ideas of example and counsel, but it also provided the context in which exemplary actions were to take place and furnished that context with a history of its own. The heroic figures of antiquity had for the most part been the citizens, magistrates, statesmen, and generals of city-states and republics, above all of ancient Rome; the republic provided the moral and political context—or, as it was often called, the theater—for their deeds. The function of action as recorded by the historian was to display heroic virtue; the function of virtue was to maintain, extend, and glorify the republic. Since the republic was typically at war, the virtue of the hero was typically that of the warrior. St. Augustine, in one way, and Machiavelli, in another, had pointed out that heroic virtue could be very unlike Christian virtue; but the warrior of antiquity had also been a citizen, who must accept the discipline of his city's laws, whether they enjoined obedience to his commanders in the field or, more important, adherence to particular forms of legality and equality in his dealings with fellow citizens. It is the tragedy of Coriolanus that he cannot accept this discipline; his warrior virtue is heroic, but he lacks civic virtue and obliges his city to expel him. The further problem is to determine whether the republic as a whole possesses sufficient virtue to elicit or compel virtue from its citizens. Virtue is not merely individual, but also public; the history of a republic is the history of its success and failure in maintaining the discipline of virtue in the relations among its citizens, and between the citizens and the laws. History at this point ceases to be merely exemplary and becomes political as well.

The opponent of virtue was often said to be fortune, a complex and half-magical figure symbolizing, first, the unpredictability of random chance or luck, especially on a battlefield; and second, the unpredictability of human behavior when its moral order is disturbed, typically in a disordered or corrupt republic. Machiavelli's republic is exposed to fortune because it is commonly at war; his prince, for the more subtle reason that he has usurped power and confused the loyalties of the citizens. But fortune was never absent from human affairs, whether in a pre-Christian or a Christian universe; the hero displayed his individual virtue, the republic its civil and collective virtue, in confrontation with this mysterious force, on whose disorders and deceptions virtue sought to impose order and form. There was a widespread (and again half-magical) belief that virtue, if vigorous enough, would not only dominate fortune but also compel it to be favorable to the hero or republic. It is testimony to the pervasive masculinity of the republican ethos that the contest of *virtus* and *fortuna* was often depicted (for example, by Machiavelli) in the image of a love-hate relationship between a man and a woman. Fortune was a goddess who enjoyed being dominated and made to serve a man (or city) of heroic virtue, but she would instantly betray him if his virtue failed or proved inappropriate to the times. Shakespeare's Cleopatra seems at moments an embodiment of the goddess Fortune, as when she cries to Antony, returning from a battle he has momentarily won:

> O infinite virtue, com'st thou smiling from
> The world's great snare uncaught?
>
> (*Antony and Cleopatra,* IV. viii. 17–18)

But Antony's *virtus* fails him because the republic of Rome is collapsing under the weight of its own empire. Coriolanus lives in the heroic period of the early republic, recorded by Livy; though the senators and tribunes around him are depicted as tough, unscrupulous, and frequently misguided and selfish, the republic will survive his tragedy and proceed to the conquest of its neighbors. Shakespeare may have shared the Livian and Machiavellian view that even the bitter struggles between patricians and plebeians had been a source of

strength to Rome at this time. The point is, however, that virtue existed under political and historical conditions that were themselves finite and transitory; they could fail and disappear, leaving nothing but the record of their glory and its shame. The historian, both in antiquity and in Renaissance Europe, was concerned not merely to record exemplary actions but also to consider the conditions that had made them possible; he investigated how these conditions had been maintained and how they had passed away, taking with them the opportunity of virtue itself. For some writers, history ceased at this point to be poetry and became more like political science; for others, probably the greater number, it remained poetic but ceased to be epic and became tragic, ironic, and satiric.

The historical image of the republic was less that of its virtue and conquests than that of its decay and replacement by the rule of the emperors. Shakespeare's Rome leaves the stage when Octavius Caesar is about to found the principate and take the name of Augustus. The next step was to dramatize the horrors of imperial tyranny, whose historian was Tacitus; Ben Jonson's *Sejanus,* however, is said to have failed in performance.

The political history of antiquity was a complex and in many ways contradictory series of images and values. Golden and exemplary images of heroic and civic virtue alternated with dark and diabolic images of virtue in corruption and under tyranny. Both images took republican virtue and freedom as their moral norm; to Thomas Hobbes, writing after the civil wars, this seemed to have been a disastrous mistake. The study of ancient history in the light of republican rhetoric, he declared, had taught young noblemen to pursue an active and competitive glory as though they had been citizens of a commonwealth instead of subjects of a sovereign. He had published the first English translation of Thucydides (more than twenty years previously) in the hope of convincing his countrymen that the motives and outcomes of action were too twisted and obscure, and the language in which they must be recounted too dark and enigmatic, to permit the heroic imitation of examples presented in rhetoric any political value. We must learn to mistrust our own personalities and leave action to the impersonal sovereign. That to Hobbes was the lesson of history properly read.

Whatever Hobbes's religious beliefs, his attitude to history arose from something more like a Christian sense of sin than a pagan sense of virtue; there were Christian virtues that were hard to connect with those of antiquity. The end of the republic and its replacement by the emperors had occurred in history at about the time of the incarnation of Christ (who had suffered himself to be condemned by a Roman magistrate) and at the end of the Old Dispensation in Rome as well as Israel; this fact deeply complicated the Christian attitude toward monarchy. The Caesars had been for the most part tyrants, warlords, and persecutors of the Christians; their empire had ended in conquest by the barbarians; even Constantine, founder of the Christian Empire, was regarded by humanists and Protestants with deep doubt and ambivalence. Nevertheless, the medieval and Tudor minds were pervaded and nearly dominated by an image of the Christian emperor (and in England, still more, the Christian king) as the guardian of an earthly order that was willed and commanded by God, with the effect that the king was God's representative and ruled by God's authority. Similarly in Jewish history, the heirs of David as kings of Israel and Judah had been unedifying and disastrous with few exceptions, yet Christ had been born of the House of David; kingship thus typified the role of God as savior as well as ruler. The Christian monarch stood for both order and redemption; he challenged the pagan virtue of the republic so deeply that it is a wonder he did not replace it. The sacred history discussed above reentered with him; but to say this is once more to ask whether the Christian kingdom had a history of its own.

The Renaissance sense of history combined pre-Christian with Christian elements under considerable pressure. The medieval equivalent of the antique hero, whose warrior virtue required the discipline of the republic, was the knight of chivalric romance. The knight had a touch of the barbarian about him, yet he accepted the authority of king and lord, the code of courtly love, and the discipline of a Christian ethic that might command him to lay down his arms and renounce the world altogether. His problems were explored at length in such semihistorical epics as the *Song of Roland* and the *Morte Darthur,* in which the medieval sensibility came as close as it could to a sense of tragedy. These great tales do not seem to have supplied plots for the Shakespearean theater. Perhaps one reason is that Renaissance humanism, the work of clerics and scholars before it was taken up by men of arms, in some ways involved an attempt to replace the knight by the counselor. The humanist

gentleman was to serve his prince as a counselor; his medium of action was rhetoric before it was warfare; he needed a knowledge of history, whereas the knight needed only song and romance.

Several consequences followed. In the first place, the humanist counselor sought to mobilize all that was known of antiquity in order to give counsel in, and about, a postbarbaric Christian kingdom. In a sense, he sought to know the ancient world the better to understand a world that was not ancient. In consequence he encountered, almost for the first time, important problems of anachronism, in understanding a world that he knew to be past but desired to treat as if it were present. The study of history began to take on its modern meaning, that of reconstructing the past and connecting it with the present. Because the humanist endeavored to read and think in classical Latin while living in a world in which it was no longer spoken, the study of history became for the first time philological, a matter of entering into past forms of language and, consequently, of thought and life. Hence, perhaps, Shakespeare's interest in the Stoicism of Brutus and the Epicureanism of Cassius; he did not have to be a scholar to share the preoccupations of his culture. Philology meant, besides, that the humanist need not study antiquity solely through reading history and other forms of rhetoric; he might study jurisprudence and philosophy, medals, inscriptions, and other monuments, thereby acquiring knowledge not only of exemplary deeds but also of all the forms of life surviving from a vanished civilization.

But, in the second place, the interest in exemplary deeds remained very strong. It was the aim of the humanist not merely to study and recount such deeds, but to perform them himself. From Thomas More to Francis Bacon, the English humanist studied and wrote history in the hope of acting in politics as a counselor to his prince; yet the ancient world to which he turned had not, at least ideally, been one of counselors and princes—least of all princes who were Christian rulers—but of citizens, senators, and philosophers debating as equals in republics. It followed that the giving of counsel became, insensibly but inevitably, identified with the display of republican virtue, with the performance of heroic actions, not confined to counsel, in which noble men sought to outdo one another in the pursuit of immortality (that is, in pursuit of a glory that would be remembered as long as the commonwealth endured—such being, in the last analysis, history's aim). A city-state was a very different society from a prince's court, but the disappointed counselor or courtier sometimes saw himself as a frustrated senator or citizen, groaning beneath the yoke of a tyrannous prince or corrupt minister; even when his disappointment was expressed in the darkest tones of Tacitean pessimism, it served to keep alive the image of republican virtue, freedom, and equality. This is how Cassius speaks to Brutus, and this is the problem on which Thomas Hobbes was to put his finger, however he may have exaggerated its importance as a cause of the civil wars. King Claudius had reason to mistrust any noble youth about his court who was more an antique Roman than a Dane.

The humanist commitment to living imaginatively in the past and practically in the present affected, but did not originate, the ways in which the English, Welsh, and Scottish subjects of King James VI and I understood the histories of their national societies. We have to deal here with both the "matter of Britain" and the separate histories of England and Scotland; all three were vernacular and postclassical societies with their roots in a past barbarous by the standards of classical antiquity. The history of "Britain" led back to the movements of Celtic peoples, both Cymric and Gaelic (the latter possibly Irish, who were considered more barbaric still); the histories of England and Scotland pointed to those of Germanic peoples like the Angles, Saxons and Jutes, and Scandinavians like the Danes and Normans. When the last-mentioned appeared in insular history, they brought a French and feudal culture that had taken shape in continental Europe and to whose history that of England and Scotland henceforth partly belonged, as it did to that of Latin Christendom from which the history of Celtic Christianity was to some extent distinct. The past perceived by inhabitants of the various insular cultures was linguistically and culturally diverse, with the result that the question of national origins became as important to historical consciousness as the provision of exemplary actions for contemplation and imitation.

Elizabethan and Jacobean historiography therefore had to find the means of presenting the barbaric past and making it acceptable in both classical and Christian terms. The "matter of Britain" was dealt with less by the reorganization of Celtic traditions than in terms of quasi-classical and medieval romance. The nations of Latin Christendom sought Trojan origins like those that Vergil had provided for Rome; the hero Brutus of Troy was held to have

settled in Britain and given the island his name. Elements of Celtic myth and medieval romance had accrued, by complex literary processes, to form a corpus of British history deduced from the landing of Brutus. Both scholars and poets had attempted with varying success to organize this into a single history or epic. Very prominent in this process was the potent figure of Arthur and the cycle of tales associated with his name; but we need not delve—as Shakespeare did not—into the complexities of Arthurian scholarship to be able to note that the "Arthur" best known in British history was a figure created less by Sir Thomas Malory than by the twelfth-century cleric Geoffrey of Monmouth. This inventive Norman-Welsh author had constructed a *History of the Kings of Britain* that had always outraged scholars but appealed to the imagination. This work blithely disregarded the few rules regulating the boundaries of history and fantasy, but provided a most satisfying basis for a national epic. In the reign of Henry VIII the Italian humanist Polydore Vergil of Urbino had infuriated the historians of Britain by dismissing all Trojan and Arthurian histories as poetic fictions, but, in part because the Welsh-descended Tudors had an interest in maintaining their Arthurian descent, both Brutus and Arthur still found their defenders in the time of Shakespeare. Lear and Cymbeline are both figures ultimately derived from Geoffrey of Monmouth; but the effect of humanist scholarship was progressively to widen the gap between history and poetry and to move the "matter of Britain" into the latter column. Before leaving Arthur, we should note that he was both an insular and a continental figure: at once the remote king of Caerleon and Camelot and a formidable emperor and conqueror in a legendary Roman Europe. His name was of service whenever Britons of any kind desired to assert the separateness of their island's history.

The decay of Galfridian history (as we term that associated with Geoffrey) went along with a decay of the "matter" (and even the idea) of Britain. To Shakespeare's contemporaries the word *British* meant little more than "Welsh." King James faced an uphill struggle in persuading his English and Scottish subjects to think of themselves as inhabiting "Great Britain." The English were the more reluctant of the two, but we are concerned here not with English ethnocentricity (misnamed insularity) so much as with the absence of any single or unified history of "Britain" after the humanist attack upon the Galfridian corpus. In its place, the two kingdoms of England and Scotland organized their historical pasts in different ways that looked back to different barbaric origins. The fathers of Scottish historiography—John Mair, Hector Boece, and George Buchanan—constructed a list of kings in which the problem of Trojan origins gave way before that of reconciling the Pictish (British or Cymric) with the Scottish (Irish or Gaelic) components of the national past. In Wales, only the Cymric element counted; but in England the situation was very different. Here a rich historical literature stressed, first, the conquest and expulsion of Romanized Britons by the Angles, Saxons, and Jutes —this was recorded in such great works of preconquest historiography as Bede's *Ecclesiastical History of the English Nation* and the *Anglo-Saxon Chronicle* —and second, the conquest par excellence carried out by the Normans in 1066. With this event, historiography in its high-medieval sense arrived in England (and later spread to Scotland). Heartily as Protestant Englishmen mistrusted the work of monks, ecclesiastical and monastic chronicles provided them with their knowledge of Norman, Angevin, and Plantagenet kingship in their country. Following the work of Bede, and a few remoter tales of Christian martyrs, the Emperor Constantine, and Irish hermits, these chronicles also served to connect both English and British history with that of the Church Universal: with Pope Gregory VII, Pope Innocent III, and St. Thomas Becket. Henry II, the most spectacular if not the most romantic of the medieval kings, was blamed for the martyrdom of Becket; but he had done much to discredit the prophecies of Merlin, and a tradition of popular literature in the end connected the names of his sons Richard and John with that of Robin Hood.

In the fifteenth century, chronicles written by monks gave way to those written by laymen, chiefly Londoners, and histories begin to appear in English. It was on these, collected or rewritten by vernacular humanists, that Shakespeare relied for his account of York and Lancaster's long wars, and for the central image of English kingship contained in the two, linked Lancastrian play cycles. These cycles elaborate the lack of civil order and the horrors of an uncertain succession—the nightmare of Englishmen living under the childless Tudors—and the extreme difficulty of correcting either problem. The necessary guilt of the Lancastrian deposition of Richard II is not expunged until the victory of Henry VII or perhaps not even until the birth of Elizabeth at the end of *Henry VIII,* the last and oddest of Shakespeare's history plays. The Tudor achievement was to reunite the heirs of the Plantagenets, rather than to unify England and Wales; although Henry V is on cordial terms with the Welsh soldier Fluellen, Shakespeare is fundamentally an English playwright operating within the frame of English history. *King Lear* is an excursion into a dark, pagan, and singularly non-Arthurian period of the matter of Britain; in *Henry IV, Part 1,* the lords of the Welsh and Scottish marches—Glendower, Percy, and Douglas—appear menacing, outlandish, and slightly absurd as they plot to carve up the English kingdom. Macbeth's Scotland is as dark as Lear's Britain; in emphasizing the role of England in overthrowing the tyrant, Shakespeare seems to identify Malcolm Canmore—as historians still do and as Scottish nationalists still deplore— as the first anglicizing king of Scotland, replacing the more Gaelic Duncans and Macbeths before him. What all this has to do with the Union of the Crowns by James VI and I is for scholars to determine.

Aided by the printing press, English humanists during the reigns of the Tudors set about reorganizing and rendering more available the knowledge that Englishmen possessed of the national and insular pasts—though it may be debated how far they did this in pursuit of a distinct objective and how far as part of a vigorous but unsystematic activity. Chronicles and poems having to do with history of every kind were printed and edited, and the humanist concern with classical purity led to a kind of backlash effect, in which neo-Latin and vernacular literature were studied critically rather than neglected. Something like a corpus of English and British historians began to take shape, although the discovery and editing of new sources—as much an ecclesiastical as a humanist enterprise—were probably at their peak in the two centuries following Shakespeare's lifetime. The histories thus discovered were narratives of the deeds of kings and other notables, with ecclesiastical worthies playing prominent roles; subject to the modifications that this introduced, they could be assimilated to the patterns of classical historiography at least to the point where they were studied for their exemplary value. A Christian king—to say nothing of a saint or a bishop—was a different being from a classical hero; he was imitated for different reasons and with different ideas of what imitation meant, since his deeds were valued for upholding the universe of divine order and grace, rather than the freedom, power, and glory of the city-state. Nevertheless, a body of exemplary literature was created, drawn from the Christian history to which England belonged; of this genre William Baldwin's *Mirror for Magistrates* (1559) has been most studied for its association with the English drama. To some extent, therefore, the medieval chronicler, even though an ecclesiastic and usually a monk, was assimilated to the model of the classical historian; he provided the record of exemplary deeds, which he or his contemporaries had witnessed. He was "the historian," and his works were "the English history"; for the modern man who studied such works to call himself a "historian," or anything he might write a "history," was an ambitious and innovative claim.

The medieval historian had been a cleric in orders and subject to a monastic rule. The modern man who studied him might be a churchman or a layman but was still more commonly a clerk rather than a nobleman or statesman: a member of the clerisy, or literati, a man of letters hoping to make, by his knowledge, a career as courtier, secretary, or poet. For all the classical dignity that robed the historian, something of the servitor clung about the humanist; his problem was to elevate his role to the dignity of the counselor. (The first classical English historian, Edward Hyde, Earl of Clarendon, was a minister to kings but was born just before the death of Shakespeare, none of whose contemporaries supposed that England yet boasted a historian in the antique sense.) The humanists, antiquaries, and others, who were in fact creating history in something like the modern sense of the word, were not historians and did not enjoy the social standing that they associated with the historian of antiquity. To some extent servants, they wrote because they were ambitious. They sometimes wrote on command and, even when they did not, they often wrote to satisfy the literary and ideological demands of the church or state. It was this role that carried the historiography they produced—whether or not it was called history—beyond the production of examples to be imitated.

A central event in the shaping of English historical consciousness had been the Reformation carried out under Henry VIII and Elizabeth I. Crown and parliament, engaged in the repudiation of the papal jurisdiction, had claimed that the realm of England was and ever had been "an empire entire and of itself," in which the crown enjoyed full jurisdiction

over all courts, secular and spiritual. The claim to empire was a claim to sovereignty, not to the possession of colonies; it was a historical claim and had to be substantiated by historical research and argument, conducted partly in the records of the English law. The claim to which it led—that the church in England had always lain outside the jurisdiction of the pope—could not be advanced without encountering Protestant and pre-Protestant arguments to the effect that the pope's supremacy in the church was a usurpation. These arguments in turn compelled discussion of the central question of sacred history, the nature of God's action in the space of time separating Pentecost from Parousia. While English lawyers searched records and chronicles for evidence regarding the independence of royal from papal jurisdiction in the past five to ten centuries, English churchmen went in search of evidence that their earliest bishops had not been subject to the papal obedience; and English ecclesiologists and theologians examined—increasingly in the light of the Protestant claim that salvation came through faith and not through works—the structure of the church itself and the persistence of that structure through time. A canon of English Protestant historiography began to take shape: Bishop John Bale wrote a play about King John in which that monarch appeared as both hero and victim of the struggle for royal independence against papal usurpation.

There might have been a British as well as an English dimension to this argument. A crucial event in English church history was obviously the arrival in Kent in 597 of the Roman missionary Augustine and the subsequent foundation of a bishopric at Canterbury; it was possible to present this as an expedition designed to extend papal control over an already existing and independent Irish, British, and Northumbrian Christianity. The Synod of Whitby in the seventh century, the Norman conquest of England in the eleventh, and Henry II's invasion of Ireland in the twelfth had all been episodes in the extension of papal authority over the British churches; their independence might have been reasserted on a Celtic foundation. As long as Canterbury remained the primatial see of the Church of England, however, it would be hard to present it as the bridgehead of Roman aggression, unless indeed one were disposed (as some were) to undermine the entire structure of episcopacy; and Englishmen were not much inclined to erect their history on Celtic foundations. Partly for such reasons the founder of Anglo-Saxon studies in England, Archbishop Matthew Parker of Canterbury, desired to establish the independence of the English church on early English foundations, to which the legends of British Christianity—the martyrdom of St. Alban or Joseph of Arimathea's bringing the Holy Thorn to Glastonbury—might be annexed if they could be substantiated. (It was in the seventeenth century that the great Anglo-Irish scholar James Ussher, Archbishop of Armagh, set about investigating the antiquity of all the British and Irish churches together.)

The question of the origins of the church in England or in Britain led to the greater question of the form in which it existed in history. The church was the mode by which Christ was present and acted in the time separating his ascension from his return—"I am with you always, even to the end of the world"—but what precisely was the mode of that presence? If Christ was present in the material, social, and historical world, the church was his body; but were the means of his presence themselves bodily or spiritual? Thought on this subject moved between two simple poles: the idea of a visible church, which could exercise authority (and own property) in the social world by means of its own magistrates, who were also the ministers of Christ's presence; and the idea of an invisible church, an association of believers held together by nothing more than Christ's spiritual presence in their hearts and minds. The latter acknowledged no spiritual authority other than Christ himself, and its members were wholly subject to the secular magistrate in the affairs of this world; its ministers were no more than preachers of God's word, the vehicle of his presence in the Spirit. These two ideas of the church underwent many combinations and modifications.

The visible church could have a history, which (thought not immediate to salvation) was part of the general history of mankind's secular affairs and which was governed by many of the same forces. The invisible church could have only a spiritual and mystical history, from which it followed that any historical agencies that had oppressed or corrupted the invisible church were themselves the work of spiritual and mystical evil; history in this sense might be the record of the doings of Satan or the Antichrist. The apocalyptic books of the Bible, especially Revelation, contain powerful imagery depicting the actions of a diabolical power intruding on a mystical city and the ultimate overthrow of this power by angelic and divine agents. These narratives were figurative; it was necessary to decode the symbolism in which they were expressed. A complex body of literature known as typology came into being, in which apocalyptic agents and actions were explained as typifying or representing agents—divine or human—and events in other processes by which men were brought to salvation or damnation. These processes might take place in more than one theater of spiritual experience. The beast with many horns and the breaking of the seven seals might typify events in the salvation or damnation of the individual soul, in the processes by which the church labored to bring souls to salvation, or in the history of the church or of the human race itself. When a dramatic actor appeared in contemporary history, it was legitimate to ask—though dangerous to answer—whether he had been typified and prophesied by one of the actors in the apocalyptic scenario. It was equally legitimate to reply that this typology should be avoided and that Christian worshipers should not claim the gift of prophecy but peaceably seek salvation in the order imposed by the Christian prince.

A Protestant church, such as the Church of England rapidly if incompletely became, committed to the doctrines of salvation through faith alone and the priesthood of all true believers, must be strongly drawn toward seeing itself as an invisible church and toward seeing history as a series of diabolic usurpations from which the true church was to be freed by an apocalyptic intervention that had been typologically prophesied. In Shakespeare's England it was widely declared that the pope was the Antichrist or one of his agents; there were many means of reading history as the record of this spiritual usurpation and of interpreting the future as the history of the promised liberation. At this point the vernacular history of the English nation entered—as the history of classical antiquity could hardly do—into the field of sacred history and became one with it. The members of the invisible church were the subjects of the secular prince, and they might see his jurisdiction, exercised throughout history, as their bulwark against the agents of the Romish Antichrist who pressed false claims to authority over a falsely visible church. The prince and his secular jurisdiction now took on a sacred character, as leading agencies in the defense of the true church, which must end in its prophesied triumph. The English kings, even such unedifying figures as King John, now became the captains and judges of the mystical Israel; as the kings of the House of David had prepared the way for Christ's incarnation, so they might prepare the way for his return at the end of days; the past and future of England could be read in this prophetic light. There is little evidence that Shakespeare thought in this way, unless typological elements can be found in Cranmer's prophecy over the infant Elizabeth at the end of *Henry VIII*; yet he lived in an England where in every parish church were increasingly to be found copies of the Bible in English and of John Foxe's *Acts and Monuments . . . ,* which became known as the "Book of Martyrs," the most famous of all the works in which the history of the English church and monarchy is apocalyptically presented. The belief of some Englishmen that their national history and their own actions in it possessed prophetic significance was to prove profoundly important in the civil wars and the Puritan revolution.

Yet the belief that England had been chosen by God to act as a second Israel—that God, as Milton was to put it, "revealed himself as his manner was, first to his Englishmen"—left unsolved the problem of the universal church. There were always those, laity as well as clergy, who wanted the Church of England to be a visible church and the crown, as its head, to be part of it, intimately connected but not quite identical with the secular political order; these had to insist that the church founded by Christ had been a visible church, of whose history that of England and the English church could have been only a limited part. The church headed by Rome might be corrupt and reformation might have been necessary, but Rome need not be considered a false church created by diabolic agency. Some thinkers of this persuasion went so far as to deny that the pope was the Antichrist and to consider his usurpation of authority as a mere incident in secular history. To the horror of many, this implied that at some point in secular time a reunion with Rome might become practically possible and spiritually desirable. At the date of Shakespeare's death, the debate between these opposed views of the Roman and English churches and their place in history was becoming furious and bitter.

A visible church must be so far involved in the affairs of this world that its workings might contain many things not in themselves necessary to salvation. Some Puritans wished to cast such things out of the church, others to sanctify them until they became part of the work of redemption. To those who were not Puritans, the church contained much that was not necessary to salvation but was necessary to good order and discipline; the church must legislate for itself in respect of such elements, which might include matters of authority, worship, and ceremony, as well as matters arising from the church's involvement in society. The secular prince, as head of all jurisdiction both spiritual and secular, must be the chief agent in such legislation and regulation; a great deal, in both church and society, was seemingly contingent on the accidents of time and was subject to regulation, reformation, and change by the secular government acting in time. The doctrine of "things indifferent" thus proved a powerful stimulant to a sense of history. There was a debate, leading to research, over what elements in the church's structure belonged in this category: were bishops, for example, spiritual officers designated by God at the church's foundation, or were they officers appointed by human congregations within the divinely founded church? There arose energetic inquiry into the history of the primitive church, and energetic controversy over the importance of history itself. To the Puritan view that the church must acknowledge no authority not contained in God's Word, Richard Hooker replied, in *Of the Laws of Ecclesiastical Polity,* that the church had been appointed to pursue its mission in social and historic time and was entitled to use all the resources of natural law, tradition, and legislative authority to do so.

Anglican thinking thus brought added emphasis to the idea that both church and society were creatures of time, to be acted upon by human authority in time; this emphasis helped to stimulate a development in late Tudor historical thought so important that it has been named the "historical revolution": that is, the increasing volume of study of the past monuments, laws, and languages of society. We have seen how the humanist concern to recover the language of classical antiquity led paradoxically to the study of philology, of language changing over time, of nonclassical Latin, and even of vernacular and barbaric speech and literature. The humanist ideal of counsel further reinforced these studies; the more the humanist knew about the realm and its antiquities, including the antiquities of its spiritual and secular government, the better qualified he was to bring advice to his prince, whether in learning, in court, or in parliament. By the end of the sixteenth century, scholars had created something like a new discipline of the mind, known as antiquarian learning because it was an inquiry into the antiquities of England and Britain. It could take a geographical form, in which the scholar traversed a countryside or cityscape, describing the antiquities that kept the past alive in the present, or an institutional form, in which he described the ancient—and, by comparison, the modern—structure of such great governing realities as the church or the law. William Lambarde wrote both a *Perambulation of Kent* and a series of works—*Archeion, Archaionomia, Eirenarcha*—in which he set forth the ancient laws of the Anglo-Saxons and the modern duties of a justice of the peace. (A copy of *Archaionomia* in the Folger Library bears the signature of "William Shakespeare," who may or may not have been the poet.)

Antiquarian learning is of significance in two ways. One is political: the antiquity of English laws, customs, institutions, and culture could be used to affirm the autonomy of the imperial realm against the universal authority of Rome, and also—with increasing vigor in the reign of James I—to affirm the autonomy of the king's law, his courts, and his parliaments against his authority otherwise exercised. Shakespeare seems to have remained untouched by the growing cult of "the ancient constitution"; his King John is humiliated by papal legates and poisoned by a monk, but he never meets his barons at Runnymede to set his seal to Magna Carta. By the year of Shakespeare's death, however, Runnymede was beginning to seem the central episode of John's troublesome reign. The antiquity of English law was being debated with animation in the House of Commons; the great lawyers Edward Coke and John Selden were at work; and King James's attempt to merge England and Scotland in one kingdom had led to much study of the legal history of both kingdoms, to be frustrated at last by the ancient slogan of the English barons, "Nolumus leges Angliae mutari" (We will not change the laws of England). The antiquity of the law and the invisibility of the church were to become revolutionary issues. A discontented humanist might well turn from the frustrations of offering advice at court to the more relaxed study of antiquities for the use of the precedent-hunting gentlemen of the country, though historians will warn us that this is to simplify the complexities of Jacobean political behavior (and Shakespeare was not that kind of political animal).

In the second place, antiquarian learning is of significance in the history of historiography. Though generated by the impact of humanism upon English culture, it was sharply at variance with the classical historiography studied and imitated by the humanists. It was not primarily the study of morally or politically exemplary actions but of laws, institutions, languages, and monuments, out of which it sought to reconstruct the detail of a past state of human society, whether or not this had been edifying, whether or not—it might possibly be added—this were of any immediate practical relevance. The past might be studied for its own sake, and what was being studied was, in any event, the past. Here is "the historical revolution," the replacement of rhetoric by archaeology. This kind of history was becoming divorced from poetry and need not fear its competition; curiosity and criticism were its watchwords. But was it history? For at least 200 years the "historical revolution" remained incomplete, for the reason that historiography in the classical and humanist sense survived almost unmodified by the new modes of study. William Camden, the greatest of the Jacobean antiquaries, founded the professorship of history at Oxford that still bears his name; but it never occurred to him that antiquities should be taught in a university, and he made his professor responsible for expounding epitomes of Roman history to undergraduates at the outset of their studies. There was no link yet between moral instruction and critical research. Even in the age of Hume and Gibbon, two centuries later, the deeds of rulers and the events of their reigns were retold in the patterns of classical narrative; the historical conditions under which these deeds and events had been acted and suffered were analyzed in digressions and discourses alternating with the narrative.

The sense of history in Shakespeare's England—with which we must link the ability to write history—was immensely diverse and vital, and it was growing and changing rapidly. It was neither classical nor modern, and we must ask whether the directions in which it was growing did not point away from the theater: away from poetry and toward prose, away from rhetoric and toward criticism, away from the court and toward parliament and the printing press. If history was moving away from its immediate relevance to the drama, this may be yet another reason why Shakespeare raised the English stage to heights that it found such difficulty in sustaining.

BIBLIOGRAPHY

Arthur B. Ferguson, *The Articulate Citizen and the English Renaissance* (1965) and *Clio Unbound: Perception of the Social and Cultural Past in Renaissance England* (1979). Levi Fox, ed., *English Historical Scholarship in the Sixteenth and Seventeenth Centuries* (1956). Frank Smith Fussner, *The Historical Revolution: English Historical Writing and Thought, 1580–1640* (1962). William Haller, *Foxe's Book of Martyrs and the Elect Nation* (1963). Denys Hay, *Polydore Vergil: Renaissance Historian and Man of Letters* (1952). Thomas D. Kendrick, *British Antiquity* (1950). Fred Jacob Levy, *Tudor Historical Thought* (1967). Arthur H. Williamson, *Scottish National Consciousness in the Age of James VI* (1979).

The Literate Culture
of Shakespeare's Audience

S. K. HENINGER, JR.

In August 1564—the sixth year of her reign, and incidentally the year of Shakespeare's birth—Queen Elizabeth set out on one of her stately progresses. It was a carefully orchestrated display of majesty, involving a large retinue of important personages. Her destination was Cambridge, and everyone at the university fell into a frenzy of preparation. There were posters and pageants to welcome her and a full program of speeches and plays to impress her with the gravity of the assembled scholars. The central feature of the entertainment was a series of disputations in the traditional disciplines of logic, rhetoric, medicine, divinity, and law, because this occasion, like most public occasions of the time, was seen essentially as a literary event. The most learned doctors of the university disputed pro and con on questions announced in advance. And after listening to three days of such contrived debate, the queen was expected to respond in kind. She more than rose to the occasion. In a wondrously skillful speech (in Latin, of course), she thanked her hosts and pointedly reminded them of the age-old interdependence of politics and language. "I would have all of you bear this one thing in mind," the youthful queen declared with a glance toward her ministers, "that no road is straighter, none shorter, none more adapted to win the good things of fortune or the good-will of your Prince, than the pursuit of Good Letters" (quoted in Bromley Smith).

The success of individual endeavor, says Elizabeth, derives directly from mastery of the language arts. The good things of fortune are won by pursuit of "good letters." And she goes on to score a political point: literacy also prepares a man to serve his monarch and, more generally, makes him better fit for service to the commonweal. Those who eventually secured Elizabeth's favor evidently shared her view. As J. H. Hexter observes, noting the change in cultural patterns for the Tudor aristocracy, "Among the great crown servants who surround Elizabeth—the Cecils, the Bacons, Walsingham, Smith, Coke, Hatton, Sydney—there is scarcely one without a university education." All were adepts in the arts of discourse, which formed the core curriculum at each stage of instruction from elementary school through the master of arts. And her most politic ministers kept a watchful eye on the teaching of what it took to get ahead. Among her intimate counselors, Sir William Cecil became chancellor of Cambridge in 1559 and the earl of Leicester assumed the chancellorship of Oxford in 1564. Both men accepted these responsibilities with the utmost seriousness and actively filled these more than honorific posts. Their involvement with the universities sent a clear message across the realm: the road to advancement in an increasingly centralized and urbanized society was paved by literacy. Shakespeare's audience had been reared in a literate culture, a culture in which the use of language was assigned a place of prime importance. All social institutions—not only government and commerce but also education, religion, learning, and the fine arts—were conditioned by this fact.

What we hear in Elizabeth's speech are the not so faint echoes of a civic humanism that many see as the hallmark of that historically elusive period known as the Renaissance. Grounded in biblical study and later in ancient philosophy, civic humanism emphasized the central position of man in the providential scheme. According to the accepted account of human history, after the expulsion of Satan and the other rebellious angels from heaven, God created man to take their place; and though Adam and Eve also fell, tempted to disobedience by the malicious serpent, that momentous event was the necessary prelude to the coming of Christ on earth. In order to understand this divine plan of sinfulness and salvation, and in order to comply with it, man had been endowed with a unique faculty known as reason. So civic humanism fostered a radical respect for the dignity of man as a rational being. Made in the image of God and enjoying a special status as the favorite of his creatures, humans most nearly approach the realization of their godlike potential through the exercise of reason. It naturally follows that man, blessed with this faculty which aligns him with the angels, has the responsibility of implementing the providential scheme by inducing in this world a political system that fulfills the religious vision of peace on earth, of universal order. With this charge, rational man sets about the mundane business of managing his day-to-day existence.

At first glance, civic humanism may appear to have been a secular movement. Eventually it released man from the constraints of a degenerate clergy and encouraged him to pursue a gratifying life in the here and now. It led to the separation of church and state, much to the detriment of the former's authority. In time the theological implications of an ordered society sloughed off as the power-greedy and money-hungry seized the opportunity to defy the weakening church, and the net effect of civic humanism was antireligious. But that result, which defines the modern era, was a later and unexpected consequence of a movement that had its origins in a biblical view of man who, to use Milton's words as he describes Adam and Eve in the Garden of Eden, is "godlike erect, with native honor clad" (*Paradise Lost,* IV. 289).

In order to further God's kingdom on earth and thereby to comply with the unfolding providential plan, the humanists enjoined an enlightened citizenry to devise workable social institutions. To that end, they reforged the old links between politics and poetry. Language as preaching had long been used in the service of religion; now it was developed as public oratory and diverted to the cause of government. Heeding the lessons of history, the humanists recognized that power could be established as well as overthrown by the clever deployment of language, so their movement is characterized—some would argue, propelled—by the study of literature. In particular, the literature that survived from the classical world was seen as an unappreciated source of profitable information about the human condition. The extant writings from ancient Greece and Rome, the humanists proposed, serve as records of a pristine culture when human achievement, girded by intellectual vigor and moral probity, was at its highest.

As a cultural force, civic humanism first appeared tentatively in Padua late in the thirteenth century and then more forcefully in Florence, where it rapidly matured as a philosophy for political organization. Determined social engineers such as Coluccio Salutati and Leonardo Bruni revised the educational system in order to emphasize what came to be known as the *literae humaniores,* the texts of the classical world, now read with a new reverence. Elizabeth's phrase "good letters"—in Latin, *literae bonae*—was a common epithet for this canon of ancient writings. In the affluent society of the Italian cities a dedicated cadre of scholars rapidly augmented the libraries of wealthy patrons by fresh discoveries of previously ignored manuscripts, which they edited with meticulous attention to philological details and interpreted with passionate intensity. By 1500 the discipline of historical and textual criticism had been firmly established, in large part by the scrupulous scholarship of Lorenzo Valla and Angelo Poliziano; and authoritative texts overseen by knowledgeable scholar-printers such as Aldus Manutius in Venice, Joannes Froben in Basel, and Henri Estienne in Paris were rolling from the presses.

By this time in the universities of Italy the *umanista,* the professional teacher of the *studia humanitatis,* had arrived on the scene. This course of study professing the Roman ideal of *humanitas,* or that which represents the human condition in its civilized state, comprised a collage of materials from the disciplines of history, poetry, and moral philosophy, which were held together in large part by their dependence upon linguistic ingenuity. In practice, the *studia humanitatis* consisted of the relentless analysis of these texts according to the verbal arts of grammar and rhetoric. The enthusiasm for such exercises reached so high a pitch that the *literae humaniores* became the substance of the curriculum at every level of education, and comprehension of literary works became its raison d'être. As Craig Thompson concludes with specific reference to the grammar schools of Tudor England, "Renaissance theory and practice of education were predominantly and complacently linguistic" (*Schools in Tudor England*).

In the burgeoning culture of the Renaissance there was no irresolvable conflict between the classical texts and Christianity. The saintly Schoolmen of previous centuries had read Seneca and Cato—and hadn't Aristotle written the *Nicomachean Ethics,* as sententious a treatise as anyone could wish? The church had long ago co-opted Vergil by dint of his messianic fourth eclogue, and even Ovid could be moralized. Cicero himself, the very model of civic humanism, was known in a not unrecognizable form in Macrobius' extensive commentary on the *Somnium Scipionis (The Dream of Scipio),* and St. Ambrose had adapted Cicero's *De officiis (On Duties)* for the use of medieval clerics. The smoothness with which the Renaissance emerged from the Middle Ages is illustrated by Brunetto Latini, the mentor whom Dante acknowledges with such affection. In his pious encyclopedia, *Li livres dou trésor,* Latini quotes Cicero on the very topic that became the prime justification for civic humanism: "Tully says that the highest science of governing the city is rhetoric—that is, the science of speech. For if there were no speech, neither cities, justice, nor human society would be established. It was for these things that speech was given to all men" (III. i. 2). As Latini indicates, medieval piety easily accorded with Renaissance polity.

Actually, throughout the Middle Ages the curriculum had been determined by the trivium, the verbal disciplines of grammar, rhetoric, and logic. The trivium had persisted from the classical world intact and had made the study of language the basis of education, although this education was directed toward morals and religion. In the new curriculum of the humanists the trivium still prevailed, and the texts were still directed toward an ethical end. The principles of pedagogy, though, were now governed by politics rather than prescribed by the Holy Scriptures. The aim of education was not so much to purify the soul for entrance into the kingdom of heaven as to prepare the mind for effective participation in God's kingdom on earth. Education was a matter of public morality, but it did not

conflict with the private virtues of the Christian religion. The arts of language, in fact, provided the means whereby private meditation could be turned most readily into public event. And what better models to follow than the classical authors, such as Demosthenes and Cicero, whom the church fathers themselves had admired and imitated?

In a society that depreciates contemplative isolation in preference for active involvement, the arts of discourse play a heightened role. Language is privileged in such a culture because it provides the means whereby man communicates with his fellow men—whereby he informs them, sways them, pleases them, controls them. Whatever must be done to achieve success in human affairs is most efficiently accomplished by language, which is at once the most concise and the most readily adaptable of semiotic systems. Humanists exploited the verbal disciplines as they had developed in the trivium during the Middle Ages and eagerly recovered the linguistic theory of the classical world. Civic humanism may be viewed, in fact, as largely a literary movement, a growing respect for and manipulation of verbal systems. And the invention of movable type was an intensifying event in this movement, one that made books more numerous and more familiar, and thereby enhanced the literariness of the culture. Marshall McLuhan has written exuberantly of the changes brought about by the introduction of the printing press, though his arguments should be revised in light of the more sober investigations of Elizabeth L. Eisenstein. In any case, as Louis B. Wright and H. S. Bennett have amply demonstrated, there were books in sixteenth-century England for every interest and taste. Certainly by Shakespeare's day a broad-based clientele supported a thriving book trade.

Many sources had fed this civic humanism of the Renaissance—some remote, others more immediate. One strong influence, both directly and indirectly, was St. Augustine, whose *De doctrina Christiana (On Christian Teaching)* had been for centuries the authoritative handbook for a decidedly Christian rhetoric. It set forth the principles for interpreting the Holy Scriptures as well as the rules for explaining them to a largely illiterate laity. The humanists read Augustine's *De civitate Dei (On the City of God)* with even graver attention, fascinated by his submission to a transcendent deity as well as by his clarity and practicality. They studied Augustine to make sure that their earthly cities remained godly, avoiding the twin pitfalls of self-love and self-indulgence.

In several well-known passages, Augustine had professed a quite definite theory of language, and his views underlay much of the semiotic theory of the Renaissance. Augustine, like most of the classical philosophers whom the Middle Ages accepted, believed that there is an objective order of being prior to the subjective order of knowing; that is, in Augustine's terms, God exists as an absolute being prior to, and independent of, man, the cognizant subject, and God is a necessary condition for our knowing anything. He is the ultimate source of any fact, and its truth can be tested only by referral back to him. Furthermore, Augustine assumed, to provide a basis for human knowledge God had revealed himself in the Holy Scriptures. This text, the word of God, translates the absolute being of the Deity into a verbal system at the level of human comprehension. It is notable that God chose to manifest himself to the degree he has in a literary medium. Of course, human language is inadequate to represent the Deity, who is actually ineffable. The Holy Scriptures, the *significans,* are not identical with the attributes of God himself, the *significata.* The Holy Scriptures at best are but a partial revelation of the divine will. Nonetheless, they are indisputably valid and by means of a verbal text reveal as much of God's intention as is allowable to mortals.

In addition, as mediation between himself and his human creatures, God had sent his son incarnated as the Word. Again the discontinuous levels of the divine and the mortal, of absolute being and cognizant subject, are bound together by a literary medium. So Augustine devised a primarily verbal theory of knowledge: what we can know rests in God as he has revealed himself in the Holy Scriptures, his written word, and in Christ, his word incarnate. Augustine believed that language, although a sense experience for the human ear, can accurately convey a prior and nonsensible entity. Although words are received as sense experience, their more significant element is comprehended as impalpable concept by the human mind. This is the basis for Augustine's Christian rhetoric, which the preacher uses to lead his charges toward an understanding of God.

Plato, "divine" Plato, as he came to be commonly called, also contributed heavily to civic humanism in the Renaissance. His dialogues were read as near-sacred texts, and the humanists soon appropriated those parts of his doctrine that the early church fathers had not assimilated. They completed the process of Christianizing Plato. In the *De civitate Dei,* had not Augustine, that most redoubtable church father, included a chapter to demonstrate that Platonism, of all the ancient philosophies, was the closest to Christianity? The dialogue especially valuable to the humanists, though, was Plato's *Republic,* his critique of existing social institutions by way of setting forth the ideal commonwealth. The Renaissance spawned a series of imitations—some caustic, some wistful—that constitute a distinct literary genre, the best-known example being Sir Thomas More's *Utopia.* No philosopher has ever interrelated politics and poetry more closely than does Plato; and while we may wince at his banishment of poets and his proposal for censorship, his arguments are difficult to counter. For Plato, as Renaissance humanists were well aware, only the *literae bonae* are to be tolerated in a just society, and even they must be cautiously monitored to prevent any noxious effect upon the young. Both the early humanist and the later Puritan could read the *Republic,* as they could read the *De civitate Dei,* with approval.

Plato expressed his views on the nature of language most succinctly in the *Cratylus,* an indecisive document which proposes several different theories of how words fulfill their significative function. Cratylus argues that words bear a natural and spontaneous relationship to the things they designate; signifier and signified are directly bonded. In opposition, Hermogenes counters that language is a set of arbitrary conventions established by common usage; there is no inviolable relationship between signifier and signified. Socrates in a fruitless effort to reconcile the disputants offers a sophisticated theory that words are a mimetic representation of the things they nominate; the signifier stands for the signified in some paraphrastic way. Each of these possibilities is proposed and defended but eventually demolished, so the dialogue ends with the validity of language very much in question. Nonetheless, the *Cratylus* underlay most discussions of linguistic theory throughout the Middle Ages and Renaissance, at least as an archaeological substratum.

Plato also gave a pointed critique of language—especially as employed by rhetors, poets, and philosophers—in the *Phaedrus,* a favorite dialogue in the Renaissance because of its discourse on love and beauty. The *Phaedrus* again calls into question the reliability of language, though in this instance Plato is concerned about the abuses that language is susceptible to when unscrupulous verbalizers seek to mislead a gullible public. But as the Renaissance read Plato—that is, a Christianized Plato—language was a trustworthy instrument of instruction because it dependably conveys a prior order of being. As Socrates professes in the *Cratylus,* "Things have some fixed reality of their own, not in relation to us nor caused by us; they do not vary, swaying one way and another in accordance with our fancy, but exist of themselves in relation to their own reality imposed by nature" (386D–E). Since the essence of the thing precedes the name, it must be the determinant of that name. It was easy to interpret this passage in a religious context, as Augustine had done, and to identify God as the prior order of being that makes linguistic meaning not only possible but mandatory. Language is the direct expression of a divinely ordained scheme. As the repetition at the human level of the divine act of creation, the use of language carries something of the sacred authority.

Despite the prominence of Augustine and Plato, the most potent influence upon civic humanism was Marcus Tullius Cicero, the much admired "Tully" of the Elizabethans. It was his concept of *humanitas,* the distinctive quality that sets man above the other orders of nature, that gave humanism its name, and his program of education proposing the *studia humanitatis* led to the notion of a university in the modern sense. From the time that Petrarch extolled Cicero as his mentor and model, this ancient jurist was approvingly cited as the noblest Roman of them all. He garnered this highest praise by virtue of having advocated the active, civic life over the contemplative, secluded life, a change in orientation that we have seen, perhaps somewhat simplistically, as characterizing the Renaissance. Queen Elizabeth in her speech at Cambridge may well have had in mind one of Cicero's most prescriptive statements: "The man who equips himself with the weapons of eloquence . . . he, I think, will be a citizen most helpful and most devoted both to his own interests and those of his community" (*De inventione,* I. i).

Being a rhetor himself and having gained his fame by skill in oratory, Cicero amply demonstrated that success in the active life depends almost exclusively upon mastery of the verbal arts—in Cicero's terms, mastery of the *ars dicendi,* the art of speaking well, and of *eloquentia,* the ability to use language eloquently in the cause of persuading an audience. Through Augustine's *De doctrina Christiana,* Cicero's influence had persisted throughout the Middle Ages and into the Renaissance, at least in a Christianized version; in fact, Cicero had established the topics of rhetoric during that long period when rhetoric flourished as an indispensable component of the trivium. But now his treatises *De inventione (On Invention)* and *De oratore (On the Orator)* were themselves recovered and studied with an unaccustomed willingness to accept verbatim the precepts of this ancient authority. Ciceronianism, both as a literary style and as an attitude toward society, dominated the schools.

For Cicero, as for Plato, politics is inextricably linked to the language arts—though for the Roman the two are even more closely intertwined than for his Grecian forebear. According to Plato, literature is a formative influence upon the immature and consequently a volatile factor in public opinion. It must therefore be controlled to protect the stability of the commonwealth. One aim of society is to produce only beneficial literature. For Cicero, however, the arts of discourse, including poetry, are the actual substance of politics. Language is the very basis of civilization, and the products of language are the means, as well as the ends, of society. According to Cicero, it is by exercise of his linguistic ability that man has risen above the beasts in the hierarchy of nature, and all of man's achievements may be attributed directly to his facility with words.

This assumption underlies and conditions most of Cicero's thinking, and it frequently surfaces. Even in his most youthful work, the treatise *De inventione,* Cicero sets forth the proposition that it was the framing of language that allowed men to leave behind the wild state of nature, in which physical strength prevails, and to consort together in peaceful communities in which *humanitas* thrives. Cicero is looking for the origin of *eloquentia,* the purposeful use of language, and he expatiates upon its honorable derivation from the human faculty of reason:

There was a time when men wandered at large in the fields like animals and lived on wild fare; they did nothing by the guidance of reason, but relied chiefly on physical strength; there was as yet no ordered system of religious worship nor of social duties; no one had seen legitimate marriage nor had anyone looked upon children whom he knew to be his own; nor had they learned the advantages of an equitable code of law. And so through their ignorance and error, blind and unreasoning passion satisfied itself by misuse of bodily strength, which is a very dangerous servant.

Fortunately for human history, at this point a euhemeristic hero, beyond identification, appeared on the scene:

> At this juncture a man—great and wise I am sure—became aware of the power latent in man and the wide field offered by his mind for great achievements if one could develop this power and improve it by instruction. Men were scattered in the fields and hidden in sylvan retreats when he assembled and gathered them in accordance with a plan; he introduced them to every useful and honourable occupation, though they cried out against it at first because of its novelty, and then when through reason and eloquence they had listened with greater attention, he transformed them from wild savages into a kind and gentle folk.
>
> (I. ii)

Cicero concludes this partisan account of how language originated with a disarming rhetorical flourish:

> To me, at least, it does not seem possible that a mute and voiceless wisdom could have turned men suddenly from their habits and introduced them to different patterns of life.

Language, Cicero insists, is essential to human society.

In the comprehensive treatise *De oratore,* a later and more mature work, Cicero is still praising *eloquentia* in much the same terms. "What other power could have been strong enough," he asks rhetorically, "either to gather scattered humanity into one place, or to lead it out of its brutish existence in the wilderness up to our present condition of civilization as men and as citizens, or, after the establishment of social communities, to give shape to laws, tribunals, and civic rights?" (I. viii. 33). Renaissance humanists never tired of repeating this Ciceronian sentiment, and the Elizabethans inherited this conviction that language has been the necessary and sufficient cause of civilization. William Webbe, for example, in *A Discourse of English Poetrie* (1586), opines, "Men were first withdrawne from a wylde and savadge kinde of life to civillity and gentlenes and the right knowledge of humanity by the force of this measurable or tunable speaking" (G. Gregory Smith, I).

George Puttenham, another English humanist, says much the same thing in *The Arte of English Poesie* (1589; G. Gregory Smith, II). In an early chapter entitled "How Poets Were the First Priests, the First Prophets, the First Legislators and Polititians in the World," Puttenham explains:

> The profession and use of Poesie is most ancient from the beginning, and not, as manie erroniously suppose, after, but before, any civil society was among men. For it is written that Poesie was th'originall cause and occasion of their first assemblies, when before the people remained in the woods and mountains, vagarant and dispersed like the wild beasts, lawlesse and naked.

According to this tradition, poets were necessarily "the first legislators and polititians in the world" because the artful use of language is a precondition of "civil society." As Philip Sidney says in *The Defence of Poesie* (1595; G. Gregory Smith, I), "Poetry . . . hath been the first light-giver to ignorance, and first Nurse, whose milk by little and little enabled them to feed afterwards of tougher knowledges." Civic humanism is predicated upon a literate culture, the study of Good Letters, as Queen Elizabeth urged.

The premises of civic humanism, especially as it derived from Cicero, are now evident. *Humanitas* is the standard of human behavior in a civilized nation, a standard that each citizen is enjoined to achieve. And the salient feature of *humanitas,* what most neatly and definitely sets man apart from the other animals, is language, his ability to use words as a means of communicating thoughts. "What in hours of ease can be a pleasanter thing or one more characteristic of *humanitas* than discourse that is graceful and well-informed?" Cicero asks in *De oratore.* And without staying for the obvious answer, he continues his advocacy of the language arts: "For the one point in which we have our very greatest advantage over the brute creation is that we hold converse one with another, and can reproduce our thought in word" (I. viii. 32). Literature is seen as the identifying feature of mankind, our central activity, our preoccupation. And literary works, what the Renaissance called the *literae humaniores* or *literae bonae,* provide the substance of education. The young must read the literary classics in order to learn what being human, what *humanitas,* entails; by reading, they are educated about what is important in life and are assimilated into society.

In the humanistic tradition inherited by Shakespeare's audience, speech and reason are interdependent. In the punning formulation that Latin allows and that Philip Sidney repeats, *oratio* is next to *ratio.* Speech is the utterance of reason. As Sidney says later in *The Defence of Poesie,* "The end of speech . . . [is] for the uttering sweetly and properly the conceits of the minde." Language is the means by which we make our reason manifest.

Cicero states this point most forcefully in his treatise *De officiis,* a noble program for transposing private virtue into public good. During the Renaissance this text was taken as the most thorough manual of morality to have come down from the ancient world, and it was sternly placed in the hands of every schoolboy. By 1553, Nicholas Grimald had translated Cicero's *Duties* into English, and by the end of the century this translation had gone through no less than eight editions. In his prefatory epistle to the reader, Grimald encouragingly notes that Cicero's text contains "the holle trade, how to live among men dyscreetly, and honestly: and so rightlye pointing out the pathway to all vertue: as none can bee righter, onely Scripture excepted" (3rd ed., 1558). The passage of greatest relevance to our argument, however, occurs rather early in Book I, where Cicero inquires into "what bee natures principles of neiborhod, and the felowship of man." As usual, he is thinking in a cultural context, in this instance looking for the basis of human society. The passage continues, "The bond whereof is reason [*ratio*], and speache [*oratio*], which by teachinge, learning, conferring, reasoning, and judging, winneth one man to an other, & joineth them in a certaine naturall felowship." Cicero goes on to reiterate the familiar distinction between man and beast on the basis of *ratio et oratio.* Brutes do not enjoy the fruits of rational discourse: "We never say, they have justice, equitie, and goodnesse," he observes, "for they bee voide of reason, and of speeche." The Roman teacher Quintilian, perhaps the most popular rhetorician during the Renaissance, follows Cicero in this sentiment and confirms it: "But reason could neither profit us so much, nor manifest itself so plainly within us, if we could not express by speech what we have conceived in our minds, a faculty which we see wanting in other animals" (*Institutio oratoria,* II. xvi. 15).

So language provides the means by which we express our reason, else a great prince in prison lies. But speech is reciprocally dependent upon the rational faculty. Many, especially those with a religious cast of mind, saw reason as a necessary precondition for human speech, and they readily identified reason with the divine spark that God breathed into man at the moment of his creation. Reason is a reminiscence of godly powers, an inner light, and therefore the faculty that links man with his maker. Since this divine afflatus, "right" reason, entered via the mouth, it is appropriately manifested through the mouth, through vocal utterance.

Not surprisingly, a seconding authority for the elevated position of language-mastering man was sought in the hexaemeron, where Adam assumes his lordship over creation by virtue of his ability to name things. A definite theory of language had emerged in the Judeo-Christian tradition, in which it occupies a place of considerable prominence. In Genesis, the initial act of Adam is to assign names to his fellow creatures (2:19–20), thereby distinguishing them one from another and endowing each with its appropriate identity. In his *Hyve Full of Hunnye* (1578), William Hunnis paraphrases the biblical text in standard fourteeners:

> And God did bringe all beastes and foules,
>   to view of Adams Eye,
> Which was to see, what kynde of name,
>   he then would call them by.
> And Adam called every Beast,
>   and every Fowle by name,
> As wee do use at this same day,
>   to nominate the same.

This act of naming extended eventually to all items in the universe, from the highest to the lowest, and it paralleled at the human level the divine act of creation that had produced our world. Adam creates a verbal universe that renders knowable (and therefore discussable) the fullness of the cosmos, which before creation had existed solely in the mind of God.

Our universe, in fact, can be conceived as a vast system of words, the names of things, translating into language what God had in mind when he created it. Hence, our world becomes a great book of nature, paralleling the Holy Scriptures and carrying a comparable authority. The Augustinian assertion that sensory data, aural or visual, lead to a knowledge of prior and nonsensible realities was confirmed by the scriptural doctrine that God can be known through his creation. "The heavens declare the glory of God," sings the Psalmist, "and the firmament sheweth His handywork." So nature becomes a vast verbal system wherein we might learn as much about God as mortals are permitted, and Adam's first chore consisted, as it were, of publishing this text. Since Adam is our first parent, the prototype of mankind, his ability to name things was attributed to the divine spark of right reason that God had breathed into him, the gift that set him above the lower orders of nature. Speech is again the product of reason, divinely bestowed.

When Adam assigned names to the things he perceived with his senses, he of course did not act capriciously or arbitrarily. According to Pierre de La Primaudaye, author of *The Second Part of the French Academie* (1594), as translated by Thomas Bowes, "If hee had not named them as he should, hee had brought in great confusion in nature." Adam was bound to accord with the innate qualities of each item as God had created it. In this tradition, as Cratylus had argued in the Platonic dialogue that bears his name, there is an inviolable relationship between words and what they designate. Language, in fact, is at basis a system of hieroglyphs, to borrow a term from the Egyptians; words make knowable the divinely decreed, though otherwise ineffable, nature of the things they signify.

Richard Mulcaster, for a long while headmaster of the Merchant Taylors' School in London, gave an authoritative nod of assent in the direction of this theory. In *The First Part of the Elementarie* (1582), which sets forth his pedagogical principles, Mulcaster declares:

> We nede not to prove by *Platoes Cratylus . . .* that words be voluntarie [i.e., express volition], and appointed upon cause, seing we have better warrant. For even God himself, who brought the creatures, which he had made, unto that first man, whom he had also made, that he might name them, according to their properties, doth planelie declare by his so doing, what a cunning thing it is to give right names, and how necessarie it is, to know their forces, which be allredie given, bycause the word being knowen, which implyeth the propertie the thing is half known, whose propertie is emplyed.

> (chapter 24)

So in this biblical tradition, language reveals the intrinsic nature of the universe. Language also gives the scholar control over those things that comprise nature because the relationship between signifier and signified is reversible. Not only does the signified control the signifier, but the word calls forth its nominee as an immediate presence. On this account, Mulcaster assigned special credence to the language arts and emphasized their teaching. They provide basic and practical skills. Witness Dr. Faustus. This religious scholar resorted to his books in search of the magic formula for controlling nature, an approvable practice; but it was the abuse of the power of words that ultimately led to his damnation. Thwarted in legitimate pursuits, he chose to summon satanic powers by uttering the name of Mephistopheles.

The potency of language in human affairs was given additional impetus by the tradition that expounded Christ as *logos*, usually translated as "the Word"—or, perhaps, Christ was perceived as the Word because of the potency ascribed to language. In any case, the motif of Christ as *logos* was a commonplace, as we have seen with Augustine, implying that Christ as the Word was God's perfect revelation of himself to man. This tradition drew its greatest sustenance, of course, from the opening of the gospel according to St. John: "In the beginning was the Word, and the Word was with God, and the Word was God. The same was in the beginning with God. All things were made by him; and without him was not any thing made that was made." From this text we conclude that language expresses the effective will of God, implies the commandments of creation, and partakes in the Trinity—all beliefs that Augustine had promulgated from his cathedral position. In this tradition, vigorously iterated by the Protestants, language performs a unique and essential function: it serves as the sacred instrument of God's intention.

This view of language is confirmed in the opening chapters of Genesis, where God proceeds through the days of creation by issuing verbal commands, such as "Let there be light." And these powers of the divine word carry over in at least some degree to human speech. Admittedly, man is a fallen creature, and his reason is seriously impaired. Nonetheless, his facility with language is by no means totally obliterated. Indeed, La Primaudaye writes poignantly about the "great providence of God, which appeareth in the framing of the voyce and speach of man, and in the nature and use thereof." Speech, the expression of God-given reason, is the clearest evidence that God has not forsaken his erring creature. Man is still made in the image of the Deity; though fallen, if he cultivates his linguistic competence, he may regain a large measure of the paradise lost.

Especially those entrusted with the souls of their

fellow men saw language as a sanctified medium of religious knowledge. Christ as Word mediated between God and men, enabling them to know God and to bear religious witness to one another in human speech. Language allowed them to spread the gospel, "God's tidings," and thereby to participate in the incarnation as Word. The gospel led to a knowledge of God in Christ. Furthermore, man-produced letters could be turned to this same end if prepared by the godly and if read with the eyes of faith. It was solemnly noted that preaching and poetry came together in the Psalms, which were obsessively translated into the vernaculars by a sequence of Renaissance poets, including Sidney. Since politics was religion—perhaps the only point on which Catholic and Protestant saw eye to eye—a pious poetry was summoned into its service. A prime example is the capacious hexaemeron versified by Guillaume Saluste du Bartas as *La Sepmaine* (1578), the successive installments and sequels of which were immediately translated and became a prominent landmark on the literary scene in England for several decades. By the late sixteenth century the priestly function of poetry had been largely diminished—or perhaps it had been diverted to civic ends by the likes of Spenser. But it persisted to some extent. Certainly George Herbert in the next century felt the onus to preach in verse. And John Milton as the elegist of *Lycidas* self-consciously garbed himself in the psalmist's guise of poet-priest-shepherd.

The conflation of the Ciceronian and the biblical attitudes toward language could be accommodated to Platonic doctrine, as Richard Mulcaster intimates and as Jean de Serres demonstrates more explicitly. In 1578 the younger Henri Estienne published a magnificent three-volume edition of Plato's complete works with a Latin translation by Serres. For each dialogue, Serres prepared an introduction; and in his preface to the *Phaedrus,* which is given its traditional subtitle, *On the Beautiful,* he states, "The true beauty is reason, by which man is conjoined with God, Who is the source of goodness." Serres continues, "Speech is the palpable agent of reason, as it were its interpreter. . . . So the true beauty of man is contained in this combination of reason and speech. . . . It is therefore the thesis of this dialogue that the true beauty of man shines forth in reason and speech." As Serres interprets the Platonic doctrine, man partakes in the essence of beauty to the largest extent when he poetizes. The centrality of speech in human affairs and its

interdependence with reason could be supported by a variety of incontrovertible authorities, including Plato as well as Augustine, Cicero, and the Bible.

This rich tradition for eloquent language is abundantly exemplified in Thomas Wilson, a sober humanist of the mid-sixteenth century who had acquired the new learning along with the new religion at Cambridge. In 1553, Wilson first published his *Arte of Rhetorique,* the most durable of the many Elizabethan handbooks for the language arts, persisting through at least eight editions by the time Shakespeare began to dream of authorship. Wilson introduces his preface by means of a caption in bold letters: "Eloquence first geven by God, after loste by man, and laste repayred by God agayne." Evidently, Wilson intends to site Cicero's *eloquentia* within the dynamics of God's providential scheme, and he touches upon all the familiar topics. He begins rather sanctimoniously:

> Man (in whom is poured the breathe of lyfe) was made at hys firste beinge an everlivynge Creature, unto the likenes of God, endued with reason, and appoynted Lorde over all other thinges living. But after the fall of our firste father, Sinne so crepte in, that our knowledge was muche darkened, and by corruption of this oure fleshe, mans reason and entendement were bothe overwhelmed.

In this reprobate condition, "destitute of Gods grace," man degenerated into the wild state of nature deplored by Cicero: "Al thinges waxed savage, the earth untilled, societye neglected, Goddes will not knowen, man against manne, one agaynste another, and all agaynste order." Wilson describes the ensuing social chaos in considerable detail: "None remembred the true observation of wedlocke, none tendered the education of their chyldren, lawes were not regarded, true dealinge was not once used." In default of reason, man fell prey to the devil. But in this darkest hour, "even nowe when man was thus paste all hope of amendemente," God extended mercy and granted the agents of his providence "the gift of utteraunce, that they myghte wyth ease wynne folke at their will, and frame theim by reason to all good order." In this version of the story, Cicero's euhemeristic hero who persuaded men from savagery to civility becomes God's "appoynted ministers," who work to the same purpose. "Suche force hath the tongue," Wilson declares, "and such is the power of eloquence and reason." As evidence of God's providence, men enjoy the gift of language, Wilson concludes, and "in this one point they passe all other Creatures livynge, that they have the gift of speache and reason." By divine decree, *oratio* is firmly established as an accessory of *ratio,* unmistakable testimony of God's love.

Because of this privileged position of language in the culture, the curriculum proposed by the humanists at all levels of instruction centered upon the verbal disciplines of grammar, rhetoric, and logic. The medieval trivium remained in force. Strengthened by the new reverence for Cicero, however, language was assigned a role in human affairs even greater than it had played during the Middle Ages. It became the acknowledged means by which society exists. Familiarity with the *literae humaniores* was therefore made a prerequisite to citizenship, and those nations that encouraged the language arts were evidently the most progressive and affluent. Soon the interest in ancient texts went beyond Homer and Vergil, beyond all those texts that could be allegorized or interpreted in a moralistic way, and study of the *literae humaniores* expanded into a comprehensive revival of classical learning in its multitude of subject matters. While education retained its compatibility with Christian ethics, the proportion between the study of sacred texts and of pagan texts shifted dramatically. Moreover, Latin and even Greek were learned in order to read the classical authors in their original languages. Zealous scholars revised the Latin of the church that had evolved over the centuries, and they struggled to reproduce the pure Latin of their ancient idols.

With this new learning came a revised concept of education, a resurrection of the old notion of *paideia* based in large part upon Plato's *Republic,* in which philosopher-kings rule, just as in Cicero's republic the citizens are orators. Once again letters became the major instrument by which succeeding generations were acculturated to social norms. The intent was to produce a gentleman—a Christian gentleman, of course, but one instructed in the learning derived from the ancient world. This idea of the gentleman went beyond the schoolroom and even the university. It became an ideal of behavior that received much lip service, at least, from those vying for political and commercial power at the courts of the powerful nobles. The courtier was defined as a cultured gentleman versed in the arts, especially the sister arts of music and poetry. In this

cult of the gentleman, the Ciceronian ideal made way for the Platonic.

In the sixteenth century, stimulated by other dialogues of Plato, there arose a literary genre, the "courtesy" book, which outlined the appropriate thoughts as well as pursuits of the courtier-gentleman. One of the earliest of these, and certainly the best known, was Baldassare Castiglione's *Libro del cortegiano,* published in 1528. Other popular examples were Giovanni della Casa's *Il Galateo* (ca. 1558), a book widely circulated throughout Europe that emphasized good manners rather than high morals, especially good taste in speaking, and Annibale Romei's *Discorsi* (1585), which in its final discourse places letters in equal stead with arms as an honorable occupation for the courtier. In these works the very format of a dialogue and the example of the interlocutors enjoin the gentleman above all to master language. Courtesy at basis is a "civil conversation," to use the phrase of Stefano Guazzo, author of the extremely popular work of that title first published in 1574. Courtesy becomes a social exchange modeled upon the reciprocity of language.

The new learning was introduced into England early in the sixteenth century, to be followed by the cult of the gentleman. Humanistic studies found a home in the famous school founded by John Colet about 1510 as an adjunct to St. Paul's Cathedral in London. There the *literae humaniores* were diligently employed in education for a Christian life. On the facade of the school near the cathedral, Colet announced his purpose by the following inscription: "Schola catechizationis puerorum in Christi Opt. Max. fide et bonis literis" (A school for the training of boys in the religion of Christ Almighty and in good letters). A curriculum was devised to produce young scholars who could write and speak correct classical Latin, and the humanist methods of textual analysis, note-taking, memorization, and repetition were rigorously followed. But Colet proposed also the reading of Christian authors, such as Lactantius, Prudentius, and Augustine, encouraging an ideal of private virtue expended for the public good. "Essential to this end," Joan Simon observes, "was a rational approach to learning, a clearing away of scholastic confusion so that grammar became a science of service to understanding, a full comprehension of those works of classical and Christian writers which incorporated the sum of human wisdom in lay and religious matters" (chapter 2). Desiderius Erasmus, the eminent educator from the Continent, was invited to visit and consult on the curriculum. He arrived with Cicero and Quintilian in hand and provided textbooks that were avidly adopted for classroom use. Their effect prevailed throughout the realm for the remainder of the century.

Although St. Paul's school was founded to educate the brightest of London's male children of all social ranks, most education of the period had elitest aims and was often directed to the ruling class, even the king himself. The prototype for the manual of royal instruction was Erasmus' *Institutio principis Christiani (The Education of a Christian Ruler)* of 1515, which carried the enormous weight of its author's prestige. Similar works abounded, and England soon possessed a notable example in its own vernacular, Sir Thomas Elyot's *Governour* (1531). For the production of magistrates required by the rapidly developing bureaucracy of the Tudor regime, Elyot advocated a demanding educational system grounded in study of the classical texts, both Greek and Latin. Drawing heavily upon the Platonic tradition as it had been assimilated by the humanists, this prescriptive treatise on political behavior served as a vade mecum for the governing class.

In her thoroughgoing study *The Doctrine of the English Gentleman in the Sixteenth Century,* Ruth Kelso examines the many facets of "this combination of soldier, scholar, and courtier, this new citizen in whose hands was to be the management of affairs." A compelling mystique surrounded this ideal of an actively involved man of letters, and many books, both foreign and domestic, catered to a public eager to participate in it. Castiglione's *Courtyer* was handsomely translated into English by Sir Thomas Hoby in 1561; della Casa's *Galateo* followed with an English version in 1576; and Romei's *Courtiers academie,* in 1598.

Among English authors, the doctrine of the gentleman was perhaps most forcefully furthered by Roger Ascham. Demonstrating precisely how the schools should prepare a genteel populace, Ascham in his influential *Scholemaster* (1570) drew upon humanistic principles to argue strongly for the complementarity between learning and Christian living. Displaying a zeal fed by the ardor of Protestant reform, Ascham was protective of learning, and of the language arts in particular, and warned against their abuse:

Looke upon the whole course of both the Greeke and Latin tonge, and ye shall surelie finde, that, when apte and good wordes began to be neglected, and properties of those two tonges to be confounded, than also began, ill deedes to spring: strange maners to oppresse good orders, newe and fond opinions to strive with olde and trewe doctrine, first in Philosophie: and after in Religion: right judgement of all thinges to be perverted, and so vertue with learning is contemned, and studie left off.

(Book II)

Ascham links the health of society to the state of the verbal arts: corruption of the latter leads to an inexorable decline in all social institutions. In a more positive vein, however, he calls attention to "the goodnesse of Gods providence for learning" and expresses thanks for those ancient authors who provide the best models for the practice of verbal skills:

Againe behold on the other side, how Gods wisdome hath wrought, that of *Academici* and *Peripatetici,* those that were wisest in judgement of matters, and purest in uttering their myndes, the first and chiefest, that wrote most and best, in either tong, as *Plato* and *Aristotle* in Greeke, *Tullie* in Latin, be so either wholie, or sufficiently left unto us, as I never knew yet scholer, that gave himselfe to like, and love, and folow chieflie those three Authors but he proved, both learned, wise, and also an honest man, if he joyned with all the trewe doctrine of Gods holie Bible.

(Book II)

For Protestant humanists such as Ascham, literacy stood next to godliness. It was prerequisite to righteousness as well as to social acceptability. Specifically, the gentleman should recognize God's providence in preserving the classical texts and should study most of all Plato, Aristotle, and Cicero—in Ascham's words, "those that were wisest in judgement of matters, and purest in uttering their myndes." In the new climate of Tudor England that encouraged individual endeavor, any Christian could choose this route to advancement.

In fact, by this time in England the title *gentleman* was no longer restricted to a particular social class. Rather, it was used somewhat loosely to designate a person who was distinctive because of accomplishments, not ancestry. Not only was the title appropriate to members of the minor aristocracy, but it was applied as well to many members of the rural gentry. Moreover, it was extended with increasing frequency to many professional men, such as lawyers, and even to successful merchants and tradesman in the cities. The only prerequisite, it seems, was a recognized proficiency in the *literae bonae.*

The high point of the tradition for courtesy books aimed at aspiring gentlemen came with the publication of Edmund Spenser's *The Faerie Queene* (1590). In the informative "Letter of the Authors" addressed to Sir Walter Raleigh, Spenser announces that "the generall end therefore of all the booke is to fashion a gentleman or noble person in vertuous and gentle discipline." The sixth book of *The Faerie Queene,* the last that Spenser completed, is designated "The Legend of Courtesie" and is especially germane to Spenser's avowed purpose. In the first stanza Spenser is careful to note that the basis of courtesy is "civill conversation," and he characterizes Sir Calidore, the exemplary knight of Book VI, as a man who is naturally courteous in thought and deed, to which he adds "gracious speach." Furthermore, Calidore actively disapproves of the abuses of language, such as "leasing, and base flattery," and consequently the Blatant Beast, repeatedly characterized by its foul mouth, is his natural enemy and the object of his quest. The Blatant Beast, for example, "did seeme a thousand tongues to have, / That all in spight and malice did agree" (VI. i. 9.3–4). This brutish threat to courtly knights and ladies epitomizes the subversion of language in social exchange; and while the Beast cannot be eradicated, as Spenser implies at the end of Book VI, he must be curbed. Spenser assumes that a poem, an exercise in verbal discourse, can fashion a gentleman; here is civil conversation in action. This vernacular epic was directed to the nationalistic generation who sat in Shakespeare's theater, and in its literacy it would have approved Spenser's intention. All literature, Elizabethans thought (prompted by Puritan preachers as well as by Plato and Cicero), should have such a moralizing design upon its audience.

Because of the literary nature of a dramatic script, then, the gentleman who came to Shakespeare's plays is likely to have expected an experience of greater import than bearbaiting or even jousting. Language was potent. His training from the earliest years supported this self-evident truth. Both educated and uneducated alike were imbued with an almost intuitive respect for the word. The untutored heard it from the pulpit, while the gentleman learned it as well in school.

The gentleman had, in fact, undergone careful instruction in a rather strict curriculum dominated by literary studies, especially Latin studies. They were the staple of the intellectual diet of every educated Englishman from his infancy. He fed, willy-nilly, upon the Latin grammars, logics, and rhetorics, the phrase books, the collections of aphorisms, the lexicons and dictionaries, the gallimaufry of sanctioned models that poured from the presses catering to the lucrative textbook trade. The schoolboy's regimen was established to accord with the pedagogical theories focused upon language and espoused by great educators like Erasmus and Juan Luis Vives, later to be modified by Philip Melanchthon, Johann Sturm, and Pierre de la Ramée. By the time he took his seat in the Globe Theater, the gentleman had completed elementary (or "petty") school and grammar school, and perhaps—those who were professionals such as doctors, lawyers, and theologians—Oxford or Cambridge.

At the age of four or five the young scholar entered petty school, so named because it accommodated what the French call *les petits.* Following procedures fairly well standardized throughout the kingdom, he there learned first to read English and later to write it. William Kempe in *The Education of Children in Learning* (1588) describes the elementary curriculum in some detail, a curriculum that persisted into the nineteenth century. The child began by memorizing his alphabet from a hornbook and then proceeded to pronounce letters, syllables, and whole words. These basics were followed by practice in actual reading in carefully prepared texts, such as Alexander Nowell's *Catechism, or First Instruction and Learning of Christian Religion* (1570), which became a required textbook in every school by order of the church. As the student advanced, there were also readings, of course, in the Holy Scriptures and probably in prudently selected secular materials. After mastering the skill of reading, the child was taught to write so that, as Kempe put it, the hand could record what the tongue expressed. Exercises in writing now accompanied those in reading.

At the age of seven or eight, knowing the catechism and primer by heart, the gifted youngster progressed to grammar school, so called because it was here that the study of Latin grammar began. In grammar school the young scholar entered a rigidly enforced curriculum devoted to the reading, writing, and speaking of Latin. The likeliest textbook was William Lily's oft-reprinted *Shorte Introduction of Grammar,* a composite of manuals resulting from the collusion of Lily, Colet, and Erasmus during the first quarter of the century—and, incidentally, the source for Shakespeare's numerous Latin tags. The schoolboy started by memorizing the rules of Lily's or a similar grammar and proceeded by translating easy texts such as simplified versions of Aesop and Cato, moralistic authors carried over from the Middle Ages. As his competence increased, he was introduced to passages from Caesar, Sallust, and Livy; to selected scenes from Plautus and Terence; and most certainly to Cicero's *De officiis.* Later he came to Horace and Ovid, and eventually to the much revered Vergil. At some point he was no doubt asked to study some Renaissance Latin poems of an edifying sort, such as the *Bucolica* (1498) of Mantuanus or the *Zodiacus vitae* (ca. 1535) of Marcellus Palingenius. After 1582, by order of the Privy Council he necessarily read Christopher Ockland's *Anglorum praelia* (1580), a patriotic volume of Latin hexameters recounting English battles from the reign of Edward III to the accession of Elizabeth.

After learning to read Latin, the student continued by learning to compose in Latin, both prose and verse, with the canon of the classics open before him. Cicero was the preferred model in prose, while Vergil and Horace served as the most admired models for verse. Here it was necessary to know not only the rules of grammar, but also of rhetoric, of logic, and of quantitative metrics for versifying. Pupils practiced their writing skills by composing essays on topics assigned by the schoolmaster and by devising arguments to support or subvert a given proposition. They also tried their hand at writing epistles, odes, and orations.

In the more advanced schools, the best students received instruction in reading and perhaps writing Greek. The favorite authors presented for study were Demosthenes, Isocrates, Xenophon, Hesiod, Theognis, Phocylides, and Sophocles—in addition, of course, to Homer and Plato. Some few schools with especially ambitious headmasters offered instruction in the sacred language of Hebrew, a practice that Milton perpetuated. Although it is difficult to estimate how many Englishmen mastered Greek and Hebrew, fluency in Latin was widespread.

While the extent of literacy should not be exaggerated—David Cressy (chapter 1) estimates that as late as the civil war of the 1640s more than two-thirds of the men and nine-tenths of the women in England could not even write their own names—nonetheless, there was a fully institutionalized educational system for the privileged and the fortunate. And even a poor child, if promising, might receive a scholarship. In his *Description of England* (1587), William Harrison observes that "there are great number of grammar schools throughout the realm, and those very liberally endued for the better relief of poor scholars"; and he adds, with ill-concealed pride, "There are not many corporate towns now under the Queen's dominion that hath not one grammar school at the least with a sufficient living for a master and usher appointed to the same" (chapter 3). The whining schoolboy, with his satchel and shining morning face, as Shakespeare describes him in *As You Like It,* must have been a common sight.

As a daily regimen, then, the Tudor schoolboy painstakingly reviewed the rules of Latin grammar until he had them by rote and intensively construed one Latin passage after another in an endless exercise of analyzing language. The school day allowed very little variation in the routine of memorizing, construing, reciting, and composing in one language or another. As a continuing assignment each student kept a "commonplace" book in which to record the phrases, idioms, and figures of speech that would encourage correct usage and the notable passages that he might later draw upon as topics in his own composition or declamation. Class time was devoted to linguistic exercises of this sort, and ability in the language arts was frequently submitted to the test of public performance. Success in education was measured primarily by the Ciceronian ideal of *eloquentia,* by the suasiveness of the spoken, and now the written, word.

After grammar school, which he left at the age of fourteen or fifteen, the young man had exhausted the possibilities for institutional education unless he went to a university. For a highly selected few, Oxford or Cambridge provided the opportunity of study for a professional career in divinity, medicine, or the law. William Harrison, a contemporary with extensive university experience, gives a firsthand account of what the universities offered. First came the four-year course of study required for the degree of bachelor of arts, a fairly wide-ranging curriculum including some mathematics and philosophy but still centering on rhetoric, logic, and "the use of the tongues" (that is, Greek and Hebrew). Next followed a three-year program leading to a master of arts degree, which retained at least vestigially the mathematical disciplines of the medieval quadrivium (arithmetic, geometry, music, and astronomy) and explored further the three recognized branches of philosophy (moral, natural, and metaphysical). Finally, to the dedicated and determined, a doctorate was available in divinity, law, or physic, requiring another seven to twelve years of intense, specialized study. "Thus we see," Harrison wryly comments, "from our entrance into the university unto the last degree received is commonly eighteen or, peradventure, twenty years, in which time if a student hath not obtained sufficient learning thereby to serve his own turn and benefit his commonwealth, let him never look, by tarrying longer, to come by any more." Understandably, very few persevered to complete this rigorous program for the doctorate.

A clear view of Latin studies in the university is provided by Gabriel Harvey. In 1575 and 1576 he delivered two Latin lectures at Cambridge that were published in 1577 with the titles *Ciceronianus* and *Rhetor.* Although Harvey is concerned largely with matters pertaining to style, his version of Ciceronianism, he nonetheless makes several assumptions about language that are revealing. Ciceronian eloquence is still for him the aim of education, and it is to be achieved by following the models in the classical canon. Furthermore, in the vein of Quintilian, the *rhetor bonus* provides the model for the *vir bonus,* so that again rhetoric, the coalescence of wisdom and suasiveness, shows the way to the good life. Harvey's orations are themselves exercises that demonstrate the approved literary mode, and his performance was calculated to impress his students with a system of values, the values of civil humanism. Perhaps more than any other Englishman, he embodied the literary code of the humanists in its purest form.

By the time that Shakespeare began to write his plays, the reading public had access to almost as much of the literature of Greece and Rome as we know today. Most of it was readily available in print at reasonable cost. Those who had completed grammar school could read the Latin texts in the original language, and a small number, no doubt with less ease, could read the Greek texts. A less well educated public clamored for readier access to these riches, and so translation flourished. The Greek works were rendered into Latin for the many who could read that language, and both

Greek and Latin works were translated into English. Translating, in fact, reached the level of an art in its own right, and some of the most acclaimed monuments of Elizabethan literature are outright translations: North's Plutarch, Golding's Ovid, Phaer's Vergil, and Chapman's Homer are only the most notable of a stunning array. The profession of translator became a viable, even respected, career, as exemplified by Philemon Holland, who englished Livy, Pliny, Plutarch, Suetonius, and Xenophon, just to mention the more ambitious of his numerous projects.

Not only were classical texts rendered into English, but translations from the vernaculars also abounded—narrative fiction as well as theological tracts and scientific treatises. Many Englishmen, however, recognized the advantages of fluency in foreign languages, especially French and Italian, and they took pains to learn them, either by travel abroad or from tutors at home. As Kenneth Charlton concludes, "There were many who would have a smattering which would serve for most occasions, just as an acquaintance with the classics had become an expected and accepted part of a gentleman's equipment" (chapter 8). Grammars and dictionaries for these languages were readily available in English, and busy men at all levels of society put them to good use. Shakespeare's audience was inquisitively aware of what was currently being written as well as of the literary past, and they supported a thriving book trade in a multitude of languages.

Since the time of Augustine, literacy in western Europe had been something of a Christian duty, especially for those who could afford the time and the cost of education. Devotion to the word of God entailed reading, praying, and spreading the gospel. In the intervening centuries, however, as a practical matter in the face of almost universal illiteracy, the biblical message had been published largely through images construed as story. The facade of a cathedral, the reredos of an altar, the capitals of pillars, even the underside of choir seats contained a veritable anthology of biblical tales. This semantic system in wood and stone had become so common and so extensive that by the sixteenth century some reactionaries questioned the need for the general populace to read the Scriptures for themselves and opposed the translation of the Bible into vernaculars on the grounds that its subject matter was already handy. After the Reformation there was the additional argument that salvation was to be achieved by faith alone or by grace, so that literacy for the layman amounted to little more than frippery.

But also with the Reformation came a rejection of images, ostensibly out of deference to the Second Commandment, but politically as a denouncement of Catholic materialism; and eventually the historiated facades, altars, and choirs were defaced. By the mid-sixteenth century there was a new emphasis on holy texts for layman and cleric alike, an evangelical insistence on reading, and literacy again became a Christian duty. Information conveyed visually was no longer a satisfactory substitute for reading. Manuals of devotion, homilies, and, later, collections of sermons became some of the most popular products of the printing industry. By the time of Elizabeth's accession, a Protestant clergy was making a strong case for literacy at a fairly high level. As David Cressy has demonstrated, it was argued that someone who could read was better able to prepare for salvation and was more likely to lead a life of duty and godliness; the illiterate, in contrast, could not fully meet the obligations or reap the rewards prescribed by the reformed religion (chapter 1). The translation of the Bible into English, performed several times during Shakespeare's lifetime and culminating in the great King James Version of 1611, was aimed at encouraging ordinary Englishmen to read for themselves and to share directly in the holy words that were the unique testimony of an imperishable heritage. This belief in the word provided a general stimulus to education, since parents had a moral responsibility to ensure the literacy of their children, and masters were similarly entrusted with the spiritual well-being of their servants. Not to read was to deny the gospel, to be somehow unchristian. In consequence, as Joan Simon concludes, "Puritanism did not wither the humanist heritage, even though schools became progressively more godly" (chapter 15).

The ability to read and write, of course, like all human faculties, could be abused and turned to pernicious ends. It could tempt the soul, confuse the mind, and titillate the body, initiating an infectious depravity. While there is little evidence of a salacious literature in Elizabeth's England, there seems to have been considerable concern, on the part of preacher and politician alike, that reading matter might prove to be a subversive force in society. The self-appointed guardians of public morals, such as Phillip Stubbes, railed against the idle tales and silly broadsides that provided the printers with a lucrative trade. In his *Anatomie of Abuses* (1583), Stubbes blusters that "bookes and pamphlets of scurrilitie and baudrie, are better esteemed and more vendible then the godlyest and sagest bookes that be" (P7–P7^v). But the scurrility and bawdry deplored by Stubbes prove to be little more than versions of Italianate *novelle.* And while admittedly the stories of Boccaccio, Bandello, and Cinthio could be said to waste the time of the simpleminded apprentice or the addlepated housemaid, the presses that printed William Painter's *Palace of Pleasure* (1566–1567) and George Pettie's *Petite Pallace of Pettie His Pleasure* (1576) were soon to publish John Lyly's *Euphues* (1578), Thomas Lodge's *Rosalynde* (1590), and Philip Sidney's *Arcadia* (1590)—not to mention Thomas Deloney's distinctly middle-class *Jack of Newbury* (ca. 1596).

In any case, language was not used casually in Elizabeth's realm. The government kept a wary eye on what was printed, and poets as well as most others felt a responsibility to use words purposefully. The continued effect that humanistic language theory had upon poetry is fully attested by George Gascoigne, who in 1575 published his *Certayne Notes of Instruction Concerning the Making of Verse.* In this pragmatic treatise Gascoigne assumes that the poet while composing will follow the example of the rhetorician, who begins with his thought, his "invention," which he then apparels in words. As Gascoigne avers in his initial note of instruction to his fellow poets, "The first and most necessarie poynt that ever I founde meete to be considered in making of a delectable poeme is this, to grounde it upon some fine invention" (G. Gregory Smith, I). Roger Ascham also saw literature as a product of the rhetorician's artistry; he anatomized the arts of discourse into the four species familiar to the humanists: poetry, history, philosophy, and oratory.

Following this same tradition, Philip Sidney thought of poetry as a species of the *ars dicendi,* and he defended it by showing its superiority to both history and philosophy. Poetry proves to be more generally applicable than history, which deals only with the particulars of what has actually occurred, while it surpasses philosophy in efficaciousness because it embodies the abstract concept in the discernible example of a "speaking picture." In its broadest terms, Sidney's defense of poetry is little more than an assertion that, by its linguistic potency, poetry leads men to virtuous action. "And so a conclusion not unfitlie ensueth," Sidney claims, "that as vertue is the most excellent resting place for all worldlie learning to make his end of, so Poetrie . . . [is] the most familiar to teach it, and most princelie to move towards it."

Shakespeare, an author eminently in touch with the men and women of his time, was also conditioned by the prevailing literate culture. He wrote not only to line his pockets or to jollify a hedonistic populace. It is likely that with Sidney he thought of poetry, including his own dramatic poetry, in a Ciceronian vein, as "this purifying of wit, this enritching of memory, enabling of judgment, and enlarging of conceyt." And no matter how it might be misdirected for intermediate purposes of raucous entertainment or pecuniary profit, "the final end is to lead and draw us to as high a perfection as our degenerate soules, made worse by theyr clayey lodgings, can be capable of."

Of course, to align Shakespeare with such a statement without qualification makes him too much the Calvinistic moralist. Indeed, this statement oversimplifies also the position of Sidney, whose practice clearly belies such a narrowly defined purpose. Nonetheless, both poets, probably the greatest of their era, were in large part products of their literate culture, and it would be perverse to dissociate them from the Protestant humanists. With Plato and Cicero, with Bruni and Erasmus, with Wilson and Ascham, they recognized the close ties between language and society.

When Shakespeare's plays are placed against this background of serious respect for language and hence for literature, several inferences may be drawn. Some will see a license to read the plays solemnly, looking for sententiousness and perhaps even a Christian morality. Others, aware of the demand that literature produce gentlemen and applying the courtesy book as a norm, will feel that drama, especially in the commercial theaters, was an ephemeral art form, only slightly above the broadside ballad or polemical pamphlet. Yet others will see Shakespeare catering to a burgeoning class of opportunists and sophisticates who recognized letters as a means of financial and political advancement, a new culture of ambitious individualists eager to open modern areas of inquiry. A few, recalling that Shakespeare went out of his way to castigate the pompous and pedantic schoolmaster such as Holofernes in *Love's Labor's Lost,* will argue that the playwright set out consciously to subvert the learned tradition, and they will exaggerate his innovativeness. No one, however, is likely to deny Shakespeare's genius. And most would agree that this genius is characterized by an exceptional ability for exploiting the arts of language to produce a verbal artifact with a nuance, a richness, and a power unparalleled in any medium.

BIBLIOGRAPHY

Thomas W. Baldwin, *William Shakspere's Small Latine and Lesse Greeke,* 2 vols. (1944). Hans Baron, "Cicero and the Roman Civic Spirit in the Middle Ages and Early Renaissance," in *Bulletin of the John Rylands Library,* 22 (1938). H. S. Bennett, *English Books and Readers, 1558–1603* (1965). J. Howard Brown, *Elizabethan Schooldays: An Account of the English Grammar Schools in the Second Half of the Sixteenth Century* (1933). Douglas Bush, *The Renaissance and English Humanism* (1939).

Fritz Caspari, *Humanism and the Social Order in Tudor England* (1954). Kenneth Charlton, *Education in Renaissance England* (1965). Marcia L. Colish, *The Mirror of Language: A Study in the Medieval Theory of Knowledge* (1968). David Cressy, *Literacy and the Social Order: Reading and Writing in Tudor and Stuart England* (1980). Elizabeth L. Eisenstein, *The Printing Press as an Agent of Change* (1979). Hanna H. Gray, "Renaissance Humanism: The Pursuit of Eloquence," in *Journal of the History of Ideas,* 24 (1963).

John H. Hexter, "The Education of the Aristocracy in the Renaissance," in *Journal of Modern History,* 22 (1950). Wilbur S. Howell, *Logic and Rhetoric in England, 1500–1700* (1956). George K. Hunter, *John Lyly: The Humanist as Courtier* (1962). Sister Miriam Joseph, *Shakespeare's Use of the Arts of Language* (1966). Ruth Kelso, *The Doctrine of the English Gentleman in the Sixteenth Century* (1929). John L. Lievsay, *Stefano Guazzo and the English Renaissance, 1575–1675* (1961). Marshall McLuhan, *The Gutenberg Galaxy: The Making of Typographic Man* (1962).

Jerrold E. Seigel, *Rhetoric and Philosophy in Renaissance Humanism* (1968). Joan Simon, *Education and Society in Tudor England* (1966). Bromley Smith, "Queen Elizabeth at the Cambridge Disputations," in *Quarterly Journal of Speech,* 15 (1929). G. Gregory Smith, ed., *Elizabethan Critical Essays,* 2 vols. (1904).

James A. K. Thomson, *The Classical Background of English Literature* (1948). Craig R. Thompson, *Schools in Tudor England* (1958) and *Universities in Tudor England* (1959). Foster Watson, *The English Grammar Schools to 1660* (1908). William H. Woodward, *Studies in Education During the Age of the Renaissance, 1400–1600* (1965) and *Vittorino da Feltre and Other Humanist Educators* (1963). Louis B. Wright, *Middle-Class Culture in Elizabethan England* (1958).

Science, Magic, and Folklore

MICHAEL MacDONALD

Cast ashore on Prospero's island, the enchanted noblemen and mariners wonder at the noises and illusions they experience. "These are not natural events," Alonso exclaims at last, "they strengthen from strange to stranger" (*The Tempest*, V. i. 227–228). Modern scholars of Elizabethan England, poring over masses of published and manuscript sources, have echoed Alonso's amazement, for it has become clear that Shakespeare and his contemporaries inhabited a realm that was almost as wonderful as Prospero's. Supernatural beings and preternatural events were commonly encountered by people of every social rank and degree of educational attainment. God and his angels inspired pious men and women and conferred upon them the power of prophecy; the devil, evil spirits, and witches imperiled the health and happiness of ordinary people; monstrous births and miraculous escapes from danger displayed the power and mystery of Providence.

Elizabethans who believed in the immediate and potent influence of the supernatural in this world were not credulous louts. Although various aspects of the manifold beliefs about the supernatural that some of them held struck some critics as incredible or impious, philosophical skepticism was rare and materialism still rarer. The categories that we are accustomed to use to classify the beliefs of our own and other cultures—magic, science, and religion—are liable to distort our understanding of Elizabethan beliefs, for the men and women of the six-

teenth century defined such concepts very differently. The cosmology that Elizabethans inherited fused natural and supernatural forces and beings into a single comprehensive scheme and legitimized beliefs that we would now stigmatize as irrational. To understand the place of science, magic, and folklore in Elizabethan thought, it is therefore essential to learn the wisdom of the moon-calf Caliban, who accepted as a matter of fact that "the isle is full of noises, / Sounds and sweet airs that give delight and hurt not" (III. ii. 132–133) as well as of forces that could inflict pain and suffering.

The Traditional Cosmology

When Elizabethans tried to explain the events that they observed or experienced, they appealed to a model of the universe that was based ultimately on classical science and medieval theology. Their world view is as mysterious to most of us as the workings of the beautiful and intricate astrolabes that they made to observe the positions of the planets. Its fundamental principles were teleology and hierarchy. The universe had been created by God at a particular moment, and its design and history were determined by a divine plan that would conclude in the Last Judgment. Everything therefore had a purpose; every event contributed to the fulfillment of God's will. Nothing simply existed; nothing simply happened. The beginning and the end of the universe and many aspects of the supernatural world were described in the Bible, but the place of particular beings and phenomena in the providential design had to be inferred. God's plans for individuals and the meaning of particular events were only partly knowable, but the structure of the cosmos and its natural laws were evident.

The ancient philosophers had discovered a great deal about the natural order; medieval theologians had elucidated the main features of the supernatural realm. Authorities agreed that the entire cosmos was structured hierarchically. Every being, from the basest mineral to the highest angel, could be defined in terms of its relationship to superior and inferior things. Classes of things shared characteristics that set them above or below other things; and even within classes, types and individuals were arranged hierarchically. In the 1460s, a century before Shakespeare's lifetime, Sir John Fortescue remarked:

> God created as many different kinds of things as he did creatures, so that there is no creature which does not differ in some respect from all other creatures and by which it is in some respect superior or inferior to all the rest. So that from the highest angel down to the lowest of his kind there is absolutely not found an angel that has not a superior and inferior; nor from man down to the meanest worm is there any creature which is not in some respect superior to one creature and inferior to another.
>
> (quoted in Tillyard, chapter 4)

Superior beings enjoyed dominion over lesser entities, which existed for their use and pleasure.

The design of the universe was often described as a "great chain of being," and the metaphor delighted poets and sermonizers alike. But it was easier to picture creation as a ranked series of planes or spheres of existence. The highest sphere was a purely supernatural realm, the heavenly empyrean, wherein dwelled God and nine orders of his angels. The scheme embodied the hierarchical principle so well that some learned writers and most ordinary people continued to visualize the heavens below the empyrean in terms of the Aristotelian system long after Copernicus' views had been accepted by natural philosophers. The celestial bodies were mounted on interlocking, concentric spheres made of a transparent crystalline substance. The outermost orb, or Primum Mobile, imparted motion to the interlocking spheres below

it, which bore along the fixed stars, the five known planets (Saturn, Jupiter, Mars, Venus, and Mercury), the sun, and the moon. At the bottom or core of the universe was the earth, a stationary globe around which the orbs of the heavens rotated daily.

There was a sharp division between the realms above and below the moon: the celestial bodies were perfect and unchanging, composed of stable combinations of the four elements or, alternatively, of a fifth, heavenly element. The objects in the sublunary world, compounded of unstable mixtures of the elements, were subject to mutation and decay. The elements themselves possessed qualities that ranked them in terms of their nobility and weight. Fire, the highest and lightest, was hot and dry; air, the next in dignity, was moist and hot; water below it was moist and cold; earth, the lowest and heaviest, was dry and cold. All four elements were influenced by the movements of the planets, which also possessed qualities of moisture and temperature; and the elements strove to attain their proper places in the sublunary world. It is difficult to appreciate that this fabulous astronomy and simple physics provided plausible explanations for most of the observable events in the natural world. Heavy bodies, for example, were supposed to fall because they sought their "natural place" at the center of the earth, the element that made them weighty.

The spatial hierarchy of the universe reflected, albeit imperfectly, the quality of the beings that inhabited it. Ariel rode the curled clouds at Prospero's bidding; Caliban dwelled in a hole in the earth. The highest plane of existence was the proper habitation of the angels, beings composed of an incorporeal substance so fine that it was normally invisible. At the other extreme of the cosmos, somewhere below the earth, was hell, where Satan and the fallen angels belonged. Among the creatures and beings of the earth, men and beasts were superior to plants and stones, for they possessed the powers of motion and sense. They sustained themselves by eating the plants, which in turn drew their nourishment from the ground below them. Each class of beings also enjoyed special powers that ranked it in relationship with the others, and each subsumed the qualities of the lesser entities. But, at the same time, each class of things excelled all of the others in some respect, because everything had its proper and particular task assigned to it by God. Beginning with the lowliest things, Richard Hooker summarized the excellencies of the principal kinds of beings: "For as stones, though in dignity of nature inferior unto plants, yet exceed them in firmness of strength or durability of being; and plants, though beneath the excellency of creatures endued with sense, yet exceed them in the faculty of vegetation and fertility: so beasts, though otherwise behind men, may notwithstanding in actions of sense and fancy go beyond them" (I, chapter 6).

A creature "of middle nature betwixt angels and beasts," man possessed both a reasonable soul and a mortal body (Bright). His dual nature, at once spiritual and physical, made him a microcosm of the universe. The translator of Annibale Romei's *The Courtier's Academy* (1598) stated the analogy succinctly: "The body of man is no other but a little model of the sensible world, and his soul an image of the world intelligible" (Bamborough, introduction). The soul or mind was commonly regarded as having three parts: the "vegetal, sensitive, and rational," which corresponded to the kinds of living creatures, plants, animals, and men (Burton, Part I, section I). The vegetal soul possessed the powers of nutrition, growth, and generation. Second was the sensitive soul, which enabled men to apprehend the world through the five outward senses, the "common sense," the imagination, and the memory, and to move their bodies by means of a mysterious power that controlled the muscles and nerves. Third was the rational soul, which contained the powers of understanding and will with which men could control their appetites and comprehend the meaning of their actions.

Just as the organization of men's minds reflected the hierarchy of the living world, so the structure of their bodies mirrored the design of the universe. The head, the highest part of the body, housed the reason and directed one's thoughts and actions, just as the heavenly realms contained the intelligent spirits and controlled earthly events. The heart, like the sun, warmed and animated the body. The organs of the nether parts, like the lesser creatures of the earth, facilitated nourishment and generation. The four humors corresponded with the four elements, with which they shared qualities of temperature and moisture. Choler, like fire, was hot and dry; blood, like air, was hot and moist; phlegm, like water, was cold and moist; melancholy, like earth, was cold and dry.

The microcosm-macrocosm analogy was repeated and elaborated by countless writers. Even the qualities and actions of the body, such as youthful beauty or noisy digestion, were compared to events in the natural world. Carried away by the metaphor, Helkiah Crooke maintained in 1618 that "the rumbling of the guts, their croaking murmurs, their rapping escapes, and the huddled and redoubled belchings of the stomach, do represent the fashion and manner of all kinds of thunders" (Bamborough, chapter 2). As arbitrary and absurd as such analogies seem to us today, they expressed the Elizabethans' fundamental conviction that there was an intimate relationship between themselves and the universal order of things. It is impossible to grasp the appeal of astrology or Elizabethan medicine or to appreciate the force of many poetic figures without recognizing that the correspondence between the microcosm and the macrocosm was a cultural axiom.

Man was potentially capable of transcending the natural order. In life he could use his will and understanding to approach nearer to God; after death he might shed his natural frame and attain eternal felicity in the company of the Lord. Conversely, because of the Fall, man was equally capable of defiling his nature. The original transgression had mutilated the mental powers of mankind forever, making it vulnerable to misfortune, disease, and death. By failing to exercise his remaining rational and spiritual powers fully, man sinned and so reduced himself to the level of the beasts, who possessed no higher faculty than the sensitive soul. In the process, man also courted eternal damnation, banishment to the regions farthest from the throne of God. Supreme among the creatures of the earth, man was therefore subject to both natural and supernatural law, the divinely ordained code that determined his spiritual condition.

In his efforts to conform to the mandates of God, man was hindered not only by his own weaknesses and predilections to sin but also by the devil and his minions. Ever since their banishment from heaven, Lucifer's legions had been scattered throughout the universe: hell was merely their headquarters. Hooker explains: "For being dispersed, some in the air, some on the earth, some in the water, some among the minerals, dens, and caves, that are under the earth; they have by all means laboured to effect a universal rebellion against the laws and . . . works of God" (I, chapter 5). Fortunately, Satan's demons were not the only supernatural beings at work in the world. God's angels also intervened in earthly events, striving to assist man to do good. In *The Faerie Queen,* Edmund Spenser declaimed their presence:

How oft do they with golden pinions cleave
The flitting skies, like flying pursuivant,
Against foul fiends to aid us militant!

(Book II, canto 8, stanza 2)

Man was thus an actor in a cosmic drama staged on earth but plotted and directed by God: the good and evil spirits were his fellow players. The precise degree of freedom that man enjoyed was the subject of intense theological debate. The significant point in this context is that Elizabethans believed the natural world to be vibrant with supernatural forces. This conviction had been greatly reinforced by the Neoplatonists, who declared that a magus might master supernatural forces by study and faith; but it rested on a bedrock of popular belief formed in the pagan and medieval past. The boundary between the natural and the supernatural realms was therefore blurred and shifting. Almost any event, even people's innermost thoughts and emotions, might have natural or supernatural causes or both.

Old and New Science

When described and diagramed in the pages of books, Elizabethan cosmology is like a butterfly pinned in a collector's case: intricate, beautiful, and unchanging. But in the minds of living people the world picture was subject to constant mutation. Philosophers, who saw both the structural coherence and the details of the system, elaborated and criticized aspects of it; laymen, who accepted without much reflection the concepts that it embodied, altered and reinterpreted it to explain their experiences. In retrospect, we can see that the old cosmology was in an advanced stage of evolution during Shakespeare's lifetime. Protestant reformers had already challenged the Scholastic theology on which its picture of the supernatural was based, and natural philosophers were becoming increasingly critical of its scientific accuracy. Having adapted successfully to the intellectual climate of the Middle Ages, classical science was being challenged by new theories that would render it extinct among the educated elite by 1700.

Historians have carefully charted the changing conditions that encouraged scientific speculation and discovery. Renaissance humanism, the Protestant Reformation, the invention of movable type, and the expansion of the European nations into new markets and new lands played a part in the scientific revolution. Ironically, some of the factors that eventually helped to doom traditional cosmology among the educated elite prolonged its survival among the common people. The revival of classical texts and the proliferation of printed books, for example, facilitated the formation of a large international community of natural philosophers and made the concepts of ancient and medieval science more accessible to literate laymen. In telling the story of the decline of the old cosmology, scholars until recently have imposed their own technology on it, emphasizing the novelty and rationalism of early modern science and ignoring the reverence for authority and mysticism that typified much natural philosophy until at least the late seventeenth century. Beguiled by the eventual success of the new theories and obsessed by the search for their origins, they have neglected the vitality of the old views and overlooked the significance of their persistence. This selective approach to the history of science has exaggerated the importance of ideas that anticipated modern scientific thought and undervalued those that did not. To understand the place of science in the minds of educated Elizabethans, one must try to avoid looking ahead and, rather, see the new developments that were occurring in their proper perspective.

The most fundamental challenges to ancient science in the sixteenth century were mounted by the astronomers and alchemists. The Copernican revolution is familiar to everyone: it is the very paradigm of scientific progress. In contrast, the renaissance in alchemical studies is frequently regarded with embarrassment. Jonson's cozening Subtle (in *The Alchemist*) broods over the pages of older treatments of the subject, and Paracelsus and his followers are still sometimes dismissed as obscurantists and mystics, at odds with the rationalistic spirit of the scientific revolution. And yet the astronomers and alchemists had much in common, particularly in England. Both groups expressed their innovative ideas in ancient guises and drew inspiration from the occult philosophy of the Renaissance Neoplatonists. Radical attacks on the Aristotelian tradition were fought under the banner of Plato and the pre-Socratics and, sometimes, of Hermes Trismegistus, the legendary progenitor of natural magic. The early stages of the scientific revolution were less a battle between the ancients and the moderns than a contest between the proponents of one set of ancients against the others. Even the astronomers, who are usually regarded as the champions of scientific rationalism, were not simply advancing the cause of novelty and reason against the entrenched forces of authority and mysticism.

Copernicus himself called attention to the ancient precedents for his theories and invoked the views of the Pythagoreans to justify them. His great *De revolutionibus orbium coelestium* (*On the Revolution of the Heavenly Spheres,* 1543) closely follows the plan of Ptolemy's *Almagest,* which it was intended to supersede. In it the doctrine that the earth turns on its axis and moves in orbit about the sun is traced to several Greek philosophers, particularly Philolaus, a disciple of Pythagoras. (Other writers quickly pointed out a closer parallel with the views of Aristarchos of Samos.) Asserting that the sun is the center of the world, Copernicus breaks into a hymn to its virtues in which many have heard a Neoplatonic strain: "For who would place this lamp of a very beautiful temple in another or better place than this wherefrom it can illuminate everything at the same time? . . . Trismegistus calls it a 'visible god'; Sophocles' Electra, 'that which gazes upon all things' " (Book I, chapter 10).

Copernicus' most notable Elizabethan exponent, Thomas Digges, also emphasized the classical pedigree of the new system. His loose translation and commentary on the key parts of *De revolutionibus,* published in 1576, was entitled *A Perfit Description of the Caelestiall Orbes, According to the Most Auncient Doctrine of the Pythagoreans: Lately Revived by Copernicus, and by Geometricall Demonstrations Approved.* To Copernicus' views Digges added the daring assertion that the realm of the fixed stars was not a single sphere but stretched as far as the spiritual heavens; he claimed, in effect, that the universe was infinite. This idea, too, had its ancient sources (Anaximander, Democritus, Lucretius) and a fifteenth-century one as well (Nicholas of Cusa). But to Digges the precedents for his theory seem to have been less important than its religious implications: God's "unsearchable works invisible we may partly by his visible conjecture, to whose infinite power and majesty such an infinite place surmounting all other both in quantity and quality only is convenient" (quoted in Johnson, chapter 6). These pious sentiments were carried to heretical extremes by Giordano Bruno, whose *Cena de la ceneri* (1584) and *De l'infinito universo e mondi* (1584) were written and published in London. The most famous of all the occult philosophers, Bruno defended the Copernican system and incorporated

it into his own vision of the universe as an infinite plurality of worlds coextensive with the infinity of God and endowed with a soul.

Despite the popularity of Digges's book, which was reprinted seven times between 1576 and 1605, enthusiasm for Copernicanism in Elizabethan England was evidently very slight. Mathematical adepts mentioned Copernicus occasionally: a very early favorable allusion to his theories appeared in Robert Recorde's introduction to astronomy, *The Castle of Knowledge* (1556). John Field expressed unqualified acceptance of Copernicus' ideas in the introduction to his ephemerides for 1557, but he did not explain them. Later in the century the inventor of a new astrolabe, John Blagrave, discussed the Copernican scheme very briefly and explained that his instrument could be employed by adherents of both the old and the new theories. Most astronomical and mathematical handbooks of the sixteenth century ignored Copernicanism altogether; and a couple of writers, Thomas Blundeville and Thomas Hill, rejected it on religious and scientific grounds. It is possible that the new astronomy enjoyed popularity among Neoplatonists. John Field and Thomas Digges were members of John Dee's circle; indeed, Digges was Dee's acolyte and referred to the great magus and mathematician as his "mathematical father." But unfortunately, Dee's own references to Copernicus are inconclusive, so it is impossible to establish that he shared his pupil's zeal for the new system.

The mystical implications that the new astronomy had acquired in the works of Digges and Bruno (and later in those of Kepler) certainly harmonized with the ideas of William Gilbert, whose *De magnete* (1600) was the single most important Elizabethan scientific publication. An early classic of experimental science, *De magnete* ranges far beyond a discussion of the physics of magnetism. Although, like Dee, Gilbert expresses no conclusive judgment on the heliocentric hypothesis, he accepts Copernicus' argument that the earth rotates on its axis and offers an explanation for it: magnetic power spins the earth, just as it does the needle of a compass. Magnetism for Gilbert is an animistic force that permeates the universe, which is infinite, and impels the orderly motions of the heavenly bodies. This remarkable theory resembles Bruno's cosmology, and Gilbert cites authorities from the Neoplatonic and occult canon to support his views —including Hermes Trismegistus, Zoroaster, and

Orpheus. Gilbert's work was very widely read in England and abroad, and its fusion of scientific observation and ancient mysticism epitomizes the temper of Elizabethan natural philosophy.

As the seventeenth century progressed, Copernicanism was accepted by more and more astronomers, navigational writers, and astrologers for mathematical and scientific reasons. The appearance of new stars and comets, Galileo's telescopic observations, and Kepler's radical revision of the Copernican system all contributed ultimately to its plausibility. But it is easy to see why the new astronomy long remained controversial among the wider public; for even as the evidence in its favor mounted, the diversity of the ideas advanced under its banner increased. Tycho Brahe proposed a compromise system championed by some prominent Jacobean almanac makers. Francis Bacon, declaring that the Copernican theory contained "many and great inconveniences," invented his own model, in which the planets were supposed to revolve around the earth in spirals (Johnson, chapter 7). Robert Burton, that magazine of conventional opinion, complained that "our latter mathematicians have rolled all the stones that may be stirred." Far from replacing a crumbling edifice with a new and sounder structure, the astronomers were agreed only on the need to repair the Ptolemaic system. "As a tinker stops one hole and makes two," Burton grumbled, "he corrects them and doth worse himself, reforms some and mars all. In the meantime, the world is tossed in a blanket amongst them, they hoist the earth up and down like a ball, make it stand and go at their pleasures" (II, section 2).

Famous for his lamentation "New philosophy calls all in doubt," John Donne believed that the innovations of the alchemists were every bit as corrosive as those of the astronomers. In his satire *Ignatius His Conclave* (1609), Donne imagines Copernicus and Paracelsus contesting for a place in hell near the throne of Lucifer, a region reserved for innovators in religion and science who have overthrown ancient truths. A quarter of a century earlier, Richard Bostocke had defended both the astronomer and the alchemist against charges of innovation with the argument that they had merely purged their disciplines of error, as the Protestant reformers had recovered the doctrines of the ancient church. Paracelsus, he asserted, "was not the author and inventor" of the chemical philosophy, anymore than John Wycliffe, Martin Luther, and their successors had invented religious dogma,

"and no more than Nicholas Copernicus, which lived at the time of this Paracelsus, and restored to us the place of stars according to the truth" (quoted in Russell).

Philippus Aureolus Theophrastus Bombastus von Hohenheim, mercifully called Paracelsus, was as closely identified with the alchemical renaissance of the sixteenth and seventeenth centuries as Copernicus was with the astronomical revolution. To Shakespeare's contemporaries, such as Bostocke and Donne, their stature as natural philosophers was equally imposing (or alarming). This may seem strange. The synonym of bombast in his own age, Paracelsus has become the epitome of pseudoscientific mumbo jumbo to ours. The revolution that he presided over in alchemy encountered greater resistance than the new astronomy, and it was less successful in establishing theories that guided future research. Alchemy was the most mystical of the Renaissance sciences and the most practical; it was profoundly religious and laboriously experimental. This compound of apparently antagonistic elements helps to account for alchemy's volatility in the sixteenth and seventeenth centuries: it is an exaggeration of qualities that were common to other varieties of natural philosophy.

Paracelsus' theories and the controversies that they detonated aroused much more interest in Elizabethan England than the new astronomy did. England had been a veritable alchemical academy in the Middle Ages, the home of Roger Bacon and of the alchemical versifiers John Lydgate, George Ripley, and Thomas Norton. At least a dozen leading physicians were licensed by Henry VI to conduct alchemical experiments, and there is evidence that such research was sustained under the early Tudors. The Elizabethan government actively encouraged alchemical investigations in order to exploit effectively the mineral wealth of the New World.

Thanks partly to the proselytizing of John Dee, alchemy became a subject of major importance among English natural philosophers in the late sixteenth and early seventeenth centuries. Dee's circle of alchemical pupils and colleagues included Sir Philip Sidney, Sir Edward Dyer, Sir Thomas Challoner, John Gwynn, Adrian Gilbert, William Blomfild, Thomas Twynne, John Chomely, and Robert Garland. One of his assistants later acted as the distiller for the "wizard earl" of Northumberland and Sir Walter Raleigh, who conducted alchemical experiments during their imprisonment in the Tower. Dee's influence was felt in the next generation as well: a chain of connections links him, his pupils, and prominent alchemical adepts such as Richard Napier, Robert Fludd, and Sir Kenelm Digby. Although few significant alchemical texts were published in English before 1600, the principles and practical results of alchemy received widespread publicity. Manuscript treatises and Latin works circulated among interested intellectuals and practitioners; vernacular medical books called attention to the implications of Paracelsianism and the virtues of chemically prepared medicines.

Alchemy inspired intense devotion and equally intense hostility. To sympathetic intellectuals like Raleigh, it was essential to the "kind of magic [that] containeth the whole philosophy of nature" (*The History of the World,* I, chapter 11). To skeptics like Ben Jonson, who was well acquainted with its principles, alchemists were simple charlatans who pretended "to commit miracles in art and treason against nature" (quoted in Jonson, Introduction). Much of the controversy about the art stemmed from the views and personality of Paracelsus. His aim had been to create a chemical philosophy that would unlock the secrets of the book of nature, just as theology unlocked the truth of the gospels. He accepted some traditional views as valid, and he greatly emphasized the significance of the correspondence between the microcosm and macrocosm. But he altered the ancient theory of the qualities possessed by the four elements and introduced a new set of concepts that explained the composition of matter and the ways in which its form and substance changed. There were three principles, or spiritual qualities, he asserted, that suffused everything in the natural world. These qualities were associated (confusingly) with the substances salt, sulfur, and mercury that symbolized them. The Paracelsian system offered an alternative to Aristotelian theories, and its inventor extended it to attack the humoral conception of disease as well. The vehemence of Paracelsus' assaults on his ancient as well as his modern competitors was famous: his intemperate condemnations of Aristotle and Galen made the charge of innovation a favorite point of counterattack by critics of Paracelsus.

The ancient philosophers whom Paracelsus cited with approval were the mystical sages of the Neoplatonic canon. An aura of secrecy had always surrounded alchemy, and the influence of Neoplatonic mysticism probably intensified it. The alchemists regarded their art as a religious quest. To onlookers confronted by its bewildering symbolism and reveries of transmutation, it appeared to be a heretical cult that lent itself to the designs of sharpers like Subtle. Certainly it was not easy to understand the symbolic significance of the quest for the philosophers' stone or of the attempt to transform base metal into gold. Furthermore, the theories and medicines that Paracelsus advocated were effective weapons in the hands of practitioners struggling against the monopolistic ambitions of the collegiate physicians. Although many doctors, including members of the College of Physicians, made pragmatic compromises between the old and new physic, especially during James I's reign, the war between the Galenists and the Paracelsians dragged on for over a century. The alchemical renaissance was inevitably controversial, for it questioned ancient truths about the natural world, fostered heterodox religious ideas, and challenged the hierarchy of prestige in the medical profession.

The arguments over the nature of the heavens and the earth had little immediate effect on laymen's faith in the fundamental principles of the old cosmology. The scientists' most radical ideas seemed less revolutionary to many contemporaries than they do to us, and the natural philosophers themselves emphasized the continuity of aspects of their theories with the beliefs of the past. Paracelsus, the most outspoken of the "moderns" of the sixteenth century, powerfully reinforced the microcosm-macrocosm analogy by providing a scientific basis for the venerable doctrine of signatures. Deeply imbedded in medieval thought and folk tradition was the notion that God had stamped on everything in nature a sign (or character) that revealed its correspondence with some part of the body. Paracelsus and his followers insisted that the "signatures" of objects were revealed not merely by their appearance but also by their chemical properties. The "quintessence" of a substance was a virtue infused in it by God, and it interacted with the virtues of all other things through the forces of sympathy and antipathy. Those forces were visible above all in the influence of the stars on the earthly realm. The highest objective of natural philosophy therefore was to discover the connections between the microcosm and the macrocosm so that the forces of universal interaction could be employed for the benefit of mankind. Thus, although much of the chemical philosophy was at odds with Aristotelianism and Galenism, it incorporated axioms from the traditional cosmology that harmonized with older views.

The belief that the new science destroyed the idols of ancient authority with the hammer of observation and experiment is still repeated as dogma in textbooks. But, before Francis Bacon, few English writers had advocated a wholesale revaluation of ancient philosophy; and those who attacked the inaccuracies of traditional learning most vehemently, notably the Paracelsians and William Gilbert, justified their iconoclasm with Neoplatonic slogans as well as with appeals to the results of observation and experiment. Most of Shakespeare's contemporaries were scientific conservatives. They were interested in the practical applications of science and mathematics, and they presumed that the old cosmology could be revised to accommodate new facts. In the course of the seventeenth century, the proliferation of new theories and discoveries for which classical science could not account did gradually enhance the appeal of the critical attitude toward ancient authority advocated by Bacon.

And yet Baconianism itself was more complex and less dominant than most textbooks indicate. Forgotten are the vast numbers of English books published in the sixteenth and early seventeenth centuries that popularized traditional beliefs about the cosmos or propagated animistic ideas that are at odds with our conception of science. Translations of medieval encyclopedias like that of Bartholomeus Anglicus, editions of ancient scientific texts, and hundreds of works of medical information and advice made the old cosmology and the Aristotelian and Galenic traditions on which it was based more accessible than ever before. Astrological almanacs, which were produced in prodigious numbers, instructed the reading public in scientific and magical lore. Their authors were among the first to publicize new developments in astronomy and alchemy, but many of them also clung to the microcosm-macrocosm analogy and other aspects of traditional cosmology and folklore. Even works that acknowledged the views of the moderns, such as Burton's massively influential *Anatomy of Melancholy* (1621), frequently devoted more space to discussing ancient and medieval authorities than they did to evaluating scientific innovations. The strongest wine of the new science was sold in old bottles, and plenty of the earlier vintages remained on the market as well.

Elite Magic

Among the ancient novelties and new inventions that excited the minds of Elizabethan intellectuals, magic and mysticism were as influential as scientific theories and discoveries. Indeed, the boundary line between magic and science was shifting and uncertain, like a shoreline eroded and restored by the sea. Throughout the sixteenth and seventeenth centuries, the terra firma of natural philosophy was periodically submerged by tides of magical thought that left behind them new land when they receded. Discoveries and techniques that proved in the long run to be scientific advances appeared first as aspects of magical and mystical pursuits. The Pythagorean and Neoplatonic mysticism of the great sixteenth-century astronomers Copernicus and Kepler has already been noticed. Kepler's reveries about the celestial harmonies are a particularly striking expression of the aspiration shared by many early modern scientists, to discover transcendent meanings in the natural world as well as to provide a more exact description of its workings. In the next century Gilbert's experiments with magnetism, the chemical discoveries and techniques of the Paracelsians and Helmontians, and even some of the scientific work of Isaac Newton were motivated by fascination with animistic conceptions of nature. The occult philosophies of John Dee and Robert Fludd subsumed mathematics and science, which they regarded as facets of natural magic; and these great magicians encouraged the advancement of mathematics, chemistry, and medicine as part of a broader quest for enlightenment. Although Bacon and Robert Boyle in some celebrated passages deplored the mystical pretensions of men who confounded natural philosophy and the occult, many other intellectuals did not regard them as incompatible.

The great tidal wave of enthusiasm for Renaissance Neoplatonism had not yet receded during Shakespeare's lifetime. Sweeping across Europe from fifteenth-century Florence, the ideas of Marsilio Ficino and Giovanni Pico della Mirandola acquired greater magical depth from the works of Johann Reuchlin, Francesco Giorgi, and, especially, Agrippa von Nettesheim. Ficino and Pico had devised a syncretic philosophy that promised the aspiring magus that he might achieve a union of earthly and heavenly wisdom by mastering natural and spiritual magic. Both writers deplored demonic magic, and there were differences between them about the legitimacy of some other magical arts, notably judicial astrology. But Ficino and Pico provided a Christianized interpretation of occult texts attributed to Hermes Trismegistus, Zoroaster, Orpheus, the Jewish cabalists, and, of course, Plato and the Neoplatonists. Agrippa, in his famous *De occulta philosophia* (*Three Books of Occult Philosophy,* 1533), organized into a handbook for aspiring magi the magical concepts and techniques that the Neoplatonists and their followers extolled. Agrippa maintained that there were three sorts of magic that unlocked the secrets of the three realms of being: the sublunary world, the celestial heavens, and the very highest domain of the angelic intelligences.

In England as elsewhere in Europe, the works of the Neoplatonists exerted a powerful attraction on pious and ambitious minds. They influenced the poets Sidney and Spenser and shaped Sir Walter Raleigh's conception of the meaning and uses of magic. Praising Pico, Raleigh maintained in *The History of the World* (1614) that legitimate magic reveals the influence of the stars on the elements in the sublunary world and "bringeth to light the innermost virtues, and draweth them out of nature's hidden bosom to human use." The true magician is an observer of divine things; his art is the perfection of natural philosophy.

Raleigh's enthusiastic vision of magic as a means to perfect man's understanding of the world and his dominion over it was shared by many educated Englishmen. The works of the Renaissance Neoplatonists as well as magical texts of all kinds were widely read in the late sixteenth and early seventeenth centuries. Citations to Hermes Trismegistus can be found in the works of authors who had little interest in practicing magic themselves, such as Hooker, Burton, and Milton. Hermes continued to be revered as an ancient Egyptian sage long after 1614, when Isaac Casaubon showed that the gnostic writings attributed to him were actually post-Christian. Among those who pursued occult studies deeply, large numbers of books and manuscripts circulated. Some adepts, notably John Dee, Simon Forman, and Richard Napier, accumulated large libraries of medieval and Renaissance magical lore; in 1629, Sir Richard Napier sent his uncle and namesake a long list of books in the Bodleian Library at Oxford on magical topics.

The extent of magical study and practice cannot be measured accurately by counting books and manuscripts, because many works were shared clandestinely by magicians and much of the evidence has been destroyed by later generations antagonistic to magic. The occultists' penchant for secrecy, which was based partly on ancient precedents and partly on prudence, is illustrated by the Rosicrucian controversy. Two anonymous pamphlets published in 1614 and 1615 seemingly revealed the existence of a secret brotherhood of magi in Europe and excited a fierce debate over the ideas and importance of the fraternity of the rosy cross. Scholars now doubt that there was really such a brotherhood, but the ideal of a clandestine circle of magical adepts was realized by networks of scholars throughout Europe. In England the most important groups were apparently those that gathered around John Dee, Simon Forman, Richard Napier, Robert Fludd, and, later in the seventeenth century, Elias Ashmole. Fascination with magic was not, however, confined to such shadowy circles, even after the Restoration: indeed, some of the leading figures and many of the minor supporters of the Royal Society pursued a medley of magical and scientific studies.

The arts that were embraced by magic were extremely varied. Agrippa's *De occulta philosophia* (1533) and Giambattista della Porta's *Magiae naturalis libri viginti* (1589) contained long lists of subjects and techniques that natural magicians were urged to master. Robert Fludd, in a figure in a treatise on the relationship between the microcosm and macrocosm, neatly simplified the kinds of magic into six major categories: prophecy, geomancy, the art of memory, astrology, chiromancy (palmistry), and the science of pyramids (mathematics). Prophecy and astrology were, of course, the most widely practiced branches of magic. Pious and respectable men of great learning aspired to predict the future of mankind, above all the moment when human history would be eclipsed by the reign of Jesus and his saints. Millenarianism exerted a magnetic force of great power on magic, science, and religion and often brought together in the work of a single thinker ideas and methods from each of those disciplines. Learned astrologers and esteemed physicians applied themselves to improving the accuracy of astrology and employing it as a means to discover correspondences between the macrocosm and the microcosm and foretell specific events. Many intellectuals sought to master the intricate mnemonic systems that were based largely on the writings of Ramon Lull, the thirteenth-century alchemist.

At the heart of all these endeavors was an aspiration to find ways to express mystical truths symbolically, so that their unity and complexity might be grasped simultaneously. John Dee's famous emblem, expounded bewilderingly in his *Monas heiroglyphica* (1564), is merely the most famous English example of magical semiotics. In appearance Dee's emblem is simple: it looks like the astrological symbol for mercury standing on arched legs. But its combination of lines and curves signified the unity of the universe, the *monas* that was the goal of astrological, alchemical, hermetic, and Christian thought. The lesser methods of divination mentioned by Fludd—geomancy, physiognomy, and chiromancy—were widely practiced by occultists. Finally, many of these arts depended on the possession of basic mathematical skills, especially arithmetic and geometry. Astrologers often referred to themselves as mathematicians, and some occultists made significant contributions to the development and teaching of mathematics. The chief example is once again John Dee, whose works on geometry and navigation were an extension of the magician's aspiration to discover the secrets of the cosmic order and put them to the general use of mankind.

The magician's highest ambition was to comprehend the future as well as the forces that affected mankind in the present. The natural world was obviously dynamic and changing; the peoples of the earth had a collective history and destiny. The varieties of learned magic provided the means to master time and to predict at least a part of God's providential plan. Spiritual or angelic magic was the most powerful and controversial method of divination. By using the Christianized rites of the Jewish cabala, the magus could converse with the angels themselves and so see truths that lay beyond the horizons of natural philosophy and theology. The basis for spiritual magic had been provided by Pico and Reuchlin; its rituals were amplified by Agrippa, who combined them with rites from works of medieval conjuring in the third book of his *De occulta philosophia*. These authorities emphasized that because the cabala employed the holy names of God and invoked angelic powers, it was the antithesis of demonic magic. Agrippa also depicted spiritual magic as a religious quest. "The greatest conjurer in Christendom," as the satirist

Thomas Nash styled him, insisted that the ceremonies he published could be used effectually and safely only by the most pious and ascetic magi. Marlowe's Faustus debases spiritual magic by alloying it with a sordid ambition to be "as cunning as Agrippa was, whose shadows made all Europe honor him" (I. i. 118–119).

Real scholars were as ravished by spiritual magic as Faustus was, and the best of them were untarnished by his lust for power and fame. Dee and his followers collected and studied medieval conjuring books as well as the texts of the Renaissance cabalists. Dee himself used the rituals in them. With the assistance of several scryers, the most notable of whom was Edward Kelley, he conducted a long series of seances in which (he claimed) he conversed with angels and spirits. The archangels Uriel and Gabriel appeared in his crystal ball; and through Kelley and his other mediums, Dee was able to receive mysterious revelations and to question the angels about scientific, magical, and religious matters. Dee's pious aspirations overreached any of Faustus' vainglorious dreams. He hoped to learn truths from the angels that would reveal the secrets of the natural world and serve as the basis for a reconciliation of the Christian churches. During his long sojourn on the Continent in the 1580s, he tried to win the support of the Holy Roman Emperor Rudolf II for his magical ecumenicalism. His failure and subsequent disgrace did not prevent younger scholars from emulating his experiments with spiritual magic.

Spirit-raising was in vogue among university students around the turn of the century, and many Jacobean occultists were charged with conjuring. In some instances such accusations must have been exaggerations or completely groundless, but the chance survival of a few collections of manuscripts indicates that interest in angelic magic was quite widespread. They show, for example, that the notable medical astrologer Richard Napier, who was the rector of a parish in rural Buckinghamshire, began to practice the art in the second decade of the seventeenth century. Napier had known Dee and had been instructed in various branches of magical practice by Simon Forman. Like Dee, he was a deeply devout and virtuous man who hoped that spiritual magic would yield truths about contentious theological problems and also enable him to perfect his medical practice. In his *Brief Lives,* John Aubrey commented that he was so pious that his knees were "horny with frequent praying." He purportedly succeeded many times in contacting the angel Raphael, who responded laconically to some religious questions and many medical queries. Once he even vouchsafed to Napier a prophecy of plague and war. Napier was utterly sincere in his conviction that spiritual magic was effective and licit, and his beliefs were shared by his intimate friends and correspondents. Some conjurers were certainly charlatans, and others sought magical power for sinful reasons. But to the now obscure scholars who followed Dee, spiritual magic was a force for the improvement of mankind, and they hoped to use it to achieve the kind of benevolent mastery that Prospero enjoyed over his realm.

Despite the pious intentions of magicians like Dee and Napier, conjuring spirits was a perilous practice. Everyone knew that Satan could assume the guise of an angel of light, and many contemporaries were convinced that spiritual magic was diabolical. Raleigh, who regarded natural magic of all kinds sympathetically, condemned it with the conventional argument. However impressively the magi cloaked themselves in piety and asceticism, they were profoundly deluded to think that the spirits with which they conversed were angels. Higher beings could not possibly be summoned and controlled by any human cunning. "Let the professors thereof cover themselves how they please by professed purity of life, . . . [they] are men of evil faith and in the power of Satan. For good spirits and angels cannot be constrained; and the rest are devils, which willingly obey" (*The History of the World,* I, chapter 11). The magi themselves acknowledged the force of this logic: some of the spells that they used to summon spirits included explicit appeals to God for protection against Satan's illusions. But the snares of the Fiend were not the only danger that conjurers faced. The church was deeply hostile to any kind of spirit-raising, and people who practiced it were liable to prosecution in the ecclesiastical courts. Parliament made conjuring evil spirits a secular crime punishable by death in 1563 and added necromancy to the roll of capital offenses in the second witchcraft statute of 1604. None of the famous magi was tried or executed as a sorcerer or necromancer, but all of them were threatened with prosecution. Lesser figures were harassed by magistrates and by the ecclesiastical authorities. The disgrace of the great Dee and the conviction of many obscure wizards in the church courts made absolutely plain the attitude of the authorities to angelic magic.

Angelic magic was as demanding as it was dangerous. The most eminent adepts therefore relied upon less controversial kinds of magic, particularly astrology, as their principal means of discovery and divination. Widely esteemed as an ancient science, astrology had an impressive intellectual pedigree: its principles and symbolism could be traced to the earliest civilizations, and they were a fundamental aspect of Western culture. As long as the traditional cosmology prevailed, the existence of astral influences was axiomatic to any attempt to understand the natural order and man's place in it. "If you do but consider the whole universe as one united body, and man an epitome of this body," explained Nicholas Culpeper, "it will seem strange to none but madmen and fools that the stars should have some influence upon the body of man. . . . Every inferior world is governed by its superior, and receives influence from it" (quoted in Thomas, *Religion and the Decline of Magic,* chapter 11).

Even the critics of astrological divination had to grant that the stars affected natural phenomena, such as the tides, the weather, and diseases. Until the second half of the seventeenth century, most educated men and women thought that it was possible to make specific astrological predictions of human actions as well as natural occurrences. Astrology was thus a means of understanding the natural world and of foretelling sublunary events. Intricate rules for determining stellar influences, devised by ancient and medieval scholars, were greatly elaborated by early modern astrologers. The stars were a kind of macroscope, in which the design of nature and the destiny of men might be seen.

Both the natural and the judicial functions of astrology appealed to men eager to discover the secret causes of things. Among the Renaissance Neoplatonists, Pico was conspicuous in his opposition to astrology. His massive attack on the discipline was motivated by his conviction that spiritual beings, angels and men, enjoyed complete freedom and could not possibly be controlled by mere bodies. Few magi shared Pico's views on astrology. His Florentine colleague Ficino regarded it as the basis of natural magic, and della Porta stressed that the natural magician must be skilled in astrology as well. Agrippa declared that all of the kinds of divination were "rooted and grounded upon astrology" (quoted in Thomas, *Religion and the Decline of Magic,* chapter 21). The hermetic texts offered a deeply mystical interpretation of stellar influences.

Medieval and Renaissance alchemy depended heavily on astrological principles and symbolism. Astrology was, in fact, the common denominator of all of the kinds of elite magic, and the leading English occultists naturally studied and practiced it. John Dee gave astrological advice to Queen Elizabeth. Simon Forman wrote a textbook of astrological medicine and maintained a huge astrological practice; his clients included many of the Elizabethan nobility. Richard Napier and William Lilly were equally successful and fashionable in the seventeenth century. Thanks to his best-selling almanacs and textbooks, Lilly was the most famous astrologer of the age. A host of lesser magicians published astrological books and provided advice to clients as well.

Astrology made men like Forman, Napier, and Lilly rich and famous. Unlike the other kinds of elite magic, astrology was a profession as well as a field of study, and the services of its leading practitioners were in great demand. Despite his mean birth and repellent personality, Forman exploited the public esteem for astrology to gratify his prodigious cravings for social prestige and sexual conquest. His success made him the object of the College of Physicians' harassment and Ben Jonson's satire, but nothing diminished his popularity. Forman and his fellow astrologers provided information and advice about a vast array of personal problems and anxieties to men and women of every social rank. The techniques of astrology permitted astrologers to forecast events that would affect everyone or to predict an individual's personal destiny. They could help their clients choose the propitious moment to act and could supply the answer to almost any specific question put to them.

Astrology had anciently been a tool of medical diagnosis, and many astrologers treated the maladies of mind and body. In the early seventeenth century, regular physicians employed astrology as well. Medical astrologers were supposed to be particularly adept at diagnosing pregnancy and foretelling the probable outcome of troubling afflictions. Astrologers also helped to solve crimes, recover lost property, resolve difficult family problems, find missing persons, and make business decisions. Many ignorant and unscrupulous practitioners preyed on the public demand for astrological advice, but the best astrologers were very skilled doctors and psychologists. The astrological profession was an essential social institution in the Elizabethan age.

More than any other kind of magic or science, astrology was woven into the fabric of early modern thought and social life. It could not be unraveled from the tapestry of contemporary belief without altering the overall design of the world picture. And yet critics repeatedly plucked at the loose threads of astrological theory and practice, hoping to rip out the impious art. Prior to the mid-seventeenth century, their iconoclasm was motivated chiefly by religious scruples and professional rivalries, rather than by scientific skepticism. Some theologians attacked judicial astrology because it allegedly presumed that man's destiny was determined by the stars and not by God's providence and man's own free will. This objection to astrological divination was very old; it had been raised by medieval writers and by Pico. But it received redoubled emphasis from Protestant divines, particularly Calvinists, who added that the techniques of astrologers resembled the rites of the papists. The clergy's opposition to astrology was motivated by professional rivalry as well, for the astrologers competed with ministers for the esteem and faith of the common people.

Medical men were also angered by the confidence that ordinary men and women placed in astrologers. They strove to depict their rivals as ignorant quacks who lured sick people to their deaths with promises of miraculous cures. Astrologers, complained the Northampton physician John Cotta, were wont to overstep the legitimate medical applications of their art and "fish for a name and fame amongst the common and easy deceived vulgars with the glorious bates of prodigious precepts" (II, chapter 3). Such religious and professional caveats encouraged a vigorous strain of antiastrological opinion among a minority of laymen, who believed in the existence of stellar influences but doubted the capacity of astrologers to predict them accurately. The most potent weapon of these critics was satire. "Astrology is an art," sneered John Melton (fl. 1609–1620) in *Astrologaster,* "whereby cunning knaves cheat plain honest men, . . . a science instructing all the students of it to lie as often as they speak, . . . that tells the truth as often as bawds go to church, witches or whores say their prayers" (quoted in Allen, chapter 3).

The objections to astrology were well known—and so were the astrologers' answers to them. The defenders of the art parried the charge that judicial astrology was impiously determinist with the stock response that the stars influenced but did not control the fortunes of men. "They do incline, but not compel," Robert Burton explained. "No necessity at all: *agunt non cogunt* [they lead but do not compel]: and so gently incline, that a wise man may resist them; *sapiens dominabitur astris* [a wise man is the master of the stars]: they rule us, but God rules them" (quoted in Allen, chapter 4). The frontispiece of William Lilly's annual almanacs was a portrait of the author holding a book on which was inscribed the legend *Non cogunt* (They do not compel). Many astrologers and some leading churchmen asserted that prayer could overcome the influence of the stars. Although these arguments did not mollify the godly enemies of judicial astrology, they seem largely to have satisfied the Elizabethan and Jacobean public. Popular dramatists, poets, and pamphleteers occasionally echoed the preachers' diatribes against astral determinism, and professional astrologers were almost always depicted as cheats; but the great bulk of the thousands of literary references to astrology assume its validity.

Popular literature was, in fact, the principal vehicle for disseminating astrological lore. Almanacs themselves outsold every other kind of secular book; by 1660 as many as one in three households purchased an almanac each year. The case for astrology and the knowledge of its principles became more and more widely known in the late sixteenth and seventeenth centuries. Even the clergy was ambivalent about the legitimacy of the art. Despite complaints about astral determinism and astrological practitioners, many clergymen, including Puritans, consulted astrologers. Other divines, of whom Robert Burton is the most famous, praised astrology and practiced it. At least until the Restoration, physicians also dulled their own polemical weapons by admitting that their adversaries' art had legitimate medical applications. Leading doctors continued to use astrology, and a few of them even published almanacs; the natural philosophers were strikingly slow to condemn astrology as unscientific. The astronomers' discoveries initially sharpened intellectuals' interest in perfecting astrology, not in disproving it. Even Bacon advocated a "sane astrology" based on sound scientific principles (Allen, chapter 4). The enemies of astrology certainly buttressed their arguments with evidence produced by the astronomers in the seventeenth century, but many scientists did not think that their discoveries invalidated the basic principles of astrology.

Despite a good deal of clerical and medical criticism, astrology therefore remained an integral feature of Elizabethan and Jacobean culture. The growth of literacy and of the book trade made it increasingly popular, and the vogue for natural magic and the discoveries of the astronomers heightened intellectuals' interest in it. Not all the claims of judicial astrology were universally accepted, but the stars retained their power over the minds of educated Englishmen until the end of the seventeenth century.

Folk Magic

The varieties of elite magic were kinds of religion and science in the eyes of their practitioners. Folk magic was similarly a part of the religion and science of the common people. Almost every English village seems to have contained people who claimed to possess some special knowledge or preternatural power that surpassed the capacities of their neighbors. Cunning men and women used their talents to ease the myriad pains and anxieties that befell people living in conditions much harsher than those that we experience. They healed the diseases of men and beasts, solved crimes, recovered lost property, salved the pangs of lovesick youth, and foretold the future. Their services were cheap and very popular. "Sorcerers are too common," grumbled Robert Burton, "cunning men, wizards, and white witches, as they call them, in every village, which, if they be sought unto, will help almost all infirmities of body and mind" (quoted in Thomas, *Religion and the Decline of Magic,* chapter 7). The evil counterpart of the wise woman was the witch, who used her powers to injure her neighbors. People spoke of white and black witches, or of good witches and bad, to distinguish between the wizards who helped and those who harmed. Sometimes the talents of the cunning were entirely natural—a gift for healing particular afflictions with secret herbs or for setting broken bones, for example. Others were popular astrologers. But most wizards used rites and spells that invoked supernatural powers. The folk magic that Burton and many other clergymen and physicians condemned embraced lore about the natural world as well as beliefs about the supernatural realm, and many wise men and women freely combined practices derived from popular science with those based on popular religion.

Folklore attributed inherent natural powers to a vast array of substances. Animals, plants, and minerals possessed secret virtues that healed diseases or had some other beneficent effect. Like their social betters, the common people believed that the world pulsated with natural as well as supernatural forces that could act between objects, as a lodestone could attract iron. The affinities between things were revealed by analogies, which established correspondences between the parts and levels of creation. The aetites, or eaglestone, for example, was hollow and contained a smaller stone inside it. Its resemblance to a pregnant woman is obvious, and contemporaries consequently believed that an aetites worn as an amulet could prevent miscarriages. Wizards who used such objects were not necessarily attempting to manipulate the supernatural: regular physicians prescribed medicinal herbs, and natural philosophers were convinced that many beliefs about sympathetic powers between objects were correct. Such beliefs were so numerous and varied that it is impossible to fit them all into a comprehensive scheme of popular science.

Neither the logic of the natural symbolism nor the number and kinds of forces that were collectively recognized by the common people is clear. It is evident, though, that many folk rituals, especially healing rites, that hostile contemporaries regarded as magical were in fact practical applications of popular beliefs about nature. Some intellectuals were intensely interested in the scientific basis of the practices of cunning folk. They collected popular lore and rationalized it. The doctrine of signatures, which had originated as a folk belief, was incorporated into Paracelsus' philosophy. The Neoplatonists explained the ability of folk healers to cure diseases with amulets as the effects of the power of sympathy. Scientific curiosity about popular wisdom continued to be intense in the seventeenth century: the early fellows of the Royal Society investigated many folk remedies and beliefs. Their attempts to find out whether particular aspects of folk magic had a natural or a supernatural basis demonstrate that even contemporary scientists found it difficult to classify many items of popular lore. It is probable that ordinary people were generally unconcerned about the problem: the cunning of wise men and women included secrets of nature as well as command of supernatural powers.

Most folk remedies and rites, however, appealed explicitly to some supernatural power for assistance. The magical techniques of village wizards were extremely varied, and it is impossible to trace the lineage of all of them or to fit them into a single explanatory scheme. Some practices were based on pre-Christian beliefs whose overall logic had vanished over the centuries. Others employed the language or sacred paraphernalia of the medieval church. The common people believed that the world teemed with spiritual beings that imperiled or protected them. The clergy had traditionally provided magical protection against the molestations of malevolent spirits by casting out demons, blessing the fields, and purifying women after childbirth. But the Protestant reformers repudiated many of the rituals of the medieval church, discarding, in effect, the ministry's role as God's wizards. Cunning men and wise women took up their mantle and supplied the public demand for magical rites that could counter the powers of evil spirits and witches. Ordinary people saw nothing wrong in seeking the help of folk magicians, for their test of legitimacy was practical, not theological. In Edward Poeton's "The Winnowing of White Witchcraft," the country bumpkin exclaims, "No sir, I don't think that I was in any fault in going to seek for help and health from such as can do one good!" (British Library, MS Sloane 1817, fol. 169r). Neither the status of the wizard nor the origins of his techniques mattered as much as the simple question of whether he used his magic to help his neighbors or to hurt them.

The distinction between good magic and bad followed from a fundamental axiom of popular religion: that there were two antithetical types of supernatural beings. The spirits of the air, remarked Robert Burton, "we subdivide into good and bad angels, call gods or devils, as they help or hurt us" (I, section 1). There was an almost Manichaean quality to this habit of thought. The tormented rustics who sought Richard Napier's help for their mental afflictions sometimes told him that they were torn between their good spirits and their bad; a woman charged with witchcraft at Northampton in 1612 confessed that she acknowledged two gods, "God the Father and the Devil." The good and bad angels who strive to influence Faustus represented literal realities to Marlowe's audience. Wicked urgings were frequently personified as temptations of Satan and his demons; deliverances from them were attributed to God and his angels. Protestant theologians sometimes complained about the heretical tendencies of popular dualism, but they and their medieval forebears had indeed helped to create it.

Learned divines taught that the supernatural powers were arrayed in two vast armies, commanded by God and by Satan. They cataloged the spiritual and earthly battalions of each force, and they tried to align the spirits of the pagan past under one banner or the other. Richard Hooker, for instance, declared that the spirits of wood and water, whom the heathens had honored as gods, were the remnants of Lucifer's scattered legions. Asked his opinions of fairies, the great Puritan preacher Richard Greenham replied in *Grave Counsels and Godlie Observations* that "he distinguished between them and other spirits, as commonly men distinguish between good witches and bad witches." The clergy's interest in popular pneumatology was evangelical: they hoped to place the beliefs of the common people in a sound theological context. They were not entirely successful. Calling her subordinates to order, Heccat in Thomas Middleton's *The Witch* lists some of the many kinds of spirits: "Urchins, elves, hags, satires, pans, fauns, . . . Kit with the candle stick, tritons, centaures, dwarfs, imps, the spoorne, the mare, the man i'th' oak, the hell-wayne, the fire-drake, the puckle" (I. ii. 297–301). It was hard to write a gloss that reconciled all the spirit lore inherited from the ancients and from pre-Christian paganism with a scheme that had plausible scriptural sanctions. Few theologians, for example, agreed with Greenham that fairies were good spirits, and some dismissed them altogether as papistic fictions. Over the centuries, however, the church had profoundly influenced the thought of the mass of the people, even though many of them were indifferent to doctrinal niceties. God and the devil, together with their angels and demons, had become the leading figures (if not the only players) in the popular conception of the spiritual world.

Shakespeare's contemporaries thus believed that invisible beings were as numerous and near as the stage spirits that Prospero commanded, and they thought that most of them were malevolent. "The air is not so full of flies in summer as it is at all times of invisible devils," exclaimed Burton (I, section 2). Every imaginable misfortune might be attributed to Satan and his minions or to the lesser spirits of folklore. Sometimes the devil or an evil spirit actually possessed a person's body and mind. The effects were awful: the victim suffered horrible fits, vomited strange objects, raved and cursed, and

spoke in the demon's voice, occasionally in learned tongues that the patient could not have known naturally.

In a widely publicized and representative Elizabethan case in 1574, a morose law student named Briggs became persuaded that he was haunted by Satan himself. After he had made several attempts at suicide, a physician tried and failed to cure his melancholy. His fits gradually worsened until he fell into a tormented trance. Speaking in a strange voice, the demon inside him tempted the victim and taunted the ministers who attended him. The struggle with Satan finally ended when Briggs succeeded in calling upon God to cast his tormenter out of him (Thomas, *Religion and the Decline of Magic,* chapter 15). Spectacular episodes like this one were very rare; they attracted much more attention than their numbers warranted. Lesser cases of demonism were commonplace. The devil obsessed the godly, tempting Puritan saints to renounce their faith and commit horrible sins. He lured ordinary people to kill themselves or perpetrate shocking crimes. Almost any evil impulse or deed could be plausibly attributed to the instigation of Satan.

Evil spirits also inflicted mental and physical diseases and brought bad luck of every kind. The devil knew how to cause or exacerbate natural disorders by disturbing the balance of the humors in people's bodies. Demons and spirits sometimes haunted persons and property, wrecking business ventures, harming crops and animals, upsetting objects mysteriously. Spirits were supposed to raise tempests, as Ariel did at Prospero's bidding. Witches, who were the human manifestations of supernatural malevolence, could inflict all of the same kinds of injuries and mishaps. Spirits and witches served, in fact, as the chief supernatural explanation for misfortune. Their malice did not exclude the possibility of a natural cause for afflictions; it added a dimension to them that made personal disaster an aspect of the supernatural contest between good and evil. The theologians declared that misfortunes were sent ultimately by God to correct and test his children, and that they should be occasions for repentance and prayer, rather than for witch-hunting and countermagic. But by their own admission their teachings were little heeded by the common people.

The powers of spirits and witches were a matter of intense discussion and considerable anxiety in the late sixteenth and early seventeenth centuries.

There were two distinct conceptions of witchcraft, one of them invented rather recently by continental demonologists and the other anciently imbedded in folk belief. The elaborate theory of witchcraft propounded by the theologians presented the crime as a kind of devil worship. "The ground of all the practices of witchcraft," William Perkins explained, "is a league or covenant between the witch and the devil, wherein they do mutually bind themselves one to other" (chapter 13). The demonologists taught that witches consorted with evil spirits and with Satan, meeting at sabbats to perform his blasphemous rites. They could perform miraculous feats, such as conjuring demons, changing their shape, and flying great distances. This highly theologized doctrine of witchcraft was particularly appealing to strong Protestants, who were convinced that the people of God were locked in a final climactic struggle with the forces of Satan. It was less attractive to the majority of laymen. Despite support for the doctrine from influential writers, including King James himself, it had comparatively little effect on popular beliefs or witchcraft prosecutions. The majority of the people, including the educated elite, continued to believe that witchcraft was above all an antisocial crime.

For centuries the English had believed that some women had the power to injure their neighbors magically. Their methods were simple—cursing, ocular enchantment, and crude kinds of sorcery—and the origins of their powers were of less concern than the harm or *maleficium* that they did. Witchcraft accusations almost always followed from an incident in which the accused was supposed to have caused one of her neighbors to suffer some illness or misfortune. Witches exhibited few distinguishing characteristics: they had familiar spirits that they suckled from a third teat or they had a witches' mark somewhere on their bodies. But familiars looked just like ordinary small animals, and the distinctive teats and marks were normally hidden. Witches could be discovered initially, therefore, only by the injuries that they caused. They were malevolent misanthropes such as Mother Sawyer in *The Witch of Edmonton* (1658), a collaborative work based on a notorious but otherwise typical case, rather than the fabulous hags of demonology such as the Weird Sisters in *Macbeth* or Heccat in *The Witch.*

English religious and judicial institutions diminished the usefulness to zealous officials of the doctrine of diabolical witchcraft and circumscribed the

actions that might be taken against accused witches. England had no inquisition; its legal traditions forbade torture to extract confessions and demanded that charges be proved in trials before juries. Witchcraft trials therefore remained rooted in the folk beliefs of ordinary people who initiated prosecutions and played a crucial role in them as witnesses and jurors; the accusations on which they were based arose out of the tensions of village life and reflected the popular fear of *maleficium.* The relationship between the supposed witch and her neighbors was the crucial factor in making her the object of suspicion.

Accused witches were typically middle-aged women of humble social standing with disagreeable personalities. A few were cunning men and women or, rarely, astrologers or conjurers. The proportion of female healers or midwives who were prosecuted for witchcraft was very small in comparison both to their numbers in the society at large and to the numbers of women charged with the crime. Suspects were seldom insane, although mental illnesses were not uncommonly attributed to witchcraft. Witches were, in sum, terrifyingly ordinary people. Typically, a woman incurred suspicion when she annoyed her neighbors for a long time, straining the customary bonds of hospitality and reciprocity beyond the breaking point. The final incident that led to a formal witchcraft charge was often a quarrel over a gift or loan of food or some other necessity. When a person who had refused a favor to a chronically demanding neighbor subsequently fell ill or suffered a misfortune, he was likely to suspect her of bewitching him. Some women even used their reputation as witches to extort gifts and favors. It is often asserted that witchcraft trials were a murderous manifestation of misogyny; the observation, while true, is inadequate. All women were potentially witches, but only an unlucky few were charged with witchcraft. The target of witchcraft prosecutions was not women in general; it was those women who had violated the norms of the community by making aggressive and threatening demands on their neighbors.

The link between social tensions and witchcraft prosecutions partially explains why they were at their peak in the 1580s and 1590s. Those decades were terrible years of acute distress for many English people, and magistrates at every level of government were obsessed by the problem of poverty and the threat of disorder. Diminished tolerance for disruptive and dependent women, however, would hardly have been expressed indirectly in witchcraft accusations, had not other factors enhanced the popular fear of witches. The quality and magnitude of the threat of witchcraft are difficult to grasp in retrospect. Bishop John Jewel warned Queen Elizabeth in 1559 or 1560, "Witches and sorcerers within these last years are marvellously increased in this Your Grace's realm" (quoted in Scot, Introduction).

The government sought to combat the apparently growing incidence of witchcraft by making it a secular crime. Statutes passed in 1542 (repealed in 1547), 1563, and 1604 made *maleficium* that resulted in the death of the victim and conjuring evil spirits punishable by death. Perhaps because of the relatively strict procedures of the English legal system and the cost of prosecutions, the number of women tried and executed under these laws was small by European standards: between 500 and 1,000 witches were put to death in the sixteenth and seventeenth centuries. But for every charge that resulted in a trial at the assizes, many witchcraft accusations were made in lesser tribunals or informally. Witchcraft cases were heard in every kind of court, secular and ecclesiastical, and accusations that never came to trial are recorded in huge numbers in the notebooks of astrologers and medical men.

Pious writers lamented the readiness of the vulgar to blame their misfortunes on witches and seek the help of popish exorcists and folk wizards. "The fables of witchcraft," grumbled the great skeptic Reginald Scot in 1584, "have taken so fast a hold and deep root in the heart of man, that few or none can (nowadays) with patience endure the hand and correction of God. For if any adversity, grief, sickness, loss of children, corn, cattle, or liberty happen unto them, by and by they exclaim upon witches" (I, chapter 1).

Complaints of defamation from women who had been denounced as witches were a staple item of business in the church courts. Many accused witches were assaulted by gangs of their neighbors intent on "scratching" them (drawing the witches' blood) to nullify their spells or "swimming" them (immersing the witches to see if they floated, a sign that the water—and God—rejected them) to prove their guilt. Mob attacks on suspected witches continued long after formal prosecutions had ceased. The last woman known to have died as a witch was beaten and drowned by a crowd in Tring in 1751.

Worry about witchcraft was thus endemic in village society, and at times, notably in the period of Shakespeare's maturity, it intensified and became a kind of prolonged collective phobia.

English awareness of the perils of witchcraft was no doubt heightened in the late sixteenth century by the works of the famous continental demonologists and the vast witch-hunts in France and Germany. But domestic ecclesiastical politics also contributed to the prevailing anxiety. The Edwardian church had unwittingly contributed to popular apprehensiveness when it discarded ritual exorcism in 1552 as a relic of popish superstition. The faithful had relied on the church for spiritual protection; the Protestant clergy that was gradually installed in local parishes during Elizabeth's reign was increasingly unwilling or unable to provide it. Preachers counseled their flocks to rely on prayer to withstand the assaults of witches and demons. It was a hard doctrine, and many resorted to Catholic priests and cunning men and women for help. Some Elizabethan divines, the most prominent of whom was John Darrell, devised a method of casting out devils and unwitching people by prayer and fasting. Even this means of ecclesiastical countermagic, which had a sound scriptural basis, was repudiated by the church hierarchy because of its antagonism to Darrell's Puritanism. The canons of 1604 forbade local ministers to conduct fasts for bewitched or possessed persons without their bishop's permission. At the same time that the clergy was laying down its most potent weapons in the fight against supernatural malevolence, it was emphasizing the powers of Satan and his minions. The doctrinal changes that accompanied the Reformation, which were intended to produce a stronger relationship between the laity and God, thus had the initial effect of making ordinary people feel more vulnerable to witches and evil spirits.

Conclusion

Science and *magic* meant very different things to Shakespeare's contemporaries than they do to us, and the term *folklore* was not coined until the nineteenth century. As useful as these terms are to distinguish between natural philosophy and occult studies and between elite traditions and plebeian beliefs, they are crude tools for analyzing early modern thought. Ever since the eighteenth century the assumption that science and magic are incompatible has dominated the thinking of the English upper classes. But Elizabethan scientists, as we have seen, were deeply interested in the occult; and although many natural philosophers rejected hermeticism and mysticism in the seventeenth century, magic continued to fascinate others. Opposition to magic in the sixteenth and early seventeenth centuries was founded mainly on the conviction that it was irreligious. Even in the Restoration there was still truth in John Aubrey's remark that occult studies were more despised by churchmen than by scientists: "The Dean of Wells would laugh at this, but Kepler and Tycho Brahe would not" (quoted in Hunter, *John Aubrey,* chapter 2). Antagonism to both elite and popular magic was ignited by the religious controversies of the Protestant Reformation and was only gradually subsumed in the educated elite's growing confidence in scientific progress. During the course of this change, the definition of magic itself was altered to meet the requirements of polemicists who contested the legitimacy of scientific beliefs and practices.

The leaders of the English Reformation regarded the Catholic clergy as little better than wizards, and they repudiated rituals and symbols to which the medieval church had attributed supernatural powers. The rites of consecration and exorcism were eliminated from the liturgy; relics and shrines, holy repositories of miraculous power, were destroyed; holy emblems were dismissed as the toys of superstition. The Mass itself was characterized as a magical rite: the miracle of transubstantiation was presented as a kind of sorcery in the overwrought language of the Protestant propagandists. Rituals that the Church of England did preserve, such as the churching of women and rogation, were transformed into commemorative ceremonies. "Surely," declared William Perkins, summing up the Protestant position, "if a man will but take a view of all Popery, he shall easily see that a great part of it is mere magic" (quoted in Thomas, *Religion and the Decline of Magic,* chapter 2). In the lexicon of the post-Reformation church, the word *superstition* meant a Catholic belief or practice. The Protestants' rejection of Catholic rituals and symbols was based on strong theological arguments, but the equation of popish rites and magic was more than just a polemical device. It expressed the reformers' conviction that magical beliefs and practices were a major obstacle to religious reform.

Godly divines assailed elite and popular magic in the late sixteenth and early seventeenth centuries, hoping to replace learned mysticism and plebeian credulity with a Protestant faith soundly based on Scripture. They charged that many of the operations of magicians and folk wizards were popish or heathen. Although overdrawn, such accusations had some grounding in fact, because magic was linked to the old religion and pre-Christian paganism by analogy and history. Elite magicians had borrowed from the church's liturgy in their efforts to Christianize the occult texts they discovered. The rituals that the Renaissance magi used were a medley of Catholic or pseudo-Catholic prayers and ancient symbols. Folk wizards had purloined the church's prayers and emblems to invoke the help of God and his angels, and they used spells and techniques that originated in forgotten cults. To Protestants, particularly Puritans, much magic was therefore extremely suspect, and some of it was anathema.

The campaign against folk magic was especially vigorous, and many of its spokesmen denied the validity of the distinction between good and bad magic altogether. Protestant writers declared that the age of miracles was over and that it was absurd to think that God conferred supernatural gifts on ignorant rustics; cunning men and women must therefore be the agents of Satan. They were worse than black witches because they seduced afflicted people away from religion just when they most needed the assistance of a spiritual physician. "The good witch," railed William Perkins, is a "more horrible and detestable monster" than the black one (chapter 13).

The clerical enemies of magic received some support from educated laymen. Physicians reinforced the attack on cunning men and women, whom they regarded as "ignorant practicers of physic." They charged that their plebeian rivals were quacks who gulled the public by selling them ridiculous remedies for diseases they did not understand. Their spokesmen echoed the clergy's complaint that popular superstitions about the supernatural made the public easy marks for charlatans. The vulgar were too eager to assign supernatural causes to entirely natural maladies. "Everything whereof every man cannot give a reason is not therefore a miracle," scolded John Cotta in 1612 (I, chapter 8). The churchmen and doctors who attacked magic encouraged dissent from the prevailing acceptance of a wide range of magical beliefs and practices.

Social critics assailed magical mountebanks who

mesmerized their clients with hocus-pocus while they fleeced them. Dramatists delighted in the terrifying perils of conjuring. Some writers asserted, or strongly implied, that the magical arts they traduced were sheer fakery. Marlowe's Mephostophilis denies that Faustus has the power to constrain him, and Jonson depicted alchemy as a magical confidence trick. Sweeping skepticism about magic itself, rather than about particular practices and their abuse, was very rare. The most powerful rejection of elite and popular magic was Reginald Scot's *The Discoverie of Witchcraft* (1584). A devout Kentish gentleman, Scot applied a highly corrosive mixture of religious and medical arguments to the entire range of contemporary magical practices. "Alas! How many natural things are there so strange, as to many seem miraculous; and how many counterfeit matters are there, that to the simple seem yet more wonderful?" he lamented near the end of his survey (chapter 41).

But it was not merely the simple who continued to believe that the world was full of wonders. The clergy itself was divided over the legitimacy of magic. Orthodox divines, such as Richard Napier, studied occult texts and conjured angels; clerical alchemists were commonplace, and clerical astrologers abounded. Even stout Calvinists patronized astrologers, and during the Interregnum the Puritan regime permitted the publication of a vast array of magical books. Natural philosophy was marbled with magic and mysticism, as we have seen. Contemporaries were aware of the new ideas and discoveries altering the cosmology that epitomized their world view. But it was not until the century after the English Revolution that the educated elite finally repudiated supernaturalism and embraced scientism.

During Shakespeare's lifetime, new philosophy called all in doubt, but ancient truths endured. Learned men and women knew that there was more in heaven and earth than any natural philosophy could explain. Much had been discovered, but much more remained mysterious—the matter of faith, not reason. Their attitude was far from uncritical, as the reformers often claimed, but it lacked the modern assumption that everything is known or knowable. In *All's Well That Ends Well*, sage Lafew summarized this outlook best: "They say miracles are past, and we have our philosophical persons, to make modern and familiar, things supernatural and causeless. Hence is it that we make trifles of terrors, ensconcing ourselves into seeming knowledge when we should submit ourselves to an unknown fear" (I. iii. 1–6).

BIBLIOGRAPHY

Don Cameron Allen, *The Star-Crossed Renaissance* (1941). John B. Bamborough, *The Little World of Man* (1952). Marie Boas, *The Scientific Renaissance, 1450–1630* (1962). John Brand, *Observations on the Popular Antiquities of Great Britain,* revised and enlarged by Sir Henry Ellis, 3 vols. (repr. 1969). Katharine M. Briggs, *The Anatomy of Puck* (1959) and *Pale Hecate's Team* (1962). Timothy Bright, *A Treatise of Melancholie,* Hardin Craig, ed. (1940). Peter Burke, *Popular Culture in Early Modern Europe* (1978). Robert Burton, *The Anatomy of Melancholy,* Holbrook Jackson, ed., 3 vols. (1978).

Bernard Capp, *English Almanacs, 1500–1800: Astrology and the Popular Press* (1979). Nicholas Copernicus, *On the Revolutions of the Heavenly Spheres,* Charles Glenn Wallis, trans. (1952). John Cotta, *A Short Discoverie of the Unobserved Dangers of Severall Sorts of Ignorant and Unconsiderate Practisers of Physicke in England* (1612). Hardin Craig, *The Enchanted Glass* (1960). Allen G. Debus, *The Chemical Philosophy,* 2 vols. (1977), and *Man and Nature in the Renaissance* (1978). Betty Jo T. Dobbs, *The Foundations of Newton's Alchemy* (1975).

Peter J. French, *John Dee* (1972). Richard Greenham, *The Works of the Reverend and Faithfull Servant of Jesus Christ M. Richard Greenham* (1599). John Edward Christopher Hill, *Society and Puritanism in Pre-Revolutionary England,* 2nd ed. (1967). Richard Hooker, *Of the Laws of Ecclesiastical Polity,* Christopher Morris, ed., 2 vols. (1963). Michael C. W. Hunter, *John Aubrey and the Realm of Learning* (1975) and *Science and Society in Restoration England* (1981).

Francis R. Johnson, *Astronomical Thought in Renaissance England* (1937; repr. 1968). Richard Foster Jones, *Ancients and Moderns,* 2nd ed. (1965). Ben Jonson, *The Alchemist,* Charles Montgomery Hathaway, Jr., ed. (1903). Paul H. Kocher, *Science and Religion in Elizabethan England* (1953). Christina Larner, *Enemies of God: The Witch-hunt in Scotland* (1981). Michael MacDonald, *Mystical Bedlam: Madness, Anxiety, and Healing in Seventeenth-Century England* (1981). Alan Macfarlane, *Witchcraft in Tudor and Stuart England* (1970). Robert W. Malcolmson, *Popular Recreations in English Society, 1700–1850* (1973). Christopher Marlowe, *Doctor Faustus,* in *The Complete Plays of Christopher Marlowe,* Irving Ribner, ed. (1963). H. C. Erik Midelfort, "Witchcraft, Magic, and the Occult," in Steven Ozment, ed., *Reformation Europe: A Guide to Research* (1982).

Marjorie Hope Nicolson, *The Breaking of the Circle,* rev. ed. (1960). William Perkins, *The Work of William Perkins,* Ian Breward, ed. (1970). Charles Phythian-

Adams, *Local History and Folklore: A New Framework* (1975). Walter Raleigh, *The Works of Sir Walter Raleigh,* 8 vols. (1829; repr. n.d.). Paolo Rossi, *Francis Bacon: From Magic to Science* (1968). John L. Russell, "The Copernican System in Great Britain," in Jerzy Dobrzycki, ed., *The Reception of Copernicus' Heliocentric Theory* (1972).

Reginald Scot, *The Discoverie of Witchcraft,* Hugh Ross Williamson, ed. (1964). Wayne Shumaker, *The Occult Sciences in the Renaissance* (1972). Eva Germaine Rimington Taylor, *The Mathematical Practitioners of Tudor and Stuart England* (1954). Keith Thomas, *Religion and the Decline of Magic* (1971) and *Man and the Natural World* (1983). Lynn Thorndike, *A History of Magic and Experimental Science,* 8 vols. (1923–1958). Eustace M. W. Tillyard, *The Elizabethan World Picture* (1944; repr. 1979). Brian Vickers, "Frances Yates and the Writing of History," in *Journal of Modern History,* 51 (1979), and as ed., *Occult and Scientific Mentalities in the Renaissance* (1984).

Charles Webster, *The Great Instauration* (1975); "Alchemical and Paracelsian Medicine," in Webster, ed., *Health, Medicine, and Mortality in the Sixteenth Century* (1979); *From Paracelsus to Newton* (1982); and, as ed., *The Intellectual Revolution of the Seventeenth Century* (1974). Robert S. Westman and J. E. McGuire, *Hermeticism and the Scientific Revolution* (1977). Frances A. Yates, *Giordano Bruno and the Hermetic Tradition* (1964) and *The Occult Philosophy in the Elizabethan Age* (1979).

Travel by Sea and Land

DAVID B. QUINN

The words *travel,* to go from one place to another, and *travail,* to toil, were the same in Shakespeare's time. To go on a journey was to make an effort, to arrive at a destination only after something of a struggle, to endure a difficult and muddy road or a creaking vessel. When Richard Madox set out in 1582 on the Atlantic voyage from which he did not return, one of his first concerns was seasickness:

> I was tawght many medcynes to avoyd the sycknes of the sea as namely a safron paper on the stomak or to drink the juse of wormwod, but I perceaved that the best things [are], to keep very warme, to be sure of hote supping often, to use moderat motion and to bear yt with a good corage til by acqueyntance you become famylier with the heaving and setting of the ship and be able to brook the seas and than the more excers[is]e with reason the better, for yf you once fawl to lasynes or unlust [sloth] than is the scarby [scurvy] redy to catch you by the bones and wil shak owt every tooth in your head.

(Diary entry for 16 April 1582)

When the journey was by road, the narrow English saddle seemed excruciating to foreign horsemen. The mud and the deep ruts, the uneven surfaces, the lack of guides and guidebooks—which meant that it was possible to get lost easily once one left the major tracks—and other hindrances are well illustrated in the travel literature of the time.

The inconvenience of travel—and its dangers too, since pirates by sea and robbers by land were considerable risks—did not prevent people from moving about England freely. The population was, indeed, much more mobile than was formerly thought, and many travelers took risks in sailing craft that might later have been considered wholly unseaworthy. Many, probably most, rural families had members who had traveled and settled many miles from home. Families moved freely from country to town and from town to city.

London was the great attraction. The conurbation doubled its population from under 150,000 to almost 300,000 in Shakespeare's lifetime, and Shakespeare was only one of many thousands of provincials to find a niche there. Many of the new settlements along the Thames were made possible by travel, specifically by the profits of piracy and privateering (the latter lawful between 1585 and 1604), in which so many men from Thameside took part.

The road system converged on London. The road to the north ran all the way to Edinburgh, but it was by no means all easy going. The section from London to Barnet became impossible, and London had to carry on long negotiations with its bishop and the local parishes before a new section could be constructed. By statute, road verges had to be kept wide, and parishes had to enroll men for a week's work on roads every year, but there was much discrepancy between theory and practice. Lack of stone, overuse by commercial traffic, and water penetration made roads a perpetual trial to their users.

Nevertheless, the late Tudor and early Stuart period saw the development of an efficient postal system. The postmasters were not only concerned with mail (particularly official correspondence) but also had a monopoly of hiring horses along the post roads. Reserves of horses and stabling facilities were developing, along with the provision of reasonably comfortable inns. Post stages were short—ten to twenty miles—but a traveler in a hurry could cover several stages a day. The road from London to Chester, with a continuation to Carlisle, followed for a part of the way the old Roman Watling Street. The road to the southwest was extensively used, especially as communications with Plymouth were vital to travel by sea as well as by land. Problems of access to the English Channel by London ships meant, it was said, that it took as much time to sail from London to Plymouth as it took to sail from Plymouth to North America.

Cross-country communications were less satisfactory. A coach could travel from London to Oxford or Cambridge with ease, but if it went directly from one university town to the other it would likely get bogged down in mud or even lose its way. A network of minor roads and lanes covered the country, but their condition depended very much on local requirements. Some rural communities could still not be reached by any wheeled transport and had to depend on packhorses.

The traveler depended largely on the postboys for travel information. Christopher Saxton's great county atlas (1579) provided guidance for journeys in England and Wales but no indication of roads. There was little that a traveler could carry with him until John Norden began his portable county descriptions, *Speculum Britanniae,* with a volume on Middlesex in 1593, continued with another on Hertfordshire in 1598 (both showing roads). But the series did not catch on, in spite of its obvious utility, and subsequent volumes remained in manuscript, though Norden did publish the first distance tables for the whole country in 1625.

Most people traveled the roads of England on foot. A man would walk several hundred miles to a city or port town with better opportunities for making a living than his country village offered. He often had to rough it, but there were cheap lodging houses too. Families moving long distances might endure hardship unless they could obtain seating on a cart or wagon. Two-wheeled carts drew most of the goods that went by road in the earlier part of Elizabeth's reign; these carts also took passengers. But the lumbering, four-wheeled wagons that were gradually displacing them for heavier goods were more suitable for poor travelers.

Horses, too, were so numerous that a man might acquire a not too reliable nag for a few pounds. The most favored travelers in England were men who could afford adequate horses of their own. Many would travel with two horses, one ridden by the traveler with heavy saddle bags, the other in reserve ridden by a young attendant. If there was one horse only and the traveler was not in a hurry, the attendant might be an Irish horseboy who ran alongside the slowly moving horse or caught up with it when it had to be attended to for the night. Post-horses were usually reliable, and most gentlemen and persons on official business traveled by post, staying at inns along the route.

Beyond the limits of the English roads, the traveler made do with what he could find. Between the principal towns in Scotland and Ireland he would find roads that were not intolerable. Off them he would have to take his chance on narrow and often dangerous tracks. The Irish "pace," or pass, was often a path through dense woodland or treacherous bog.

It must not be thought that travel within England and the British Isles as a whole was solely by land; coastal traffic by small vessels, moving from port to port, was very considerable. Passengers could often have a more comfortable journey by sea or river than by land, though shipwrecks were not uncommon. Along the Bristol Channel and up the river Severn to Shrewsbury and beyond, the sailing vessel was the usual means of transport. The Humber-Trent basin was a route favored by travelers from the east coast. There were parts of the coast that were difficult to traverse, among them the English Channel. The Irish Sea was often impassable and so rough that a contemporary satirist said that "it would engender weasels in a bitch." The North Sea coast in winter was also notorious for danger and discomfort.

The overseas voyager had well-traveled routes to follow. He would often go down the Thames by tilt boat to Gravesend and take a ship from there, or cross the river and take a horse to Dover. In good weather the English Channel crossing took hours rather than days, though there were times when landing was impossible and the vessel was forced to turn back. Access to the Netherlands was easier: we read of voyages from Flushing to the customhouse in London that took precisely forty-eight hours. Voyages to west German ports were equally commonplace. But to embark on a longer voyage to Russia by way of the North Cape to St. Nicholas (Archangel)—from which Anthony Jenkinson made his trans-Caspian and Persian travels—was an arduous and dangerous affair. Most English trade was carried down the Channel from London, but contrary winds very often forced shipping to accumulate at anchor at the Downs, off the Kent coast, until the wind changed and a whole fleet could proceed to western France, the Iberian countries, the Mediterranean, and the oceans beyond.

The range of English commerce, and hence of the possibilities of sea travel, was expanding almost continuously throughout the period. Ships on long voyages in the mid-Elizabethan period might be as little as 100 tons burden. Before 1616 they could be very much larger, 300 to 400 tons for a Levanter, 500 to 600 tons for an East Indiaman. As ships became larger, their accommodations improved, but sailing vessels offered little sustained comfort for the traveler, who had to put up with the creaking and groaning of masts and timbers, rolling and pitching on stormy seas, and cramped quarters. Sir Walter Raleigh described cabins as "but sluttish Dens that breed Sickness."

For the upper classes, *travel* in this period had a limited connotation. It was the discipline favored by families for their sons, especially their younger sons—a kind of finishing school, a means of acquiring education and sophistication. Handbooks, many of German origin (since Germans seemed most addicted to this particular form of activity), laid down serious objectives for the traveler. He was urged to work up the elements of some foreign languages before he set out on what was usually a year-long tour. He was also given sensible advice about travel, lodging, money, and the religious and social sensitivities of foreign peoples—advice that was also valuable to merchants and government officials.

As for the gentleman traveler, he was usually advised to acquire a speaking knowledge of three languages. (It was often assumed that he could make himself understood to educated men in Latin.) He should spend three months each at the places where the best style of language could be learned—Orléans or Blois for French, Florence or Pisa for Italian, Leipzig or Heidelberg for German. Then he was expected to seek out and admire the relics of antiquity: the buildings, paintings, sculpture, manuscripts, and other achievements of Renaissance rulers.

Pioneer works in English were *The Traveiler of Jerome Turler* (1575), translated from the Latin, and Albertus Meierus' *Certaine Briefe, and Speciall Instructions for Gentlemen* (1589). These two works set the didactic style of such manuals—indeed, overdid it, since no young man could possibly have followed all the recommendations given in any one year's progress. It was assumed, of course, that a traveler would at least make contacts with persons of learning and high social rank.

William Bourne, in *A Booke Called the Treasure for Traveilers* (1578), began with some general advice on conventional travel, but he was aiming at a somewhat different readership: young men who might find travel or employment at sea to be their metier. Most of Bourne's book was concerned, then, with supplying necessary information about elementary mathematics so as to enable his readers to proceed to the study of navigation. Bourne believed that without this kind of knowledge, the traveler could not find his way around, even on land. Of course, with more and more travel into new, unknown, or unexplored areas, there was much to be said for his approach. Similarly, John Davys, in *The Worldes Hydrographical Description* (1595), informed the queen's Privy Counvil that it must sponsor travel into the northern region of the world for what we would describe as scientific, economic, and political objectives.

Sir John Stradling, in *A Direction for Travailers* (1592), relied on a book of advice by Justus Lipsius, written as long ago as 1564. He clearly addressed himself to the upper class: "The best and wisest, the chief and noblest men have always travelled," he wrote. Sir Robert Dallington, author of *A Method for Travell* (1605), knew both France and Italy well, and could say, sensibly:

> He therefore that intends to Travell out of his owne country, must likewise resolve to Travell out of his country fashion, and indeed out of himselfe: that is, out of his former intemperate feeding, disordinate drinking, thrift-lesse gaming, fruit-lesse time spending, violent exercising, & irregular misgoverning whatsoever: he must determine, that the end of his Travell is his ripening in knowledge; and the end of his knowledge is the service of his country, which of right challengeth, the better part of us.

But there were other voices. Joseph Hall's *Quo Vadis?* (1617) opposed foreign travel for the very reasons that Dallington thought it advisable: to travel made good men bad, kind men vicious, sensible men vain, and careful men spendthrifts. It also put them in danger of contamination by Romish practices.

Richard Hakluyt's *Principall Navigations* (1589) and his three-volume *Principal Navigations* (1598–1600) inspired many men to travel by sea. Later, Francis Bacon, thinking no doubt of Hakluyt, complained in his essay on travel (1625) that "it is a strange thing that in Sea-voyages, where there is nothing to be seen but Sky and Sea, Men should make Diaries, but in Land-Travile, wherein so much is to be observed, for the most part, they omit it; As if Chance were fitter to be registered than Observation." In fact, the land traveler was often so absorbed in what he was doing that any diary he kept tended to be cursory and hence of insufficient interest to circulate or publish.

Thomas Coryate, in his European travels, followed such an orthodox route—through France, Italy, Switzerland, parts of Germany, and the United Netherlands—that it was impossible to get his journal published. But because he had walked most of the 2,000 miles, he was determined to get into print. He therefore induced his friends to enliven his straightforward, if occasionally eccentric, narrative with "Panegyricks" in verse and a flippant title, *Coryats Crudities. Hastily Gobled up in Five Months Travells* (1611). Coryate advertised his walking prowess by hanging up his boots in Odcombe Church. It is clear that at least one of his readers considered this an ungentlemanly exhibition, because he commented sarcastically on "Tom Coryat in his socks sweaty" in a copy of Samuel Purchas' *Pilgrimes* (1625). But Coryate was indeed a traveler extraordinary. In 1612 he sailed to the Levant and from there walked to India, where he learned Oriental languages at Ajmer. He died at Surat before returning to put his full narrative into print, but selections of his letters were published in *Thomas Coriate . . . Greeting. From the Court of the Great Mogul* (1616) and *Mr. Thomas Coriat to His Friends . . . from Agra* (1618). These letters were addressed to his friends in the Mermaid Club, including John Donne and Ben Jonson.

Elizabethans were fascinated by the sea travels of sailors and gentlemen. They read John Hawkins' cautious narrative of his disastrous voyage of 1567–1568, *A True Declaration of the Troublesome Voyadge of M. John Hawkins to the Parties of Guynea and the West Indies* (1569), and they also read of voyages in search of the Northwest Passage, most notably in George Best's *A True Discourse of the Late Voyages of Discoverie, for the Finding of a Passage to Cathaya* (1578). Publications like these incited gentlemen as well as merchants to take part in expeditions outside the normal scope of commerce. For instance, Hawkins helped to inspire the sea war (totally illegal until 1585) against the Spanish Indies.

Drake's remarkable circumnavigation of the earth in 1577–1580 so struck the popular imagination that his *Golden Hind* was preserved as a national monument at Deptford. Even after Shakespeare's death, it was pointed out to foreign visitors, though little of it then remained. At the same time, official caution prevented any popular narrative of the voyage from being circulated: only reluctantly was Hakluyt allowed to include a short account in 1589. But references to the voyage in the literature of the time show that it had a very wide influence. It inspired a successful circumnavigation by Thomas Cavendish in 1586–1588 and several unsuccessful attempts thereafter.

Global voyages were dangerous: only one of Drake's ships and one of Cavendish's completed the passage. Yet hardened seamen were not the only ones who made such voyages, for some gentlemen also were only too eager to volunteer their fortunes and their lives. To some this type of travel represented a new chivalry—something to test their manly endurance as well as to satisfy a growing curiosity about the world outside western Europe.

The New World also offered a chance for wealth. Young gentlemen who might have made their European tour and then exploited it at court, in law, or in continental warfare now let their aspirations run farther afield. Many were younger sons, with little hope of fortune at home. The Indies offered romance and plunder for some, failure or death for others. Meanwhile, it was the cautious merchant promoters and the hardy professional seamen they employed who gained the most from the long war of plunder (1585–1604) of the Spanish empire. By the end of that war, much of the romance of sea travel had faded, but the memory of it colored much of the popular literature of the Jacobean age.

Commercial travel now took the place of romantic privateering. The East India Company, from 1601 onward, was sending ships to what is now Indonesia and to India itself, primarily for trade. There was a place for gentlemanly enterprise in this context too, as we have seen in Coryate's case. The

Shirley brothers, Francis and Robert, traveled to Persia almost as a matter of course, and Robert to India too, on gentlemanly adventures and intrigues. Sir Thomas Roe, on his diplomatic mission to India (1614–1618), made it an excuse to obtain so much information about the country (from Coryate among others) that on his return voyage he was able to provide information sufficient to have a map of India made that remained standard for many years.

In 1604 peace was concluded with Spain. Although trade and piracy in the Caribbean continued, the English shifted to colonizing voyages to North America. John Brereton (*A Briefe and True Relation of the Discoverie of the North Part of Virginia,* 1602) and James Rosier (*A True Relation of the Most Prosperous Voyage Made . . . in the Discovery of Virginia,* 1605) began to turn public attention to this new area of English travel, as did Christopher Newport's 1607 colonizing expedition to the Chesapeake. In 1607 and 1608, Englishmen explored the James River well into the Piedmont, and John Smith brought his barge into each of the great river estuaries of the northern Chesapeake. Gentlemen, almost too many of them to balance the working colonists, proved willing to travel to Virginia and settle there, even though it soon became known that settler mortality was high.

The strange adventures of Sir Thomas Gates stirred the imagination of Englishmen. Destined for Virginia in 1609, but wrecked on Bermuda instead, Gates miraculously appeared at Jamestown the following year in improvised craft. Gates's story caused Michael Drayton to add to the prefatory poems in Coryate's book an ironic reference:

Of the Bermudos, the example such,
Where not a ship until this time durst touch;
Kep't as supposed by hels infernall dogs,
Our Fleet found there most honest courteous hogs.

A poorly written tract by John Smith, *A True Relation of Such Occurrences . . . as Hath Hapned in Virginia* (1608), served to satisfy public curiosity concerning the new colony until his more sophisticated *Map of Virginia,* bound with *The Proceedings of the English Colonie in Virginia,* appeared in 1612. But exploration soon gave place to economic exploitation, and within a few years most of what was known about Virginia centered around publicity for the Virginia Company of London's lottery (1613–1621).

Far northern Canada became the new objective for English explorers. Even the tragic story surrounding the discovery of Hudson Strait in 1611–1612, when Henry Hudson was cast adrift by his crew, did not deter further attempts to find the elusive Northwest Passage. Newfoundland was visited by hundreds of English fishermen every summer, but after Anthony Parkhurst in the 1570s and Sir Humphrey Gilbert in 1583, no one attempted to survey its rugged coasts until Bristol merchants launched a colonizing venture in 1610. The colonists made a living there for some years, explored the coast to the north, and made contacts with the Beothuk Indians. But lacking sufficient support from England, this colony withered, and from 1617 onward gentlemen began to acquire title to parts of the territory. Little was published about the island until Richard Whitbourne's *Discourse and Discovery of Newfound-land* (1620). Lord Calvert tried to live there (1628–1629) but found the winter climate intolerable, and thereafter interest in Newfoundland as a colony declined sharply.

The spectacular travels and conquests of the Spanish in the New World created much interest among the English in the sixteenth century, so it is not surprising that some Englishmen traveled there in search of adventure and riches. Sir Walter Raleigh wanted to oversee the settlement of much of eastern North America, but Queen Elizabeth forced him to do his exploration there by proxy—through Ralph Lane, Thomas Harriot, and John White, who traversed and surveyed a substantial part of Virginia. In the 1590s, Raleigh was carried away by reports of a gold-rich kingdom on the Orinoco in South America, and he insisted on going up the Orinoco himself in 1595. Though he never found his Eldorado, his tract *The Discoverie of the Large, Rich and Bewtiful Empyre of Guiana* (1596) described these regions in dramatic and eloquent language. Unfortunately, duty and later misfortune held Raleigh back from fresh attempts. Only in 1616, the year of Shakespeare's death, was he released from thirteen years' imprisonment in the Tower of London to make a last journey to his golden kingdom. This 1617 voyage was a tragic fiasco, leading to Raleigh's execution in 1618.

Guiana and the Amazon continued to interest English travelers in the early seventeenth century. Many small expeditions went to Guiana, mostly to grow tobacco. Sir Thomas Roe made a long voyage up the Amazon in 1610 to see what secrets that almost unknown region held. Though he did not return there, he financed some settlements in the Amazon basin for several years.

In the later sixteenth century, English travelers in Europe were confined largely to Protestant areas, but France was never wholly closed, and Italy, the greatest objective of the grand tour, was usually safe enough for Protestants if they were careful not to disclose their hostility to the Roman church. Spain and Portugal were closed to English Protestants from 1585 to 1605; and even afterward, the Scottish traveler William Lithgow, a more dedicated and widely ranging walker even than Coryate, was imprisoned and tortured by the Inquisition.

From 1604, for nearly twenty years, travel in Europe was much easier. More and more young gentlemen went to the Continent, and a few ventured much farther, to Jerusalem, Egypt, Algiers, Morocco, Persia, and India. No Englishman before 1616 is known to have set foot in China, but the sailor William Adams, shipwrecked from a Dutch ship, made himself something of a celebrity in Japan. East India Company factors attempting to trade with the Spice Islands and with adjoining lands against Dutch competition often journeyed into Cochin China, Siam, and Burma, as well as into the heart of India; but none of them traveled, as Coryate did, for travel's sake.

While so many men were traveling and trading overseas, some important changes were taking place in Jacobean England. The coach, which made its appearance around 1575, was at first a curiosity, a luxury used only by a handful of the richer nobility. In the seventeenth century, coaches were much more widely used. They became a feature of the principal roads in the southeast and, by 1616, in other parts of the kingdom as well. In London they blocked the narrow streets as they jostled with heavy country wagons.

River travel was also becoming more sophisticated. The tilt boats on the Thames were bigger and grander. Wherries across the river were larger, busier, and more often in collision. Traffic along the Severn estuary and upstream from Bristol also developed, with more spacious and comfortable vessels. Family visits between distant country houses by horse, coach, or sailing vessel became commonplace.

The posts were also improved. Leasing of privileges along the post roads generated income for the crown; post-horses became more numerous; the quality of horses on many roads improved as the demand for them increased; inns became better adapted to a wider range of customers. Improvement of the roads themselves was slow but tangible.

Jacobean England may have had growing social problems, but England was a much more vigorous and active country in 1616 than it had been in the 1560s. The lot of the traveler was easier, and the range of his travels was wider. There were still wild parts of Wales and wilder parts of the Highlands where few dared to venture, but beyond the British Isles much of the wider world had been opened to exploration.

BIBLIOGRAPHY

Ernest Stuart Bates, *Touring in 1600* (1911). Peter Hume Brown, ed., *Early Travellers in Scotland* (1891). Thomas Coryate, *Coryats Crudities* (1611; repr. 1905). Robert Coverte, *The Travels of Captain Robert Coverte,* Boies Penrose, ed. (1931). Arthur H. Dodd, *Life in Elizabethan England* (1961). Sir William Foster, ed., *Early Travels in India, 1583–1619* (1921). Richard Hakluyt, *The Principall Navigations* (1589; repr. 1965) and *The Principal Navigations* (1598–1600; repr. 1903–1905). Virginia LaMar, *Travel and Roads in England* (1960). William Lithgow, *The Totall Discourse of . . . Nineteene Yeares Traveyles* (1906).

Richard Madox, *An Elizabethan in 1582: The Diary of Richard Madox,* Elizabeth Story Donno, ed. (1976). Fynes Moryson, *Itinerary* (1617; repr. 1907). Allardyce Nicoll, ed., *Shakespeare in His Own Age* (1964). John Parker, *Books to Build an Empire: A Bibliographical History of English Overseas Interests to 1620* (1965). Joan Parkes, *Travel in England in the Seventeenth Century* (1925). Boies Penrose, *Travel and Discovery in the Renaissance, 1420–1620* (1955). Samuel Purchas, *Hakluytus Posthumus; or, Purchas His Pilgrimes* (1625; repr. 1905–1907).

David B. Quinn, *The Elizabethans and the Irish* (1966); *England and the Discovery of America, 1481–1620* (1974), and as ed., *The Hakluyt Handbook* (1974). William Brenchley Rye, *England as Seen by Foreigners* (1865). John Walter Stoye, *English Travellers Abroad, 1604–1667* (1952). Thomas Stuart Willan, *River Navigation in England, 1600–1750* (1936).

"Style Is the Man": Manners, Dress, and Decorum

LACEY BALDWIN SMITH

Sir Walter Raleigh's oft quoted dictum "Style is the man" confronts the cultural historian with an apparent paradox. What kind of style, let alone what kind of proper man, is compatible with those starched and showy Elizabethans who strutted and preened like so many self-satisfied peacocks, dressed in clothing that was not only vulgar, exhibitionistic, and hopelessly impractical but also condemned by almost everyone as un-English, immoral, and economically harmful to the kingdom? Raleigh himself was one of the worst examples of Tudor sartorial and theatrical ostentation, but when he spoke of style, he was stating a sixteenth-century ideal that had little to do with "the spirit of perpetual dressing up" or even with the social philosophy that maintained that it was "comely that every estate and vocation should be known by the differences of their habits." Instead, he voiced the conviction that the essence of civilized behavior was the ability to enact gracefully and convincingly upon a public stage the role that fate had selected for the individual. It was not the clothes that made the man; it was the quality of the wearer's performance—his style and "grace"—that set him apart from the rest of mankind.

The making of a civilized man was the aim and aspiration of Tudor society and the climax of its educational and social system. Everyone agreed with Giovanni della Casa that "a person who proposes to live in a civilized place among other men, rather than in a desert or a hermitage, will find it most useful to know how to behave with courtesy and tact." Shakespeare's Desdemona described Lodovico as "a proper man" on the grounds that he spoke well, and no Elizabethan doubted that eloquence was "the fairest gift of providence to man" and the divine instrument through which civilization itself had been forged; but true propriety, style, and "grace" involved more than melodious words and persuasive conversation. They entailed the whole man—grace of movement, choice of words, command of manners, respect for others, sensibility to circumstance, knowledge of the situation, and, above all, the ability to make words and actions appear fresh, spontaneous, and appropriate both to the man and the occasion.

In short, the cultural goal of society was the application to life of the principles of decorum, the essence of which was laid down by the ninth earl of Northumberland for the benefit of his son. "Certain works," he wrote, were

> fit for every vocation; some for kings; some for noblemen; some for gentlemen; some for artificers; some for clowns; and some for beggars; all are good to be known to everyone, yet not to be used by everyone. If everyone played his part well, that is allotted him, the commonwealth will be happy; if not then will it be deformed.

The ability to play one's role well, especially to make the part appear easy and spontaneous, might for a fortunate few be a gift from heaven, but for most Elizabethans it was a process learned partly at

19. Sir Walter Raleigh (1598), wearing a deep ruff, sleeveless and heavily embroidered and bejeweled open jerkin with skirt, revealing a plain shirt with jeweled buttons, a "Spanish kettledrum" or onion trunk hose, and plain canions.

school, partly from courtesy books, and partly from daily life. The aim of Tudor education was holistic: as T.W. Baldwin put it, "the tender little mind" was to "imbibe impregnation in piety," be taught to "love and master liberal disciplines," be instructed "in the duties of life," and be "habituated to civility of behavior" on the grounds that "the unity of the state exists not merely in its houses or its streets but . . . in the agreement of its minds."

For the members of the ruling elite, who sought to pass on to their offspring the good things of political and economic life and whose own position in society was based more on kinship, birth, and patronage than on innate talent, it was more important to educate their children in propriety and piety than in technical knowledge. As a consequence, wherever the child turned—the classroom, the home, the households of the rich and powerful—

he discovered that the educational goal had been agreed on by his elders: "To catechize him in religion truly, frame him in opinion rightly, [and] fashion him in behavior civilly."

Central to fashioning polite behavior was training in "decorum," which went by a host of other names—seemliness, decency, propriety, comeliness, appropriateness. In part, decorum involved a proper understanding of, and respect for, those social symbols dictated by a hierarchical and deferential society, such as when to bend the knee and doff the cap, and how to address one's elders and betters. More important, decorum embodied the final Tudor educational product, the "well fashioned mind," which through years of discipline, exposure to virtuous examples, and the development of good habits was able to discern what was proper in relationship to "things, places, times, persons." In education, decorum represented the triumph of reason and self-control over emotions and bodily appetites. The young gentleman possessed of decorum was, at least in theory, capable of attaining the educational ideal of John Colet, dean of St. Paul's: the ability to "see the where, when, how, why or wherefor thou speakest, doest or biddest any thing to be done."

In language, *decorum* meant the judicious selection of the appropriate word, suitable both to the subject and the speaker. Thus, it was unbecoming for the historian to write that a king or emperor who was engaged in battle "ran out of the field and took [to] his heels . . . and fled as fast as he could." Only mean soldiers or captains were cowardly and took to their heels. At all times the decorous man sought to weave thought, word, and action into an artistic and harmonious whole, searching always to make his speech accord with his life. The diplomat and scholar Thomas Elyot described decorum as that "majesty" which is "the foundation of all excellent manners." The man possessed of such majesty had "a beauty of comeliness in his countenance, language and gesture apt to his dignity and accommodate to time, place, and company."

Sixteenth-century decorum went deeper than simply insisting on those arbitrary rules of etiquette that enabled strangers to meet and do business on the basis of shared social signals. Instead, it was a rigid syllogistic logic that linked actions and thought, insisting that "ill-doings breed ill-thinking" and arguing that from "corrupted manners spring perverted judgments." Manners, style, and proper word usage, in the opinion of the educator

Roger Ascham, were so central to civilized behavior that he interpreted the rise and fall of civilization itself on the basis of decorum and claimed that the fate of Greece and Rome was proof of what happens when language becomes indecent and lacks decorum. "Mark all ages," he said, "look upon the whole course of both the Greek and Latin tongue, and ye shall surely find that when apt and good words began to be neglected and properties of those two tongues to be confounded, then also began ill deeds to spring, strange manners to oppress good orders, new and fond opinions to strive with old and true doctrine."

The same principle applied to contemporary events, and Sir William Paget counseled Edward Seymour, duke of Somerset, who, as lord protector under young Edward VI, was standing in for royalty, that if the duke wanted to be accepted as a king, he had first to behave like one and conform his words and actions to his office—"for a king do like a king." On a less lofty level, James Cleland, author of *The Institution of a Young Noble Man* (1607), offered his readers the same advice: "Walk manlike with a grave civil pace, as becometh one of your birth and age." Only servants and apprentices rushed about and sweated.

In a sense, the thrust of Tudor education in general and decorum in particular was training in role playing, in performing on a public stage a part that suited both the actor and his audience. Hamlet's instructions to his hired actors set the standards for his century: "Be not too tame neither, but let your own discretion be your tutor. Suit the action to the word, the word to the action, with this special observance, that you o'erstep not the modesty of nature" (III. ii. 15–18). Possibly no cultural ideal has ever been so wildly optimistic in what it expected of both pupil and teacher, for decorum assumed not only that a suitable and appropriate response existed for every social situation but also that the formula for success could be written down in a textbook, memorized, and successfully applied by the student. Henry Peacham confidently entitled his instructions *The Compleat Gentleman* (1622), in the expectation that everything a young gentleman needed in order to enact his role in life could be found within the pages of his text. And when Richard Brathwaite brought out a new and improved pocket version of *The English Gentleman* (1630), rather than abridge his material, he urged his readers to enlarge their pockets.

Underlying Tudor education and supplying the

philosophical principles on which decorum rested was the study of rhetoric, which had as its goal the manipulation of words and ideas in order "to produce a particular effect in relation to a particular place and time, having regard to the particular speaker and listener." The inspiration for sixteenth-century rhetorical training came from Cicero's *De oratore,* and every grammar school boy was exposed to intensive and exhaustive drill in the three essentials of classical rhetoric: copiousness *(copia),* or richness of expression; invention *(inventio),* or the discovery of material to exemplify a poem, theme, or oration; and structure *(dispositio),* or the organization of ideas according to exact rules that reflected the order assumed to exist within the universe. "I know," wrote Thomas Wilson in his immensely popular *Arte of Rhetorique* (1553), "that all things stand by order and without order nothing can be, for by an order we are born, by an order we live, and by an order we make our end." If God's universe possessed order, it followed by indisputable logic that there was a correct order or organization for every theme and oration, and an equally correct and decorous rule for sentence structure and word order. Thus, Wilson warned that an untutored student might inadvertently "set the cart before the horse" and write, " 'My mother and my father are both at home,' even as though the good man of the house wore no breeches or that the grey mare were the better horse."

Following fixed organizational formulas, schoolchildren discussed at length the link between the universal principle and the concrete episode, thereby extracting the moral meaning hidden within any event or statement. Scarcely a tale existed that did not include "something that pertaineth either to the amendment of manners, to the knowledge of truth, to the setting forth of Nature's work, or else to the understanding of some notable thing done." Every written or spoken word was scrutinized and weighed for its literal as well as metaphorical and symbolic meaning; every sentence was inspected for its shape, balance, and design relative to the position or role that the speaker had assumed. As Wilson pointed out, it would have been a violation of decorum and a denial of all social order to have placed the wife before the husband.

Equally essential to rhetorical training was the development of a literary style overflowing with images, metaphors, comparisons, and examples, and the ability to manipulate words and ideas in

order to achieve a desired effect and to dazzle an audience with "forms and fashions of speech." At the same time, this copiousness of style, as well as the slavish attention to structure and organization, had to appear natural and uncontrived. Consequently, the Tudor schoolboy labored equally hard at spontaneity, or what the manuals called *sprezzatura,* the art of naturalness that conceals the long hours of hard work and practice needed to guarantee a performance appropriate to time, place, and circumstance. At its best, rhetorical training produced the brilliance, versatility, control, and naturalness of Shakespeare; more often, it degenerated into the stiff, stylized writing and vulgar, overblown verbiage of the hack writer. Indeed, no violation of decorum was so universally condemned as the verbal exhibitionism of so many Elizabethan authors, especially the use of "such bombasted words, as seem altogether farced full of wind, being a great deal too high and lofty for the matter," as George Puttenham put it.

Education in decorum, especially as it applied to good manners, was available to anyone who cared to consult the mountain of courtesy books that laid down the rules of etiquette on everything from table conduct to the exquisitely fine points governing social recognition and deference. Hugh Rhodes, in his *Boke of Nurture, or Schoole of Good Maners: For Men, Servants, and Children* (1577), codified the minimum standard for deportment at table and produced a list of behavioral prohibitions and exhortations, which were repeated endlessly throughout the century and indicate that decorum existed far more as an ideal than a social reality: "Don't answer your parents back," "Wash your hands," "Walk demurely," "When your master speaks to you, take off your cap and stand up," "Don't dip your meat in the salt cellar," "Belch near to no man's face," "Don't pick your teeth with a knife," "Don't fill your mouth too full or blow out your crumbs," "Don't throw your bones under the table," and "Don't look at what comes out of your nose or break wind."

On a somewhat higher level was the courtesy manual with the modest title *The Courte of civill Courtesie: Fitly furnished with a plesant porte of stately phrases and pithie precepts: assembled in the behalfe of all younge Gentlemen, and others, that are desirous to frame their behavior according to their estates, at all times, and in all companies: thereby to purchase worthy praise, of their inferiours: and estimation and credite amonge theyr betters* (1582). It explained that if a young man of rank should find himself in the company of an inferior who was older and esteemed for his wisdom and experience, the gentleman should give place to him "but yet with such a modest audacity mingled with a smiling grace and courteous speech, neither too low or whispering, as the rest of the company may well perceive." In Tudor England it was always important to receive credit for any decorous modification of the rules of social hierarchy.

Training in decorum continued in the households of the great and mighty, reinforcing what could be learned by the socially ambitious in a multitude of courtesy books. Katherine Howard, Lady Berkeley, insisted that those essential gestures so necessary for maintaining the habit of respect in a deferential society be done with decorum. When young John Smyth failed to make a proper bow as he hurried past her while balancing a covered dish of food in his hand, she ordered him back, made him kneel before her one hundred times, and actually performed the bow herself, lifting "up all her garments to the calf of her leg that I might the better observe the grace of drawing back the foot and bowing of the knee." In the Berkeley home it was evidently not sufficient to know the rituals of deference; it was necessary to perform them well and in a fashion appropriate to one's status in life. "A man," as Giovanni della Casa urged, should "not be content to do things well, but must also aim to do them gracefully."

Decorum was accepted as "the universal rule" of existence and was discerned in the harmonious and balanced operation of the heavens, in the organic metaphor describing the proper relations of the various parts of the body politic, and in the cultural ideal of the well-fashioned individual who possessed a finely "tempered style" and who could make his actions fit his words and his words his actions. In the breach, it also explained all disorder, violence, usurpation, unnaturalness, and murder.

Most of the great Shakespearean tragedies are in effect dramatic homilies on the wages, not of sin, but of indecorous behavior whereby kings and usurpers, lovers and fools failed to conduct themselves or use language appropriate to their character or their status: "The baby beats the nurse, and quite athwart / Goes all decorum" (*Measure for Measure*, I. iii. 30–31). Both Richard II and Bolingbroke "sin against courtesy." Richard II forever violates the dignity of his office by overstating his regal powers in showy, high-flown language "full of wind" or by actions and words unbecoming majesty; and, as York observes, Bolingbroke's behavior and thoughts rarely correspond—"Show me thy humble heart and not thy knee, whose duty is deceivable and false" (II. iii. 83–84). Polonius' "words, words, words" are models of rhetorical excess and indecorous phrases, and Hamlet lives in a world, both real and imagined, that has lost its balance, form, and decorum. Othello is "eaten up" with passion "most unsuiting such a man" (IV. i. 77), and Iago's entire purpose is to destroy not only Othello but also the very essence of God's harmonious universe and man's ordered society, the bonds of trust, loyalty, marriage, and human love. And finally Macbeth's usurped title hangs increasingly "loose about him, like a giant's robe upon a dwarfish thief" (V. ii. 21–22), as he shrinks and wizens within himself, becoming more and more unfit for office.

While wantonness of language was a sure sign "of a sick mind," rashness, impropriety, inconstancy, and "excess of feasts and apparel" were, according to Ben Jonson, "the notes of a sick state." Thomas Drant, archdeacon of Lewes, expressed the frustration of all Elizabethans versed in decorum when he complained that "matrons are lightly apparelled, or harlots so gravely, that things are blundered and confounded." Why, then, did Elizabethan clothing so completely fail to conform to the cultural ideals of society and instead develop a vulgarity and flamboyance that stood in direct opposition to everything the sixteenth century held sacred? If there is one area where church, state, and school utterly failed to maintain the rules of decorum it was in the riot of dress and ornaments with which all Elizabethans, great and small, bedecked themselves. As stated by della Casa, the social and political ideal was clear: "Whatever you wear, it must suit you and be compatible with your calling." It was, according to that strict Puritan divine Mr. Philip Stubbes, inappropriate for "private subjects" to festoon themselves in silks, velvets, and silver cloth lest there be a confused "mangle of apparel," which would make it impossible "to know who is noble, who is worshipful, who is a gentleman, who is not." The nobility and gentry might discreetly "innoble, garnish and set forth their births, dignities and estates," and magistrates might "demonstrate the excellency, the majesty and worthiness of their offices and functions" by fine attire; but even they were expected to display restraint both for the good of their souls—"pride of apparel . . . induceth the whole man to wickedness and sin''—and for the kingdom's economic well-being. It was highly inappropriate, warned *The Institicion of a Gentleman* (1568), that a gentleman's apparel ''exceed in too much costly array'' or fail to ''be clean and comely made, keeping always a good manner or fashion.''

Sporadic efforts to regulate both food and dress had a long history and in England went back as far as the fourteenth century, but all over Europe in the sixteenth century attempts to legislate and control fashions were revived and intensified as part of that holistic approach to life and society which argued that ''corrupt manners'' engendered ''perverted judgments'' and that ''all things stand by order.'' Proper clothing, even if it did not make the man, at least marked him and introduced into society a tidiness and order appropriate to a hierarchical world. Attempts to dictate fashions reached their height under Elizabeth, and early in her reign, on 20 October 1559, the Privy Council ordered all lords and masters within the City of London to examine the clothing of their servants and apprentices and to confiscate the unlawful attire unless the culprits were too poor to replace the offending garments; under these circumstances they were permitted to wear the clothing until it was worn out. At the same time, instructions were issued to prevent baseborn men and women from breaking the spirit of the law by bedecking their legal apparel with expensive ornaments and frills. On the following day, in order to advertise what was appropriate to each social rank, the government published a brief schedule summarizing what the previous statutes of 1533 and 1554 had legislated. They had ordered that ''none shall wear in his apparel'' any ''cloth of gold, silver or tinsel,'' silk or sable except a nobleman of the degree of earl or higher. ''Woollen cloth made out of the realm,'' furs, and crimson, scarlet, and blue velvet were forbidden to all except dukes, marquises, earls, barons, and knights of the garter. Embroidery was limited to a baron's son, a knight, or a gentleman worth £200 a year. And only the sons and daughters of a knight or those higher in rank could display silk in their hats, bonnets, nightcaps, girdles, hose, and shoes.

Tudor sumptuary laws were motivated only in part by a passion for decorum and a sense of universal and social order. Economics and morality joined hands in the conviction that extravagant and ostentatious display was harmful. Men and women who wasted their patrimonies on gaudy attire and wore entire estates on their backs made bad subjects.

Greed, pride, and bankruptcy were linked in a chain of infamy that inevitably led to theft, treason, and perdition. Ben Jonson spoke for his century when he argued that ''of sloth cometh pleasure, of pleasure cometh spending, of spending cometh whoring, of whoring cometh lack, of lack cometh theft, of theft cometh hanging.'' To make matters worse, many fashions, at least in the eyes of legislators and moralists, were dangerously foreign, and almost without exception the sumptuary statutes sought to curb ''excess of apparel and the superfluity of unnecessary foreign wares'' imported into the country to the detriment of the home economy, especially the woolen industry.

Gloriana's war against extravagance and her insistence on ''degree, priority, and place'' in dress continued throughout her reign. In 1562, orders were issued to local magistrates in Surrey to inspect all female apparel for sumptuary violations. In the same year, the amount of material that could be used in the manufacture of male trunk hose was set at a yard and three-quarters, and gilded spurs, swords, rapiers, and daggers were limited to men of knightly position. A decade later the government was bewailing the decay of the kingdom's wealth as a consequence of the importation of costly silks and other fabrics, and ''the wasting and undoing'' of young gentlemen who mortgaged their lands and ran into debt to pay for their vanity.

In 1597 the government faced up to more practical concerns—the practice of servants who wore their masters' cast-off clothing and the right of heralds and liveried retainers to violate the sumptuary codes. Unfortunately, nothing worked. Neither the crown nor the various towns and guilds succeeded in dictating what an Englishman wore, and the government in its final endeavor in 1597 to curb ''the inordinate excess in apparel'' in effect admitted failure when it stated that, notwithstanding a host of previous proclamations, partly through the negligence of its own officials ''and partly by the manifest contempt and disobedience of the parties offending, no reformation at all hath followed.'' Four years later the inevitable occurred: scarcely twelve months after Elizabeth died, Parliament repealed all of the sumptuary legislation. Henceforth, English men and women were free to become, as Mr. Stubbes had so direly predicted, ''a laughing stock to all the world for their pride'' and ''very caterpillars to themselves in wasting and consuming their goods and treasures upon vanities and triffles.'' Such, however, was the perversity of the species that within a generation, men and women ceased to squander their estates upon their backs; and clothing, although responding to the universal principles of hierarchy and seduction, returned to a more normal level of extravagance and artificiality.

Decorum demanded restraint and control, but in clothing the odds in the sixteenth century were heavily weighted against both. Medieval sumptuary legislation had had two advantages over Tudor efforts at control: there was little vertical or horizontal mobility, and there was even less that money could buy. As a consequence, even the aristocracy had relatively little choice in what they could wear. By the sixteenth century everything had changed. Wealth had increased, as had social and geographical mobility, and materials and styles were abundant. Apprentices and journeymen aped their betters, merchants dressed like princes, Englishmen copied Italians and Turks. Fashion books, circulating throughout Europe, permitted the imaginative and the ingenious to design their own clothes. Not only did Elizabethan dress eventually display a degree of "personal finery" as "has never before nor since occurred in the history of English costume," but also the young gallant became "a walking geography of clothes . . . French doublets, German hose, Spanish hats and cloaks, Italian ruffs, Flemish shoes" (Brooke, 1950; Calthrop, 1906).

The mania for new styles reached England, like most things Renaissance, rather late, attaining dazzling heights of imagination and fantasy only in the second half of the sixteenth century. By Elizabeth's reign both sexes could draw on the earlier "German fashion" of the generation of Henry VIII; the Spanish influence that commenced with the reign of Philip and Mary; the drawings published in Paris in 1562 by the Italian costume engraver Enea Vico, who depicted in ninety-eight plates the apparel of "all the nations upon the globe"; and, later, the works of Cesare Veccellio, whose costume illustrations were on display in most of the bookstalls of Venice, that pleasure city of the sixteenth century.

English, as well as continental, fashions for both men and women evolved out of the basic late-medieval wardrobe. Men wore an undershirt; a short, form-fitting doublet or gipon; a jerkin or outer jacket; and tight hose. Women dressed in a shift, a kirtle or underdress, and a gown. Both sexes wore a cloak or coat. Throughout most of the fourteenth and fifteenth centuries male attire emphasized the legs, crotch, and buttocks; and female

doublet

jerkin with medium-length skirt

points

hose

20. Basic medieval look.

plaited and folded hair

form-fitting kirtle with attached tippets above the elbow

21. Basic medieval look.

22. Henry VIII (ca. 1560–1570), dressed in a fur-lined gown with puffed and padded shoulders, a jerkin with attached skirt, opened to reveal a slashed and puffed doublet with similar sleeves emerging from beneath the gown, trunk hose with prominent codpiece, and square-toed and slashed shoes.

apparel stressed the breasts, held high by a tight bodice, and the sculptured torso, accented by a skirt that was molded to the hips and fell in an unbroken vertical line.

Under Henry VIII this medieval look was, at least for men, fundamentally changed by the introduction of the German look, with its heavily accentuated shoulders, "slashed" doublet, and long-skirted jerkin. As the shoulders and sleeves grew monstrously large and puffed out, the doublet and jerkin exploded into a riot of pleats. The pleated jerkin with skirt now required seven or eight yards in contrast to its medieval predecessor of only two yards, and both doublet and jerkin were opened in the front to display an enlarged codpiece, which grew so immense that on occasion, and even in the presence of ladies, it was used to carry money or to store bits and pieces of food. Slashing or blistering, whereby the outer garment was cut either to reveal the underlining or to bring the underclothing through the opening, produced an even fuller and puffier look. The further slashing of the upper portions, or trunk, of the hose and the use of heavily brocaded and furred cloaks completed the inflated and boxlike effect.

Although women's attire did not change as dramatically as men's and was not as colorful or varied, it manifested the same heavy, layered look and expansion of yardage, as skirts became fuller and fuller and sleeves grew so voluminous that they often reached the ground. The outer gown frequently opened in front to reveal the kirtle below, and the bodice was cut low at the throat in order to display the shift, or chemise, underneath. Only the headdress grew smaller as the horned, padded, boxed, sugarloafed, and conical adornments of medieval fantasy gave way first to the gabled effect associated with royalty pictured on playing cards, and later to the French hood worn well back on the head, which allowed a lady of fashion to display her hair.

Moralists and legislators regarded all of this ostentation and extravagant aping of German dress as thoroughly immoral and perversely un-English, but the surge of fashion was irresistible, and with the introduction in the late 1550s of the Spanish style, the tide became a flood. The new fashion continued to favor the broad-shouldered and slashed appearance of Henry VIII's reign but introduced for both men and women a tight, wasplike waist and a rigid and starched torso. Central to the new look was the ruff and the corseted waist for both sexes; the far-

thingale, or hooped skirt, for women; and bombasted breeches for men. Underlying the new image were two technological innovations: the introduction of starch from Holland in 1564, which made possible the stiff, extended ruffles formed into a series of figure eights around the neck, and the development of knitting whereby silk hose or stockings could be made skintight and formfitting, in contrast to medieval tights, which, contrary to illuminations and illustrations, tended to bag about the knees and ankles.

At the same time, the vastly increased use of interchangeable parts of clothing made it possible to mix and match colors and materials as never before. Late-medieval attire, especially the hose and doublet, had been held together with ties and eyelets called points. Eventually sleeves were also tied to the doublet, skirts to the jerkin, and, in women's apparel, sleeves and skirts to the bodice. As the use of points grew, clothing began to break up into separate parts. The medieval male "long-stocked hose," equivalent to modern tights, divided up into two, occasionally three, segments:

tight bodice; high breasts

heavy gown

ca. 1520

ca. 1540

French hood

tight-corseted bodice

funnel-shaped sleeves

gown open to reveal the kirtle

23. Women's clothes of the early Tudor period.

24. Robert Devereux, 2nd Earl of Essex (ca. 1596), dressed in modest ruff, doublet with peascode belly and rolled wings and short skirt, puffed and embroidered sleeves, trunk hose heavily bombasted and attached to plain canions, stockings, and a single decorative garter.

the trunk segment, or breeches; canions, which were thigh sleeves generally covering the lower thigh, or "nether-stocks"; and stockings from the knees down. The lady's kirtle separated into a skirt and bodice, which in turn divided into the modern blouse or jacket, a corset, and a stomacher. The desired effect, especially for men, was a riot of conflicting colors and materials, and the well-appointed Elizabethan gallant might have displayed a sartorial ensemble consisting of five or six different materials tied together by points.

In order to accentuate the narrowness of the waist, the new Spanish fashion puffed out the sleeves, lowered the waist by elongating the rib cage, and inflated the hips so that they extended as far as, or even farther than, the shoulders. The ballooning was achieved with bombast, literally cotton padding but in practice horsehair, wool, flax, bran, or any leftover material. To complete the effect, the doublet was stiffened by quilting, buckram (coarse linen hardened with glue), or bone stays in order to achieve a long pointed waistline and an armored appearance. The neck was encased in a ruff that might extend out over a foot and had to be wired into place; and the crotch retained its still fashionable but less conspicuous codpiece, which by the end of the sixteenth century disappeared entirely. Finally, the entire array of stays, quilting, bombast, and slashing was set off by a short or long cloak and a hat, which was evolving from the Henrician bonnet into the tall-crowned, stiff, and cylindrical structure of late-Elizabethan style. How long it took a gentleman to be outfitted, to have his points tied and his ruff adjusted so that it would stay straight and firm, is impossible to guess. All that can be said with confidence is that the process was made even longer by the wide variety of choices available and that the cost was astronomical.

Available to the young man of fashion were puffed sleeves so bombasted that they substituted for pockets, doublets with stiff peascod bellies that extended so low they displaced the codpiece, jerkins with rolls or grotesquely enlarged shoulder wings that covered up the points by which the sleeves were attached, and padded waistcoats worn under the doublet. Below the waist he had three choices. Spanish trunkhose shaped like either a conic section or a pumpkin, Venetian-style trunks resembling inflated modern breeches, and German "plunderhose," which fell below the knees and had slashing so extensive that the effect was a series of panes or ribbonlike strips joined at the top and the bottom. Like Malvolio, he might also go cross-gartered at the knees or wear a single ribbon above the knee to hold up his stocking. (Malvolio almost always appears on the stage incorrectly garbed: cross-gartering is not from the ankles to the knees, as he is usually portrayed, but literally a garter above and below the knees, crossed at the back of the knee and tied in a bow at the front.) He might have a short Spanish cape with or without a collar, a long French cloak with or without a hood, or a sleeveless mandilion; but whatever the style, he had to have at least three outer garments, one for morning, one for afternoon, and one for evening. He also possessed one or two ornamental handkerchiefs, wore pointed shoes with heels and soles of varying heights, and bedecked himself with as much jewelry as he could afford. A fine embroidered silk shirt might cost as much as £10, and a proper hat ran to £2 in an era when it was possible to survive on £3 to £4 a year. Sir Walter Raleigh was rumored to have worn jewels on his shoes worth 6,600 gold pieces and to have adorned his jerkin, breeches, cape, and cap with 60,000 precious gems. His portrait presents him wearing a pearl-covered doublet and cloak and an immense pearl in his ear.

The total effect of Elizabethan fashion was prodigious: a display of wealth, contrasting colors (black was used to offset silver, gold, and ruby), and rich materials unparalleled in sartorial history. The clothing must also have been extremely uncomfortable to wear. Stubbes, with his fierce Puritan bias, was not an uncritical observer, but given the starched and rigid attire of the Elizabethan male, he could not have been far off the mark when he acidly commented that bombasted and quilted doublets were designed to neither "work, nor yet well play in . . . through the excessive heat thereof." The heavily stiffened and upholstered peascod fronts, which weighed four to six pounds, made it impossible to either "stoop down or decline . . . to the ground." The Houses of Parliament had to construct special seats to accommodate the pumpkin- and onion-shaped trunks known as "Spanish kettle-drums," and it must have been a nightmare when a seam gave way and the stuffing, which was often bran, began to run out of a gentleman's breeches. "Men," William Harrison rather sourly commented in *The Description of England,* were "transformed into monsters."

If men had become monsters, women, at least in the eyes of some contemporaries, had "become

men," donning doublet, jerkin, and ruff; tightening their bodices; padding their shoulders; and expanding their hips to achieve the low, hourglass waist and armored exterior so admired by both sexes. At the same time, they exposed so much of their hair to public view that hair styling became the rage. The ruff was important to both sexes, for it, above all other articles of clothing, demonstrated the hierarchical principle of dress, creating the desired haughty and disdainful angle of the chin. Unfortunately, it did little for sexuality because it limited the women to high-cut bodices that concealed the breasts. The Elizabethan compromise was to open the ruff in front, expose the neck and breasts, and offset the ruff with stiff gauze butterfly wings at the back of the head. A similar compromise was achieved by retaining the complete ruff but lowering the cut of the bodice and covering the upper chest and shoulders with a partlet ("fill-in"), often of a highly transparent material.

As the century advanced, the female waist grew not only narrower but also more pointed, and the stomacher, which was worn over the bodice, became more rigid in order to force down and tip forward the immense hooped skirts or farthingales favored by Elizabeth during the final decades of her reign. A lady of fashion had three choices: the Spanish vardingale, which produced a funnel or bell-like appearance; the French or catherine-wheel farthingale, which was fashioned rather like a drum; and the more humble skirt supported by the inelegant bum roll, a sausage-shaped tube of padding around the hips worn with a slight upward tip at the back—"a bolster for their buttocks." Over these rigs, constructed of wood, bone, or metal, were placed heavy brocaded and ornamented skirts or kirtles. Worn outside the bodice and kirtle was the gown, often open below the waist to expose the underdress and usually worn with a wide variety of attached sleeves. Such bulky elegance was not only heavy but also expensive; a dress might require anywhere from seventeen to thirty yards of material and cost as much as £13.

Then the court lady donned an array of extravagant accessories. She required a mirror attached to her fan or girdle, a silk mask, high-heeled shoes of soft leather or cloth, and, depending on how daring she was, a hat modeled on masculine fashions or nothing but a kerchief or piece of lace covering her head. Finally, she was ornamented and bejeweled from head to toe. She wore earrings and necklaces, and rings on all four fingers and thumb. Every inch

25. Elizabeth I (1592), dressed in a butterfly ruff with wired head rail, low-cut bodice with lace-edged chemise displayed, embroidered-bombasted sleeves with extra-long hanging sleeves attached to the shoulders, pointed stomacher, and bejeweled French farthingale skirt.

of her dress and gown was embroidered with birds, serpents, flowers, and insects and was plastered with jewels; and she covered her face with red and white lead-based cosmetics. As one contemporary said of the female of his species, you "have periwigs to curl your hair, colours to paint your face, art to square your shoulders, holsters to fashion your waist."

Experimentation, individuality, and exhibitionism were the hallmarks of Elizabethan costume, and it is customary to point to such exuberance as yet another example of Renaissance dynamism and further evidence that wealth, daring, and individuality were corroding the restraints and inhibitions of the medieval past. Gaudy display and extravagance, much as they were criticized by sixteenth-century divines and moralists, were not, however, seen as denials of an ordered and hierarchic society. On the contrary, they were visual confirmations of the principles of "degree, priority, and place," for Tudor England did not question the right of society's natural leaders to attire themselves in clothing appropriate to their station or to spend money on ostentatious display. The mark of a nobleman was, as it had always been, his liberality and willingness to spend money. High fashion was reserved for the aristocracy. The ruff was meant to be worn only by gentility; blue was the color associated, in theory, with the serving masses, while deep red was reserved for royalty; and hats and caps of velvet were prohibited to men "under the degree of a knight, or of a lord's son." Degree, priority, and place required that the elite dress not only well but distinctly, so that power could be recognized and revered. It was not until the final decades of the nineteenth century that political and economic authority discovered that it was far safer to hide behind the obscurity of a gray flannel suit.

Possibly at no time in history has the principle of hierarchy been so vividly and self-consciously demonstrated as in sixteenth-century dress. Almost every article of clothing proclaimed to the world that it was owned by people of wealth and rank who did not work for a living and who required a cadre of servants to dress their bodies and staff their wardrobes. What appears to the twentieth century as nouveau-riche vulgarity was for the sixteenth century perfectly natural behavior. Tudor sumptuary legislation, although it decried waste and extravagance at every level of society and deplored all fashions that undermined the nation's economic health, was only incidentally directed at the upper

ranks. It primarily sought to prevent indecency and indecorum among the multitude, where ostentatious dress was deemed inappropriate to a well-ordered commonwealth.

That aristocratic dress also lacked comeliness, with its blatant self-advertising of rank and status, was not so much a violation of the principles of decorum as it was a misapplication and overemphasis of one of the basic ingredients of sixteenth-century rhetorical training from which all seemliness and appropriateness were presumed to stem. Rhetoric sought to achieve a balance between richness and variation of expression (copiousness) and the control of thought and organization (structure). As in literature, where Cicero had warned that "to those who are inexperienced, turgid and inflated language often seems majestic," so in dress inexperienced courtiers allowed *copia* to get out of hand and believed that costly, modish, and ostentatious clothing made the man. Like the hack writer who indulged in the "vain pomp of words," the shallow young gentleman displayed his foppish fineries and fashions without regard for the full meaning of "decorum," which involved the whole person—thoughts, words, countenance, and gestures, as well as time, place, and circumstance. The concept of a civilized and decorous style in language, dress,

26. Bum roll (early seventeenth century), a padded roll for distending the skirt at the hips.

and behavior nevertheless remained constant, and in the hands of a Shakespeare or a Raleigh—although both men violated the rules of decorum —the idea that "style is the man" found full expression.

BIBLIOGRAPHY

The three basic modern studies on the Tudor cultural ideal are Ruth Kelso, *The Doctrine of the English Gentleman in the Sixteenth Century* (1929); John E. Mason, *Gentlefolk in the Making: Studies in the History of English Courtesy Literature and Related Topics from 1531 to 1774* (1935); and Louis B. Wright, *Middle-Class Culture in Elizabethan England* (1935).

Shakespeare's contemporaries wrote prolifically on the subject, but the key works are Roger Ascham, *The Schoolmaster* (1570), Lawrence V. Ryan, ed. (1967); Giovanni della Casa, *Galateo; or the Book of Manners,* R. S. Pine-Coffin, trans. (1958); James Cleland, *The Institution of a Young Noble Man* (1607), Max Molyneux, ed. (1948); Thomas Elyot, *The Book Named The Governor* (1531), Stanford E. Lehmberg, ed. (1963); Henry Peacham, *The Complete Gentleman* (1622), Virgil B. Heltzel, ed. (1962); Thomas Hoby, trans., *The Courtyer of Count Baldessar Castilio* (1561); Henry Percy, Ninth Earl of Northumberland, *Advice to His Son* (1609), G. B. Harrison, ed. (1930); Hugh Rhodes, *The Boke of Nurture, or School of Good Maners* (1577), reprinted in Frederick J. Furnivall, ed., *The Babees Book* (1868); and Philip Stubbes, *The Anatomie of Abuses* (1583).

Crucial to an understanding of decorum are T. McAlindon, *Shakespeare and Decorum* (1973); and George Puttenham, *The Arte of English Poesie* (1589), Gladys D. Willcock and Alice Walker, eds. (1936).

On the educational curriculum and rhetorical training, see Thomas W. Baldwin, *William Shakspere's Petty School* (1943) and *William Shakspere's Small Latine and Lesse Greeke* (1944); Kenneth Charlton, *Education in Renaissance England* (1965); Richard Mulcaster, *Positions Wherein Those Primitive Circumstances Be Examined, Which Are Necessarie for the Training Up of Children* (1581), Richard DeMolen, ed. (1971), and *The First Part of the Elementarie Which Entreateth Chefelie of the Right Writing of Our English Tung* (1582), Ernest T. Campagnac, ed. (1925); Walter Ong, *Rhetoric, Romance, and Technology* (1971); Joan Simon, *Education and Society in Tudor England* (1966); Juan Luis Vives, *On Education,* Foster Watson, ed. and trans. (1913); and Thomas Wilson, *The Arte of Rhetorique* (1553), Robert H. Bowers, ed. (1962).

The best works on Tudor dress and clothing are Frances E. Baldwin, *Sumptuary Legislation and Personal Regulation in England* (1926); Max von Boehn, *Modes and Manners,* vol. II, *The Sixteenth Century,* Joan Joshua, trans. (1933); Iris Brooke, *A History of English Costume,* 2nd ed. (1946), and "Dress," in J. E. Morpurgo, ed., *Life Under the Stuarts* (1950); Dion C. Calthrop, *English Costume,* vol. III (1906); and Cecil W. Cunnington and Phillis Cunnington, *Handbook of English Costume in the Sixteenth Century* (1954).

Daily Life in City, Town, and Country

GEORGE P. GARRETT

Our Elizabethan and Jacobean ancestors are so distant from us in time that we must exercise an active imagination if we are to summon them up out of the long dream of history. Yet they are near enough, in contrast with, for example, the pre-Christian world, so that we must likewise resist an easy temptation to consider them as close kin to ourselves. They are close enough, yet alien also; and their world is unfamiliar enough that it would be a serious mistake to try to put ourselves in their shoes—shoes that we would find comfortable and well made but a little strange on our feet, since both shoes and boots were made to be interchangeable, with no difference in shape or form between left and right. It would also be wrong to assume that, in the absence of the scientific method, lacking the guidance of Darwin, Marx, and Freud, the Elizabethans were intellectual primitives or that their daily lives were inevitably crude and almost devoid of necessary comforts and amenities. That is to say, there are assumptions about the Elizabethans that we must unlearn.

For instance, maritime historians once regarded the Elizabethans' square-rigged, high-charged, shallow-draft galleon-type vessels as a crude transitional stage in the development of the full-rigged sailing ship of the late eighteenth and nineteenth centuries. Viewed from that perspective, the sixteenth- and early-seventeenth-century ships seemed extremely awkward and unwieldy, evidently designed by people whose concepts of sailing were rudimentary and whose amazing achievements

were more accidental than the result of any skill. It was believed, from the general principles of sailing, that a galleon was hard to handle in winds and tides and that it would have been almost impossible to hold to a course except by running with the wind.

In principle, these suppositions are true; but in practice, skilled Elizabethan mariners, with much experience to draw on and with somewhat different goals than later seamen had, found that these ships worked very well for their purposes. Contemporary yachtsmen have tried their hands at sailing authentic replicas of Elizabethan and Jacobean ships (like the *Mayflower*) that were built as exhibits and tourist attractions. Unlearning some of their own habits and learning old skills simply through trial and error, modern sailors have found that by crafty use of the sails in various riggings and combinations, they can handle a galleon with considerable ease and subtlety, much more so than had once been believed. True, those ships do not handle well in a real gale; but they can be turned up into the wind, with sails struck and masts stepped down, and then they can ride out the roughest weather, hull down and surprisingly dry. Elizabethan ships might pitch, roll, and bob wildly in storms, but very few of them were victims of weather alone.

The greatest fear of a galleon crew, hundreds or even thousands of miles from any home port, was to be becalmed. The absence of wind was far more dangerous than the worst weather. Crude and simple in all its parts, a galleon could be easily patched and repaired, indeed completely rebuilt, wherever timber was available. It was made for long voyages and was the ideal vessel for exploring far and often unknown places. Not drawing much water, it could venture into shallow waters. It seldom ran aground, and if it did, it was easily floated.

On long voyages there were problems and diseases of one kind or another that often devastated a crew. Yet, unlike sailors a century or so later. Elizabethan and Jacobean seamen seldom suffered from scurvy. Drake, Hawkins, and the other great sea captains carried limes and other citrus fruits on board, knowing that they somehow or other inhibited scurvy. It was less a matter of science than magic—but it worked. In similar fashion, navigation, mostly dead reckoning based on severely limited and often inaccurate data, should have sent Elizabethan seamen far from their destinations; and it is true that weather, together with a multitude of variables, often dictated radical changes of course. Yet elaborate courses were charted, and exact landfalls and rendezvous halfway around the world were achieved so frequently as to baffle the modern navigator.

Elizabethans were much more knowledgable and skilled than we usually give them credit for, but many of their skills and crafts were in the nature of "mysteries": secrets passed on not, as they might be today, by books and formal schooling but directly and by masters to journeymen and apprentices in a given field. It was a system that worked well enough until the social fabric of England was ripped apart, first by Cromwell's revolution, then by the Restoration, and finally by the Glorious Revolution of 1688–1689. These social upheavals broke the continuity of many skills and crafts and made it necessary to reinvent the wheel: it is not accidental that the triumph of the scientific method dates precisely from the time when England began to recover from its long season of internal broils.

More than the continuity of mysteries and crafts was broken. Many aspects of daily life, some virtually unchanged for a thousand years, had vanished from the scene, and so had many of the familiar things of Elizabethan and Jacobean life. To imagine our ancestors, we have to skirt around the period that came after them, and often the bits and pieces of evidence are even more fragmentary than those of earlier ages.

Much that was rare and wonderful in Elizabethan times was also very perishable. For example, except for tombs, where stone and brass were traditionally used, much Elizabethan sculpture was wooden and painted. (Our own cigar-store Indians are an odd survival of that tradition.) Almost all of that wooden sculpture has vanished, and even museums have very few examples.

Elizabethan costume has also not been well preserved, though well-to-do Elizabethans spent fortunes on their clothing. For a single outfit, a courtier ordinarily spent as much as a modern man spends for a very expensive automobile. For special occasions, that courtier might dress in splendidly tailored silks, satins, and velvets, enriched with jewels and elegant accessories and costing more than a fine manor house and farm or a sailing ship fully equipped for a long voyage. Among the gentlemen and ladies of the court, then, clothing was a major investment and status symbol. The plain Puritans, who railed against this habit in many a book and sermon, were not exaggerating when they described young courtiers as wearing their fortunes on their backs like snails. In the half-century reign of Queen Elizabeth millions of pounds were spent by ambitious men and women on their clothing. Yet almost none of it survives. We can see it in portraits. There are a few dusty and fading examples in museums, the best of which are some Elizabethan dolls dressed in the "rags" from good clothes.

Our capacity to recapture the age is limited not only by our ignorance, our inexperience, and the uneven or even missing evidence but also by myths, judgments, and fabrications of our own that we must unlearn at the beginning. For example, it is still widely asserted and taught that London was a dirty city, odiferous and noisy, crime-ridden and crowded beyond relief. None of this appears to be true. It is unquestionably true that many Elizabethan and Jacobean writers vociferously complained about the city and especially about the noise, the dirt, the stink, and the crowding. We know that London was growing rapidly and extravagantly during this entire period. We know that there were urban problems which deeply concerned not only the lord mayor, the sheriffs, the aldermen, and the guilds but also the queen and her council. And we know from fascinating and impeccable sources, like William Harrison's *The Description of England* and especially John Stow's *Survey of London,* how "pestered" the city became by overcrowding and overbuilding and how different it seemed to such writers from the city they had known in youth.

And yet, there is every evidence that we would

not pass the same judgments upon the place. We certainly would not be entitled to do so. All of the noise and clamor of which Shakespearean London was capable could not begin to equal the aural assault of a modern industrial city; neither, as a number of scholars have pointed out, could the dirt and stench of London have ever approached the pollution and squalor of even our most salutary urban environments. The Elizabethans were, by and large, fastidious in these matters and outspoken in their concern for cleanliness. We know now that they were apt to bathe more often than had once been thought. Their well-known fondness for perfumes, pomanders, and nosegays; the scenting of leather and clothing; and the strewing of "sweetening" herbs and flowers indicate that their complaints about smells, while genuine, were also traditional and reflexive. Much evidence indicates that they would have found the odors of our world to be intolerable, while we might, in truth, be delighted by theirs. We know now, too, that the wealth of laws and regulations about cleanliness were rigorously enforced.

As for crime, there appears to have been enough to keep visitors wary and the law courts and prisons busy, but murder and other crimes of violence seem to have been very rare when measured against modern statistics. Most of the physical violence in and around London was the work of the law imposing its harsh punishments for every kind of crime. In short, by any standards we know of, Shakespearean London was clean, calm, and safe, though it appears to have been a very lively place indeed.

Another myth that could stand some correction concerns the general health and physical well-being of the Elizabethans. True, the rate of infant mortality seems to have been high. Also, the Elizabethans were afflicted by many diseases, some obscure and evidently vanished, like the "sweating sickness"; others now preventable or easily curable, like smallpox, diphtheria, and typhoid; others, like the bubonic plague, terrifying and baffling. These pestilences carried off many people, especially young people. Smallpox was so prevalent that only milkmaids (for reasons that would one day lead to the development of a vaccination for it) were said to have perfect, unblemished complexions. With all these diseases to contend with, those who arrived at middle age appear to have been tough survivors.

Yet, as best we can judge, mature adults tended to live out a life span close in length to our own.

The population was growing rapidly, and those Elizabethans who reached adulthood were much taller and healthier than their own grandparents had been or than their grandchildren and later descendants up to the edge of the present generation would be. Medieval people had been fairly small, judging by such obvious standards as armor, beds, chairs, and doorways, and nineteenth-century industrial workers also tended to be short. But for a time, chiefly the Elizabethan age and a little afterward, people were much taller, sturdier, and healthier than before or later. It appears that there were many men who stood six feet and over. At roughly six and a half feet, Sir Walter Raleigh was considered tall but no giant. He was captain of the guard at a time when, as now, all of the queen's guards stood over six feet. These facts should not surprise us. There are many examples in the modern world. The post–World War II generation in Japan measures nine inches taller than the prewar generation, a difference attributed to diet and life-style.

Medicine, for the Elizabethans, was a primitive craft, and they knew it. From queen to ratcatcher they wisely distrusted doctors and did as much as they could for themselves by means of what we have named preventive medicine. Their conclusion, which agrees precisely with the latest reports of medical science today, was that diet and exercise are the keys to good general health. Except in rare times of famine, even the poor had a fairly well balanced, high-protein diet; and most Elizabethans had a much more active physical life than we usually have today. Regular practice with the longbow was required of every ablebodied man long after the longbow ceased to have any serious military value, because the Privy Council conceived of the requirement as good outdoor physical exercise and also as a diversion less dangerous to health and welfare than many others.

One of the chief myths of the period—one that seems to have been as widely accepted by Shakespeare's contemporaries as by modern historians and one that can give us some indication as to how the truth of imagination can sometimes triumph over cold facts—is that the long period of Queen Elizabeth's reign, taken together with the first years of the reign of James I, was a time of peace and prosperity. It is true that, following the failure of the rising of the northern earls in 1569, most of England, except for the Scottish border, was free of warfare. There were many plots against the queen and her council, culminating in the brief and ill-fated rebellion of the earl of Essex in February 1601, but no other conspiracy advanced beyond the planning stages. Thus, while the continental European nations were torn apart by wars and rebellions, England was spared the worst excesses of the times. Though England was often threatened from outside, especially by the power of Spain, peace at home permitted the nation to build and to grow.

Yet that domestic sense of peace and calm was purchased by English blood and treasure, by continual involvement in the wars and affairs of others. Throughout this entire period English armies saw action in the wars of the Netherlands and France, sometimes in Spain and what had been Portugal, always in boggy Ireland; and English mariners fought for prizes and for their lives over all the seas. Compared to the actions of other nations, these ventures were mostly conducted on a small scale. Even so, the expense was great and ultimately (as James I would discover when he came down from Scotland to receive the English crown) grievous and irreparable. We need to recognize that the casualties, while never overwhelming in number, were serious enough. Throughout the reign of Elizabeth the towns and villages of England furnished young men for foreign graveyards, and there were wounded veterans everywhere with scars and crutches or wasted by disease, which took more soldiers' lives than any battlefield.

Still, it seemed to the English people that they were enjoying a period of real domestic tranquility, of peace in a real sense. This interpretation of events was, of course, encouraged by the government. But the most important fact is that it was believed by the people, of all ranks and stations—and not only believed in but also lived by. That is, they tried to live, and to a large extent succeeded, as if the myth were true; and, somehow, it became so. The power of this myth was reinforced by the vague memories of elders, memories that extended back to the Wars of the Roses and on through the brutal and unsettled times of Henry VIII, Edward VI, and Bloody Mary. Later, sentimental remembrances of "merrie England" would be a conventional reaction to the confusions and upheavals of the century following the death of Elizabeth. But even allowing for all that and for all the other factors, the prevalence of the myth of peace is nearly inexplicable except as an enormous testament of public faith in the queen: she proclaimed that she

had preserved peace and brought prosperity to her people, and she believed—or surely seemed to—that she had done so. Most important, her loving and loyal subjects generally believed her and believed in her.

Significantly, except for a few hundred personal guards, whose functions were as much ceremonial as practical, and a handful of troops to maintain the few operational fortresses left in England, there was no professional standing army in England. The Elizabethans made much of this contrast between themselves and the rest of the world, and so have historians since then. Of course, there was no way that the English could have afforded to maintain a standing army: all the riches of the New World were insufficient to defray the costs of Spain's great military machine. The queen was a scrupulously frugal custodian of England's limited wealth, and in times of danger she would not keep her citizen-armies mobilized for one day longer than necessary. After all, the troops had to be supplied and had to be paid something—not a salary like professionals and mercenaries (and there had been mercenaries in England up until the reign of Elizabeth) but a bare daily subsistence allowance. In 1588, during England's hour of greatest danger, with the Spanish Armada battling the Royal Navy in the English Channel and the issue still very much in doubt, the queen gambled and dismissed the largest army ever assembled in England until that time, sending her thousands of citizen-soldiers home from their camp at Tilbury, thus saving money for other purposes or, anyway, another day.

It would be a mistake, however, to judge from these facts that England was largely free of the military experience. In the absence of a large number of professional soldiers, the queen depended on her able-bodied citizens, for whom military training and regular musters were expected service and a common part of daily life. Her people were trained in the use of the basic weapons of the time. Though they may not have been well armed, they were still an armed populace (and thus a trusted populace), unique in Europe except for the cantons of Switzerland and some of the little city-states of the ramshackle Holy Roman Empire. Their training appears to have been fairly rudimentary: except for tactical situations requiring heroic defense, at which the English seem always to have excelled, the English citizen-soldier and his mostly amateur leaders were no match for German, French, and Spanish professionals. Yet, on its native ground, a large armed population presented a formidable obstacle to an invader. Practical Spanish military strategists of the period (as distinguished from King Philip II, who sincerely believed that God would side with him to overcome all difficulties) estimated that the conquest of England would require at least eight full-scale pitched battles—never mind the number of fixed sieges, skirmishes, and ambushes—and that the Spanish would have to win every battle. They reckoned that, with their trained and experienced men and excellent equipment, they could subdue the English, but only at an appalling cost of thousands of casualties, so many that even total victory would be nearly suicidal. The Spanish generals were greatly relieved that they never had to deploy an army in England. Reasonably, they determined that the murder of the queen and of certain key members of her court and council was the most practical and feasible strategy.

Throughout this period, the English also generally believed that they were enjoying prosperity; and there are sound arguments to be made that this was, indeed, a time of economic growth and expansion, of building and thriving, of great fortunes made, of a marked improvement in the standard of living. This last fact was duly noted by many contemporary writers. Harrison, in *The Description of England,* portrayed a better and easier life enjoyed by the two generations of Englishmen who came to maturity during Elizabeth's long reign. Some observers, however, believed that this improvement was undermining the physical and moral fiber of the English people. Harrison argued that breathing smoke (before the houses of England replaced the smoke hole with fireplaces and chimneys) was good for body and soul; that thick, opaque windows of horn were morally superior to glass, which allowed easy looking out and looking in; that hard beds and a plain and simple diet had helped to shape men and women of better character. His was the venerable argument that the fruits of prosperity are not salutary.

Very few people questioned the perception that things were getting better all the time. And yet much evidence, accessible then and now, indicates that economic and social conditions were much more complex and contradictory than the expressed perceptions of the times allow. Inflation was a serious grievance, virtually uncontrollable despite strict wage and price controls, and was eating away at gains and wealth at all levels. Care of the poor was a constant and unsolved problem,

engaging the government at every level from the parish priest and the local justice of the peace to the queen, whose summer progresses permitted her to see for herself that all was not well. There were periodic crop failures throughout her reign and especially in the last dozen years or so, some of them resulting in actual famine conditions in outlying shires. As new crafts and industries flourished, especially in London and in the southern and western ports and shires, other regions and enterprises deteriorated. Sheep raising continued to disrupt traditional agriculture, as it had for a century. The older ports of the north were silting up and falling into disuse. As London drew everything to it like a magnet, ancient cities settled into decline. In the north, poor people who could afford only dry dung for fuel dug coal that was shipped off to keep Londoners warm. In the midst of seeming plenty, then, there were poverty and hardship all around.

As for the seeming plenty, perhaps a perfect image of it is expressed in the celebrated jewels of Queen Elizabeth. At the end of her reign she was surely the most glittering and bejeweled monarch in the world. Much was made of this, and none of it was lost on James of Scotland, who dreamed for years that one day he would come into the affluence and plenitude that those jewels represented. When he came to the throne in 1603, he discovered that Elizabeth's treasury was almost empty and that most of her jewels were, in truth, paste—excellent copies. She had long since secretly pawned and sold her real jewels, but she maintained the outward and visible appearance that she clearly believed to be an urgent necessity.

Throughout Elizabeth's reign, prodigy houses, most of them really palaces of pleasure, were built by her nobility and gentry all over England, literally spreading and sharing, as well as showing, the vast wealth they were enjoying. It is true that these shining structures—equipped with rich glass windows, glittering gold weather vanes, glorious and fantastic gardens, collections of gold and silver plate, and precious things from all corners of the earth—asserted peace and plenty all over the land, but many of them nearly bankrupted their builders. Several of the queen's favorites, on whom she lavished incredible wealth—men like Leicester, Hatton, and Essex—died so deeply in debt (often to her) that there was never any possibility of repayment. Ironically, Sir Walter Raleigh, who had gained riches through her favor, was able to preserve some of that wealth by falling out of favor in

1592. Left alone, with no need for show, he managed to keep his fortune sufficiently intact so that it would attract the interest of James I in the next reign.

This great season of building was accomplished at a time when most English fortifications and the old castles (castles that, as Oliver Cromwell was to learn in the next century, were still formidable defensive positions, artillery or no) were allowed to decay for lack of funds to repair and maintain them. It was also a time when very few new churches were built and many old churches deteriorated. The supreme symbol of this policy of indifference was the great wooden spire atop old St. Paul's, which had made it the tallest cathedral in the world. In 1560 the spire was struck by lightning and burned. This event became a subject for many sermons, and all through Elizabeth's reign there were plans to raise the money to rebuild the spire. These plans were still unrealized when the great London fire of 1666 so damaged old St. Paul's that the entire cathedral had to be replaced. Meanwhile, Sir Thomas Gresham built his huge and expensive Royal Exchange, a kind of archetypal shopping center, only an easy walk away. In short, the architectural prodigies and wonders of the age, which are in fact singularly dazzling, were achieved at the expense and neglect of other things.

Never mind; the English, in what looks more like an act of faith than anything else, chose to take the times they lived in as blessed by peace and prosperity. And their faith has remained mostly unquestioned ever since except by some implacable scholars and by skeptics whose reflexive revisionist impulses make their conclusions at least as debatable as the conclusions of those who insist that the age was the best that England has ever known.

How, then, do we know the Elizabethan English, and how can we begin to imagine their daily lives? We know them, of course, through their buildings, furniture, arts, and crafts, through the objects that have somehow managed to survive succeeding generations—generations that were often hostile to the aesthetic interests and principles of those times. We know them through their tombs and through the solemn, often enigmatic portraits that endure. Because so much else has been lost to us, we know them chiefly through the wealth of words—from the innumerable official and semiofficial documents, records, and transcriptions. Diaries and precious caches of letters—letters like those of the Lisle family, edited by Muriel St. Claire Byrne—

come as close as anything we have to telling us how they really talked to each other, what daily speech was like. The published literature of the time, when printing was new and exciting to the world, included pamphlets and broadsides, sermons, textbooks, books of practical advice and general counsel, fiction, poetry, and plays, which combined fiction and poetry to create a popular literary form of the period. Above all, we have the work of the greatest poet of the language and the age, William Shakespeare, whose unimaginable energy and genius can so kindle our imagination that we may believe, only half deceiving ourselves, that we are capable of conjuring up an accurate picture of Elizabethan society on the strength of his plays alone.

Country Life

Daily life in the country followed an immemorial cycle of labor through the seasons of planting, growing, harvesting, and slaughtering, and then the brief waiting through the worst part of winter until it was time to begin planting again. The calendar was based on the parallel seasons of the ancient Christian calendar, as outlined in the Book of Common Prayer, where rituals, readings, and prayers were, of course, the same in city and country and, in fact, would be read at precisely the same time each Sunday and holy day throughout England. With the parish of the Church of England as a constant center of their lives, and with no real choice about this, for it was a matter of law, town and country moved together through the schedule of fast days and fixed and movable feasts in the seasons of Advent, Christmas, Epiphany, Septuagesima, Lent, Easter, and Pentecost.

Life was not so different in the towns, for the country grew up close to the walls and gates of the cities, and the markets and fairs regularly brought the countryman into town to sell his wares. Towns and cities—even huge London, which is still a surprisingly green city to this day—were greener then, for no house was considered a worthy dwelling place without a garden for pleasure, herbs, and vegetables. Urban people relished the pleasures of country life and aspired to own a house and some land in the country. Land was wealth, and as soon as the city dweller—gentry or merchant, adventurer or entrepreneur—managed to make and save some money, chances were that it was invested in land. The manor houses and prodigy houses of the period brought townspeople into the heart of the country. (Law and social custom required landowners to go and maintain "hospitality" at their places during certain times of the year.) They brought with them urban fashions, habits, and attitudes.

The typical country village—with its manor house and parish church, its common (or village green), its dovecote, its bakehouse, brewhouse, and smithy—was a nearly self-sustaining corporate unit. Most essentials could be made locally. Luxuries and special skills were regularly provided by familiar itinerant visitors from the city—the limner and the bookseller, the dentist and the scissors grinder. Royal and private post riders, those messengers who could ride a hundred miles a day and sometimes more, if they had to, changed their spent horses for fresh mounts in the yard of the village inn, bringing with them the news and rumors—all that was included in the fine old word *bruit*—of the city. No doubt, in the brief moments before saddling up and riding on, these messengers picked up at least the major news from the village.

A great deal has been written about the state of the roads and highways of Shakespearean England, and the consensus is that they were mostly in deplorable condition. There is some question about the truth of this judgment. Certainly the condition of the roads varied widely, for maintenance was a local responsibility; but, until later in the seventeenth century and especially in the eighteenth century, weather was more of a problem than anything else. The principal highways of England were still the great Roman roads, built by extraordinary engineers to last forever. The truth is that they lasted very well until huge wagons and coaches for traveling became commonplace. The roads had been built for the traffic they had to bear: people moving on foot and on horseback, livestock being driven to market, and some wagons, usually having two high wheels and pulled by four (or sometimes six) horses. Heavy loads—timber, coal, ore from the mines of Cornwall and Wales—were shipped by boat and barge as much as possible, using the natural network of rivers.

Coaches were very few and far between in Elizabeth's reign. Her own little coach, first acquired in 1564 and complete with a Dutch coachman, created something of a stir. Not until the last years of the century did coaches become the fashion and a serious problem in the streets of London, most of which, like the streets of other ancient towns, had been made mainly to serve horseback and foot

traffic. Judging by what we know about the movement of goods and people—including a number of major military operations—the main roads and highways held up very well. Lesser roads, often scarcely more than footpaths or cattle trails, were more troublesome. Repair of bridges seems to have been a problem in many localities, yet many medieval and Elizabethan bridges are still in place and functioning well enough with heavy modern traffic.

If the roads were less than ideal, travel was greatly eased by the presence, practically everywhere, of excellent inns. English inns, at that time, were the best in the world and much better than they would be later. They offered comfortable chambers, good sturdy beds with clean sheets, and uniformly adequate food and drink. Every village seemed to have at least one inn, and each town had several. In England, the inns were far more numerous than the monastic lodgings for pilgrims and travelers that they replaced after the dissolution of the monasteries. Innkeeping was a profitable and flourishing business—evidence that more people were using the English roads than we earlier imagined.

For the most part, those roads were reasonably safe: the age of the highwayman came later. There were some complaints about safety on the roads, but rape and robbery seem to have been rare. Thus, for the most part and for most of the year, travel between town and country was uninterrupted. The exchange between town and country was active and constant. But probably most important of all was the complex of attitudes that town and country had toward each other, particularly shared attitudes, assumptions deeper than intellectual constructs or concerns. The natural environment, then as now, was much "tamer" in England than in America, where there is still much open space and preserved wilderness. There was some wild country in Shakespearean England, what was termed "waste" land. There were also mountains and moors, forests and marshland; the Fens, still undrained, were enormous. There were uninhabited places, but no part of the nation could be called unknown. Nature was familiar, well used, and generally well cared for.

Almost everything growing, wild or cultivated, had its use. Very little was wasted. For example, almost every kind of tree, native or newly introduced (and many new trees and other plants were brought into England in Elizabeth's time), had a practical value. Oak was marvelous for buildings, ships, and furniture; supple willows made lobster and crab pots; hazel was used for hoops for casks; from the yew came posts believed to outlast iron; boxes were made from the soft, light wood of the poplar; ash made the best oars and the handles for tools; lime was used for musical instruments; box for other wooden instruments and for engraving; hornbeam served as a slow-burning fuel; alder made the best charcoal for gunpowder; leather tanners made use of birch bark; and the hawthorne's leaves were the favorite food of oxen. Birch and beech ("nursing trees") were used to assist the growth of other trees.

Timber of all kinds was a valuable crop; and so, though the great forests of England had dwindled, a serious effort was made to preserve what was left by careful forestry. The contrast with Scotland, which had been one of the world's most heavily wooded areas in the Middle Ages, is instructive. By the time of Elizabeth, Scotland was virtually denuded of trees. Timber had to be imported. Even firewood was scarce and often had to be bought or stolen from England.

Herbs and flowers, in the garden and growing wild, were more than purely aesthetic: the Elizabethans used them to make symbolic statements, to provide nourishment, and to fulfill many kinds of medical purposes. All parts were used—seeds, roots, stems, and flowers. Traditional Elizabethan salads, rich with greens, nuts, and fruits, added flowers also. Roses, violets, primroses, nasturtiums, dandelions, hawthorne flowers, and many kinds of tree blossoms were common salad ingredients. Flowers, herbs, and spices were used for strewing, to "sweeten" the chambers of houses.

Elizabethans seem especially to have enjoyed distilling things, and they used the "still room" to concoct a variety of medicinal potions and cordials made of herbs, flowers, and spices. Nutmeg was for the spleen, clove for the sinews, the leaves of agrimony for the liver. Mints had many uses—peppermint for the stomach and bowels, spearmint for headache, apple mint for "falling sickness" (epilepsy). Wild strawberry made lotions and gargles, raspberry treated sore throat, rue was for infection, angelica was highly regarded for dog bite, rosemary restored the memory, and lemon balm was believed to make a merry heart. Among the familiar flowers, the Elizabethans used lavender for palsy, violets for inflammation of the lungs and insomnia (and to ward off evil spirits), the peony for toothache, marigold for bee sting, and the gillyflower (carnation) for ailments of the heart. Juniper

was reported to be excellent for gout, hemorrhoids, worms, cramps, and convulsions. The pansy was a cure for the French pox, and the daffodil was thought to be good medicine for some fifty-one different disorders.

Disregarding the debatable merits of this system of pragmatic medicine (are our own health-food fads and fears any more valid?), we can at least acknowledge that these practices are evidence of a habit of very close, if unscientific, observation of nature. The Elizabethans knew their herbs and flowers very well and clearly believed that virtually all natural things had some beneficial use in the large scheme of things, if only we were privy to the secrets of them. As in the case of their basic political, social, and religious assumptions, this assumed conception of the meaning and significance of nature was shared by both countrymen and townspeople. This habitual assumption had a scriptural basis: man, like Adam, was viewed as the steward for the garden of this world. That garden was good because God had made it so; and the world, with all its infinite multitude of things, was an intricate, subtle, elaborate pattern of mysteriously interrelated parts. Like the surprised Adam, the Elizabethans tried to study and give names to everything. It was this conception of the world that gave Elizabethan arts and crafts their richness and complexity: everything that could be was decorated with allusions to other things. It was a deeply simple view of reality, for it assumed that all things are kin to each other, a choir singing the same music in many voices.

This cosmology was rooted in the experience and perception of nature by country people. It is no wonder that the pastoral poem, with its echoes of Vergil and Theocritus, was regarded as the most elegant literary form of the age: Spenser wrote out of that tradition in *The Shepherd's Calendar* and *The Faerie Queene*. As the towns and cities, and especially London, grew and changed, becoming complex and international, the pastoral dream—the memory of the country with its rough edges smoothed and its rude surfaces painted over—became more and more important to urban people, particularly the queen and her court. By the end of Elizabeth's reign the fashion of the court was country dancing, and in her last months the queen was seen in her chambers dancing in the old English fashion to the tune of a pipe and the rhythm of a tabor. Her summer progresses brought the fabulous court out into the country to be seen and, it was hoped and imagined, to be refreshed and restored with rural virtues. Country customs were reintroduced to the city in the form of holidays such as May Day and Midsummer's Eve.

Eventually, this easy and natural revival degenerated into an official program of enforced preservation. The government tried, without much success, to stem the tide of country people who came to the cities and towns to change their lives for the better. Elizabeth's last progresses were thinly attended, and it became increasingly difficult to make a new generation of landowners stay in the country for long. More than anyone consciously knew or could admit, the lives of the inhabitants of town and country were becoming more distinct.

Facts of Daily Life

City or country, the day was as long as there was daylight. Elizabethans rose in the dark, dressing by such artificial lights as they could manage, and worked through the daylight hours. They allowed a civilized hour or more around noon for dinner (the chief meal of the day) and for digestion, and they went to bed soon after the fall of darkness. This schedule made for long days in summertime, when people rose as early as 3 A.M. to be dressed and ready for business with the rising of the sun. In the dead of winter they sometimes dawdled until 5 A.M. before rising to face the cold and damp. For lighting they had the fitful flare and shadow of the fireplace. (Someone had to get up earliest of all to lay the day's fire, to stoke and blow on the banked coals to kindle a flame.) They also had candles (the most expensive made with perfumed beeswax and the cheapest with tallow) and oil lamps. Most ordinary people, except on festive occasions, burned only the cheapest sort of fat candles or, frequently, used sputtering and smoky rushes that had been dried and dipped in grease so that they would burn like torches. Rising, they washed with water from a basin or ewer. The well-to-do had their water warmed by a servant and scented with the essence of flowers and some floating petals, and they washed with soft and gently perfumed soaps.

Elizabethans, rightly concerned about the pollution of streams and wells, used water for washing and cooking and cleaning, but they were very careful about the water they drank. At all ages, they drank mostly beer and ale, and sometimes cider, perry, or other forms of fermented fruit juice, a gallon or so a day to slake their thirst. The beer and ale, having roughly the same alcoholic content as our own, were not considered intoxicating but healthy and nourishing. For serious beer drinking they turned to "double beer," which had been double-brewed to increase its strength, or the formidable and fairly expensive "double-double," readily available in tavern and marketplace under such descriptive names as "Mad Dog" and "Father Whoreson" and "Dragon's Milk." Early in her reign the queen forbade the brewing and serving of double-double beer at her court, which indicates that the effects of the drink must have been distinctly noticeable. Roughly sixty full-time brewers produced about 600,000 gallons of beer a year for the queen and court. As Madge Lorwin points out in her invaluable *Dining with William Shakespeare,* "Even in William Harrison's modest home—he was rector of a small Essex village church—two hundred gallons of beer were brewed and consumed each month" (chapter 3). There seems to have been a distinction in the drinking habits of town and country: beer was newer to England than ale and was more popular in the towns, while ale, made more simply and without hops, was the country drink.

There were many servants at all levels of society except the lowest, for it took many hands working together to accomplish the basic subsistence chores, and groups larger than immediate family had to join together to survive. In a sense, the whole group, masters and servants, and the whole hierarchy of the latter group, from kitchen turnspit to the butler, were considered as "family." The system was benignly (ideally) paternalistic, in the great manor houses as well as the more humble establishment of the country yeoman; actual wages were minimal, but the responsibility of the master for the health and well-being of one and all of his servants was real. In return labor, obedience, and loyalty were expected. Just as each master was theoretically the servant of some higher master, all were servants of the queen; and she was God's servant. Thus, in greatly altered circumstances, feudal ideas persisted. Those who were not servants of some sort or another, the ones whom Elizabethans called "masterless men," were considered a danger to good order.

And so it was the servants who rose in the dark and the cold to try, briefly, to banish both for the benefit of the others.

English men and women rose and cleaned their teeth in the morning with a sweet toothpaste and a soft cloth. A soft cloth was probably better for the care and preservation of tooth enamel than the brush that we use today. For cleaning after meals, Elizabethans regularly and openly used toothpicks. For the well-to-do, a fancy gold toothpick was often in order.

Clothes for men—whether the formal and elegant clothing of courtiers and gentry for formal and elegant occasions or rough-and-ready clothing of wool and canvaslike cloth and leather—was much the same in design, if not in fashion. That is, the fashions changed often and sometimes radically, but the essential form persisted, and that form was very different in concept and purpose from our own. For one thing, long trousers had not yet come into general use: they were worn by some English troops to protect against the mud and chill of the bogs of Ireland but were almost completely unknown. Elders and important public figures wore robes and gowns for public and official occasions. Younger men wore doublet and hose, which (to oversimplify greatly) consisted of something very like shorts of varying length, sometimes with a short skirt, and long, tight-fitting stockings resembling a dancer's tights. The doublet was like a jacket, more or less form-fitting and modeled after upper-body armor. Sleeves were often separate, and for work or hard exercise a sleeveless jerkin was frequently worn. Shoes were light and soft, not altogether unlike modern running shoes except for the materials. Boots were worn for riding, brogans for hard outdoor labor, and feather-light slippers for dancing.

The important things to know and remember are not the intricate details of Elizabethan costume—which, in any case, baffled most contemporaries except for tailors—but the essential design. Allowing more freedom for legs and arms than later fashions, it was an ideal costume for all kinds of vigorous physical activity, better than almost any modern outfit except for specific athletic clothes. It was easy to run, jump, climb, ride, and dance in a doublet and hose. Clearly, much physical activity was expected of a man. Indeed, it was really required, for to cut a handsome figure in those clothes, a man had to keep himself trim and fit.

Elizabethan men and women alike wore many individual parts of clothing joined together—usually by tight lacing, tying of "points," buttons, and snaps, some of them brightly on display and others carefully concealed from sight. Thus, within the limits of the purse, one had a potential for much more variety than is possible today. It appears that Elizabethans very seldom preferred "matching" or "color-coordinated" outfits in the modern sense. They liked a clashing counterpoint of many colors and textures. The model they aspired to seems to have been the rich profusion of an English flower garden in springtime. With their clothing, built upon and around a simple and unchanging basic design, they made themselves intricate and thus, in their view, "natural."

Elizabethans, to look right and to wear their clothes well, required the help of others in both dressing and undressing. Thus, it was assumed that there would almost always be others nearby and able to assist. The Elizabethans enjoyed precious little privacy, but they seem not to have missed it much. The desire for privacy was viewed as suspicious, perhaps a symptom of mental instability, and there was very little loneliness. The intricate design of clothing reflects the fact that from the cradle to the grave, people were always close by other people and were prepared, each according to station and vocation, to help each other and to be helped.

Awake, washed, dressed, having said or read the morning's prayers, most likely in a small group, the Elizabethans sat down to a brisk, light breakfast—usually bread, butter, and cheese, perhaps some leftover cold meats, all washed down with beer or ale. In the country there might well be something warm—a thick, rich soup or a porridge—that was always kept simmering in a large pot in the kitchen fireplace. Breakfast was casual compared to the other meals, but the same general etiquette obtained. A man who sat at table kept his hat on. Drinking vessels—whether of glass (in the finest houses), pewter, stoneware, wood ("treen"), or blackjack leather—were kept on a sideboard or shelf and brought and served only when asked for and then returned to their original place when the person had finished drinking. Elizabethans ate out of bowls or off plates of various materials, rich and humble. They used spoons and a knife, often a knife of their own that they carried with them. There were no forks at the table. Already in use by European aristocracy, forks had appeared on royal tables in England long before Elizabeth; she owned at least one set of gold forks but evidently never used them. Forks were not common tableware in England for almost a century. There is some indication that their reputed Italian origin made Elizabethan English suspicious of forks, a sort of guilt by association that made the implements seem effete and vaguely immoral.

Many descriptions of daily life in Shakespearean times give the unimaginative impression that in the absence of forks, table manners of the period were crude and clumsy—that the Elizabethans needed forks but did not know it. On the contrary, it appears that, by and large, table manners were formal and, depending on place and occasion, quite as elegantly correct as our best modern etiquette. It is true that fingers had to be used a bit more than is usual today, by carvers and servers as well as those seated at table; but because this was so, cleanliness was stressed and made easy. All who sat down to eat first washed and dried their hands. Ewers of water and clean towels were made available throughout the meal. Carvers and servers washed their hands each time they carved or handled any food. A contemporary analogue to this—deriving, in fact, from the period and its manners—is found in the celebration of the Eucharist by Roman Catholic and Anglican clergy. Having prepared the sacrifice of bread and wine on the altar (much as bread and wine might have been prepared at a sixteenth-century table), the priest turns to an acolyte who pours clean water over his hands and offers him a towel to dry himself. It is hard for us to imagine eating without a fork, and when we try to do so, we can only picture ourselves as clumsy and inept. It does not follow that there was anything clumsy about the Elizabethan craft of forkless dining.

Just as the first light of day appeared, the Elizabethans went to work. Here, except for a shared concept of the meaning and value of hard work, the daily life of city and country was quite different. Of course, everywhere in England, town and country, young students went off to school for a long day of learning. Most of them learned the same subjects: the classics, grammar, literature, basic arithmetic, and all that was included in Shakespeare's "small Latin and less Greek." While not enough to earn anyone the reputation or perquisites of a scholar or a "university wit," this curriculum was a more than adequate introduction to the humanities.

Actual figures—the numbers of students and schools—are still being compiled, insofar as they can be in the absence of complete records; but we have reason to believe that, at least by the end of Queen Elizabeth's reign, most young English men and women had the benefit of a fairly standard and generally adequate education. Even apprentices who were training in skills or crafts were also required by law to spend some hours every day in conventional schooling. We know that there were regulations concerning the education of children and that those laws were generally enforced. Clearly, education mattered to the authorities, and it mattered a great deal to the queen. It is quite possible that the audience for whom Shakespeare's plays were performed was about as literate, as informed, and as well educated as any English-language audience has ever been, before or since. The social separation between the "groundlings" and the gentry may have been real enough in fact, but they rubbed elbows at the Globe, and the difference in their educational backgrounds was not so great.

As to the Elizabethan work ethic, the nobility were spared some forms of labor but were compelled to assume certain heavy social obligations not required of lesser folk. Everyone else was expected to work for a living. Abstractly, work was not considered intrinsically ethical or especially edifying; but not to work for one's living, at whatever calling and in whatever station one found oneself, was considered definitely unethical. Neither work nor good works could, of themselves, save one's soul, but too much leisure and idleness could put a soul at hazard.

Everybody went to work, then—some to the many domestic tasks required to maintain a household, large or small. In towns and cities, most merchants and shopkeepers lived and worked in the same building: the ground floor was used as a shop, and the floors above were the dwelling place of the family. But new centralized workplaces, such as the Royal Exchange and the New Exchange, were beginning to change that custom. Some craftsmen went to places where their fellows commonly plied their trade; for instance, in London you would find candlestick makers in Lothbury, bell founders in Aldgate Ward, butchers at Smithfield, poulters at St. Nicholas Shambles, fishmongers along Thames Street close by Bridge Street or Billingsgate. And for all the herbs and spices you might need you went to the great gathering of grocers and apothecaries in Bucklersbury.

In the country, labor was harder and more continually demanding. Dorothy Hartley's *Lost Country Life* brings together a fascinating treasury of knowledge about rural tasks and trades. Those tasks were not only hard but also practically endless, meaning they could never be entirely finished, except for the time being. Building on the framework of the familiar Elizabethan farming calendars of Thomas Tusser (the first edition of his *Hundred Points of Husbandry* appeared in 1557), Hartley shows us a long year of almost constant labor, broken up by ancient country holidays and church festivals. Throughout this period the legal beginning of the year fell in March, but for most country people the new year was marked by an old holiday on the first Monday following Twelfth Night and the end of Christmastide—Plow Monday. This rural year ran on until the next Christmas season, from the first plowing and planting (as early as weather and frost allowed) and the breeding of animals, until the fall harvest and the slaughter of all but the breeding stock in November, known as the Blood Month.

Since almost everything the country family had was made from materials at hand, maintenance was careful and ceaseless. Country people saved and used almost everything, even dung from the hen roost and dovecote and manure from animals and the privy. Most parts of slaughtered animals had uses—bladders for containers, for example, and horns for cups and spoons. Straw was made into rope, baskets, tubs, and brooms. For special skills, rural people depended on the cooper and the thatcher, the smith and the mole catcher.

The very shape of the land was swiftly changing, in appearance as well as use, from the old customs of feudal strip farming and unenclosed land to a somewhat more efficient mixture of cropland and pasture, often demarcated by hedges. To contemporaries the most obvious transformation was the increase of pasture land for sheep at the expense of crops. This change had been going on for a long time and continued throughout the Elizabethan period in spite of a good deal of complaint and criticism. To an extent sheep raising was beginning to displace the labor-intensive habits of the farming culture.

Herding and farming both demanded knowledge of many different crafts and skills that had not changed greatly in a thousand years or more. In this respect, agriculture was distinguished from the crafts and trades of the towns and cities, where there were a fairly high degree of specialization, a desire for the improvement of skills and products (where possible), and an impulse toward the development of more efficient, labor-saving devices. Where profit was a real possibility and where what we have called upward mobility was not beyond aspiration, if still not often an easy transformation

of one's original station and condition, clearly there was no good purpose in the unquestioned effort to master and to practice old ways.

For all rural people except the large-scale and often absentee landlord, from the common farm laborer to the honorable yeoman with his own acreage, the basic rational goal was subsistence. The requirements for survival, aside from hard work and some good luck, were essentially conservative —to continue, by and large, as one's ancestors had done, doing many of the same things in the same place. The countryman's subsistence depended on doing well with the things at hand and doing without extraneous and newfangled luxuries. In the town and city, where more and more displaced country people resettled, the emphasis was much more on the new, on improvement, and (where such magic could be worked on the consumer) on turning today's luxury into tomorrow's necessity.

Thus, in a deep sense, townspeople and country folk were already working at cross-purposes. Of course, poets and preachers extolled the country life, with all its rigor and fatigue and simple pleasures. It was not farmers but townsmen, trained in schools and universities, who celebrated the benefits of a life of sweat and toil, coarse brown bread, old English ale, and plain "white meats" (beans, cheese, poultry, and fish). But there were also more sophisticated and skeptical voices, among them Marlowe and Raleigh in their "shepherd" poems and Shakespeare, with his country bumpkins in *A Midsummer Night's Dream* or *Love's Labor's Lost.* Busy townspeople might look on country life from a fairly sentimental perspective, but they were ruthlessly unsentimental in the elaborate use and abuse of both land and the people on it. More and more well-to-do city dwellers put their profits into land, as a commodity and as an investment; and they bought, sold, and traded real estate in bits and pieces. Once the country people had been largely at the mercy of the lord of the manor, but that lord had been deeply rooted in the same place and the same traditions. Now the manor, often empty most of the year except for the servants who maintained it and oversaw the local tenants, might be the property of several strangers in a lifetime.

If rural labor was hard, it was usually performed at a somewhat easier pace than work in the town or city, for where work is never really finished, there tends to be a slower, steadier rhythm of labor. Both town and country followed the church bells that tolled the hours from cockcrow to curfew and on through the hours of the night. In a coded language that often differed from town to town and from one shire to another, the bells signaled alarms and celebrations, births and deaths, marriages and funerals. Both town and country enjoyed, sometime after 11 A.M., a long dinner hour and respite, followed by another session of work until the end of the day. But in cities and towns, and especially in London, there were more distractions of all kinds, from bowling greens and alleys and archery butts to street shows and the pleasures of cookhouse and tavern, calling the worker to hurry with chores so as to enjoy fully the possibilities of recreation. Ironically, it was precisely the range and availability of leisure activities that made the pace of urban life more hurried. To the country people, the life of the towns, however appealing, seemed almost frantic, a chaos of color and noise peopled by crowds of clever strangers whose chief aim, it seemed, was to part a poor man from his money.

If hard, though often different, forms of labor were a common characteristic in both town and country, and if both shared a common profession of the values of work, at least all those except for the rare and lucky few to the nobility and manor born, leisure also played a very large part in their lives. There were the great holidays of the calendar, each with its own special customs and traditions. Though the Christian calendar had been altered by the Reformation and subjected to Puritan pressures for more drastic change all through Elizabeth's reign, it still included the feast days and fast days, the former to be celebrated and the latter to be observed.

First, in the Christian calendar of the year, came the crowded sequence of days beginning with Christmas Eve and including St. Stephen's Day on 26 December, St. John's on 27 December, and Childermas or Holy Innocents on 28 December, a curious mixture of festival and mourning for the children of Judea slaughtered by King Herod. Though the shrine of St. Thomas à Becket was demolished by Henry VIII and his feast day was officially dropped, many more-than-secret Catholics still honored England's saint of Canterbury on 29 December. The first day of January, a day for exchanging gifts at court and all over the country, was also the feast of the Circumcision. Epiphany, the day of the Magi, was celebrated in England as Twelfth Day; the evening before it was Twelfth Night and the end of the holidays of Christmastide.

On St. Agnes' Eve, the night of 20 January, a young maid who went to bed without supper, followed a series of conventions, and finally fell asleep while praying, might dream of her future husband. On 2 February came Candlemas, the day of the presentation of Christ in the temple. Before the Reformation the immemorial custom had been to bless and to distribute candles to the congregation, and in Elizabethan times there was still a procession with candles and torches. This day also marked the time for taking down all the greens—holly and ivy, bay and mistletoe and rosemary—that had been put up as Christmas decorations. Next was the popular St. Valentine's Day (14 February), on which wives gave gifts to husbands, as did young women to escorts chosen by lot.

The forty days of Lent, beginning with the Ash Wednesday fast, were preceded by Collop Monday (the last day when meat was to be eaten until the great feast day of Easter) and Shrove Tuesday, a carnival day of feasting and public sports that began and ended with the ringing of a pancake bell. The Sundays of Lent had their traditions, many of which fell into disuse after the Reformation, though in the north of England some of these old Catholic practices persisted: for example, the fifth Sunday of Lent was called Carling Sunday, on account of the custom of eating "carlings" (parched peas) on that day. On Palm Saturday, all over England, it was customary to go out and gather willow branches to decorate houses and to carry to church on Palm Sunday. Maundy Thursday of Holy Week was a time for charity (in recollection of Christ's injunction to the disciples to love one another), with the giving of money, food, and clothing to the poor. It was also the occasion when the sovereign of England knelt and washed the feet of a number of poor people equal to the sovereign's age, just as Christ had washed the feet of his disciples. This was a ritual regularly observed by Queen Elizabeth. Good Friday, once also known in England as Long Friday, lost most of the Roman Catholic customs associated with it, but it remained a fast day and, in the Book of Common Prayer, a day for the celebration of Holy Communion. It was also the day for which hot cross buns were baked and eaten at breakfast. Holy Saturday, or Easter Even, was a strict fast day ending with a midnight service in church heralding the beginning of Easter.

Easter remained the greatest feast day of the ecclesiastical year and, except perhaps for the "harvest home" feasts in the country, the chief day for feasting in England. Two ancient customs continued—the eating of small cakes riddled with bitter herbs (rue, tansy, and wormwood) and the painting and eating of paschal eggs. Holy Thursday (Ascension Day), the fifth Thursday after Easter, was usually, in the towns and villages, the day for the "beating of the bounds." There was a ceremonial procession, including all the local children, all around the boundary stones that marked the limits of the parish. Children were symbolically "beaten" so that they might remember the bounds.

The next great feast of the church, Whitsunday, marked the beginning of the season of Whitsuntide, or Pentecost. In England, beginning in the Middle Ages, Whitsunday had been a time for raising money for the maintenance of church buildings. The parish customarily sponsored a Whitsun Ale—a large, happy party with food, drink, and sports contests, all of it fueled by strong ale that the church sold to raise money. This was a day of drunkenness for the most pious reasons, much deplored by Puritans and much enjoyed by parishioners, especially in the country. Whitsun ales and regular church ales, usually celebrated on the day of the saint for whom a parish church was dedicated, were hearty and rowdy occasions associated with the life and seasons of the country parishes.

Trinity Sunday survived the Reformation as a significant feast day for the English. In country parishes the children wore garlands. In London the lord mayor and the aldermen, together with judges, gathered at St. Paul's and were preached to by the lord mayor's chaplain. Corpus Christi (the festival of the Transfiguration) and many saints' days fell victim to the reforming spirit of the sixteenth century, as well as to an official concern that the calendar was too cluttered with holidays to allow the work of the world to be well done. But enough holy days remained, through custom and usage or the official sanction of the Book of Common Prayer, to offer leisure time at regular intervals throughout the whole year except for Lent. St. George, the patron saint of England since the reign of Edward III, had his fixed feast on 23 April. St. John the Baptist's vigil, falling on 23 or 24 June, continued as Midsummer Eve, a time of late-night bonfires, pageants, and military parades. Michaelmas Day, celebrating St. Michael the Archangel, on 29 September, and St. Martin's Day, on 11 November, were days for a feast of roast goose. Halloween, the last night of October, was a vigil rich with superstitious notions concerning ghosts and witches, followed by the pleasures of All Saints' Day on 1 November.

Church holidays dominated the calendar, but there were also ancient secular and pagan holidays like May Day, with its traditional morris dancers and maskers, its maypole dancing, and its queen of the May. There were great public holidays like Accession Day (17 November), honoring Elizabeth's coming to the throne, with bonfires, bell-ringing, music, and fireworks; the queen herself presided over elaborate chivalric pageants and tournaments at the Tiltyard of Whitehall Palace, for which expensive tickets were sold to the general public. There were special civic occasions like the ceremonious and public election of the sheriffs and the lord mayor in October, followed by the extravagant pageantry and public festivity of the Lord Mayor's Show in November. There were the queen's progresses and royal entries, with shows and holidays accompanying her. And in London there were executions of the greater and lesser enemies of the state: beheading usually for the nobility and the bloody butchery of hanging, drawing, and quartering for common traitors. On these occasions a holiday would often be allowed so as to edify the populace and satisfy the law. Altogether, taking into account the ecclesiastical, secular, and civic holidays and not overlooking the regular routines of market days and market fairs, there was enough leisure time built into the Elizabethan calendar so that later generations could look back on the era as that of a mythical "merrie England" with genuine envy and some justice.

Whether on a holiday or not, Elizabethans of all ages were greatly fond of pastimes, good company, games, and competitions. In the country the outdoor pleasures were, of course, somewhat rougher and more dangerous: football, wrestling, cudgel play, and fighting with the old English broadsword, which was a far cry from the clever rapier-and-dagger tactics taught to young gentlemen. There were also fowling and fishing for all classes and hunting and hawking for the gentry. In cities, and sometimes in the great country palaces and manors, the gentry enjoyed the pleasures of court tennis and bowling. Onlookers freely made wages on the games, for the Elizabethans seem to have been willing—indeed, eager—to bet on almost anything. At the royal court and in the village alehouses, from the queen in her chambers to the turnspit in the kitchen, they loved to play at dice and at cards, gambling on a variety of ancestral games with names like primero, gleek, noddy, and triumph.

It seems that everyone in England loved music—even the Puritans delighted in singing metrical versions of the psalms. The music varied according to class and social context, from the country shepherd's homemade pipe to the elegant technique of the professional lutenists maintained for the queen's pleasure. Not counting her choirs of children and male singers, the queen had roughly sixty musicians in her service at all times. In those days the professional musician had to be very skilled and gifted, for the level of ordinary amateur performance, both at singing and at many musical instruments, was quite high. Waits wandered the streets and played for what they could earn. Shops and taverns kept a stock of musical instruments for their customers to pass the time with, much as today's reception rooms offer magazines. Sheet music in several parts was to be found in most houses, even the most lowly, and it was shameful and embarrassing not to be able to join in and sing a part at sight.

Elizabethans also loved to dance, but here town and country, court and commoners, parted company. In the villages, out on the greens, the old English jigs, hornpipes, and country dances were carried on. In the halls and galleries of palaces and great houses and especially at the court of the queen, the dancing was international in source. It was physically demanding and thus was deemed to be excellent exercise by people whose regular physical exertion was quite strenuous. Lessons and practice with a dancing master were required by most people. We know the music for the dances—the stately and ceremonious pavane, the allemande, the quick and lively galliard and courante. We also have some idea, from paintings and from descriptions, of the nature of the dancing that accompanied the music. Much remains cloudy, but what is clear is that much of the court dancing was akin to what has become ballet; that is, it was rigorously demanding and called for considerable skill. In the last years of the queen's reign, court variations of the English country dances became all the rage: native music and movement challenged (if not actually replaced) the continental traditions. Perhaps this fashion was, in part, a celebration of their own nation, its culture and identity; but it also seems to have represented a nostalgia for something—

namely, the timeless, ageless quality of English country life, which was just beginning to disappear.

The great public entertainments and spectacles seem to have delighted all classes, excepting always those sober and pious precisians of ethics and Holy Scripture whose hunger for purity earned them the (then) ironic appellation *Puritan.* In London, apprentices and courtiers, Southwark and Lambeth whores, as well as fine ladies from Westminster, often crowded together to enjoy cockfighting, bearbaiting, and bullbaiting. These sports sometimes took place at country houses, in market squares, or on village commons; but it was in London (in the suburbs to be sure) that some thousands of people would pay well for the privilege of watching and gambling on blood sports.

Theater had been a part of English life for centuries. The great religious pageants, the miracle and mystery plays produced by the guilds for holy days, were swiftly vanishing from the scene; but in the country there were still the morris dancers, mummers, and maskers, all of them amateurs, who played their parts at Christmastide, Whitsunday, May Day, and Midsummer Eve. Schoolchildren acted in educational plays, from which practice developed the professional companies of child actors like the Children of St. Paul's and the Children of the Revels. In the colleges of Oxford and Cambridge young scholars regularly acted out parts in Latin dramas. At the Inns of Court there were masques and dramas for the chief holidays. In the country there were minor traveling companies of players, usually safe in the patronage of some noble lord. Sometimes the better-known London companies traveled when the theaters were closed by the plague. Traveling companies went to fairs and markets, where they mingled with and vied for attention with the fire-eater, the sword-swallower, the juggler, the acrobat, and the rope-dancer, or they played in innyards, guildhalls, and the halls of great houses.

At court the queen's men were expected to be able to speak some memorized lines of verse as they sang and danced, together with a few professionals, in masques and shows. The pageants and shows at the Tiltyard on Accession Day and during the queen's progresses were elaborate and extravagant, calling for some lively performances to please and to surprise the queen. Moreover, the best and most popular professional companies came, by order and under the arrangements of the lord chamberlain and the master of revels, particularly during the festive nights of Christmastide, to present some of their latest plays to the court.

Like professional musicians, the players in the theaters had to be very skilled to earn applause and their bread. Just as in the probably more popular entertainments of bearbaiting and bullbaiting, the large theater audiences of several thousand were a curious mixture of people from all walks of life, from all stations and vocations. Generally, the public behavior of these heterogeneous crowds seems to have been cheerful and good-mannered; those who objected to the theaters as incitements to bad behavior had only a few, often repeated, examples to cite. A modern rock concert seems to be far more dangerous to civil order than any afternoon performance at an Elizabethan theater.

Perhaps, however, the city fathers were correct in their fears that during epidemics, these large crowds were a health hazard. People from all over the world came to London, and when they did, they usually attended the theater—which, together with St. Paul's, the Tower, Goldsmith's Row on Cheapside, the palace at Whitehall, and London Bridge, was one of the "sights" one had to see in London. With them they brought many kinds of diseases and infections, as did Englishmen returning from military service or long voyages.

What city and country people feared most, and with good reason, was the plague. Never wholly absent throughout the sixteenth century (it has never been entirely absent ever since), the plague lingered in the slums and dark corners of the city, suddenly spreading to epidemic levels without any apparent cause. The worst times were during the reign of James I, beginning in the summer of his accession in 1603 and delaying his coronation. There were also serious plagues in London, each causing many deaths, in 1563, 1570, 1574, 1583, 1592–1593, and 1602–1603. Smaller towns, especially the ports, from time to time were decimated when foreign travelers or returning soldiers and mariners brought the sickness with them.

When there was a serious epidemic in London, the theaters were closed. Companies of players, along with the court, the council, and everyone else who could afford it and had some place to go, left for the country to escape the danger. Rural people rightly feared that these fugitives might carry infection with them. Inns would be closed, their large colorful signs taken down. Markets and fairs were curtailed. At the queen's court, wherever it had

assembled, strict regulations were enforced to fend off anyone, courtier or commoner, who had been exposed to the disease. To emphasize the point a gibbet was set up before the gate of whatever royal palace the queen was occupying. That gibbet was used, and it seems to have been an effective deterrent. The Elizabethans had to live with dangerous diseases about which they knew next to nothing except the symptoms and the consequences. They endured with style and vitality, taking their pleasures where they could and, it seems, finding them sweeter and more precious because life itself was always so vulnerable.

In a literal sense, the Elizabethans loved to sweeten everything. They mixed native honey and imported sugar into most of their foods and nearly everything they drank. They consumed a great deal of wine and distilled spirits flavored and sweetened into cordials more potent than any modern cocktail. Drunkenness was common, but the remarkable thing is that there was not much more of it, that the problem was not overwhelming. The Elizabethans seem to have been able to hold their liquor well; though the wealth of sugar ruined their teeth, their livers appear to have been tougher than ours.

In a larger sense, this fondness for sweets of all kinds, together with a habit of flavoring foods and sauces with sweeteners and elaborate combinations of herbs and spices, reflects the attitude of Elizabethans toward the created universe. According to the religious teaching of the time, they were the responsible custodians and stewards of the world. They brightened, painted, sweetened, perfumed, and, above all, decorated. They were deeply conscious of their duty to protect and preserve natural things, not for the sake of the things themselves but for the use and pleasure of mankind and for the glory of God. They left their mark on everything they touched, not changing its essential nature but altering, sometimes radically, its appearance. There was a kind of simple, childish joy in this, and it fostered some childish habits. Elizabethans loved to leave their names and initials where they could, even carved in the soft lead of the roof of St. Paul's. The queen herself left her mark on windowpanes, etching her words with a diamond.

We tend to forget that the church was, among many other things, a powerful and popular form of entertainment in this period. Compulsory attendance, enforced by law, may lead us to imagine that the Elizabethans viewed the services as an interruption in their lives, that they obeyed the law only reluctantly. It is true that many Roman Catholics suffered openly or inwardly from the requirement to attend the Church of England; it is also true that the Puritans despised the vestments, candles, altars, and much of the Book of Common Prayer as vestiges of popery, indicating that the queen was a papist at heart. But most priests and ministers conformed. The overwhelming majority of Englishmen attended regularly and cheerfully enough, offering a stark contrast with the riots, brawls, and rebellions that had troubled the years before Elizabeth.

In the country, the parish church was the chief civic building of the community—except for the manor house, which was, after all, more or less private and open to all only on very special occasions. In the towns there were guildhalls, and in the cities there were many public buildings of all kinds, but in the villages of England the church was the principal building. Its bells marked the hours and events of daily life. Its spire or tower, always the tallest structure, distinguished the village from the perspective of nearby fields or forest or from the highway. The church offered music, brightness, color, and the words of the Book of Common Prayer and of the Bishops' Bible, from which the psalms and passages of Scripture were taken for the prayerbooks. Still new enough to outrage many at the outset of Elizabeth's reign, the words and services, by calm and constant use, became familiar and finally ingrained in the public consciousness. The majority of English people kept a Geneva Bible of 1560 at home, but in church they listened to the cadences of the Bishops' Bible and the Book of Common Prayer.

They listened to sermons also, by the hour, and they seem to have enjoyed them as, among other things, another form of entertainment. Books of sermons became best-sellers. A village priest might mind his own business and stick close to the standard homilies of the Church of England, but in the larger towns and in the cities there were preachers who attracted large crowds. This was, of course, especially the case in London, to which the most celebrated preachers came. It was a popular diversion to attend a sermon at Paul's Cross in the large, bustling yard of St. Paul's.

Clearly, from everything we can know about them, the English of Shakespeare's age loved words. Poetry was everywhere a part of their lives, from the rhyming street cries of London vendors and the call of the bellman marking the night hours, to the high rhetoric of the Westminster law courts and the royal proclamations announced by trumpets and read aloud by a herald. The theater, and its greatest artist among many good and gifted poets, created a tapestry of language worthy of the world it depicted. The Elizabethans left us a great imperishable gift of language—a language renewed, brightened and sweetened, richly decorated as never before or since. At the center of their lives were the ritual words of the Book of Common Prayer, which became a constant of the language, a music more substantial than what we call "background music," much more like the ground bass line above which Elizabethan authors improvised elaborate counterpoint. If we had lost all other ways to know and remember them, the rhythms and words of the Book of Common Prayer would allow us to hear what they heard, to believe in them whether or not we can or dare to believe what they believed.

BIBLIOGRAPHY

George P. V. Akrigg, *Jacobean Pageant; or, The Court of King James I* (1962). Andrew B. Appleby, *Famine in Tudor and Stuart England* (1978). Felix Barker and Peter Jackson, *London: 2,000 Years of a City and Its People* (1974). David M. Bergeron, *English Civic Pageantry, 1558–1642* (1971). Mary Cathcart Borer, *The City of London: A History* (1977). Carl Bridenbaugh, *Vexed and Troubled Englishmen, 1590–1642* (1968). Ivor Brown, *How Shakespeare Spent the Day* (1963) and *Shakespeare and His World* (1964). Anthony Burgess, *Shakespeare* (1970). John Burke, *English Villages* (1975) and *Life in the Castle in Medieval England* (1978). Elizabeth Burton, *The Pageant of Elizabethan England* (1958) and *The Pageant of Early Tudor England, 1485–1558* (1976). Muriel St. Clare Byrne, *Elizabethan Life in Town and Country*, 8th ed. (1961).

Kenneth Charlton, *Education in Renaissance England* (1965). Peter Clark, *English Provincial Society from the Reformation to the Revolution* (1977). Olive Cook, *The English Country House* (1974). Madeleine Pelner Cosman, *Fabulous Feasts: Medieval Cookery and Ceremony* (1976). Leonard W. Cowie and John Selwyn Gummer, *The Christian Calendar* (1974). Charles G. Cruickshank, *Elizabeth's Army*, 2nd ed. (1966). Roland Mushat Frye, *Shakespeare's Life and Times: A Pictorial Record* (1967). Joseph Gies and Frances Gies, *Life in a Medieval Castle* (1974). Mark Girouard, *Life in the English Country House* (1978). Richard L. Greaves, *Society and Religion in Elizabethan England* (1981).

William Harrison, *The Description of England,* Georges Edelen, ed. (1968). Dorothy Hartley, *Lost Country Life* (1979). Cyril Walter Hodges, *The Battlement Garden: Britain from the Wars of the Roses to the Age of Shakespeare* (1980). Pearl Hogrefe, *Tudor Women: Commoners and Queens* (1975) and *Women of Action in Tudor England: Nine Biographical Sketches* (1977). William Ingram, *A London Life in the Brazen Age: Francis Langley, 1548–1602* (1978). Alan C. Jenkins, *A Village Year* (1981). Peter Laslett, *The World We Have Lost,* 2nd ed. (1971). Norah Lofts, *Domestic Life in England* (1976). Madge Lorwin, *Dining with William Shakespeare* (1976). Richard Muir, *The English Village* (1980). Allardyce Nicoll, ed., *Shakespeare in His Own Age* (1964). Wallace Notestein, *The English People on the Eve of Colonization, 1603–1630* (1954).

Lu Emily Pearson, *Elizabethans at Home* (1957). Colin Platt, *Medieval England* (1978). Alison Plowden, *Tudor Women: Queens and Commoners* (1979) and *Elizabethan England* (1982). A. G. Robertson, *Tudor London* (1968). Alfred L. Rowse, *The England of Elizabeth: The Structure of Society* (1950); *Sex and Society in Shakespeare's Age: Simon Forman the Astrologer* (1974); and *What Shakespeare Read —and Thought* (1981). Lorna J. Sass, *To the Queen's Taste: Elizabethan Feasts and Recipes Adapted for Modern Cooking* (1976). Samuel Schoenbaum, *Shakespeare, the Globe, and the World* (1979). Adelma G. Simmons, *Herb Gardens of Delight* (1974). Lawrence Stone, *The Crisis of the Aristocracy, 1558–1641* (1965); *Social Change and Revolution in England, 1540–1640* (1965); and *The Family, Sex and Marriage in England, 1500–1800* (1977). John Stow, *Survey of London,* H. B. Wheatley, ed. (1956).

Joan Thirsk, ed., *The Agrarian History of England and Wales,* IV: *1500–1640* (1967). Geoffrey Trease, *London: A Concise History* (1975). Alice Venesky, *Pageantry on the Shakespearean Stage* (1951). Henry J. Webb, *Elizabethan Military Science* (1965). Frank Percy Wilson, *The Plague in Shakespeare's London* (1927). John Dover Wilson, ed., *Life in Shakespeare's England: A Book of Elizabethan Prose* (1911; repr. 1969). Penry Williams, *Life in Tudor England* (1965). Louis B. Wright and Virginia A. LaMar, eds., *Life and Letters in Tudor and Stuart England* (1962).

Shakespeare and Foreigners

JOHN L. LIEVSAY

Islanders are notoriously (and by definition) insular in their outlook, and the inhabitants of Britain in Shakespeare's day were no exception. Within the island itself, the metropolis of London was almost another island. For the ordinary Londoner, the world beyond the fringe of the Great City, and certainly that beyond the seas—even merely across the Channel—was "outlandish," or foreign. Except for the two universities and, possibly, the archiepiscopal see of York, the Londoner saw the rest of his island, and Ireland as well, as cultural wasteland. To him, T. S. Eliot's perspective would have seemed madly eccentric or the jest of an arrant knave. The nonacademic Elizabethan drama was primarily the product of the city, and the concern of the dramatists was mainly with London and its environs.

Nevertheless, between the accession of Elizabeth in 1558 and the closing of the theaters in 1642, for a number of reasons—national self-interest among them—the English developed an increasing awareness and knowledge of the culture, language, and history of other countries. This nascent consciousness of otherness, of differences, was quite naturally reflected in the drama produced by "the Elect Nation" (William Haller's phrase), by "God's Englishmen" (Milton's). By contrast, it served to heighten the Englishman's awareness of his own national identity and singularity. This patriotism resounds in the swelling rhetoric of *Henry V* and breathes more quietly, but firmly, in the closing speech of the Bastard Faulconbridge in *King John*.

Casual mentions of foreigners, of no particular characterizing or individualizing value, occur in Shakespeare's plays by the score, if not by the hundreds. They serve mainly to indicate that his was a mind fully stored with the current lore and that for him the world did not end with Henry V's "We few, we happy few, we band of brothers," but extended beyond the wave-washed cliffs of Dover. Shakespeare's imagination embraced the sheeted dead of ancient Rome, Norwegians pursuing the sledded Polack, a Norman praised for horsemanship *(Hamlet)*, pretended Muscovites *(Love's Labor's Lost)*, Antony's "serpent of old Nile" and attendant Egyptians *(Antony and Cleopatra)*, "the noblest Roman of them all" *(Julius Caesar)*, Turks, Moors, Cypriots, Venetians *(Othello)*, Burgundians, Dutchmen, Athenians, Spaniards, Tyrians, assorted Frenchmen and Italians—a whole congeries of nationals, ancient and modern. He took his good where he found it and found humanity everywhere.

Knowledge of the foreigner and of distant lands crept into the English consciousness through various routes. The age was one of expansion and exploration—the "age of Reconnaissance," as J. H. Parry calls it. Sir Francis Drake was but one of those venturesome and often piratical Elizabethan-Jacobean seamen who opened up brave new worlds to their countrymen and wrested from the Spanish,

Portuguese, and Dutch the mastery of the "ocean seas." Frobisher, Hawkins, Gilbert, Grenville, Cavendish, and Raleigh were names to conjure with, and the drama of their exploits found reflection on the stage. Sir John Millais' painting *The Boyhood of Raleigh* (1870), showing the youngster, dockside, gazing into the sea of England's triumphs and of his own troubled future, is more than an idealized biographical statement: it captures a moment in the life of a nation mesmerized by the vision of its own greatness. Empire and "the white man's burden" would lie just over the horizon.

How much Shakespeare and his fellow dramatists drew directly from the lips of returned voyagers is a matter of conjecture. But it is conjecture based upon their ample opportunity at the wharves and harbor taverns of London, Plymouth, and Bristol to hear strange tales such as Othello told:

> Of being taken by the insolent foe
> And sold to slavery. . . .
> And of the Cannibals that each other eat,
> The Anthropophagi, and men whose heads
> Do grow beneath their shoulders.
>
> (I. iii. 137–145)

The annual Jesuit "Relations," recording the unusual happenings and the natural wonders of their distant missions, were not fuller than sailors' yarns of such quaint lore—some of it authentic. Of the latter sort, apparently, were the exotic details of setting (I. iii) and customs in Fletcher's *The Island Princess* (1621), that Jacobean prototype of *Anna and the King of Siam*. Gleanings of exotica from beyond the seas were also to be fetched from conversations with the merchants, factors, and seamen involved in the business of the great trading companies: the Levant Company, the Muscovy Company, the Virginia Company, and the Merchant Adventurers. It was these last who had supplanted the centuries-old association of Hanseatic merchants, specially privileged and protected traders from certain North German free towns (Lübeck, Hamburg, Rostock, and others) who had established footholds in various English seaports and whose London headquarters were the Steelyard.

But one did not need to have "swam in a gundello," or have sailed the Spanish Main, or even have talked with sailors to have come by such materials. They were at hand, richly, in printed accounts of voyages and travels. The greatest of the Elizabethan compilations, Richard Hakluyt's *Prin-*

cipall Navigations Voiages and Discoveries of the English Nation (1589), was the work of an armchair traveler. Hakluyt was abroad only once, having "passed . . . the narrow seas into France," where he dwelled for five years—long enough to be prodded by invidious comparisons into drawing together the notable voyaging exploits of his own countrymen. His vast assemblage was supplemented by two works of Samuel Purchas, *Purchas his Pilgrimage* (1613) and *Hakluytus Posthumus, or Purchas his Pilgrimes* (1625), compilations more extensive even than Hakluyt's own. To these could be added, among English accounts, such individual land travels as Thomas Coryate's *Crudities* (1611), William Lithgow's *Delectable Peregrination* (1614, with later expansions), and Fynes Moryson's *Itinerary* (1617). For those who knew Italian, the vast and frequently reprinted collection of Gian-Battista Ramusio's *Navigationi e viaggi* had been available since the mid-sixteenth century. John Day's play *The Travels of Three English Brothers* (1607) was based primarily on accounts of Sir Anthony Shirley. Thomas Heywood's *The English Traveler* (ca. 1624) has little to do with such travel accounts despite its title.

Few of the dramatists, an impecunious lot shackled to Henslowe's busy production line, could have had the means, time, or opportunity for travel abroad. Their information came necessarily from printed sources or from casual encounters at home. Several of these writers, nevertheless, may have had some modicum of firsthand knowledge. Anthony Munday was in Rome in 1578. Ben Jonson fought briefly (and vaingloriously) in Flanders as a young man. A John Webster (not necessarily the dramatist) is listed in 1596 among English actors playing in Germany. Cyril Tourneur is said (Schelling, I) to have "spent many years in the Low Countries." He is known, also, to have gone on Wimbledon's expedition to Cádiz in 1625 and to have died in Ireland. Dekker, although born in London, seems to have been of Dutch descent; the cranky Marston was part Italian. Attempts to prove that Shakespeare ever went abroad have not been convincing. There is, however, not the slightest doubt that he fully appreciated the broadening value of travel. How else does one learn to "lie by authority"? In *Two Gentlemen of Verona* Panthino observes of the homebody Proteus that his spending more time at home

> . . . would be great impeachment to his age
> In having known no travel in his youth.

To this the young man's father replies:

> I have considered well his loss of time,
> And how he cannot be a perfect man,
> Not being tried and tutored in the world.

(I. iii. 15–21)

Almost alone among the popular dramatists, John Fletcher and Francis Beaumont were of a social station (though hardly of means) to have taken what came to be known as the Grand Tour; but we have no evidence that they did so.

With Shakespeare and his fellows occurs a case like that of Muhammad and the mountain—in reverse: if they did not go abroad to observe the foreigner, they would learn from the foreigner when he came to England. There, if they had the inclination to observe and inquire, they had varied opportunities to pick up information. A company of traveling Italian players ("tumblours"), possibly one of those active in Paris in the 1570s and probably of the *commedia dell'arte* variety, visited England around the middle of Elizabeth's reign. Some of the older playwrights may have seen their performances then; some may even have encountered members of the noted Andreini family. At any rate, the stock characters of their improvisations—their *pedanti* (teachers), *zanni* (clowns), *pantaloni* (old men), *capitani* (swashbuckling soldiers), and ingenues—themselves descendants of the type characters of Roman comedy—were known to the English by the end of the century. It is such a group of wandering players that the Prince makes use of at Elsinore (*Hamlet,* III. ii) and another such that figures in *The Taming of the Shrew* (Induction and *passim*). It would be too much to say that Shakespeare's better-fleshed type characters derive from the *commedia;* but there are touches suggestive of the *capitano spavento* (a swaggering, fearsome soldier) about the bombastic Don Armado of *Love's Labor's Lost* and even in that more splendid creation, Falstaff. Don Armado, indeed, doubtless with some exaggeration, calls himself "a soldier, a man of travel, that hath seen the world"; he is matched with another type character, Holofernes, styled in the play "Pedant." Armado and Falstaff have a cousin-german in the braggart Huanebango of George Peele's English-oriented *Old Wives Tale* (post-1591), relevant here because Huanebango is almost certainly a satire of Gabriel Harvey, the most notoriously "Italianated" Englishman of his time.

Throughout the Elizabethan-Jacobean period casual visitors and naturalized aliens afforded the dramatists opportunity for contact with foreigners. The court was frequently enlivened with visits by foreign royalty, nobility, or civic dignitaries. The playwrights and actors probably had little contact with most of these grand personages, beyond the attendant public pageantry and the presenting of plays for their entertainment; they may have had more with the servants and lesser figures in the retinue. Similarly, Londoners might be in touch, if not with the ambassadors themselves, at least with members of their households; English Catholics, though restricted by government regulations, might at their peril attend mass in the embassy chapels. Both the French (Huguenots) and Italians in London were permitted a Protestant church of their own where services were conducted in the native tongue, permitting curious island-bound Englishmen to acquire a smattering of French or Italian. The scraps of these languages scattered through the plays of the period may in some instances have been of no more arcane origin. Dutch craftsmen (generally resented) and Dutch religionists—particularly those of the Family of Love—were also present and were given satiric attention by the playwrights. The latter is seen in Middleton's *The Family of Love* (ca. 1607); and the romantic Lacy, disguised and speaking broken Dutch, is introduced as a "scomawker" in Dekker's vigorous *Shoemakers' Holiday* of 1600.

Some strictly conventional English attitudes toward foreigners are expressed in the exchange between Nerissa and Portia (*Merchant,* I. ii) concerning the suitors at Belmont: the stolidity and inebriety of the Germans, the boastfulness and capering lightness of the French, the devilish complexion of the Moors—blackamoors, as they were generally called. But if Portia shied away from the darkness of the Prince of Morocco's skin, Desdemona found an attraction in this exotic aspect of Iago's "old black ram" (*Othello,* I. i. 88); and Claudio would accept Hero "were she an Ethiope" (*Much Ado About Nothing,* V. iv. 38). In fairness, it should be remarked that Portia's satiric characterization of "Falconbridge, the young baron of England" most probably represents a typical reaction of cultivated foreigners to the English travelers of 1600:

> You know I say nothing to him, for he understands not me, nor I him. He hath neither Latin, French, nor

Italian; and you will come into the court and swear that I have a poor pennyworth in the English. He is a proper man's picture, but alas! who can converse with a dumb-show? How oddly he is suited! I think he bought his doublet in Italy, his round hose in France, his bonnet in Germany, and his behavior everywhere.

(Merchant, I. ii. 63–70)

Visiting or naturalized foreigners of high public visibility served to heighten the Englishman's patronizing or satiric view of outlanders, particularly if scandal attached to their names. The unfortunate Michael Florio, for instance, John Florio's father and Waldensian pastor of the Italian Protestant church in London in 1550, was dismissed on charges of immorality and became a stereotype for Italian "lechery"—a suitable fellow for the Iachimo of *Cymbeline.* Jean de Simier, Alençon's pockmarked, precious, and unsuccessful proxy suitor to Queen Elizabeth in 1579, had the additional bad luck to be satirized as the Ape in Spenser's *Mother Hubbard's Tale.* Dr. Lopez, the Portuguese-Jewish physician to Queen Elizabeth executed in 1594 for high teason on suspicion of plotting to poison the queen, became at once a type figure for Catholic and Iberian treachery. One of several Italian teachers of fencing—the *duello*—in Elizabethan London was Vincentio Saviolo, whose advocacy of the rapier over the traditional English broadsword and buckler, and of various positions over the plain English slash and parry, roused animated opposition in George Silver's *Paradoxes of Defense* (1599) and provided ample material for unsympathetic comment in the drama. The loci classici in Shakespeare are the duels in *Hamlet* (V. ii) and in *Romeo and Juliet* (III. i). In the latter, Mercutio satirically refers to his opponent's *passado* and describes him as "a braggart, a rogue, a villain, that fights by the book of arithmetic." Setting and character are foreign, but the sentiment is authentically English. A similar mocking comment is that of the Host, who comes to see the failed fencing of Sir Hugh Evans and Doctor Caius and showers the French Doctor with a spate of the duelist's jargon: "To see thee fight, to see thee foin, to see thee traverse; to see thee here, to see thee there; to see thee pass thy punto, thy stock, thy reverse, thy distance, thy montant" (*The Merry Wives of Windsor,* II. iii. 21–24).

We do not know where Shakespeare learned the French that amusingly appears in several of the plays (for example, *Merry Wives,* I. iv; *Henry V,* III.

iv, IV. iv, V. ii), but he need not have learned it in France. Living in London were a number of refugee or expatriate teachers of languages, French and Italian. Prominent among them were Pierre Erondelle, Claudius Holyband (Claude de Sainliens), and John (or Giovanni) Florio. Besides translating Montaigne's *Essaies* (1603), Florio compiled two useful Italian-English dictionaries, acted as language tutor to some of the nobility, taught French and Italian in Oxford, composed dialogue manuals for students of Italian, and was apparently in friendly association with the dramatists. Both Jonson and Shakespeare have been thought to be indebted to him. From the two often printed French-English dialogue manuals of Holyband, *The French Schoolemaister* (1573) and *The Frenche Littleton* (1576), as well as from others of his publications, Shakespeare could easily have learned such French as he possessed. But, for the charmingly Gallicized "fractured English" spoken by Doctor Caius and by the Princess Katherine *(Henry V),* he must have had recourse to the French themselves.

Impressions of French topography, customs, and character could have been derived by the dramatists from a great variety of sources, but one of the most likely was *The View of Fraunce* (1604) by Sir Robert Dallington. The following year Dallington published a useful similar work for Italy, *A Survey of the Great Dukes State of Tuscany.* In the former work, after providing a workable paradigm—"a pattern of a method"—for any English tourist, Dallington turns his attention to an analysis of the French "nature and humour." In these he finds (sigs. V4–X4) "impatience and haste in matter of deliberation"; wavering wits full of legerity and suddenness; "lightnesse and inconstancie"; quarrelsomeness at home and abroad, but quickness in making (and losing) friends—"a childish humour, to be wonne with as little as an Apple, and lost with lesse then a Nut"; poor supervision of their wives; boldness; unclean habits; troublesomeness; vain pride and boastfulness: in brief, like a character described by Plutarch, of a "boldnesse and saucy impudency . . . the only subject in this time for all Satyricks and Commedians to worke upon" (sig. X3). Here indeed was a veritable bonanza for the dramatist. The notion of French inconstancy is perfectly mirrored in the Pucelle's speech, though spoken in an aside and out of character: "Done like a Frenchman—turn and turn again" (*1 Henry VI,* III. iii. 85).

Besides their light-heeled dancing, of which he

patently disapproves but hesitates to charge with "lightnes and immodesty in behaviour," Dallington finds the French, even the poorer people, passionately given over to another pastime: they play tennis—"A thing," he says, "more hurtfull then our Ale-houses in England, though the one and the other be bad ynough. And of this I dare assure you, that of this sort of poore people, there be more Tennis Players in France, then Ale-drinkers, or Malt-wormes (as they call them) with us" (sig. V1 verso). Readers of *Henry VIII* will recall the scornful anti-French speech of Lovell (I. iii) and the bandying of insults over tennis balls between the Dauphin and King Henry in *Henry V* (I. ii). On another score, the mercurial French, though ever shifting their fashions, are fastidious in their dress. The point is made by the sententious Polonius:

Costly thy habit as thy purse can buy,
But not expressed in fancy; rich, not gaudy,
For the apparel oft proclaims the man,
And they in France of the best rank and station
Are of a most select and generous chief in that.

(*Hamlet,* I. iii. 70–74)

English travelers, whether of the armchair variety or of that more fortunate group who enjoyed the enlightenment of the Grand Tour, were familiar with the Low Countries, Germany, France, and Italy. Generally, except in war, they avoided Spain. It was unhealthy terrain for Englishmen, especially Protestants—witness the unhappy experience of poor Thoms Coryate, who fell afoul of the Inquisition and was fortunate to escape with nothing more than maiming. The English knew even less, authentically, about Africa, but that did not prevent the dramatists from using indigenous settings and introducing Moors and Negroes in their plays and other dramatic entertainments. At least four of Shakespeare's plays did so: *Titus Andronicus* (Aaron and the black Child), *The Merchant of Venice* (Prince of Morocco), *Othello,* and *Antony and Cleopatra.* Perhaps a score or more, lost or extant, of other plays before 1642 made use of African settings or characters, though seldom with anything more than the conventional misconceptions. The playwrights' shaky information, when it did not come from Plutarch or Herodotus, or from the modern but hardly more dependable *Travels* of Sir John Mandeville, was likely to be derived from Leo the African, whose *Geographical History of Africa* was translated into English in 1600 by John Pory. The similarity

between Pory's biographical sketch of Leo and the character of Othello has been held to be striking (Jones, 1971), but despite the greater authenticity of Leo's account, the old clichés were perpetuated: Africans, whether "Moors" or Negroes, were depicted as idle, carefree, lustful, and treacherous. They led lives of ease and sensuality, which was part, apparently, of Pistol's notion: "I speak of Africa and golden joys" (*2 Henry IV,* V. iii. 98). Images of burning heat, of mysterious darkness and evil, hovered over the continent; and, although the English had some firsthand experience of North African piracy, capture, and slavery, they made little distinction between the dusky ("tawny") Moor and the black African, even though numbers of both North Africans and west-coast Africans could be seen in London (Jones, 1971). Queen Elizabeth's decree of 1600, which required the exportation of Africans from the realm, lumps them together as "Negars and Blackamoors." Is it possible that Shakespeare's Dark Lady could have been among them?

One of the more notable plays and entertainments that involved African characters, settings, history, or allusions was Marlowe's *Tamburlaine* (acted 1587; published 1590). Techelles, King of Fez, presents Tamburlaine

with the crown of Fez,
And with an host of Moors trained to the war,
Whose coal-black faces make their foes retire.

(I. iii)

Others were Peele's *Battle of Alcazar* (ca. 1589); the anonymous *Lust's Dominion* (1600); Jonson's *Masque of Blackness* (1605); and Heywood's tedious two-part *Fair Maid of the West* (1631). The barbarous cruelty of the Moors in Rowley's *All's Lost by Lust* (ca. 1619) is of a key with that of the Turks and other Easterners in *Tamburlaine* and *The Jew of Malta.*

Less exotic but of more than common interest to Londoners, although resident somewhat after Shakespeare's period of greatest productivity, were two unsavory characters from the Continent, the Dalmatian renegade archbishop of Spalato (modern Split) Marc'Antonio de Dominis, and Diego Sarmiento de Acuña, more commonly known as Count Gondomar, Spanish ambassador to James I. Deceived by the former and not at first aware of his greedy ambition, the king unwisely granted Dominis extraordinary status and favors—

to the disgust of some of his more perceptive subjects. Intent on effecting a Spanish match for Prince Charles and on establishing peace with the traditional enemy Spain, the king involved himself in demeaning intrigues with Gondomar that displeased loyal Englishmen. The always venturesome Thomas Middleton, in *A Game at Chess* (1625), mercilessly satirized both foreigners for what passed as their personal and national defects, Dominis as the Fat Bishop and Gondomar as the Black Knight. The play had an unprecedentedly long London run of nine successive days before being suppressed by the scandalized authorities. The actors were summoned before the Privy Council and severely reprimanded; Middleton, who had prudently made himself scarce, was lucky to escape with his ears and an unslit nose. Other than this play, the most effective English drama dealing with contemporary foreign characters and history was the Fletcher-Massinger *Sir John Van Olden Barnavelt* (ca. 1620).

Few of the foreigners who visited England in Shakespeare's time traveled so widely, were such diligent observers, or so fully recorded their impressions as did English travelers abroad. An exception to this rule was Paul Hentzner, a learned German who in 1598 acted as tutor and guide for a small group of German aristocrats on a tour through Europe that included, unusually, a trip to England. Hentzner carefully preserved his observations in a Latin *itinerarium;* the part that described England was translated into English by Richard Bentley and was edited in the eighteenth century by Horace Walpole as *A Journey Into England in the Year 1598.* The prime objective of these, as of other visitors, was the city, with the magnificence of which Hentzner was duly impressed. He noted that his countrymen in London, the merchants of the Hanse, were customarily charged with the care and defense of Bishopsgate in the North Wall, observed the existence and practice of pickpockets at Bartholomew Fair, and recorded the presence "without the City [of] some *Theatres,* where *English* actors represent almost every day tragedies and comedies to very numerous Audiences; these are concluded with Music, variety of Dances, and the excessive applause of those that are present."

Hentzner also visited Windsor and the universities of Cambridge and Oxford, whose individual colleges he faithfully described and commended. He was generally enthusiastic about what he saw in England, though his comments were mainly concerned with places, buildings, and ceremonies. His account concludes with a brief generalized estimate of the people and their manners—a tourist's-eye view of Shakespeare's contemporaries:

> The *English* are serious like the *Germans,* lovers of Show, liking to be followed wherever they go by whole troops of servants, who wear their masters arms in silver, fastened to their left arms, a ridicule they deservedly lay under. They excel in dancing [like Dallington's light-heeled French] and music. They are active and lively, though of a thicker make than the *French;* they cut their hair close on the middle of the head, letting it grow on either side; they are good Sailors and better Pirates, cunning, treacherous, and thievish; above 300 are said to be hanged annually in *London;* beheading with them is less infamous than hanging. They give the wall as the place of honour. Hawking is the general sport of the gentry. They are more polite in eating than the *French,* devouring less bread, but more meat, which they roast in perfection. They put a great deal of sugar in their drink. . . . They are powerful in the field, successful against their enemies, impatient of anything like slavery, vastly fond of great noises that fill the ear, such as the firing of cannons, drums, and the ringing of bells, so that it is common for a number of them, that have a glass in their heads, to go up into some belfrey and ring the bells for hours together for the sake of exercise [Falstaff and Shallow, *2 Henry IV,* III. ii. 203–205]. If they see a Foreigner, very well made or particularly handsome, they will say, *"It is a pity he is not an Englishman."*
>
> (*Journey,* 77–78)

Not until Shakespeare was dead, civil war at hand, and the Puritans ringing down the curtain on English drama did such another observant and diligently recording foreigner, Vincenzo Armanni, appear in England.

Current clichés could have supplied Shakespeare and his contemporaries with notions about other foreigners. The Dutch were butter-box money grubbers in baggy breeches; the Russians (Muscovites) were frozen-witted, wife-beating louts; the Danes—even before the drunken debauch of James's brother-in-law Christian IV at the Theobalds (1606)—were noted as mighty soakheads. This national vice is subjected to bitter comment by young Hamlet, who says of the King's midnight wassailing in Rhenish wine:

> This heavy-headed revel east and west
> Makes us traduced and taxed of other nations.
> They clepe us drunkards and with swinish phrase
> Soil our addition.
>
> (I. iv. 17–20)

The American natives, occasionally alluded to by the Elizabethans, had not yet figured appreciably on their stage and certainly were not conceived of as the noble savages of Rousseau and later generations. But the patent and well-known connection of *The Tempest* (II. i) with Montaigne's essay "Of Cannibals," as well as with "the still-vexed Bermoothes" of the Bermuda accounts, written by the earliest English visitors to those islands, suggests that Caliban and other unsavory spirits of Prospero's island, though transplanted from "Argier," were intended to represent those New World savages.

As for those native outlanders, the Scots, the Welsh, and the Irish, their ubiquitous presence was, to Londoners, most unpleasant. Before the union of the two kingdoms in 1707 under the Stuarts, the Scots were traditionally enemies of the English—and they remained so even afterward. Years of border incursions, the pre-Knoxian Catholicism of the northern kingdom, the alliances with France, the character and activities of Mary Stuart, the rivalry of English and Scottish settlers in northern Ireland, and, above all, the tide of needy Scots who flooded London and the court in the wake of James I as rivals with the English for favors and place—all these factors were conducive to little esteem on the part of the dramatists. The collaborative *Eastward Hoe* (1605) of Chapman and Jonson, although only mildly satirical, drew down the wrath of the Scottish courtiers and landed the authors in jail. Shakespeare, in those plays where he dealt with the Scots *(1 Henry IV, Henry V, Macbeth),* treated them with respect as courageous and honorable fighters. The Douglas of the first play is a worthy and forthright soldier, of whom Prince Hal generously says:

> His valors shown upon our crests to-day
> Have taught us how to cherish such high deeds,
> Even in the bosom of our adversaries.

(V. v. 29–31)

Of Captain Jamy of *Henry V,* the testy Fluellen's praise is a sufficient description: "Captain Jamy is a marvellous falorous gentleman, that is certain, and of great expedition and knowledge in th' aunchient wars, upon my particular knowledge of his directions. By Cheshu, he will maintain his argument as well as any military man in the orld in the disciplines of the pristine wars of the Romans" (III. ii. 70–75). In the same scene, Fluellen's opinion of the military skills of the Irish Captain Macmorris is somewhat lower: "By Cheshu, he is an ass as in the orld! . . . He has no more directions in the true disciplines of the wars, look you, of the Roman disciplines, than is a puppy-dog" (64–67). Short on theory the Irish may have been, but when trained on the Continent they proved excellent fighters. Amusingly, the three captains—Scottish, Irish, and Welsh—speak in their own dialects, and Shakespear obviously relishes the quaint un-Englishness of their speech; so, no doubt, did his audience. Falstaff (*Merry Wives,* V. v. 139–140), pinched by the disguised "fairies" of Sir Hugh Evans, reacts to Sir Hugh's "seese" and "putter" (cheese and butter) in typical scorn of the "mountain-foreigner's" garbled English: "Have I lived to stand at the taunt of one that makes fritters of English?"

These particular "foreigners," proud, irascible, pugnacious, boastful—witness Glendower *(1 Henry IV)*—may be viewed with aversion, with condescension, or with mild tolerance; but, in general, they were seen as comic types. That Shakespeare was able to individualize and differentiate them so effectively is a mark of his astounding genius.

Like many of his fellow dramatists, Shakespeare liked his plots and settings ready-made and took them, along with incidental motives, from a variety of foreign sources, mainly classical and Italian. He did not have a taste for dabbling in contemporary or near-contemporary foreign history or biography. His plays offer no counterparts to Marlowe's *Massacre at Paris* or *Jew of Malta,* Chapman's *Byron* and *D'Ambois,* Barnabe Barnes's lurid *Divils Charter* (1607), or even the semihistorical *White Devil* (ca. 1611) and *Duchess of Malfi* (ca. 1613) of Webster. When he wrote history plays, Shakespeare drew his materials from the remote (classical) past, like his rival Jonson, or from the history of his own country. For him, a foreign setting had little essential significance, reflecting little of national characteristics. The scenes might be laid in Elsinore, in Verona, in Venice or Cyprus, in Bordeaux or the never-never Forest of Arden, in a wood outside Athens, on the equally fanciful seacoast of Bohemia, or along the sunny banks of the Nile—the principals in the action remained much the same. A change of place, a change of name, a change of costume—these things mattered little. Beneath an infinite variety of surface appearances, the enduring sameness of humanity remained. This is not to say that Shakespeare did not endow his non-English characters with individualizing personalities, for this he did masterfully, as he would have done had they been his London or Stratford friends and neighbors. The inns and taverns of the imagined foreign places are those with which he was familiar at home; the servants and minor characters are such as he rubbed shoulders with in the Strand, in Eastcheap, or in Southwark. The melancholy Jaques is no Frenchman; Gobbo (despite the name) is no Italian; Autolycus is such a rogue as might figure in the coney-catching pamphlets of the envious Robert Greene. Shakespeare's foreigner holds only a suggestion of the alien; the essence is English.

BIBLIOGRAPHY

Geoffrey Bullough, *Narrative and Dramatic Sources of Shakespeare,* 8 vols. (1957–1975). Edmund K. Chambers, *The Elizabethan Stage,* 4 vols. (1923; repr. 1951).

Samuel C. Chew, *The Crescent and the Rose* (1937). Sir Robert Dallington, *The View of Fraunce,* W. P. Barrett, ed. (1936). Selma Guttman, *The Foreign Sources of Shakespeare's Works* (1947). Paul Hentzner, *A Journey into England in the Year 1598,* Richard Bentley, trans.; Horace Walpole, ed. (1757; repr. 1881). Charles Hughes, "Land Travel," in *Shakespeare's England,* 1, Charles Talbut Onions, ed. (1916).

Eldred D. Jones, *Othello's Countrymen: The African in English Renaissance Drama* (1965) and *The Elizabethan Image of Africa* (1971). Victor von Klarwill, *Queen Elizabeth and Some Foreigners* (1928). John L. Lievsay, *The Elizabethan Image of Italy* (1964). Boies Penrose, *Urbane Travelers, 1591–1635* (1942). John Davenport Rogers, "Voyages and Exploration: Geography: Maps," in *Shakespeare's England,* 1, Charles Talbut Onions, ed. (1916). Felix E. Schelling, *Elizabethan Drama, 1558–1642,* 2 vols. (1908). John Walter Stoye, *English Travellers Abroad, 1604–67* (1952).

Painting and Other Fine Arts

WYLIE SYPHER

Shakespeare and the Continental Arts

We may never satisfactorily explain how Shakespeare was able to represent so full a measure of human experience in drama derived from a provincial England. Amid the upsurge in Renaissance arts England often seemed an enclave apart, a society inhabited by aggressive provincials, intensely chauvinist in opinion and conduct, marauding at sea, and on land fond of spectacular pageantry—so fond, indeed, that their most ghastly executions were a public ritual of barbaric cruelty transformed into art. When we read in *Titus Andronicus* the stage direction "Enter . . . Lavinia, her hands cut off, and her tongue cut out, and ravished" (II. iv), we think of the blinding of Gloucester or of Lear crying that he is "bound upon a wheel of fire" (IV. vii. 47), or we recall the hideous allusion to beheading when Escalus in *Measure for Measure* (II. i. 5–6) urges:

> Let us be keen and rather cut a little
> Than fall and bruise to death.

Such savagery is counterpointed with the licentious revels of Falstaff in Eastcheap, resembling the low-life riotous genre scenes in Pieter Brueghel (Shakespeare's vulgar comedy is Flemish, while his tragedy and romance are often Italian or pseudo-classical.) In any case Shakespeare has a detached ecumenical view of life, holding in impartial focus characters as unlike as Prospero, Iago, Benedick, Prince Hal, Coriolanus, Imogen, and Lady Macbeth.

In contrast with Shakespeare's cosmopolitan, if not Olympian, view of man, the English were emphatically parochial in their prejudice against foreigners, particularly Spaniards like Armado and Italians like the "yellow Iachimo." Their very scorn of Italianate culture testifies that Shakespeare and his audience were familiar with arts and manners on the Continent. Mercutio ridicules Tybalt's foreign ritual in dueling by the book of arithmetic: "the immortal passado! the punto reverso! the hay! —one, two, and the third in your bosom" (*Romeo and Juliet*, II. iv. 23–26). Portia has contempt for her suitors, even for the Englishman who is Italianate: the Neapolitan prince, the County Palatine, the French lord Monsieur LeBon, Falconbridge with his French hose and German bonnet, the Scots noble, and the sottish German. The glare of Venice must be offset by moonlit Belmont, an English dreamworld adjacent to the Rialto.

The English were even more provincial in painting, valuing portraits alone. For dread of damp the walls of great country houses were decorated with tapestries, not frescoes. The English attraction to portraits was perhaps related to their abiding attention to character, a concern heightened by a growing Puritan and Protestant focus on individuality. John Buxton reports that in 1601, Hardwick Hall had about 70 portraits and fewer than 10 other paintings. Leicester left 200 paintings, about 130 of which were portraits. It is understandable that

Shakespeare reaffirmed this accent on the limning of character in all its human wealth. Around 1600 Nicholas Hilliard, the only major English painter of the time, wrote the treatise *The Art of Limning,* insisting that portraits must show clear lines to indicate human character.

In spite of the English sensitivity to nature, landscape painting did not arrive in England until well after its appearance on the Continent, where the Austrian Alps had inspired Albrecht Altdorfer to become a pioneer landscapist. In England landscape remained auxiliary to the portrait. Yet the English were devoted to the garden as a retreat to satisfy their landscape instinct until Inigo Jones provided scenic effects for courtly masques. The builder had no canon; English architecture was an unorthodox composite of renovated Gothic castles, Italianate Renaissance palaces, and traditional, native half-timbered structures decorated by Flemish strapwork.

For the English the word was the beginning: in literature they were incomparably superior, belying their provincialism. This superiority was partly due to their drama, their numerous poets, and their devotion to music. The English gentleman was able to read a score at sight and to sing it properly. He was expected to command a repertory of dance figures learned as a boy. Dancing at court followed styles executed on the Continent.

In view of the special character and limitations of the English arts, how can we use any canon of style for Shakespearean drama, ranging as it does over a full spectrum of genres—usually defined as tragedy, comedy, history, and romance—that often intersect? In speaking of style, especially in Shakespeare, we must recognize, first, that a style exists not so much for the artist as for the critic or historian, who, aided by hindsight, tries to define modes of representation. The writer may be trying only to give form and pressure to his time. Doubtless Shakespeare did not try to write a play to conform to a style. But we may nevertheless detect a style in what he wrote.

And what he wrote does have some relation to the Renaissance arts in Italy, where artists were very conscious of their purposes and methods, and, unlike most northern artists, formulated nearly doctrinal theories in a criticism that was a basis for changing styles. These different styles reappear sooner or later (mostly later) north of the Alps, but not with Italian clarity. Defining styles in the north is complicated by the fact that a whole century may

elapse between what happened in Italy and what happened farther north. Another difficulty is that the north preserved many traits of Gothic art in spite of the innovative talents of a whole group of artists whose painting had no theoretical basis: Jan van Eyck, Hieronymus Bosch, Matthias Grünewald, Pieter Brueghel the Elder, Dürer, and Holbein. Because of the many contacts between England and the Low Countries, Shakespeare must have known something of Holbein, for example. And like Shakespeare's theater, northern painting retained its medieval heritage and forms in Renaissance guise. Yet in the large context of Renaissance arts, we must place Shakespeare in some relationship with Italian art history.

On the evidence of the Italians themselves, art historians have distinguished three intersecting (sometimes concurrent) styles in painting, sculpture, and architecture, appearing between 1450 and 1650: Renaissance (including High Renaissance), the interim style called (after much debate) mannerism, and finally baroque, which is an extravagant magnification of High Renaissance, creating melodramatic illusion. However doctrinaire it may seem, this threefold grouping of styles is helpful in treating the diversity of Shakespeare's performance in, for example, the complexity of *Hamlet.*

Shakespeare, like Milton, seldom repeated himself, and strictly speaking, we should refer only discreetly to the corpus called Shakespearean drama. In their enormous variety there are only Shakespearean plays—possessed of certain recurring themes but differing in approach, structure, meaning, and language. Grouping by genre (comedy, tragedy, history, romance) may blur relationships between actions as different as *A Midsummer Night's Dream, Troilus and Cressida, Othello,* and *Cymbeline.* The span of character and situation is composite, extending from *The Comedy of Errors* to *The Tempest,* which is masquelike.

Shakespeare and Three Discernible Styles

Modern art history is helpful in treating the various modes of Shakespeare's performance. Drawing largely on Italian works that laid down patterns followed by northern artists, Heinrich Wölfflin's influential *Principles of Art History* contrasted Renaissance and baroque styles in painting and other arts. By a binary grid of opposing forms, Wölfflin identified an early Renaissance style structured by symmetry, balance, and stable order and held in closed space. Painting, sculpture, and architecture in Italy had a linear clarity and a decorative design on the surface. The closed perspective was formulated geometrically by Leon Battista Alberti in 1435 and again by Piero della Francesca about 1485 in a treatise using theories that he had applied in his strictly proportioned painting *The Flagellation of Christ* (1456–1457). The stable, symmetrical structure, so instantaneously readable, appears in the uniform rhythms of the nave of Santo Spirito, Florence (about 1435); it reappears in the perfectly controlled harmony of the facade of the Rucellai Palace (about 1450) and in the exactly articulated groups of figures in Perugino's *Christ Giving the Keys to St. Peter* (1481). This strong sense of orderly composition was maintained in the High Renaissance, as Raphael's great *School of Athens* (1510–1511) shows.

Then, according to Wölfflin, the baroque brought a new and grand illusion into art, magnifying the clear Renaissance order by turning from the linear to the painterly, from surface design to projection into distant space, from isolated decorative detail to urgent organic rhythms. The baroque is a frankly emotional art, often devotional in its declarative and energetic spectacle—public, confident, seductive in its acceptance of the flesh, which it can transfigure by its alchemy (Cleopatra becomes fire and air in a secular assumption). It inherited from Michelangelo, Raphael, and the High Renaissance its vigorous classical contours, its breadth, the security of its convictions, its doctrinal tone, its vision of a world beyond, its elaborate illusions created on the domes of Roman churches and in visions of Mary's Assumption. The baroque resolves problems with large orthodox public gestures; its celestial world invites entrance by its excess, its unabashed theater.

Certain Shakespearean plays seem to fit at least loosely into Wölfflin's twofold categories of style. The tidy scheme of coincidence and character in *The Comedy of Errors* would correspond crudely to the early, often overrationalized balance in Renaissance arts. *Twelfth Night* has a similar but more tactful design. *Love's Labor's Lost* shows the same balance behind its decorative rhetorical surface, its pattern of equations in euphuistic artifice. This pattern of contrasts carries over to *Romeo and Juliet,* with its closed space—Romeo saying, "There is no world without Verona walls" (III. iii. 17). Similar contrasts inhere in *The Merchant of Venice* and in

Measure for Measure. As for the baroque, *Antony and Cleopatra* transfigures lust as the play moves from Rome to Egypt, to an envisioned Elysium "where souls do couch on flowers" (IV. xiv. 51). The movement is not scholastic but a powerful projection of the flesh and history into another, transcendent world, an elevation that is public and spectacular. *Othello* has a baroque vigor sweeping through its classic proportions that is doubtless inherited from Christopher Marlowe's heroics. Wölfflin's two categories do provide an approach to Shakespeare.

However, Wölfflin ignored a style more directly relevant to the problematic Shakespeare: mannerism, which now seems generally recognized as a style (or at least a mentality) characteristic of the arts from about 1520 to 1600. *Mannerism* is a term no longer pejorative; it bears some of the meanings that earlier criticism linked with tragedy. Mannerism is now seen as a reaction from, or a revision of, the High Renaissance symmetry, stability, and care for structural clarity and order. Deriving from the Italian *maniera* ("style," "stylishness"), *mannerism* may be an equivocal term—one of those words that are vague in themselves but amenable to exact usage. It is particularly useful as a way of indicating the restlessness of the arts during the sixteenth century and the interim directions evident between the styles of Renaissance and baroque. John Shearman sees mannerism as an inevitable and easy sequel to Renaissance art, not as a sign of intellectual crisis. Yet in his more provocative plays Shakespeare raises more problems than he (or we) can readily resolve. In sum, if the baroque dominates the seventeenth century, mannerism is at its height in the sixteenth.

The development of mannerism is more apparent in Italy than north of the Alps, where, as Nikolaus Pevsner says, a new style in France or England "was already a style of the past in Italy." Besides, in Germany and the Low Countries painters were establishing supremacy in portraiture, landscape, and devotional art: Bosch, Brueghel, Dürer, and Hans Holbein the Younger. On both sides of the Alps a residue of Gothic elements made no style completely pure; yet the context for Shakespeare's more problematic plays is a pervasive and international mannerist mentality disturbing the Renaissance equilibrium.

E. M. W. Tillyard has noted how belief in a cosmic order was especially needed in an age frightened by mutability. The affirmation of this order is phrased by Ulysses in *Troilus and Cressida* (I. iii. 85–126) when he asserts that the very heavens "observe degree, priority, and place," so that any disruption of this hierarchy results in chaos (as it does in *Lear*). Ulysses might be referring to the new frightening politics of power described in Machiavelli, a view of statecraft that was rapidly unsettling the feudal order. The medieval world was being shaken by what Arnold Hauser calls a mentality of crisis. Martin Luther had defied the Roman Catholic church, an act that later led to savage religious wars. Montaigne had prompted a skepticism echoed in Hamlet's appraisal of man as the "quintessence of dust" (II. ii. 304–305) and in old Gonzalo's yearning for the primitive in *The Tempest* (II. i. 143–152). Meanwhile, the cosmic order itself was revised by Copernicus and again by Galileo, causing John Donne in his "First Anniversary" to fear that "all coherence" was gone from the universe now that proportion was broken. Kepler tried in vain to recover order by a dubious compromise. A break with the past seemed to follow the sack of Rome by the Spanish in 1527; and of course the plague was a present threat, like the Spanish Armada of 1588.

Such disturbances at the core of the sixteenth century and of the Jacobean years led Hiram Haydn to write *The Counter-Renaissance,* and art historians have used the term *mannerism* to denote the unsettling of Renaissance visual and plastic forms. Clifford Leech has described the insecurity of Elizabethan and early Jacobean dramatists:

> Standing between a belief in natural order and a growing perception of chaos, between the Renaissance enthusiasm for living and an ever-darkening disillusion, between the twin poles of Fate and Chance, of predestination and free will, they went through mental experiences of a peculiar intensity, knew the darkness and the terror all the more keenly for the light that still remained in a diminishing fragment of the heavens.
>
> (chapter 2)

Leech's comment reminds us of the difference between art that is merely mannered by a stylish or postured glamour and genuine mannerism, where distortion or violation of form signals some psychic complication of a private, individual nature. Whether or not the Sonnets are autobiographical, there is an authentic mannerist disturbance behind Sonnets 95 ("How sweet and lovely dost thou make the shame"), 110 ("Alas, 'tis true I have gone here and there"), and especially 129 ("Th' expense of spirit in a waste of shame") and 138 ("When my love swears that she is made of truth"). So there are two different mannerisms: the affectation that offends Berowne in *Love's Labor's Lost,* and the disturbed and disturbing erratic responses of Hamlet, who is indeed apt to quarter his thoughts and look on (or for) truth "askance and strangely," in the words of Sonnet 110. The flaming distortions in El Greco are kindred mannerist art.

However, what we see as distortion may be only a new, unexpected kind of order. The arts, especially drama, have often been most powerful exactly when an establishment was being dismantled. A cultural earthquake may bring, along with a revision of past forms, a new and initially unintelligible vocabulary. Like Euripides, Shakespeare wrote in a world shaken by instabilities. At its most penetrating, drama can thrive on perceptions that are unexpected, if not shocking—in Hamlet's case a sense of the rotten state of Denmark, which is prelude to Lear's world, in which Gloucester says, "We have seen the best of our time. Machinations, hollowness, treachery, and all ruinous disorders follow us disquietly to our graves" while "love cools, friendship falls off, brothers divide" (I. ii. 104–112). Tempering such despair, Lafew in *All's Well That Ends Well* shows the tension in the age: "They say miracles are past, and we have our philosophical persons, to make modern and familiar, things supernatural and causeless. Hence is it that we make trifles of terrors, ensconcing ourselves into seeming knowledge when we should submit ourselves to an unknown fear" (II. iii. 1–6). If mannerism is not a formal style, it is at least an expression of a quest for personal accommodation to changes eroding traditional forms—another version of Hamlet's quest.

Raphael's High Renaissance classicism prompted a recoil toward eccentric, unstable, seemingly irrational figuration in Pontormo, toward the experimental perspective of Parmigianino's self-portrait in a convex mirror (1524), and toward the clogged tumult of Rosso's Michelangelesque violence. The chill reserve of Bronzino's elegant portraits has the bloodless, arbitrary temper of Peruzzi's flimsy facade for the Palazzo Massimo alle Colonne. Cellini's Perseus-Medusa statue seems risky, if not impudent, in technique. The expressionist convulsion of Tintoretto's figures, like El Greco's vibrant *contrapposto,* is a ghostly spasm from Michelangelo's *figura serpentinata.* El Greco sees with his mind's eye (*disegno interno* is the mannerist term). The mannerist has his own sophistication, for he is aware not only of his virtuoso talent but also of his role as experimenter or rebel against an establishment that is being exhausted. Again, Hamlet is painfully aware that he is alone in his quest for a code by which he can exist in an alien world; he can live only by his repulsions, which become a negative ethic forcing him toward the art of playing roles as a command of life. But this drama does not work.

Here is the most significant effect of mannerist reaction against the High Renaissance majesty of Raphael's *School of Athens.* With its uneasy sense of the limits of the medium being used, mannerism marks the onset of a modern aesthetic—an art view of life. The mannerist is always testing and exploring the possibilities and deficiencies of his own medium in an inquisition about the relevance of art to life and actuality. Shakespeare is never more modern than when he is questioning his own technique: in play after play (as early as *Love's Labor's Lost* and *A Midsummer Night's Dream* and as late as *The Tempest*) he boldly invites us to inspect dramatic illusion, mere role playing as a fragile surrogate for life. Though Hamlet is obsessed with taking his cue, he is forced to test whether the play's the thing to catch the conscience of a criminal Claudius. His dilemma about the validity of drama is one cause of Hamlet's paralysis: his need to play the role correctly (which is why he cannot kill Claudius while praying) and his perception that he cannot exist in roles, as can the strolling player in speaking of Hecuba (II. ii. 535–544).

Because Shakespeare had doubts about the legitimacy of his medium, he had an advantage over the dramatist who trusts realism as a reliable mirror of life. Like Cervantes, Shakespeare discovered the infidelity of his fictions, which are vulnerable theatrical enactments. To indicate to his audience the treachery of theatrical illusion, Shakespeare adopted a tactic of mannerist painting: presenting within the representation itself a figure who faces directly out of the space of the painting toward the space of the beholder, thus breaking the plane of the fiction by addressing what is beyond the composition. This figure is known by German critics as the *Sprecher* ("speaker") and is an intermediary between art and life, urging the beholder to appraise the representation in what is now called metatheater, where an actor calls attention to the success of his role playing.

The *Sprecher* appears at the opening of *Richard III,* where Richard himself uses the daring mannerist tactic of informing the audience that he is going to play the villain—with what success they can judge. (Iago uses the same tactic, which looks forward to Luigi Pirandello and Bertolt Brecht.) The *Sprecher* consciously (or defiantly) violates the logic of Renaissance perspective, which pretends to avoid seeming in order to establish an illusion of being. In the prologues to Acts I and IV of *Henry V,* Shakespeare achieves metatheater by warning that the audience is not to see any adequate enactment of the Battle of Agincourt but only a disgraceful action by "four or five most vile and ragged foils" in a parody of warfare: "Yet sit and see,/ Minding true things by what their mock'ries be." Shakespeare has a mannerist awareness that instead of offering actuality, the theater can only stimulate the audience to imagine true things by their mockery in art. Shakespeare seems to endorse what Leontes says at the close of *The Winter's Tale* when he thinks he sees the statue of Hermione come alive: "We are mocked with art" (V. iii. 68).

One of the mockeries of art is Shakespeare's use of the mirror effect of the play-within-the-play when the audience watches an audience. This mannerist tactic appears in Velázquez' *Las Meninas,* presumably a royal portrait, where Velasquez himself appears looking out at us from the pictorial space; behind him is a mirror reflecting the king and queen entering the space where Velázquez stands before his painting (with its back to us), his attention being on the invisible royal couple; and in an open door far behind the Infanta and her attendants, a figure is evidently entering or leaving the studio. Here is a painting about seeing—watching, being watched and observed, the figures observing each other, and us (as in *Hamlet*). It is a painting about painting, a calculated scrutiny of the medium that takes priority over the mere subject or motif.

In similar ways Shakespeare incorporates the play-within-the-play as a parody of drama: the inset playlets like the Nine Worthies, Pyramus and Thisbe, and the Mousetrap, and the masquelike interludes in *Cymbeline* and *The Tempest.* Indeed, *Hamlet* itself can be read as a running mannerist comment on the problematic nature of art, for Hamlet's venture in converting his moral impulses to artistic form is a sequel to Jaques's view of life as a succession of roles played out on the world as a stage (where Hamlet feels he must take his cues). In light of Jaques's "All the world's a stage" (*As You Like It,* II. vii. 139–166), Hamlet's aestheticism seems like a parody of life because of the available roles one can play. In fact, the tendency to parody inheres in mannerism. Parmigianino's *Madonna with the Long Neck* is an elegant (perhaps even a witty) parody of the Renaissance Virgin—a suave experiment in disproportion. El Greco can be said to parody Titian. *Troilus and Cressida* is Shakespeare's parody of Homeric nobility, as *Measure for Measure* seems a parody of purity. And parody requires awareness of how the medium can be used.

One of the most extreme mannerist experiments in Shakespeare's time is like a parody of Renaissance perspective: a weird distortion of image known as anamorphosis, a by-product of the age's intense analysis of the optics of Renaissance recessional space. Anamorphosis occurs when a figure is seen from such an acute angle that it takes intelligible and recognizable form only when seen from that required angle. Seen frontally, there seems to be only a bundle of elongated splinters without discernible contours. Only from an arbitrary approach at right or left does the figuration unexpectedly come into focus. Anamorphosis is a painter's technique for expressing Shakespeare's experience in Sonnet 110, where he says,

> I have looked on truth
> Askance and strangely.

The most famous anamorphosis in English painting is by Holbein the Younger, who worked in England in 1533, when he painted *The Ambassadors*, a half-allegorical portrait of Jean de Dinteville and his friend Georges de Selve standing behind what looks like a shutter of paint. Only when seen from a sharp angle on the right does a skull appear as a sign of mortality. Another anamorphic painting is a portrait of disputed identity, possibly of Edward VI at nine years by Guillaume Scrots in 1546. The fracturing of features, completely unintelligible when viewed straight-on, becomes, when seen from a prescribed angle, a very sensitive, lifelike head of a youth tenderly posed in profile. Anamorphosis was sometimes useful in conveying hermetic meanings.

Such anamorphic perspective is one of the more egregious mannerist distortions, and yet this contrived violation of normal perception has a certain bearing on Shakespeare's portrayal of characters like Shylock. According to the logic of the action, Shylock ought to be a wolfish monster; but seen from the angle of theatrical gesture, he suddenly becomes illogically and outrageously humanized when he asks, "If you prick us, do we not bleed?" (III. i. 56). This speech gives Shylock a convincing but merely verbal human dimension. On stage Shylock mutates before our eyes into a riveting human being, an anamorphic creature at the core of dramatic illusion, by a mannerist shift of perspective.

In his total satanism Iago is a kindred anamorphic creation, existing on stage as a frightening, lively image of every human malignity, unexplained yet effectual—mistrust, ambition, jealousy, obscenity, envy. Anamorphic perception accounts for some of Hamlet's mystery: on the basis of the text Hamlet is so fragmented, so contradictory, so fractured in his responses and acts, so irresponsible in thought and unpredictable in mood that we cannot summarize his erratic experience by any entirely consistent explanation; rather, we see him momentarily from a succession (rather than a sequence) of arbitrary angles no one of which suffices but each of which is convincing. (This need for a rotational approach to the *figura serpentinata* is required in Cellini's statue of Perseus, with its multiple profiles, none being definitive.)

This essentially mannerist suspension of declared meaning characterizes Shakespeare's problem plays; figures like Angelo and Isabella need to be seen from a double, inconclusive angle. In his extreme anguish, even Lear seems anamorphic, existing credibly only within the perspective of a drama that arbitrarily posits a nature so chaotic as to be grotesque. Doubtless Shakespeare was aware of the distorting mirror of an art that reaches truth only by mockeries of nature.

R. A. Foakes speaks of the arbitrary nature of *Cymbeline* and *The Winter's Tale,* in which "Shakespeare learned how to liberate himself from a commitment to characters presented with psychological and linguistic consistency, in order to achieve special kinds of effects in his later plays, and particularly as one means of distancing his audience from the characters and preventing identification with them" (Introduction).

Later, Foakes observes that "given the deliberately arbitrary nature of the action, as not dependent on cause and motive, and as flaunting its theatricality and rejection of ordinary narrative continuity and expectation, there is no need for a stable and consistent portrayal and development of characters" (chapter 4).

Anamorphic trickery (which continued to fasci-

27. The French ambassadors: Jean de Dinteville, lord of Polisy, and Georges de Selve, bishop of Lavour, by Hans Holbein (1533); oil and tempera on wood.

nate the seventeenth century in the form of the *camera lucida*) is one result of the strenuous Renaissance efforts to organize space by means of optics inspired by Brunelleschi's experiment with mirror images in 1425. (Did Shakespeare know that Brunelleschi actually did hold a mirror up to the Florentine Baptistry to study our perception of space?) The development of theories of perspective brought not only the painter's orthogonal (vanishing point) space but also the new, scientific Mercator projection in cartography, linking art with commerce and exploration.

In England the unsystematic but adaptable space of the Globe gave Shakespeare certain special advantages that enabled him to manipulate theatrical effects at will. Inherited from medieval painting and persisting during the Renaissance even in Italy, especially in devotional painting, was the so-called beam structure, providing a way of mediating between the local scene and the cosmic order. In Italy and in the north the beam structure appeared in representations of the Adoration of the shepherds and the Magi. The figures of Mary and Joseph with the Christ child are grouped with the shepherds or Wise Men under a scaffolding of pillars or rafters, arches or beams, like the skeletal architecture of the modern crèche. Behind and beyond the skeletal architecture opens a vista of sky and limitless landscape, a poetic *paysage.* After it appeared in the porchlike area of Fra Angelico's *Annunciation* (Florence, ca. 1449), Botticelli set his *Adoration of the Magi* (1475) in this reduced phantom architecture, already traditional in the north.

The stage at the Globe was, in effect, a modified beam structure, in part a precious heritage from medieval religious iconography. It provided a space amenable to the local and the cosmic, the macrocosm or microcosm, a symbolic space capable of being organized in many ways, released from the geometrically closed grid of the painter's vanishing-point composition severely defined in Piero della Francesca's *Flagellation.* The stage of the Globe—with its thrust apron, its pillars supporting the "heavens," and probably some inner-stage nook and balcony—suited action in all directions without the confining fiction of a proscenium arch.

The beam structure protected the lyrical climate created by Shakespeare's poetry. Belmont in *The Merchant of Venice* exists in a magical atmosphere established by Lorenzo's saying:

> And bring your music forth into the air.
> How sweet the moonlight sleeps upon this bank!
>
> (V. i. 53–54)

By poetry Shakespeare sets the climate in Macbeth's sinister Dunsinane, in Hamlet's nocturnal Elsinore, or on Lear's apocalyptic heath. And the platform stage projecting into the audience made possible an intimacy in prologue and soliloquy, which used rhetoric to gain a three-dimensional, nearly plastic value of the sort seen in Renaissance freestanding statuary. The freestanding statue offered multiple perspectives unavailable even to the painter. But in fact the Globe thrust stage with its optional angles of vision, was in its way as mobile as the cinema, which exploits alternative perspectives.

How Shakespeare knew about the intensive Renaissance analysis of optics that led to anamorphosis is unexplained; yet he shows an acquaintance with the problem of perspective, a topic of continuing interest on both sides of the Alps (Alberti and Piero della Francesca in Italy, and Dürer in the north). Sometimes his plays suggest a Sophoclean concern with vision and blindness, as in *Othello* and *Lear,* but he surely knew about recessional composition in painting, as is reflected in Sonnet 24:

> Mine eye hath played the painter and hath stelled
> Thy beauty's form in table of my heart;
> My body is the frame wherein 'tis held,
> And perspective it is best painter's art.
> For through the painter must you see his skill
> To find where your true image pictured lies.

Scattered through the plays are passages indicating this same interest in perspective. One thinks, for example, of the casual remark of the French King to Hal, who says that a French maid so stands in his way that he cannot see many fair French cities, whereupon the King replies, "Yes, my lord, you see them perspectively" (*Henry V,* V. ii. 307). In trying to comfort the Queen in *Richard II,* Bushy advises her that

> sorrow's eye, glazèd with blinding tears,
> Divides one thing entire to many objects,
> Like perspectives, which rightly gazed upon,
> Show nothing but confusion—eyed awry,
> Distinguish form.
>
> (II. ii. 16–20)

Obviously Bushy is referring to anamorphic painting. At the close of *Twelfth Night,* when Sebastian and Viola appear together, the duke exclaims:

> One face, one voice, one habit, and two persons—
> A natural perspective that is and is not
>
> (V. i. 208–209)

Scandalously, when, in *All's Well That Ends Well,* Bertram tries to justify his abandoning Helena, he explains to the King how his vision was distorted:

> The impression of mine eye infixing,
> Contempt his scornful perspective did lend me,
> Which warped the line of every other favor,
> Scorned a fair color or expressed it stol'n,
> Extended or contracted all proportions
> To a most hideous object.
>
> (V. iii. 47–52)

The most hideous anamorphic distortions were contrived by warping the images of objects in a circular mirror, as Bertram, by extending or contracting the image of Helena, transfigured her. Mannerist disproportion seems to revise Euclidean space.

The non-Euclidean space of the Globe stage illustrates Henri Focillon's distinction between space as limit and space as environment. The geometric space of orthogonal perspective specifies a grid of space to determine locus. But space as environment creates another nongeometric space that might be termed "scene" instead of "topography." The space of scene is atmospheric and can escape rationalizing. It is the space of Giorgione's *Tempest* instead of Alberti's cartoglraphy. A map does not generate atmosphere; atmosphere results from the poetry of space, suspending precise location within pictorial composition. Atmospheric space is not only setting; it is also a harmony or pictorial climate that seems to convey a psychic tonality that saturates the scene.

It is harder to rationalize color and the play of light than to rationalize locations. The modulations of light can transpose geometric setting to scenic landscape, as happens in Bellini's *Allegory of Purgatory,* with its poetic architecture. Space is bathed in the same scenic tonality in northern paintings by Albrecht Altdorfer, Joachim Patinir, or Henri met de Bles. And in Leonardo there opens behind the foreground figures the so-called blue distance that transposes the valley of the Arno into the charmed climate of a dream. Shakespeare also can immerse local space in a poetic atmosphere that does more than any realistic setting. There are magical transformations by light in the Midsummer Night forest, in the coming of dawn in Hamlet's Elsinore, in Othello's groping in darkness, in Lady Macbeth's nocturnal excursions, and in the light that thickens over Dunsinane.

Each Shakespearean action has its own tonality—from the harsh glare of *Troilus and Cressida* to the twilight of *Richard II* and the high noon of *Antony and Cleopatra.* The Renaissance landscape with figures is immersed in a luminescence gently diffused from the classic pastoral. The pastoral itself is established in some provisional domain between court or city and the tranquil climate of the dream. *As You Like It* is a pastoral that somehow lacks the full transposition to scene attained in the more poetic fêtes champêtres of Giorgione or even

A Midsummer Night's Dream, where Demetrius remarks:

> These things seem small and undistinguishable,
> Like far-off mountains turned into clouds.

> (IV. i. 186–187)

In a landscape with figures we are indeed mocked with art, and pastoral is justified by Touchstone's claim that "the truest poetry is the most faining" (*As You Like It,* III. iii. 16–17).

Some of the best feigning in Renaissance painting, as in Shakespeare, occurs in the pastoral or in the landscape with figures, a poetic dream that is a cultural resource. Yet Shakespeare seems to have no illusions about poetry, for in *A Midsummer Night's Dream* Theseus is ambiguous, if not condescending, about the airy nothings that are a basis for the poet's fantasies. Shakespeare is entirely aware that drama is the stuff of dreams, a momentary sea change. In play after play he implies that we cannot live in dreams, yet he also reminds us that without the dream we impoverish our lives. As if answering Theseus' skepticism about the poet, Hippolyta says that the midsummer madness

> More witnesseth than fancy's images
> And grows to something of great constancy;
> But howsoever, strange and admirable.

> (V. i. 25–27)

Looking back on her own aberration, Hermia is changed in her vision:

> Methinks I see these things with parted eye,
> When everything seems double.

> (IV. i. 188–189)

This midsummer dream is one sign of Shakespeare's ability to shift toward baroque illusion. Baroque is a style best expressed in the sumptuous painting, architecture, and sculpture of Rome. Nevertheless Shakespeare does offer certain illusions characteristic of baroque art, which, like Hermia, has its double vision. In baroque, the very excess of the all too solid world in its fleshly splendor opens upon a supernal world that is equally resplendent—a world able to make the flesh seem ethereal. This split between two worlds is a baroque illusion or transfiguration appearing not only in the many visions of the Virgin's Assumption but also in Shakespeare's baroque vision of Cleopatra amid her full Elizabethan splendor:

> The barge she sat in, like a burnished throne,
> Burned on the water: the poop was beaten gold;
> Purple the sails, and so perfumèd that
> The winds were lovesick with them.
>
> (*Antony and Cleopatra,* II. ii. 192–195)

As Shakespeare says, she

> beggared all description: . . .
> O'erpicturing that Venus where we see
> The fancy outwork nature.
>
> (II. ii. 199–202)

(Did Shakespeare know the Venus of Giorgione and Titian?)

Baroque has the ability to immerse even the most outrageous extravagance in what we have termed scene (not mere setting). Baroque illusions are majestic in scale and melodramatic in vigor, publicly inviting entrance to the celestial realm so exhilaratingly affirmative in iconography. Baroque waives the mannerist privacy and intricacy in favor of its theatrical scenography, offering large, plain solutions to problems inherited from Michelangelo's tormented titanism. *Othello* is, like much baroque action, melodrama on a humanized and powerful scale: simple in design, imperative in movement, physical in texture, classic in stature, elemental in its psychology. The baroque scene is realized in its captivating fleshly splendor (which had been already apparent in crude physicality in *Venus and Adonis*).

Shakespeare very subtly slides from one kind of illusion to another, from mannerist reservations about the validity of his medium to the baroque splendor of *Antony and Cleopatra,* an action that expands from Rome to Egypt, then from Egypt to a vision of Elysium, a new blue distance—in this instance not a double but a triple escalation. A baroque tactic in painting and architecture was to establish a foreground boundary and then to open a spacious vista behind it, breaking through to a triumphant expansion of another domain where there is a release from mannerist tension and constraint. *Antony and Cleopatra* exemplifies this baroque movement of breaking through limits into

another realm—from Roman duty to Nilotic pleasure, to a prospect of eternal redemption.

The play opens with Cleopatra's cynical query about how much Antony can love. Antony replies that there is beggary in love that can be reckoned. Then Cleopatra teasingly avers that she will set a bound on how far to be loved—whereupon Antony argues that she must then find a new heaven and earth. They both eventually find that they can envision such a new heaven in their illusion of the Elysium beyond their world-weary infatuation and defeat. Their irrepressible vitality projects them beyond the negation of the death that overtakes Romeo and Juliet. Before his death Antony catches a glimpse of a blue distance where the world of imperial power and policy becomes vaporized into "black vesper's pageants" by metamorphosis of vision:

> Sometime we see a cloud that's dragonish;
> A vapor sometime like a bear or lion,
> A towered citadel, a pendant rock,
> A forkèd mountain, or blue promontory
> With trees upon't that nod unto the world
> And mock our eyes with air.
>
> (IV. xiv. 2–7)

Already Antony, like Prospero, sees that we are the stuff of dreams, so he is able to die with the prospect of a scene where souls couch on flowers. This baroque double vision is impossible in Lear's world, which retains only the terror of the baroque energy, like Michelangelo's *Last Judgment.*

The Personal Accent in Elizabethan Arts

But there is the memorable figure of that honorable and humane cynic Enobarbus as evidence of Shakespeare's unremitting sense of the contradictions (and the absurdities) in human behavior and its capacity to surprise—in Berowne, Benedick, Falstaff, Posthumus, and Hal. Whether or not this strong emphasis on individuality is due to the Protestant and Puritan tradition, English painting from the first was committed to portraiture. Like English painting, English literature centered in portraiture not only in Shakespeare but also in an unbroken tradition from Chaucer through Fielding, Austen, Dickens, and George Eliot—a tradition often almost obsessively populated by eccentric characters. Shakespeare's plays are inhabited by personages as vivid and singular as Macbeth, Caliban, Desdemona, Lady Macbeth, Parolles, and Hotspur—a galactic assemblage of human beings in all their divergent existences. Perhaps Shakespeare's most conclusive comment on the human species is phrased by Benedick at the close of *Much Ado:* "For man is a giddy thing, and this is my conclusion" (V. iv. 106–107).

The first native and visiting painters in English Renaissance art were portraitists: the miniaturist Hilliard, Holbein the Younger, and Antonio Moro. Hilliard worked on a very small scale. His fragile, melancholy *Portrait of a Young Man Leaning Against a Tree Among Roses* (ca. 1588) has the postured elegance and preciosity of *Love's Labor's Lost* —a refined, overbred mannerism. Portraits by Isaac Oliver are less sophisticated. The grave and monumental Holbein portraits of Thomas More and of Christina of Denmark (who sat for only three hours) have a human dimension lacking in the calculated figures of the Florentine Bronzino, whose people are unapproachable, like Shakespeare's Troilus. If the English fall short in painting, their characterizations in literature compensate —notably Hamlet, the most inward and complex character ever presented, a provocation to multiple readings open to inconclusive interpretations.

One English vehicle for characterization was available in tomb sculptures, whether in the altar tomb or on the wall tomb used when the nave was filled with altar tombs. The features of the deceased were faithfully recorded in a sculpture sensitive to the pathos memorialized in the gisants, especially husband and wife. Unlike Italy, England produced no important freestanding statuary. The mannerist *contrapposto* of Giambologna has no corresponding form in England; and it is perhaps significant that Shakespeare seemingly knows about painting but makes the mistake of thinking that the popular painter Giulio Romano was a sculptor. When the gentleman in *The Winter's Tale* wants to praise the realism of Hermione's statue, he says it is "a piece many years in doing and now newly performed by that rare master, Julio Romano, who, had he himself eternity and could put breath into his work, would beguile Nature of her custom, so perfectly he is her ape" (V. ii. 90–94). (Shakespeare had the excuse that Giulio was known for his unusually plastic and sculptural forms.) The titanism in Italian

imitators of Michelangelo does not appear in English sculpture, although it could take literary form in Marlowe's heroics rather than in Shakespeare, who seems to speak through Hamlet when the prince enjoins the players to avoid a whirlwind rhetoric that tears a passion to tatters (III. ii. 9).

English tomb sculpture was a heritage of medieval art but was often encrusted with classical medallions affixed to Renaissance tombs by visiting Italian artists like Pietro Torrigiano. Like English architecture, English sculpture was impure in style in its continuing use of medieval forms, the Italianate elements adhering to previous structures and themes with a notably English conservatism. This conservatism reappears in Shakespeare himself in *Timon of Athens* (which resembles a morality play) and even in the figure of Falstaff, who is not only the classical *miles gloriosus* but also a shadow of the old medieval morality-play character Gluttony.

The same intersection of past and present is confirmed in English architecture, which is more visibly composite than literature or painting. Like the changes that occurred in dramatic structure as Shakespeare's company moved from the Globe to Blackfriars, architectural features changed as English baronial castles were renovated in the interests of warmth and comfort, the great country house emerging by alterations in portals and fenestration. But again there is no uniform style for the great sixteenth-century country houses like Longleat, Blickling Hall, Hardwick Hall, Wollaton, Burghley House. Each had its own plan, accommodating a variety as wide as the various plays of Shakespeare. In spite of ambitious builders like Robert Smythson and John Thorpe, the great houses were renovated or designed by English craftsmen, not by architects with Italianate theories, though Vitruvius and Serlio were known. The native half-timber house existed along with late-medieval modified perpendicular styles evident in the pinnacled facade at Richmond Palace, Surrey (1499), and in the fan vaulting of King's College Chapel, Cambridge (1446–1515), wholly at odds with the semiclassical court of Burghley House, Northamptonshire (1585); the chaste facade of Blickling Hall, Norfolk (1620); the half-timber at The Ley, Weobley, Hertfordshire (1589); and Wollaton Hall, Nottinghamshire (1580–1588), whose Gothic conflicts with the Flemish roof lines at Lilford Hall, Northamptonshire (1635). The influence of Serlio and Palladio was brought to bear on English architecture by Inigo Jones at the White-hall Banqueting House (1619–1622). The similarity of this architectural medley to Shakespeare's eclectic Italian, classical, and English sources is obvious.

The Italians may have offered principles, but the English masons and other craftsmen relied on ad hoc methods and improvised their way to an unacademic style of structure and decoration, ornamenting ceilings with intricate Flemish strapwork, a form of architectural euphuism. James Lees-Milne remarks that the work of the first known English architect falls somewhere between the doctrines of Serlio and Palladio. After the Reformation, foreign artists left England, and English nobles began to visit Italy, which fostered ideas of beauty and harmony. But the very diversity of English architecture can be seen as evidence of an intransigent individuality.

Except for the simple design of *A Comedy of Errors, Romeo and Juliet,* and *Timon of Athens,* the structure of Shakespeare's plots, like English great houses, does not lend itself to easy definition. It seems more profitable to use the analysis of Mark Rose, ignoring for the moment the total plot structure and division into acts and attending to the arrangement of individual scenes, which fall into a pattern of contrasts in events and characters. In fact, Shakespeare often seems to have conceived his actions in diptych or triptych patterns, in a nearly Gothic contrast of successive scenes. This diptych or triptych design clarifies the meaning of the action as well as the balance in total composition, bracketing situations by preceding and following scenes.

This is one way of dealing with the complexity and privacy of *Hamlet,* treating it as a succession of episodes arranged in double or triple units that are more significant than the whole action. The Renaissance care for symmetry and order may be more evident in the segments than in the completed movement. Especially in plays in which the ending is obviously reached under the theatrical exigencies of a performance and the demands of an audience, the parts seem greater than the whole. We can find the same sort of de-composition in Elizabethan architecture, where striking features are more effective than the uncertainty of the whole composition.

Academic criticism of Shakespeare's plays is wont to look for larger unities of character, action, and time as proof of an overarching decorum and logic, which, in a play like *Lear,* Shakespeare seems as ready to ignore as the Elizabethan builder was willing to violate Italianate theory. *Lear* ruptures academic proportions: the crisis in plot comes within the first 265 lines as Lear commits himself to Goneril and Regan, exiles Cordelia, and yields his royalty. Such disproportion belies the usual pattern of rising action, climax, and denouement as *Lear* becomes a long, unendurable anguish and the denouement consumes the play. The interminable suffering of Lear, unlike the gradually mounting blindness of Othello, is a disproportionate falling action. The tragic rhythm is broken, and the tragic ethic denied or at least seen askance and strangely. *Lear* might be taken as a violently mannerist distortion of plot and a terrifying experiment in the collapse of Renaissance art form, appearing at some intersection between mannerist disturbance and explosive baroque energy. Customary categories fail, as they usually do in Shakespeare.

Yet the Elizabethans could still hear (or believed they could hear) harmonies in heaven, for they had an auditory bias, as their very language proves. The rhetoric of *Love's Labor's Lost* defeats the modern ear; how did actors ever learn or speak, or the audience ever follow, the quick, witty shimmer of a dialogue that, as Costard says, "comes so smoothly off, so obscenely as it were, so fit" (IV. i. 142). Quite aside from such preciosity in language, the discourse of the time was always approaching music in its rhythms. Even prose in Shakespeare must be heard, ranging from Iago's bleak obscenity to Falstaff's dionysiac praise of sherris sack and his catechism on honor, each in contrast to Hamlet's last monosyllabic judgment: "If it be now, 'tis not to come; if it be not to come, it will be now; if it be not now, yet it will come. . . . Let be" (V. ii. 209–213). There is also the Iago discord—"I'll set down the pegs that make this music" (II. i. 198)—in contrast to what is called *Othello*'s music, his symbolic poetry ("Put out the light").

In *The Merchant of Venice,* Lorenzo phrases a Shakespearean premise:

> The man that hath no music in himself,
> Nor is not moved with concord of sweet sounds,
> Is fit for treasons, stratagems, and spoils.
>
> (V. i. 83–85)

However far the English painter, sculptor, or architect lagged behind Italy and the Continent, English music was admittedly in the vanguard, especially since the break with Rome required a new sacred music. Like her father, Elizabeth enjoyed playing the virginals and had some sixty musicians in her service, including those in the royal chapel. The devotion to music was classless, from the popular catches and psalm singing by Puritans to Henry Peacham's wish that the gentleman both sing and play: "I desire no more in you than to sing your part sure, and at the first sight, withal to play the same upon your viol, or the exercise of the lute privately to yourself" (Buxton, chapter 5).

It was the age of the madrigal and ayre, a time when English composers like Thomas Morley, Orlando Gibbons, and William Byrd were internationally ranked with Italians like Ferrabosco. The songs and ayres that John Dowland published in 1597 gave him fame in Germany and Italy. Sonnet 8 in *The Passionate Pilgrim,* whether by Shakespeare or not, is evidence of Dowland's reputation:

If music and sweet poetry agree,
As they must needs (the sister and the brother),
Then must the love be great 'twixt thee and me,
Because thou lov'st the one, and I the other.
Dowland to thee is dear, whose heavenly touch
Upon the lute doth ravish human sense;
Spenser to me, whose deep conceit is such
As passing all conceit, needs no defense.

There was an English school of lutenists and virginalists, and music, instrumental and vocal, greeted Elizabeth everywhere during her progress at seats like Kenilworth. But there was prejudice about a gentleman's playing wind instruments because they distorted the face. A similar curious prejudice was held against vocal music in tragedy, for vocal music was ordinarily expected from the clowns or fools in a drama. Shakespeare ignores such prohibitions: Hamlet may intend to humiliate Guildenstern by asking him to play a recorder (III. ii. 331–342), and Ophelia and Desdemona sing in tragic situations.

Shakespeare may have blundered in mistaking Giulio Romano for a sculptor, but he was thoroughly informed about the music that he uses some one hundred times in his plays—catches, airs, ballads, street songs, and ditties, with many stringed and wind instruments available for special effects: the virginals, a variety of citerns, lutes, hautboys (oboes), fifes, recorders, and, for military episodes, cornets and trumpets for alarums and sennets. Instrumental mood music accompanied dumb shows. Like the Italian intermezzo, Elizabethan the-ater was not only allowed but expected to incorporate music in the action, which was followed by a jig, danced to music.

Shakespeare uses songs freely to indicate or sustain the tone of the action itself or to suggest the nature of the singer or the atmosphere in which he appears. Orsino's first words in *Twelfth Night* indicate his sentimentality:

If music be the food of love, play on,
Give me excess of it, that, surfeiting,
The appetite may sicken, and so die.

(I. i. 1–3)

A strange sexuality inheres in Desdemona's song about the maid Barbary (IV. iii. 40–51); it is as troubling as Ophelia's mad pathetic-cynical song suggesting some injury after an unidentified sexual episode (IV. v. 23–66). The Fool's songs express the absurdity of Lear's world, and Hamlet's jingles reveal a hysteric tension behind his jests. Pandarus' nasty, cloying song about tickling the sore is an index to the corruption of a classic world where love is only hot deeds (III. i. 107–116). The songs in *Love's Labor's Lost* are themselves a commentary on the preciosity of the little Academe. More symbolic is Ariel's song about the sea change worked by Prospero's magic in an isle filled with sounds and sweet airs (I. ii. 397–405). As for comedy, the ditty sung to the Nurse by Mercutio is an obscene reference surely appreciated by the groundlings: having sung the jingle about the old hare hoar, he waves the Nurse out with the refrain of "Lady, lady, lady" from the song on Chaste Susanna (II. iv. 126–136). More surprising, when in *Lear* Edmund mentions how "these eclipses do portend these divisions. Fa, sol, la, mi" (I. ii. 132–133), he may be referring to what musicologists call the devil's interval, or *diabolus in musica* (the tritone). Shakespeare's incorporation of music is, then, not to be seen as an impurity but as another facet of the auditory wealth of English literature.

The masque provides a bridge between music, literature, and pictorial art in Shakespeare's later plays, such as *Cymbeline, The Winter's Tale,* and *The Tempest,* each with its scenic context and its sensitive lyrics. The court masques allowed the scenic effects of the indoor theater, which became spectacular under Inigo Jones and the patronage of Queen Anne in the years when Ben Jonson was poet of the revels. The original occasion for the court masque was to welcome some visitor: a group of masked

28. "Queen Elizabeth Confounding the Three Goddesses," by Hans Eworth (1569).

persons would enact some flattering text (often allegorical) and then descend from the stage to dance with the audience in revels. But the masque became an institution at the court on Twelfth Night as the revels were elaborated by the antimasque, adding the grotesque to the action. The height of the spectacle was reached in 1609 with the Jonson-Jones *Masque of Queens.*

M. C. Bradbrook gives us some notion of the extravagance of the earlier *Masque of Blackness* to please Queen Anne after *Othello.* The queen had asked Jonson to write the text of a masque in which she and eleven other ladies became blackamoors. "It cost over £3,000, and was modelled by Inigo Jones upon a masque of the Medici. Each of the ladies wore jewels worth thousands of pounds" (chapter 9). In the masque twelve Daughters of the Niger seek to whiten their skins (which they believe will happen in England). In the all-night dancing after the masque, the actors joining their audience, we have another version of the play-within-the-play, breaking the plane between the

fictional world of Jones's extravagant baroque perspective scenery and the (equally fictional) world of the revels, which themselves became a ritual.

Indeed, the court masque was rooted in the age-old rites of masking, primitive mummings, the disguising of fertility celebrations, and the morris dance. Enid Welsford, in *The Court Masque,* traces the changes that allowed primitive rites of masking and mumming to be domesticated by the English talent for poetry. The wearing of the mask, with all its psychological implications, is treated again and again in Shakespeare's many disguisings, not only in Hamlet's antic disposition but also in the academe in Navarre, in *Measure for Measure,* in *Lear,* in comedies like *Much Ado,* in *Cymbeline,* in the Forest of Arden, and in Iago's satanism. And these disguises often appear with masque interludes in which gods or other supernatural beings appear with magical pageantry. In Imogen's case the mountains of Wales become, like Prospero's masquelike isle, an ethical landscape. The appearance of Jupiter and the ghosts in *Cymbeline* (V. iv) converts the masque to a brief morality play. Caliban is a figure strayed from the antimasque into *The Tempest.*

The plays at the Globe, like the masques at court, were followed by dance, one of the most elemental arts. (Aristotle at the opening of the *Poetics* remarked how rhythm alone can represent men's characters.) Like music, dance was indigenous to Elizabethan life and theater—a theater providing jigs performed by Richard Tarlton or Will Kempe. The dance, like masking, mumming, and disguising, was a folk activity, a popular fertility rite underlying the morris dance, so thoroughly English in its traditional characters: Maid Marion, the Hobby Horse, the Fool or Clown, and Friar Tuck, most of whom danced their roles and are mentioned in Shakespeare.

This sort of folk dance persisted in the local saturnalia long after aristocratic dances were formalized in Italian courts. While traditional popular sword dances continued parochially, dancing at court was becoming a studied art, specifying the many figures and positions to be executed by the fashionable. The so-called Age of the Galliard (1500–1650) produced formal discourses on modes of the dance, including the pavane, slow and stately; the bergomask; the saraband, called licentious; and the cinquepace (listed by Sir Toby in *Twelfth Night* for Sir Andrew). Evidently the galliard required ability to leap, and it is said that when she was in her mid-fifties Queen Elizabeth took her morning exercise by dancing six or seven galliards (Sachs). Elizabeth herself delighted in the clownish dancing of Tarlton (who may be Hamlet's Yorick). In England dancing was a sturdy affirmation of national muscular superiority over effete foreigners. In *Henry V* a French duke complains of the English:

> They bid us to the English dancing schools
> And teach lavoltas high, and swift corantos,
> Saying our grace is only in our heels
> And that we are most lofty runaways.
>
> (III. v. 32–35)

In many comedies Shakespeare refers to popular dances: Beatrice values her "measure in everything," since "wooing, wedding, and repenting is as a Scotch jig, a measure, and a cinquepace" (*Much Ado,* II. i. 63–65); and *Love's Labor's Lost* asks whether love is won by a "French brawl," or *branle* (III. i. 6–7). In *Henry VI, Part II,* John Cade is said

to "caper upright like a wild Morisco" (III. i. 365); and there is Hamlet's dreadful accusation that women jig (III. i. 144). One of the celebrated Elizabethans was Morocco, the "dancing" horse reputedly trained to count by John Banks (*Love's Labor's Lost,* I. ii. 52). Will Kempe, the low-comedy star trained by Tarlton, in 1600 for sake of a wager did a morris dance from London to Norwich and said, "I have daunst my selfe out of the world."

The pleasures of the Elizabethans—like their blood sports and their laws—were often coarse, if not brutal. This coarseness is not only a sign of their provincialism but also, particularly in Shakespeare, a token of an art based on a robust acceptance of all ranges of human nature. As many earlier critics (like A. C. Bradley) proposed, the axis of Shakespeare's plays is parallel to the axis of English painting—that is, portraiture or the depiction of character. Bradley is justified in taking Shakespeare's plays as studies in actions based on character, but he expected character to be consistent and was concerned to establish a logic of behavior.

The importance of mannerism in Shakespeare is here, for Shakespeare is thoroughly aware of the violations of logic and consistency in his characters and also of the fragility and treachery of his medium. Thus, Fabian says in *Twelfth Night,* "If this were played upon a stage now, I could condemn it as an improbable fiction" (III. iv. 119–120). A character can be powerfully convincing without being consistent, a situation common in portraiture as well as in Shakespeare, who, like Holbein, centers his art on a person's individuality, regardless of consistency, as in Hamlet's case. The consistency comes from the angle of vision only, as in anamorphic painting.

The wholly consistent character tends to become an abstraction, dehumanized to a personification instead of a person. Wallace Stevens has defined poetry as "an unofficial view of being," and the masque is dehumanized by its official characters who become personifications. Queen Anne enacts the goddess Athena. In 1569, Hans Eworth painted *Elizabeth and the Three Goddesses,* showing the queen as a female Paris holding an orb (instead of an apple) to be awarded to herself, not to the disconcerted Juno, Pallas, or Venus. This is to dehumanize Elizabeth into a figure like Viola's "Patience on a monument, smiling at grief" (*Twelfth Night,* II. iv. 113–114).

In contrast to such masquelike personifications

Shakespeare's characters are persons, even those clowns who have strayed from the antimasque: Costard, Bottom, Feste, Lear's Fool, Caliban, Touchstone, and brutes like Cloten or liars like Parolles. If the root of drama is human character, Shakespeare stands alone in the art of portraiture with his own version of Renaissance humanism.

As to whether one can properly speak of a Shakespearean style, in view of the differences among the plays the best we may be able to do is to take their full register of human experience as a conglomerate where categories hardly suit the case. Using the categories of art history, however, one can discern a tendency toward mannerist problems and a mannerist mentality. At least, *Hamlet* may be the most significant mannerist work in literature. In any event, Shakespeare, by commanding the resources of action, gesture, music, scene, and language, has created a drama that is total.

BIBLIOGRAPHY

Anne Barton, *Shakespeare and the Idea of the Play* (1977). Jacques Bousquet, *Mannerism: The Painting and Style of the Late Renaissance*. S. W. Taylor, trans. (1964). Muriel C. Bradbrook, *Shakespeare: The Poet in His World* (1978). John Buxton, *Elizabethan Taste* (1963). Oscar James Campbell and Edward G. Quinn, eds., *Reader's Encyclopedia of Shakespeare* (1966). Kenneth Clark, *Landscape into Art* (1949). Anthony B. Dawson, *Indirections: Shakespeare and the Art of Illusion* (1978). Samuel Y. Edgerton, Jr., *The Renaissance Rediscovery of Linear Perspective* (1975). Philip Edwards, *Shakespeare and the Confines of Art* (1968). Robert Egan, *Drama Within Drama* (1975).

Reginald A. Foakes, *Shakespeare: The Dark Comedies to the Last Plays; from Satire to Celebration* (1970). Henri Focillon, *The Life of Forms in Art*. C. B. Hogan and G. Kubler, trans., 2nd ed. (1948). Timon H. Fokker, *Roman Baroque Art: The History of a Style*. 2 vols. (1938). Sidney J. Freedberg, *Painting of the High Renaissance in Rome and Florence* (1961) and *Painting in Italy 1500–1600* (1970). Walter F. Friedlaender, *Mannerism and Anti-mannerism in Italian Painting* (1957). Frederick Hartt, *History of Italian Renaissance Art*, 2nd ed. (1979). Arnold Hauser, *Mannerism: The Crisis of the Renaissance and the Origin of Modern Art* (1965). Harriett Hawkins, *Likenesses of Truth in Elizabethan and Restoration Drama* (1972). Hiram Haydn, *The Counter-Renaissance* (1950). Cyrus Hoy, "Jacobean Tragedy and the Mannerist Style," in *Shakespeare Survey*. 26 (1973).

Emrys Jones, *Scenic Form in Shakespeare* (1971). Clifford Leech, *Shakespeare's Tragedies and Other Studies in Seventeenth-Century Drama* (1975). Fred Leemann, Joost Elffers, and Mike Schuyt, *Hidden Images*, Ellyn Childs Allison and Margaret L. Kaplan, trans. (1976). James Lees-Milne, *Tudor Renaissance* (1951). John H. Long, *Shakespeare's Use of Music* (1972). John Rupert Martin, *Baroque* (1977). Frank Jewett Mather, Jr., *Western European Painting of the Renaissance* (1948). Nikolaus Pevsner, *An Outline of European Architecture*. rev. ed. (1945).

Franklin W. Robinson and Stephen G. Nicholas, Jr., eds., *The Meaning of Mannerism* (1972). Mark Rose, *Shakespearean Design* (1972). Daniel B. Rowland, *Mannerism: Style and Mood* (1964). Curt Sachs, *World History of the Dance*. Bessie Schoenberg, trans. (1963). John K. G. Shearman, *Mannerism* (1967). Alastair Smart, *The Renaissance and Mannerism in Italy* (1971) and *The Renaissance and Mannerism in Northern Europe and Spain* (1972). F. W. Sternfeld, *Music in Shakespearean Tragedy*. rev. ed. (1963) and "Shakespeare and Music," in *New Companion to Shakespeare Studies*. Kenneth Muir and S. Schoenbaum, eds. (1971). Thomas B. Stroup, *Microcosmos* (1965). John L. Styan, *Shakespeare's Stagecraft* (1967). Wylie Sypher, *Four Stages of Renaissance Style* (1955).

Eustace M. W. Tillyard, *The Elizabethan World Picture* (1943). Enid Welsford, *The Court Masque: A Study in Relationship Between Poetry and the Revels* (1927; repr. 1962). Rudolf Wittkower, *Architectural Principles in the Age of Humanism*. 3rd. ed (1962). Heinrich Wölfflin, *Principles of Art History*. M. D. Hottinger, trans. (1932; repr. 1950) and *Classic Art*. Peter Murray and Linda Murray, trans. (1952).

Forest, Field, and Garden: Landscapes and Economies in Shakespeare's England

JOAN THIRSK

Creative artists draw their ideas from the world around them. No matter how transmuted, masked, or distorted in a finished work, the assumptions of the age lurk somewhere below the surface, forming a recognizable part of the common inheritance in that period of man's historical development. What then can we identify as the common inheritance of attitudes to the natural world that Shakespeare shared with his literate contemporaries? His work abounds with references to the growing cycles of plants, to man's activities in growing plants, and the life of man in the countryside. All critics agree in stressing the strong influence of country life on Shakespeare's imagery; indeed, this influence is far more obvious in his case than in that of any of his contemporaries. His work does not express timeless attitudes but rather those peculiar to the sixteenth and early seventeenth centuries. New ideas and attitudes enabled Elizabethans to see the countryside around them in a fresh way. Their influence can be observed, setting the scene of some of Shakespeare's plays and governing the words uttered by his characters.

Because attitudes toward the natural world cannot be guessed at until they are written about, the limited sources surviving from the medieval period yield only fragmentary glimpses of the age's perceptions. But for those living in the sixteenth century and for historians retrieving the past from their writings, the situation was transformed with the appearance of printed books. More people took up their pens to express a view, and their views circulated more widely and crystallized more readily, so that more has survived for the historian of ideas to interpret.

A veritable revolution was inaugurated when books in considerable numbers became accessible to literate men, a revolution that may be likened to the advent of television in the middle of the twentieth century. Books publicized a host of ideas relating to many different facets of human experience. A great variety of tastes was catered to, and true Renaissance men counted on savoring them all. Not least among the many books placed at their disposal were works on the land and its cultivation.

The earliest such books were the works of the classical authors, published first in Latin and then in English translation. A fresh breeze blew through musty, long-closed corridors when gentlemen landowners, many of whom had neglected or totally abandoned demesne farming for a century or more, began to read the works of such writers as Cato, Varro, Columella, and Palladius, and were told how satisfying and worthwhile was farming as an occupation. The writings of these four Romans first appeared in a compendium entitled *Rei rusticae scriptores*, published in Venice in 1470. By 1504 another eleven editions had appeared, and between 1513 and 1521, another six. Meanwhile, Xenophon's *Oeconomicus (Of the Household)*—a work concerned with the management of a landed estate, including its home farm—was published in Latin translation in 1508; by 1526 it had appeared four times more, and in 1532 it was translated into English.

The classical writers taught men to regard farming as an education as well as a means of livelihood. To watch the changing landscape through the seasons, to observe the growing habits of plants and animals, and to take a hand in assisting the process, it was argued, were tasks for watchful eyes and intelligent minds. The land could be made to yield more bountifully if the stages of growth were carefully observed and if men intervened to plow, weed, and harvest at exactly the right moment. Farming was a noble occupation, bringing great rewards and satisfactions. Moreover, the discipline that it imposed trained men for yet higher duties. When called, some men had left the fields to rule kingdoms. Socrates had spoken truly when he called husbandry the mother and nurse of all the other sciences.

Thus, the classical works of husbandry taught novel but eminently serious lessons about the virtues of country life, which were not lost on their readers. Increasingly in the course of the sixteenth century, country gentlemen absorbed and acted upon them. They managed their estates more professionally; they took an active part in running their home farms; and not a few of their younger sons chose farming as a career, welcoming toil on the land in the spirit in which the classical authors had written. Indeed, some of them eventually became writers themselves, voicing the same respectful attitudes to husbandry and so demonstrating the effectiveness of their classical reading.

The consequences of this intellectual revision of attitudes were diverse. High-ranking gentlemen in their off-duty moments enthusiastically discussed farming matters with each other. When at home, they positively relished the time and care given to managing their land. Interest in plant and animal life required them to develop an eye for detail, as a result of which their appreciation of the skill and lore of the countryman was sharpened. Some humanists went even further, advocating respect for the peasant because of his deep practical knowledge of such matters. Formerly disdained by the well-to-do, who viewed him as a dull-witted boor, the peasant came to be regarded as a storehouse of common sense and well-tried experience. But this more extreme point of view did not carry much weight until the middle of the seventeenth century. The other arguments were more immediately influ-

ential—that gentlemen should read books, use their eyes, and experiment for themselves, and in this way advance knowledge and understanding of the natural world as well as improve the yield of their land.

Against this background, it is not surprising that a new genre of books appeared—practical manuals of husbandry, written from the outset in English rather than in Latin and setting a high standard in the accuracy of their advice. They rendered good service to gentlemen in their farming routines. In literature the same influences were noticeable in the use of metaphors and similes that revealed how discerning an eye had indeed been directed at the landscape, observing subtle changes in the shape, color, and demeanor of plants and animals as the seasons turned.

An associated theme, drawing inspiration from the same source, emerged in the literature of the sixteenth century: men began to commend the life of the countryman far above that of the courtier. The proposition was most influentially and effectively argued by the Spanish humanist Antonio de Guevara, who had been a cleric, chronicler, counselor, and companion of the emperor Charles V. He clearly wrote from personal experience when he described the life of "we courtiers . . . much cumbered with tediousness." Who better than he knew the "many men in this court loitering, superfluous, idle, vagrant, and evil-tongued"? These pungent words were written in his *Epístolas Familiares (Familiar Epistles),* published in Spain (1539–1541) and translated into English in 1574.

But earlier than this, in 1548, another of Guevara's works had been translated into English as *A Dispraise of the Life of a Courtier and a Commendation of the Life of the Labouring Man.* A humanist text with an argument that is sufficiently conveyed in its title, its message evidently met with considerable sympathy in literate circles from Spain to Germany and England, for it was much read and plagiarized. The English translation was reissued in 1575. Four years later it reappeared in a new version entitled *Cyvile and Uncyvile Life.* This time the original author was nowhere named (this was a period of mounting anti-Spanish sentiment), but it bore clear traces of its Spanish origins. In it the gentleman upheld the country life for the deep contentment it offered: people were more neighborly and kindly to one another; gentlemen's households were self-sufficient and continued the old traditions of hospitality. The courtier, on the other hand, defended his more civilized life and attacked the new-style country gentleman as covetous and clownish. His present mode of living filched the role of the working farmer and deprived him of his living. The gentleman, argued the writer, should keep his due place in society and either buy his food at the market or have it brought to his gate by others.

The result of all this literary flurry was a sharpened awareness of the merits of country life, which gentlemen in high office at Westminster in Elizabeth's reign strove to enjoy by performing the two roles at one and the same time. *Cyvile and Uncyvile Life* was dedicated to Sir Francis Walsingham, who was one such example. But the tension between the committed courtier and the dedicated country gentleman persisted, and more than once Shakespeare's characters bring it to mind. In *Henry VI, Part 2,* Iden asks:

> Lord, who would live turmoilèd in the court
> And may enjoy such quiet walks as these?

> (IV. x. 18–19)

Or again in *As You Like It,* Duke Senior, living in banishment, recognizes the merits of the beguiling life that he encounters in the Forest of Arden:

> Hath not old custom made this life more sweet
> Than that of painted pomp? Are not these woods
> More free from peril than the envious court?

> (II. i. 2–4)

In James I's reign, when gentlemen had more reason than ever to turn from the court in disgust and settle for the satisfactions of country life, the debate was revived yet again, this time by Nicholas Breton, who published *The Court and Country, or a Brief Discourse Dialogue-wise* (1618).

The notion that country life brought more serenity than the hazardous intrigues of the court, and the promise of deep satisfaction for the man who worked his land to the best of his ability, became part of the stock of accepted ideas animating the lives of sixteenth-century literate gentlemen. With these notions mingled the associated idea of patriotism, of pride in the English landscape and men's achievements in taming it. It showed itself in a new curiosity about the shape of England and its many provinces. A search for a more exact knowledge of the geography of the kingdom ensued, springing in part from a growing sense of Britain's distinctive

identity. The Reformation, which broke England's connections with Rome, fostered this sense of separation. But, paradoxically, the perception of differences was intensified by the closer contacts with the Continent that Englishmen were establishing in other fields of interest. People traveled abroad in larger numbers, some perforce staying away as refugees for several years at a time.

It became almost routine for Englishmen journeying overseas to look for foreign models before laying any plans for new developments at home, whether they were economic, political, administrative, or financial. While this established a closer feeling of association with Europe, it enhanced Englishmen's appreciation of their own country. Its variety over short distances was evident to every traveler, but individuals who observed it only through seeing a few closely placed, local examples or disjointed, widely scattered ones wanted a more comprehensive picture. The cloth merchants who regularly journeyed from Kendal to Southampton, for example, saw the West Midlands but not the East Midlands or East Anglia. The fishing fraternity that regularly moved for a season from Rye to Yarmouth knew southeastern England and Norfolk, but had any of them seen the Forest of Arden or the Pennine Hills? The pieces of the jigsaw had to be fitted into a larger whole before men could grasp Britain's significance as a whole country and distinguish its characteristics from those of Europe—and, for that matter, the continents of Asia, Africa, and America. Many garbled reports of these fantastic places filtered through from sailors and adventurers who told their tales in the inns and alehouses of their home ports. How could these stories be put into perspective if one did not know the full variety of the English scene?

The need was satisfied when writers began to compose comprehensive descriptions and surveyors compiled surveys and maps. The first steps toward building up a word picture of the English landscape were taken by John Leland during the reign of Henry VIII. He was deputed in 1533 to search monastic and collegiate libraries for forgotten "monuments of ancient writers." When the dissolution of the monasteries followed, this mission assisted the removal of monastic manuscripts and books to Henry VIII's own library. But the task and the traveling undertaken by Leland had lasted about ten years and had aroused his interest in the topography of England and Wales. "Inflamed by their writings to see all parts of this realm," he devoted another six years to further travel, intending to convert his notes into a full description of the realm. In 1546 he planned to complete his project within a year, but it was crowded out by other writing not altogether dissimilar in its aspirations, since it was designed to expound and support the glory of the British nation and the Tudor monarchy. Leland's manuscript notes, however, survived, to become a quarry for a new generation of topographers, possessing the same pride of country as Leland.

The first and most influential of the county historians was William Lambarde, author of *A Perambulation of Kent, Conteining the Description, Hystorie, and Customes of That Shire* (1576). He was followed by Richard Carew, who modeled his account of Cornwall (1602) directly on Lambarde's. Meanwhile, in the same decade William Camden was at work on a larger canvas, preparing a chorographical description of the whole of the British Isles, which was published as *Britannia* in 1586. Three English editions and one German appeared in four years, bearing witness to the lively interest that it evoked. Fulsome appreciation was expressed by Richard Carew: Camden, he said, had "illumined the obscurity of Britain with the brilliant light of his genius."

With Camden's panoramic view at hand, county surveys could be fitted into place against the larger background. Sampson Erdeswicke began to write on Staffordshire in 1593, though his manuscript was not published until 1723. In the 1590s, John Norden was accumulating wide knowledge of English regions through his work as a surveyor in the service of landowners wishing to know the full extent and potential of their newly acquired estates. With encouragement from the Cecil family, he set to work on a *Speculum Britanniae* (1593), and between 1590 and 1599 he completed surveys of several counties, though he never completed them all. Some of his maps, together with his book *The Surveyor's Dialogue* (1607), admirably exemplify the level of refined detail that his surveys attained.

Through the work of the surveyors and mapmakers (Christopher Saxton's first county maps appeared in 1574) greater precision was given to the image of the English landscape. The science of surveying was being much improved in the period, and printing presses were capable of producing attractive maps. Gentlemen showed themselves eager to adorn the walls of their rooms with the elegant results. By the middle of Elizabeth's reign,

the English possessed a much clearer notion of the outlines of their native country, with its contrasts between mountain and vale, fen and forest, park and field.

People now appreciated more clearly than ever the significance of the terms *woodland* and *champion,* commonly used to contrast the regions of England. Their use goes back a long way, though it is difficult to say how far. It was a distinction not between small pieces of woodland and adjoining fields of arable crops but, rather, between two fundamentally different regional landscapes. *Woodland* meant areas in which the economy was pastoral, trees were numerous (though they did not form dense forest, for many clearings were present), and people were likely to live in scattered, small hamlets rather than in large villages. In many cases, though not all, the woodland was subject to forest law, which prevented grassland from being freely converted to arable and restricted farming routines at certain times of the year in order to preserve the game. *Champion* meant countryside in which the plowland was the central support of the agrarian economy, the arable fields were extensive (usually cultivated under the common-field system), and people were more likely to live in villages than in scattered hamlets or farmsteads.

When Thomas Tusser published *A Hundreth Good Pointes of Husbandrie* (1557), a textbook in verse that was expanded into *Five Hundreth Pointes of Good Husbandry* in 1573, and became the best read farming manual of the century, he differentiated the farming conventions of woodland and champion. In champion country, for example, farmers entered on the fallow land of their farms at Lady Day (25 March); whereas in woodland country, where the pasture farmer set greater store by the grazing of the fallow field, tenants did not yield up their farms until Michaelmas (29 September). Later in the century, John Norden penetrated to yet deeper layers of difference. The inhabitants of these two contrasting landscapes were distinctive: "The people bred amongst woods are naturally more stubborn and uncivil than in the champion countries." In a more general way, the same idea was enunciated by a near contemporary, John Barclay, in *Icon animorum* (1614): "There is a proper spirit to every region, which doth in a manner shape the studies and manners of the inhabitants."

By the seventeenth century the distinct personalities of different regions were taken for granted, and administrative and political problems seemed to follow and confirm the same lines of division. More rural unrest was centered in the woodlands than in the champion, though clumsy government interference to improve the land in woodland and other pastoral areas like the fens without much regard for the inhabitants' well-being was largely responsible. Later still the distinction was given yet another dimension when Puritan sentiments were specially ascribed to woodland communities.

The term *woodland* thus collected a number of attributes that went well beyond the plain agricultural description of its pastoral concerns. The woodland harbored a less law-abiding—some would have said lawless—fraternity than the champion. This did not mean that people were also poor, or poorer than the poorest in champion country. All the evidence suggests otherwise. Some woodland country was enclosed and therefore readily adapted to another use if the economic climate changed. Other tracts were underused and readily available for new enterprises. Land was not unproductively managed, and since the natural resources of woodland were more varied, the poorest inhabitants had many alternatives at their command. In champion country, in contrast, the creation of arable land had reduced the grassland, virtually eliminated all wasteland, and diminished the variety of resources. Worse than this, the boundaries between intermingled arable strips were a source of endless quarrels and gave rise to much pilfering.

Thus, a contemporary image of woodland country solidified, with the help of repeated statements in print, depicting a place where proud individuality found full rein, where men led simple but not abjectly poor lives, freed from irksome controls. Among these forest areas, the Forest of Arden in Warwickshire was a prominent example. It was the forest with which Shakespeare was most familiar from his childhood, for the town of Stratford-upon-Avon straddled the boundary between the two types of landscape. To the south lay the champion, or, as it was called in Warwickshire, the Felden. This was described by Leland as "somewhat barren of wood but very plentiful of corn." To the north lay the Arden, "much enclosed, plentiful of grass, but no great plenty of corn." Leland explained how the distinction between Arden and Felden was pointed out to him by local people when he visited Warwick; in other words, it was part and parcel of local lore long before Shakespeare was born.

It was therefore totally appropriate for Shake-speare's forest inhabitants to speak with forthright and fearless directness to their betters. And since the Arden was dairying-fattening country, it is possible that Shakespeare had one particular dairyman-grazier in mind when he put into the mouth of Gremio in *The Taming of the Shrew:*

> I have a hundred milch-kine to the pail,
> Sixscore fat oxen standing in my stalls,
> And all things answerable to this portion.

> (II. i. 359–361)

It should be said that by Elizabethan standards Gremio was farming on a very large scale, more usually found in the later seventeenth than the later sixteenth century.

For gentlemen to find themselves roaming the forests in Shakespeare's day, there were more reasons than escape to the wild wood or banishment. Forests (and fens, too) came to the forefront of discussions on land improvement. As the population of the later sixteenth century increased rapidly, so the demand for food grew and farmers had to devise new ways of producing more from the land. They first of all improved the management of their good soils. But by the end of the century, they were animatedly discussing the possibilities of improving their poorer lands. Out of these debates came schemes to drain fenland, embank marshland, and disafforest the forests. All such projects were first mooted during Elizabeth's reign and more determinedly carried into effect in the early seventeenth century. As a result, many gentlemen became considerable investors in these ventures. Shakespeare's literary devices were thus entirely in step with economic realities when he directed his unfortunate courtiers to seek their salvation in what had once been for them totally unfamiliar territory in the forests. Gentlemen had customarily set up their residences on downland, on wolds, or in well-cultivated vales, where the plow for centuries had reigned supreme.

When land improvement became one of the slogans of the age, the opportunities to engage in such enterprise were unusually numerous. Land was up for sale in every quarter of the realm, some of it being dissolved monastic land and some of it crown land put on the market by an impecunious monarch. Such land, which had often lain comparatively neglected for several decades, offered a challenge both to those who wished to redeem it for traditional agricultural uses and to those with an urge to experiment. At the other end of the spectrum, the zest for improvement took another form—a fascination with the more delicate art of gardening.

Gardening represented not one but three newly invigorated branches of land cultivation, which excited much effort and ingenuity in the sixteenth century and, still more, in the seventeenth. It involved the cultivation of flowers for decorative purposes, vegetables and herbs for medicinal and culinary use, and fruit and nut trees to supply a greater variety of foodstuffs to the table. Since gardening did not require large amounts of land or, necessarily, a large expenditure of money, different types of gardening captured the energy and enthusiasm of all classes. But the fashion was set by kings and noblemen, followed by gentlemen, and it was they who strove for the highest standards of achievement, regardless of the expense. They not only procured exotic plants from all parts of the world but also went to great lengths to hire experienced gardeners, which often meant bringing them from France or Holland. Their skills were bought dear, and so they had relatively high status in gentlemen's houses. At the very least, they were regarded as skilled craftsmen; at best, they talked with their masters on equal terms.

Gardening was so much in vogue in upper-class circles in Shakespeare's day, especially in southern England, that no one could fail to be aware of the ramifications. And its procedures bulk so large in Shakespeare's imagery—his mind, said C. Roach Smith, was "richly stored, almost to overflowing, with horticultural learning"—that some critics have plausibly suggested that he had served an apprenticeship as a gardener on a gentleman's estate. It is not impossible. In many quarters agricultural work continued to be despised as a lowly occupation, despite the exhortations of humanists to the contrary. And if Shakespeare's references to peasants are a reliable guide to his own views, then he did, indeed, see them as base, dull creatures rather than proud men with skills. But gardening was in a different class. If Shakespeare's father had planned for his son a better future than his own, he could have done worse than choose the trade of gardening, for it could open the doors into the houses of great men and bring young apprentices regularly to the attention of their masters. Following the advice of Columella, gentlemen took a personal interest in their gardens, kept a close eye on every decision relating to their design, visited them continually, and sometimes worked in them. A

more than casual acquaintance with gardens and orchards may be needed to explain why they form the background scenery on twenty-nine occasions in Shakespeare's plays.

The consuming interest in gardening developed out of a conjuncture of circumstances. It was not a new art; rather, it was raised to a new level of achievement. The monasteries had devoted skill and attention to their gardens throughout the Middle Ages. They were not intended to be decorative so much as useful; plants were essential as medicines and in the kitchen. But interest can be maintained at many different levels, and it is clear that an outburst of enthusiasm of another order characterized the sixteenth century, transforming the whole enterprise into something qualitatively different.

William Harrison during Elizabeth's reign described past and present thus: gardens of the useful kind had been plentiful in Edward I's reign, but in time they had become neglected. For some two hundred years herbs, fruits, and vegetables had been despised as fit food "for hogs and savage beasts" rather than food for men. Then a new age dawned. Harrison did not explain why, beyond commenting on man's restless search for novelties and the readiness of foreigners to supply them, but we can see a number of contributory factors at work. When gentlemen started to read the classical books on husbandry, they were introduced to fresh notions on horticulture, showing it in a wholly new light. They noted first of all the attention paid to it fifteen centuries earlier by Columella. He devoted a whole book of *De re rustica* to the matter and explained his reasons thus: in the past it had been carried on halfheartedly and negligently, whereas it "is now quite a popular pursuit." Such words accurately described the situation in England by the end of the sixteenth century. But the bookish advice of ancient writers was not the only stimulus to the new fashion. Englishmen traveling abroad were encountering new vegetables and new varieties of old vegetables at the tables of their hosts in Italy, Spain, France, Holland, and Germany. Gardening at the beginning of the sixteenth century was much more advanced on the Continent, and the taste for vegetables and fruits was already well established among the upper classes. Englishmen found themselves lagging behind.

During Henry VIII's reign, if not earlier, king and courtiers had further reasons for feeling impelled to remedy their backwardness. Henry VIII's first queen, Catherine of Aragon, had spent much of her youth in Granada, where Moorish horticultural skills were taken for granted. Legend has it that she made her own contribution to the improvement of gardening in England. France's king, Francis I, was actively promoting horticulture in his country, promising financial rewards to men who brought plants and seeds from abroad.

Just how much interest in England was aroused by Spanish and French enthusiasm is a matter for speculation, but the foreign influences impinge at every turn of the historian's investigation. When, for example, Henry VIII encountered globe artichokes for the first time, he developed a gluttonous appetite for them, wishing to enjoy them whenever opportunity offered. When a visit to Calais was planned for him in July 1534, his host, the lord deputy, Lord Lisle, received a letter from London ordering him to buy every available artichoke in the neighborhood "for the king's pleasure." This was his "special commandment." By the early seventeenth century one might well find in the immediate environs of a gentleman's house a whole garden allocated to artichokes, like "the artichoke garden" on the estate of Henry Oxinden of Great Maydeacon in Kent, mentioned in an account of work done there in 1640.

Henry VIII was among the leaders of fashion, both in planting and eating vegetables and fruit. He was responsible for commissioning his fruiterer in 1533 with the task of establishing a fruit orchard at Teynham, Kent, granting him some 140 acres of land and thereby putting the stamp of royal approval on the enterprise. Richard Harris accordingly imported quantities of young trees from France and the Low Countries. The range of Harris' varieties was not the only novelty in this orchard: the trees had to make a geometrical pattern that was pleasing to the eye. In other words, the new concept of the orchard was intellectually, as well as botanically, different from the old; and when farmers imitated Harris in neighboring parishes in Kent, their new-style cherry orchards were all "beautifully disposed in direct lines."

Enthusiasm for gardening was intimately connected with the appreciation of new flavors in foodstuffs. When herbs, vegetables, and fruit were eaten with new relish, the diets of the fashion-setters in society underwent change. The trend was highlighted in the work of Konrad von Heresbach, a high-ranking official and prominent humanist at the court of the duke of Cleves. He published *Rei*

rusticae in 1570, which was especially influential in England because it was rapidly translated as *Four Books of Husbandry* (in 1577) by an English landowner and government administrator, Barnaby Googe. Heresbach expressed pride in his home-produced foods and advocated the eating of vegetables and fruit as a healthier diet for the rich than the fare that usually adorned their tables; in this respect, he maintained, they had a lot to learn from the poor. Thus, new food fashions spread outward from courtly circles. Before long, they had sufficiently influenced the middle classes in England to foster market gardening as a commercial enterprise. They also encouraged the publication of books on horticulture.

Just how compelling was the whole subject in all its facets may be judged from Blanche Henrey's opening remarks in her bibliography of horticultural literature (1975). "Many years of the sixteenth century went by before a book was published in English on a botanical or horticultural subject," she writes. An anonymous work on grafting and planting had made a lonely appearance around 1520 from the press of Wynkyn de Worde. In the next thirty years followed Richard Banckes's herbal and two of William Turner's three works on herbs. Then the steadily swelling tide of interest erupted in a wave of high enthusiasm between 1590 and 1600; many books appeared, and thereafter gentlemen spared no pains to adorn old gardens or make entirely new ones. Gardening, whether for flowers, herbs, vegetables, or fruit, had captured their imagination.

The attention paid to fruit growing can be gauged from the planning in Hertfordshire of the gardens of Hatfield House by Robert Cecil. Beginning in 1609 a huge orchard was laid out, featuring pears, plums, mulberries, cherries, nectarines, figs, and quinces. Trees were bought from abroad or received as gifts; 500 fruit trees were, in fact, given by the queen of France. Even orange trees were not excluded, for rich men were unwilling to admit failure in growing anything, no matter how exotic. A symbolic act of high significance had taken place in Whitehall in 1604, when the Spanish constable of Castile, Juan Fernández de Velasco, had sat at a banquet in the course of peace negotiations between England and Spain. He was presented by James I with a melon and half a dozen oranges on a green branch, grown in England. James drew attention to the Englishmen's achievement, and Don Juan ceremoniously shared the precious melon between himself, James, and his queen. Even the mulberry trees in Cecil's new garden (also planted in Shakespeare's own garden at New Place in Stratford) had a significance for contemporaries that could be overlooked if we did not have a record of the supreme efforts expended by James I in popularizing them in order to feed silkworms and so support a silk industry.

More conventional fruits, such as apples and pears, received equally attentive study from those who took satisfaction in multiplying the varieties growing in their orchards. Shakespeare refers to a number of them: crab apples, codlings, pippins, leathercoats, applejohns, bitter sweetings, pomewaters, and costards. But these were probably only a tenth of those available. Each had its particular merits and use. Subtle differences in flavor were noted, as well as differences in the keeping qualities of each variety. And as techniques of cultivation became more sophisticated, so the books encouraged higher aspirations. A wealth of meaning therefore lay behind Justice Shallow's invitation to Falstaff in *Henry IV, Part 2:* "Nay, you shall see my orchard, where, in an arbor, we will eat a last year's pippin of my own graffing, with a dish of caraways" (V. iii. 1–3). Gentlemen were exhorted to perform grafts for themselves, for, as John Parkinson explained in his gardener's handbook, *Paradisi in Sole* (1629), they did a better job than when buying trees grafted by others.

As for storing last year's pippins, Shakespeare's reference draws attention to the problem of long-term storage, which was as much a challenge as successful grafting. Some fruits could best be kept by leaving them on the tree. Others, like the applejohn, tasted best when the fruit was picked and the skin had shriveled. (Of this fact Shakespeare was plainly aware when he described Falstaff's skin as "withered like an old apple-john.") A book of instruction on gathering, packing, carrying, and storing, *The Fruiterers Secrets,* by an anonymous Irishman, came to the rescue in 1604 and served as the best manual on this score for many a long day.

Flowers and herbs were as much the object of skillful cultivation and experiment as were vegetables and fruit. They continued to be grown for practical use in medicine and in the kitchen, but pleasure and beauty became objectives in "the garden of delight" for those who could afford such luxury. As William Harrison explained, gardeners helped nature by coloring flowers and enlarging their blooms. Considerable success was achieved with the gillyflower, and all double blooms were

especially prized. Thus, the playgoer who heard the lines in *The Winter's Tale* about carnations and streaked gillyflowers, "which some call nature's bastards" (IV. iv. 83), would instantly have recognized the reference to a myriad of experiments currently under way among the gardeners.

Every traveler overseas was urged to bring back plants from India, the Canary Islands, the New World, and elsewhere. One result was the garden of medicinal herbs, seen by William Harrison, containing three or four hundred plants, of which half bore names unknown forty years before. And the list of varieties lengthened annually, each one being tested for new uses, as medicaments, in cooking, or as "nose herbs." They also had a role as emblems; rosemary, it will be recalled, was for remembrance.

Horticulture developed so many dimensions in this period that it is impossible to do justice to all its intricacies. Every successful fashion involves much subtlety in the choice of objectives, the shaping of styles, and usually some snobbery in the judgments applied to the different manifestations of that style. Since this was as true for horticulture as any other fashion, it is difficult at this distance in time to perceive all the abstruse niceties embedded in the achievements of the men who kept up-to-date with the mode of the moment.

Thus, certain fruits and vegetables were ranked higher in esteem than others. Oranges and melons were a tour de force, for obvious reasons if home-grown, but less so if imported. Onions, leeks, and garlic had long been a traditional mixture in poor men's pottage, which might have condemned them all to a lowly place in the vegetable hierarchy. But English writers commented that these three commonplace items made acceptable food at tables in Muscovy and Turkey. This could have elevated them all to a higher place. As it happened, onions and garlic were welcomed at gentlemen's tables; indeed, a fastidious taste for special varieties may even have developed, thereby explaining why select quantities of onions were regularly imported from abroad. But leeks, for some reason, became unacceptable. "Our dainty age," wrote John Parkinson, "refuses them," allowing them to be eaten only during Lent. The one place where they were more generally consumed was in Wales, where vulgar gentlemen enjoyed them and endured the Englishman's scorn. Shakespeare's jibe at Fluellen's leeks in *Henry V* can be fully appreciated only in this context. At the same time, individual vegetables were liable to move down the scale of preferences as they became more plentiful. Shakespeare was not drawn to mention Jerusalem artichokes; but we know from other comments that when this new vegetable, introduced about 1617, became plentiful forty years later, the price fell, and the London populace disdained to buy it.

The ingenuity shown by gardeners out of doors demanded the same inventiveness among those indoors who were to put flowers, vegetables, fruit, and herbs to practical use. Plants ranked alongside a miscellany of other items, now made available in increasing abundance, to beautify or otherwise introduce additional comfort into domestic life. These amenities reached into dwellings well below those of the nobility and gentry, bringing elegance into the homes of yeomen in the country and of merchants and higher-class craftsmen in the towns. William Harrison went further, believing that such luxuries had descended "even unto the inferior artificers and many farmers." Alongside chests and chairs distributed in living rooms and tapestries hung on walls, herbs were used to create pleasing, sweet-smelling interiors by spreading them on the floors and at windows. Yet more elaborate were the series of tasks devised in order to exploit fully all the new plants that were available. Of prime significance for the future was the distilling of herbs. Distillation became as fashionable an occupation indoors as was gardening out of doors. Like gardening, it was an ancient skill, reinvigorated by a new enthusiasm, which turned it into something qualitatively different.

The great practitioners of distillation of aromatic waters, essences, and alcohol had been the Arabs from the eighth to eleventh centuries. Their processes were used in Europe in the Middle Ages but were known to only a small circle of people, mainly doctors and apothecaries. Improved methods of distillation in the fifteenth century inaugurated a new phase of public interest. The publication in 1519 by Hieronymus von Braunschweig of a treatise (in German) on distilling represents a landmark, signaling more publicity for its potential. For Hieronymus, a Strassburg physician who had read the classical authors and acquired practical experience of his own, the possibility that he welcomed most was the chance to enable the poor, who lacked the money to pay doctors' fees, to cure their illnesses—though he cannot have expected them to read his book. John Parkinson in *Paradisi in Sole* (1629) clarified this last point: books were read by gentlewomen, who would then be able to help the poor to the remedies.

Hieronymus' substantial tome was soon translated into English as *The Vertuose Boke of the Distyllacyon of All Maner of Waters of the Herbes* (1527). It explained how to distill the essences of innumerable plants and described the virtues of each for curing different ailments. The labor that distillation entailed may be judged from the long list of plants from which distillates were ordered to be prepared for the household of the Percy family (earls of Northumberland) at their castles of Wressell and Leconfield in Yorkshire. A *Book of Regulations* governing all branches of domestic management was begun in 1512 and subsequently enlarged. It is likely that the orders for the preparation of distilled waters were inserted later than 1512, perhaps as much as twenty or more years later. At all events, twenty-eight different distillations were called for, from plants as varied as borage, columbine, fennel, parsley, sage, marigolds, and wild tansy.

Distilling duties in the Percy household are a relatively early illustration of the new wave of interest in herbal essences. When John (or Anthony?) Fitzherbert published *The Boke of Husbondrye* in 1523, he had something to say on fruit growing but nothing further on horticulture and nothing on distillation. Yet when his book was newly corrected and amended for publication in 1598, significant additions were made in wholly new chapters. In an account of gardening and planting, the importance of growing garden produce for health and profit was underlined, though the new editor refrained from going into detail, as much was by then available in print elsewhere. But since, he said, many people did not know about the distilling of herbs, he took more space to expand on this theme. Twenty-nine pages were filled with advice on the distillation of walnuts; fruits such as apples, grapes, and quinces; and other plants like angelica and hops.

A fashion had plainly taken hold, which was mirrored in the building of distilling rooms on gentlemen's estates. In the 1580s, Sir Christopher Hatton, who kept up to date with every kind of new fashion, introduced into the layout of his gardens at Holdenby, Northamptonshire, "a distilling house," alongside his "many delightful trees of fruits, and artificially composed arbours." It stood at the west end of the garden and drew on a nearby pond of water brought by conduit pipes from a field a quarter of a mile away.

Distillation had become a conventional routine in smart gentlemen's establishments. By 1594, when Sir Hugh Platt published *The Jewell House of*

Art and Nature, practical experimenters with distillation were calling for more precise hints on the best methods. Platt explained from his own trials that flowers of sage, thyme, rosemary, lavender, and the like yielded more oil than the leaves or seeds and that by drying them for five or six days beforehand, the yield of oil was increased. Apart from their medicinal use, oils were commended for washing and in the preparation of food. Sage oil, for example, was used to flavor butter, and attar of roses was used for preserving bottled fruit. In 1602, Platt had more advice to offer, which he pointedly directed this time to the ladies, who had evidently taken charge of these matters. *Delights for Ladies* offered information on herbal distillation "after a new and excellent manner" (among other things, copper vessels were now deemed important in place of pewter); preserving and candying flowers; preserving oranges and cherries; and making violet syrup, marigold paste, and pomanders. A pulp of fruit that would keep all year was recommended, and a way of keeping artichokes a long time was described, as well as a method of keeping cherries by packing them in layers in hay. All these activities, if successful, introduced greater variety into the foods that were available at different seasons and added artistry at the table as well.

More distilling, of course, led to the production of more alcohol, which now came to be more liberally consumed as a convivial, and not just as a medicinal, drink. Refugees from the Low Countries popularized the everyday drinking of spirits and flavored their liquors with as many ingredients as ingenuity could devise. The countrywoman Margaret Hoby recorded in her diary her domestic occupations in the garden and, among her morning tasks indoors, her "stilling." It is most likely that this devoutly Puritan Yorkshire woman was preparing spirits for medicinal use only. Shakespeare too refers to aqua vitae only in this sense, used by midwives and seafarers to keep out the cold. But in London other uses had been found.

Since the distillation of oils, waters, and spirits in the home had become women's work, this may explain Shakespeare's sparing references to skills that he did not know at first hand, in contrast with all he seems to have known of gardening. But Hamlet's father was killed by a distillation of hebona (possibly henbane; *Hamlet,* I. v. 62), and "a man distill'd out of our virtues"—words used by Nestor in *Troilus and Cressida* (I. iii. 350–351)— seems like an echo of the words of Hieronymus von Braunschweig, whose book began with a definition of distillation as "the purifying of the gross from the subtle" and claimed thereby to teach "the high and marvellous virtue of herbs."

All around him the stroller through London saw signs of the skills that made ingenious use of plants to produce consumer goods with a difference. In this respect, perfumed gloves were symbolic of a whole array of similar wares. The art of perfumery had made its way to the Continent in the fifteenth century, along with the art of distillation. Rich men and women, notably in Italy, France, and Spain, where the climate produced the strongest scented herbs, readily fell victim to the perfumer's arts. Perfumes were on public display in Paris in 1548 when aromatic plants were used to perfume the waters of public fountains during festivities. But in England at that date French perfumes and perfumed gloves were regarded with contempt, as symptoms of the frothy French economy that was totally at variance with the solidly based English one, which was built on the use of such natural resources as wool, lead, and coal. In *A Discourse of the Common Weal,* written in 1549 by the secretary of state, Sir Thomas Smith, as a debate on the country's economic ills, perfumed gloves were named with painted cloths and papers, oranges, pippins, and cherries as "trifles" from abroad that politicians thought could be "clean spared." In fact, they were destined to be numbered among life's necessities by those who could afford to indulge in the luxuries of a burgeoning consumer society.

Edmund Howes, who chronicled the novelties, regarded 1572–1573 as the significant date for the introduction of perfumery, for in that period the earl of Oxford returned from Italy with perfumed gloves and bags and a perfumed leather jerkin. The queen herself then acquired a pair of perfumed gloves, and they became suitable gifts for presentation to her on official occasions. For years after, people spoke of the earl of Oxford's perfume. By the end of the century, even peddlers dispensed it. The description by Autolycus of a chapman's wares in *The Winter's Tale* neatly enumerates some of the most desirable consumer goods then on sale, including

> Gloves as sweet as damask roses,
> Masks for faces and for noses,
> Bugle bracelet, necklace amber,
> Perfume for a lady's chamber.

(IV. iv. 218–221)

In the course of Shakespeare's life, Englishmen's perceptions of the country in which they lived were transformed by new knowledge, new values, and new success in exploiting its potential. People were given a better view of the whole kingdom as a geographical entity. They were inspired with a new sense of power in manipulating the land, which was made to bear another harvest of previously neglected or unknown plants. The cultivation of land with the spade was tested and deemed beneficial, if not more beneficial than the plow. For some men an almost religious zeal lay behind their efforts to make the land more productive and so help to overcome the threat of food shortages that had plagued them in the past. The success of efforts long under way was most manifest during Elizabeth's reign, when the slow revolution gathered momentum. The land was tamed for a variety of new uses—to yield more food, more variety of foods, more healing medicines, and some exotic luxuries. The luxuries did not yet touch the lives of the poorest in society, but they were available in unwonted abundance. Some were now being made at home instead of being imported, and so could serve more than the very rich. They enhanced the lives not only of gentlemen in their manor houses but also of the middle classes and of some lowlier folk in their service. Such goods were distributed comparatively rapidly to the far corners of the realm, so that fashions reached towns in the northern counties only a few years after they reached London.

Thus, the cultivation of forest, field, and garden in new ways not only changed the rural landscape but also expanded the range of domestic comforts, added to the domestic duties of women, and multiplied the consumer goods displayed in the towns and brought to the villages on the backs of peddlers. Fresh attitudes and material goods of a new kind so altered the world view of Elizabethan citizens that every sentence they spoke harbored references to things that they might take for granted but that belonged peculiarly to that period. In this respect, Shakespeare's use of the English language combined an intellectual and imaginative command with a multitude of revealing comments on the aspirations, assumptions, and fashions of the age.

BIBLIOGRAPHY

D. M. Barratt, "A Second Northumberland Household Book," in *Bodleian Library Record*, 8, no. 2 (1968). Muriel St. Clare Byrne, ed., *The Lisle Letters* (1981). Lucius Columella, *On Agriculture*, I, H. B. Ash, ed. (1941), and II–III, E. S. Forster and Edward H. Heffner, eds. (1954–1955). Anthony Fitzherbert, *Fitzherbert's Booke of Husbandrie*, W. W. Skeat, ed. (1882). Robert J. Forbes, *Short History of the Art of Distillation* (1948). Frederick J. Furnivall, ed., *Harrison's Description of England in Shakespeare's Youth*, 3 vols. (1877–1881). George E. Fussell, *The Old English Farming Books from Fitzherbert to Tull, 1523 to 1730* (1947).

Blanche Henrey, *British Botanical and Horticultural Literature Before 1800*, I: *The Sixteenth and Seventeenth Centuries* (1975). William Davis Hooper and Harrison B. Ash, eds., *Cato on Agriculture, Varro on Agriculture* (1967). Ruth Kelso, *The Doctrine of the English Gentleman in the Sixteenth Century* (1929). Hilda Leyel, *The Magic of Herbs* (1932). James K. McConica, *English Humanists and Reformation Politics Under Henry VIII and Edward VI* (1965). Dorothy M. Meads, ed., *Diary of Margaret, Lady Hoby, 1599–1605* (1930). Victor Morgan, "The Cartographic Image of 'The Country' in Early Modern England," in *Transactions of the Royal Historical Society*, 5th ser., 29 (1979).

Bishop Thomas Percy, ed., *The Regulations and Establishment of the Household of Henry Algernon Percy, the Fifth Earl of Northumberland, at His Castles of Wressle and Leconfield in Yorkshire* (1905). Eugene Rimmel, *The Book of Perfumes* (1865). Eleanour Sinclair Rohde, *Shakespeare's Wild Flowers* (1935). Charles Roach Smith, *The Rural Life of Shakespeare as Illustrated by His Works* (1874). Lucy Toulmin Smith, ed., *Leland's Itinerary in England and Wales* (1964). John M. Steane, "The Development of Tudor and Stuart Garden Design in Northamptonshire," in *Northamptonshire Past and Present*, 5, no. 5 (1977).

Joan Thirsk, *The Agrarian History of England and Wales*, IV–V (1967–1985); *Economic Policy and Projects: The Development of a Consumer Society in Early Modern England* (1978); and "Plough and Pen: Agricultural Writers in the Seventeenth Century," in T. H. Aston, et al., eds., *Social Relations and Ideas: Essays in Honour of R. H. Hilton* (1983). Keith Thomas, *Man and the Natural World: Changing Attitudes in England, 1500–1800* (1983). Ronald Webber, *The Early Horticulturists* (1968).

Sports and Recreations

ROGER PRINGLE

A consideration of how the Elizabethans enjoyed most of their leisure provides valuable clues about their society, and if the attempt is a reminder at times that little has changed in four centuries, it more often jolts us into realizing how distant Shakespeare's world is. Sports and recreations fulfilled many functions, but their obvious purpose then, as now, was to help people to cope with the pressures and routines of daily life by periodically escaping from them. We appreciate the point easily but fail perhaps to perceive how vital that need was for most of Shakespeare's contemporaries.

About a third of the population lived a simple peasant existence, rarely moving any distance from the villages where they lived and worked and owning few possessions beyond their clothes, tools of trade, and some rudimentary cottage furniture. The vast majority of working people, dwelling in the country and the towns, labored at the same tasks for very long hours, basically from dawn to dusk, six days a week. Misfortune, whether in the form of economic depression, harvest failure, or disease, was always close to hand. The expectation of life was short. These harsh realities, far from lessening the desire to make merry, were an incentive to seize the existing chances to fleet the time carelessly. Sports and recreations, whether physical or sedentary, crude or sophisticated, were a means of forgetting, even defying, a world where the struggle to survive was constant.

For the upper classes, insulated from material privation but not from illness or other buffets of life, leisure activities also provided a release from tedium and worry. The correspondence of Lord Burghley, one of the hardest-working politicians of the time, breaks off from dealing with affairs of state to report to the Earl of Leicester on the performance of a hound the Earl had given him. "She maketh my hunting very certain," he wrote. "She hath never failed me; and this last week she brought me to a stag which myself had strucken with my bow" (Fortescue). Queen Elizabeth's exceptional capacity for undertaking governmental work was matched with a zest for enjoying her leisure hours. By taking regular exercise she kept in excellent health most of her life and was better able to shoulder the heavy burdens of her office for so long. She often rode ten miles or more a day until her final months and maintained her legendary reputation as a dancer, footing a coranto shortly before her last illness.

The value of exercise in promoting mental and physical health was generally recognized, although physical education in schools was still largely ignored. It was partly to remedy this defect that Richard Mulcaster wrote his book *Positions*, published in 1581, which advocated a program of physical activities to complement the academic side of school life. He stressed the interdependence of mind and body and believed that if the whole human personality were to be developed, hard exercise should accompany hard study. The medical benefits of various exercises were explained. "Moderate running," presumably the equivalent of our jogging, strengthened "the natural motions"; dancing, he considered, drove away "numbness and certain palsies" and was an aid for "weak hips, fainting legs and freatishing (chilled) feet."

Some of Mulcaster's views echoed opinions expressed fifty years earlier in Sir Thomas Elyot's *Governour,* in which a chapter was devoted to "Exercises whereof cometh both recreation and profit." Individual activities were identified by Elyot with particular benefits, some sports being recommended for strength, some for agility, and others for speed. Later writers also gave emphasis to the health motive for taking exercise. Henry Peacham's popular *Complete Gentleman,* published in 1622, praised archery because "it openeth the breast and pipes, exerciseth the arms and feet with less violence than running, leaping, etc." Leaping, he agreed, also had its value but should not be practiced "upon a full stomach or to bedward." A year before Peacham's book, Robert Burton's discussion of recreation in *The Anatomy of Melancholy* had reflected some of the views of Shakespeare's time. Burton considered that exercise was "nature's physician" and a cure for melancholy, especially amongst scholastic persons who often "have no care of the body." Energetic sports like wrestling, swimming, and football were not, he believed, the only way to ward off anxiety and depression. Gentler pleasures might be a better solution, such as "to take a boat in a pleasant evening and with music to row upon the waters."

Others underlined the therapeutic value of mild exercise. A tract about the spa at Buxton, written by a Dr. John Jones in 1572, forwarded bowling as one of the most salutary occupations for patients. In *Richard II* the lady companion of Richard's sad Queen suggests bowling as an antidote to her melancholy (*Richard II,* III. iv. 1–5). Shakespeare's scene is set in a garden, and the cultivation of gardens for pleasure as well as profit was an increasingly popular recreation, encouraged by the publication of many books. Most of these writings stressed the beauty and solace of a garden as much as its practical function of providing a vital supply of vegetables, fruits, and herbs. Francis Bacon in his *Essays* rated a garden as "the greatest refreshment to the spirits of man." John Gerard, whose splendid herbal appeared in 1597, affirmed the visual delights of flowers and asked in true Renaissance spirit, "Who would look up dangerously at planets that might look safely down at plants?" Robert Bur-

ton celebrated the joys of walking "amongst orchards, gardens, bowers, mounts and arbours."

The connection between pastimes and military training was made by various writers, including Mulcaster, who listed "war and service" among the main purposes of exercise. Since the Middle Ages, wrestling, jousting, and archery had been valued as useful preparations for the battlefield. The longbow had been the secret of English victories over the French in the Hundred Years War and was also revered for its association with Robin Hood, most famous of folk heroes, and with yeoman virtues generally. In the sixteenth century the popularity of archery declined, partly because rival sports competed favorably with it, and partly because changes in the nature of warfare, especially the increasing use of gunpowder and artillery, began to make the bow obsolete. Nevertheless Tudor governments continued to regard the availability of large numbers of trained archers as indispensable to national defense and vigorous efforts were made to reverse the diminishing interest in bowmanship. An Act of 1541, reconfirmed in Elizabeth's reign, made it obligatory for all able-bodied men under sixty to own and practice with a bow and to make male servants and children do likewise.

In Shakespeare's time, therefore, most of the male population were archers by compulsion. Towns and villages had public butts where citizens and country folk went shooting on Sundays and holidays. Gentlemen of means practiced in their own grounds. Contests were held and virtuoso performances given: Richard Carew in his *Survey of Cornwall* (1602) describes an ace archer called Robert Arundell "who could shoot twelve score (arrows), with his right hand, with his left, and from behind his head." Shakespeare's references to the use of the bow, both for military and sporting purposes, show his knowledge of a national pastime that gave his language many lasting words and phrases: "highly strung," "bracing" oneself, "being a butt," knowing the "upshot."

The 1541 Act also banned various popular recreation from being played by the lower classes in the hope that they would devote more leisure time to archery and thus be trained for war service. The recreations declared unlawful included tennis, bowls, dicing, and cards. The prohibitions applied to the mass of ordinary working people defined as any "artificer or handycrafts man of any occupation, husbandman, apprentice, labourer, servant of husbandry, journeyman or servant, or artificer, mariner, fisherman, waterman, or any serving-man." Excluded from the restrictions, however, were "all men of worship which may dispend 100 pounds yearly and upwards." The Act seems to have been largely ignored but in the attempt to make certain pastimes the exclusive right of the wealthier classes it reflects the hierarchical nature of Elizabethan society. Leisure pursuits, as well as patterns of work and degrees of political responsibility, were clearly related to social rank. How men and women played and rested depended to a significant extent on their status.

The linking of recreations with social objectives derived impetus from the process that saw the medieval ideal of the chivalric knight give way to that of the cultivated gentleman. The cult of gentility owed much to Baldassare Castiglione's *Courtier,* the most influential of many Renaissance books that defined the training appropriate for the ruling class. Apart from being a man of social grace, martial skill, and artistic ability, Castiglione's ideal courtier excelled in recreations suitable for one of his position. The English books that transmitted Castiglione's ideas and gained for them a wide currency in Shakespeare's time made accomplishment in certain sports an essential requirement for those who aspired to be gentlemen.

Sir Thomas Elyot's *Governour* advocated a program of physical activities designed to foster qualities of character expected of a gentleman, quite apart from the development of his physique. Class considerations influenced Elyot's choice of appropriate pastimes. Whereas running, wrestling, swimming, horse riding, hunting, hawking, and tennis were approved, other recreations associated with the lower classes were ruled out. Football, he thought, was "nothing but beastly fury and extreme violence"; skittles and quoits were to be "utterly abjected of all noble men." That Elyot recommended some activities for the way they reinforced differences of social status is shown by his praise of horse riding. He considered this to be the most honorable of exercises because the sight of a rider astride a prancing steed "importeth a majesty and dread to inferior persons."

Shakespeare's age saw the ranks of the gentry enlarged by those who had grown wealthy through land or trade. Many of these arrivistes assiduously cultivated the role of the country squire and were eager to assimilate the tastes and habits that distinguished the gentleman's style of life, including his sports and recreations. Paramount among these

29. The falconer, from George Turberville, *The Book of Falconry* (1575).

pastimes were hawking and hunting, and the social snobbery attached to them became a target for satire in plays and pamphlets. In Ben Jonson's *Every Man in His Humour* (1598), Master Stephen, who is setting up as a country gentleman, boasts: "I have bought me a hawk and a hood and bells and all. I lack nothing but a book to keep it by. . . . Why, you know, an' a man have not skill in the hawking and hunting languages nowadays, I'll not give a rush for him."

Specialist manuals catered to those for whom social respectability meant mastering the language and skills of falconry, or at least employing professional falconers who trained the birds on their behalf. The standard work was George Turberville's *Book of Falconry or Hawking* (1575), expressly written "for the only delight and pleasure of all Noblemen and Gentlemen." A companion volume, *The Noble Art of Venerie or Hunting,* published anonymously in the same year, was an authoritative treatise on the other main sport of the country gentry. Only the leisured classes had the money and opportunity to indulge in the full rituals of these sports. The purchase of hawks and hounds, with the equipment required to train and keep them, was costly, and the actual business of flying birds or hunting was time consuming. Such constraints, however, did not exclude many ordinary people from taking an interest in these pastimes, and judging by the number of allusions to them in contemporary literature, their terms were a familiar part of everyday speech.

Shakespeare's plays indicate that his audience had a considerable knowledge of hunting and hawking, and his references point to both the privileged status of these sports and their sophistication. He often made brilliant figurative use of the technical language to give vivid expression to the thoughts and feelings of his characters. All aspects of falconry were drawn upon, including the training of hawks. In *The Taming of the Shrew* (IV. i. 180–185) Petruchio describes Katherine as a "haggard," meaning an untamed hawk, and his plan of action to "curb her mad and headstrong humor" (196), which involves denying her food and sleep, is precisely the training to which a falconer would subject an undisciplined bird until it submitted to his will. In an anguished moment Othello, suspecting Desdemona's unfaithfulness, envisages her as an inconstant "haggard" and uses the word "jesses," the term for leather straps tied to a hawk's legs so that it could be held, to signify the bond of love that will break if her guilt is proved:

> If I do prove her haggard,
> Though that her jesses were my dear heartstrings,
> I'd whistle her off and let her down the wind
> To prey at fortune.
>
> (*Othello,* III. iii. 260–263)

In the early stages of taming a hawk its eyes were often "seeled" or temporarily blinded by stitching the eyelids with a thread until the bird became accustomed to being handled. Antony uses the term when he bewails man's blind endeavors before heaven:

> The wise gods seel our eyes,
> In our own filth drop our clear judgments, make us
> Adore our errors, laugh at's while we strut
> To our confusion.
>
> (*Antony and Cleopatra,* III. xiii. 112–115)

As with his hawking images, Shakespeare drew on his extensive knowledge of hunting to create metaphors of beauty and power. Often an elaborate ritual, hunting was enjoyed as an opportunity for social display, apart from its value as exercise and entertainment. In Shakespeare's plays the most detailed hunting scenes are those involving high-ranking persons. In *A Midsummer Night's Dream* (IV. i. 111–125), Duke Theseus and his bride-to-be, Hippolyta, compare the qualities of their hounds, with the Duke boasting of the harmonious cry made by his dogs as they pursue their quarry. In *The Taming of the Shrew* (Induction, i. 14–27) a lord argues with his huntsman over which is the best hound in the pack. In *Love's Labor's Lost* (IV. i) a deer shoot is arranged as a divertissement for the Princess of France. In these scenes and others scattered through the plays, many of which now require explanations of their terminology, Shakespeare confirms the sophisticated and privileged nature of hunting in his day. Like other refined sports, such as court tennis, fencing, and jousting, both hunting and hawking demanded a measure of time, affluence, and expertise beyond the resources of ordinary people. By means of these pastimes the upper classes not only passed their leisure time pleasurably but displayed their wealth and asserted their social ascendancy. Not everyone applauded the rich at play. Godfrey Goodman, a clergyman, was one of the few who considered the feelings of those for whom the hunt might be a sober reminder of their lowly position on the social ladder. In *The Fall of Man* (1616), discussing the effect of hunting, he described "the cry and the curse of the poor tenant, who sits at a hard rent and sees his corn spoiled," and he sympathized with the "servants and followers, who must attend their lordships and partake with them in their whole sport, but not in any part of their pleasure."

Despite the gulf between the sports of the gentry and those enjoyed at a popular level, simple forms of hunting, hawking, and other country sports were widely pursued for reasons that had little to do with cultivating an image, amusing oneself, or keeping fit. Some field sports were undertaken for the all-important purpose of obtaining food. The large country houses, accommodating many servants in addition to the owner's family and dependents, relied on hunting to supply some of the household provisions. William Harrison in his *Description of England* (1577) recorded an impressive range of dishes served in noble households, including "red or fallow deer, besides great variety of fish and wild fowl.'' Further down the social scale many country folk also made use of nature's larder.

Game laws were designed to restrict deer hunting to the wealthy landed class, but poaching was widespread and venison sometimes appeared surreptitiously on the tables of ordinary people. Though the gentry often had private ponds and controlled the rights to some waters, fishing was normally open to everyone. The rivers were plentifully stocked with fish of all kinds: trout, roach, carp, perch, salmon, bream, grayling, and eel. Household accounts testify to the popularity of fish and reflect the fact that it was a necessary part of everyone's diet because of the legislated fast days and fish days.

Hawking was not a sport entirely for the rich. Although the keeping and flying of the grander falcons was an aristocratic pastime, people of more modest standing owned smaller hawks that were used to capture prey for eating. In *The Merry Wives of Windsor* (III. iii. 204–205) George Page, a member of the town's bourgeoisie, tells his friends that after breakfast "we'll a-birding together: I have a fine hawk for the bush." Birds used on such occasions were the short-winged goshawks or sparrowhawks that were capable, over short distances, of catching pheasants, partridges, and rabbits to fill the kitchen pot.

Those who could not afford any kind of hawk might ensure a varied food supply by fowling. Small birds of the fields and hedgerows, as well as game birds, could be taken by several inexpensive methods. A popular practice was to capture birds by liming, or smearing twigs with a sticky substance. Nets, snares, and traps of many kinds were common devices. Birdbolts were blunted arrows fired at the prey; stone bows shot pebbles. Shakespeare's references to all these means of capture indicate their widespread use. Firearms, which led to the decline of fowling and hawking, were beginning to be used, although they did not become reliable or extensively carried until the late seventeenth century.

Though a townsman, Shakespeare's Master Page enjoyed hare coursing as well as hawking. Slender remarks, rather tactlessly, to him: "How does your fallow greyhound, sir? I heard say he was outrun on Cotsall" (*Merry Wives,* I. i. 79–80). As with the citizens of Windsor, the great majority of the urban population lived close to the countryside in fact as well as in spirit. Even in the largest cities of London, Bristol, and Norwich, the countryside was a short walk from their centers. Although growing

30. Hunting the deer, from *The Noble Art of Venerie* (1575).

numbers of town lawyers, merchants, businessmen, and artisans lived away from the land, there was in many respects no fundamental division between urban and rural styles of life. This certainly applied to most forms of recreation.

As the word *holiday* indicates, recreation had been closely linked in the Middle Ages to the church calendar with its many saints' days and other observances. Although the Reformation reduced the number of these occasions, the church continued to be at the center of social life. An Act of 1552 decided the holiday arrangements that ap-

31. Fowling for partridges, from Henry Peacham, *Minerva Brittana* (1612).

plied to the working population of Shakespeare's time. In addition to Sundays, twenty-seven feast days were spaced at intervals throughout the year, so that, apart from Christmas, when most people of all classes enjoyed several consecutive days free from work, the modern notion of a holiday being a sustained period of unbroken rest did not exist. Nor were holidays for the majority a time to move away from one's usual environment for a change of air and situation. They were essentially local celebrations bound up with the life of the parish. Church wakes, held on the anniversary of the church's consecration or on the feast day of its saint, were celebrated in many districts with the rush-bearing ceremony. Decorated carts, preceded by morris dancers and musicians, brought green rushes to strew on the floors of the church. After a service there would be dancing, feasting, and many sports, which might include wrestling, running, football, and other ball games. Such occasions helped to generate the sense of togetherness that, in a vulnerable world, gave strength and cohesion to the community. "Game" is derived from a word meaning participation or gathering.

Drinking was a key element of any holiday occasion, especially of the church ales that raised money for the religious needs of the parish by the sale of food and drink. Births and marriages provided further pretexts for local merrymaking. The intense

delight with which the Elizabethans seized their holiday opportunities is caught in Joris Hoefnagel's painting (1590) of a marriage feast. His animated scene shows a banquet being prepared and the wedding guests breaking into dance. Music and dancing were favorite diversions of all classes. Morris dances, jigs, rounds, and many other folk dances were part of almost every country celebration. In aristocratic circles there were the stately dances of the pavane and allemande, in contrast to the energetic steps of the galliard, the cinquepace, and the coranto. Books of part-songs and madrigals were easily available, and it was customary for ordinary families to entertain themselves and their guests by singing and music-making, indoors or outdoors, depending on the time of year.

Religious feast days often coincided with festivals linked to the cycle of the country year, many of which were pagan in origin but had been absorbed into the Christian calendar. The beginning of spring, midsummer, the end of harvesting, and other main events of the farming world were marked with appropriate revels. Tradition largely dictated the form taken by the entertainments. Shrove Tuesday, followed by the abstemious period of Lent, was associated with feasting and combative sports such as tug-of-war, football, and cockfighting. The ancestral link of the May Day festivities with fertility rites was apparent in the

32. May Day festivities, from Edmund Spenser, *The Shepherd's Calendar* (1586).

ceremonial erection of the maypole, which aroused the wrath of Puritans like Phillip Stubbes:

> They have twenty or forty yoke of oxen, every ox having a sweet nosegay of flowers placed on the tip of his horns; and these oxen draw home this maypole (this stinking idol rather), which is covered all over with flowers and herbs . . . with two or three hundred men, women and children following it with great devotion. And thus being reared up with handkerchiefs and flags hovering on the top, they strew the ground round about . . . and then fall they to dance about it.
>
> (*The Anatomie of Abuses*, 1583)

Everyone's holidays were bound up with agrarian rituals and religious observances, whether they lived in the towns or countryside. John Stow, in his *Survey of London* (1598), recalled that on May Day in London milkmaids paraded through the streets with their pails and garlands, morris dancers performed, and maypoles were put up. This fundamentally rural outlook of city dwellers allowed Shakespeare to write plays for his London theater audiences that were full of references to country ways and pastimes.

Dramatic spectacle of various kinds was a regular part of holiday activity. At Christmas, masques featured as popular court entertainments, as did the plays of Shakespeare and other leading dramatists. Elsewhere in the country many festivals were associated with a less sophisticated tradition of pageants, disguisings, mummings, and folk plays. There was a strong theatrical element in the custom of electing a Lord of Misrule to preside over feasts in noble households or to lead the village revels. Stubbes describes how "all the wildheads of the parish . . . choose them a grand captain (of all mischief)" whom they then crown as a mock king and lead to the churchyard in the company of a rowdy crowd of morris dancers. The custom of Misrule allowed the revelers a temporary freedom to mock secular and religious authority by counterfeiting monarchs, noblemen, bishops, and mayors. Through the experience, tensions and antagonisms were released and the revelers returned better able to face the rigid disciplines of their daily lives.

The value of some pastimes in contributing to social stability was recognized by James I. In his "Book of Sports," written to defend his subjects' rights to "lawful recreations and honest exercises,"

33. "A Fete at Bermondsey," by Joris Hoefnagel (1590).

he argued that the Puritans' desire to see recreations prohibited on Sundays would breed discontent. Certainly some of the more vigorous pastimes must have been useful safety valves for the release of energies that might otherwise have been diverted to more dubious moral or political ends.

Football was a notoriously boisterous game, widely played on Sundays, at wakes, and at festivals like Shrovetide. Not yet confined to a special playing field, it was practiced in fields and streets. Rules were practically nonexistent except for the object of scoring a goal. Teams were composed of an indeterminate number of players and the game often became one of mass participation involving two villages or rival factions from within a community. Goals were sometimes miles apart, with the parish constituting the playing field, regardless of rivers and other obstacles. Stubbes condemned it as "a bloody and murdering practice" and gave graphic details of the violence and injuries suffered by the participants. In line with all the literature concerned with exercises suitable for gentlemen, James I's *Basilicon Doron* (1599), a book of instructions for his son, excluded football, regarding it as "meeter for laming than making able the users thereof." When James watched *King Lear* at his court a few years later, he must have approved of Kent's insulting dismissal of Oswald as "a base football player."

Closely allied to football were hurling and campball, primitive types of rugby in which the ball was carried or thrown. Richard Carew described wild

34. The country swains at football, from Henry Peacham, *Minerva Brittana* (1612).

interparish matches of hurling where the goals were two gentlemen's houses or villages set several miles apart.

Other hand and ball sports were enjoyed, along with their more sophisticated derivative, the racket and ball game. Handball was popular either in a form of fives or tennis or as a general game played in the open countryside. John Nichols' *Progresses . . . of Queen Elizabeth* (1788) records a kind of hand tennis played by teams of several players for the entertainment of the queen:

> The same day after dinner, about three of the clock, ten of my Lord of Hertford's servants, all Somersetshire men, in a square green court, before Her Majesty's window, did lay up lines, squaring out the form of a tennis court, and making a cross line in the middle. In this square, they (being stripped out of their doublets) played, five to five, with the hand ball.

A less restricted form of hand game called *balloon* is described by Gervase Markham in *Country Contentments* (1615) as being "a strong and moving sport in the open fields, with a great ball of double leather filled with wind, and driven to and fro with the strength of a man's arm armed in a bracer of wood." Tennis developed from being played with the bare hand, to the wearing of a stringed glove, to the use of a racket. It was already fashionable during the late Middle Ages and, as played on royal and private enclosed courts, remained a popular game for the privileged in Shakespeare's time. In London some public courts were attached to taverns and gaming houses for the recreation of the middle classes, but, as John Stow commented in 1598, "the people of meaner sort" continued to play their versions of the game "in the open fields and streets."

The mass of people on lower incomes had been banned from playing bowls by the 1541 Act. As with the other prohibited pastimes, the law was honored more in the breach than in the observance, and bowls flourished at all levels of society. Ordinary folk played it in alleys, on open ground, and on village greens. It was a popular gambling sport with the leisured classes whose gardens often incorporated their own greens and turfed alleys. Judging by the number of bowling terms in Shakespeare's plays, such as "bias," "kiss," "Jack," and "rub," it is likely that he was as proficient a player as Sir Nathaniel, the curate in *Love's Labor's Lost,* who is vouched to be "a very good bowler." There were many forms, too, of pin-bowling. In kayles the wooden pins were knocked down with a stick; in closh a bowl was used; in loggets, as Hamlet knew, bones took the place of pins and another bone served as the throwing weapon, hence his question in the grave-digging scene: "Did these bones cost no more the breeding but to play at loggets with 'em?"

Many other diversions occupied the Elizabethans during their Sundays, saints' days, and festivals. A woodcut illustrating the famous Cotswold Games, held at Whitsun, shows the contestants engaged in various activities, including pitching the bar, tossing the hammer, doing handstands, cudgel-playing, and shin-kicking. Many simple games, some still played by children today, had a broad appeal: hoodman-blind (blindman's bluff), leap-frog, top-whipping, and barley-break were all enjoyed. Merels or nine men's morris could be played outdoors on a square cut into the turf (which might become filled up with mud, as Titania says in *A Midsummer Night's Dream*) or indoors on a small board or a square scratched on a table.

Since horses were the chief means of transport,

35. Bowling, from *Le Centre de l'amour* (1680).

36. Tennis, from *Le centre de l'amour* (1680).

277

COTSWOLD GAMES.

37. Country sports at the Cotswold Games, from *Annalia Dubrensia* (1636).

it is to be expected that horse riding and racing were pastimes. Apart from the pleasures of exercise and fresh air, horsemanship gave rise among courtiers to the art of manage, or dressage. Horse races, closely identified with gambling, were part of many annual festivities, like the Cotswold Games, and were also promoted in their own right by some town corporations, as at Chester and Doncaster. If horse racing was not a high-society preserve, those who took part in the spectacular jousts and tournaments, in which mounted knights contended with lance and sword in the lists, were strictly aristocratic. Intended to revive the chivalric traditions of the Middle Ages, the tourneys were highly ceremonious occasions held in the tiltyards attached to the royal palaces or the great houses of the nobility. One of the knightly contests, riding at the quintain, had become a popular game of strength and skill. The rider's target was usually a shield or dummy figure hung on a revolving crossbar attached to a post, with a sandbag tied to the bar's other end that could swing round and hit the incompetent tilter. John Stow recalled seeing "the youthful citizens" of London who "made

great pastime," in summer and winter, running at a quintain at Cornhill.

Our image of Shakespeare's "Merry England" is mainly conjured from verbal and visual pictures of outdoor jollity. Yet in the long, dark, winter months and during periods of bad weather, a wide range of indoor pastimes kept people amused and restored their spirits. Maw (a kind of piquet), ruff (a precursor of whist), and the highly fashionable primero (an earlier form of ombre) were favorite card games among the gamblers at court or in the taverns. Tables (the ancestor of backgammon) was popular, and there was a proliferation of dice games. Shovel-board, draughts, a kind of billiards, and chess were all well-established diversions. Needlework, including intricate embroidery, was one of the most common indoor pastimes of women. Several diary entries attest to the pleasure it gave, as well as to its usefulness.

In a highly oral culture, centuries before television monopolized living rooms, storytelling had the status of a pastime, especially within a family circle. Many were the children whose imaginations were fired by the legends and adventure stories

38. "Four Gentlemen of High Rank Playing Primero," by John Bettes, sixteenth century.

279

told by their parents and grandparents; and some of those children, like young Mamillius in *The Winter's Tale* (II. i), enjoyed impressing their elders with their own versions of sad or merry tales. Nor should the delights of reading be minimized. Edward Topsell, author of a wonderbook on animals, *The History of Four-footed Beasts* (1607), which included incredible accounts of dragons, intended his work to be good Sunday reading. In his preface he envisaged that the readers of his book would "pass away the Sabbaths in heavenly meditations upon earthly creatures." Poorer folk who could not afford a folio volume might attend a local fair or feast and fall for the sales talk of a peddler who, like Autolycus in *The Winter's Tale*, was hawking broadsheet ballads that told of extraordinary happenings.

Those who went to see Autolycus on the stage of the Globe enjoyed a pastime that occupied the same cultural framework as the bull and bear-baiting contests that took place close by. Baits appealed to all classes and attracted large crowds, whether staged in market squares, on village greens, or in city arenas like the famous ones on London's Bankside where Shakespeare's theater stood. Some theater companies actually shared the same arena as blood-sports promoters. Playgoing was a robust experience, enjoyed in much the same spirit of holiday merriment as the dramatic shows that were often a part of festival entertainments. The license granted by the queen in 1574 to a group of actors (including James Burbage, who later put up the first theater building in London) to perform throughout the country viewed the purpose of their playing as "the recreation of our loving subjects." Theatergoing was not a rarefied, "artistic" experience; seeing a play was more in the nature of an afternoon's sport than a cultural experience. When Lady Anne Clifford, countess of Dorset, described how her husband had amused himself in London in 1616, she mentioned his theatrical visits in the same breath as various rugged entertainments: "He went much abroad to cocking, to bowling alleys, to plays and horse races."

If the earl of Dorset had seen *Hamlet* he would have heard a children's company of actors described as "little eyases," young hawks, and a company of adult actors referred to as "a cry of players," a pack of hounds bent on pursuit of their dramatic quarry. It was fitting that the greatest Elizabethan theatrical scriptwriter described his profession in terms of two other of the most popular recreations of the time.

BIBLIOGRAPHY

Anon., *The Noble Art of Venerie or Hunting* (1575). Edward A. Armstrong, *Shakespeare's Imagination* (1946). C. L. Barber, *Shakespeare's Festive Comedy* (1959). Dennis Brailsford, *Sport and Society: Elizabeth to Anne* (1969). Robert Burton, *The Anatomy of Melancholy,* Lawrence Bobb, ed. (1621; repr. 1965). Muriel St. Clare Byrne, *Elizabethan Life in Town and Country* (1925; rev. ed. 1961). Baldassare Castiglione, *The Book of the Courtier,* Sir Thomas Hoby, trans., J. H. Whitfield, ed. (1561; repr. 1974). Sir Thomas Elyot, *The Book Named the Governor,* S. E. Lehmberg, ed. (1531; repr. 1963). J. W. Fortescue, et al., "Sports and Pastimes," in *Shakespeare's England,* 2, Charles Talburt Onions, ed. (1916). William Harrison, *The Description of England,* Georges Edelen, ed. (1577; repr. 1968). T. R. Henn, *The Living Image* (1972). Christina Hole, *English Sports and Pastimes* (1949). W. G. Hoskins, "Provincial Life," in *Shakespeare Survey,* 17 (1964).

Reginald Lennard, ed., *Englishmen at Rest and Play: Some Phases of English Leisure, 1558–1714* (1931). D. H. Madden, *The Diary of Master William Silence: A Study of Shakespeare and of Elizabethan Sport* (1897; new ed. 1907). Richard Mulcaster, *Positions,* R. H. Quick, ed. (1581; repr. 1888). John Nichols, *The Progresses and Public Processions of Queen Elizabeth,* 3 vols. (1788–1805). Henry Peacham, *The Complete Gentleman,* V. B. Heltzel, ed. (1622; repr. 1962). A. L. Rowse, *The Elizabethan Renaissance: The Life of the Society* (1971). Lilly C. Stone, *English Sports and Recreations* (1960). John Stow, *A Survey of London,* C. L. Kingsford, ed. (1598; repr. 1908). Joseph Strutt, *The Sports and Pastimes of the People of England,* William Hone, ed. (1801; repr. 1876). George Turberville, *The Book of Falconry or Hawking* (1575). Marcia Vale, *The Gentleman's Recreations: Accomplishments and Pastimes of the English Gentleman, 1580–1630* (1977). Christopher Whitfield, ed., *Robert Dover and the Cotswold Games* (1962).

WITHDRAWN

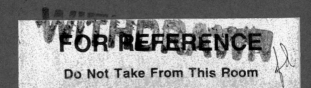

FOR REFERENCE

Do Not Take From This Room